GÖRING
A BIOGRAPHY

GÖRING

A BIOGRAPHY

DAVID IRVING

AVON BOOKS ◆ NEW YORK

AVON BOOKS
A division of
The Hearst Corporation
105 Madison Avenue
New York, New York 10016

"A Thomas Congdon Book"
Copyright © 1989 by David Irving
Front cover photograph courtesy of The Bettmann Archive
Published by arrangement with William Morrow and Company, Inc.
Library of Congress Catalog Card Number: 88-21776
ISBN: 0-380-70824-8

First Avon Books Trade Printing: May 1990

AVON TRADEMARK REG. U.S. PAT. OFF. AND IN OTHER COUNTRIES, MARCA REGISTRADA, HECHO EN U.S.A.

Printed in the U.S.A.

OPM   10   9   8   7   6   5   4   3   2   1

To Thomas B. Congdon,
who has helped me so much

CONTENTS

PART 5: THE BANKRUPT

PART 6: THE SURROGATE

ARREST THE REICHSMARSCHALL!

The place reeked of evil. Standing in the wet darkness of this wrecked bunker in Berlin, Captain John Bradin of the U.S. Army snapped his cigarette lighter shut, scooped an untidy armful of souvenirs off somebody's desk, and groped his way back up the dark, winding staircase to the daylight.

In the warm sun the haul seemed disappointing: a brass desk lamp, cream-colored paper with some handwriting on it, blank letterheads, flimsy telegrams typed on Germany Navy signals forms, and a letter dictated to "my dear Heinrich."

Bradin took them home and forgot about them. Forty years passed. In Berlin the bunker was dynamited, grassed over. The lamp ended up dismantled on a garage floor, the yellow sheaf of papers moldered in a bank vault in South Carolina. Bradin died without knowing that he had saved vital clues to the last days of Hermann Göring's extraordinary career—papers that reveal all the hatred and envy that his contemporaries in the Nazi party had nursed toward him over twelve years and their determination to see his humiliation and downfall in these last few thousand minutes of Hitler's "Thousand-Year Reich."

The desk that Captain Bradin had found was Martin Bormann's. Bormann

had been the Nazi party's chief executive—Hitler's predatory Mephistoph-
eles. The handwriting was Bormann's too—desperate pages that mirrored
the atmosphere of hysteria in the bunker as the suspicions grew among its
inhabitants that Göring had betrayed them.

The first telegram that Bormann had scrawled onto the cream-colored paper
was addressed to SS Obersturmbannführer [Lieutenant Colonel] Bernhard
Frank, commander of the SS detachment on the mountain called the Obersalzberg that was Göring's last retreat:

> Surround Göring villa at once and arrest the former Reichsmar-
> schall Hermann Göring at once. Smash all resistance.
>   ADOLF HITLER

It was the late afternoon of April 23, 1945. Russian troops had already
reached Berlin's seedy Alexander-Platz district. The bunker was filling with
battle casualties, and the scent of treason was mingling with the mortar dust
in the air. There were whispers of betrayal by Albert Speer, the young,
ambitious munitions minister, and by Foreign Minister Joachim von Ribbentrop as well. And now strange messages signed by Göring himself had
begun reaching the bunker's signals room.

As heavily bandaged officers clomped about the constricted tunnels clutching dispatches on the battle outside, Bormann swept his desk clear of debris
and scribbled a second signal to the SS unit on the Obersalzberg:

> You will pay with your lives if Führer's order is not executed.
> Find out where Speer is. . . . Utmost caution, but act like
> lightning.
>
>   BORMANN

He was in his element. For Germany a nightmare might be ending, an ordeal
in which the dark hours had blazed with air raids, and nearly every family
had suffered the agony of bereavement, imprisonment, deportation, or persecution. But in the caged mind of Martin Bormann the entire battle had
narrowed down to this: a final settling of scores with Göring. For four years
he had labored to depose Göring, conspiring, hoping that the fat air-force
commander would make one mistake too many—and now he had, and the
telegrams were piling up on Bormann's desk to prove it.

Bormann dashed off a third vengeful directive, this time to Paul Giesler,
the party's gauleiter in Munich:

> Führer has ordered immediate arrest of Reichsmarschall Göring
> by SS unit Obersalzberg because of planned high treason. Smash
> all resistance. Occupy Salzburg, etc., airfields immediately to

prevent his flight. Advise all neighboring gauleiters, SS, and police at once.

BORMANN

Bormann's own days might be numbered, but at least he would have cooked Göring's goose as well.

Berlin was dying, Hitler and Bormann were trapped there, and Göring was doing nothing at all about it. With his plump wife, Emmy, and their little daughter, Edda, he was in his lavishly appointed mountain villa on the Obersalzberg, three hundred miles to the south. It was April 23, three days since he'd seen either the Führer or his once all-powerful secretary. Sucking a cigar, he motioned to his valet, Robert, to pour out another cognac. Then he kicked off his boots, revealing ankles clad in exquisite red silk stockings, leaned back, and reflected.

At first he had half-expected Hitler to join him down here, but late the day before, his adjutant had woken him with a garbled message from Berlin: General Karl Koller, chief of air staff, had just phoned from Kurfürst, air-force headquarters, to report that the Führer had "collapsed" and planned to stay put. "Collapsed"—might that not mean that Hitler was already dead? That possibility had brought Göring wide awake. "Phone Koller," he ordered his adjutant. "Tell him to fly down here at once."

The Reichsmarschall knew that Hitler had always regarded him as his successor. Now was the time to make it happen.

Koller strode into the Obersalzberg villa at noon the next day, saluted, and at his commander in chief's behest read out his shorthand notes of the previous day. Air Force General Eckhard Christian, he said, had phoned him from the bunker with the cryptic message, "Historic events. I'm coming straight over to tell you in person." When Christian arrived, he told Koller, "The Führer has collapsed and says it's pointless to fight on. . . . He's staying on in the bunker, will defend Berlin to the last and then do the obvious." General Alfred Jodl, chief of the armed forces' operations staff, had confirmed all this to Koller at midnight. Hitler had turned down Jodl's suggestion that they swing all the western armies around against the Russians—"The Reichsmarschall will have to do that!" was all he had said. Somebody had suggested that there wasn't one German who would fight for Göring. "There's not much fighting left to be done," Hitler had said bitterly, "and if it's a matter of dealing, the Reichsmarschall is better at that than I am."

Göring whistled, then acted with a decisiveness that he had not displayed for years. He sent for balding, pettifogging Dr. Hans Lammers, the chief servant of the Reich; Lammers always carried around with him a dossier of the constitutional documents relating to the succession. Göring also sent for his close friend Philipp Bouhler; Bouhler, former head of Hitler's Chancellery, had masterminded the Nazi euthanasia program, but now, like Göring, he had fallen out of favor. Finally, Göring ordered the flak and Waffen SS defenses around the villa reinforced, and he instructed his adjutant to check out everybody coming through this cordon.

When they had all assembled, Lammers explained in his precise, fussy manner that after President Hindenburg's death in 1934, a secret law had conferred on Hitler the right to nominate his own successor; in April 1938 a further law had defined who should deputize for him. Since then, Lammers continued, Hitler had written certain codicils, and they had been sealed in an official envelope.

Göring impatiently asked to see it. Lammers was uneasy about unsealing the Führer's will before he was known to be dead, but he opened the metal casket. The envelope inside bore the legend "Führer's Testament. To be opened only by the Reichsmarschall."

Göring broke the wax seals and plucked out the contents with bejeweled fingers. He perused the documents silently, almost furtively, then beamed and read out loud the first decree, which said:

> In the event that I am impeded in the discharge of my duties by sickness or other circumstance, even temporarily . . . I denote as my deputy in all my offices the Reichsmarschall of the Greater German Reich, Hermann Göring.
>
> Führer's Headquarters, June 29, 1941

A second decree directed that "immediately after my death" Göring was to have both government and party resworn in his name.

It was a tricky position. Was Hitler de facto dead? Or had he perhaps recovered from his collapse? Suppose Bormann had persuaded him to draw up a new will in some rival's favor?

"Send him a radiogram," suggested General Koller. "Ask him what to do."

Göring dictated one, and it went off at 3:00 P.M. on April 23:

> Mein Führer!
> Acting upon information furnished by Generals Jodl and Christian, General Koller has today given me a version of events according to which in the context of certain deliberations you made reference to my name, underlining that if negotiations should become necessary then I would be better placed to conduct them than you in Berlin.
> These statements were so startling and serious in my view that I shall consider myself duty-bound to infer that you are no longer a free agent if I do not receive an answer to this by 10:00 P.M.

I shall thereupon consider the conditions of your decree as satisfied, and act for the good of nation and fatherland.

"May God protect you," he concluded, "and see you through . . . Your
faithful Hermann Göring."

The noblest prize of all now glittered ahead of him—head of state at last!
He cabled Hitler's air-force adjutant: "It is your personal responsibility to
ensure that the radiogram is delivered to the Führer in person. Acknowledge,
so that in this grave hour I may act in harmony with the Führer's wishes."

Meanwhile he radioed to Field Marshal Wilhelm Keitel, chief of the high
command, to fly to the Obersalzberg if by 10:00 P.M. they were no longer
getting direct orders from Hitler. "A government must be in existence,"
reasoned Göring, "if the Reich is not to fall apart." A further radiogram
notified Ribbentrop, the foreign minister, that he, Göring, was about to
succeed Hitler "in all his offices," and that if Ribbentrop had not received
orders to the contrary by midnight, either from Hitler or from Göring himself,
he was to fly down to Göring without delay.

These were the suspicious signals that Hitler's radio room had monitored in
Berlin. But Hitler had recovered from the suicidal depression that had seized
him the day before. With hollow eyes he shambled around the cement cor-
ridors clutching a soggy, tattered map of Berlin, waiting for the relief attack
promised by SS troops from the north.

Bad enough for Göring that his most serpentine enemies—Bormann, Speer,
and Ribbentrop—all chanced to be in Hitler's bunker on this afternoon of
April 23 as his string of radiograms was intercepted. It was Bormann who
carried them in to Hitler's study and pressed the flimsy naval signal forms
into Hitler's palsied hands. "High treason!" shouted Bormann.

Treachery!—Hitler had seen it as the cause of every defeat since the attempt
on his life nine months before. Now his own chosen successor was a traitor
too. He turned to Bormann, his face expressionless. "Arrest the Reichsmarschall!" he commanded.

Porcine eyes twinkling with anticipation, Bormann hurried to the radio
room and seized more sheets of paper. To navy commander Grand Admiral
Karl Dönitz, based now at Flensburg in Schleswig-Holstein, he wrote:

Urgent! On Führer's orders: Reich government is not to fly to
Bavaria. Prevent any flight from Holstein, move like lightning.
Block all airfields.

And to the SS barracks on the Obersalzberg itself:

(1) Führer awaits news mission accomplished fastest.
(2) Have you taken Lammers and other ministers into custody?
Arrest Bouhler too.

Glimpsing Speer, his face bright with intrigue even at this desperate moment—he had been flown in by a sergeant pilot in a light aircraft that had landed him near the Brandenburg gate—Bormann added another radio message to the Obersalzberg:

Speer has meantime arrived here.

These were the pages that would be found ten weeks later, still on Bormann's darkened desk in the bunker ruins. Among them was a copy of a letter dated April 24, which Bormann had sent to "my dear Heinrich"—Himmler—describing Göring's "treachery":

In the Führer's opinion he must have been plotting to do this for some time. On the afternoon of April 20—the day he drove down south—G[öring] told Ambassador [Walther] Hewel [Ribbentrop's liaison officer to Hitler], "Something's got to be done and now. We've got to negotiate—and I am the only one who can do it. I, Göring, am not blackened by the sins of the Nazi party, by its persecution of the churches, by its concentration camps . . ."

He said that obviously our enemies can't deal with somebody unless he's totally blameless and has even, as Göring has himself, condemned many of these things right from the start.

The wording of the messages he sent summoning the others [to the Obersalzberg] show clearly enough, in the Führer's view, what he has been working up to. *He* [Göring] issued an ultimatum giving him liberty to act in internal and foreign affairs; he even sent for a mobile broadcasting truck. Our detailed investigations are continuing. It's significant that since quitting Berlin our former Reichsmarschall has not taken one step to help the battle for Berlin, but has devoted his entire time to preparing his little act of treachery.

In our opinion, anybody else in his situation would have done his level best to prove his loyalty to the Führer by rendering swift help. Not so Göring! It doesn't take much to imagine how his broadcast would have run; quite apart from anything else it would have led to an immediate and total collapse of our eastern front.

At 10:25 P.M. that evening Bormann phoned Dönitz to repeat Hitler's orders that no government elements were to be allowed to fly south to join Göring. "It's got to be prevented at all costs," he said. Speer sent a similar message to General Adolf Galland, commander of Germany's elite Me 262 jet-fighter squadron. "I ask you and your comrades to do everything as discussed to prevent Göring from flying anywhere."

Not that Göring was leaving the Obersalzberg that night. As darkness fell across the mountainside, a breeze whipped a thin veil of icy snow across the sloughs around Göring's villa, covering the tracks of the shadowy figures who were quietly drawing an armed cordon around the buildings. He now had a chilling response to his 3:00 P.M. telegram to Berlin. "Decree of June 29, 1941, takes effect only when I specifically authorize," Hitler had radioed. "There can be no talk of freedom to act. I therefore forbid any step in the direction you indicate."

So Hitler was still alive! Panicking, the Reichsmarschall penned telegrams to Ribbentrop, Himmler, and the Wehrmacht high command rescinding the messages he had sent out at midday. But it was too late. At 8:00 P.M. his telephone lines went dead. By eight-fifty a force of SS men had surrounded the villa, and at ten o'clock SS Obersturmbannführer Bernhard Frank marched in, saluted, and announced, "Herr Reichsmarschall, you are under arrest!"

Göring's 264-pound frame quivered with anger and indignation. He guessed that it was the word *negotiations* in his telegram that had irked his Führer. "Hitler always hated that word," he conceded to interrogators later. "He feared I might be negotiating via Sweden."

The Reichsmarschall spent a disturbed night. At 9:00 P.M. Frank returned with another telegram from the Berlin bunker. In this one Bormann accused Göring of betrayal but promised he would be spared provided that he agreed to resign for reasons of ill health. Göring was swept with feelings of childish relief, not because his life was to be spared but because Hitler seemed not to have stripped him of any offices other than air-force commander: He was still Reichsmarschall, or so he could argue. Nonetheless, the guard was not removed, and his troubles were only beginning.

Twenty-four hours later, while he lay in bed half awake, he sensed the windows beginning to vibrate—gently at first, then with increasing amplitude. A deafening roar swept along the valleys toward the mountainside. Plates fell off shelves, a closet door swung open, and the floor began to heave. "The English!" cried one of the guards.

There had been no radar warning to the villa, because the phone lines were still cut. A hundred yards down the slopes a heavy flak battery bellowed into action as the four-engined Lancaster bombers came into sight. Smoke generators belatedly pumped out artificial fog that snaked lazily down the mountainside as thick as a San Francisco pea-souper, and through its pungent fumes came shattering explosions, trampling closer and closer to the villa.

His face chalk white, Göring leaped to his feet. Clutching his silk pajamas around him, he shouted, "Into the tunnels!" But an SS officer waved him back at gunpoint.

As a second wave approached, the guards' nerves cracked too. They bundled Göring and his family into the dank, damp tunnels drilled into the limestone beneath the villa, rudely pushing him as they stumbled pell-mell down the 288 steps into the subterranean labyrinth. The lights failed, the

ground trembled, and Göring shuddered too. It was symbolic of the pow-
erlessness of his air force that enemy bombers could parade over southern
Germany like this.

As the massed Russian artillery began slapping armor-piercing shells and
high explosives into the Reich Chancellery Building above his bunker, Hitler
was still counting on his "trusty Heinrich" Himmler to relieve Berlin. Bormann, meanwhile, continued to indulge in sweet revenge. "Kicked Göring
out of the party!" he sneered in his diary on April 25. And when General
Hans Krebs, the last chief of the general staff, notified Keitel, chief of the
high command, by radiophone that Hitler had stripped the Reichsmarschall
of all his offices, Bormann grabbed the phone and shouted, "And that includes Reich chief gamekeeper too!"

If Berlin now fell, Bormann wrote to Himmler, Germany would have to
accept peace terms. "The Führer could never do that, while a Göring no
doubt would find it quite easy. At any rate, we stay put and hold out here
as long as possible. If you rescue us in time, it's going to be one of the
war's major turning points: because the differences between our enemies are
widening every day. I, for one, am persuaded that once again the Führer has
made the right decision. Others are less convinced or choose to offer comfortable advice from a safe distance. There's not much of a rush to come
into Berlin to see the Führer now."

A few hours later, however, the bunker's teleprinter rattled out the stun-
ning news that Himmler had offered peace talks to the British through Stockholm.

"Obviously," fulminated Bormann in his notes on the twenty-seventh.
"H.H. is wholly out of touch. If the Führer dies, how does he plan to
survive?!! Again and again, as the hours tick past, the Führer stresses how
tired he is of living now with all the treachery he has had to endure!"

Four days later Bormann's writings would be entombed in the deserted
bunker and he, like Hitler, would be dead.

The British bombers had lifted Göring's luxurious villa off the mountainside.
Among the ruins lay the torn envelope with shattered seals that had contained
the Führer's testament. In the tunnels one hundred feet beneath the cratered
landscape languished Göring with his staff and family—still held at gunpoint
by the SS. "By the guttering light of a candle," recalled his personal aide,
Fritz Görnnert, a few days later, "they threw him into one of the tunnels
and left him there. Nothing was brought to eat, nobody was allowed out."

His wife and daughter shivered in their night attire. Göring tried to send
a telegram to Berlin setting the record straight, but his captors refused even
to touch it. He was now a nobody, like the thousands of politicians, trade-
union leaders, and newspapermen whom he had himself incarcerated over
the last twelve years. Hungry and unwashed, and craving opiates to kill the

pain of ancient injuries, he wallowed in self-pity. He had no doubt that "Creature" Martin Bormann was behind all this—"I always knew it would come to this," he wailed to Görnnert. "I always knew Bormann would grow too big for his boots and try to destroy me."

As the days passed, however, he saw the guards fidgeting uneasily, arguing quietly among themselves. The residual authority that Germany's top-ranking soldier still exuded was something not to be trifled with. On April 25, SS Standartenführer (Colonel) Ernst Brausse, one of Himmler's legal staff, arrived. He promised to send off Göring's signal, but the atmosphere was still unnerving. "Nobody could contact anybody else," said Görnnert later. "There were dreadful scenes, with everybody crying—even the men. At the end the whole thing was downright shameful."

Late on April 26, a new SS unit took over and removed Göring from his military staff. As they parted, Göring, tugging off some of his rings to give to the men as mementos, suggested that evil was afoot. It seems likelier that Himmler had decided to take the Görings out of Bormann's personal domain. The Reichsführer SS undoubtedly realized that, in the final *Endkampf*, a live Reichsmarschall was a more readily negotiable trump than a dead one.

Whatever the reason, the escort relaxed. Göring was even asked where he would like to be confined. He affably mentioned Mauterndorf Castle, forty miles beyond Salzburg. Early on April 28, he took leave of his bodyguard with a "God be with you until we meet again," climbed in the back of his armor-plated Maybach limousine with little Edda while Emmy sat in the front, and waved grandly to the chauffeur to drive off. A short while later, escorted by an SS platoon in trucks, the cavalcade rattled over the Mauterndorf drawbridge and into the castle yard.

He had spent part of his childhood here at Mauterndorf. It had belonged to his Jewish godfather. He promptly resumed his pasha life-style, and something of the old Göring bonhomie returned. Fine wines and a case of Dutch cigars were brought up from the cellars for Göring to share with Colonel Brausse. Emmy made only one appearance in the great halls of the castle, and on that occasion she spent the whole evening weeping to Hermann about everything they had lost. Once Brausse saw Göring flicking through a diary he had written as a boy; and once Göring fetched his family genealogy and showed Brausse how he could trace his bloodline back to most of the country's emperors as well as Bismarck and Goethe.

There was, of course, an animal cunning in all this. The prisoner wanted to establish rapport with his captor. In this he at first seemed to have succeeded. Visiting General Koller a day or two after the arrival, Brausse assured him, "You know, Göring's a splendid fellow. I won't do him any harm."

All the time Göring kept his ears and his pale blue eyes wide open. On the radio he heard Berlin announce his "retirement"—but still there was no mention of his losing the Führer succession. On April 30, Brausse showed him a new signal from the bunker: "Shoot the traitors of April 23 if we should die." Göring murmured dismissively, "Bormann's handiwork again!" and saw Brausse nodding in sage agreement.

But on May 1, when the radio announced Hitler's death, the SS colonel did, in fact, telephone Field Marshal Albert Kesselring, commander in chief in the south, to inquire if he should now execute Göring. Kesselring advised him not to—but nobody wanted to order the Reichsmarschall's release, either.

Humiliated, Göring sent his doctor to plead with General Koller. Koller passed the buck to Kesselring, and Kesselring passed it on to Grand Admiral Dönitz, who vouchsafed no reply. Dönitz, no friend of the once-haughty Hermann Göring, probably relished his humiliation now.

That afternoon, May 4, an air-force general drove past Mauterndorf with an air-signals regiment and saw the unmistakable shape of Göring strolling along the fence with his SS captors.

Göring beckoned him over. "Tell Koller to act now!" he hissed angrily. "Tell him that I, as Germany's most senior general, must be sent to meet Eisenhower. Tell him I am the most popular of our generals, particularly in the United States." Koller still did nothing.

On the sixth, Kesselring finally ordered the Reichsmarschall's release. Characteristically, Göring romanticized this most undignified end to his custody into a more heroic version: His own air-force troops, pulling back in exhaustion from Italy, had routed the SS unit and freed their beloved commander in chief. "While he was standing there," said a British interrogator a few days later, reporting Göring's account, "surrounded by SS men, members of Number 12 Air Signals regiment passed by. Upon seeing him, they ran forward to greet and cheer their beloved commander. Göring, swiftly sizing up the situation and finding that the Luftwaffe men outnumbered the SS, ordered them to charge. . . . 'It was one of the most beautiful moments of my life [Göring said to the interrogator] to see them present arms to their commander in chief again.' "

Once freed of the SS, Göring sent a radiogram up to Admiral Dönitz, offering to handle the negotiations with the enemy.

Grand Admiral!
    Are you fully aware of the deadly intrigue hatched by Reichs-leiter Bormann to eliminate me? . . . Bormann waged his campaign against me entirely by means of anonymous radiograms . . . to SS Obersturmbannführer Frank on the Obersalzberg. . . . Reichsführer Himmler will confirm to you the outlandish scale of this intrigue.
    I have just learned that you are planning to send Jodl to Eisenhower for talks. I consider it absolutely vital . . . that parallel to Jodl's negotiations I approach Eisenhower unofficially as one marshal to another . . . I might create a suitably personal at-

mosphere for Jodl's talks. In recent years the British and Americans have displayed a more benevolent attitude to me than to our other political leaders.

The fighting had all but ended. Göring sent his adjutant off by car to contact the Americans, bearing a laissez-passer and two secret letters, addressed to "Marshal" Eisenhower and U.S. Army group commander General Jacob L. Devers.

The letter to Eisenhower, verbose and tedious, read in part:

Your Excellency!

On April 23, I decided as senior officer of the German armed forces to contact you, Excellency, to do everything I could to discuss a basis for preventing further bloodshed . . . On the same date I was arrested with my family and entourage at Berchtesgaden by the SS. An order for us to be shot was not carried out by our captors. I was simultaneously expelled from the National Socialist party. The public was informed by radio that I had been retired as air-force commander in chief because of a severe heart ailment . . . Under the decree appointing me deputy Führer I had the law on my side. I have only today managed by force of circumstances and the approach of my own air-force troops to regain my liberty . . .

Despite everything that has happened during my arrest, I request you, Excellency, to receive me without any obligation whatever on your part and let me talk to you as soldier to soldier. I request that you grant me safe passage for this meeting and accept my family and entourage into American safekeeping. For technical reasons I would propose Berchtesgaden for this purpose. . . .

My request may perhaps appear unusual to Your Excellency, but I make so bold as to state it, since I am reminded that the venerable marshal of France, Pétain, once asked me for such a meeting at an hour of similar gravity for his own country. . . . Your Excellency will understand what emotions inspire me at this most painful hour, and how very grieved I was to be prevented by arrest from doing all I could long before to prevent further bloodshed in a hopeless situation.

The accompanying letter asked Devers to radio this message to Eisenhower immediately. It is unlikely that Eisenhower ever received it.

Göring then sent Eisenhower a message suggesting Fischhorn Castle at Zell am See, fifty miles away, near Salzburg, for their historic meeting. He lingered at Mauterndorf, claiming to be awaiting a reply, but in fact he hated to leave this castle—childhood memories of his parents and of games of knights in armor clung to its walls. Besides, Russian troops, Austrian Communists, or Bormann's assassins might be lurking beyond the castle keep.

At midday on May 7, an irate Koller phoned and told him that a top American general, the deputy commander of the 36th (Texas) Division, had put on all his medals and finery and driven through the lines to Fischhorn Castle. "You asked for that rendezvous," said Koller. "Now keep it." Grumbling and hesitant, Göring climbed into the twelve-cylinder Maybach and set off with his family and what remained of his staff. He was uniformed in pearl gray, with a tentlike greatcoat that flapped open over his fat paunch to reveal a small Mauser pistol on his belt.

Some thirty miles short of Salzburg they encountered the American posse. Tired of waiting, the American officers had set out to fetch him. Both convoys stopped, facing each other. Brigadier General Robert I. Stack, a burly, white-haired Texan, met Göring, saluted smartly. Göring returned the courtesy, using the old-fashioned army salute, not the Hitler one.

"Do you speak English?" asked Stack.

The Reichsmarschall smiled wearily. His face was flabby and lined, the famous John Barrymore profile betraying a hint of his eagerness to meet Eisenhower, mingled with sorrow that a long adventure was over.

"I understand it better than I speak," he apologized.

He apologized again, for not being better dressed. The G.I.'s pealed with laughter at his vanity.

Emmy began to cry. Her husband chucked her under the chin and said that everything was going to be all right now—these were Americans.

Stack motioned toward his American sedan. As Hermann Göring clambered in, he muttered something under his breath. "Twelve years," he growled. "I've had a good run for my money."

PART 1
THE OUTSIDER

1
A TRIANGULAR AFFAIR

Hermann Göring—the Führer's chosen successor; last commander of the legendary Richthofen Squadron; commander of the storm troopers and of the German Air Force; speaker of the German Parliament, prime minister of Prussia, president of the Prussian State Council; Reich master of forestry and game; the Führer's special commissioner for the Four-Year Plan; chairman of the Reich Defense Council; Reichsmarschall of the Greater German Reich; chairman of the Scientific Research Council—Hermann Wilhelm Göring, holder of all these titles, styles and dignities, architect of the Gestapo, the concentration camp, and the giant industrial conglomerate bearing his name, was born in Bavaria on January 12, 1893.

His father was a haughty German colonial official, his mother a simple peasant girl, his godfather a Jew. Dutiful researchers would trace his ancestral line back to one Michael Christian Gering, who in 1659 was appointed economic controller (*commissarius loci*) to His Majesty, Frederick the Great, king of Prussia, and to Andreas Gering, who had been a pastor near Berlin a hundred years before that.

His parents had married in London in May 1885. For Dr. Heinrich Ernst Göring, then age fifty-six, it was the second marriage. For Franziska ("Fanny")

Tiefenbrunn—Catholic, open-faced, flirtatious, and over twenty years his junior—it was the first. Dr. Göring, Protestant, grave, tedious, was a former judge like his father, Wilhelm. He already had five children by his first marriage and he would have five more by Fanny, with Hermann the second of her two sons.

Under Prince Otto von Bismarck, Heinrich had become a colonial governor. In 1884 the Iron Chancellor had launched Germany on a brief era of colonization in Africa, northern China, and the South Pacific. Bismarck had sent Dr. Göring to London to study the problems of colonial empire, then to German Southwest Africa (today's Namibia) as minister resident, or governor. He rendered the mineral-rich, beautiful colony safe for traders—there is a Göring Strasse in its German-speaking capital, Windhoek, to this day —struck up a friendship with Cecil Rhodes, the British imperial pioneer, then left with Fanny to a new posting as consul general in the disease-ridden former French colony of Haiti. Fanny produced their first child, Karl-Ernst, in 1885 and bore two daughters, Olga and Paula, before returning to Bavaria carrying Hermann in her womb.

It was in the Marienbad Sanatorium at Rosenheim that the remarkable subject of our story entered the world in January 1893. Six weeks later his mother returned to the Caribbean, leaving him to spend his infancy in the care of a friend of hers at Fürth near Nuremberg; this friend, Frau Graf, had two daughters, Erna and Fanny, some three years older than Hermann.

Three years later Dr. Göring brought Fanny back to Germany to retire. Hermann told one psychiatrist some months before his death that this was his earliest memory—as the lady introduced to him as his mother stooped to hug him, he pounded this stranger's face with both tiny fists.

In March 1895 a younger brother, Albert, had been born at Rosenheim. Albert remained the black sheep of the family. He became a thermodynamics engineer, fell out with Hermann as the Nazis came to power, and moved to Austria, where he applied for citizenship in the hope that this would put a safe frontier between himself and his domineering brother.

In 1896 Hermann's father retired from government service and they moved to Berlin. Göring told Nuremberg psychiatrist Paul L. Schroeder fifty years later that he recalled riding in a horse-drawn coach to Berlin—a passing farm cart broke one window, and he remembered seeing a man badly cut, with trickling blood. Three years old by then, he had only the vaguest memories of life in the pleasant Berlin suburb of Friedenau. His older sisters spoiled him, and his father indulged his whims as though he were the favorite; Hermann venerated rather than loved the old gentleman—there were sixty-four years between them, and his father was as old as the grandfathers of his friends.

As he grew up, Hermann noticed something else. In Africa Dr. Göring had befriended the corpulent, dark-haired doctor who attended Fanny's first confinement, Hermann von Epenstein; he had probably named Hermann after this Austrian Jew. Epenstein had used his wealth to purchase his title, sexual favors, and prestige. He became godfather to all the Göring children and may have imprinted on the young Hermann's character traits that were not always wholesome—the conclusion, for instance, that money could buy everything, and a contempt for morality.

But it was Epenstein's castle in Franconia—the countryside around Nuremberg—that left its most powerful mark on Göring's childhood. A towering jumble of castellated walls, built and rebuilt over nine hundred years on the site of an old fortress fifteen miles from the city, Veldenstein Castle had begun to decay during the nineteenth century. In 1889 stones had crumbled on to four houses beneath, and the then-owner, Nuremberg businessman Johann Stahl, decided to unload it onto some unsuspecting purchaser. "Army physician Dr. Hermann Epenstein" (no von then), "property owner of Berlin," bought it for twenty thousand marks on November 29, 1897; over the next forty years, until it was formally deeded to Field Marshal Hermann Göring on Christmas Eve, 1938, this philanthropic gentleman would pour one and a half million marks into the renovation and reconstruction of its keep, its roof timbers, its inner and outer fortifications. Veldenstein Castle was the romantic setting for Hermann's boyhood. Undoubtedly Epenstein had provided it to the Göring family out of a sense of obligation to the elderly former colonial governor, Dr. Göring, whose young wife he had taken quite openly as his mistress.

This bizarre triangle would persist for fifteen years.

With the approach of manhood it dawned on the young Hermann that it was not without carnal purpose that his godfather, Epenstein, had retained for himself the finest of the castle's twenty-four rooms, close to Fanny Göring's comfortably appointed bedroom—forbidden territory now to his cuckolded Papa, who was consigned to meaner quarters on the ground floor.

It was altogether a rare experience, growing up at Veldenstein. What boy of spirit would not have thrilled to live in this ancient pile, surrounded by dramatic mountain slopes and forests of dark conifers? Playing knights-in-armor at age eight, Hermann would look down from the battlements and have visions of Roman chariots and of plumed warriors galloping in the valley. "You must come and see Veldenstein Castle," his sister Olga would tell people in later years. "Then you will understand him better."

When he was five, his father had given him a Hussar's uniform. And when his father's military friends came to stay at the castle, Hermann would play with their caps and swords in his bedroom at night. He saw himself in sword and buckler, jousting, crusading, triumphing—always triumphing in the end.

He was a robust child who suffered only tonsillitis and scarlet fever. As a young man he developed arthritis, but this would vanish never to return after his 1923 groin injury. The education begun in his parental home was continued at Furth in 1898; his collected papers included reports from Furth Private Boys' School dated March 21 and July 12, 1902. It was a Catholic school, (he was born and confirmed, in 1908, as a Protestant), but it was the closest to the castle. He did not take easily to formal education, became something of a malingerer, and mentioned later that he was taught by a private governess after leaving Furth. Packed off to boarding school at Ansbach in 1905, he stood it for three distasteful years, then absconded back to Veldenstein. School's only lasting legacy was an abiding dislike of intellectual pursuits, which inspired his scathing witticism, "When I hear the word *culture* I reach for my Browning!"

Years later a psychiatrist would note that he played no team sports and preferred singles matches in tennis, and that he preferred too the lonelier masculine pursuits like mountaineering. In his youth he was known to lord it over the farmhands' sons, and became their natural ringleader.

A change came over him when his father entered him at one of Germany's best officer-cadet schools, at Karlsruhe. He flourished like a failing plant newly placed in a window. He wore a crisp uniform, and when he visited the Graf sisters and his own sister Paula, who were attending finishing school nearby, he clicked his heels, presented their headmistress with flowers, and invited the girls to a local pastry shop, where he found he had no funds to pay.

In 1910 Hermann Göring progressed to the military academy at Gross Lichterfelde, outside Berlin. It was Germany's West Point. He luxuriated in the social life of the Prussian officer, imagined his manly breast already ornamented with medals, and willingly submitted to the disciplinary straitjacket that was the price for what he coveted—power over the destinies of others.

He sailed easily through his finals in March 1911. Although at loggerheads with the civilian teacher of academic subjects, he had got on famously with the military instructors and scored 232 points (or so he later claimed), one hundred more than needed and the highest in the history of the academy. The surviving record shows that he gained a "quite good" in Latin, French, and English, a "good" in map reading, a "very good" in German, history, math, and physics, and an "excellent" in geography. On May 13, 1911, his forty-four-year-old company commander at the academy signed this report to Hermann's proud father:

> I beg to inform Your Excellency that your son Hermann recently
> passed the ensign examination with the grade summa cum laude.
> Baron [Richard] Von Keiser

After the examination Göring joined his pals on a sightseeing trip to Italy. He kept a careful diary in a gray quarto-sized notebook, illustrating it with picture postcards of the art and architecture. The little group hit Milan on April 1. Hermann chuckled over the way the cathedral clergy cadged for tips, he sought and found Leonardo da Vinci's "Last Supper" ("it has been well repaired," the eighteen-year-old Göring noted, "but it has lost its original beauty"), and he remarked upon the garrison character of Milan. As he gazed, on the following day, upon the city's other famous works by Rubens, Raphael, Titian, and Bellini, there stirred within him the first signs of appreciation that would make him, thirty years later, one of the world's most discerning collectors. He noted in his diary:

> For two hours we went from painting to painting, but scarcely even began. There were magnificent pictures, and several sculptures on display as well. At midday we stood once more before the cathedral, taking in the magnificent metal portals that we overlooked yesterday.

A train journey that was first class only in name, across the lowlands of Lombardy ("interesting," he commented, "only for its numerous battlefields"), brought the little group to Verona.

> APRIL 3, 1911 (SUNDAY). Passing through the Porta Nuova we had our baggage closely checked. They think anybody arriving with a camera is a spy. Went first to the famous ancient Roman arena. It made a colossal impression. These gigantic monoliths, these immense walls that threaten to collapse at any moment, the sheer scale of the amphitheater—all vivid evidence of the great Roman age . . .
> In a German restaurant we called for some Munich Löwenbräu beer, then turned in at eleven P.M.; but it was some time before we could get any sleep as a loud altercation began between a lot of men and women right outside our hotel, and it was conducted with authentic Italian vigor.

This youthful diary is in a U.S. Army archives in Pennsylvania. A subsequent diary, written by Göring four months later during the mountaineering holiday he took in the Bavarian Alps, is now in private possession in New York.

The diary, inscribed "Hermann Goering, German-Austrian Alpine Club, Salzburg," describes an eight-hour climb to the summit of Salzburg's famous Watzmann Rock and mountaineering exploits in the Dolomites, including his pioneering ascent of the twin Wild Sander peaks south of Lienz with his two friends Barth and Rigele, probably Friedrich Rigele, the Austrian lawyer who married Olga Göring. Several locations that figured later in Göring's life are featured in this diary's pages—among them, the Bürgerbräu beerhall, Berchtesgaden, and the Hotel Geiger. The adventure began, as did so many for him, at Veldenstein:

> JULY 16, 1911. At exactly four A.M. the alarm clock rattled me out of my splendid dreams of soaring mountains, glaciers and

chimneys in the Dolomites. . . . I sallied forth from the old castle as the first rays of the rising sun shone upon it. Everybody was fast asleep instead of rejoicing in this lovely Sunday morning. The train left Neuhaus [Veldenstein's station] just before five A.M. and puffed off through the Jura mountains toward Nuremberg. . . . At eleven we were in Munich. I made my way to the Bürgerbräu first to seek refreshment in a mug of Munich beer. . . . At the station hobnail climbing boots rang on the paving, well-stacked rucksacks were on every back, in short you could see this was the start for the Alpine travelers.

JULY 17. A shopping spree through Salzburg—Alpine Club membership card, climbing boots, irons, etc., had to be obtained, and my mountain boots needed renailing. . . .

JULY 18. Wakened at three-thirty A.M. Straight to window to look at the weather, it was clear and the Watzmann and its "children" were standing there in such splendor that they kindled great hopes in my breast. It was by no means certain we'd get to the summit, as the weather could thwart us at any moment. At four-thirty we set off from the Hotel Geiger. . . . The path climbed gradually to the first Watzmann hut, mostly through forest. In one clearing we glimpsed a deer grazing peacefully without paying us the slightest attention. After two and a half hours we reached the Mitterkaser pastures, where the steeper meadows began. The path snaked uphill in long, winding bends. A couple with a nine-year-old boy followed us from the Mitterkaser, dressed from head to foot in city suits. These simple-minded Saxons clambered straight up, pouring with sweat, without of course making any faster progress than we did.

After eight hours Hermann Göring had reached the Watzmann's summit. As his little party descended, he rejoiced in the view of the König See, surrounded by mountains bathed in the sunset's glow and crisscrossed by the wakes of two white motor boats. Then he set off for the main climbing adventure in the Tyrol, overlooking the Italian frontier:

JULY 19. We strolled through Lienz and purchased what we needed. Lienz is very well placed as a starting point for the Dolomites, the Schober Group and Kals; a pretty little town in the Puster Valley. Like all towns in the southern Tyrol it is a garrison for the Imperial Rifles (Kaiserjäger). . . .

On the next day they climbed to the Karlsbad Hut at 2,252 meters (7,500 feet) in the Dolomites.

JULY 20. We had a lively talk about mountains, Alpine Club, guides, huts and the Bohemian question. . . . A wonderful sight: The little hut nestles between two dark green lakes in the middle of the Laserzkar, framed by the sheer rockfaces of the Lienz dolomites. A desolate mountain wilderness extended beyond it, with the proud twin peaks of the "Wild Sander." . . . Tomorrow we plan to climb it. As the two peaks are joined by a narrow ridge, we want if possible to climb both.

The next day they struggled onward to the ninety-three-hundred-foot summit.

JULY 21 . . . . After half an hour's rest we put on the forty-meter rope and began the traverse of the south face of the Seekofel. This is endless, as it goes round the whole mountain. The ledge we were on was very good and relatively wide, but very long.

Finally we found ourselves in a fissure. . . . The first bit of chimney was all right but then overhanging rocks blocked the way and forced Barth to work round them. We crossed over into the left branch of the chimney, but this was considerably narrower, wetter and more difficult. I left my rucksack here, tucked some cramps and pitons into my pockets and climbed up to Barth, who was inside a fissure and trying vainly to get out; the crack was extremely narrow, overhanging, and lacked any handhold. As we wormed up it we had the unpleasant feeling that it was squeezing us out. Barth tried again and again without any luck.

So we did it like this: We hammered in two pitons to which Barth tied himself and then climbed on up as far as he could; I climbed up after him inside the fissure and wedged myself in so that my hands were free to give Barth a leg up. With this kind of human ladder Barth managed to get past the smooth bit. His left hand found a hole he could use as a handhold after clearing out the pebbles. Then he doubled around (very difficult) and thus got into the main chimney. I wasn't too well placed, as the entire rubble Barth was clearing out landed on my head and he was standing on my hands. I then climbed back down to the bottom of the fissure, releasing the rope from the fastening and climbed after him. After hard work and a lot of exertion I too overcame the fissure, and was gratified to find myself in the broad chimney, as I felt suffocated in the narrow crack. This was probably the reason why this route had never been climbed before. . . .

We had to step out onto a ledge barely a hand's breadth, with a sheer drop down into Laserzkar. The hut and lakes seemed tiny down there—boy, it was windy up here! Straddling the knife-edge ridge like a horse, I crossed between the two peaks.

The twin summit conquered by an as-yet-untried route, nothing remained but to return. "I had a frantic thirst," he wrote in his diary, "and ordered Barth's own well-tried drink—red wine mixed with hot water and sugar."

Exhausted, he flopped into bed that afternoon.

"How splendid everything was from up here," he mused on July 23, 1911. "Alone with Nature and nice people, I thought of the hot, dusty cities, particularly of Berlin; I thought of the bare walls and drab parade ground of the corps, and thanked God I could enjoy the heights of nature."

He ended this illuminating (and hitherto unpublished) diary with the words, "Every morning, incidentally, I discovered I had dreamed all night of the events of the day before."

Dreamy, physically brave, and romantic, young Hermann Göring was inducted into the infantry as a subaltern in March 1912. The war academies were overflowing. He remained at Gross Lichterfelde and passed the officer examinations in December 1913. He would write in his curriculum vitae that he spent his spare time watching the airplane-acceptance flights at Habsheim Airfield. "My interest in flying," he pointed out, "was always very pronounced."

On January 20, 1914, he joined his regiment. "If war breaks out," Lieutenant Hermann Göring assured his sisters, "you can be sure I'll do credit to our name."

War did break out that August. It is not easy to unravel the truth about Göring's personal contribution to it from the skeins of legend that he afterward encouraged—lively accounts of his exploits in command of small infantry platoons skirmishing with the French, riding bicycles into the enemy lines, commandeering horses, plotting once to kidnap a French general, hiring airplanes, jousting with (almost) equally brave airborne enemies.

Sadly, his personal papers were looted from his private train at Berchtesgaden in May 1945, among them the two war diaries that he wrote in August 1914, a private diary kept intermittently between September 1916 and May 1918, and five flying logs recording all his flights from November 1, 1914, to June 1, 1918; one of these private diaries is known to be in private American hands, but the owner has refused to let anyone see it. However, in 1941 "court historians" began working on his military biography and filled four green files with selected World War I documents; these green files, which figure in the inventory of the Berchtesgaden train, are now in U.S. Army hands in Pennsylvania. They include Göring's complete personnel record since 1905, forty-four selected air-reconnaissance reports, and extracts from war diaries and personal-mission reports.

The unrelenting evidence of these documents is sometimes difficult to reconcile with the flattering Göring biographies. The personnel file shows him as a junior infantry officer of 112 Baden Regiment (the "Prince Wilhelm"), garrisoning Mühlhausen, close to the French border, that August of 1914. It was a quiet sector, and he saw only leisurely action as a platoon commander in the battles of Vosges, Seenheim, and Lorraine, and then as battalion adjutant in the fighting at Nany-Epnaul and at Flirey. He was awarded the Iron Cross Second Class, but only five weeks into the war he was stricken down with arthritis and evacuated from Thiacourt to Metz on September 23. From here he was sent to the rear for further treatment in southern Germany.

This seemingly inglorious beginning changed his life. Convalescing at Freiburg, he struck up a friendship with Bruno Loerzer, a dashing young army lieutenant undergoing flying training. Listening to Loerzer's tales, Göring rediscovered his interest in flying. "I applied," he stated in his personnel record, "for posting as an airborne observer." Authorized biographer Erich Gritzbach wrote that having been rejected for observer training, Göring nevertheless moved with Loerzer to Darmstadt and started flying as his observer in defiance of all rules and regulations. In fact, he was routinely posted to 3 Air Reserve Detachment at Darmstadt for observer training on October 14.

The Gritzbach legend maintained that Göring "stole a plane" to join Loerzer at 25 Field Air Detachment. The personnel file shows this (regular) posting beginning on October 28, with Göring flying as Loerzer's observer at Verdun until the end of June 1915, but again it makes no mention of any stolen plane. The detachment's war diary shows that by mid-February Loerzer and Göring were flying an Albatros, No. B990; they had picked up photographic equipment at Trier, and Göring had taken a rapid radio and Morse signaling course.

Their mission reports gave both men a first-class opportunity of mingling with the top brass. Herman pasted into his album snapshots of the Prince of Hohenzollern with him on Vouziers Airfield, General von Knobelsdorff with Loerzer and himself, and other visiting notables. On the last two days of February the war diary mentioned that Lieutenant Göring had taken the reconnaissance reports "in person" to brigade or corps headquarters. After particularly valuable reconnaissance flights over the dangerous armored gun battery at Côte de Talon, the two intrepid aviators were summoned to the royal presence on March 25 and personally decorated by the crown prince, who commanded the Fifth Army, with the Iron Cross First Class. "The air-force lieutenants Göhring and Lörzer [sic]," recalled the prince in his 1923 memoirs, "were among those who displayed conspicuous dash and zeal."

Göring became a frequent visitor in the royal mess. When he strolled in, all eyes went to this handsome, broad-shouldered young man with the penetrating blue eyes and square jaw. He was good at his job, as the excellent reconnaissance photographs testify—clear, dramatic pictures of the enemy airship hangar at Verdun, the spreading maze of enemy trenches, the enormous craters left by tunnel mines. On June 3, when enemy planes bombed the headquarters at Stenay, it was Loerzer and Göring, now flying a 150-horsepower Albatros, who although unarmed managed to force one of the raiders down. "The two officers were rewarded," the war diary records, "with an invitation to His Imperial Highness the crown prince."

The legend has it that he took flying lessons at his own expense, but once again the personnel file is more mundane. It shows that he was posted to the flying training school at Freiburg (where he first met Loerzer) at the end of June 1915, and returned to the Fifth Army in mid-September. He flew his first operational sortie as a fighter pilot on the third day of October—a 140-minute patrol after which he nonchalantly wrote in his report that he had "fought off seven French planes one after the other."

The planes were primitive, the pilots daredevils and gladiators; their life expectancy was not long, but if they shot down an enemy officer the man might be dined for days afterward in the German messes. There was a chivalry toward a defeated foe then that did not recur in other arenas or in later wars.

On November 16, 1915, Göring was credited with his first official "kill," a Farman shot down at Tahure. For the Fifth Army's great assault on Verdun, which finally began three months later, he flew fighter No. G49, one of the big three-hundred horsepower AEG planes. In this fast, heavily armed fighter, with its superior rate of climb, he shot down a French bomber on March 14. His observer's action report reads:

> Air battle with three big French warplanes, Caudrons. After fifteen minutes managed to shoot down one . . . It went down toward the French lines in a steep glide with its port engine on fire and Lieutenant Göring giving chase; we managed to force it to land behind our lines (southeast edge of Haumont Woods). We circled overhead at 150 feet until we observed them taken prisoner . . . Their plane had about a dozen hits. The crew, an officer and a sergeant, were both uninjured.

On June 20, 1916, he was given a new Halberstadt plane, No. D115. He had been comfortable at Stenay Airfield—he pasted into his album pictures of himself at his well-appointed writing desk and even better-appointed dressing table—but from July 9 he flew sorties from Metz over the Third Army's front. A typical action report six days later records four missions by him: In one dogfight over Côte Claire he fired five rounds into an enemy Voisin, killing the observer, then lost his quarry as it plunged into the clouds. Gradually his score increased, although some claims were disallowed. "I regret," wrote the lieutenant colonel commanding the Fifth Army's air element, "that I am unable to credit to Lieutenant Göring the plane shot down on July 24." He was, however, credited with a twin-engined Caudron destroyed at Mameg on the thirtieth (his third kill).

For three months after that the Göring file recorded only a series of new postings—back to 25 Field Air Detachment, then back again to Combat

Squadron (*Kampfstaffel*) Metz, and three weeks after that, on September 28, to 7 Fighter Squadron (*Jagdstaffel*). Bored as the fighting stagnated, he asked to be posted to 5 Fighter Squadron; the crown prince gave permission, and on October 20, again with his buddy Loerzer, Göring made the transfer. Here he flew mainly escort duty for bombers until his luck ran out, on November 2, 1916; he incautiously tackled an English Handley-Page bomber without realizing that it had powerful top cover from fighters. A machine-gun bullet embedded in his hip, Göring nursed his crippled plane back to his own lines and made a crash landing in a cemetery.

"Plane in need of repairs," recorded the unit war diary. The same was true of its pilot, and he spent four months in hospitals at Valenciennes, Bochum, and Munich.

The legend would have it that he was ordered to report to Böblingen to convalesce but returned directly to the front claiming he could not find the town on the map. Be that as it may, the more prosaic personnel records show him being posted as a fighter pilot in mid-February 1917 to Bruno Loerzer's 26 Fighter Squadron in the Upper Alsace. Ten days later, on March 16, Göring signed this combat report:

> Took off [in Albatros III, No. D2049] March 16, 1917, with First Lieutenant Loerzer on pursuit mission. At about four-thirty I saw three Nieuports attacking two German biplanes. I immediately closed on the nearest hostile and loosed off a few short bursts at it. I then attacked the second Nieuport, which suddenly lost height and made off at low altitude.

On April 23, the record shows, he shot a British biplane out of a flight of four and saw it go down in flames northeast of Arras. Five days later he reported a dogfight with six Sopwiths over St.-Quentin: He expended 370 rounds of ammunition and had the satisfaction of seeing one Englishman spinning out of control into the German lines.

On the twenty-ninth, Göring shot down a Nieuport, watched it crash, and learned later that the British pilot, a Flight Lieutenant Fletcher, survived with a bullet in his leg. "As I flew on to Behain at three hundred feet," he reported that night, "a second enemy single-seater swooped down, pursued by an Albatros. The Englishman briefly attacked me and shot out my rudder . . . I could not see what happened then as I had my hands full flying my plane without a rudder."

These dry reports give something of the flavor of air combat in those days.

On May 17 he had been given command of 27 Fighter Squadron, operating from the same field as Loerzer at Iseghem near Ypres. As the grim and bloody battles of Arras and Flanders dragged on, the rivalry between pilots was intense:

JUNE 8, 1917: Attacked a Nieuport that engaged me from above. I gave chase. In a protracted duel he kept recovering and attacking me. Finally I forced him down at Moorstedt, where he flipped over and caught fire. The dogfight had been watched by the entire 8 Fighter Squadron either from the ground or from the air, so . . . there can be no question of any other plane claiming this one. . . . Five hundred rounds expended.

This victory was credited to him, but not others. On July 7 he engaged a Spad, lost sight of it as hot oil sprayed into his face, then believed he saw it crashing west of Ypres; but he was denied the credit. Nine days later he attacked a patrol of Sopwith single-seaters and shot one down on the second pass:

Immediately after that I had to take on a second hostile, which I forced down to about six hundred feet, but my engine had caught some bullets and suddenly began to race; it just spun in its mounting, and my plane at once went into a spin. I put the plane down behind our third line of trenches and flipped over. The second hostile therefore got clean away . . . [signed] Göring.

He was allowed the next claim, a Martinsyde destroyed south of Paschendaele on the twenty-fourth. That was number ten. On August 5 he downed his eleventh, another Sopwith:

At 8:15 P.M. I attacked an enemy force of nine single-seaters with my squadron. They were fast biplanes. I dived on the leading hostile . . . closed right in to about 150 feet and opened fire. Suddenly flames and thick smoke belched out of the plane and the hostile spiraled down into dense cloud. I plunged in after him, but could not find him beneath the clouds as there was a lot of haze at the lower levels. I had clearly seen the plane on fire. Fired 260 rounds. [signed] Göring.

It pained Göring that his slim-waisted aviator's uniform still lacked the highest Prussian decoration—the blue-enamel cross of the Pour le Mérite, the "Blue Max," but as a fighter ace he was still way down the "league table." On November 1, 1917, the top air ace was the "Red Baron," Manfred von Richthofen, with sixty-one kills; Göring and Loerzer had scored fifteen each, and their friend Ernest Udet one fewer. Thirty years later, Loerzer would snicker to fellow generals that his buddy Lieutenant Göring had inflated his mission claims. "Do the same," Loerzer claimed Göring had urged him, "otherwise we'll never get ahead!"

Despite his robust good looks, his general health caused more problems than his war injuries. In February 1918 he was hospitalized with a throat infection for several weeks. In his absence, the Germans began stitching their fighter units into larger formations, using four squadrons in a wing (*Geschwader*). Von Richthofen was given No. 1 Wing, and Loerzer No. 2. Göring was consumed by an envy that was only partly allayed by the kaiser's award, at last, of the Pour le Mérite on June 2, 1918.

Richthofen had been shot down and killed on April 21, but Göring was passed over as his successor. He now had eighteen official kills. On June 5, he gunned down a biplane near Villers and four days later, flying a Fokker distinguished by white engine cowling and white tail, he poured two hundred rounds into a Spad prowling at low level along the front lines—"He plunged vertically like a rock from thirteen hundred feet and impacted at the north-western corner of the horseshoe wood south of Coroy behind our front lines. I circled several times over the crash site."

That was number twenty. On June 17, he destroyed another Spad near Ambleny.

A few days later Richthofen's successor was killed, and the squadron's adjutant, Lieutenant Karl Bodenschatz, formally handed to Hermann Göring the wooden cane that symbolized command of the famous fighter unit at a parade on July 14. (Bodenschatz, a burly, talkative twenty-seven-year-old, had been injured four times already in the Boelcke Fighter Staffel; he would remain Göring's chief aide until 1945.) The days of easy kills were now over. On the day after taking over, Göring attacked a Caudron at point-blank range, and saw the bullets just bouncing off the armor. On the sixteenth, he claimed his twenty-second victory, sending another Spad spiraling down into woods near Bandry. After that—perhaps prefiguring his later career, in which dazzling bursts of activity would give way to a deadly lethargy—Göring awarded himself ten days' leave and departed, assigning temporary command to Lothar von Richthofen, Manfred's brother.

When the world war ended the morale of these German aviators was high. Lieutenant Göring refused to turn his equipment over to the victors. Ignoring the armistice terms, he evacuated his planes to Darmstadt and demobilized his men on the premises of a paper factory at Aschaffenburg. At a farewell binge in the town's beer hall he spoke about Germany's bitter lot with an eloquence that surprised him. "Our time," he declared, "will come again!"

He was uncertain about his future. For a while he stayed with fellow fighter ace Ernst Udet in Berlin, then returned to his widowed mother, Fanny Göring, in Munich. A British air-force officer, Frank Beaumont, had been charged with the local enforcement of the armistice terms. As luck would have it, Göring had ensured that this officer was treated with more than customary chivalry when he had been shot down, and Beaumont now returned that kindness in various ways; this softened the transition from the unreal wartime world of heroism and adventure to the harsher reality of postwar Munich.

Seeing no future for military aviation here, he sought his fortune in Scandinavia. The Fokker company invited him to demonstrate their latest plane in Denmark, and Göring agreed—provided he could keep the plane as payment. That spring of 1919 the Danish government asked him to recommend which aircraft their forces should purchase. His reputation as the Richthofen Squadron's last commander was high, but his life had an undeniable aimlessness now. He staged aerobatic displays with four former Richthofen Squadron pilots. On another occasion fawning Danish pilots paid him twenty-five hundred kroner and "all the champagne he could drink" for two days aerobatics over Odense. Emboldened by the liquid portion of the honorarium, that night Göring switched around all the guests' shoes outside their rooms at the Grand Hotel and carted several young ladies about in a wheelbarrow singing loudly; his sponsors had to retrieve him from the local police station.

He had broken several maidens' hearts; one now broke his. At Mainz in 1917 he had fallen in love with Käthe Dorsch, a young actress appearing on the local stage; blond and blue-eyed, this Garbo-like creature would become one of Germany's most illustrious performers, although she would remain in people's memories for her wit and presence rather than for any conventional beauty. For three years Lieutenant Göring courted her, and when she announced her intention of marrying the actor Harry Liedtke, Göring swore revenge and threatened to strangle Liedtke with his bare hands. Käthe's photograph traveled in his luggage long after, and in the subsequent sad years of Europe's nightmare this modern Joan of Arc would often turn to him, intervening to rescue acquaintances from persecution.

In the summer of 1919 he flew on from Denmark to Sweden. At Malmstät he sold off his Fokker plane and joined the embryonic Swedish airline Svenska Lufttrafik, whose joint owner Karl Lignell preferred war veterans as pilots because of their vast flying experience. A Swedish license to fly passenger planes, dated August 2, 1919, soon joined Göring's prized possessions.

He had political ambitions even then. At the end of September the German legation in Stockholm reported to Berlin that Lieutenant Hermann Göring was now describing himself as a "candidate for the post of Reich president."

A mere lieutenant was not enough for him, and he soon learned that even a captain (*Hauptmann*) was worth more in society. Writing from Stockholm on February 13, 1920, he applied for demobilization from the army with the desired rank of captain and permission to wear the air-corps uniform; if granted this request, he said, he would forfeit his rights to any pension and disability allowance. "It is absolutely essential for my further station in life," he explained, writing to his regiment twelve days later, "that my request for discharge be processed as rapidly as possible." In a further letter on April 12, he again offered to sacrifice his pension rights, explaining now that the rank of captain would be "of particular advantage in my civilian career."

The army granted his request two months later.

It seemed therefore that Captain Hermann Göring, distinguished German aviator and knight of the Order of Pour le Mérite, might spend the rest of his life in Sweden. He bought Langenscheidt's dictionary of Swedish, and started to learn the language.

With his dazzling good looks and his courtly manner he was a killer in Swedish society, but he found no woman who could fill the gap left by Käthe Dorsch until February 20, 1920—the night that a young and wealthy Swedish explorer, Count Eric von Rosen, chartered Göring's plane for a flight up to his castle, Rockelstad. After a bumpy, stomach-pitching flight through gathering blizzards, Göring landed expertly on the frozen lake next to the castle and accepted the count's invitation to spend the night. He had always liked castles. Balloons of cognac in their hands, Hermann and Eric strolled through the great structure, pausing once before a giant stuffed bear—the rugged beast reached out stiffly at the Norseman who had slain it with his spear. By coincidence there were several swastika emblems embellishing the castle. The swastika had yet to appear on the flags and armbands in drum-beating parades across Nazi Europe, and Hermann had never seen one before; Count Eric had discovered the swastika emblem on rune stones in Gotland, and had incorporated this harmless Nordic symbol of the rising sun everywhere at Rockelstad—embossed on the hearth and iron firedogs and on one wall of his shooting box in the grounds.

As Göring puzzled at the emblem, he was distracted by a rustling sound, as a statuesque, auburn-haired lady glided down the stairs. This was Carin, Countess von Fock; her sister was Eric's wife. Upright, round-faced, and tenderhearted, Carin was the thirty-one-year-old daughter of a Swedish officer and his Irish wife. She was bored with life in general and her officer husband, Nils von Kantzow, in particular: She was eager for adventure and hungered for romance. It is not impossible that having noticed a prominently featured interview of Göring published in the *Svenska Dagbladet* two weeks before —he had commented on a recent airplane crash—she and Eric had actually plotted to arrange the aviator's enforced sojourn at their castle.

Whatever the origins of their meeting, Göring fell deeply in love with Carin von Fock. She was nearly five years older; she was different from any other woman he had set eyes on. She showed him the tiny chapel of the family's private Edelweiss Order nestling behind the castle, and Hermann detected in her something of the maternal feeling that he had always missed in his own mother. Before flying back to Stockholm the next morning, he wrote in the guest book: "Hermann Göring, Kommandeur, Jagdgeschwader Freiherr von Richthofen, February 21, 1920."

Afterward, he penned these emotional lines, betraying a depth of feeling found scarcely anywhere else in his writings:

> I would like to thank you from my heart for the beautiful moment that I was allowed to spend in the Edelweiss chapel. You have no idea how I felt in this wonderful atmosphere. It was so

> quiet, so lovely, that I forgot all the earthly noise, all my worries,
> and felt as though in another world. . . . I was like a swimmer
> resting on a lonely island to gather new strength before he throws
> himself anew into the raging torrent of life. . . .

Her sister Lily had married a German officer (he had died on the battlefield),
and now Carin decided to divorce Nils and to marry a German officer too.

Between stolen weekends with Carin von Fock in Stockholm or at the
castle, Göring maintained his humdrum existence piloting air taxis for Svenska Lufttrafik. In their files is one report he wrote in March 1920: "When
the warmer weather set in," this read, "there were more requests for round-
trip flights, so it would be worth advertising these on Sundays." He added
his criticisms of their current organization: "There is much confusion about
who gives orders, distributes jobs, and takes responsibility."

A few days later, on April 11, 1920, *Svenska Dagbladet* reported that
Captain Hermann Göring, "who has for months been one of Stockholm's
most popular air chauffeurs," had shown off his white-cowled wartime Fokker fighter plane with its 185-horsepower BMW engine at an aerobatics
display.

Meanwhile his love affair with the married Swedish countess grew into a
public scandal in the straitlaced city. If anything at all sanctified it then, it
was the depth of the emotion that each felt for the other. This becomes clear
only now that the letters they exchanged have surfaced in the United States.
(From a surviving inventory of his most precious documents, stored in an
empty wine crate in the air-raid shelter at "Carinhall" in February 1944, it
is clear that they included her intimate letters to him, as well as his diaries;
they were among the cache plundered from his private train in Berchtesgaden
in 1945.) Carin's letters to Captain Göring hint at the mounting opposition
that her adulterous affair with an itinerant German aviator had aroused in
her parents; the estrangement from her father would last until her death.

That summer of 1920 Hermann and Carin traveled to Germany. (Nils was
away, taking a course at France's Saint-Cyr Military Academy.) Hermann's
older brother, Karl-Ernst, met them at the Munich railroad station. Carin
looked at the two brothers and decided they were both "German to their
fingertips." Hermann had gallantly filled her hotel room with roses, and he
took her to meet his mother, Fanny Göring (whom the Swedish countess
also described as "Germanic"). Fanny scolded Hermann like a small boy
—he had stolen Carin from her husband and from her seven-year-old son,
Thomas von Kantzow. Hermann stuck out his jaw, turned on his heel, and
took Carin defiantly into the mountains with him. They spent a few idyllic
weeks at Bayrischzell, in the depth of the Bavarian mountains. The photographs show her in a peasant costume, towering over her young lover, with
the pastures and mountains of Bavaria in the background.

As his marriage crumbled, Nils von Kantzow showed a heroic stoicism, and even a generosity that Carin surely ill deserved. He wrote to her parents saying that he still loved her; when he met her briefly in Berlin on August 4, she assured him that all she wanted from life was her mother, husband, and little Thomas, but when she returned to Sweden she added Hermann to that list and made it plain she wanted her German lover to come and live with her, even though it meant losing her husband. To her uncomprehending sorrow, Nils declined to let her salvage Thomas from the family collapse along with the other jointly owned property at No. 5, Karlavägen.

She wrote to Göring from that address on December 20, 1920, thanking him for two letters and telegrams from Berlin and Munich:

> Darling! You really need not have any concern for me. Nils is so nice to me, and no one else is angry with me. It is so terrible for me without you, my only eternally beloved. I feel more and more how deeply and warmly and sincerely I love you. I don't forget you for a minute. Thomas is my consolation. He is so sweet and dear and loves me so faithfully and deeply. He has gotten so big, and he laughs and kisses me every time he sees me. Today was his last day at school and he got the highest marks in every subject. He was so happy, he had two sweet tears in his blue eyes!

Her mother-in-law, she continued, "that old witch," had phoned Nils two days ago to ask for her address; Nils had said she was back in his home in Karlavägen, and his mother had congratulated him and written Carin a cloying letter reproaching her, which evoked from her only a scornful comment, written to her distant lover, "Isn't she a conceited, idiotic old monkey???"

> You asked me [wrote Carin to Hermann] about writing from Bayrischzell. Yes, darling, always write me at Karlavägen. It is after all better to be open about it. I told Nils the whole truth the first day I was back. I told him you were with me at Bayrischzell and that you had rented our house for me. He took it all very calmly and even said he was glad to know I was happy and hadn't been all by myself.

On the following day she wrote more, lamenting that Nils and her own family never left her alone—"Nils always wants to talk to me and in spite of the fact that he is nice and friendly, I am bored to death!" She went on:

> Darling, oh, how I long for you! . . .
> Moreover Nils still hasn't given me a cent. What a nerve! He knows I don't have anything. Today I told him, "You'll have to

give me a little money, I want to give Mama and my sisters
something for Christmas!"

"No, Carin dear," says he, "no need for you to do that: I'll
give presents to your relatives and friends!

"Have you ever heard anything so dumb? . . . This ignorance
makes him seem like a scoundrel, but at the same time like an
angel or a child. I get so nervous I can hardly stay in the same
room or house with him.

More and more I realize how much you mean to me. I love
you so much. You are everything to me. There is no other like
you. To me you are really my ideal in everything. You do everything so sweetly . . . You remember me with so many little things
and that makes my life so happy. Now, for the first time I realize
how accustomed I have become to you. It is difficult for me to
say it . . . I want you to feel it in your dear beloved heart! If I
could only say that with kisses and embraces, darling! I would
like to kiss you from one end to the other without stopping for
an hour. Do you really love me as much as you say? Is that
possible??

My thoughts are with you. You must feel my love everywhere,
in every little corner, table and chair; in my thoughts I kiss everything that is near you—that dear ugly old floor in the kitchen,
your bed, your chair. I am crying, I love you so much. I think
only of you, and I am true to you in everything.

The remainder of this letter makes plain that her disapproving sister Fanny
had chaperoned them in Bavaria. Fanny was scornful. "Look how he's
compromised Carin!" she exploded over one meal. "In Germany it's a
scandal for a woman to live the way she did and to do the things she did.
He was placing her in an impossible position in German eyes, and as a
German officer he must have known it."

"Carin is the one you should be angry with," their mother retorted. "Not
Göring."

Her cuckolded husband, Nils, continued to support her, but their curly-
haired boy, Thomas, was often crying, sleepless, and worried. "Nils could
not live without Thomas now," Fanny reproached her sister Carin. "Oh,
Nils . . . He is one of the noblest men I know."

Deaf to this reproach, Carin invited Göring to live with her in Stockholm
quite openly. He obeyed her call. Heedless of her parents' protests, they
took a small apartment in Östermalm. Uneasy at this irregular union, which
may have reminded him of his mother's liaison with Von Epenstein in his
own childhood, Göring pleaded with her to divorce Nils but she refused,
fearful of losing her son. Thomas lived with his father, torn between the two
ménages. He slipped off after school to visit his mama and "Uncle Göring."

Nils pleaded with her to return. Once he invited her to bring Hermann to lunch; young Thomas listened round-eyed as Göring dominated the table with tales of the "Red Baron" and aerial combat. The little boy noticed that his mother never took his eyes off the handsome aviator.

Unable to take the wagging tongues in Stockholm any longer, Hermann and his mistress left for Germany. They began a romantic existence in a little hunting lodge at Hochkreuth, near Bayrischzell, some miles from Munich. He registered at the university to study economic history, she earned money with painting and handicrafts. (There exists in the village to this day a painted cupboard door signed with her initials.) He found it was not easy for a retired army captain in his thirtieth year to embark on higher education; they were penniless, and when she fell ill he had to pawn her fur coat to pay the doctor's bill (Nils heroically cabled her the money to redeem the coat—and buy a ticket back to Stockholm.) Her mother tried to lure her home by offering the family's summer house near Drottningholm; in her reply, inviting her mama to Munich instead, Carin added the eloquent assurance: "Mama would not have to see Göring—even at a distance."

"Bavaria," she wrote in this letter, of May 11, 1922, "is a lovely countryside, so rich, so warm and so intellectual and strong—so unlike the rest of Germany. I am very happy here and feel very much at home. When I feel homesick for Sweden, it is really only a longing for Mama, Nils, the little boy, and those I love. But just that painful, insane longing means that I am nearly always melancholy. Oh, my own dear Mama, if only one didn't have such powerful love within one."

2

STORM TROOP COMMANDER

Two planets pass, so close that each is fractionally deflected by the other's course. So it is, sometimes, with humans too.

For Hermann Göring this celestial episode came late in 1922. The orbit of this out-of-work war hero intersected briefly with that of Adolf Hitler, unknown demagogue, one Saturday in October or November of that year, in Munich's Königsplatz. A demonstration had been called to protest the latest Allied demands on defeated Germany. Göring, who was himself trying to raise a small political party of ex-officers, heard shouts for a Herr Hitler to speak; people standing around told him that this Hitler headed a small National Socialist German Workers' party. Hitler, standing a few yards away from him, declined to speak, but something about this callow, slightly built man in his early thirties must have fascinated Göring, because he visited Hitler's regular Monday evening political at the Café Neumann two days later.

The topic was "The Versailles Peace Treaty and the Extradition of the German Army Commanders." Göring was much impressed by what Hitler said. Hitler explained that no Frenchman was likely to lose much sleep over the kind of language talked by the other speakers at the Königsplatz demonstration—"You've got to have bayonets to back up any threats!" he exclaimed. "Down with Versailles!" he shouted.

Goddammit, thought Göring, that's the stuff, he enlisted in Hitler's new party the next day.

Hitler told him he needed people just like him—famous, highly decorated—in the party. For Göring, Hitler also filled a need. Meeting Hitler, he had at last found a replacement for his dead father, his godfather, and the kaiser.

The attraction between them was mutual. Impressed by the fiery speech that Captain Göring delivered at the Café Neumann—about how officers put honor first in any conflict of interests—Hitler recalled twenty years afterward, "He'd been to those evenings of mine several times, and I found I liked him. I made him commander of my SA."

At that time the Sturmabteilung, or storm detachment, was, as Hitler was the first to admit, just a "motley rabble." These two thousand unemployed roughnecks had the job of stewarding Hitler's meetings and disrupting his rivals'—but he had military ambitions for the SA that went far beyond this.

The SA was only one of several semi-legal private armies that had sprung up in the aftermath of Versailles. The Bavarian authorities not only tolerated this but colluded with them to a degree that becomes clear only from the three thousand closely typed pages of the Hitler trial that followed the unsuccessful Nazi coup of November 1923. This bloody fiasco had its origins in January 1923. Since Germany was unable to pay reparations, France and Belgium sent in their armies to occupy the rich Ruhr industrial region. Regular army officers in Berlin and Munich—men like the scar-faced army captain Ernst Röhm—itched to take action against the French and saw in the private political armies a reservoir of semi-trained military personnel. Fifteen days after the invasion of the Ruhr, Lieutenant General Otto von Lossow, the new army commander in Bavaria, granted Hitler his first interview, because Hitler's SA "army" was by now one of the largest.

Göring took Carin along to the SA's first big rally two days later, on January 28, 1923.

He had moved with her into a villa in Reginwald Strasse at Obermenzing, just outside the boundary of Munich, in November 1922, soon after Hitler gave him command of the SA. Carin had at once set about furnishing this, the first home they could call their own.

Nils, whose munificence surpasses comprehension, had sent her the money to furnish this villa. One room was lit by a tinted pink window—the rose-hued sunlight played across a bowl of red roses to where her white harmonium stood amid the pink and white fur rugs beneath her mother's portrait. Her bedroom had pink curtains and a bed canopied in blue brocade and veiled in white lace. There was nothing of this femininity in Hermann's quarters —his room was heavy with carved oak furniture and lit by a window painted with knights in armor. A concealed cellar had an open fireplace and oak cupboards around the walls.

They married in February—probably under pressure from the prudish Adolf Hitler. Although Hermann Göring would later encourage biographers to believe that they had married one year earlier, the family papers show that her divorce had only become absolute in December 1922, and the registry at Munich's city hall confirms that the marriage was solemnized at Obermenzing on February 3, 1923. His private papers contained proof of a civil ceremony in Stockholm on January 25; the marriage certificate, which was looted along with his other papers in 1945, has now been donated anonymously to the Institute of Contemporary History in Munich, and shows the date February 3, 1923. His comrades of the old Richthofen Squadron formed the guard of honor.

This second marriage changed Carin's life. "God!" she enthused to a friend. "How wonderful it is to have a husband who doesn't take two days to see the point of a joke." Nils now had little to laugh about; years later he would still refer to Carin as his "lost treasure." Carin did not care.

> Aunt Mary [she wrote to her little boy Thomas that spring of 1923] will have told you that I am now married to Captain Göring . . . You know, the raw climate in Sweden was none too good for my health . . . We have known Captain Göring since that time in Stockholm, you will remember, and he was so kind . . . to your mama when she was lonely in a foreign country.
>
> And then I found that I was beginning to like him so much that I wanted to marry him. You see, sweetheart, he has made your mama very happy. And you mustn't be upset about it, and it won't interfere with our love for each other, dearest Thomas.
>
> You see, I love you best of all . . .

Deepening his ties with the private armies in Bavaria, General von Lossow agreed to Hitler's request that the SA troops should be given clandestine army training. "Hitler's well-known powers of charm, persuasion, and eloquence," the general would wanly admit, "were not without effect on me."

Göring had armed and enlarged the SA far beyond the boundaries of Munich. Four years younger than Hitler, he was still more of a drifter and adventurer than political agitator. He would later recall the first pitched battle with the Communists in Munich (on March 1, 1923) only for the beerhall bruises given and received. "Boy, how those beer mugs flew!" he reminisced twenty years later to American historian George Shuster, without a trace of apology. "One nearly laid me out!"

A few days previously Berlin had advised General von Lossow that in May the army would begin operations against the French occupying the Ruhr. Lossow made preparations under the code name *Spring Training* and informed Göring that the SA and other "patriotic bodies" would be recruited for the campaign.

Hitler was uneasy. He argued that this sequence was wrong. "There's no point," he told the general, "in staging an attack on the external enemy before the domestic political issue has been dealt with"—by which he meant disposing of the feeble, "Jew-ridden" central government in Berlin.

Von Lossow paid no heed. To the aristocrats who ruled Bavaria, Hitler cut an unimpressive figure at this time. He was so poor that during one Easter outing Göring was seen giving him pocket money—in fact, Göring and his new wife sank much of their own money into the party. The two men were inseparable, however; on April 15, when Hitler took the salute at the big review of his troops, he stood in Göring's new car, a twenty-five-horsepower Mercedes-Benz 16, with his arm outstretched for an hour as the thousands of SA men trooped past in uniform (field-gray ski caps and windbreakers with swastika armbands).

"Today," wrote Carin proudly to little Thomas von Kantzow in Stockholm after watching this thrilling, ominous spectacle:

> the Beloved One paraded his army of true young Germans before his Führer, and I saw his face light up as he watched them pass by. The Beloved One has worked so hard with them, has instilled so much of his own bravery and heroism into them, that what was once a rabble—and I must confess sometimes a rough and rather terrifying one—has been transformed into a veritable Army of Light, a band of eager crusaders ready to march at the Führer's orders to render this unhappy country free once more . . .
>
> After it was over, the Führer embraced the Beloved One and told me that if he said what he really thought of his achievement the Beloved One would get a swollen head.
>
> I said that my own head was already swollen with pride, and he kissed my hand and said, "No head so pretty as yours could ever be swollen."

The Bavarians were ready for action against France, but Berlin had cold feet. Worse, when Hitler and Göring tried to force the Bavarian government's hand by holding a provocative anti-Communist May Day parade in an arena north of Munich, General von Lossow called in all the army weapons that he had previously allowed the SA to carry. "What mattered," explained the general to the judges one year later, "was this: Who was in charge in this country? . . . This first trial of strength ended with Hitler's defeat, and we had nothing more to do with one another."

It was a serious loss of face for Hitler, Göring, and the SA.

"An officer never breaks his word!" Göring told Hitler, perplexed.

In August 1923 his widowed mother died. This was a watershed in his career, and he committed himself recklessly from this time on to the Nazi movement. On August 24, Hitler issued to him his first Vollmacht, or supreme authority to act in his behalf. The work was hard, but Göring thrived on it. "Often," he bragged a year later to an Italian correspondent, "I was on the go until four A.M. and was back at the office at seven A.M. the next day. I didn't have a moment's respite all day. One visitor followed the other . . . You know we Germans are great beavers for work. Out of twenty-four hours we will work twenty-three! Believe me, I have often—very often—come home dead tired at eleven P.M., spent fifteen minutes grabbing some tea or supper with my wife and then, instead of going to bed, reviewed the day's activities for two or three hours; the next morning at seven A.M. the first adjutant would come to report."

Hitler became a frequent visitor to the Göring household, and Carin heard them endlessly discussing the same old topics—Chancellor Gustav Stresemann, his "Jew government" in Berlin, and the economic crisis since Versailles. Robbed of the Ruhr industries, the economy had toppled into an abyss. In the Ruhr, the French occupation troops sent to the firing squad any Germans who offered resistance. Currency had become virtually valueless: On August 1, one American dollar equaled three million German Reichsmarks; by late September it would buy 142 million Reichsmarks—people had to pay even the smallest bills with suitcases of overprinted and double-overprinted paper money.

Hitler and Göring, the SA, and the other private armies were restless for action—any kind of action. But Berlin refused now to act; *Spring Training* was off.

Envious of Benito Mussolini's recent March on Rome, Hitler and Göring hatched grandiose plans to raise all Bavaria for a March on Berlin. But time was running out. Feeding on the economic chaos, Communist revolutions had broken out in Saxony and Thuringia, to the north of Bavaria. Hitler urged Bavaria to act and offered his "troops" in support.

Göring, however, had, other preoccupations now. Carin had contracted a lung infection at his mother's funeral and returned to Stockholm, where heart problems forced her into the Vita Kors Nursing Home at Brunkeberstorg.

Göring remained in Germany at Hitler's side. Early in October 1923 he wrote to Carin's mother, adopting the ornate style customary in her family. "I sense your gentle aura, and kiss your sweet hands!" he wrote. "Then a profound stillness comes over me and I sense your helping prayers."

"Over here," he continued, turning to the political crisis in Bavaria, "life is like a seething volcano whose destructive lava may at any moment spew forth across the country . . . We are working feverishly and stand by our aim: the liberation and revival of Germany." He concluded by begging the countess to take care of his Carin—"She is everything to me."

Countess von Fock replied sending Göring twenty gold crowns ("from Carin") and a food parcel containing rarities like coffee and butter.

Still ailing, Carin returned to her Hermann a few days later. "I have a slight cold," she wrote to Thomas from Munich, "and am writing this in bed, where the Beloved insists I must stay until I am better. He is very busy these days and great events are in the offing, but until I am better he insists that I mustn't bother myself with them. He looks tired and doesn't get enough sleep, and he wears himself out traveling miles just to see me for a few moments."

They were both homesick for Sweden, but a sense of destiny kept Hermann in Bavaria. "Times are grim here," he wrote to Carin's mother on October 23. "Strife and deprivation ravage the country, and the hour is not far off when we must take responsibility for the future."

At a Nuremberg rally early in September 1923 Hitler had pronounced, "In a few weeks the dice will roll!" At this rally he and the right-wing paramilitary organization had set up the "Combat League" (*Kampfbund*): Colonel Hermann Kriebel, who had served on the staff of the redoubtable General Erich von Ludendorff, took military command, and Dr. Max von Scheubner-Richter, a pharmacist, was secretary general. The Combat League united the private armies in Bavaria—Göring's SA, the Reich War Flag (*Reichskriegsflagge*) headed by Ernst Röhm, and the Highland League (*Bund Oberland*); by the end of September 1923 the latter two had agreed to obey the directives of the SA and Adolf Hitler.

On September 26, in the rising economic emergency, the Bavarian prime minister had appointed a General-Staatskommissar with dictatorial power, and, like Hitler, this man, Dr. Gustav von Kahr, began talking of using force to install a right-wing dictatorship in Berlin. General von Lossow was initially dubious. But neither the general nor Kahr could afford to hold the Nazis—Hitler's National Socialists—at arm's length for long. When Berlin ordered Lossow to prepare to send Bavarian battalions to quell the Communist uprising in Saxony, Kahr instructed General von Lossow to resume his previous fruitful contacts with the right-wing organizations to fill the gaps in his army.

Lossow eventually went further. He updated the operational plan called *Spring Training* and gave it a new code name, *Autumn Training*. It shortly became clear that the enemy was neither the French occupation force in the Ruhr nor the Communists in Saxony, but Stresemann's regime in Berlin. Kahr's deputy made this plain in a rabble-rousing speech to right-wingers on October 20: "We don't say 'Let's Dump Berlin!' " he declared. "We're not separatists. What we say is, 'Let's March on Berlin!' For two months Berlin has spouted one lie after another. What else can you expect from such a gang of Jews? Fall in behind Kahr!" he appealed. "As from today we're marching side by side with Hitler."

All of this came out at the later trial. "The authorities," Hitler testified there, "the state policy, and the army, now resumed the training of our

Sturmabteilung in their barracks.'' To rub this point in he added, ''From Day One our troops were training in launching a mobile war of attack northward,'' i.e., against Berlin.

Hitler and Göring emphasized in their instructions to the Combat League that they would be marching side by side with the army. In his ten-minute speech to Göring's SA commanders on October 23, at Nazi party headquarters in Munich, Hitler underlined that there must be the closest collaboration between the Combat League, the army, and the police. ''I would be an idiot,'' he stated, ''to attempt anything against them.'' Göring for his part outlined in detail how the Combat League ''troops'' would be spliced into the nationalist army for the March on Berlin. General von Ludendorff would march at their head.

Gregor Strasser, commander of the SA battalion at Landshut, later testified that Göring harped on the need to act in ''total conformity'' with the regular army. When Strasser objected that his battalion's weapons were all rusty and unusable, Göring assured him that the army had agreed to clean and restore the guns in time. On the next day Lieutenant Hoffmann, at the 19th Infantry Regiment barracks, indicated that the march would take place in two weeks' time, and Strasser arranged to deliver seven hundred rifles to the barracks for servicing before then.

That same afternoon, October 24, 1923, Lossow told the officers of these private armies, assembled at his headquarters, that they were not going to follow a narrow, Bavarian line, but the nationalist black-white-and-red one. One of the army colonels present, Etzel, heard him talk quite openly of a March on Berlin (at the Hitler trial Lossow would deny it). The Bavarian Army now issued order No. la-800 to the Combat League commanders, including Göring, directing them to provide trained paramilitary personnel to the army preparatory to operation *Autumn Training*.

By this time, it must be stressed, the Communist uprisings in Saxony and Thuringia had been put down, so this army order can only have been for a March on Berlin. ''Our impression,'' testified one recipient, ''was that the army district headquarters and the National Socialists had now reached agreement.''

Feverish activity began. Rifles were serviced, museums scoured for artillery pieces; SA and Oberland men, volunteering for *Autumn Training*, were detailed to report to the ''sports commander'' at the infantry regiment barracks on November 11.

Göring had reason to believe that the police would be on Hitler's side. The Bavarian police commander, Colonel Hans Ritter von Seisser, was the third member of the blue-blooded triumvirate that ruled Bavaria. His green-uniformed state police (*Landespolizei*) lived like soldiers in barracks and were equipped with heavy weaponry. Hitler had established contact with Seisser on October 25, delivered a speech attacking the parliamentary system, argued that only a military dictatorship under Ludendorff could save Germany, and held out the alluring prospect that Seisser would take over the Reich police force.

Seisser objected that Ludendorff, a militant nationalist, was anathema to foreign countries.

"I need him to win over the Reichswehr," Hitler explained, referring to the puny, post-Versailles German Army. "There's not one German soldier who will open fire on Ludendorff."

Two days later Seisser told his officers to get ready for the March on Berlin.

> In Berlin [he pronounced in this speech] there's a Jew-boy gov-
> ernment. It is quite incapable of restoring the Reich to good health.
> So Mr. von Kahr's intention is to heal Germany, taking Bavaria
> as the starting point. The Reich government is going to be over-
> thrown and replaced by a dictatorship of a handful of nationalists.
> For the March on Berlin we shall make units of the state police
> available with immediate effect.

Police Captain Ruder took a shorthand note of these words. Since Hermann Göring and dozens of others would be scythed down by state-police machine-gun bullets only a few days later, they took some explaining at the Hitler trial—as did the fact that Seisser had ordered on October 28, 1923, a massive increase in munitions output, which could only have been in anticipation of the March on Berlin.

There was quite evidently no time to be lost. German currency was inflating to galactic figures. At the end of October 1923, one U.S. dollar would cost 270,000 million Reichsmarks.

After visiting General von Lossow, SA Commander Hermann Göring told his officers, "Lossow is with us. We're on our way!"

Almost at once, however, Hitler detected signs that the triumvirate was getting cold feet. Lossow inexplicably banned his public meetings after October 30. To cheering Nazi supporters packing the Krone Circus amphitheater that evening Hitler declared, "The German problem will be solved for me only when our red-white-and-black swastika banner is fluttering over the [presidential] palace in Berlin."

The next day he learned that Bavarian police chief Colonel Seisser was about to travel to Berlin for talks with the central government.

"If you don't act when you get back," Hitler warned the colonel at a private meeting, "I shall consider myself at liberty to take action for you!"

Seisser reminded him that he had promised not to do anything against the army or state police.

Hitler retorted that Göring's SA and the other "troops" were already straining at the leash. He repeated: If the triumvirate did not march when Seisser came back, he would withdraw all undertakings.

What did happen in Berlin is not clear. Whatever it was, after Seisser returned to Munich on the morning of November 4, he and the other two triumvirate members cold-shouldered Hitler and the Combat League. Summoning the latter's officers and those of the Highland League to his own headquarters on the sixth, Gustav von Kahr advised them not to indulge in flights of fancy. "We are all agreed on the need for a new nationalist government," he said. "But we must all stand shoulder to shoulder. We must proceed to a well-thought-out, adequately prepared, and uniform plan."

General von Lossow took the same negative line. He promised to stand by Kahr and to back any scheme that promised success. "But," he sniffed, referring to two recent revolutionary fiascos, "don't expect me to join in, if it's going to be just another Kapp Putsch or Küstrin Uprising." He pulled a notebook out of his pocket and wagged it at Colonel Kriebel (Combat League) and Dr. Weber (Oberland). "Believe me," he intoned, as the secret conference ended, "I want to march too. But I won't do it until my little notebook tells me we've got at least a fifty-one percent chance of pulling it off."

One week before, Hitler had threatened not to tolerate any further procrastination by the triumvirate. Now, on the evening of November 6, he called his men together and set the ball rolling. They would march on Sunday the eleventh. The next morning, meeting with Göring and Kriebel, Hitler sketched out the broad outline of the planned coup: Their "troops" would seize the major towns, railroad stations, telecommunications buildings, and city halls throughout Bavaria. It sounded so easy that they brought forward the zero hour. Why not strike the very next day, November 8, 1923?

The odor of revolution, faint but unmistakable, drifted into Lossow's office at the Army Headquarters Building in Schönfeld Strasse that afternoon, November 7. There were telephone intercepts and police agents' reports too.

The general's chief of staff, Lieutenant Colonel Baron von Berchem, told his assembled officers that Kahr was talking of acting in fourteen days' time, but that Lossow believed Hitler no longer intended to wait, in which case they, the army, would have to stop him. "He has yet to prove," interrupted Lossow, "that he is the German Mussolini he seems to think he is."

The Nazi coup began to roll. That evening Kahr received an unscheduled invitation. "On the night of November 7," he would testify:

> I learned to my surprise that the right-wing patriotic organizations were planning a major demonstration at the Bürgerbräu beer cellar on the eighth, and that they were expecting me to come and make a speech.
>
> I was a bit queasy about this and made some inquiries. They told me that demand had been enormous—they had tried to book an even bigger hall, they said, but only the Bürgerbräu was available. So really I had no alternative but to comply.

Seduced and blinded by this unsubtle flummery, he ordered his press chief to provide free beer for the three thousand people he expected to turn up. Had he known that the reason the other halls were not available was that the Nazis had booked them all too (as revolutionary assembly points) and had he known that he was in fact being invited to attend a revolution, Gustav von Kahr might well have preferred to stay away.

3
PUTSCH

November 8, 1923, was to be a painful turning point in the lives of both Hitler and Göring. Icy cold and bitterly windy, the dawn broke to the unfamiliar sound of marching feet in Munich; strange uniforms were seen; there seemed to be ancient carbines and revolvers everywhere. Trucks disgorged Göring's ski-capped SA men. The railroad stations rang with mountain boots as Weber's men arrived from the Alpine highlands, sporting helmets and Edelweiss insignia.

Göring's wife was still laid low with the pneumonia she had caught at Fanny Göring's funeral. He knelt at Carin's bedside, kissed her, and said he might be late that night; then he drove downtown in the Mercedes-Benz, taking the shiny black leather coat and steel helmet with him. Carin knew nothing of what was afoot—nor did most of Göring's commanders.

By 10:00 A.M. he had issued orders to a trusted handful of them. Wilhelm Brückner, a lanky ex-marine gunner, was to take two SA "battalions" to the Bürgerbräu that evening to await further orders; others would muster at the Arzberger and Hofbräu beer cellars. The one-hundred-strong elite force, the Adolf Hitler Shock Troop, was to stand by at the Torbräu. Rohm's organization had already booked the Löwenbräu beer hall across town.

Some word of all this reached the triumvirate, but it failed to trigger adequate alarm. At Kahr's request Colonel von Seisser had that morning briefed his state police. "I told them," he testified, "that some people intended to set up a Reich dictatorship with its base here in Munich, and to carry it northward by force. And I said that this was bound to lead to catastrophe."

At 3:00 P.M. Dr. Weber telephoned Seisser to ask if he was definitely going to be at that evening's "support demonstration" at the Bürgerbräu. Seisser confirmed that he would be there.

They all drove across the River Isar that evening to the great beer hall— Seisser, Kahr, his deputy, and a police major in one car, and General von Lossow in another. Kahr was queasy again when he saw the way the audience was overflowing onto the sidewalks outside the packed beer hall, and the hundreds of political uniforms among them. He recognized many of his friends, looking equally perplexed. Later he learned that the Nazi conspirators had invited Bavaria's entire government and military elite.

"Herr Hitler has said he's coming too," apologized one organizer, Kommerzienrat Eugen Zentz. "But you are please to start without him. He'll be here shortly."

Seldom can sheep have herded themselves so obligingly into the shearing pen. Kahr elbowed his way through the five thousand people jammed into the cavernous, two-hundred-foot-long hall, climbed onto the rostrum, and unfolded his notes.

Hitler arrived in the foyer. Rather oddly, he was wearing a black frock coat with his Iron Cross. He and Scheubner-Richter of the Combat League had difficulty getting in: Police were already sealing off the building because it was so full, so Hitler went outside again to await the arrival of Göring and the shock troop from the Torbräu. They arrived at 8:34 P.M. Leaving one man behind with a machine gun to cover the doors, he took three men with him, flung open the doors, and plunged into the hall, drawing his Browning .08 revolver. ("You're hardly going to go in waving a palm branch!" he scoffed to his later judges.) An uproar broke out. Kahr faltered in midsentence, then dried up. People climbed onto chairs to look. Police Chief Seisser heard voices shouting, "It's Hitler!" and he saw a wedge of armed, helmeted men pushing through the hall toward them. Two paces from the rostrum Hitler halted, glared at Kahr, pocketed his revolver, and climbed onto a chair.

The din was thunderous. Kahr just gasped, clutching his half-finished speech. As Hitler swung around to face the audience, they could see him shouting but could not hear what. Impatient, Hitler tugged the Browning out of his back pocket again, cocked it with his left hand in a swift move, and loosed off a shot into the ceiling. "The national revolution has begun," he screamed. "I have six hundred heavily armed men surrounding this hall. Nobody is to leave!"

There were shouts of anger and disbelief.

"If you don't quiet down," he shouted, "I'll have a machine gun set up in the gallery."

His voice forced and unnatural, he rounded on Kahr and ordered him off the rostrum. Then he told the three Bavarian leaders to accompany him outside, promising, "I can vouch for your safety."

They filed out meekly behind him—Kahr, Lossow, and Seisser—leaving consternation behind them. They saw no sign of six hundred men surrounding the building, just a handful of city police lolling around the foyer and a dozen SA storm troopers under Göring's command. The former air-force captain had unbuttoned his black leather coat to reveal the blue enamel of his Pour le Mérite.

"A fine mess your police have let us get into!" Kahr snapped to Seisser.

"Put on an act," advised General von Lossow, sotto voce.

More police were coming, but not to help them: When the commander of the thirty-strong police detachment sent to the hall had appealed to Göring for help, the latter had merely tapped his watch and said with a broad grin, "Wait till eight-forty. Frick's coming then." (Wilhelm Frick, chief of Munich's political police, had been a Hitler supporter for some time.) At that very moment the Nazis' code word, *Safely Delivered*, was being telephoned to Frick at police headquarters—and to a pay-phone at the Löwenbräu beer hall, where Ernst Röhm had assembled his Reichskriegsflagge men. The audience there saw Röhm's chauffeur whisper to him, then Röhm took the stage and announced that the government had been overthrown and that a new one was being formed. He instructed his "troops" to form up outside for the march across town to join Hitler at the Bürgerbräu.

Over at the Bürgerbräu beer hall Hitler's captive audience was growing restless as his deliberations with the triumvirate dragged on. There were loud shouts of "Scandal!" and jeers of "South America!" (in mocking reference to that continent's frequent petty revolutions). Colonel Kriebel ordered Göring to restore order; Göring put on his helmet, drew his gun, and waded in through the throng. To most of the audience, the young man who mounted the stage was unknown. Witnesses spoke later of an officer, an aviator, an air-force captain. Blue eyes blazing, jaw thrust forward, he glared at the five thousand faces and shouted for silence, then he too loosed off a pistol shot into the ceiling. Bellowing at the top of his voice, he promised that no harm was going to come to the Bavarian leaders—the ones who were going to be got rid of, he declared, were "the wretched Jews (*elende Judenschaft*) in Berlin." (At this, there were faint cheers.) "At this very moment," he continued, "units of the army and Landespolizei are marching out of their barracks with colors flying to join with us."

That sank in. A hush fell across the cavernous hall.

Meantime, he apologized, nobody could leave the building.

"Be patient," he cried jovially. "You've all got your beer!"

It was going to be a long night. Colonel Kriebel instructed Göring to use his SA men to supervise the feeding of these five thousand, and sent a motor cyclist to head off Röhm's troops and send them to Lossow's headquarters, where they were to greet the general with a guard of honor on his return from the Bürgerbräu. "I reported first to Herr Hitler," testified Lieutenant Brückner at the later trial, "then to my superior officer, Captain Göring. He told me to march my troops into the Bürgerbräu, where everybody was to rest and be victualed. That took up most of the night."

Hitler himself was making little progress in his attempts to win over the angry triumvirate. Göring left General von Lossow in little doubt of his private opinion of him. "What does an old general have to do, anyway?" he sneered. "Just sign a few orders . . . I can do anything he can. I can be a division commander too—let's sack him here and now."

The threat of dismissal had little effect. As Hitler pleaded and cajoled with Kahr, Seisser, and Lossow, the angry hubbub from the hall arose again. Leaving Göring to continue the argument, Hitler pushed through to the front of the hall again, mounted the rostrum, and delivered a speech that was described by historian Alexander von Müller, who witnessed it, as a masterpiece of rhetoric. "It turned that vast assemblage inside out," said Professor von Müller, "smoothly as a glove."

The triumvirate, Hitler announced, were all but won over. He proposed that General von Ludendorff become the "reorganizer" of the national army, and that Lossow and Seisser take command of the Reich's army and police. Hitler pronounced the dismissal of the Bavarian government, and loftily threw in the dismissal of Reich President Ebert and Chancellor Stresemann for good measure. "I therefore propose," he concluded, "that I take over political leadership of this provisional national government." He appealed to them all to fall in behind Kahr, Lossow, and Seisser if they backed the revolution.

This did the trick. Frenzied cheers greeted the announcement. Hitler had the three men brought back in—to renewed frenetic applause—as though they were a vaudeville act.

Their faces were a picture. Professor Müller described Kahr's as like a mask, Seisser's as agitated and pale, Lossow's as "mocking and foxy." Kahr spoke a few brave words of acceptance, stuttered something—to more storms of applause—about taking over the destiny of Bavaria as regent for the monarchy that "disloyal hands" had struck down five years before. Seisser also spoke a few words, and then Lossow—nudged into reluctant oratory by Hitler.

By this time war-hero Ludendorff had arrived, fetched by Scheubner-Richter in Hitler's Mercedes. The audience rose to its feet to cheer the general. Up on the stage, Hitler shook each man's hand—as he clasped Gustav von Kahr's right hand the latter dramatically placed his left hand on top, to seal their bargain. As if conducted by an unseen baton, five thousand throats burst forth into the national anthem. As Hitler stood at attention, ramrod stiff, his face illuminated by a childlike ecstasy, Ludendorff joined him and stood, ashen with suppressed emotion, at his side.

Outside, the thump and blare of brass bands announced the arrival of one thousand officer cadets; they had marched over from the infantry school with swastika flags fluttering at their head. Ludendorff and Hitler went out to give the salute. Word came that the railroad station and telegraph office were in the hands of Bund Oberland men, that Lossow's army district was firmly in the hands of Röhm's "troops." Hitler was euphoric: The revolution seemed to have succeeded. Göring sent word of his triumph to Carin on her sickbed that same night.

All too carelessly, Göring now accepted the word of Kahr, Lossow, and Seisser, and allowed them to return to their ministries while Hitler and Ludendorff were momentarily called away. Kahr seemed to have been won over, and the two others were officers whose word was surely not in doubt; besides, Göring and the young former fighter pilot Rudolf Hess had taken half a dozen Bavarian ministers as hostages from the audience in the beer hall, and they were even now being whisked off to a safe house in the suburbs.

Kahr at first went along with Hitler's revolutionary intent that night. But then, during those wee small hours of the morning in which men lose faith and enterprise, the revolution began to fall apart. Kahr and Seisser joined General von Lossow in the safety of the 19th Infantry Regiment barracks (since Lossow's own building had been occupied at midnight by Röhm), and they began to backtrack on the promises they had given to Hitler. They ordered their press chief to ensure that not one Munich newspaper appeared, and at 2:50 A.M. they issued a bulletin to all German radio stations under the heading "General Staatskommissar von Kahr, General von Lossow and Colonel von Seisser repudiate Hitler putsch." "The opinions expressed by us at the Bürgerbräu assembly," the brief bulletin explained, "were extracted at gunpoint and are invalid. Watch out for misuse of above names."

Ten minutes after that they issued a further radio bulletin: "Barracks and most key buildings are in army and Landespolizei hands. Reinforcements are on their way. City quiet."

Puzzled by the failure of General von Lossow to arrive at army district headquarters, Röhm ordered his guard of honor to stand down. By 6:00 A.M. it was dawning on the Nazis that they had been double-crossed. Hitler and Ludendorff could find no sign of the missing triumvirate, while over at the Bürgerbräu Captain Göring was remarking uneasily to his lieutenant, Brückner, "It is odd that none of them can be reached." Guessing that this meant trouble, he sent Brückner out to barricade the bridges across the River Isar. As Hitler and Ludendorff drove back from visiting Röhm, they saw billposters at work across the whole city, putting up, on Kahr's orders, placards repudiating the Hitler putsch as "senseless," banning the Nazi party, and promising ruthless punishment of the guilty.

Something had clearly gone wrong. Back at the Bürgerbräu beer hall Hitler and Ludendorff conferred with Göring, as the Nazi storm troopers mingled with the infantry cadets and party men, all hungry and unshaven. General von Ludendorff faced a dilemma: He told an intimate friend later that day, "It was clear that the Nazi movement was to all intents and purposes finished. It was quite plain to me where my duty lay. I would have been a cowardly dog if I had left Hitler in the lurch now."

Göring urged Hitler to retreat to Rosenheim, south of Munich, and regroup there. Ludendorff would not even hear of it. "Now is the time to show what we're made of," he stoutly declared. "Let's show we're worthy of leading the nationalist movement."

Thus Adolf Hitler, revolutionary and would-be statesman, prepared on this dull, overcast, chilly November 9 to meet his destiny. He, Ludendorff, and Göring decided to march their men into the city center to prove that they were not finished. They were sure of the people's backing. Hitler had the infantry cadets lined up outside the beer hall and delivered a powerful speech to them. They swore allegiance to him. He felt immortal. His hour had come. He sent armed men into the city to requisition funds; they took 14,605,000 billion Reichsmarks from the Jewish bank-note printers Parvus & Company, and gave a Nazi receipt in exchange. Meanwhile, Hitler acted to maintain order. Learning that one Nazi squad had ransacked a kosher grocery store during the night, he sent for the ex-army lieutenant who had led the raid.

"We took off our Nazi insignia first!" expostulated the officer—to no avail, as Hitler dismissed him from the party on the spot. "I shall see that no other nationalist unit allows you to join either!" Göring goggled at this exchange, as did a police sergeant who testified to it at the Hitler trial a few weeks later.

The march into the city center would begin at noon. Göring meanwhile sent shock troops to pick up still more hostages. They burst into the city-council chamber at 11:00 A.M., singled out the Burgomaster and nine terrified Socialist councillors and frog-marched them outside. "They had it coming to them," said Hitler later, without a trace of remorse. "In that same town hall a few months earlier we had heard them say that Bismarck was the biggest swine and gangster in Germany's history." The hostages were not treated gently. "We ran the gauntlet of punches, oaths, and human spittle," protested Socialist majority leader Albert Nussbaum at the trial, "all the way across the square until we were tossed into a truck and driven off to the Bürgerbräu."

Hitler ran his eye over Göring's ten new hostages without enthusiasm. He said nothing, but ordered a lame hostage released.

A few minutes before noon the Nazis and storm troopers formed up into a marching column outside the beer hall. Hitler took his place in the front rank flanked by Göring and Ludendorff. "We leaders went out in front," he proudly testified at the trial, "because we're not cast from the same mold as the Communists. They like to lag behind a bit, while somebody else goes over the top of the barricades."

As they marched off, somebody shouted to the storm troopers guarding the hostages—it was probably Göring himself—"If the army opens fire on us, you'll have to bayonet them or smash their skulls with your rifle butts!" (Colonel Kriebel had ordered all firearms to be unloaded to avoid any accidental shooting.) The two thousand or so marchers were led by two flag-bearers carrying the colors of the Nazi party and the Bund Oberland, each flanked by two helmeted troopers with fixed bayonets or drawn sabers. The Oberland column headed by Weber was on the right, the column of SA and shock-troop men headed by Göring and Hitler was on the left. Göring was marching at Hitler's immediate left. There was no clear plan of action, nobody knew where the march was heading. As they reached the river, they saw ten green-uniformed *Landespolizei* officers forming a thin cordon across the Ludwig Bridge. An hour earlier their officer had formally warned Göring and Brückner that he would not allow any march to pass over his bridge into the city center. They saw the *Landespolizei* clap ammunition drums into their machine guns, but the first ranks of marchers began lustily singing the national anthem, while others shouted, "Don't shoot!" and "We have Ludendorff with us!"; the sheer momentum of the march carried it right through the cordon before the order to open fire could be given.

Munich's burghers poured into the streets to watch the unforgettable spectacle. Hitler's two thousand doubled as the citizens fell in behind. The marchers now broke into SA battle songs. Passing the city hall, they could see its façade now draped with the pre-Weimar colors, and there were loud cheers; a swastika banner was run up its captured flagpole. "As we came through the arch," Colonel Kriebel testified, "we were greeted by universal enthusiasm. The whole square was black with people, and everybody was singing patriotic songs. They all fell in behind, there were shouts of Heil, and then more singing."

Many thought that the march would halt right there.

The first volley cut down the front rank of marchers instantly. Dr. Weber saw a broad-shouldered man, Hitler's bodyguard, bound forward. "Don't shoot!" he called out before a bullet felled him too. "It's Ludendorff!" The general had dropped with all the animal reflexes of a trained infantryman. Hitler had been pulled violently to the ground by the dying Kampfbund leader Scheubner-Richter, who had been shot through the heart. Police swarmed down the steps of the Feldherrnhalle to finish off the injured. "I saw one Landespolizei officer," Kriebel alleged at the trial, "put a round at three paces into somebody lying on the ground—it was either Ludendorff's valet or Hitler's bodyguard. Then he reloaded and fired another bullet into him so that the body kicked into the air."

As the rattle of rifle fire ended, Hitler picked himself up. Fourteen of his men, and four policemen, were dead. As for Hermann Göring, Carin's sister Fanny glimpsed him lying motionless in a widening pool of blood and thought that he too had been killed.

It was a tragic and senseless outcome. Cursing themselves for their own folly, Hitler and Ludendorff realized in retrospect how weak their allies had been. "The hopes that inspired us all on the evening of November 8," said the general, "hopes that we could save our fatherland and restore the nation's will, were dashed because Messrs. Kahr, Lossow, and Seisser lost sight of the main objective: because the Big Moment found only little men within them."

What had become of Göring?

A police marksman's bullet had pierced his groin, only millimeters from an artery. Some of his own men found him and carried him to the first door showing a doctor's nameplate in the nearby Residenz Strasse. Years later his adjutant Karl Bodenschatz would reveal, "The people on the ground floor threw him out, but there was an elderly Jewish couple upstairs, and they took him in." Ilse Ballin, wife of a Jewish furniture dealer,* gave Göring first aid, then, helped by her sister, carried him round to the clinic of a friend, Professor Alwin Ritter von Ach. He found the entry and exit wounds still foul with mud and gravel, and did what he could to ease the pain.

Friends took word of Hermann's misfortune to Carin who bravely came to hold his hand and plan his escape. She took him by car down to Partenkirchen, seventy miles south of Munich, where he was hidden in the villa of a wealthy Dutch sympathizer, Major Schuler van Krieken. Clearly he could not stay long, and plans were laid to smuggle the Görings out of the country. Kriebel published two obituary lists, including the name of "Göhring," to draw the heat off him, but the police authorities were not deceived and issued a warrant for his arrest on the morning of November 10. A Lieutenant Maier of the Garmisch-Partenkirchen police station telephoned orders to the frontier post at Mittenwald ordering Göring's apprehension if he showed up there.

Göring shortly did. In his personnel file is a contemporary account by the driver who tried to smuggle him across the frontier, Nazi storm trooper Franz Thanner:

> Around ten P.M. I drove off by car to the frontier post at Griesen with Göring, his wife, a doctor Maier of the Wiggers Sanatorium

*"When they [the Ballins] were due to be arrested by the Gestapo," recalled Bodenschatz, "Göring told me: 'No, Bodenschatz, we'll get them out of the country despite Himmler.' I took care of that myself."

and myself as driver . . . Checking the passports the customs
men on duty drew attention to the ''Göhring'' one and asked if
this was Captain Göring of Munich. I said I didn't know but
didn't think so.

The customs official sent for the police. Thanner continued:

> When they arrived, Frau Göring began to scream. They directed
> that the car was not to be allowed through, and we were escorted
> by the police back to Garmisch.
> An official of the local police precinct was waiting for us there.
> He notified Captain Göring that . . . he might stay in a Garmisch
> sanatorium of his choice, but under strict supervision, as they
> were still awaiting the arrest warrant.

Göring had no intention of waiting, and when the police returned to the
Wiggers Sanatorium barely an hour after leaving him there with Carin, they
found that the bird had already flown. ''A police detective came from Munich
to arrest H.!!!'' she wrote in her diary. ''Room inspection! They came back
three times.'' The indignant local police said later that he had given his word
of honor not to escape. His brother, Major Willi Göring, issued a statement
to the press denying it, but the allegation continued to occupy the libel lawyers
for the next ten years.

> They had instructed me [driver Franz Thanner recorded] to
> drive off but to stand by not far away. A short time later I was
> instructed to drive back as quietly as possible and wait around
> the back of the building. With my engine switched off, I pushed
> the car around to the back exit with the help of some Bund
> Oberland men. Captain Göring was carried out and bedded down
> in the car. The captain's lady stayed behind—only the doctor
> came with me. I was told to drive Captain Göring over the frontier
> at Mittenwald without fail, as the warrant was already being
> phoned through from Munich.

The mountain roads were dark as pitch. At the frontier the striped barrier
pole was up. Thanner blipped the horn and slammed his foot on the gas,
catapulting the car through into Austria before the German guards could stop
him. On the Austrian side he showed a false passport for Göring, borrowed
from a doctor at Garmisch, then drove on to the Golden Lamb, an inn at
Seefeld. They carried him upstairs but there was a noisy firemen's ball going
on down below, which prevented any sleep. At Göring's behest, Thanner
went back for Carin, and on Monday the twelfth they all drove on to

Innsbruck, where they checked into the Hotel Tyrol, owned by one of the many local Nazi sympathizers.

Thus the Görings were beyond the reach of German law. Hermann would not return to Germany for four years; and when he did he would be a changed man.

He was now delirious with pain from his groin injury, and they took him straight over to No. 9 Bahnhof Platz, where the pediatrician Dr. Sopelsa checked his injuries. They were suppurating badly, and the doctor rushed him to hospital late on the thirteenth.

> A multitude of people [described Carin in a hitherto unpublished letter written the next day] gathered outside as four Red Cross men carried Hermann out into the ambulance. Everybody shouted Heil! and sang "Swastika and Steel Helmet."
>
> Later in the evening, after I left the hotel, a crowd of students gathered . . . and staged a torchlight procession and sang beneath our hotel balcony.
>
> Today there was an even bigger demonstration in Munich. Leaflets have been published saying that Hermann is dead. The university has had to close. All the students have declared themselves for Hitler.

Over the next ten days she wrote several more letters betraying not only her excitement but also her blind devotion to the Nazi cause. The Görings' situation was not enviable. Munich was placarded with wanted posters, the police were keeping watch on their villa at Obermenzing, their mail was being impounded, their beautiful Mercedes-Benz 16 had been confiscated.

Carin kept all this from Hermann. Gradually his fever declined, but he had lost a lot of blood and seemed frighteningly pale. The disappointment that he had suffered kept him awake, and he brooded incessantly over the events of the past weeks.

> Our car [lamented Carin] has been confiscated by von Kahr. Our bank account has been frozen. But even though it sometimes seems as though the world's entire misfortune is about to descend upon Hitler's work and us, I have a firm belief that everything will turn out all right in the end.
>
> The work goes on, and thousands of new followers are joining us daily . . . furious at Kahr's treachery. There are various [SA] regiment commanders who are having daily political conferences with Hermann either in person or through couriers.

In these letters to her worrying parents Carin more than once embroidered on the distressing truth, such was her anxiety to impress them with the wisdom of her new marriage. But as the days went by, she noticed that her family maintained an icy silence in Stockholm; only her mother continued to send food parcels to them—the parcels were smuggled across the mountains by the courier who carried the secret letters that were now being exchanged between Göring and Hitler, who had been committed to Landsberg Prison pending his trial for treason.

Harassed by Communists, who stoned her in the street, breaking a bone in one foot, Carin moved into the hospital to be with Hermann. His condition fluctuated badly. On November 26, just as the wound had closed, it broke open again. To muffle the searing pain, the doctors began injecting morphine twice a day. "Hermann is in a terrible state," Carin wrote to her mother on the last day of the month. "His leg hurts so much he can hardly bear it."

> They operated on him under a general anesthetic, and for the past three days he's been running a high temperature. His mind wanders, he weeps, he has nightmares of street fighting, and all the time he is in indescribable pain. His whole leg is a mass of rubber tubes to drain off the pus.

As Hermann Göring bit his pillow and groaned incessantly, Carin sat help-lessly at his side. "I have to watch him suffer in body and soul," she wrote one month after the shooting, "and there's hardly anything I can do to help . . . His pain is as bad as ever, despite his being dosed with morphine every day."

A stream of visitors and well-wishers came to the hospital, including Hitler's sister Paula ("a charming, ethereal creature with great soulful eyes set in a white face, quivering with love for her brother"), Houston Stewart Chamberlain, and Siegfried Wagner, son of the composer. Wagner had tried to buy Hermann's photograph in Munich—the famous one with a helmet— but the photographers had sold out the entire stock of forty thousand they had printed the week before. Through the Nazi underground, meanwhile, they received clothes and other necessities, and then more friends like Ernst "Putzi" Hanfstaengl and Karl Bodenschatz came to bring him news of the coming trial.

Göring sent a message to General Ludendorff, asking whether he should surrender to Kahr's police in the interests of the party. Ludendorff advised him not to, since Göring was more useful at large.

> Here in Austria [Carin wrote, starry-eyed, to her mother on December 20] National Socialism is especially strong, and I am sure that when Hermann is well again he will find something to do here. A party of a million members and "storm troops" of 100,000 armed men cannot be put down at one stroke.

Hitler's methods have thus far only been for decency and chiv-

alry. That is why he is so beloved and admired and has the whole
of the masses behind him. . . . Hitler is calm, he is full of life
and faith now, after the first few days when he was apathetic,
refused to eat . . .

It was Carin's tenderness that kept Göring going through those painful weeks
before Christmas of 1923. Each time he lifted his head on the hospital bed
and opened his eyes he saw her radiating peace and affection. On Christmas
Eve he was allowed back into the hotel, but it was a ghastly Christmas. The
local SA troops had sent over a small Christmas tree with candles beribboned
in red, white, and black, but Göring was still a sick man, deathly white and
trembling like a leaf.

"Dead tired," wrote Carin a few days later, "he tried to drag himself
around on crutches." The hotel was empty—all the guests were celebrating
elsewhere, except for a Scroogelike character who sat at the far end of the
dining room, and two young men in the company of females of dubious
profession. Seemingly star-crossed lovers, like Wagner's Tristan and Isolde,
the Görings shared this, their first married Christmas, in a gloom that not
even Carin's party dress could lighten.

In her thoughts she was far away: At her parent's home in Sweden, with
young Thomas, with gifts and feast and open fire. At eight o'clock she could
stand it no longer—she threw a coat over her shoulders and went out to get
some fresh air. It was blowing hard outside, but she scarcely noticed. All
at once she heard the sounds of an organ and violin from an open window
above their own hotel apartment, playing "Silent Night." "I cried, of course,"
she wrote her father afterward, "but recovered my confidence and peace of
mind again. I went back in to Hermann, and I was able to cheer him up
again. Two hours later we were both fast asleep."

She expressed a vague alarm at the metamorphosis that seemed to be
coming over her husband. "I hardly recognize him now," she wrote in the
same letter to her father. "The whole man seems to have changed. He barely
utters a word—so utterly depressed at this betrayal, so miserable. I never
thought Hermann could get so low."

In Munich the Bavarian government prepared to put Hitler on trial. Göring
could only watch impotently from afar. "I threatened," he claimed to historian George Shuster, "that if they held the trial in camera I would appeal
directly to the German public by newspaper articles."

In the weeks before the trial Hitler remained in close touch with him.

Yesterday and the day before [wrote Carin on January 2] Hitler's lawyer was here. He came direct from the fortress where
Hitler is held, full of the latest news and bringing letters from
him. The lawyer visits Hitler every day. Perhaps there won't
be any trial. If there is, it won't be to Kahr's liking, because

he'll be in the dock with the other two scoundrels [Seisser and Lossow] . . .

Money was becoming a real problem, although the hotel was proud to have them as guests; they gave Göring a 30 percent discount on everything and allowed him to run up a bill. "The waiters are nearly all storm troopers," said Carin in a letter dated February 20, 1924. "They worship Hermann." The Görings hated being thrown on the charity of their friends. Their poverty fed their anti-Semitism. "I would rather die a thousand times of hunger," Carin wrote, "than serve a Jew." And Hermann, writing to her mother on the twenty-second, explained their plans thus: "I want to stay here until the [Hitler] trial is over; but if there is then no prospect of us returning home [to Munich], we should like to go to Sweden." There he hoped to find work—"Because I only want to go home to a strongly nationalistic Germany, not to the present Jew-ridden Republic."

The trial of Adolf Hitler et al. began four days later. The Görings could not put Hitler and the other defendants out of their thoughts.

> While I am writing this [noted Carin that morning, February 26] my Hermann is stalking up and down the room, occasionally leafing through a book, jotting something down, glancing at the clock, looking at the ceiling, sighing out loud, laughing, tossing a smile at me . . . but beneath all that I can feel so keenly how he is shaking within, trembling for Hitler!!!

The Munich trial ended with short prison sentences. In Innsbruck the Görings lunched that day with Paula Hitler and tried to look on the bright side.

> The more we think about Hitler's sentence [wrote Carin on April 1] the better it looks to us . . . When he is released, he can pick up where he left off, but with hundreds of thousands of new followers who came to him during the trial because of his wonderful, noble character and intellect! . . . He received a brand-new automobile yesterday as a gift from Director Bechstein— you know, the piano and airplane manufacturer. It is a Benz eight-seater, one-hundred horsepower, specially ordered and built for Hitler; and when the amnesty comes there will be another exactly the same waiting for Hermann, a six-seater presented by Bechstein.

On March 5, the Innsbruck authorities had issued a passport to Göring. But then Carin, who had been disturbed by his increasing depression resulting from the injury and his inglorious role as a voiceless exile during the trial, took a step that was again to change their lives. After paying a farewell visit to Hermann's empty villa in Munich on April 5, she decided to see Hitler himself in jail. Afterward, the incarcerated Führer would inscribe a photograph to her "in memory of your visit to Fortress Landsberg." Hitler gave to Carin Göring important instructions to take back to her husband in Innsbruck: He was to establish contact immediately with Benito Mussolini, whose Fascist movement had come to power in Italy two years before.

4

FAILURE OF A MISSION

The ten months that Hermann and Carin Göring spent in Italy from the first days of May 1924 have been widely misinterpreted by historians. It is plain that Hitler had appointed Göring to act as his plenipotentiary in Italy, with the special mission of raising a 2-million lire loan from Mussolini to help the Nazi party to regain its lost momentum. It is equally plain, however, that Göring did not see the Italian dictator.

Göring embarked on this task all too naïvely. He established immediate contacts with the up-and-coming Fascist diplomat Giuseppe Bastianini and with the former Munich correspondent of the newspaper *Corriere d'Italia*, Dr. Leo Negrelli, who a few weeks later joined Mussolini's personal staff. The many biographers who have accepted that the young German aviator actually secured the audience he desired with Mussolini are wrong, as Negrelli's private papers make quite clear; and if Carin's unpublished letters give the impression that he did see Mussolini, this is in fact a tragic reflection on the relationship that existed between them as this, the most harrowing period of their life, began. Injured in his vanity, Göring evidently concealed his failure from her: In her letters home, she described in touching detail his (nonexistent) visits to the Italian dictator. It is worth noting that when Göring sanctioned the publication of some of these letters after her death, all such embarrassing embroideries on the truth were scrupulously removed.

In fact, his 1924 mission to Italy was an ignominious failure—the certain origin of his barely concealed later contempt for the Italian Fascists, of his decision to slink away from the political scene for the following three years, and of his slide into the total oblivion offered by morphine.

The mission had started promisingly enough. In Innsbruck, the owner of the hotel waived his bill as a contribution to the Nazi cause, and recommended to them the Hotel Britannia, situated right on the Grand Canal in Venice.

For a week they vacationed there. Carin was in transports of joy at being "in Venice," as she put it, "en route for Rome." She found herself cruising the canals in a gondola while silken threads of romantic music drifted around the ancient buildings.

> The whole canal [she wrote to her mother] was thronged with gondolas, each decked out with a different-colored lantern, and there was singing everywhere. Soothing, surging—oh God, how romantic it all was! On many of the gondolas there were castanets, and virtually all of them had a guitar . . . Whenever we see something as beautiful as this, we think, "Why can't Mama see this?"

For a few days he browsed around the art galleries as he had as a boy thirteen years before, admiring the paintings at Sienna and ogling the sculptures in Florence before moving on to Rome late on Sunday, May 11. They booked confidently into the expensive Hotel Eden, and the very next morning, while Carin was still puttering around in pajamas, Göring set about his mission.

"Hermann," Carin wrote proudly, "has been going at full speed for an hour already. He's going to look up Mussolini's adjutant first and settle a time to meet M. himself."

Göring wanted a quick decision. He knew his wife was homesick and longed to fold little Thomas into her arms again. His intent was to dazzle Mussolini with his Pour le Mérite, charm the big loan out of him for the Nazi party, then leave Italy for good, sailing via England and Norway or Denmark back to Sweden. Carin's father tried to dissuade them, cautioning her that Göring would never find a job, and her mother warned her too about Nils, her former husband, who was showing signs of dementia: The presence of the Görings in Stockholm would not make things any easier for·him. Carin did not care and said so. "Consideration for him," she expostulated to her mother, "must have its limits! Hermann and I have had a long talk about this, and we see completely eye to eye."

But her husband's troubles in Italy were just beginning. Although armed with a personal letter from Hitler and a signed authorization (*Vollmacht*) to negotiate—both documents now, unfortunately, lost—he found that Mussolini showed no inclination whatever to receive him. Why, indeed, should he enter into talks with a defeated German political movement whose pleni-potentiary was himself a fugitive from justice? The only useful contact that Göring made was with Giuseppe Bastianini, to whom Negrelli introduced him during May.

As funds ran low, the Görings had to move out of the Eden into a cheaper hotel. "I took up residence in the Hotel de Russie," he reminisced candidly in 1945, "and as a hotel guest I saw the Fascists celebrating their great [election] victory with a banquet there. That's where I first set eyes on Mussolini, though I didn't speak to him. Later, down in the bar, I got to know quite a lot of the Fascist party's leaders."

As the new Italian Parliament opened on May 24, 1924, all that his doting wife saw was the panoply and pomp of Mussolini and the royal courtiers in ceremonial dress.

"Right here in the hotel there was a state banquet for eight hundred people," Carin wrote to her mother the next day, "—all the royalty, Mus-solini, all the ministers with their wives etc. . . . I hardly believe that we can get away from here yet, because Hermann has to work with Mussolini himself on all the agreements and negotiations between Mussolini and Hitler . . . This is a huge responsibility for him. But I believe it's all going far better than even Hitler imagined in his boldest dreams."

She obviously had not the faintest idea that Hermann had lied to her—that Mussolini was refusing to see him. "Mussolini," she gushed in the same letter, "is a strong personality but in my opinion a bit theatrical and very spoiled in his manner. That may be explained by the nauseating flattery that surrounds him. The merest word he utters is regarded by this disgusting crowd as if it had emanated from God Almighty!!!! To me, Hitler is the more genuine; above all he is a genius, full of the love of truth and a burning faith." She referred to the similarities between their two political movements, and concluded, "Sympathy here for Hitler and his work is tremendous. You cannot imagine how enthusiastically the entire Fascist party here receives Hermann as Hitler's representative."

For Carin Göring, as a letter written a few weeks later shows, Adolf Hitler was Germany's last hope of a place in the sun. "We have not had such a man in the world in one hundred years, I believe. I worship him totally . . . His time will come."

> Mussolini told Hermann [so Carin reassured her worried mother
> on July 27] that he had had to overcome many more difficulties
> than Hitler . . . The Fascists here had many dead and thousands
> wounded before they pulled it off, but Hitler has had only thirty
> dead. Mussolini has absolute faith in Hitler alone in Germany,
> and will not sign one single treaty, or meet with anyone, or in

particular deal with any government of which Hitler is not the head.

All this was not even near the truth. Her husband had introduced into the preliminary negotiations with Bastianini an extraneous element that rendered them certainly vexatious to the Italian government and probably hopeless from the start. The part-owner of the Grand Hotel Britannia, where they were staying in Venice, was one Rudolfo Walther, who although born in Venice was a German national; under the Versailles Treaty of 1919, Rome had declared his share of the hotel forfeit; and although Göring now pleaded Walther's case for exemption with an obstinacy worthy of a better cause— he had no option but to sing for his supper in this way—neither Bastianini nor Negrelli would humor him.

Throughout the early summer of 1924 Göring stayed in Rome, badgering Bastianini and Negrelli about the hotel in Venice, about the loan to the Nazi party, and about the terms of a secret deal to be signed between Mussolini and Hitler, the extraordinary history of which was later summarized in a letter by Bastianini to Mussolini:

> In May [1924] I established contact with Mr. Hermann Göring,
> a member of the Reichstag [this was not so] and Adolf Hitler's
> alter ego, introduced to me by Negrelli. He expressed to me the
> strong wish of his Führer and of his party to arrive at an agreement
> with the P.N.F. [Fascist Party] because they are convinced of the
> need for a close co-existence between Italy and Germany on the
> one hand, and between the nationalists of the two countries on
> the other.

Bastianini continued that Göring and Negrelli had between them drafted two secret agreements, which they hoped Mussolini and Hitler would sign. "Your Excellency," Bastianini would remind Mussolini in November, "accepted them in substance but rejected them in form."

Unfortunately for his larger purpose, Göring continued to pester Bastianini about the Walther hotel case, urging him to take it up with Guido Jung, the politician who had the power to arbitrate in such sequestration cases. When Bastianini fobbed him off with solecisms, Göring became obnoxious and even more importunate, writing to Negrelli anti-Semitic remarks about Jung and the Banca Commerciale, the financial institution that was trying to dis-possess the unfortunate Walther, until finally, in Bastianini's eloquent words to Mussolini, "Göring . . . at our request departed from Rome for Venice, where he is at the present time."

If Göring recognized this as a first-round defeat, he kept it all from Carin.

Nevertheless, the change in mood is unmistakable in her last letter written home from Rome:

> We don't get so much news from Germany. I expect things are gloomy there. Hitler has gone into complete seclusion and is writing his first book, "Four and a Half years' Struggle against Stupidity, Lies and Cowardice" [soon to be changed to *Mein Kampf*]. . . . Hermann, who is in command of all the armed troops, also has his share of troubles: now that he's not there himself, everything has to go through other hands.

During his last days in Rome Göring drafted two important secret agreements. The first was to Mussolini as prime minister, and addressed the thorny problem of the South Tyrol—the beautiful mountain region, populated largely by Germans, which had been turned over to Italy after the war and renamed "Alto Adige." In this remarkable deal, Göring and Hitler were secretly offering to Mussolini to sell out the South Tyrol in return for an Italian loan and official recognition for the Nazi party upon its revival. With Hitler's written authority, Göring offered in this first document:

> 1. To make unmistakably clear that it [the Nazi party] does not recognize that there is any Alto-Adige question and that it recognizes absolutely and without hesitation the status quo, i.e. Italian possession. . . . The NSDAP [Nazi party] will do everything possible, starting right now, to discourage the German people from revisionist thoughts in regard to Alto Adige.
> 2. To argue that our reparations obligations toward Italy as imposed by the Versailles Treaty must be properly fulfilled.
> 3. To instigate an immediate campaign in the press at our disposal for a rapprochement between Germany and Italy . . .

In return for this valuable real estate, Göring's letter politely asked the dictator to "help out" Hitler by giving certain undertakings:

> 1. That, in the event that the NSDAP comes to power in Germany, whether by legal or illegal means, the Italian Government will refrain from putting military pressure on this new German Government and will not join in if such moves are initiated by third powers. . . . The P.N.F. will render prompt aid to the NSDAP by every means (including press coverage, speeches by Members of Parliament, and loans);
> 2. That, with regard to Italy's guarantee of the Versailles Treaty (especially toward France) . . . she will not set herself up as a

champion or defender of any demands or claims submitted by
other states against the new German Government.

In the second secret document, which was addressed to the Italian Fascist
party headquarters, Göring asked outright for a confidential loan to keep
Hitler's moribund party alive. "The most total secrecy will be observed,"
he promised. "The agreement will be known on our side only to the Führer
of our movement, to the trustee assigned by our party, and to the under-
signed." Göring suggested a loan of two million lire, payable in installments
and repayable over five years, with "the entire chattels and real estate (cash,
property, cars, etc.)" of the Nazi party as collateral. To justify the loan,
Göring explained that the party was now shaping up for its crucial fight
against the wealthy democratic system and against a rising Communist tide
in Germany, awash with funds from Moscow.

Hermann Göring posted these letters by registered mail to Negrelli for
him to deliver to Mussolini in person and left with Carin for Venice on
August 11, 1924. They were now cruelly impoverished. "Hermann has
learned a lot here," she had written in her last letter from Rome, two weeks
earlier. "I think much of it has been painful to his soul, but it has certainly
been necessary for his development."

Back at the Grand Hotel Britannia in Venice, he waited for a response to
the two letters: None would ever come. Meanwhile he became even more
beholden to Rudolfo Walther, whose interest was in neither Germany, nor
Italy, nor the South Tyrol, but in his beautiful hotel. "You can stay as long
as you want," Walther tempted the two Görings: "Months, if you wish!"
But they could not overlook the eagerness with which Walther waited for
official word about the fate of his hotel. Hitler had vaguely promised to send
them money, but he was still in jail and no money came. "The hotel says
nothing," Carin wrote guiltily to her mother, begging more money, "but
one feels it in the air."

In an astoundingly ingenuous attempt to twist Mussolini's arm, Göring
inflated the hotel claim to a test case to prove "Fascist sincerity" toward
the Nazi cause. If deprived of his hotel, argued Göring, Walther would have
to emigrate—but the Nazi party needed him where he was. "Our party would
regard this as a very special favor and as proof that our negotiations are
being treated with the kind of importance that we are entitled to expect."

Evidently the Görings were still planning to leave soon, because they
obtained a new passport in Venice on August 26. While waiting for word
from Mussolini, Göring strolled around the island city. A street photographer
snapped the already quite stout Hermann with his surprisingly tall wife as
they fed the pigeons in a piazza on September 5. In the Italian political crisis
that flared up after Fascist thugs murdered the Socialist Matteotti, Göring
adopted a different tack. His letters became effusive. Hearing that leftists
had retaliated by butchering Casalini, one of Mussolini's lieutenants, he

scribbled an offer to Negrelli to place himself "as a simple fascist" at Italy's disposal in any showdown with the Communists that might result now: "I'd be very sad," he wrote, "if I couldn't join in when the balloon goes up. Please pass on my request to Bastianini or your commander. I beg you to do all you can so I can help the fight: at very least I could go along as a liaison man to our own movement. And if things got really hot, as an aviator!"

He sent a similar letter to Mussolini the next day. Impatient at receiving no reply to any of these letters, on September 19 he picked up his pen again. "I'd be very grateful," he wrote tersely to Negrelli, "for a few urgent lines as to . . . how far the matter has got and what steps are being taken to expedite it. In fact I should be glad to hear that anything at all was coming of our negotiations."

He continued this letter with an important insight into the way his political thinking was developing:

> The attitude of Austria [he wrote, referring to the South Tyrol issue] is of no consequence, since this little state—70 percent of whose people want Anschluss [union with Germany] anyway—will be incorporated into Germany as soon as we are strong again. Thus Germany will be more or less obliged to face the . . . issue of the South Tyrol. If, when that time comes, a party that is hostile to Fascism is in power in the German Reich, the resulting tilt toward France will produce a lineup hostile to Italy . . .
>
> So Italy must cast around for what helpers she can: and what better helper than a National Socialist Germany under Hitler's leadership? Just picture the advantage if a German government voluntarily crushes any South Tyrolean revisionism and freely guarantees Italy's northern frontier!

Göring added that he himself was drafting a pamphlet explaining to his party friends why Alsace-Lorraine (both German provinces that France had annexed), as well as West Prussia and Danzig (claimed by Poland), were far more important to true Germans than the South Tyrol and its "tiny towns" of Merano and Bolzano.

As a quid pro quo, however, he wanted proofs of Italian sincerity, and these, he told Negrelli, would be:

> 1) the final signing of our agreement;
> 2) payment of finite installments on the loan in return for which we shall place our [Nazi party] press at the disposal of your Fascist propaganda; and
> 3) a friendly attitude toward our representatives.

By "our representatives" he meant, of course, hotel-owner Rudolfo Walther in Venice. Göring also asked for the first installments to be paid up front, before Hitler publicly "sold out" the South Tyrol. "This," he reminded Negrelli, "would only cost you a loan of two millions. In return you receive an invaluable mouthpiece in our press. Besides, you will get your two millions back within five years at the most."

Again there was no response from Rome. In a crusty letter to Negrelli on September 23, Göring voiced suspicions that for all their fine promises neither he nor Bastianini had done anything even about Walther's hotel, and he rudely alleged that "the Jewish Banca Commerciale" was at the bottom of it—"it wants to take it over in a typically vile Jewish way." For months now, Göring grumbled, they had been negotiating: Surely, he pleaded, Mussolini or Jung must have half an hour to spare ("When you talk to Jung, remember that he's a Jew!")

His plan to emigrate to Sweden now took on more concrete form. He applied for jobs there and disclosed this to Hitler in a letter.

Carin began hunting for somewhere to live in Stockholm, but it was not easy: "We can't live with my parents," she wrote to an old friend there, "as they have only one room each and a dining room. Likewise Fanny, likewise Lily." (She made no mention of her third sister, Mary, who lived in the von Rosens' castle, Rockelstad.) "If only," she wrote, "I knew somebody who would rent one or two rooms to us."

Plagued by poverty, she begged her parents for cash while Hermann did what odd jobs he could around Venice. Their German friends looked the other way. Promising to use his family connections in Sweden, General Ludendorff wrote thin words of consolation: "I know that a Hermann Göring will always fight through!"

"The trouble is," explained Carin to her mother, "Hermann can not possibly nor will he join a firm where there is one iota of Jewish blood . . . That would bring disgrace on his whole position and on Hitler and his entire philosophy. We would rather starve to death, both of us."

Unemployed and in fact unemployable, given his worsening condition, Göring spent the last two days of September describing their plight in an unvarnished letter to Hitler. On October 1, he went out for a stroll around the city, hoping that this was the day that Hitler would be released from Landsberg: because then, he was sure, Hitler's book, Mein Kampf, would be published, and Hitler would become rich enough to repay to them what they had sunk into the party. "Hitler won't leave us in the lurch," wrote Carin that day. "Not us who have sacrificed everything for him and the fatherland." But Hitler remained in jail. From Olga and Paula Göring, Hermann received these lines: "You can live with us as long as you wish. That would be the greatest joy you could give us." But he knew that his sisters were poorer than himself. His eyes were still on Sweden; a leading airplane manufacturer had asked him to mail his résumé, and he was dealing with Carl Flormann, the Swedish air pioneer who had just formed an aviation company called A. B. Aerotransport in Stockholm.

Carin's father begged her in a harshly worded letter not, for God's sake, to return to Sweden without a firm job for Hermann. She kept the letter to herself and told her husband only of the little money that she had received from her mama that day. She thanked her mother immediately.

> All that we had was used up over a week ago. We have gone through such hard times lately. I cannot tell you how it was. Never in this life was it so hard to exist in spite of all the happiness I have with my darling Hermann. . . . If I didn't have him, I could never have stood it all. . . . He always consoles me when I whine.
>
> Hitler can do nothing. He himself is penniless and everything that the party had was confiscated—every stick of furniture, every automobile, the lot! . . . For a long time I have had deep down a very positive feeling that God will help us, he won't forget us. But sometimes life is difficult!!!

Unable to afford a ticket to anywhere, the Görings were trapped in Venice. It was no longer a pleasure for them. One can almost hear Negrelli groan at the opening words of Hermann's next letter on October 15: "As you can see, we are still here. . . ." In this letter Göring angrily complained at being "led by the nose" and demanded as the accredited representative of a movement with four million voters and eight million supporters to be taken seriously. He indicated that when released, the Führer, Adolf Hitler, would want to visit Rome with Göring to continue the Fascist-Nazi party negotiations in person. "However, he would not come unless he could be sure of an audience with Mussolini," warned Göring—and the querulous tone shows once more how tenuous were the contacts that he had established with Rome. For good measure, he threw in a lecture for Negrelli on the importance of a crusading anti-Semitism for nationalist movements everywhere. "The Jews," he wrote, "must be fought in every country."

Göring had an added reason or impatience with Rome now. Acting on his advice, Hitler had issued an official Nazi party declaration expressing a lack of interest in the South Tyrol. The consequences had been the most immediate and widespread condemnation of the party by other nationalist groupings and by the entire German press. Hitler had been stripped of his Austrian citizenship, and all those Nazis who had taken refuge in the Tyrol after the beer hall putsch had been summarily expelled. Yet all that Göring could extract from Rome were the vaguest unofficial expressions of goodwill.

Hermann had been on the run for nearly a year now, and it pained him to see Carin withering away in this Venice hotel with its red plush trappings and pretentious menus in kitchen French—the "consommé à la Butterfly" and the "volaille à la Chanteclair." Munich and the brouhaha of November 1923 seemed part of another world. "How many fine dreams have gone their worldly ways," sighed Carin in a letter written on the anniversary of the putsch, "and how many 'good friends' too." She longed for a home of her own again:

> At home I could set the table myself with a few flowers from the market, I could speak naturally without the next table eavesdropping on every word, I could laugh out loud, I could jump up and plant a kiss on Hermann in the midst of everything . . .
>
> When shall we be spared the monotony of three fresh towels neatly hung over the wash basin each morning, instead of hearing Hermann's voice—half reproachful, half apologetic—calling out, "Carin, perhaps it is time for me to have a fresh towel, I've had this one for ages," and to quarrel, just a tiny little bit!

Between them they developed a plan for her to sell off the villa at Obermenzing, while Hermann traveled to Sweden by a roundabout route through Austria and Poland to avoid arrest in Germany. But how to buy the tickets? Sitting in the hotel lobby while Carin brooded upstairs, Hermann composed a letter in painful, prosaic Swedish to her mother on October 22, 1924: "For one year we have grappled with our singular fate. Often we are in despair, but our faith in God's help has fortified us. Carin is so brave, so sweet to me and such a great comfort that I cannot thank her enough."

Unstinting in his flattery of her mother, since this was an emergency, he added: "We long for our beloved, wonderful Mama and hope to God that we shall see our Mama again as soon as possible and can sit down together and describe our eventful life this last year . . . and can start a new life full of sunshine!"

The money came, but they postponed their departure for Sweden once again. Perhaps it was because Leo Negrelli, bombarded by Göring with press clippings proving the damage that the Nazi party had suffered because of its sellout of the South Tyrol, had come to Venice to see them. He offered to speed up the outstanding matters and warmly approved of plans that Göring now outlined to stand as a Nazi candidate for the German Reichstag. In a letter on November 28, however, Göring once again voiced ill-concealed anger at the Italian government's failure to enter any agreement with him. "To date," he wrote, "we alone have kept our promises to the letter, incurring a lot of unpleasantness in the process." Possibly hinting at his imminent departure, he concluded: "For other reasons too this is becoming urgent!!!!!!"

On December 3, 1924, Carin sat in their room upstairs alone, because Hermann had gone off for "important conferences" (or so he had told her).

The skies above Venice had opened and the rains lashed down on gray lagoons and canals as far as the eye could see. Life in this hotel was not dull, she reflected—among the guests was composer Franz Léhar, and they got all the opera tickets they could use. When tenor Rafaelli Giuseppe sang, they both wept like children, and returned to their hotel existence to listen to an American, a Mrs. Steel, loudly boasting of her life in Chicago and of the automobiles owned by her husband, herself, her daughter and her son. "We never walk a step," she exclaimed. Another guest was the former queen of Spain, a frail, pale-skinned creature with jet-black hair; surrounded by her fawning exiled retinue. She had had to pawn her pearls, and she handed out signed photographs in return for little favors.

But Carin too was living a fantasy herself, here in the Grand Hotel Britannia. "Have I told you about our meetings with Mussolini?" she wrote wistfully to her mother. "It is a wonderful thing to be with him . . . Hermann has two important conferences today."

On that same day Göring was complaining in a handwritten letter to Leo Negrelli once again about the Fascists' failure to respond, and his letter mentions nothing about any "importance conferences" that day.

They did not spend that Christmas of 1924 together, because Hitler had now been released from prison and Göring had sent his wife posthaste to Munich to lay bare their plight to him and extort what funds she could from him or the other Nazi potentates.

Göring himself had now abandoned all hope of any secret agreement with the Italians despite Hitler's public sacrifice of the South Tyrol. Carin repeated this gloomy prognosis to the Führer. Hitler was evidently more understanding than Göring's erstwhile Nazi comrades. Ernst Röhm had languidly sought contact with Göring soon after Röhm's release from prison, but Carin warned Hermann in a letter on January 13, 1925, against having anything to do with this flabby homosexual. "Please don't put too much trust in him!!!!" she wrote. "Now he's only seeking contact with you because he's feeling rather alone."

As for the other Nazis, Max Amann, who was to publish Hitler's *Mein Kampf* in three months' time, had only words of censure for Göring; the Hanfstaengls "only talked of their own money troubles"; and Hitler was still waiting for funds to arrive from a man (either an Italian or millionaire piano manufacturer Bechstein) whom Carin's letter of the seventeenth identified only as "Bimbaschi":

> They [the Hanfstaengls] told me that Bimbaschi was supposed to
> have given Hitler a firm promise of a sizable donation . . . Bimb.
> had told H. that he wanted nothing more to do with the party,
> and that this sum was for Hitler personally! In addition Bimb. is
> said to have complained a lot about you, saying you had written

> him "harsh letters" and he had sent you over four thousand . . .
> Hitler is expecting the money any moment and he has promised
> me positively, time after time, that he will let me know imme-
> diately when the money is there.

In the rest of this letter from Bavaria, Carin gave her exiled husband advice
on how to approach Hitler with his idea of transferring operations to Sweden,
which people in the party might well find hard to swallow. He should write
the Führer a concise letter ("because he has so very much to do"), and
above all gloss over the failure in Italy. "Please," she cajoled him, "don't
be too pessimistic about Italy and his plans there."

"At our first meeting here before Christmas [Carin wrote] I told Hitler
about your talks with the gentlemen in Rome. He knows also that the transactions were about an alliance, about the two million lire, and about the
South Tyrol question."

If, she continued, Hermann now admitted to Hitler that Mussolini's men
were refusing even to see him anymore, Hitler would surely dismiss her as
"muddle-headed." She had mentioned the negotiations only so that Hitler
could see how hard her husband had slaved for him—"So that he wouldn't
think you were incompetent," she told Hermann candidly, adding hastily,
"I adhered strictly to the truth just as you told me." Thus Hermann's letter
to Hitler should explain that while at the time the loan had seemed feasible,
the fact that the Nazi party had recently suffered an electoral setback suggested
that there was nothing to be gained from any kind of deal with the Fascists.

> I would indeed advise you [Carin wrote] to include in your letter
> to Hitler the treaty proposals drafted at the time so that he can
> see for himself the trouble you went to and will readily pay the
> expenses you incurred . . . Emphasize that personally you stand
> very well with the gentlemen [in Rome]! . . .
> If you were to begin now suddenly telling Hitler only of the
> impossibilities in Italy and of your own plans in Sweden (my
> native country), he might easily get the impression that you are
> prompted by purely personal motives, that you mean to go to
> Sweden at any price and are abandoning all hope of securing an
> understanding with the Fascists . . . In that case he won't pay us
> anything . . .
> Hitler is our only salvation now (with the exception of the sale
> of the villa). Everyone is waiting impatiently for the funds from
> Bimbaschi. You can be certain I am watching out for them too!
> They want to get the better of you and certainly don't want you
> to get any of the money, because they want it all for themselves.
> I don't believe that we have one single unselfish friend!

Leo Negrelli had in fact duly passed on to Bastianini in Rome the newspaper clippings about Hitler and letters that Göring sent him, but he had not bothered to inform Göring in Venice. When he now wrote to Göring mentioning the Nazis' poor election showing, Göring was stung to send back his most truculent letter yet. "Elections," he pointed out, "have nothing to do with a promise that has been given. I am convinced that M[ussolini] will be very upset when he hears how we have been given the run-around. . . . Either you have the authority to approach M. directly, in which case you could have done so long ago, or you do not. . . . It puts me in a hideous position now, because I am being blamed for letting myself be duped—because on my advice we have done everything, and have received nothing in return." Cutting a very small figure now, Göring pleaded with Negrelli to secure for him at least a press interview with the Duce, claiming to be writing a book about Mussolini and his party—"Otherwise we shall both earn a reputation for being bunglers and dilettantes who are all talk and no action." He concluded this letter (which of course made plain beyond peradventure that he had not yet seen Mussolini) with a reminder that was more threat than promise: "Don't forget one thing. There is a future, and we shall not forget those who did something for us." He added the postscript: "My wife has already been in Munich for some weeks."

Already packing to leave for Sweden, Hermann Göring was a disappointed and humiliated man. Negrelli had not even bothered to send back the press clippings about Hitler to him. "I have just received word from Hitler," Göring chided the Italian on February 12, 1925. "He says you should have told me straight out if you couldn't get access to M." He gave Negrelli "one last chance" to reap the rewards of success himself—"Otherwise," he continued, abandoning pride for candor, "I am afraid that H. will send other negotiators who will get to M. direct, and that will leave me looking pretty stupid."

This time Negrelli did claim to have shown the letter to Mussolini. Inspired with fresh optimism, Göring rushed a packet of books on Hitler for Negrelli to show to the Duce. "If only I can speak with M.," he wrote, "I shall be able to work everything out. . . . So please arrange the interview rapidly. You might say that I've got to leave and it is important for me to have spoken with M. first because I really am writing a little book about him and the fascio for propaganda in Germany. It would look dumb then if I have never seen him."

This poignant letter to Negrelli was typed in clumsy capitals—evidently by Hermann Göring himself. Perhaps he did not want Carin to see it, with its shaming admission that he had lied about seeing the great Italian dictator. Moreover, the letter's wooden phrasing hints at the inroads already made into his mental stability by their humiliating plight and, of course, by the pain-killing injections of morphine that he was now getting several times a day.

This lowering darkness was now pierced by one ray of light. A telegram came from Negrelli: Its text is lost but Göring replied with alacrity to him at Mussolini's Press Office: VENICE FEB 13 2315 + THANKS FOR TELEGRAM EVERYTHING ALLRIGHT (the last word was in English).

Negrelli marked the telegram: "Duce."

At last the indolent mandarins in Rome seemed to be stirring, probably aroused by the unexpected revival in Nazi fortunes in Germany: Hitler had firmly resumed control of the party and had ousted all usurpers and pretenders to his throne like General von Ludendorff. On February 16, 1925, the Nazi party was again legalized (though the SA was still banned). On that day Carin paid Hitler a secret visit in Munich, and reported to Venice the next morning what the Führer had said:

> 1. He is of course ready to go to Mussolini and he's already having his papers (passport, etc.) put in order . . . However he will come only if he can deal personally with Mussolini himself. He does not want to speak with any of the underlings . . . 2. With regard to the South Tyrol question he takes exactly the same stand as ever—that for him there is no problem; 3. He wants to confer with M. only after he has sufficient backing . . . At present his authority does not extend beyond the four walls of his little apartment at No. 41, Thiersch Strasse [in Munich]. In a few days he will have himself acclaimed Führer again . . . [and] he will represent two million people, in a people's movement.

"He leaves it to your judgment," continued Carin, "to size up the situation with Mussolini. He asks you to make clear to M. that this is a populist movement and not a parliamentary setup . . . He was very cordial," she wrote, "kissed my hand again and again, sends you his best wishes, etc."

Göring sent Carin's report straight to Bastianini, who forwarded it to Mussolini with the eight-month dossier of letters from Göring, the press clippings, and the tedious memoranda on the Walther hotel affair. He guiltily reminded Mussolini that, acting on the Duce's instructions, he had clearly given Göring to understand that the Fascists accepted the spirit of his proposals, though not without reservations.

> Since then [Bastianini advised his prime minister] the situation in Germany has undergone remarkable changes. Once persecuted and unrecognized, the Nazis have now recovered their material and political rights; their capo, Adolf Hitler, has been restored to freedom and to the Führership of his movement. Göring has now stated in a letter to Negrelli that they are no longer thinking in terms of an agreement . . .

He therefore recommended that Mussolini humor the German's residual requests, given the unquestionably pro-Italian Nazi line on the South Tyrol, namely the request for an interview and the desequestration of Rudolfo Walther's hotel. "To allow the matter to go by the board would," Bastianini submitted, "create a disastrous impression of Italian and Fascist loyalty." Concluding that the luckless Hermann Göring had now been awaiting a decision in Venice for six months, Bastianini urged Mussolini to grant him an interview. "He only asks not to be sent away without moral satisfaction after his hopes have been aroused."

Mussolini—this much is plain—did not unbend and see Göring even now. The hotel affair wasn't settled, either.

That spring of 1925, depressed and defeated, the Görings scraped together enough money to leave for Sweden. Carin had sold the villa and shipped their surviving furniture to a little apartment at No. 23, Ödengatan, in Stockholm. From Sweden her downhearted husband sent one last picture postcard to Dr. Leo Negrelli in Rome, expressing his joy at seeing familiar surroundings again and inquiring whether he should write to "M." again in connection with the Walther affair. "We often think with gratitude," his postcard ended, "of beautiful Italy and of our friends there."

5
ASYLUM FOR THE CRIMINALLY INSANE

For the remaining twenty years of his life Hermann Göring would wage a grim and not always successful struggle against the evil dictatorship of the morphine addiction to which his Austrian surgeons had introduced him. It was not a public battle. He fought, lost, and won this tragic campaign in the privacy of his own soul. When he assured Erhard Milch in 1933 that he had defeated the craving, it was probably true; but when his air-force generals saw him in later years, his eyes glazed and face masklike, it was clear to them that the tyrant morphine had occupied his body once again.

To those familiar with the drug's effects on the human frame, the case of Hermann Göring provided all the circumstantial evidence they needed. Morphine is capable of rendering a person of honest character completely untrustworthy, of producing delusions that in turn result in criminal actions, of increasing glandular activities, and of generating side effects like outpourings of immense vital energy and what the pharmaceutical textbooks describe as "grotesque vanity." The morphine addict may find his imagination stimulated, his oratory more fluid, but then a state of languor supervenes, followed on occasions by deep sleep. As General Helmut Forster would be heard telling fellow air-force generals four days after World War

II ended, "I've seen the Reichsmarschall nod off in midconference—for instance, if the conferences went on too long and the morphine wore off. That was the commander in chief of our air force!"

In Stockholm the Görings had moved into a modest apartment in the neighborhood where Carin had once lived with Nils. If she was startled to find Thomas, now thirteen, almost as tall as herself, her family was shocked at the change in her once lithe and handsome husband, now in steep physical and mental decline, his body consumed by the vital opiate that he craved. He was listless, overweight, and short-tempered to the point of physical violence.

Carin sent him out alone to make friends with her own old circle, an odd experience that Stockholm lawyer Carl Ossbahr would still recall nearly sixty years later:

> A rather stout gentleman turned up, wearing a white suit that looked somewhat out of place on him. It didn't go with his physique at all, and I wondered who he could be. He introduced himself as Hermann Göring, and then I knew that he had got the Pour le Mérite—and you didn't get that for nothing. I suppose he did the same with Carin's other friends.

Ossbahr had them to dinner several times. The German visitor talked politics most of the time, but not in the manner of an agitator at all. He left Ossbahr some books to read, including *Mein Kampf*, but the lawyer never got around to reading it. On one occasion Göring admitted that he was addicted to morphine, but he said he was fighting back. "I have such great tasks ahead of me," he said, "that I simply have to be cured."

Ossbahr found Carin a changed woman. She was now "a bit peculiar, something of a mystic." He was mildly taken aback when she insisted on reading his palm. The atmosphere around the couple left this lawyer with a feeling of "something somehow unreal"—it was hard to describe. "Her wish was his command. He wasn't her slave, but almost. Göring was clearly even more deeply in love than she." After 1925 Ossbahr lost sight of the couple, never dreaming then that Captain Göring of No. 23 Ödengatan would one day become the great Hermann Göring of Germany.

For months the ingratitude of the party gnawed at Göring's mind. He had written to Hitler about resuming command of the SA once the ban on it was lifted, but Hitler had tartly responded that the SA was his own business and that Göring should keep his nose out of it. Göring then reminded Hitler of the party's indebtedness to him, and "carefully filed away" this correspondence, as he disclosed in an embittered letter to Captain Lahr, the veteran who had bought the Obermenzing villa. The letter, written from Stockholm on June 26, 1925, seethed at the hypocritical "nationalist [*völkische*] circles" and "party hacks" around Hitler; the Nazi party, grumbled Göring, had ruined him by its "utter brutality and ruthlessness." "It has shown," he added, "not one spark of conscience or comradeship." He advised Lahr to profit from his own experience. Gone was his previous "blazing admiration" for the Führer, Adolf Hitler. "I wrote to the Führer but got back just empty words of consolation. To date I have still not received one pfennig from either Ludendorff or Hitler—nothing but a load of promises and photographs signed 'in deepest loyalty.' "

Göring took a job as a pilot with a new company, Nordiska Flygrederiet, operating between Stockholm and Danzig. But it lasted only a few weeks —perhaps his drug addiction was found out. It was an expensive habit, and the funds that Carin had brought from Germany ran out. She had to be hospitalized with heart trouble and tuberculosis. They pawned furniture, and her sister Lily sold her piano to pay the medical expenses and buy more morphine for Hermann. He made no secret of his addiction. One of Carin's girl friends would later recall walking with them in the hills outside Stockholm (he was anxious to lose weight). For a while, she noticed, Hermann looked taut and odd; then he disappeared briefly and returned looking visibly better and talking freely.

His decline steepened. On occasions he became so violent toward Carin and Thomas that she fled to her parents. Once, he opened a window and threatened to kill himself. "Let him jump, Mama!" screamed Thomas, white with fear. The family physician, Dr. Fröderström, recommended that he should enter a drug-withdrawal clinic for a month, and he registered voluntarily at the Aspuddens Nursing Home on August 6, 1925.

For a while all went well. On the twentieth, he wrote to Carin's girl friend, vacationing in Norway, looking forward to joining her for some long stiff walks:

> I want to regain my former health and trim figure by climbing mountains, since the cure that I am successfully undergoing here has eliminated the main causes of my unnatural bulk. I am vain and coquettish about this—usually a female prerogative.
>
> But this is merely an excuse. I go quite wild when I think that my trusty old ice pick will soon be clattering on Norwegian glacier ice. I also believe that my old energy and zest for life will return. What is it like in the evening at your hotel, by the way? Does one have to wear a dinner jacket?

He never found out. Ten days later he suffered a violent relapse, and Carin herself would sign the necessary papers for him to be committed to a lunatic asylum.

The extraordinary Swedish medical dossier recording Hermann Göring's committal to Långbro Asylum tells a desperate tale. Nurse Anna Tornquist reported how the behavior of "Captain von [sic] Göring" during the last two days of his stay at the clinic left no choice but to commit him:

> Until then things had gone calmly although he was easily irritated and insisted on his doses. On Sunday, August 30, Captain Göring's craving for Eukodal* became much greater, and he insisted on getting the quantity he himself determined. At about 5:00 P.M. he broke open the medicine cupboard and took two shots of the two percent Eukodal solution himself. Six nurses could do nothing to stop him, and he behaved in a very threatening manner. Captain Göring's wife was afraid that he might even kill someone in his frenzy.

By Monday he had quieted down. The medical superintendent, Dr. Hjalmar Eneström, ordered him given a sedative and a shot of morphine. Göring told him he was willing to adhere to the prescribed doses.

> At about 10:00 A.M. on Tuesday [September 1, 1925] however, the patient became troublesome and again demanded medication. He jumped out of bed, got dressed and shouted that he wanted to go out and meet death somehow, since somebody who had killed forty-five people had no other choice now than to take his own life. As the street door was locked, he could not get out; so he ran up to his room and armed himself with a cane, which turned out to contain some sort of sword. The patient was given the additional injections, and remained in bed demanding still more.
>
> When police and firemen arrived at about 6:00 P.M. he refused to go along with them. He tried to resist but soon found it futile.

Wrapped in a straitjacket he was taken by ambulance to another hospital, the Katarina. They opened a case-history file:

> Göring, Hermann Wilhelm: German Air Force lieutenant. Cause of illness: abuse of Morphine and Eukodal; severe withdrawal symptoms. Was removed by governor's office from Aspuddens Nursing Home on certificates issued by Drs. G. Elander and Hjalmar Eneström.
>
> The patient holds a prominent position in the "Hitler party" in Germany, took part in the Hitler putsch, during which he was

---

*Eukodal, a controlled substance under the Reich Narcotics Act, was the synthetic morphine derivate *dihydro-hydroxy-codeinon hydrochloride*, to be injected intravenously.

injured and hospitalized; says he escaped from there to Austria, was given morphine by the doctors at the hospital, after which he became addicted to morphine. Admitted to Aspuddens, the patient manifested violent withdrawal symptoms (in spite of his nurse allowing him more morphine), during which he became threatening and so violent that he could no longer be kept there. Threatened to take his own life, wanted to "die like a man," threatened to commit hara-kiri, and so on.

Compulsorily committed, with his wife's consent. Upon arrival here [at the Katarina Hospital] on September 11 in the evening he was sedated with Hyoscin and soon fell asleep, but after a few hours he woke and became quite restless. He protested at his loss of freedom, said he intended to send for his lawyer, and so on, and demanded to be given sufficient Eukodal "for the pain."

On coming to, he was talkative, lucid, and in full possession of his faculties; considered himself badly wronged.

No violence as yet.

September 2 [1925]: Indignant conversation with Dr. E. on his rounds today about the illegal manner—according to him—in which he was brought here. Refuses to take Hyoscin, as he believes he will be certified insane while in an anesthetized condition. Expressed broad sympathy with opinions of *Fäderneslandet* [a notorious scandal sheet] on psychiatrists.

Committed to Långbro Asylum later that day, Hermann Göring had his wits about him enough to know that his life was now entering into a tunnel whose very blackness might spell finality. He found himself in a small ward known to outsiders simply as The Storm—he was alone in a cell with a bed bolted to the floor and no other furniture. Panicking, he shouted at the first doctor he saw, "I am not insane, I am not insane!" Realizing that his whole future was in jeopardy, he refused to be photographed for the asylum's dossier.

The doctors had seen it all before. For the next five weeks they calmly recorded his maniacal ordeal:

September 2–October 7, 1925: [The patient was] troublesome, depressed, groaning, weeping, anguished, tiresome, constantly demanding, irritable and easily affected (i.e., NaCl [common salt] relieved the pain); dejected, talkative, target of a "Jewish conspiracy," malevolent toward Dr. Eneström because of his committal, [says] E. bribed by the Jews; thoughts of suicide; says he himself is a "a dead man politically" if word of his commital gets out in Germany; exaggerates withdrawal symptoms; hysterical tendencies, egocentric, inflated self-esteem; hater of the Jews, has devoted his life to the struggle against the Jews, was Hitler's right-hand man. Hallucinations—saw Abraham and Paul, "the most dangerous Jew who ever existed"; Abraham offered him a promissory note and guaranteed him three camels if he would give up the fight against the Jews; onset of visual hallucinations, screamed out loud; Abraham was driving a red-hot nail into his back; a Jewish doctor wanted to cut out his heart; suicide attempt (by hanging and strangulation); threatening, smuggled an iron weight in as a weapon; visions, voices, self-contempt.

The doctors' confidential reports spoke of his weak character—"One never knew how he would react," wrote one. "But since he had been a German officer he found it easy to obey." Another qualified him as a "sentimental person, lacking in fundamental moral courage."

Then, on October 7, 1925, his ordeal was over. He was discharged from Långbro with a certificate that he had obviously begged the professor in charge to sign:

> I hereby affirm that Captain H. von [sic] Göring was admitted into Långbro hospital at his own request; that neither upon admission nor later did he show signs of mental illness; and that upon discharge now he also does not show any symptoms of an illness of this kind.
>
> Långbro Hospital
> October 7, 1925
> OLOF KINBERG,
> PROFESSOR

Won almost at a greater cost than his famous war decoration, though not a prize that he was so anxious to display, this vital certificate of sanity would be among his most precious possessions for the next twenty years.

His return to Carin's little apartment triggered fresh troubles. Since his crazed outbursts were now a thing of the past, Thomas often came over from school at Östermalm. Nils warned Carin that the lad was playing truant, and his schoolwork was suffering. Overreacting, she sued Nils for legal custody. His defense lawyers hired a private detective, and he dug up evidence of Göring's drug addiction. On April 16, 1926, Dr. Karl Lundberg, a court-appointed doctor, certified that neither Hermann nor Carin—who was, he said, an epileptic—was fit to provide a home for Thomas, and on the twenty-second the court dismissed her petition.

Planning to appeal, she persuaded Hermann to return to Långbro and complete the withdrawal cure. He gloomily reentered the asylum on May 22. The hospital's dossier on him states only, "Subdued, fluctuating moods, egocentric, easily affected, back pain.'' Afterward, Dr. C. Franke, the assistant medical superintendant, issued this new certificate:

> Captain Hermann Göhring [sic] of No. 23 Ödengatan, Stockholm, was admitted to Långbro Hospital in May 1926 at his own request and treated there by the undersigned. During his stay there he underwent a detoxification cure from the use of Eukodal, and when he left the hospital at the beginning of June, he was completely cured from the use of the above and free from the use of all types of opium derivatives, which fact is herewith certified on my honor and conscience.

On August 23, he wrote a pathetic letter to the court stressing his former status and acts of wartime heroism, and declaring his willingness to submit to medical and psychiatric examination. The court still refused to grant Carin custody of Thomas.

Göring's movements after this are something of a mystery. Unlike Hitler, he seldom reminisced about the more barren years of his existence. He clearly intended to regain high office in the Nazi party, but three years had passed since his inglorious exile, and the party now had no time for him. His name was scratched from the membership register, and he had difficulty later in reclaiming an early number (his party file shows that his ''second membership'' was grudgingly backdated only to April 1, 1928).

Eventually the BMW motor works gave him a job in Sweden, selling its airplane engines in Scandinavia. But he knew that his political fortune lay in Germany. In January 1927 he returned therefore to the land of his birth, holding a concession from the Swedish automatic parachute company Tornblad.

Carin was to stay behind in Sweden. As his train pulled out of Stockholm's central station, she collapsed into her sister Fanny's arms. Her heart gradually fading, she was taken to the Vita Kors Nursing Home at No. 11 Brunkebergstorg.

Each of them was half convinced they would never see the other again.

6

TRIUMPH AND TRAGEDY

Alone and penniless, Hermann Göring did not find it easy to rebuild
his career in Germany. The Richt-
hofen Veterans Association had blackballed him—their own last commander!—because of unresolved allegations about his war record. For Carin's sake, Ernst Röhm asked Munich musician Hans Streck to give the
returning prodigal a roof over his head. Göring settled down on the Strecks'
sofa, rising before the cleaning lady came each morning to put on his black
kimono embroidered with gold dragons, manicure his hands, and then sally
forth to put out feelers to the ungrateful party.

His first meeting with Hitler was unpromising. The Führer coldly recommended that perhaps his most useful accomplishment would be if he could
establish a foothold in Berlin society. Göring obediently rented a room in a
hotel off Berlin's Kurfürstendamm. He struck up a friendship with Paul
Körner. Körner, ten years his junior, would become like a son to him: a
small self-important Saxon wearing a polka-dot bow tie and single-medal
ribbon earned in the artillery, he attached himself to Göring as unpaid secretary and chauffeur. It was an ideal partnership—he had some money but
no ideas, Göring the reverse. Chauffeuring his own Mercedes, Körner drove
Göring around as he tried to sell parachutes. There were, Körner later said,

hard times that neither of them would ever forget, and the old craving gradually overwhelmed Göring again.

Occasionally a thin, pathetic voice came from the Stockholm sanatorium where Carin had piously placed herself in God's hands. The doctors had now told her that her condition was hopeless, and she wrote and told Göring that on January 26, 1927, soon after he left. "You have a right to know the truth," she wrote, "because you love me and have always done everything for me."

> I have no fear of death . . . I want only that His will be done, because I know that what He wills is for the best for everyone. And, darling, if there is no God, then death is only rest, like an eternal sleep—one knows no more of anything. But I firmly believe that there is a God, and then we shall see each other once more up there.
>
> Naturally I should like to live so that you have no sorrow and for Thomas's sake, and because I love you and Thomas above everything else and want—yes, I want it terribly—to stay with both of you.

Without her rapturous love, sensed by Göring from afar, he would probably have foundered forever in the twilight Berlin world of addicts and down-and-outs. But she threw her fragile weight into the battle for his survival, writing letters that are among the most moving documents in the Hermann Göring story.

> My darling's health is my greatest concern [she pleaded]. It is in far, far greater danger than my own. Darling, darling, I think of you all the time! You are all I have, and I beg you, make a really mighty effort to liberate yourself before it is too late. I understand full well that you can't break free all at once, particularly now when everything depends on you and you are hounded and harassed from all sides. But set yourself limits. Abstain from taking it for just as long as you can stand it.
>
> Make the interval as long as possible. You must suffer, you must be uncomfortable—but for my sake, because I love you so endlessly.
>
> I want so much to be with you when the time comes that you quit altogether . . . And after that, place your trust in me. This time tell me if you feel the craving coming back. Don't keep it from me. This time tell me, "I can't hold out—I want to take it again."
>
> Then we can talk with the doctor or go away for a few days or you can go alone to the mountains so that you escape the urge.

> You are a great spirit and fine man, you dare not succumb. I
> love you so strongly, with my whole body and soul, that I could
> not bear to lose you: to be a morphinist is to commit suicide—
> day after day you lose a small part of your body and soul. . . .
> You are ruled by an evil spirit or force, and your body gradually
> wastes away. . . .
>   Save yourself and with you, me!

Despite all his efforts, Göring was again losing the battle. Under interrogation
eighteen years later he would hint at otherwise unexplained excursions he
made to Turkey in 1927 and to Britain in the same year or the next. It is
fair to comment that Turkey was one of the leading opium-producing nations.
The Swedish record shows that from September 7 to 26, 1927, Göring was
again admitted to Långbro Mental Hospital for "abuse of morphine, dosage
of 40 to 50 cgm per diem."

   The story of Göring's struggle to overcome his accidental morphine addiction remained a closed book for some years. Then, in June 1933, at a
wedding dinner at Rockelstad Castle, Göring, by then a powerful German
minister, boasted to Count Eric von Rosen's new son-in-law, Dr. Nils Silfverskjoeld, that the Nazis would "gradually destroy" (*vernichten*) the Communists in Germany. Silfverskjoeld, himself a Communist, laid hands on
the Långbro dossier and publicized it in the Communist newspaper *Folkets
Dagblad* on November 18, 1933; the left-wing newspaper *Social-Demokraten*
also published references to Göring's hospital treatments. The war between
Göring and the Communists was by then one in which neither side gave
quarter.

   Göring spent Christmas with Carin in Sweden but left her still on her
sickbed in January 1928 to return to Berlin. He now shared an office in
Geisberg Strasse with Fritz Siebel, who was also in the aviation business.
Parachute sales were slow, but Göring had his eye on bigger game. On May
20, the all-important elections to the Reichstag (Parliament) would be held.
With the recklessness of a man with little more to lose, Göring blackmailed
the Nazi leadership into including him among their candidates. Secret backers
had provided the funds that enabled Hitler to enlarge his party to a membership of millions. Göring bluntly threatened to sue the party otherwise for
every pfennig it had owed him since 1922. Hitler capitulated, promising him
a seat if more than seven Nazis were elected. Göring rushed around to his
friend "Putzi" Hanfstaengl, whooping with glee. To be a Nazi candidate
under these circumstances was like money in the bank.

   Suddenly Göring was no longer a pariah. He brashly looked around for a
more imposing apartment, and begged Carin to travel to Berlin in time for
the elections. She arrived in mid-May, a few days before the poll. By that
time he had rented a little apartment at No. 16, Berchtesgadener Strasse. On
the seventeenth, three days before the election, he carried Carin into the

large corner room he had prepared for her, with its sun-drenched balcony smothered with white lilac. Sick though she was, she was in ecstasy to be with him again.

"I had a bath," she wrote to her mother, "and Hermann unpacked for me, I rested an hour, then three of Hermann's best friends came and invited us to a fine, stylish luncheon with champagne and *Schwedische platte*."

They dined at sunset on the shores of a Berlin lake, "amid the most revolting Jews!" They lunched with chopsticks at a Chinese restaurant where "slant-eyed" waitresses in kimonos served strawberries, and they talked excitedly about Sunday's polling day:

> They've already begun shooting it out. Every day the Com-
> munists parade with their crooked noses and red flags with the
> Star of David . . . and meet Hitler's men carrying their red ban-
> ners with swastikas (but without the crooked noses). Then there's
> a pitched battle, with dead and injured. Oh, if only things go well
> for Hermann, we would have some peace for a long time . . .
> just think!!!

She followed this letter with a telegram on the twenty-first:

HERMANN ELECTED YESTERDAY: MOTHER, YOU UNDERSTAND.

Hitler's party had attracted enough votes nationwide for twelve deputies to be returned to the Reichstag. So Göring was in, with a guaranteed income, influence—and friends. "It is awful," Carin wrote on the twenty-third, "to see how all those who kept away while he was having a hard time now come and assure him that they always believed in him, and why didn't he tell them he was in difficulties?"

He was overwhelmed with commissions for newspaper articles: He would earn five hundred Reichsmarks per month as a deputy, and eight hundred more as a party orator—and that was just the beginning. Their poverty was finally at an end: They could begin to pay off ancient debts, settle doctors' bills, redeem the things they had pledged at the pawnbrokers. As Carin's little white harmonium and all the other furniture that had been discreetly hocked was carried up to their third-floor apartment again, Hermann smiled indulgently. He was looking forward to a general settling of accounts all around.

"In the Reichstag," he told historian George Shuster, "we were the Twelve Black Sheep."

He took Carin along to the ceremonial opening on June 13, 1928.

"It was quite uncanny," she wrote the next day, "to see the Red Guard gang. They throw their weight about colossally. They were all wearing uniforms adorned with the Star of David—that is, the Soviet star—red armbands, etc. Young, most of them, and just raring for a fight. And some of them downright criminal types. How many in all these parties except Hitler's are Jews!''

Göring immediately claimed the Nazi party's transport "portfolio." It was no secret that since 1924 the general staff had been nurturing an embryonic aviation effort despite Versailles, and that the government's subsidies to the Lufthansa Airline played no small part in this. Captain Ernst Brandenburg, the ex-bomber pilot who was looking after this concealed army aviation effort, advised Lufthansa's director, Erhard Milch, as the subsidies came under increasing Communist attack, to "fix" a few gentlemen in the Reichstag. "They're all wide open to bribery," said Brandenburg. "Send for one man from every leading party, give them some cash, and they'll authorize the full subsidy the next time."

Milch evidently acted immediately, because Carin Göring was already mentioning "a contract with the Reich Transport Ministry" (i.e., Brandenburg) in a letter dated June 17, adding in the same letter that Hermann had already received the first payment under it and the thirty-four hundred marks that he wanted as a down payment on an even grander apartment in a new building at No. 7, Badensche Strasse, in Berlin's select Schöneberg district. Milch confirmed (to this author) that Lufthansa was bribing Göring and a handful of other deputies (Cremer, Quaatz, and Keil) with one thousand marks per month; only the Communists refused to accept Lufthansa money. It became common knowledge. "Milch," suggested one lieutenant colonel later, "had Göring in his pocket because he could have blown the whistle on him at any time." The record shows that in the next two years Göring addressed the Reichstag only once—and then it was to demand higher subsidies for civil aviation, and to ask why Germany had no aviation minister, a post that he clearly coveted for himself.

After the election Hermann and Carin flew to Zurich, Switzerland, to lecture and demonstrate parachutes. But he now had far better sources of income. The funds were beginning to flow to him from German industry. He was shortly retained as a "consultant" by BMW and by Heinkel, and the records of young Willi Messerschmitt's Bavarian aircraft company would show at least one payment by a director, Fritz Hiller, entered as "one-time dispensation to G." Steel magnate Fritz Thyssen donated to him the decor and furnishings for the new apartment.

Greedy for more, Göring shortly asked Lufthansa for funds to set up an office, to pay Pili Körner's wages, and to hire a first-rate secretary too. Soon the airline found it was paying him fifty thousand Reichsmarks a year.

> I hardly ever see Hermann [lamented Carin that summer]. He goes to the office [on the corner of Friedrich Strasse and Tauben Strasse] early each morning and we usually lunch together, but mostly with a lot of other people who are invited or invite them-

selves. Then Hermann has the exhibition [the 1928 World Air Fair] or committees, and then dines hardly ever alone.

He is rarely ever home before two or three A.M., and he usually starts at eight in the morning . . . It is mainly his nervous energy and his interest in everything that drives him on. And the Reichstag session hasn't even begun yet!

He has an excellent stenographer and typist, and that is a great help. Today he got seventy-four letters! Yesterday fifty-five! . . . And yet he always has time if I need him.

Hitler is coming here on Friday. I haven't seen him since the old days [1925]. I'm agog!

She became an excellent society hostess in Berlin, though she hid her failing health only with difficulty. In November 1928 their new corner apartment in Badensche Strasse was ready for them to move in. The walls were white, the carpet wine red. The building had a basement garage, so the rich and influential could be transported up by direct elevator with the utmost discretion. Among their regular guests was the stocky Lufthansa director Milch, who now studiously entered Göring's birthday—January 12—in his pocket diaries. By December Milch would be entertaining Göring with lavish luncheons at the swank Kaiserhof Hotel; sometimes he would arrive in the basement garage, bringing the money Göring needed with him. "Carin Göring was present," he has told this author. "She radiated a wonderful charm. I could see that at heart he was a soft man who tried to conceal his softness by bluster."

Relieved momentarily of financial worries, Göring threw himself behind the party's recruiting campaign. "This evening," wrote Carin on February 21, 1929, "he's speaking to students of all parties at Berlin university. More than half of them are Nazis already, and I hope he'll manage to convert the rest. Tomorrow he's speaking at Nuremberg, and then he's off on a ten-day, twelve-lecture tour of East Prussia. Our home's swarming with politicians . . ."

He learned a lot about parliamentary procedure that session. The Reichstag was dominated by the Social Democrats and Communists. As the latter threat to Germany grew, Göring found he was able to raise his price. The Ruhr industrialists willingly paid it when they found that he had their interests at heart. It was coal magnate Wilhelm Tengelmann who had introduced him to the steel king Thyssen, to their mutual advantage.

This new source of funds was timely, because Lufthansa's bankers had begun to squirm. The Deutsche Bank archives show at least one ten-thousand-mark check in Göring's favor in June 1929, and a letter from Milch to the bank explaining, "As far as the deputy Mr. Göring is concerned, his position before the election was one of adviser to Lufthansa—that is, he was a paid consultant in the American sense." Appointed commercial director in July

1929, Milch chose as his first action to tackle Göring about the whole "unseemly" bribery business. "You can't carry on like this," he pointed out, "if you have any hopes of rising to important positions in public life later." He suggested that they pay him one hundred thousand marks now as an advance on his services as a consultant until the present Reichstag session was over. "Milch," exclaimed Göring, who was a year his junior, "I'm very grateful. That is far more acceptable to me, and besides, my freedom of action is now greater. Thyssen," he explained with childlike openness, as Milch recalled in 1945, "has opened an account of fifty thousand Reichsmarks on my behalf. I can draw as much as I like. . . . It will always be replenished."

Covering all bases, the Lufthansa director indicated that he wanted to join the Nazi party. Hitler asked him—and other key aviation figures like Göring's old flying comrade Bruno Loerzer—to lie low. To "come out" as Nazis now would vitiate their usefulness. "Accordingly," noted party chief Rudolf Hess five years later, "both [Milch and Loerzer] agreed not to join until the party came to power . . . and they handed their [secret] applications in to Göring."

Göring held no Nazi party office, and never would, but Hitler now shifted him onto the stage of high politics in his behalf, ordering him to win over Berlin's high society while Joseph Goebbels fought the battle for the streets. Aided by his Swedish countess wife, Göring drew easily on his blue-blooded wartime contacts, and the Nazi movement snowballed. The crown prince had been his army commander; the prince's younger brother, Prince August-Wilhelm ("Auwi"), fell for Carin and joined the party after Göring introduced him to Hitler; dressed in the uniform of an SA colonel, Auwi would stomp the election platforms at Göring's side. Soon the portly figure of Prince Eitel-Friedrich was also decked out in party uniform.

Carin described the social whirl in name-dropping letters to her mother. "Neither of us," she wrote loftily on the last day of February 1930, "would bear common parties today. The Wieds"—Prince Viktor and Princess Marie-Elisabeth zu Wied—"want to get their whole circle of friends interested in the Hitler movement and Hermann is absolutely bombarded with questions, opinions, and comments. Everybody tries to spot flaws in Hitler and criticize his program. Poor Hermann has to talk, talk, talk and answer questions until he's fit to drop. But all the time I can see that the circle around us is expanding, and that we've won over a lot of them to Hitler and his cause"—and she went on to mention one prince who was forty, chairbound, and paralyzed, "the poor fellow," but always got wheeled in to the meetings that Göring addressed.

Sometimes, those audiences were twenty thousand or even thirty thousand strong. Göring's style was demagogic rather than analytical, but, with unemployment touching four million, audiences found style less important than content now. "We shall flatten our opponents!" he would roar, and sit down to thunderous applause. He took to wearing the party's now-universal brown shirt, with his blue Pour le Mérite slung nonchalantly over a dark brown leather necktie. Ploughing his furrow across the German election landscape, he spoke at Magdeburg, Frankfurt, Plauen, and Mannheim, pulling himself together so as not to crack up during each speech, as Carin—whom her mother had urged to join him in Germany—wrote on June 2. "But he collapses like a wounded man afterward."

Later that summer she fell ill again. He transported her to the hospital at Bad Kreuth, on Lake Tegernsee, and took her son under his wing, walking and climbing with him in the mountains.

The rival parties were now fighting over 577 seats in the Reichstag. Göring's speeches took on a more combative style. On August 8, police agents reported that speaking at the Krone Circus in Munich Göring had defamed the Weimar Constitution and the present government. "He called the minister of the interior a bottom-spanker [*Steiss-Trommler*]," reported one scandalized police official. "He referred to the foreign minister [Dr. Julius Curtius] as 'that guy Curtius,'" he added; and as for the defense minister, General Wilhelm Groener, Göring had scoffed that his only combat experience so far had been to advance from desk to desk. To hoots of laughter from his mass audience, the police report said, Göring had advised Groener to take the salute at the Constitution Day parade in two days' time "with a slouch hat on his head and a peacock's feather sticking out of a certain part of his anatomy." For this lèse majesté the courts fined Göring—soon to become one of the richest men in Europe—three hundred marks.

The Nazi campaign paid off. On election day, September 14, 1930, they won 107 of the seats. It was a landslide.

Taking Thomas von Kantzow with him, Hermann went to congratulate Hitler at Jena the next day. In his little green pocket diary the lad wrote an amusing vignette of his stepfather's sly tactics:

> Hitler is here. Hermann speaks from a balcony and everybody is so enthusiastic that they could have thrown themselves at the feet of Hitler and Hermann, so the police have their work cut out.
>
> Hitler is very busy, so it is difficult for Hermann to speak to him. "Wait, watch this!" says Hermann and goes chasing after a tall, pretty blond actress from Munich, whom he takes over to Hitler. She is tickled pink and Hitler gets a delightful moment of relaxation . . . They chat for some time, after which Hermann finds it easier to approach Hitler about the important questions he has.

During those exhilarating weeks Göring had not seen much of Carin. He had ridden the political tide, but had left her more or less stranded in her sanatorium. Later that summer, the doctors let her go home, though with strict reservations (to which she paid little heed).

As the second-largest faction in the Reichstag now, in the autumn of 1930 the Nazi party was entitled to the office of deputy speaker (*Vizepräsident*). Hitler gave this plum job to Göring, which betokened his growing importance to the movement in Berlin. He appointed Göring his political trustee in the capital—which was, as Göring later pointed out, a very important post, enabling him to exploit his contacts there. "I was on the best of terms with Hindenburg, the armed forces, big industry, and the Catholic Church," he claimed; Hitler had authorized him to begin "wheeling and dealing," because the party now meant to win power by legitimate means: "Precisely how was irrelevant—whether with the help of the left or the right."

When the new Reichstag opened on October 13, 1930, he marched in at the head of the 107 Nazi deputies, all wearing brown shirts, and took his seat in the deputy speaker's chair. Afterward, the party's leadership and financial backers celebrated in the Göring apartment. "Reichstag opening," wrote airline-director Erhard Milch in his pocket diary. "Tumult. Evening at the Görings' with Hitler, Goebbels, August-Wilhelm of Prussia, Prince zu Wied and wife, the Niemanns, [chief photographer Heinrich] Hoffmann and daughter [Henrietta], the Hesses, Körner, Frick and Epp."

The only blight on Hermann's blossoming political career now was the failing health of Carin, the all-important hostess at these gatherings. On Christmas Eve she fainted as the presents were being unwrapped and rolled off the sofa onto the floor. For days after that she languished in bed with a fever, but she managed to struggle to her feet, waxy-featured and frail body trembling, for a dinner party on January 5, 1931, in honor of Hitler, Thyssen, and steel King Alfred Krupp, together with the country's leading men of finance. Banker Hjalmar Schacht, knowing nothing of her illness, was struck at the bareness of the repast—pea soup with pork, followed by Swedish apple pie. She retired to a sofa afterward, listening apathetically to their conversation.

Göring steeled himself against her physical decline. The political battle remained paramount to the Nazis, and they took support from whatever quarter they could get it. The harassed chancellor, Dr. Heinrich Brüning, later alleged (in a letter to Winston Churchill) that he found out that the Nazis were being financed by the Jewish general managers of two big Berlin banks, "one of them the leader of Zionism in Germany." On January 16, 1931, Göring joined Hitler's discussions with Brüning, who was vainly trying to hammer out a deal with the Nazis; then he and Carin left to visit the former kaiser at his place of exile, Doorn in Holland.

"Hermann and Mama have just left," wrote Thomas, who was visiting Germany again, in his green pocket diary. "It is eleven P.M. I went to the [Berlin] Zoo station with them and waved good-bye. We hope to profit by winning the kaiser over to the party, the kind of thing Hermann is adept at."

The former empress was horrified at Carin's condition—so weak that she could hardly climb the stairs—and pressed a wad of bank notes into an envelope for her to recuperate at Altheide, a spa in Silesia. Carin found the seventy-year-old kaiser sprightly for his age, but quick to lose his temper at Göring. "They flew at each other at once," she wrote in a letter afterward. "Both are excitable and so like each other in many ways. The kaiser has probably never heard anybody voice an opinion other than his own, and it was a bit too much for him sometimes." The adjutant made a note that the kaiser toasted the "coming Reich"; while Göring murmured a response to the "coming king," he was careful not to tag a specific name, given the several contenders.

A week later Carin seemed to have died. The doctors in Berlin could find neither pulse nor heartbeat. Hermann knelt in desperation as they injected stimulants. Lying at peace (she told her sister Fanny afterward), she could hear them announcing to her husband that it was all over. She sensed them prying open her eyelids. She was aware only of standing before a tall gateway, lustrous and beautiful. "My soul was free," she wrote to Fanny, "for this one short instant of time." Then her heart flickered and her eyes opened into Hermann's sorrowing gaze again.

> If Mama had died [commented Thomas in his diary] Hermann would have broken down completely. He himself says he doesn't know how he would have coped. Oh, I think it could have been dangerous given his smoldering temperament. He says I was the stronger . . . and that we must take this lesson to heart and start leading a healthier, more regular life.

Goebbels, Hitler's gauleiter (local Nazi party governor) in Berlin, frowned at Göring's flamboyant methods. After talking things over with him on February 18, 1931, Goebbels made a private note that the man was too much of an optimist—"He banks too much on doing deals. We're only going to get results by consistent hard work." But Göring was already dealing on many levels in Berlin. Behind the back of the government he was talking with the Italian ambassador, Baron Luca Orsini, and Brüning's agencies intercepted one telegram from the baron to Rome, sent on October 30, 1930, revealing that Göring had apparently leaked secret proceedings of the Reichstag's foreign-affairs committee (on disarmament and the Young Plan) to the embassy.

Göring airily denied the allegations, but when he traveled to Rome in May 1931—instructed by Hitler to assure the Vatican that the Nazi party was not pagan in intent—he had no difficulty in seeing Benito Mussolini in person. It was all very different from his humiliation at the hands of the Italians six years before.

Hermann had a wonderful time in Italy [wrote Carin on May 30]. For three weeks he was the guest of the king!!! He met Mussolini several times, and [air-force general Italo] Balbo too, and Sarfatti, Mussolini's "girl friend," who still has a great political influence.

He saw the pope and almost all the influential Vatican scoundrels as well. He had Mussolini's or the king's box every evening at the opera, a motor car was permanently at his disposal.

On this occasion he was not lying about seeing Mussolini, because he brought back a signed photograph for the Führer (which Mussolini only gave in person). But Göring had not seen the pope, or even Pacelli, the cardinal whom Hitler had specified. The Vatican had let him see only Giuseppe Pizzaro, a somewhat humbler functionary.

Göring had left Carin at the Altheide Sanatorium, and sometimes even put her out of his mind. For one last time she wrote to her mother in mid-July 1931, a long letter expressing cautious hope for her own eventual recovery:

But great news! Hitler has given us a wonderful car. Hermann only has to go and collect it himself. It will be a splendid specimen that was exhibited at the last Automobile Show in Berlin—a Mercedes, gray outside, red leather inside, long, elegant, and stylish! They made only one car of its kind. . . .

Hitler told us he always felt bad about the way the Bavarian authorities took away our car (you remember, 1923) and he has always wanted to give us a new one. He has done it from the royalties of his book, so it is an entirely personal gift!

Göring felt they both needed a vacation. He was drained. He spoke that month to an audience of thirty thousand farmers. "He was so moved to see all these people in need," wrote Carin. "There they all stood, singing 'Deutschland Deutschland uber Alles,' most of them with tears streaming down their faces. . . . How his nerves stand it beats me."

Her life was coming prematurely to its end, while her husband's, as though he had been born again, was just beginning. Carin von Fock would love Hermann Göring to her dying day, which was not many months away, and he would never forget the debt that he still owed her: Thanks to her, he had beaten off the fateful addiction long enough to reach the very threshold of absolute power.

Knowing perhaps that she had not long to live, he packed her at the end of that August 1931 into the swanky new Mercedes, and they set off with swastikas fluttering from each fender to tour Germany and then Austria, where his sister, now Paula Hueber, was christening a daughter. He and Pili

Körner took turns at the wheel, while Carin sat in front wearing a light gray coat, her face as pale as death but framed in a rakish motoring helmet of leather. She watched Hermann triumphantly signing autographs everywhere, but she was so weak that meals had to be carried out to her.

Suddenly and unexpectedly Carin's mother died on September 25. Ignoring the warnings of her doctors, she returned to Stockholm for the funeral: with newly hired, beige-liveried chauffeur Wilhelm Schulz driving, they all set out in the Mercedes from Berlin, but by the time they arrived at the wind-swept, bleak churchyard at Lövo near Drottningholm, the coffin was already in the ground. It was the last time that Carin's embittered father, Baron Carl von Fock, would ever seen his five daughters together, because on the following night, at the Grand Hotel, Carin collapsed with a heart attack.

Once more Hermann was told that these were her last hours. She had no will to live on, now that her mother had gone, but for several days she lingered, while Göring sat at her bedside clad in a red silk dressing gown, or crept away to shave or snatch a meal. Once her eyes fluttered and she whispered, "I did so hope I was going to join Mama."

Occasionally Hermann turned to Thomas, sitting bleakly in a darkened corner of the room, and tears were glistening in his eyes.

And then the telegram came recalling him to Berlin. With unemployment now topping five million, the Nazi clamor to take over from the hapless Brüning had become too loud for President Hindenburg to ignore. He wanted to see the Nazi leadership about forming a new government. Herr Göring was required to return at once.

For five more days he stayed at Carin's bedside, his conscience torn between duty and desire. The nurse, Märta Magnuson, would recall years later that his hands were soft and feminine—on first glimpsing him with his head bowed and long hair hanging down she had thought it was a woman. The couple barely spoke. Once Carin asked for the bed to be moved so she could look across the water to the palace where she had been presented at court in 1909 and had danced at the royal balls.

"I am so tired," she whispered to her son when Hermann was out of the room. "I want to follow Mama. She keeps calling for me. But I cannot go. So long as Hermann is here, I cannot go."

Guilelessly Thomas told her of the telegram that had come from Berlin on the fourth, and when Hermann came back in she took the big man's head close to her lips and whispered faintly but urgently to him.

Her sister Fanny came in.

"Hermann has been called back to Berlin," Carin said. "You must help him to pack."

Hitler and Göring were shown into President Hindenburg's presence on October 10, 1931. The ex-corporal subjected the great field marshal to a lecture on Germany. This failed to impress, and nothing came of the interview. Disappointed, the two Nazi leaders threw themselves back into the general political fray.

It was back to tactics and point-scoring again. Göring forced a vote of no confidence in the government. Brüning managed to survive it, on October 16, but only by twenty-five votes.

Jubilant and confident of eventual victory, Göring telephoned the clinic in Stockholm the next morning and spoke to the nurse Märta. She broke it to him that Carin had died that morning at 4:10 A.M.—the clinic's telegram had not yet reached him. Consumed with remorse, he made the long journey back to Stockholm, supported by Pili Körner and his older brother Karl, to say adieu at last to his beloved wife. Thomas watched him kneel weeping by the open coffin in the Edelweiss chapel where their great love affair had begun, then stood at his stepfather's side as the white, rose-covered coffin was lowered into the ground next to her mother's freshly planted grave.

Young Thomas was overwhelmed with boyhood memories. He recalled once meeting his stepfather and Carin at the railroad station in Stockholm. Hermann had alighted first, and turned to lift her down. He had draped his greatcoat around his shoulders, and the empty sleeves fell around her neck as he embraced her so that for one instant it had seemed as though he had four arms to hold her with. "She put her arms around him," said Thomas later, "and tucked her head into his shoulder, and it looked just as if a chubby bear were fondling its cub." This image would recur to Thomas each time in coming years that people spoke ill of the Reichsmarschall.

"I once asked Göring straight out," said young Birgitta von Rosen, Carin's niece, "how his frightening megalomania really began. He told me quite seriously and calmly, without being the least affronted, that it must have been when Carin left Thomas and her own family [in 1922] to follow him to Germany. He had no position, no money, and no means of offering her a secure future. On the contrary, Carin had had to raise funds by selling off her home." He had then told Brigitta of one auction he had witnessed at their Ödengatan home in Stockholm; while the heartless auctioneer had called for bids on her ancient family heirlooms, and his hammer rose and fell, Göring had sat next door listening to the whole ordeal (it was at the lowest point of his morphine addiction). "Something," he said, "snapped inside me. From that moment on I determined to do all I could so that my Carin should live as well as she had before, and better." Thus his debt to Carin had grown. By marrying him, she had lost everything. "And that," he confided to Birgitta von Rosen, "was how my 'megalomania' began."

How would he survive without Carin? Would he revert to his old and unbecoming ways? Back in Berlin he closed the apartment in Badensche Strasse, with its pink-and-white decor and its fragrant memories of his Swedish countess bride, and moved into the masculine, mahogany-and-leather world of the Kaiserhof Hotel.

This was where Hitler made his command post whenever he was in Berlin.

7
THE SPEAKER

For fifteen months following Carin's death Göring hurled himself into the Berlin effort. That way he had no time for sorrowing. When it was all over and he was asked to reflect upon this period, he remembered first the thrills, the drama, and the trickery—the political backstabbing in which he took such obvious delight. Hitler was fighting for the future of Germany: to Göring, however, it was the means that mattered far more than the aim.

Something of the flavor of those months is caught in the files of Göring's attorney, the later-notorious Hans Frank. Göring, it seems, would issue libel writs at the drop of a hat. Thus, when Bruno Loerzer mentioned on May 12, 1932, that at lunch that day at the Aviators' Club he had heard a Major Baron Ugloff von Freyberg declaim in front of the assembled aviators, "I can no longer regard Göring as a man of honor!", Göring at once exacted a written apology and costs. A few days later the files show Göring suing a Munich editor, Dr. Fritz Gerlich, for having claimed that Göring had broken his word of honor by escaping after the beer hall putsch. As the summer election campaign began, another typical suit on the attorney's file was being brought by Göring against a Count Stanislaus Pfeil for having stated in public that Göring was once heard to shout "Waiter, a bottle of champagne!" from his sleeping compartment in a train in East Silesia. It seems clear that Göring had developed the monumental vanity of which the pharmaceutical textbooks on morphine had spoken.

Meanwhile, Brüning's government had collapsed, and for want of a better alternative Franz von Papen, a reputable officer who was otherwise a non-entity, had been appointed interim chancellor; at the end of May 1932 Hitler grudgingly agreed to support Papen, but only until the elections were held two months later.

Before leaping into the election melee, Göring went to the Mediterranean island of Capri to recover from the obsessive melancholy that still seized him, nine months after Carin's death, whenever he thought of her, entombed now in Sweden. From Capri he sent a telegram to a blond German actress he had recently met in Weimar, Emmy Sonnemann, saying he hoped to see her when he returned there during the election battle. Separated from her husband, the actor Karl Köstlin, Emmy was a domestic, unsophisticated Hamburg woman. Perhaps not as well versed in politics as she might have been, she at first confused Göring with Goebbels when they met, but in the spring of 1932 Hermann had contrived a second meeting in Weimar, where she was on the stage, and she had been oddly impressed by his frequent and tender references to his deceased wife.

Although Emmy would become Göring's second wife, the ghost of Carin von Fock was to dog them everywhere. His first gift to Emmy would be a photograph of Carin; later, he would name their two yachts and a forest palace after her. Emmy would find that he had not only installed Carin's old housekeeper, Cilly Wachowiak, at his newly rented third-floor apartment at No. 34 Kaiserdamm in Berlin, but that he was setting aside one room there as a permanent shrine to Carin's memory, with her white harmonium and a painting of her. Placid and tolerant, Emmy put up with these intrusions, although she confessed to friends that the apartment's furniture was not to her taste—it was ponderous and expensive, with no particular style.

On Emmy's first evening at Kaiserdamm Göring threw a big reception. She caught sight of the kaiser's nephew Prince Philipp of Hesse, whom Hermann had now lured into the party (Göring had been at cadet college with one of the prince's brothers, later killed in action), along with another brother, Prince Christoph (who would meet an untimely end in 1943 as head of Göring's signals intelligence agency, the Forschungsamt.)*

In Berlin the election battle had begun—and the word *battle* was literal in this case. Pistols and machine guns took the place of words, fists, and libel actions. During the final month, July 1932, thirty Communists and thirty-eight Nazis would die in the election skirmishes. The Nazi party seemed unstoppable. Its private army, the SA, numbered 445,000 men—over four times the size of the regular army.

*He was killed in an October 1943 plane crash. For the Forschungsamt, see Chapter 9, Göring's Pet.

When the votes were counted on July 31, the Nazis had attracted 13,732,779. Entitled therefore to 230 seats in the Reichstag, they became the biggest party, but still Hindenburg offered Hitler only the vice-chancellorship, coupled with the appointment of Göring, his principal lieutenant, to the Prussian ministry of the interior. Göring seemed disposed to accept these terms, because on August 5, he telephoned Lufthansa's Milch and talked about making him his Staatssekretär (undersecretary of state). But Hitler demanded all or nothing, and when he and Göring went in to see the venerable old president on the thirteenth, he did not get his way. In vain Hitler lectured the field marshal again—about unemployment, agriculture, national unity, and alleged Jewish domination of the German way of life. Hindenburg had been distressed by the Nazi party's uncouth behavior both in the Reichstag and in the streets (although he told his secretary the next day that he had found much to admire in both Hitler and Göring). Yet during the months of ensuing political intrigue, Hindenburg would remain in touch with Göring, often using Pili Körner, Göring's dapper adjutant, for this purpose.

With the necessary support of the Center party and the Bavarian People's party, the Nazis unanimously elected Göring as speaker (*Präsident*) of the Reichstag when it opened on August 30. The office gave him direct access to Hindenburg. Göring would retain it in fact until parliament's heart ceased to beat in Germany ten years later. "I thus occupied," he would emphasize, "the third-ranking position in the Reich."

Von Papen's position as chancellor without an effective majority was impossible right from the start, and the Nazis did nothing to make it easier. In fact, he would be the only Reich chancellor in history who never managed to speak from the floor of his House. In a meeting of the top Nazis at Göring's apartment on the last evening in August, they plotted how to humiliate Papen and hound him out of office. The opportunity to do so came on September 12, the very first session. The Communists had tabled a vote of censure. "Papen," recalled Göring amusedly years later, "rushed over to Hindenburg and fetched his authority for the decree to dissolve the House. . . . I could see he had the red dispatch box tucked under his arm, and I knew of course what that meant, so I speeded up the calling of the division." Papen frantically tried to attract his attention, but Göring looked the other way: "Gentlemen, we shall take the vote!" Papen sprang to his feet and dumped the dissolution decree in front of Göring—who recognized, without looking, the signatures of Hindenburg and Papen on it.

"Mr. Chancellor," he admonished Papen. "You'll have to wait. Not until the vote is over!"

Grinning elfishly, he turned the document around so that he could not read it. In the ensuing vote of censure, Communists and Nazis joined forces: Papen attracted only 42 votes, to 513 votes against him. After announcing the result, Göring picked up the document and read it out to guffaws all around the chamber. "I informed Papen," he recalled in 1945, with huge enjoyment, "that he could not dissolve the Reichstag as he was no longer chancellor!"

The upshot was yet another libel action. Papen furiously wrote accusing Göring of violating Article 33 of the Constitution by preventing him from speaking. "The Reichstag was dissolved," his letter of that same day claimed. "But you continued the session and took a vote, both of them actions that violated the Constitution." Since he published his letter, Göring sued him for libel. Papen apologized, but only in private, and the episode left feathers ruffled on both sides.

Hindenburg was equally unamused by Göring's parliamentary prank. Overriding Göring, he left the Reichstag dissolved, by presidential decree, with Papen still in office.

The episode showed how rapidly Göring had mastered the intricacies of parliamentary procedure. "If I had hesitated for one instant," he bragged afterward, "the whole maneuver would have flopped. As it was, Papen was finished."

He was developing two personalities, and reveling in both of them—the beer hall adventurer of 1923 and the lion of society of 1932. He became a famous host and a much-sought-after guest for dinners and hunting parties. Wealthy landowner Martin Sommerfeldt, who invited him to hunt that autumn on his estate in the province of Brandenburg, noticed that the dichotomy in his former aviator persisted, "torn between the blustering and rowdy revolutionary and the visionary grand seigneur—between the SA's brown shirt in the forenoon and the snug-fitting dinner jacket at night."

Fresh elections had been called for November 6, 1932. A real electoral cliff-hanger was beginning. In this new poll Hitler lost two million voters, and the number of Nazi deputies in the Reichstag was trimmed accordingly from 230 to 196. Hitler sent Göring urgently to see Mussolini, possibly to raise cash for the exhausted Nazi party coffers; the Bavarian frontier police reported on the thirteenth that Göring "mentioned casually at the currency checkpoint that they were not carrying very much cash, as they had been invited as guests to Rome"—and the "they" included former Reichsbank governor Dr. Hjalmar Schacht, who had assured Hitler in a secret letter on August 29 that the Nazis could count on him. The news of Papen's resignation as chancellor four days later reached Göring when he was actually dining with Mussolini; he rushed back to Berlin as the Führer's personal delegate to revive the horse-trading with Hindenburg. Hindenburg sent for both the Nazi leaders on the nineteenth, and again over the next few days. ("Herr Hitler," he boomed, "I want to hear what your ideas are!") The politicking continued until the end of November, with Göring backing Hitler all the way in his unflinching demand for the supreme office of chancellor, and Hindenburg equally obstinately refusing so long as the Nazis did not command an absolute majority in the Reichstag.

At one stage General Kurt von Schleicher, who had assured the aged president that he could split the Nazis, offered Hitler the vice-chancellorship. Again Hitler refused. The final lineup was that on December 1, 1932, Hindenburg appointed Schleicher as chancellor with Papen as vice-chancellor. This regime would survive only two months. Göring called it the most wretched that Germany had ever suffered. It was a testing time for the Nazi rank and file: They were on the threshold of power, and many could not understand why Hitler and Göring would not accept the half-loaf that Schleicher had cunningly offered to them. Gregor Strasser, the leader of a rival leftist faction within the Nazi party, had played an unfortunate and destabilizing role in those weeks, and neither Hitler nor Göring could forgive him for that: Strasser would eventually die on the same day as Schleicher, and in the same way. "A movement like ours," wrote Göring that year, "can pardon many things, but not disloyalty toward a leader."

Göring in these days was nagged by insomnia, and he found himself occasionally yearning for more tranquil times. His soul was now torn between two women—one cozy, warm-blooded, and alive, the other intellectually vastly her superior, but dead. He spent that Christmas of 1932 with the former, Emmy Sonnemann, then left to commune with the other, spending the New Year with Carin's relatives at Rockelstad. The letter that he wrote to Emmy from the Swedish castle, penned that New Year's Eve by the light of candles and an oil lamp as he sat before an open fire, betrays a certain fondness; but there was no trace of the intensity of the devotion he had felt for Carin:

> My darling!
> I'm listening to songs on the Swedish radio. . . . What pleasure the radio set you gave is giving me. I had a concert all the way from Berlin to the Sassnitz ferry despite the rattling of the train. I can pick up thirty or forty stations here. Yesterday I was able to get Stuttgart for a while. . . .
> For hours every day I go for long walks by myself in the most beautiful forest you've ever seen. I'm sleeping eight or ten hours a day; I just hope I can stay on a bit longer. They all speak so charmingly of you here, they're all very nice to me.
> My dear, I want to thank you from my heart for all your love and unselfish sacrifice and for everything you've done for me. Let's hope the New Year is just as kind to us.

A few hours later, the new year, 1933, began: Göring's year of destiny, and Europe's too. He was obsessed with Gregor Strasser and his treachery. "At midnight," wrote Goebbels, campaigning with Göring in an important election at Lippe on January 13, "Göring came. Strasser is the eternal subject of our discussions." But then, just when it seemed impossible that anything productive would emerge from the weeks of grubby intrigue, the Nazis began to emerge victorious after all. The vice-chancellor, Franz von Papen, met Hitler furtively at the house of a Cologne banker and, in a reversal of his former position, agreed to serve under the Nazi Führer; they carved up the future Cabinet portfolios between their respective parties. Papen then arranged a secret meeting between Hitler and the president's influential son, Colonel Oskar von Hindenburg. Göring attended this secret meeting—held in the villa of champagne-company director Joachim von Ribbentrop at Berlin-Dahlem—and claimed much of the credit himself for its successful outcome. At any rate, after listening for an hour to Hitler urging that every week his father waited was a week lost for Germany's destiny, the colonel took a cab back to the presidential palace visibly impressed.

President Hindenburg now moved rapidly to dissolve Schleicher's government. On January 23, he refused the general's request for dictatorial powers. He instructed Papen to negotiate with Hitler. Hitler in turn told Göring to start bargaining with the other parties, and Göring started dealing out Cabinet portfolios to entice them. On Hitler's instructions he selected General Werner von Blomberg, the staid, uncomplicated military commander of East Prussia, to take over as minister of defense.

His position now hopeless, Schleicher resigned on January 28. The next day the last obstacles to Hitler's chancellorship were removed, and Göring had the good fortune to be the one to convey the welcome news to him. "In the afternoon," recorded Goebbels, "while we are taking coffee with the Führer, Göring suddenly comes in and announces that the Führer is to be appointed chancellor tomorrow." Goebbels conceded that Göring had "diplomatically and cleverly" prepared the ground for Hitler in "nerve-racking negotiations" that had lasted several months; thus it was only right that Göring, "this upright soldier with the heart of a child," should bring to Hitler the greatest news of his life. Göring's face was wreathed in smiles. He was now savoring an opiate as sweet as any forbidden narcotic—the prospect of power, and of the material wealth that would go with it.

PART 2
THE ACCOMPLICE

8
BONFIRE NIGHT

itler and Göring came to power on January 30, 1933. On that day began the twelve-year "good run for my money" of which the latter would make wistful mention when delivered into the hands of his captors in 1945. He was about to enjoy great power and the privileges that went with it—access to immense riches and the ability to repay to others something of the physical pain that he had suffered since the beer hall putsch ten years before.

There were still snags, of course. Germany was on the brink of political anarchy. Six million people were now unemployed. The same number of disgruntled Communists showed no sign yet of accepting defeat. And Hitler, still heading only a minority party in the government, was allowed to fill only two of the Cabinet posts with Nazis. Prima facie there was little to prevent Hitler, with only Wilhelm Frick as minister of the interior and Göring as minister without portfolio, from being washed overboard like Schleicher and Papen before him.

It looked like an unpromising start. "Shortly after midday," wrote Count Schwerin von Krosigk in his diary—he would be retained as finance minister—"we were called into the president's room."

I found the whole future Cabinet assembled there—Hitler (on whom I set eyes for the first time); Frick; Göring; Papen [vice-chancellor]; Seldte; Hugenberg; Blomberg; Neurath [likewise retained as foreign minister] . . . The Old Man welcomed us with a brief speech expressing his satisfaction that the nationalist right wing had at last united. Papen read out the list of ministers.

Hitler had already taken one determined step to consolidate the Nazi seizure of power. He had appointed, as was the chancellor's prerogative, the new minister of the interior in Prussia—Hermann Göring. In the first instance, this enabled Göring to ban the Communist protest demonstration threatened for that evening, but in the longer term it would provide the means to make the Nazi party's stranglehold on power impregnable. At the very first Cabinet meeting, held at 5:00 P.M. on that January 30, 1933, while crowds swayed and chanted in the street outside, roaring the national anthem up to the Cabinet Room windows, Göring predicted that the existing laws and police forces might prove inadequate; from the misgivings that he now voiced about the "present civil service structure" of his Prussian ministry, it is obvious that he was already planning a purge there too.

At this first Cabinet session Hitler and Göring adopted a more moderate line than the non-Nazi ministers when the possibility of banning the Communist party altogether was considered. Hitler felt, as Schwerin von Krosigk recorded later that day, that "a new Cabinet ought not to begin with immediate confrontations that would lead to bloody fighting, and probably a general strike and economic paralysis." The Cabinet minutes show that Göring backed Hitler and successfully suggested that they call a new general election immediately and hope for the two-thirds majority that would grant to the Nazi party the constitutional power to pass an enabling act making Hitler dictator.

That night Hitler and Göring stood at the Chancellery windows and took the salute as the SA and other Nazi formations staged a drum-beating, blaring, intimidating torchlight victory parade.

Göring had given Emmy a revolver to protect herself that night against any last-minute revenge attempts. He was worn out, but asked her before falling asleep next to her to do a favor for him the next morning. "Buy the Führer some flowers," he said. "He will like that."

The new elections were to be held on March 5, 1933. That did not leave much time. Working, living, eating, and sleeping in the Ministry of the Interior Building, Göring began a bare-knuckles purge, determined to cleanse the entire ramshackle structure of dissidents and replace them with men who were 150 percent dedicated to the new cause. On the very next day Schwerin von Krosigk remarked in his diary, "With his ruthless hiring and firing, Göring seems without question to be the Danger Man."

But Hitler was a man in a hurry, and relied on Göring's nerve. Ten years later he would still describe him admiringly as "ice cold in times of crisis," and add: "I've always said that when it comes to the crunch he's a man of steel—unscrupulous."

Neither of them had any intention of losing office. "No living force," Hitler told his cronies, "will get me out alive."

Vice-Chancellor Franz von Papen, formally vested by Hindenburg with the powers of chancellor of Prussia, still hoped to exert some checks on Hitler and Göring. "As Prussian police minister," the German press was reassured in a confidential circular on February 2, "Herr Göring is also subordinated to Papen."

But Göring saw things differently and crowed to Papen, echoing Hitler's boast, "You will only get me out of this room flat on my back!"

Throughout February, while the election battle warmed up, Göring plotted, planned, and purged. Foreign Minister von Neurath called him "a dreadful man," and told Britain's bibulous ambassador Sir Horace Rumbold that Papen was quite unable to control him. "Göring," advised Neurath, "is regarded as the real Fascist in the Hitler party."

In broad outline Hitler's eventual plan, if he won the coming election, was to restore Germany's economic health, rebuild her armed forces in defiance of Versailles, and then start making history.

Göring would have a key part in this too. On February 2 Hindenburg had appointed him Reich commissar for aviation. Göring appointed Lufthansa's bustling chief executive, Erhard Milch, as his deputy. On the sixth the two men explained to a dubious Defense Minister von Blomberg that they intended to build up a military air force under cover of expanding Germany's civil aviation. Hitler hinted at this to his Cabinet on the eighth—this project would provide work for the unemployed. "Everything for the armed forces!"— that was the paramount principle that Hitler suggested to this Cabinet session, and on the next day they voted an initial 40 million Reichsmarks for the aviation budget. A week later they voted to increase that figure, and when the finance minister stoutly objected, Hitler advised him that what they were doing was to help the German people, "by camouflaged means," to acquire the air force that Versailles had denied them.

That much is in the Cabinet minutes (which, like the Swedish hospital dossiers, routinely spelled Göring's name wrong). The military records bear it out. "Our air-force officer corps," Hitler told Blomberg, "is to be an elite. The other services will have to lump it." By November 7, 1933, as Milch's private diary shows, Göring would have secured a 1.1 billion-Reichsmark budget for the coming year. The aim was to create a "risk air force" by late 1935, that is, a force strong enough to burn the fingers of any neighbor who interfered with Hitler's intentions.

As uncrowned king of Prussia, Göring commanded the largest police force in Germany. Addressing the assembled staff of the ministry, he traded heavily on the memory of his father as a former Prussian official and demanded that all Communists hand in their resignations. Out of thirty-two city police chiefs in Prussia, he later bragged, he removed all but ten. He fired hundreds of inspectors and thousands of sergeants, and filled their desks with trusty comrades drawn from the ranks of the SA and Heinrich Himmler's SS.

On February 4, he had dissolved the Prussian State Parliament. (He would replace it with an advisory State Council packed with political cronies and the occasional elder statesman or lawyer, to pacify President Hindenburg.) "Göring," wrote Goebbels in an approving diary entry on the thirteenth, "is mopping up in Prussia with a zeal that warms the cockles of your heart. He's got the wherewithal to do some really radical things." He banned the Communist election meetings; his hired thugs terrorized the other parties' gatherings.

The police, of course, no longer intervened. "My actions," he told police officials at Frankfurt-on-Main, "are not affected by legal considerations. You must become accustomed to the idea that I am not in office to dispense justice—but to destroy and exterminate!" "Shoot first and ask questions afterward," one of his first directives to police officers read. "Any mistakes that my officers make," he told assembled policemen at Dortmund, "are my mistakes. The bullets they fire are my bullets."

"You can't carry on in your ministry like a pasha!" Papen gasped to him. But carry on he did, and Papen shortly learned that Dr. Erich Gritzbach, his own principal private secretary, was in Göring's pay as well as his.

The Italian consul general Giuseppe Renzetti reported to Rome from Berlin, "Göring is the driving force in the Cabinet and is waging a merciless fight against the left."

Had she still been alive now, Carin would not have recognized her husband. Hair slicked back, he sat behind his ministerial desk wearing a somber suit, and prepared to embark upon his first criminal adventures, convinced of the sanctity and rectitude of his own cause. With Emmy hovering in the background—because once again he was living with another man's legal wife—Göring hosted the party's vital fund-raising functions in his Kaiserdamm apartment or in the speaker's official residence. On February 20, he invited twenty-five wealthy Ruhr industrialists to meet Hitler and make one last major cash infusion for the coming election. Banker Hjalmar Schacht acted as master of ceremonies. Sixty-three-year-old Gustav Krupp, head of the steel-making dynasty, brought with him the big names like Kauert, Winterfeld, Tengelmann, and Albert Vogler, while top I.G. Farben executives Dr. Stein, Carl Bosch, and Georg von Schnitzler were also definitely present. Hitler shook hands all around, took up his stance at the head of the table, and delivered a speech that—to judge from the record in Krupp's files— lacked nothing in candor.

> We've got [Hitler said] to seize the instruments of power first
> of all if we are to floor the enemy permanently. . . . You must
> never strike until you are at the summit of your might—until you
> are sure that you are at the peak of your power growth.

He described the coming election fight as stage 2 in his attack on the Communists. "There will be no turning back for us," he promised these men of money, "even if there's no clear election result. It's a case of either/or: Either the result is cut-and-dried, or we shall force a showdown some other way.

"I have only one wish for the economy," he continued, "that it enter upon a peaceful future, in parallel with our reconstruction at home. The question," Hitler added, "whether we raise a Wehrmacht [armed forces] or not will be decided, not at Geneva, but in Germany. But first we shall proceed through domestic peace to domestic strength—and there can be no peace at home until Marxism is finished."

Handsome and urbane, Göring spoke a few words, assuring them that the German economy would recover rapidly once political peace was restored. "There will be no experiments," Hitler's right-hand man promised.

"Göring," the Krupp transcript states, "led his argument adroitly on to the need for those circles not engaged in the political arena at least to make some financial sacrifice."

"Industry," he concluded, with a brazenness that suggests that he knew his remarks would be well received, "will I am sure be happy to make this sacrifice once they realize that the coming election of March 5 will be Germany's last for ten years—and perhaps for one hundred!"

Twenty-five pairs of heavily ringed, manicured hands applauded. Krupp thanked the forty-three-year-old Hitler for "having given us such a vivid insight into the way your mind is working." The Führer left Göring's apartment amid the rustle of checkbooks (Schacht had indicated that three million Reichsmarks was the kind of campaign fund they had in mind).

Stepping up the fight against their opponents, four days later Göring's police officials swooped on the Communist party headquarters in Berlin. He claimed that they had found incriminating documents in what he picturesquely called its "catacombs." "I was told," he later recalled, "that the Communists were winding up for a major coup. I had lists of all the Communists drawn up so that we could arrest them immediately when the balloon went up." For the moment these lists were kept on ice, since President Hindenburg had already proven unreceptive to the Nazis' radical measures, like a new law proclaiming their swastika to be Germany's national flag.

All such reservations were dramatically dispelled a few days later. At 9:30 P.M. on February 27, 1933, as Göring was toiling at his desk, reports reached him that his Reichstag Building was ablaze. He threw on a voluminous camelhair coat and jumped into his car. He pulled up outside his official residence, across the street from the Reichstag. He could see flames already shooting up through the building's glass cupola, and the first fire engines were on the scene. His first thought was for the heirlooms that he had inherited from his father—some of them were hanging in the Speaker's Office. He was also heard to shout, ''We must save the tapestries!'' as he dashed into the tunnel that connected the speaker's residence with the blazing Reichstag Building. He came up inside the latter to find the big session-chamber already a furnace—sucking in air from outside so violently that, although not of negligible bulk, he found himself being dragged forward into the flames.

It is now generally accepted by reputable historians that the Nazis were not the instigators of this blaze—fortuitous though it proved for their campaign and cause. Göring, toppling helplessly toward the flames, would certainly have cursed his own misfortune if they had been. ''As I opened the door,'' he told George Shuster years later:

> I was all but drawn into the flames by the hot draught. Fortunately my belt snagged in the door [of a phone booth] and that stopped me from toppling forward. Just at that moment the huge cupola came crashing down . . . I saw self-igniting firelighters on the benches and chairs in the chamber that had eaten through the leather upholstery and set them on fire.

His office was still intact. He met Hitler and Goebbels there, joined shortly by Rudolf Diels, chief of his political police, and Vice-Chancellor von Papen, who had been dining over in the cliquish Herrenklub with President Hindenburg when the shocking news of the fire came. One of the security men told Hitler that the last person he had seen leaving the chamber was Ernst Torgler, the senior Communist deputy. In fact, Torgler had left over an hour previously, which did not prevent Göring from claiming mischievously in his conversation with George Shuster, ''I saw Togler there, carrying a briefcase.''

Shortly, a more convincing suspect was apprehended, trying to get away through the south door. Naked to the waist and streaming with sweat, this young man of twenty-four made no attempt to conceal that he had started the blaze, using his own clothes and four packets of firelighters for the purpose. A burly, stooping bricklayer with tousled hair and vacant eyes, he was identified as Marinus van der Lubbe, a member of a Dutch Communist splinter organization. In a crazy one-man protest against the new government for ''oppressing the workers,'' this Dutch youth had already tried unsuccessfully to burn down three other buildings, including Berlin's City Hall, castle, and a welfare office.

For Göring, who had hoped for proof of an immense Communist conspiracy, Van der Lubbe, ''a halfwitted Communist pyromaniac,'' was a poor exhibit. Discussing it at the Chancellery later, however, that same evening,

Hitler and Goebbels saw it very differently. If they extracted every ounce of publicity from this "godsent beacon," as Hitler called it, they could walk away with the March 5 election.

"Now we'll show them," cried Hitler, purpling with excitement. "Anybody who stands in our way now will get mown down!"

In a further meeting at Göring's own ministry, Hitler instructed him to make immediate use of the arrest lists that they had so fortuitously drawn up during the past few days.

A draft presidential decree suspending civil liberties was also taken out of its file, ready for Hindenburg to sign.

Small wonder that when his ministry's press chief now diffidently laid before Göring his draft communiqué, announcing Van der Lubbe's arrest and police beliefs that "a hundredweight" of incendiary materials had been used, he exploded with frustration, swept his desk clear of the accumulating telegrams and police reports, grabbed a blue pencil, and shouted, "Rubbish! One hundredweight? Ten—no, one hundred!"

The official stammered that Van der Lubbe could hardly have carried in all that alone.

"Nothing is impossible!" cried Göring. "There were ten—no, twenty men!"

He dictated a new communiqué to his secretary, Fräulein Grundtmann, scrawling his own outsized "G" at its foot.

He adhered to the same standards of accuracy in reporting to the quailing Cabinet ministers the next morning:

> Admittedly the man arrested [Van der Lubbe] was maintaining that he had perpetrated the outrage on his own, [said Göring according to the Cabinet minutes], but this statement was not to be credited. He, Reich Minister Göring, was assuming that there had been at least six or seven attackers. The arsonist was definitely observed some time before the fire consorting with the Communist Reichstag deputy Torgler; both are reported to have walked around inside the building.

All of this was quite untrue, as was the rest of Göring's report to the Cabinet, about the seizure of Communist plans to set up terror squads, burn down public buildings, poison communal soup kitchens, and kidnap the wives and children of leading ministers.

Playing the role to the full, Göring announced that he had closed every museum and castle, had banned every Communist and Social Democrat newspaper in Germany, and had arrested the Communist officials. The world press was already indignantly proclaiming that the Nazis themselves had torched the Reichstag. Göring was privately facetious about the allegation. "The next thing we know," he sniffed, "they'll be claiming I stood and watched the blaze wearing a blue toga and playing the violin!'' Not least among the administrative problems that the fire had caused him was that he now had to relinquish Prussia's best theater, the Kroll Opera House, to provide a home for future Reichstag sessions.

Perhaps some Cabinet ministers still voiced misgivings about the evidence, because on March 2, Göring would assure them that further documents had been seized during the night, proving this time that Moscow had given the Communists in Berlin a mid-March deadline to take action or forfeit their Soviet cash subsidies in consequence. Suffice it to say that never in later years, and least of all to subsequent interrogators, did Göring repeat these claims; nor did he ever produce the documents—''captured maps'' locating the electric-power installations, subway, and transformer stations that were to be blitzed. (''One map,'' he had convincingly claimed, ''was found at [Communist] party headquarters, the other had been cut up and distributed to the individual hit squads.'')

The Reichstag fire was the first occasion on which he resorted to such truly monumental falsehoods. But the lies served their purpose, because they enabled him to lock up three thousand political opponents before election day. Among the Communists to be apprehended were three Bulgarians— Vassil Tanev, Blagoi Popov, and Georgi Dimitrov. Together with Torgler and the luckless Van der Lubbe, they were accused of responsibility for the Reichstag fire and committed for trial. Göring reserved his venom particularly for Dimitrov, who was a leading member of the Comintern (the Soviet directorate of international subversion). ''Dimitrov,'' he snorted years later, ''was a murky figure. Wherever he turned up, you could be sure there was dirty work afoot.''

When the Reichstag fire trial began at Leipzig late in September 1933, Göring attempted to turn it into a crusade against the Communists and was humiliated. He appeared in person as a prosecution witness, clad in brown tunic, riding breeches, and polished jackboots. He would never forget the resulting confrontation with Dimitrov on November 4.

''My opinion is different,'' retorted the Bulgarian at one stage.

''Logical,'' conceded Göring. ''But mine's the one that counts!''

''I continue,'' said Dimitrov. ''Is it known to Mr. Göring that the party with what he calls this 'criminal ideology' is a party that rules one-sixth of the earth's surface? Namely, the Soviet Union?''

''What they do in Russia,'' Göring broke in after a further lecture by the defendant, ''is a matter of indifference to me. I am concerned only with the Communist party in Germany and with the alien Communist scoundrels who come here and set our Reichstag on fire.''

There were shouts of ''bravo'' from the public benches.

''This bravo-bravo,'' mimicked Dimitrov. ''Of course. Say bravo. To wage war on Communist party in Germany is your good right. Like right of

Communist party in Germany to live illegally and fight your regime and keep fighting!''

"Dimitrov," snapped the judge, bringing down his gavel, "I forbid you to make Communist propaganda here!''

"He is making Nazi propaganda here!'' was the fearless retort.

Once Göring snapped, "Listen! I'll tell you right now what the German people is aware of. It's aware—'' and his voice rose to a hysterical shriek —"it's aware that you're acting like a thorough scoundrel. You come trotting over here to set our Reichstag on fire, and then have the gall to spout such arrant nonsense to the German people! I didn't come down here to have you level charges at me! In my eyes you're a scoundrel and should have been strung up on the gallows long ago.''

The judge murmured a rebuke, and Dimitrov nodded appreciatively. "I'm quite content," he said, "with Mr. Göring's utterance.''

Cool and sovereign in the knowledge that he was winning, the Bulgarian turned to Hermann Göring. "Are you afraid of my questions?'' . . .

Beet red, Göring screamed at him, "You will be afraid if I ever come across you outside this courthouse, you scoundrel!''

All four hard-line Communists were acquitted. The Dutchman alone was found guilty and submitted to the guillotine on January 10, 1934, without a flicker of remorse. Remorse, if any, was displayed by Göring. "It was too stiff a sentence for Van der Lubbe," he reflected twelve years later. "He did not deserve so much notoriety, or such a punishment.''

Two days after the Reichstag fire a discreet ex-sailor, Robert Kropp, answered Göring's advertisement for a gentleman's gentleman. Göring ran his eye over the blue folder of testimonials. Kropp had been an infantryman for four years and a sailor for eight. Göring fired off a string of questions. "Can you drive? Handle a launch?" (Göring had no boat but he was thinking ahead.) "I'll do most of the driving myself," he added, without waiting for an answer. "But you can take over the wheel from time to time.''

Kropp asked for 140 marks a month, but settled for less with a promise of more. "Four weeks' notice," said Göring. "If I'm not happy with you, then you're out on your ear. Out through the hole the bricklayers left. Get it?''

"Yes," stammered Kropp. "The door.''

Göring softened. "You start at ten," he said, and waved an apologetic hand at his own cramped quarters here in Kaiserdamm.

"We'll be moving into the prime minister's residence later on," he said.

9
GÖRING'S PET

Toward midnight on election night, March 5, 1933, the Nazi party notables came together in Göring's Kaiserdamm apartment to await the results. Industrialists in evening dress, like Thyssen, and princes in SA rig, like August-Wilhelm, rubbed shoulders with Richthofen Squadron aviators and brown-shirted party infantry, stuffing themselves with canapés and free liquor. But the voting figures were still nothing to celebrate. With 288 Nazi seats this time, backed up by Hugenburg's 52, they were still a long way short of the 432 that Hitler would have needed for a two-thirds majority.

For several days Hitler and Göring pondered ways and means of bridging the gap. In the Cabinet on March 15, Göring suggested, according to the minutes, "that the majority could be attained by ordering a number of Social Democrats out of the Chamber." In the end, by ensuring that the Communist deputies did not attend (all 81 were on the run or in custody), Hitler scraped together enough votes when the Reichstag opened to see the all-important Enabling Act, which would give him dictatorial powers, passed by 441 votes to 94. (The opposition came mainly from the Social Democrats, who alone braved Göring's boisterous threats thundered at them from the speaker's chair: "Quiet! Or the chancellor will deal with you!'') "Weimar,'' Göring declared flatly, "is finally dead!''

For a while he turned to domestic issues, of which law and order had become the most urgent. On February 20, two weeks before the election, he had set up an auxiliary police force (*Hilfspolizei*) of fifty thousand men drawn largely from the SA and the SS, and these "auxiliaries'' had done everything possible to steer the voters in the right direction; the most dangerous opponents had been steered straight into two "concentration camps'' that Göring had set up at Oranienburg and Papenburg. His original intention, he later explained, had been to use these camps to rehabilitate political delinquents, but now that the elections were over, the terror system gained a momentum of its own as the hordes of rootless and unemployed SA men ran wild and even set up concentration camps of their own.

For a while Göring lost control, that is clear. "You can't make an omelet,'' he would philosophize under interrogation, "without breaking eggs.'' Typical of the casualties was Otto Eggerstedt, forty-six, who had been the left-wing police chief of Altona City. Arrested and thrown into Papenburg, he would be "shot while trying to escape'' in October 1933. By that time, according to the estimate of Gestapo Chief Rudolf Diels, no fewer than seven hundred opponents of the Nazis had been bludgeoned or otherwise done to death in the "wildcat'' concentration camps set up by the SA. Occasionally—very occasionally—Göring intervened. That summer he had Ernst Thälmann, the imprisoned national leader of the German Communist party, brought before him. Thälmann confirmed that he was being maltreated. Göring had the manhandling stopped and boasted that ten years later, in 1943, the grateful Communist wrote to thank him. (Göring might have added that in August 1944 a phone call from Himmler sufficed to have Thälmann shot).

Göring had the dubious honor of having founded not only the concentration-camp penal system but also the Gestapo, the secret state police. The latter creation had come about after his friend Admiral Magnus von Levetzow, the police chief of Berlin, had raised his voice against the brutality of the SA; Ernst Röhm, whom Hitler had appointed his SA "chief of staff,'' and the Berlin SA commander Karl Ernst, had hit back at the admiral, pointing out that he was not a Nazi party man and should accordingly be replaced immediately. While protecting Levetzow as long as he could, Göring had as a precaution transferred the admiral's political police department ("Ia'') to his own Prussian Ministry of the Interior, as the first step in fact toward establishing his own Hausmacht or private army, loyal only to him. This was how Rudolf Diels, at that time head of Department Ia, came to Göring's staff—although he was already the ministry's specialist on "political extremism.''

On April 26, Göring appointed Diels, a sallow six-footer of thirty-two with slicked-back, dark brown hair and an assortment of dueling scars, as his deputy, in charge of the secret state police, shortly to be known and feared as the Gestapo. Under Göring and Diels, the Gestapo, staffed primarily with lawyers and intellectuals, became a precision instrument in the fight against political opponents. "I founded it originally," Göring explained to Shuster in 1945, "on the model of other [countries'] state police forces, and solely to combat Communists." Diels would testify to the British in 1946 that he received most of his orders for the "elimination" (*Ausschaltung*) of political opponents from the minister, Göring, in person. A year later, when the Gestapo passed into the hands of Heinrich Himmler and the SS, the word *elimination* would be taken more literally.

From the first moment of Hitler's new regime, Hermann Göring was privy to the long-term strategic intentions. In the Cabinet on April 4, he had heard Hitler once again set them out in pristine clarity. "Frontier revisions," the chancellor had declared, "can be undertaken only when Germany has restored her military, political, and financial integrity. . . . Our principal objective" Hitler had continued, "is the redrawing of our eastern frontier."

He was grooming Göring for supreme office. More than once he assured him that when Hindenburg died and he, Hitler, became head of state, then Göring should become chancellor. Unable to persuade his foreign minister, Constantin von Neurath, to drop his frigid attitude toward Italy, Hitler resorted to Göring as a special emissary. Early in April he asked Göring to establish new friendly ties to Mussolini and the Vatican, and to convince the Duce that Germany no longer had designs on Austria. To lend weight to Göring's mission, Hitler sent him a telegram on April 10, the day he arrived in Rome, appointing him prime minister of Prussia.

No German record exists of Göring's ten days of talks in Italy. He met Mussolini three times, and the pope at least once, greeting His Holiness with the Fascist salute. However, a German decrypt of a confidential cable from the Italian ambassador in Berlin to Mussolini a month later gives a powerful clue. On May 12, it revealed, an angry Neurath "reproached Göring in Cabinet for his overweening trust in the Italian government." Göring assured the Italian ambassador that in the face of this attack he had strongly emphasized his faith in Italian friendship.

> Göring repeated to me [the intercept continued] what he had already told Your Excellency [Mussolini] verbally, that there is no truth in the claim that there are differences between Italy and Germany over the Austrian question, because in its policy on Austria Germany is resolved to follow whatever path Your Excellency indicates. . . .
>
> Göring added that should Your Excellency so desire he would undertake to ensure that there would be no further talk of "An-

schluss'' [union of Austria with Germany] just as there is no
longer to be any talk of the South Tyrol.

As Staatssekretär in the Prussian Prime Minister's Office Göring had appointed his friend Paul Körner, the bachelor with wispy, receding hair who had until now been his poorly remunerated dogsbody and chauffeur. Göring took a paternal interest in Körner, and moved him into the mansard attic of the prime minister's gloomy official residence on Leipziger Platz, built during the Bismarck era.

Göring disliked this palace and picked for his own future residence a villa in the grounds of the Prussian Ministry. He sent for the chief civil service architect Heinz Tietze and directed that the villa be rebuilt. When Staatssekretär Friedrich Landfried of the Prussian Ministry of Finance flatly refused to sanction the projected cost, some 720,000 Reichsmarks, Göring bellowed, "I do not intend to begin my dictatorship by allowing the Ministry of Finance to lay down the law to me!" He got his way.

Among the new building's appointments would be a roomy lion-pit for his pet lion cub.

It will be appropriate at this point to contemplate Göring's other finely sinewed and highly intelligent animal, his Forschungsamt (literally, Research Office). Created on April 10, 1933, the Forschungsamt (FA) was perhaps the least known, but most significant, of all his agencies. Its role in entrenching his position in Hitler's power structure, surrounded by increasingly envious enemies, was considerable; and its extraordinary output over the next twelve years—nearly half a million* reports, coyly termed "research results," on intercepted telephone conversations and deciphered signals—would affect the political history of the Reich.

Small wonder that Göring jealously guarded access to this agency. He had, like Hitler, a healthy contempt for the other Nazi intelligence-gathering agencies like the Abwehr (he once said, correctly, that Admiral Wilhelm Canaris and his "boatload of pirates" had contributed nothing). With the possible exception of the Foreign Ministry's code-breaking section (Pers-Z), Göring's FA was unquestionably Hitler's best general intelligence agency, with cryptanalytical sources ranging from the Vatican to Switzerland. Thus the FA read the cipher of the U.S. legation in Berne continuously until 1942, when one of his Prussian officials, the traitor Hans-Bernd Gisevius, sold the information to the U.S. government and the leak was plugged.

Instinctively neither Hitler nor Göring trusted human agents. When military code-breakers Gottfried Schapper and Georg Schröder had first proposed a

*Each FA intercept had a serial number prefixed N (for *Nachrichten*, intelligence). Surviving references run from N28,000 in November 1935 to N425,140 in January 1945.

"Reich Intelligence Agency," Hitler had turned the project over to Göring, stipulating only that the agency was to make no use of agents, but to rely exclusively on what is today called signals intelligence (wiretapping and cryptanalysis). This was clear evidence of the trust that he reposed in Göring: It was like the absolute trust a blind man must have in his guide dog. Funded initially by Göring's Prussian state government, the harmless-sounding Forschungsamt began with four code-breakers, expanded to twenty by July 1933, and employed thirty-five hundred or more, operating throughout Germany and the occupied countries, over the next twelve years. Its senior officials were dedicated Nazis, and only one FA employee—Oberregierungsrat Hartmut Plaas, a close friend of Canaris and the former adjutant of Freikorps Commander Ehrhardt—was caught leaking FA secrets (he was shot).

Soon after it was set up, Göring handed over general supervision of the Forschungsamt to Paul Körner. Körner approved its budget and staff appointments. When the FA moved into its first cryptanalytical workshop, in an attic in Behren Strasse in the heart of the government district, the FA chief was Hans Schimpf, a quiet navy lieutenant commander who had until recently been attached to the army's code office.

All except Schimpf survived the coming war, but after the surrender they lay low, scared of being treated as Nazi agents. They volunteered little information, and the records of that era vanished. Scattered around the world, however, are a few items that clearly betray FA provenance, and they show beyond a doubt that it was one of the most efficient and accurate intelligence-gathering agencies of its time, its integrity guaranteed by the rigid civil-service standards imposed on its staff and by the extraordinary character of Hermann Göring as its ultimate master.

Hitler had granted to him the absolute Reich monopoly on wiretapping. Göring protected this monopoly fiercely. A big "G." scrawled at the foot of a warrant, forwarded to him by Pili Körner, would suffice for the tap to be applied. But that "G." was not easily attained, and he gave Himmler's Gestapo a particularly hard time. "If," recalled one FA official, "as was usually the case with the Gestapo's applications, the reason given for the wiretap was too vague, then the minister [Göring] simply disallowed it; and if he did permit it, he forbade any results to be forwarded [to the Gestapo] until he had given his express authority in each case."

Walter Seifert, head of the FA's evaluation section, who had joined straight out of Jüterbog Signals School in August 1936, would recall that Reinhard Heydrich, chief of the Gestapo under Himmler, hated having to submit every wiretap application to Göring—"But without that 'G.' on it I wasn't allowed to order the tap." Over the years he and Himmler would advance every possible argument for taking over the Forschungsamt. The Führer merely told them to take it up with Göring.

The first chief, Schimpf, lasted only two years. A cheerful womanizer, he became amorously entangled with a lady in Breslau; he solved the matter by shooting her and then (being a gentleman) himself on April 10, 1935. Göring appointed Prince Christoph of Hesse,* and he retained this top Nazi intelligence job for the next eight years.

During Göring's regime, the Forschungsamt moved into magnificent new premises in Berlin's Charlottenburg district; housed in a sprawling complex of former residential buildings set discreetly back from Schiller Strasse, near what Berliners call "the Knee," the hundreds of specially sworn officials and language specialists sat at their equipment in halls patrolled by armed guards and subject to the most stringent security regulations. Every scrap of paper, from the duplicate pads used by the telephone monitors to the brown paper of the "research results," was number-stamped and logged. Recipients of the Brown Pages signed oaths of secrecy subjecting them to the death penalty in the event of violation. The Brown Pages were conveyed only in red double-thickness envelopes inside locked pouches or pneumatic-mail canisters; handled only by special FA couriers; signed for in triplicate by their authorized recipients. (Milch signed for his new pouch key on April 27, 1936, promising "in the event of loss to notify the FA immediately and pay all costs for the replacement of the pouch.")

"The work of the FA," warned Prince Christoph, who had the rank of Ministerialdirektor in Göring's Prussian Ministry, "will have both point and profit only if its secrecy is safeguarded by every possible means. Inadequate security will result in the enemy," whom these February 1938 security regulations did not identify, "taking precautions, and our sources drying up." Thus the "results" were never to be explicitly referred to in documents, nor discussed by phone except on the special secure-telephone network installed by the FA throughout the government district, or on the secure teleprinter system. Recipients, regardless of rank, had to return each and every Brown Page intact to the FA. Even Hitler had to toe this line. FA chief Gottfried Schapper wrote to Hitler's adjutant Paul Wernicke in May 1938 peremptorily demanding the return of seven numbered "results" delivered to the Führer on the day that German troops entered Austria.

By 1937 the FA had grown so costly that Göring switched it to the budget of his Air Ministry, where secrecy was easier. As camouflage, all FA officials now wore air-force uniforms. The FA maintained five hundred wiretaps around the clock in Berlin alone, primarily on foreign embassies, legations, journalists, and suspected enemies of the Reich. The Charlottenburg rooms were divided into "regions" (*Bereiche*)—one each for English, American, Italian, Portuguese, Dutch, Polish, Czech, and the other languages of the moment. Dr. Gerhard Neuenhoff, one linguist who was assigned to the French (and Belgian) "region" on September 15, 1936, found himself just one of a thousand other specialists, strictly limited in their mobility in the FA

---

*Born in 1901, he had married Sophie Battenberg, one of the six German sisters of the present duke of Edinburgh (who fought against the Germans in WWII).

complex: He was never allowed up to the top floor, where Section IV's code-breakers were at work with the Hollerith punched-card computers and the other tools of their trade. Neuenhoff was set in front of a standard hotel-type switchboard, monitoring forty lines including the Belgian legation, the French military attaché, and French correspondents in Berlin. He soon learned to recognize who was speaking—the French ambassador André François-Poncet, with his slow, pedantic enunciation, or the French journalist Madame Tabuis, with her shrill tones.

It is important to accept that these FA monitors were incorruptible civil servants, with neither the means nor the motive to falsify "results." They jotted down what they heard on paginated duplicate pads, in longhand, or recorded it on wire recorders; tossed the completed note, already headed "State Secret" (*Geheime Reichssache*) onto a conveyor belt; within minutes it was typed up, evaluated, cross-indexed, and issued—either by FA dispatch rider or vacuumed with the speed of a rifle bullet through Berlin's pneumatic-mail system into the very anteroom of the authorized minister or his Staats-sekretär. Each canister had its own address code on it—three narrow rings in blue guided it, for example, to Milch's private office at the secret Air Ministry Building.

The Forschungsamt gave Göring an edge over every rival contender for power in Germany. Not one international cable crossed Reich territory or its adjacent waters without being tapped by the FA. There were FA field units in every amplifier station. Fifty synchronous teleprinters installed in the cavernous basement at Charlottenburg churned out "results" twenty-four hours a day. Göring's SigInt specialists "looped into" the great Indo-Cable that carried all London's telegraphic traffic with India. ("At first," recalled FA specialist Walter Seifert, "that was quite bountiful.") The cable from Paris, France, to Tallin, Estonia, navigated the Baltic Sea; Göring's frogmen tapped that, and of course the landlines between Vienna, Prague, Moscow, and London—all of which crisscrossed Reich territory.

The biggest customers for the Brown Pages were Hitler's new Propaganda Ministry and the Ministry of Economics. An intercept of any story being filed by a foreign correspondent in Germany enabled Goebbels to plant an immediate reply in rival foreign newspapers overnight. The FA could also supply inside economic information with a speed and reliability that assisted Göring and the Reich to make dramatic "kills." Seifert's evaluation section built up a card index of names and subjects; his subsection 12-C kept tabs on every spoken or enciphered reference to vital raw materials like rubber, nonferrous metals, wood, and newsprint. Göring's secret agency made him an expert in everything from international egg prices to the yield of low-grade iron ores.

He had laid down two rules: He was to be supplied automatically with copies of everything; and all FA intercepts of his conversations were to be drawn to his attention to enable him to check his own phone security. Surviving data shows that he used the system well, as a routine check on the Reich's ponderous and inefficient bureaucracy. Two typical Brown Pages that came rattling through the pneumatic tube in December 1944 were number N400,611 about German explosives manufacture, entitled, "Managing Director Dr. Müller complaining about lack of official cooperation from Berlin"; and N400,784 about aircraft production: "Ernst Heinkel Aircraft Works, Vienna, having serious problems getting raw materials for He 219 construction."

There were those who considered such eavesdropping not *korrekt*—somehow ungentlemanly. And often there was a prurient element. When Mussolini paid his first state visit to Berlin in September 1937, an FA team manning the switchboard at Castle Belvedere monitored his calls to his mistress, Clara Petacci. When the duke of Windsor came to Salzburg with his American duchess a month later, Hitler ordered Göring to tap their phones as well.

Such tidbits lightened the darker watches of the night at Charlottenburg. A monitor would cry out "*Staatsgesprach!*" ("State talks!") and throw the switch that poured the intimate conversation into every switchboard in the room. Down the tube came transcripts of the titillating conversations between one of the most eminent Catholic prelates in Berlin and a nun—"Compared with him," Milch snickered, "Casanova was a wimp!" Göring had ordered General von Schleicher's phone tapped, of course. "What is it?" the general's wife was heard teasing a friend. "With an *i* everybody wants to be it. Without an *i*, nobody!" "Give up? *Arisch*!" she triumphed. "Aryan!"

Göring read it out to Gestapo Chief Rudolf Diels, roaring with laughter, and ordered the wiretap continued.

His Forschungsamt gave to Hitler and his experts a certain deftness, a sureness of touch when they played their diplomatic poker. A French trade mission arrived: An FA "flying squad" took over the switchboard at the Hotel Bristol, monitored even their room-to-room calls, a Brown Page reporting the rock-bottom price they had instructions from home to accept was blow-piped across Berlin to the Ministry of Economics in time for the afternoon's vital conference. After Germany remilitarized the Rhineland in 1936, Chief Evaluator Seifert took to Hitler the Brown Pages (numbered around N34,500 now) reporting the hysterical foreign-press reaction; Hitler said calmly, "They'll settle down again." In 1938 the FA intercepts (numbered around N83,000) would tell him that Britain was not coming to the aid of Austria in March, nor Czechoslovakia in September.

The sense of sovereign power that this quiet agency gave to Göring cannot be underestimated. It put him a cut above the rest of Hitler's henchmen. Noiseless taps were put on the phones of Gauleiter Julius Streicher, the widely disliked gauleiter of Franconia; on Hitler's female English admirer Unity Mitford; on his talkative adjutant Fritz Wiedemann, and Wiedemann's globe-trotting girl friend Princess Stefanie von Hohenlohe; and on Goebbels's bedmate, the lovely Czech actress Lida Baarova. After obtaining clear proof from the FA of the intrigues of Roosevelt's ambassadors in Warsaw, Brussels, and Paris, Göring instructed the Forschungsamt department chief Dr. W. Kurzbach to publish a stinging but anonymous exposé in Berlin's authoritative newspaper, *Börsenzeitung*.

Seifert, who often had to deliver the Brown Pages to Göring in person, found him a hard but not unfeeling employer. On the one hand, he had no sense of time or place. He might summon Seifert at dawn to Budapest, then leave him waiting for hours without any breakfast. But, Seifert found, the minister sometimes gained as much pleasure from distributing his growing wealth as from accumulating it. One FA courier could not afford the treatment needed for his child's infantile paralysis. Seifert wrote a message for Göring on that day's FA summary, and it came back that night with a scrawled reply: "Of course I shall pick up all the bills."

Once, Seifert took the locked pouch in person to Göring's new domain, "Carinhall," in the forests outside Berlin. Göring left him standing in front of the mammoth desk for longer, perhaps, than was polite. As Seifert waited patiently to begin the FA briefing, he felt something nibbling at his leg: It was a lion cub, its fangs still fortunately petite.

"Proceed!" roared Göring, enjoying the situation.

The lion was a pet that he could openly display; the Forschungsamt, however, was a pet that he could not.

10
RENAISSANCE MAN

Göring had appeared at the great Aviators' Club Ball in February 1933 in white tie and tails and, close to tears, had repeated to his fellow Great War aviators the solemn pledge that he had made on disbanding the Richthofen Squadron in 1918— that the German Air Force's time would come again. He pledged too that the first fighter squadron of the reborn air force would bear the name Richthofen. He kept his word in both respects. On May 2, 1939, his generals would inform him that Germany now had an air force that was the most powerful in the world.

Creating it in the face of all the international prohibitions placed on any kind of German military aviation had been quite a problem, but the Weimar Republic had already laid some foundations, establishing in the Soviet Union, far from prying eyes, bases and proving grounds for airplanes, artillery, gas warfare, and even submarines. The young army officer Kurt Student had selected a primitive airfield at Lipetsk, in southern Russia, as a suitable experimental site: Another officer, Heinz Guderian, had begun studying tank tactics nearby, and many later famous names like Hans Jeschonnek and Hermann Ploch passed through this secret training base at Lipetsk in the twenties. As recently as September 26, 1932, Milch—still a Lufthansa executive then—had visited the German Aviation Research Institute's secret laboratory at Yagi, outside Moscow.

Göring's plan in 1933 was to raise initially a small, well-camouflaged air force under cover of amateur flying clubs and civil aviation, and then, from the autumn of 1935 until the autumn of 1938, rapidly build a full-scale armada of the air. It is unlikely that anyone but Göring could have raised an air force with such speed. Göring had Hitler's trust, and the Führer gave him a free hand that he would not have given to any other politician. Throughout the embryonic air force the stock phrase became "Money is no object!" The finance minister shuddered when he saw Göring approach. When General von Blomberg protested, Göring simply said, "It's not your money, is it!"

The first secret Air Ministry was set up on March 11, 1933, in the offices of a bank that had defaulted in Behren Strasse. Göring rarely visited the building, preferring the pomp and splendor of the Prussian prime minister's lair he was building a few hundred yards away. Milch, whom Göring was happy to leave running the ministry, coaxed him into visiting the experimental aeronautical station at Rechlin, west of Berlin, on March 29, but when they both flew down to Rome that April, Göring left it to Milch to confer with Italian Air Force General Italo Balbo, while he himself concentrated on the Duce. Back in their hotel, Milch told him that he had explained to Balbo that the German Air Force would concentrate on building bombers at first, as a deterrent.

"*Ja, ja,*" interrupted Göring impatiently. "Do as you think best."

A few days after their return, on April 25, Blomberg agreed to their insistence that the air force be independent and not a branch of either the army or the navy, as in other countries. On May 6, Milch issued contracts for the manufacture of one thousand planes—the purpose of businessman Milch, "nimble as a weasel," as Bruno Loerzer enviously called him, was plain: to lay the foundations of an aircraft industry, regardless of the quality of planes; Germany's need was for trained aircraft workers above all else. At that time the industry employed only thirty-five hundred workers, and Junkers, the largest factory, could manufacture only eighteen Junkers 52 transport planes a year.

To Göring's ex-aviator friends this seemed to be the happiest year of his life. He appointed his old pal Loerzer, now forty-two, commissioner for airships, and then put him in charge of amateur flying clubs (sport flying): The clubs had a uniform that became the basis of the Luftwaffe's uniform. Loerzer apart, Göring's other personnel appointments could scarcely have been bettered. As de facto chief of air staff he selected one of the army's finest colonels, Walther Wever; Blomberg sadly agreed to the transfer, lamenting, "I'm letting you have a man who could have been the next commander in chief of the army." Göring picked another army colonel, Albert Kesselring, an officer with a permanent tombstone grin, to run the administration side of the new secret air force. None of these men had ever flown, nor had the officer Göring appointed on July 1, 1933, as chief of air-force personnel, Colonel Hans-Jürgen Stumpff.

Stumpff, never one of Göring's critics, found him "packing a colossal punch" in those days. "He was bursting with ideas," the colonel later recalled. On Hitler's orders, the other services had to release their best material to Göring's new air force. During the first year Stumpff recruited 182 officers from the army and 42 from naval aviation. A rapid-training program began. When Stumpff proudly reported the training of the thousandth pilot, Göring congratulated him: "Now on to the next thousand!" he bellowed.

"You left every conference with him," said Stumpff afterward, "boosted to an extra thousand rpm."

The real architect of the secret air force was Milch. A year senior to his minister, he was ambitious, loud-mouthed, and every bit as ruthless. Milch had trampled many of his business rivals in his climb to power, and he never enjoyed Göring's perennial, inexplicable popularity. Göring could hardly overlook Milch's naked ambition. Several times in May and June 1933 it was Milch and his minister who had attended the Cabinet meetings, and Göring heard that his Staatssekretär was saying, "The real minister is me!" Milch suspected that Göring had succumbed to morphine again, and tackled him about it. It was a strained, rambunctious relationship, not made easier for Göring by the knowledge that Milch was indispensable to him. Once he telephoned Milch, sitting in that first secret ministry building in Behren Strasse: Milch listened only briefly to Göring's ill-tempered outburst before hanging up on him.

Göring phoned again. "We were cut off," he said.

"No," snapped Milch. "I put the phone down on you. I don't want our switchboard to get the impression that our minister has no manners."

What Göring never took into account, Milch explained to this author, was time: "That was beyond him." Milch methodically pulled together all the strands that, entwined, go to make an air force—civil aviation, meteorological services, aeronautical laboratories, flying schools, ground organization. In mid-August he signed the orders setting up *Fliegerwaffen* schools for specialist training in navigation, air-to-air combat, gunnery, flight engineering, and naval aviation. When he took the dates and deadlines in to his minister, Göring just roared with laughter. "You're planning to do all this over the next five years?" he bellowed. "You've got six months."

Among the very highest air-force officers, there were powerful and often unusual forces of cohesion. Each had something on the other.

But deadliest of all was the file being built up on Milch by rivals like SA Brigadier (*Oberführer*) Theo Croneiss in Bavaria. Milch had bankrupted his little airline in the twenties, and now Croneiss put it about that the Staatssekretär's father, Anton Milch, was really a Jew. The words flew around the Nazi hierarchy. Gauleiter Joseph Terboven told his friend Göring, who tackled

Milch that August as they were driving back from the Obersalzberg, where they had just inspected the site for Göring's new luxury villa. Milch was shocked and investigated his own blood ancestry. By October 4, when they met again to inspect the secret uniform being designed for the new air force, he had established the truth—which Milch saw as a vindication. Milch handed to Göring a letter written by his mother, establishing beyond doubt that his biological father was not Anton Milch, but in fact her own uncle. That he was the product of incest was not a pleasant discovery, but for a Staatssekretär in Nazi Germany, it was preferable to being a half-Jew. On October 14, Göring reprimanded Croneiss for the slander. Two weeks later he discussed the letter with Hitler, Blomberg, and Hess. "It's all okay," Milch noted in his diary on November 1.

Versions of the story percolated around the air force for the next twelve years. Lieutenant Colonel Erich Killinger told fellow officers that Milch's brother was still a Jew. "Milch," added Killinger, "proved—or claimed— and his mother, who's still alive has confirmed it, that she had had an affair with a Christian and that Erhard [Milch] was the product. So Milch," guffawed Killinger, unaware of the awful truth, "branded his own mother a whore so as to become a Christian."

Göring shielded Milch against the slander and never revealed what he knew, even years afterward under interrogation in the shadow of the gallows.

Sovereign, unimpeachable, arrogant: Some idea of the breathtaking scope of Göring's ambitions in 1933 is given by a letter to the minister of culture, Bernard Rust, expressing indignation at the appointment of a "Reich bishop" without consulting him.

> I was astonished [Göring wrote] to find that the appointment is a fait accompli.
> In my view, so long as we have only regional [Protestant] churches and not one Reich Church, no Reich bishop can be appointed. Until the [1918] revolution, the King of Prussia was the summus episcopus of the Church of Prussia. In my opinion these prerogatives now devolve upon the Prussian State Ministry, i.e., upon the Prussian prime minister . . .

The Prussian prime minister was, of course, Hermann Göring himself. This open letter, in which he neatly claimed to be legal successor to the king of Prussia and head of the Protestant (Evangelische) Church as well, was published in the first edition of the *Deutsche Allgemeine Zeitung* on June 27 but expunged from all later editions.

The dispute over the Reich bishop had a Forschungsamt sequel that illustrates how Göring did not hesitate to use the Brown Pages to manipulate his Führer.

The background was this. Disturbed by the increasing factionalism within Protestantism, Hitler had tried first reconciliation, and then, when that failed, subversion, setting up a new church, the "German Christians," as a Trojan Horse operation. At an April 1933 convention, these worthies had dutifully called for a united Reich Church, with twenty-nine regional bishops to choose a Reich bishop as their leader. More or less democratically they had elected Ludwig Müller of Königsberg to the job.

Thousands of disaffected Protestant pastors had thereupon chosen an opposition candidate to Müller, the roughneck pastor Fritz von Bodelschwingh. The leader of this opposition faction was an opportunistic and implacable clergyman, Martin Niemöller, a former U-boat commander who had been a zealous Nazi until this Müller business.

After initially sharing their dismay at Müller's appointment, Göring found it more useful to back him, however, and his temporal cunning outwitted the spiritual conniving of the clergymen. On January 9, 1934, he began assembling a police dossier on Niemöller's opposition group, the Pastoral Emergency Pastors' League (*Pfarrer-Notbund*). Meeting with Hitler on January 19, Göring found him still characteristically undecided on what to advise President Hindenburg on this issue, so he suggested that the Führer meet a dozen of the clergymen in person. The meeting was set up for January 25, and Göring ordered wiretaps placed on Niemöller's phone meanwhile.

At 1:00 P.M. on the appointed day the rival bishops and pastors formed up in two lines facing the desk in Hitler's reception room. They had barely begun to argue their case ("with mealy mouth," as Hitler later nastily described, "and many quotations from the Scriptures") when Hermann Göring rushed in, brandishing a red file, from which he extracted several Brown Pages.

"*Mein Führer*," he cried, "as prime minister of the largest German province, I request permission to read out a phone conversation just conducted by"—and here he pointed at the culprit—"the director of the Pastoral Emergency League."

Niemöller, crew cut and lean-featured, stepped forward in military fashion as his name was mentioned.

"Read it out," invited Hitler.

"We've done our 'mine-laying,' " declared Göring, seemingly reading Niemöller's words. "We've submitted our memorandum to the Reich president. We've fixed him good and proper. Before today's conference on church affairs, the chancellor's going to be hauled before the president and get his comeuppance—the last rites!"

Hitler glared at Niemöller. "Do you really think that by backstairs intrigues you can drive a wedge between the Reich president and myself, and threaten the very foundations of the Reich?"

Niemöller attempted to reply—he had been motivated, he said, only by his "cares for the Church, for Jesus Christ, for the Third Reich, and for your German people."

"Kindly leave 'caring for the Third Reich' to me," snapped Hitler.

Göring read out more of the alleged Forschungsamt intercept. "We ladled so much holy oil over him, [meaning Hindenburg], that he's going to kick that bastard out."

Hitler was speechless at this language—it was the language of the conning tower, not the pulpit.

Niemöller found his voice and fired off a flustered denial, but this only angered Hitler more. ("Result," recalled Göring eleven years later, wiping tears of laughter from his eyes: "Painful collapse of stout brethren!") The extent of his impromptu falsification is evident from the archives of the Reich Chancellery, which contained the actual—and very rare—Brown Page concerned:

> Jac. Re.
>
> (Strictly Confidential)
>
> Berlin, January 25, 1934
> Re: Church Conflict
> Niemöller talks with unidentified person and tells him among other things that Hitler has been ordered to Hindenburg at 12:00. The Reich president receives Hitler in his dressing room. The Last Rites before the conference! Hindenburg receives him with our memorandum in his hand. The approach via the ministry of the interior has also turned out well. (FA comment: How, was not explained.)
> "I'm glad that I brought—? here and that I rigged it all so well with Meissner [Hindenburg's Staatssekretär]. If things go wrong—which I don't anticipate—we've got a good start for a free church. Give me a call late afternoon. I'll know more then." (Monitored 10:15 A.M.)

The deception sealed Niemöller's fate. Göring's police searched his house later that day—nothing incriminating was found—and two days later he was suspended from all further office.

On the last day of August 1933 President Hindenburg had appointed this cheeky former air-force captain, Hermann Göring, to full general (*General der Infanterie*). Göring in turn rewarded Hindenburg with the gift of an estate in Germany's amputated eastern province, East Prussia. Göring's servile aide Erich Gritzbach, passing through Allenstein, in East Prussia, on his way to arrange Göring's "state visit" to the president, indicated casually to the local burgomaster that his minister, General Göring, would like to be made an honorary citizen of the town—despite the short notice—and he recommended the Berlin jeweler who would be able to provide the kind of gift that Göring thought he should receive to embellish the ceremony.

* * *

By summer of 1933 handpicked pilots like the twenty-year-old Adolf Galland—later one of Germany's most famous fighter aces—were being given fighter training in Italy. Other air crews were practicing long-distance night flying, operating a night air-parcels service between Berlin and East Prussia for the Reich railways. On August 25, Milch inspected the prototype of a new bomber, disguised as a passenger plane, the Heinkel 111. Soon Junkers alone had nine thousand men working in its airplane assembly plant, and forty-five hundred more making aircraft engines; and two million workers were laying out airfields and barracks for the new squadrons, concealed behind harmless names like "Reich Autobahn Air Transport Center."

On Göring's instructions, the Reich nationalized the Junkers factories, and he appointed one of industrialist Friedrich Flick's right-hand men, the bull-necked, choleric Dr. Heinrich Koppenberg, to run them. Koppenberg attended the new industry's first meeting at the secret Air Ministry Building on October 20, 1933. The climax came, he wrote shortly afterward, when Göring appeared, greeted by the industrialists rising silently to their feet and offering the Hitler salute. Göring revealed to them that the Führer had commanded him to revolutionize their position in the air "within one year."

Later that day, Göring flew up to Stockholm for four days to visit Carin's grave—it was two years since her death—and her relatives. Angry Communists protested that he was holding a "big Nazi get-together" at Count von Rosen's castle, and the Communist daily newspaper *Folkets Dagblad* claimed he had "issued directives to his relatives on how the Swedish Nazis should set about . . . introducing a Nazi dictatorship." "Minister Göring," the Communists complained, "can travel all over this country with his fellow Nazis, and nobody lifts a finger against them." Coming out of a Stockholm theater, he was jeered by an organized mob, who shouted, "Down with Göring, murderer of the workers!"

Not in the most tactful style, he left on Carin's grave a swastika-shaped wreath before returning to Berlin and Leipzig (for his confrontation with Dimitroff at the Reichstag fire trial). The Communists trampled the flowers and painted a message on the gravestone. "Some of us Swedes," it said, "take offense at the German Mr. Göring's violation of the grave. His dead wife may rest in peace—but spare us the German propaganda on her tomb."

"They desecrated the grave of my late wife," said Göring to American historian George Shuster years later. "Thereupon I arranged for her mortal remains to be brought to Germany." He ordered in Stockholm a massive and ornate pewter sarcophagus, big enough to contain both Carin and himself when the time came.

Her memory would forthwith be permanently enshrined in "Carinhall." He had found a site for this country lodge, to be built in the Norse style, on the Schorf Heath, an undulating Prussian terrain of lake and forest extending from northeast of Berlin almost to the Baltic coast and Poland. He marked out a site for Carinhall on a bluff overlooking one of the lakes, Dolln See, and sent an architect to Sweden to make drawings of a timber-hunting lodge that he had admired on the von Rosen estate. In her memory, he intended to make the new building the center of a wildlife sanctuary for endangered species—species like the elk and buffalo, the deer and wild horse and, indeed, himself.

He wanted Carinhall to have the best of everything. He called in two Prussian court architects, Hetzelt and Tuch, and gave them ten months to have the main lodge complete. Eventually Carinhall would cost the taxpayer 15 million Reichsmarks, borne equally by the Air Ministry and Prussian government budgets. It would become over the next twelve years an extraordinary, baroque palace—oversized, vulgar, and faintly ludicrous, in the image of its builder. He approved every detail of its design down to the lavish door handles. He selected the furniture, designed the green-and-gold livery for the foresters and footmen, brought back gaudy bric-à-brac from his later forays into occupied Europe. The buildings spread and multiplied around the center courtyard, with steep thatched roofs, fountains, statues, and avenues of trees. The rooms were embellished with the costliest crystal chandeliers, Flemish tapestries, and priceless Old Masters. "Magnificent," he would later exclaim to Heinz Guderian, by then a Panzer general, showing him the works of art at Carinhall. "I really am a Renaissance man. How I love opulence!" Whereupon he took the visitor by the arm and led him to the drawing room, flanked by two anterooms called the Gold and Silver rooms, where the gifts made to General Göring by the judicious, the wise, and the ambitious were on permanent display.

Throughout those early years the rumors, abetted by Communist propaganda, that Göring was back on narcotics would not go away. Prussian lawyer Count Rüdiger von der Goltz observed him as though in a trance during one speech at Stettin. Morphine intake might explain the speed with which Göring abandoned the norms of honesty and solicited both gifts and bribes. Making amends for his property confiscated in 1923, the state of Bavaria had allowed him to buy a prime site on the Obersalzberg mountain, right next to Hitler's famous chalet. Among his papers in 1945 was the deed of another plot of land at Hochkreuth, near Bayrischzell, given him by Consul Sachs on Bavaria's behalf on March 3, 1935. The speed of his transformation from Goebbels's "upright, childlike soldier" of January 1933 to the murderous, grasping Göring of 1934 took even his friends' breaths away. Whatever the occasion, paintings, sculptures, vases, embroidery, and furniture poured in for him—bronze lions, trinkets of gold and ivory, silver, and amber.

His staff rapidly perfected and systematized the bribery. Fräulein Grundtmann meticulously listed all gifts—donors, dates, and occasion. Some were innocuous, like the gifts from his childhood friends Erna and Fanny Graf; others were heavy with unspoken intent—presents from future allies and enemies, from ambassadors and agents (the British colonel Malcolm Christie gave him *Sporting Anecdotes*), from aristocrats and Reich ministers (for

Christmas 1937 Rudolf Hess thoughtfully gave him a volume of Hess's own collected speeches). The Grundtmann lists record the donations of generals, directors, publishing moguls, industrialists; there were major corporations like C. & A. Brenninkmeyer,* Lufthansa, the Hamburg-Amerika Line, and I.G. Farben, and minor ones like the Fritz Siebel Aircraft Works, and the Ufa and Fox movie companies. North German Lloyd would give him three sea voyages. The Phillip Reemtsma Tobacco Company gave him a Spitzweg painting of "The Sunday Huntsman" (Göring marked it "Keep for the Führer"). Into the early Grundtmann lists crept names of future note—the Swedish businessman Birger F. Dahlerus, boss of Electrolux, is glimpsed giving him a dishwasher as early as 1936 (the name of Dahlerus would figure prominently in Göring's life and trial). In 1937 one Albert Speer, architect, donated a flower basket, followed in 1938 by a brass goblet.

Every municipality in Germany, from Aachen, Altena, Berlin, Cologne, Düren, and Düsseldorf through the alphabet to Zossen made regular gifts to him. There were presents from friends and relatives and in-laws—from both Carin's and Emmy's families—and from people Hermann did not regard as properly in his family at all—in 1937 his unwanted cousin, Herbert Göring, and his wife gave him two small Meissen hunting figurines and in 1938 a small bronze vase. The German Colonial Veterans League gave him a marble doorplate inscribed with his father's name. Baroness von Epenstein (his godfather's widow) gave him a door from Veldenstein, his childhood castle.

Invited to Göring's birthday on January 12, 1934, the banker Schacht had brought along a modest painting of a buffalo for him. In pride of place next to Göring, however, he found a publisher who had donated a complete shooting brake with four horses.

Soon the first stage of Carinhall would be ready, a simple timber lodge. Out here among the dark Satanic forests of pine, beech, and oak, Göring felt like a Teutonic knight of old. He would carry a spear, and command Robert to dress him in red top boots of Russian leather with golden spurs, in floor-length coats like a French emperor, in silk blouses with puffy sleeves.

Emmy or no Emmy, his waking thoughts were still overshadowed by the morbid memory of Carin. Her ghost haunted him more than ever now that the workmen were constructing Carinhall. Down by the lakeside, on the far shore, he ordered them to excavate a macabre mausoleum, with five-foot-thick walls of Brandenburg granite. In a few months' time it would be ready to receive the pewter sarcophagus from Sweden.

One day he expected to lie in it by his devoted Carin's side—to spend all eternity with her beneath these moaning pines.

---

*Their gift paid off. Göring's office files reveal that he authorized C. & A. to set up their big Leipzig department store despite the local gauleiter's protests that this violated Nazi vows to protect small traders.

11
MURDER MANAGER

What were the factors that propelled Göring into the sink of criminality from which he would emerge, on the middle day of 1934, with the blood and gore of political murder clinging to his bejeweled hands? Self-preservation? Cowardice? Or the fatal arrogance inspired in leading National Socialists by the belief that their movement's undoubted achievements in the revival of Germany somehow put them above common law?

Like all bullies, and despite his Pour le Mérite, Göring was physically a coward. But Professor Hugo Blaschke, the Philadelphia-trained dentist who treated Göring, was struck by the general's quivering fear of pain. "You got the feeling," Blaschke recalled years later, "that you were dealing with a megalomaniac. Your own life was worth nothing."

There is also no doubt of Göring's belief in Nazi righteousness. On February 26, 1933, he had visited Dortmund to speak to fifty thousand working men in the election campaign and had seen the starving children with his own eyes. Returning now, a year later, on March 17, 1934, to the same steel towns in his luxuriously appointed railroad coach, he saw children with pink in their cheeks and laughter in their eyes. The Nazis were succeeding where Weimar had failed—they had brought back national unity, economic prosperity, and employment, and they were feted everywhere they went.

Nobody was celebrated with greater enthusiasm than Göring. "Göring," Herbert Backe, the level-headed deputy to the minister of agriculture, told his wife after touring eastern Germany with the general in mid-May, "arrived at Breslau wearing a white air-force uniform. The citizenry went wild." The cheers gave Göring the feeling of immortality: He was Germany—he was the law. The increasingly odd, sometimes even effeminate garments (many of them designed for him by Carin) were a part of his public image. He was at heart almost a transvestite, certainly an exhibitionist. "Herbert," Frau Backe wrote in her diary, "says that out in the Schorf Heath [around Carinhall] he always has a spear with him."

A few weeks later, on June 30, Hitler and Göring liquidated their former friends and comrades, now deadly rivals, Ernst Röhm and Gregor Strasser, along with scores of other real or imagined obstacles to their retaining absolute power in Germany.

Ernst Röhm, the pallid, paunchy, scar-faced homosexual SA chief of staff—against whom Carin had so astutely warned Hermann Göring nine years earlier—had become increasingly dissatisfied with the character of the Hitler revolution and with the role assigned within it to himself and his two million Brownshirts. Hitler and Göring had willingly made use of Röhm and his thugs during the last months of the struggle, but now the violent genie refused to go back into the lamp. Röhm, with more men under arms than the constitutional forces of law and order, made no secret of his ambitions. He wanted to become defense minister himself. "It was obvious," said Göring later, discussing this, "that we could not have suggested his name to Hindenburg, as Röhm's private life and sordid proclivities were too well known." Röhm had no intention of taking this lying down. He and his cronies began muttering about staging a "second revolution"—after which General von Schleicher would replace Hitler, Theo Croneiss would become air minister, and the SA as a whole would replace the army.

Initially, Göring and Hitler saw no option but to appease Röhm. In October 1933 Göring had allowed the SA to attach "special agents" (Sonderbeauftragte) to his various offices and agencies; and on December 1, Hitler had appointed Röhm a Reich minister, and published a fulsome letter to him—using the familiar Du—expressing his gratitude to the SA, "my friends and comrades." But then Röhm casually posted an SA guard unit outside Göring's ministry, and it became common knowledge that the SA was buying up arms from abroad, although Hitler had ruled definitely that only the regular army, the Reichswehr, would be allowed to bear arms. At this point the anti-Röhm coalition began to take shape. General von Blomberg, his chief military assistant General von Reichenau, and the commander in chief of the army,

General Werner von Fritsch, all let Göring know that they took a dim view of Röhm and the SA.

Unquestionably, Göring himself was leader of the coalition against Röhm. As he looked around for allies of the requisite ruthlessness, his gaze fell upon Heinrich Himmler, the deceptively inoffensive-looking chief of the SS, the black-uniformed elite bodyguard personally sworn to Hitler's protection. With his metal-rimmed eyeglasses Himmler, ten years younger than Göring, appeared no more lethal than a provincial schoolmaster. Ten years earlier, as a young agriculture student, he had carried Ernst Röhm's standard during the beer hall putsch in Munich that had left Göring with such a painful legacy. By early 1934 he already controlled every police force in Germany except one—the Prussian police under Göring. So each man needed the other: Himmler wanted the Prussian police, and Göring wanted Himmler. Hesitating to strike the bargain, Göring appealed doubtfully to Richard Walther Darré, Hitler's minister of agriculture: "You know Himmler," he said. "What do you think of him?"

"All I know," replied Darré, "is that when we get together he just talks about his magnificent 'guardsmen' and about our peasant stock. I can't see anything wrong with him."

Still Göring, for the first three months of 1934, hesitated to join forces with Himmler. He probably had little confidence in the new Gestapo chief, Dr. Rudolf Diels, if it came to the crunch. Until 1934 the Gestapo was Göring's own property; he had created it. Now Diels was running it, and Diels was an ambivalent character. He seemed more and more to favor crossing over to the SS or the SA. In September 1933 he had accompanied the SA gang that lynched the imprisoned Communist murderer of a Nazi "martyr," Horst Wessel. A few weeks later he had failed to uncover a Trotskyist conspiracy to assassinate Göring—fortunately for the latter, the chief of Himmler's political police, Reinhard Heydrich, thwarted the conspiracy.

Age thirty-two, Diels was unstable, even paranoid. Believing his life in danger, he had once fled to Czechoslovakia and returned only when Göring personally pleaded with him. Then Göring obtained evidence that Diels was double-crossing him with the SA. "Diels," his minister warned him, "you're hobnobbing too much with Röhm. Are you in cahoots with him?"

"The chief of your Gestapo," replied the oily civil servant, "has his finger in many pies!"

Göring smiled and said nothing. A few minutes later, however, he rose and apologized to the generals that they would have to lunch without him. "Something urgent has come up, demanding my attention," he explained. That afternoon, the 5:00 P.M. edition of the *Berliner Zeitung* announced that Diels was to resign, and take over a new position offered to him by Göring—Regierungspräsident (Lord Lieutenant) of Cologne.

In 1941 Diels would marry one of Hermann Göring's nieces. Later he divorced her. Later still, he swore a stack of annihilating affidavits against Göring for the war-crimes tribunal, most of which must be read with the utmost caution, given the vulnerable position in which the first chief of Göring's Gestapo must have fancied himself. In one, he claimed that he and Göring took a dossier on SA atrocities down to Hitler on the Obersalzberg early in January 1934. "Herr Göring," exclaimed Hitler, "these are common knowledge. This entire clique around Röhm is rotten to the core. The SA has become a haven for riffraff and scumbags." Hitler, said Diels, had then instructed Göring to see that certain "traitors"—and he mentioned Schleicher and Strasser by name—vanished from the scene.

Oblivious of the closing ranks against him, Ernst Röhm tossed off during February 1934 several arrogant statements that alarmed the army and clearly explained why their top generals were conniving with Göring behind club-house doors. Röhm declared to Blomberg that Germany's defense was purely the SA's concern, and he lectured Fritsch that the future army would be restricted to training the SA for that job. Uneasy now, Hitler ordered Röhm to sign a document, dictated by the army, agreeing to restrict his SA to purely political tasks. Röhm signed but made scathing remarks in private, which Viktor Lutze, his sworn enemy within the SA, promptly repeated to Hitler. On March 22, Göring was among party leaders who heard Hitler vow never to let a "second revolution" occur, of the sort that Röhm had in mind.

Thus the alliance between Himmler and Göring was consummated on April 20, 1934: Göring put on the blue-gray uniform that he had designed for his secret air force, marched into the Prussian Ministry Building with saber aclank at his side, and ceremonially handed over his Gestapo to Heinrich Himmler and the SS. No dullard in power politics, however, Göring retained one special unit of the green-uniformed *Landespolizei* for his own protection. From this tiny seed, in time, would grow the crack "Hermann Göring" Division and Panzer Corps.

It was going to be a long, sultry summer. Göring lingered at Carinhall, perspiring profusely in the Central European heat, bathing frequently in the marble baths, or submerging himself in the cool waters of Carin's lake.

On June 10, he invited forty foreign diplomats out to envy him. Their motorcade drove the fifty miles from Berlin along the Prenzlau highway until they reached the checkpoint that guarded access to his domains. The land-scape was dotted with ponds and lakes, around which wound the eight miles of new tarmac road leading to Carinhall itself.

He met them at the southern edge of the Heath at the wheel of his two-seater sports car. He was dressed, according to British ambassador Sir Eric Phipps, in aviator's garb of India rubber, with high boots and a large hunting knife stuck in his belt. Oblivious of the snickering asides, he took a mega-phone and launched into a lecture on the elks and other fauna that he had imported from East Prussia and elsewhere. He was particularly proud of his new bison reservation and attempted to persuade one bison to mate with another, but the bull took one glance at the cow, had reservations of his own, and fled the forty pairs of invited eyes.

Göring met them all again at Carinhall itself, dressed now casually in white with a green leather jerkin. When curious eyes alighted on the shapely blonde, Emmy Sonnemann, he introduced her to them as "my private secretary"—one of his less harmful inexactitudes.

Maneuvering for greater status, Göring had begun acting as Hitler's alternate foreign minister. His three missions to Rome in 1933 had not been wholly successful. Talking to the British ambassador on October 11, 1933, Mussolini had unkindly apostrophized the German general as "a former inmate of an asylum." On November 6 and 7, Göring conducted what proved to be his last talks with the Italian dictator for three years. He had brought a private letter from Hitler and again assured Mussolini that the Reich was willing to declare in writing that Germany did not desire to annex Austria. Mussolini, however, went one stage further, and in March 1934 he signed the Roman Protocols with Austria and her neighbor Hungary, effectively guaranteeing Austria's independence. This was not what Hitler had wanted at all, and he thereafter put Rudolf Hess in sole charge of developing the Austrian affair.

Outflanked here, Göring swiveled his attention to Poland and, later, southeastern Europe (the Balkans), and in both regions he scored personal successes.

The new Polish ambassador in Berlin, Józef Lipski, was a passionate huntsman like himself, and through him Göring cadged an invitation to the Polish State Hunting Ground at Bialowiéza in March 1934. Enlarging the contacts he made there, he used his dictatorial powers in Prussia to do the Poles little favors, as when a Ukranian nationalist killed the Polish minister of the interior and fled to Germany in mid-June. Göring arbitrarily loaded the wretched assailant onto the next plane back to Warsaw, an act of dubious legality that won him immediate acclaim from the Poles (and an annual spring visit to Bialowiéza thereafter until 1938).

He extended this unorthodox diplomatic style to the mineral-rich Balkans, hitherto neglected by both Hitler and the foreign ministry, undertaking in the spring of 1934 the first of a series of spectacular swings through the southeast. He often noised it around that he was conveying special hand-written messages from Hitler, or that he was traveling on Hitler's personal instructions—which flattered these smaller, half-forgotten nations but only dismayed Italy the more, since she regarded the Balkans as an Italian preserve.

Regardless of Italian feelings, on May 15, 1934, General Göring set out with Milch, Korner, Kerrl, and Prince Philipp of Hesse on a ten-day "vacation" tour of the southeast. Rather tactlessly, he took along his (still-married) lady friend Emmy Sonnemann, causing scandalized comment that

Goebbels was not slow to call to Hitler's attention. Even less tactfully, Göring had announced that the tour was to begin with Rome, then smugly announced just before takeoff that they would not be calling there after all, a calculated affront that left the Italian welcoming party empty-handed at the airport and Mussolini spluttering with anger.

To the delight of the Hungarians, Göring stopped briefly at Budapest instead, allegedly for technical reasons. On the sixteenth, further "technical reasons" caused him to dally in Belgrade, where he hinted that he would like to see the king (who was, however, genuinely absent). In ten days Göring succeeded in convincing all of southeastern Europe as far as Greece and the Aegean Sea that Nazi Germany (highly visibly personified by Hermann Göring) would not abandon them to Mussolini's Italy.

It was altogether an odd episode, for Hitler was due to pay his own first state visit to Rome in three weeks' time. Mussolini unleashed his newspapers on Germany, and he confidentially indicated to the Foreign Ministry in Berlin that Herr Göring would not be made welcome if he accompanied Hitler on the trip. It was a calculated affront, since Göring had, as Dr. Renzetti, the Duce's personal emissary to the Nazis, pointed out on the fourteenth, labored hardest since 1924 at German-Italian relations, "in conditions that were certainly not easy, and attracting the fury of many politicians."

Göring, anxious to demonstrate that his position had not slipped as the number-two man in the Reich, secured the Führer's personal attendance at a macabre ceremony at Carinhall immediately upon his return from Italy.

It was June 20, 1934, the day that Göring had appointed for the reburial of Carin's remains in the lakeside mausoleum he had built for her. Few pharoahs' wives can have been buried with more solemn ceremony. A special train bore the pewter sarcophagus across northern Prussia from the Swedish ferry to the railroad station where Göring and Hitler, both hatless and somber, awaited her arrival. At Göring's command, towns and cities along the train's whole route were cast into deep mourning. Teenage Hitler Youth units stood at attention on their local railroad platforms, the League of Maidens lined the bridges, saluting and showering flowers; flags were dipped as the train slowly passed, and thousands of women lined the railroad tracks to pay homage to their prime minister's long-dead wife.

The scene at Carinhall itself was like the setting for a Bayreuth opera— the thin summer mists steaming slowly off the still waters of the lake, the ranks of soldiers standing in motionless array, while Richard Wagner's rich funeral music throbbed and droned among the hazed conifers.

Göring had invited Carin's relatives, along with hundreds of diplomats and politicians, to witness this moving evidence of how beholden he still was to her memory. To the blare of hunting horns and trumpets and the answering bellows of Hermann's future trophies grazing in the forests, a dozen strong men groaned and strained to manhandle the sarcophagus down into the granite mausoleum. Afterward, Göring led Hitler down the steps alone. Both men had known Carin well, both were saddened that she had not lived to see the National Socialists triumphant. Göring's most intimate accomplices—Himmler and Körner—looked on. With him these two men were to become, in Darré's compelling phrase, the "managers" of the coming Night of the Long Knives.

In a secret meeting in the great hall of Carinhall, surrounded by the hunting trophies and Gothic furniture that he had already begun to assemble, Göring now persuaded Hitler to act against Ernst Röhm and the SA before it was too late. As a thousand hands slapped rifle butts in chiseled unison outside, and heels slammed together in salute, Göring escorted the Führer to his car. "The first revolution," he declared at the Prussian State Council's meeting the next day, June 21, "was begun by the Führer. If the Führer desires a second revolution, he will find us ready and waiting. If not, then we are equally ready and willing to act against any man who dares lift his hand against the Führer's will."

The confrontation with Röhm and the SA had drawn steadily closer. Heinrich Himmler was now a regular caller at Göring's villa in Leipziger Strasse. Göring applied Körner and the Forschungsamt to keeping Röhm under close surveillance. Meanwhile he drew up his own "hit list" for the day of reckoning, and he gave that to Körner for safekeeping. In his red linen-bound pocket diary Göring jotted sinister reminders: "Krausser [SA Gruppenführer Fritz von Krausser] on Röhm's staff. Extreme caution. Agitating particularly against me."

He had ordered the FA to tap the phones of other SA leaders, rebellious figures on the staff of Franz von Papen (still, in name, Hitler's vice-chancellor) and the former chancellor General von Schleicher. The FA, already routinely wiretapping French diplomats, had evidently found them conniving with Schleicher and his former military assistant Major General Ferdinand von Bredow, because Joachim von Ribbentrop, head of the party's private "Foreign Office," remarked to an aide as they visited Paris at this time, "The time has come to deal with them." (The aide was an anti-Nazi. He tipped off his friend, Deputy Foreign Minister Bernhard von Bülow, that Bredow and Schleicher were under Göring's surveillance. The naïve von Bülow immediately telephoned to warn them—and thus von Bülow's name too went onto a "hit list.")

For several more days the Berlin ministries and clubs crackled with the static electricity of rumor and counter-rumor. On June 23, the army instructed lower echelons to provide guns and transport to the SS for any coming operation against the SA. Göring, Himmler, and Heydrich instructed their police forces to go onto the alert.

Göring went about his affairs seemingly unconcerned. His private photo album shows him with Bodenschatz and Julius Streicher at a children's party at Dinkelsbuhl on June 24, then holidaying briefly on the island of Sylt, where Emmy had a summer house, on the twenty-sixth. On the twenty-seventh, a photographer snapped him landing at Cologne, and driving, on the twenty-eighth, through the Rhineland city. That day he met with Hitler, who had flown to Essen to attend the wedding of Göring's friend Joseph Terboven, the gauleiter and newspaper owner. Hitler had brought with him Viktor Lutze, who he intended should take over the SA after he had "expelled" Röhm from it. By that time everybody had seen documents—or knew of people who had seen them—"proving" that Röhm was up to no good. Hitler decided on one last attempt at reconciliation, and told Röhm's deputy, SA-Gruppenführer Fritz von Krausser on the twenty-ninth, "I want to try and dispose of all these misunderstandings."

Then the evidence against Röhm suddenly seemed to harden. Hitler got a telephone call from Himmler in Berlin; disturbed, he retired to his hotel room taking Göring and Lutze with him. After a while Paul Körner came into the room, having just flown to Essen from Berlin, bringing still more evidence that seemed to clinch the case against Röhm; Körner later told Milch that the evidence consisted of Brown Pages (Forschungsamt wiretaps); and from surviving members of the FA staff we know that a chief evaluator called Rudolf Popp later discreetly bragged that he was the one who had provided the Brown Pages, intercepts of Röhm's telephone orders to his SA commanders to meet him at a secret rendezvous, at Bad Wiessee in Bavaria. "I've seen enough," announced Hitler, grimly adding, "I'm going to make an example of them."

He flew to Munich that same night, after ordering Göring to return to Berlin with Körner immediately. Hitler gave Göring dictatorial powers to strike in Prussia, as soon as he received the code word *Kolibri*—"hummingbird"—to strike against the SA leaders in Prussia.

Not without prudent forethought, Hermann Göring had located his imposing Berlin villa in the center of a fortresslike block of public buildings. "You go in through the entrance of the old Herrenhaus," wrote one visitor, "and after being marched by soldiers through endless halls and past endless sentries find yourself in a garden of four or five acres, in the middle of which his house stands." Here Göring and Himmler had just one day, June 29, to prepare the massacre that was to become known as the Night of the Long Knives. It was like Oscar Night in Hollywood, but with only the deadliest prizes in their gift.

The lists were taken out of the various safes, and last-minute adjustments made—here an additional "nomination," there a reprieve. Göring handed one list to a senior Gestapo official and sent him by private plane to Breslau with a letter ordering SS-Gruppenführer Udo von Woyrsch—the "SS commander, southeast" and one of the nastiest of Himmler's blue-blooded, black-sheathed thugs—to stand by to pounce on their opponents.

On Göring's orders Milch whistled up six hundred troops, undergoing secret air-force training at Jüterbog Airfield, and brought them into Berlin to guard the three airports and the air ministry building.

What happened on the morning of June 30, 1934, in Bavaria is history. Hitler had moved the SS Leibstandarte "Adolf Hitler," an elite unit of thirteen hundred men, to Bavaria, planning to rush them in the trucks provided by the regular army to Bad Wiessee, where Röhm and his henchmen were understood to have converged on an inn. From Berlin, Göring and Himmler prodded and cajoled their irresolute Führer along, by telephone, telegram, and courier. Wilhelm Brückner, Hitler's slow-witted but devoted adjutant, recalled later that their messages painted the crisis in "increasingly dark hues." By the time Hitler's plane landed at Munich, around 3:30 A.M., the word was that hundreds of Röhm's men had spent the early hours rampaging mindlessly around the city. Hitler decided to go on ahead to Bad Wiessee and have it out with Röhm then and there.

In Berlin, the whole area around Göring's villa had been barricaded and sandbagged by his troops. His personal Landespolizei-Gruppe "General Göring" were manning machine-gun positions in the streets.

At 8:00 A.M. Goebbels phoned from Munich with the code word, "Kolibri." For a moment Göring's actions were guided by compassion. He sent for his trusty henchmen, the "murder managers," but he also offered sanctuary to a little cluster of old friends and foes toward whom he bore no ill will. Wilhelm Frick was one—now Reich minister of the interior; he slunk into the villa that morning, "as pale as a vomited-up pea," as Göring uncharitably recalled. He also feared for Franz von Papen's safety; he had crossed the vice-chancellor's name off one "hit list," but sensing ill omens Göring ordered Karl Bodenschatz to summon Papen "on a matter of extreme state urgency." Failing to grasp the very real danger he was in, Papen dawdled at his office, and at 8:45 A.M. Göring had to phone him himself, telling him to come to the villa at once.

> In his room [related Papen to a British officer in 1945] I meet
> him and Himmler. "Something very grave is happening in Mun-
> ich," he says. "A revolution has broken out. The Führer has left
> me in complete charge here in Berlin."
> "Herr Göring, I want to know what's going on—what counter-
> measures we're taking."
> "I can't go into detail. Fighting has broken out."
> "Then mobilize the army!"
> "That has been done."

Papen snapped to Göring that he was Hitler's deputy, and not Göring.

"You'll have to leave me alone now," said Göring, indicating that their interview was at an end. "My head's bursting. We've got to see how we can crush this thing."

He whispered something to Himmler, who got up and left. As a *Landes-*

polizei officer came in to escort Papen home, Papen heard Himmler's voice shouting over a phone somewhere nearby, "You can go in now!"

All over Prussia, Göring's men were "going in." He himself led the party that raided Berlin's SA headquarters in Wilhelm Strasse.

"I asked," he would relate, "whether they had got arms. Their commander denied it, but then I glanced out of the window and saw with my own eyes our trucks being loaded with machine guns."

He never tired of relating this episode, although the details varied:

> I went to that SA captain and said, "Do you have any weapons?" "Why no, *Herr Polizeichef*," the swine says. "None except the pistol for which you gave me a permit!" Then I found an arsenal in the cellar bigger than the whole armament of the Prussian police force!

"In a case like that," Göring boasted, smiling broadly, "there was only thing to do: Execute!"

And execute they did. All day long from his office at his villa—a chamber big enough to stage an Indian durbar—lolling behind a fifteen-foot table, a massive chunk of oak four inches thick, in an outsize gold-trimmed chair upholstered in cerise velvet, Göring presided over the liquidation of his enemies. He kept President Hindenburg *au courant* all day, shouting into the phone that there had been a plot to make Röhm defense minister and Schleicher chancellor. Thronging through Göring's palatial salons, displaying unashamed relief at the destruction of the SA, were the monocled army generals Fritsch and Reichenau; the air-force chief of staff, Wever; Himmler and Körner, and Staatssekretär Milch, who had hurried over from Staaken Airfield, where he was taking a flying lesson. Once or twice Defense Minister Blomberg himself appeared, handsome, upright, but unsmiling. Göring assured him that Röhm and Schleicher were to be arrested and tried for treason.

General von Schleicher was, however, already dead. Göring had sent his *Landespolizei* to deal with the general—but an unidentified "hit squad" of five assassins in plain clothes had beaten the green-uniformed police to it. They had burst into the general's Babelsberg villa at midday and shot the general to death in a hail of bullets—seven bullet wounds were found, and five cartridge cases. They had then slain the general's wife as well. Unabashed, Göring instructed his staff to describe the killing as a suicide. Down the tube into his private office, however, there rattled an FA intercept that scotched that plan. Using the dead general's own desk telephone (which the FA was tapping) an overzealous detective had reported to the ministry of justice (which was still in non-Nazi hands): "Former Reich Chancellor von Schleicher has been shot in a political assassination." Without faltering in his stride for an instant, Göring coolly phoned Franz Gürtner, the justice minister, and advised him that he planned to issue a wholly different official version—that General von Schleicher had been "shot resisting arrest." Having propagated this fiction, Göring characteristically came to believe it, and would repeat it with wide-eyed innocence until the end of his life (although the truth is clear from the ministry files, beyond peradventure).

Throughout that Saturday, June 30, 1934, the lists shortened, the killings went on. Thirty men headed by three of Heydrich's Gestapo officers burst into the absent Papen's offices looking for his press chief, Herbert von Bose (who had been overheard, probably by the FA, plotting against the regime). They led him into an empty conference room, and his appalled colleagues heard ten shots fired in rapid succession, followed by an eleventh some moments later.

What does the board meeting of a Nazi "Murder, Inc." look like? Milch saw it in session that afternoon and described it to this author: Himmler was slowly reeling off names from sweaty and tattered lists. Göring and Reichenau, the army's deputy chief of staff, were nodding or shaking their heads. Körner was carrying their duly considered "nominations" outside—with the addition of one ominous word, *Vollzugsmeldung* ("Report back!"). Rudolf Diels: Göring shook his head; Bernhard von Bülow: He vetoed that name as well. Somebody in this all-male company jested that they should nominate Baroness Viktoria von Dirksen while they could. At the mention of this, one of the more tedious females around the Führer, everybody heaved with nervous laughter.

It is not hard to recognize the "Oscars" that Göring himself awarded, or at least nodded to. Who else had any score to settle with Erich Klausener, whom Göring had sacked as head of the Prussian Police Department in February 1933? Who, other than Göring, would have ordered the pickax murder of seventy-one-year-old ex-dictator Gustav von Kahr and Munich journalist Fritz Gerlich? Kahr had betrayed the 1923 beer hall putsch; Gerlich had claimed that Göring broke his word of honor to escape: Göring had sued him for libel and lost. Now both those old scores were settled, permanently.

At 10:00 P.M. the day's bloody business came to an end. Himmler nonchalantly ordered all SS documents relating to the purge destroyed. Göring took Milch and Körner out to Tempelhof Airport in his black Mercedes saloon, to await Hitler's return from Bavaria. As they waited, a Junkers 52 from Bremen touched down, and Karl Ernst, the Berlin SA commander, was led in manacles out of its corrugated fuselage. He had been aboard a ship about to sail from Bremen. Years later, still incorrigible, Göring would continue to maintain that Ernst had been "trying to abscond with eighty thousand Reichsmarks." In truth, the unfortunate man had just set out on a belated honeymoon voyage with his wife. Now the baffled SA Gruppenführer was hustled away to a brief and merciless ceremony at Göring's old military academy at Lichterfelde. Facing an SS firing squad was not a good start to anybody's honeymoon.

Hitler's plane landed, and he emerged, deathly pale and grim-faced. He nervously complimented Göring on the honor guard, of four hundred hand-picked air-force troops drawn up on the tarmac, wearing their still-secret Luftwaffe uniform. "The men are a good racial selection," he commented.

At the Chancellery he told Göring that he had ordered the execution of all Röhm's senior henchmen but proposed to spare his longtime friend Röhm, for old times' sake. Göring gagged on this sentimentality. All the next day, Sunday, July 1, he and Himmler badgered Hitler to carry through the purge to its ruthless and logical conclusion. When Darré arrived at Göring's ministry that Sunday afternoon, he found Göring and Himmler still arguing with Hitler. Once, Hitler insisted on being put through by phone to Röhm's former deputy, Krausser (he had consulted this distinguished cavalry officer two nights before). Too late—on Göring's orders, Krausser had received his "Oscar" at Lichterfelde a few hours earlier. By the time Milch arrived at the ministry, from a leisurely sporting afternoon spent at Berlin's Karlshorst racetrack, the argument was over and Röhm too had been shot to death in his Munich prison cell.

Eighty-four people were known to have been liquidated in the purge. "Of course," Göring airily conceded later, "in the general excitement some mistakes were made." There was the unknown musician Willi Schmidt, gunned down in mistake for Willi Schmid. And there was the air-force Pour le Mérite holder Daniel Gerth, on whom Göring took compassion. This SA lieutenant was driven off, like all the others, to Lichterfelde . . . propped up before the SS firing squad . . . reprieved on Göring's orders . . . then shot an hour later.

Tabula rasa, a clean sweep. Hitler was out of his league in such company. It dawned only slowly on their private staffs that Göring and Himmler had duped their Führer completely, in order to settle private scores. Brückner was present as Himmler read out the final tally. Hitler was speechless with grief at some of the victims' names.

With his accumulated enemies thus largely neutralized, Göring recommended that the killings should stop. He would later suggest that he had to plead with Hitler all that Sunday:

> Finally I hurried around to the Führer and begged him to put an end to the shootings, as there was a danger of the thing getting out of hand. The executions then halted, even though this meant that two of the Führer's worst enemies—[Werner] von Alvensleben and [Dr. Leon Count] von Moulin-Eckart [Röhm's adjutant] escaped with their lives.

A remorseful Hitler, bilious after the bloodletting, ordered compensation paid for the "mistakes" and pensions for all next-of-kin. As for Göring, his gargantuan appetite was unaffected. On Monday evening he organized a celebratory crab feast and invited his fellow "managers" Blomberg, Himmler, Körner, and Milch to crack claws with him. A telegram came from the aged president, Hindenburg, congratulating him on his "energetic and victorious action," while a more chastened letter arrived from Franz von Papen, still believing himself under house arrest. Göring had quite forgotten him, and telephoned effusive apologies. "So sorry," he said. "Big misunderstanding. I only meant you to be given a guard for Saturday evening, until you were out of danger." (In Bucharest nine years later Papen would chance upon the Gestapo man assigned to assassinate him in 1934—"Göring prevented it," the man grumbled.)

By that odd inversion of public ethics that characterized the decade, the National Socialist regime emerged from the Night of Long Knives with its domestic popularity enhanced. Göring and Himmler would henceforth collaborate with a verve born of prudence and mutual respect.

By way of reward Göring invited the Gestapo to celebrate at his expense at the Hubertusstock, the old imperial hunting lodge around which Carinhall was taking shape, on July 7. A whole page of photographs in his private album shows him surrounded by Heydrich's staff, signing autographs for eager hands. Busloads of informers, jailers, and lawyers, with their female secretaries and girl friends frisking at their sides, debouched into the special beer garden that Göring jovially erected for them at Carinhall. But this was not Otto Horcher's gourmet restaurant, nor were these the dignified, middle-aged veterans of the Richthofen Squadron. The celebration deteriorated into an orgy. Across the lake, to Carin's silent mausoleum, drifted drunken cheers and the sound of breaking glass and furniture.

Göring may well have feared what Carin would have thought of his new friends—at any rate he discouraged future sightseeing excursions by Himmler's Gestapo to his hallowed heath. When he rewarded the Gestapo in the future—for instance, after what he called "an exceptionally important investigation" in 1942—he would send over an envelope containing one hundred thousand marks to be distributed to "particularly meritorious" officials.

12

OPEN DOOR TO A TREASURE-HOUSE

"There was no point in thrashing the whole thing out in court," said Göring, blithely dismissing the eighty-four murders committed in the June 1934 purge. "Their treason was as clear as day. . . . After all, there had been a plot against the Führer's life. The whole point was to act fast, as a deterrent."

He resumed his posture of fearless Defender of the Good and Persecutor of the Malign. When Austrian Nazis ran amok in Vienna and brutally gunned down Chancellor Engelbert Dollfuss later that summer, it was Göring who persuaded Hitler to dismiss their leader, Theo Habicht, and to send Franz von Papen to Vienna as his personal ambassador, thus killing two birds with one stone.

Then he sent for Theo Croneiss, Röhm's would-be air minister. Croneiss slunk in, with a pistol concealed in his pocket and his dossier on Milch's father deposited in a safe place as "life insurance."

Göring rose to his feet. "I might as well give up my chair," he said, with a mocking bow. "You were to be my successor, I believe?" (Croneiss was allowed to return to his job with Messerschmitt and died in his bed in November 1942.)

Those who knew Göring believed they saw the signs of narcotics addiction returning. Leading criminal lawyer Count von der Goltz met him one evening in July 1934 at a hunting festival in Pomerania and tackled Göring—who was wearing a white toga and a glazed, trancelike look—about the notorious criminality of the local Nazi gauleiter, the former lawyer Wilhelm Karpenstein.

"Karpenstein?" echoed Göring vaguely. "Out!" (That is, he was about to be arrested.)

"And Koch?" pressed Goltz. (Erich Koch was the notorious gauleiter of East Prussia.)

"Not yet decided," responded Göring. "Actually, the Führer wanted to have him bumped off too during the Röhm business, but others spoke up for him. . . ."

The choice of words shocked Goltz. Bumped off? Too? Göring drove him to Carinhall afterward, but the lawyer could not extract one coherent word from him. At the forest mansion Emmy Sonnemann was waiting for them.

"I'll make tea," she volunteered.

Göring grunted something and vanished, to reappear swathed in silence and a floor-length robe. He plodded off without a word toward his beloved lake and plunged in stark-naked. Throughout the drive back from Pomerania, Goltz realized, this prospect, of swimming in Carin's lake, had been obsessing Hermann Göring. He found himself somehow hurting for this melancholy widower.

On the day after Hindenburg died in August 1934, one hundred of Göring's officers were summoned to the Air Ministry. Göring marched into a little clearing in their midst, drew his sword, and announced that the armed forces were to swear their allegiance to Hitler, as Hindenburg's designated successor. (The old oath had been sworn to the Constitution, but nobody was given time for reflection.) Milch stepped forward and slapped his hand onto the blade of Göring's sword. Bodenschatz read out the words of the new oath, and the officers chanted it after him.

Later that month Göring and Milch went over the defense budget with Hitler at Berchtesgaden. Hitler approved a total of 10.5 billion marks for the next four years, the lion's share of it going to the air force. He gave the job of raising these unheard-of sums to Dr. Hjalmar Schacht. "We're going to need thirty billion marks to complete our armament," he disclosed to Göring afterward, "but I didn't dare tell Schacht that. He would have fainted."

That October 1934, without asking Hitler, Göring decided to attend the state funeral of the murdered king of Yugoslavia, as representative of the German Wehrmacht (armed forces). He played his hand well. Knowing that there was worldwide speculation that Italian Fascists had been behind the assassination in Marseilles, Göring made a public declaration that no German hand was to blame: This attracted favorable comment in Belgrade—and dismay in Rome. Göring arrived at Belgrade's airport in Lufthansa's imposing new airliner the Hindenburg, and allowed all Yugoslavia to learn that the wreath he brought from the German armed forces was inscribed to the king as "their heroic former enemy." The local German minister conceded enviously that Göring had stolen the whole show, while his British colleague, Nevile Henderson, agreed that Göring had converted Belgrade to the German cause simply by being the only foreign dignitary to use an open car in the funeral procession.

The professional diplomats in the Wilhelm Strasse, who had never valued the Balkans highly, looked down their noses at Göring's methods, but Hitler didn't. By a secret law he now appointed Hermann Göring the second man in the Reich, signing two decrees to this effect on December 7, 1934: One nominated Göring his deputy "in the event that I am impeded in the execution of the offices of Reich president and Reich chancellor combined in my person"; the other specified Göring as his successor.

After this, Göring's megalomania knew few bounds. Thomas von Kantzow, his stepson, visiting him that Christmas at the Reichstag speaker's palace, heard about all the new buildings Göring was planning and warned him he was well on the way to becoming another King Ludwig II of Bavaria—"the mad king who had the idea," as Thomas noted in his diary on December 23, "of building one castle after another."

> Hermann [he added] has already rebuilt the speaker's palace. The hall we were in before is now completely different. He went to the window and pointed to the Reichstag Building, and said he intends to build an Air Ministry five times as big, where airplanes can land and take off from the roof.

In January 1935 he laid the cornerstone of the new Air Ministry. It would occupy a four-hundred-thousand-square-foot site off the Leipziger Strasse. Hitler personally checked each façade in plaster miniature. Its central longitudinal block and side wings would house four thousand bureaucrats and officers in its twenty-eight hundred rooms. Throughout 1935 the country's finest architects and sculptors chiseled at heroic reliefs with motifs like "Flag Company," designed by Professor Arnold Waldschmidt of the Prussian Academy of Fine Arts. The Berliners made smug comments about this extravagance—"Pure and simple, and hang the expense!" was one; "just humble gold" was another.

Göring also became the leader in high society. His annual ball became the event of the winter season. But when the first was held, on January 11, 1935, in his State Opera House on Unter den Linden, Nazi purists wrinkled their noses. "Göring's Opera Ball," sneered Darré in his diary. "Wrong. The old Court Ball—do we have to put on airs like this?"

Those were the days when the Nazis were riding high. In Berlin Leni

Riefenstahl's spine-chilling film of the party rally, *Triumph of the Will*, was packing movie theaters. A thrill of military awakening was surging through the Reich. "We have a vital task before us," Blomberg told fellow generals one day after Göring's winter ball. "For the moment we are just erecting the scaffolding." Everybody understood that. Milch's papers show him building aircraft factories and aircraft-engine factories, expanding pilot training, commissioning synthetic-rubber and gasoline plants, and planning smoke-screens for the Ruhr. Addressing gauleiters early in 1935, Göring bragged that in two years he had turned a once-defenseless country into a major power. "Germany," he concluded, "will possess by this coming autumn the most powerful air fleet in the world." Soon they could start doing deals with their neighbors. Milch learned the planning figures and jotted them in his diary: "[German] navy: thirty-five percent of the British. Air: one hundred percent, assuming British Air Force equals French. We are banking on British—against Russia."

That was Hitler's ultimate intention, to expand northeastward, with Poland's connivance, into Soviet territories. He gave to Göring the job of wooing the Polish government. When Marshal Józéf Pilsudski, the Polish dictator, invited Göring to hunt wolves at Bialowiéza later that January, Hitler briefed him in secret on the twenty-fifth to tell his hosts that Germany was

> willing to recognize by treaty that the [Polish] Corridor question
> was not a bone of contention between our two countries. . . .
> Germany can expand, in collusion with Poland, to the east: Poland
> would have the Ukraine as its sphere of interest, and Germany
> the northeast.

In quiet intervals during the four days of strenuous hunting in Poland, Göring outlined this cynical German offer. Praising Poland's "strength and dynamic force," he scoffed at any notion that Hitler might ever do a deal with Stalin at Poland's expense. "A common German-Russian frontier," he assured the Poles, "would be highly dangerous to Germany."

Pilsudski, however, demanded a German guarantee of noninterference with Danzig—which he did not get—before he would agree to any summit meeting with Hitler.

Neither Hitler nor Göring would ever abandon these long-term strategic aims. After one internal conference in the Behren Strasse Air Ministry Building, ex-naval aviator Friedrich Christiansen confided to his fellow officers, raking one hand across the map of Central Europe, that Hitler had plans to expand in 1938 eastward into Galicia and the Ukraine. "We must be so powerful by then," said Christiansen, "that nobody dares to oppose us. We'll square things with Britain—they'll give us a free hand in the east, and in return we'll drop our claim to our former colonies." Russia would just disintegrate, Hitler had said. "And then," Christiansen continued, his hand sweeping over all the countries north of the Black Sea, "we'll inherit all of these too."

The new secret German Air Force was cautiously unveiled. To an English nobleman brought to him by the British air attaché, Göring blandly admitted that yes, he had built an air force. "One," he added flirtatiously, "that I should call little." A few days later he enlarged on that concept to the attaché, Group Captain Frank Don: By "little," he meant a first line of fifteen hundred bombers. It was a shameless exaggeration, but the officer nearly fell off his chair.

"There will be calls for an increase in the RAF," he said.

"I should welcome any increase," responded Göring evenly, according to the interpreter's recollection. "In the next war we shall be fighting side by side to save Europe from communism."

He bade the attaché a courteous good-bye. "Mark my words, Group Captain!" he said.

At about the same time Hitler dropped broad hints that it was time for Göring to make an honest woman of Emmy Sonnemann, whose divorce had now come through. One day in February 1935 Göring suggested a quiet weekend in Weimar, and sent her on ahead with a note, which he instructed her not to open before getting there. He had written: "Will you marry me at Easter? The Führer will be our witness."

He announced her change of status from "private secretary" at a "little" dinner party on March 15, held in the white marble dining hall of his rebuilt villa. Sir Eric Phipps was among the forty guests Göring had invited, as were the Joseph Goebbelses and the Heinrich Himmlers and most of the diplomatic corps. "I am only marrying her," he explained disarmingly to Lady Phipps, "at the behest of the Führer. He feels there are too many bachelors among us Nazi high-ups"—and he glanced across at the army's bachelor commander in chief, Baron von Fritsch, standing alone and frigid with his monocle palely reflecting the illuminated tapestries. His voice booming above the invisible string orchestra, Göring mentioned some of the extravagances in the villa, like the 150-foot swimming pool that he was building; and after dinner he showed off the Old Masters that he had prevailed upon the Kaiser-Friedrich Museum to lend him—"The director did object," he grinned, "but I threatened to take twice as many if these were not brought over here first thing in the morning." After that he invited the guests to watch two "stag movies"—the films showed only stags, apart from a General Göring briefly discovered by the cameras at Carinhall, wearing a leather suit and brandishing a harpoon in the Wotan-style living room.

What he felt for Emmy was probably not physical attraction. At the end of 1935 he would reveal to Staatssekretär Milch his belief that the groin injury had left him impotent. Probably he regarded his blond fiancée as merely another dazzling bauble for his collection.

His lust for precious stones and metals was notorious, and he had begun to adorn himself liberally with jewel-encrusted artifacts. Darré once witnessed him preparing to receive a Balkan minister. The valet brought in a cushion on which twelve rings were arrayed—four red, four blue, four green. "Today," the great man mused, "I am displeased. So we shall wear a deeper hue. But we also desire to show that we are not beyond hope. So we shall wear the green."

His private staff turned a blind eye on these eccentricities, but not those whom he affronted. Schacht would regale friends with the image of Göring in thigh-length boots, leather jerkin, and billowing white sleeves, with a Robin Hood hat and a man-sized spear. "His greed was boundless," he testified, "his lust for jewelry, gold, and silver plate unimaginable." One lady invited to tea found him wearing a toga and jewel-studded sandals, while his fingers were heavy with rings and precious stones, and his lips seemed to have been rouged.

The palace at No. 11a Leipziger Platz in Berlin was a dramatic example of his extravagance. He had purchased from former Crown Prince Wilhelm a large, valuable rug and had to order one of the rooms enlarged to fit it. As this work progressed, he decided on still more modifications until the final bill came to seven hundred thousand Reichsmarks (in addition to the 1933 renovation). The Prussian minister of finance, Johannes Popitz, approved without demur—not for nothing had Göring ordered the Finance Ministry alone preserved after the laws unifying the rest of the Reich. The building was later destroyed, but the architect's plans have survived and show the palace to be a rambling edifice with drinking and smoking rooms, several suites of kitchens, and a den for his pet lions at mezzanine level, while circular dining rooms, conservatories, drawing rooms, ambassadorial reception rooms, and hunting-trophy rooms took up the ground floor, along with Göring's cavernous, colonnaded study.

The same extravagance was evident in his expanding collection of medals. It was Göring who had proposed in the Cabinet (on April 7, 1933) the reintroduction of honors and distinctions: "The Weimar Republic," he argued, "went under precisely because of its dearth of honors and medals." At the time, Hitler agreed with him; but as Germany's misfortunes grew, the Führer's patience would wear thin. Ten years later he would ask Göring's heavy, brilliantined adjutant Dr. Ramon von Ondarza to remove himself from the bunker, loudly calling him "a perfumed sink of corruption"—while fastening his glare on Göring. It was like accusing the house dog of flatulence, while glaring at a guest. But that was a decade hence, and in 1935 the silent-hatred phase between the two men had yet to begin.

For the new air force Göring had designed a uniform that was almost as baroque as his palaces. Deciding upon the trinkets of rank, his imagination had run wild, and he ordained that the ceremonial parade uniform of air-

force officers would include two-handed sabers and daggers—neither, seemingly, of much use in modern air-to-air combat. Göring presented to each
new general a fine sword, signed by himself. The generals became rich and
corrupt in his own image. Ribald fighter pilots would tell each other the tale
of two starving jungle lions: One left to seek his fortune in the Reich capital
and returned to the forest, paunchy and licking his chops. "You just have
to hang around the Air Ministry," he growled. "It isn't long before you've
got yourself a fine fat-*Arsch* of a general to sink your teeth into."

Most dazzling of all the swords was the one that his generals commissioned
to commemorate his marriage to Emmy Sonnemann. The blade of finest
Solingen steel was engraved with the words FROM THE REICH AIR FORCE TO
ITS COMMANDER on one side, and FAITHFUL TO THE FÜHRER PEOPLE, AND
REICH on the other. The pommel featured his Pour le Mérite and the Göring
crest; the scabbard was covered with sharkskin of air-force blue.

He was a rare bird in the Berlin of 1935, and this was his real value to
Hitler. He did not even have any function in the party. "I was never particularly interested in the party," he said, "just in the state. I used the one
to attain position in the other. A person of my upbringing," he added loftily,
"did not really fit into the party."

On the morning of April 10, 1935, massed bands serenaded the Göring villa,
and all Berlin was halted to celebrate his wedding to Emmy Sonnemann.
Thirty thousand troops lined the route as he drove past in an open car awash
with narcissus and tulips. Associated Press correspondent Louis P. Lochner
wrote to his daughter: "You had the feeling that an emperor was marrying."
"A visitor to Berlin," echoed the British ambassador, sitting in the diplomatic
gallery facing the floodlit marble altar, "might well have thought . . . that
he had stumbled upon preparations for a royal wedding."

Insensible to Nazi party feelings, Göring had insisted on a religious ceremony (although he granted the Reich bishop, Müller, only five minutes for
his sermon). The wedding album shows Hitler standing bareheaded behind
him in the cathedral, his postman's hat nonchalantly upended on the floor
beside him, his hands clasped in their familiar station below his belt-buckle.
Göring's hair was neatly smoothed back, a broad sash dividing the areas of
saucer-sized medals covering his chest. As the newlyweds emerged from the
cathderal, two hundred planes flew overhead, followed by two storks released
by an irreverent Richthofen Squadron veteran.

At the modest wedding breakfast at the Kaiserhof Hotel the world's society
reporters glimpsed among the 320 friends and supplicants, Swedish in-laws
and German relatives, princes and princesses, field marshals and lieutenants,
gauleiters and manservants. There was Viktoria von Dirksen, whom Göring's
fellow "managers" had yearned to nominate for extermination ten months
before. There was Fritz Thyssen, whom he would shortly commit to prison

for high treason, and Rudolf Hess, who would enter upon forty-six years of incarceration just as Thyssen was leaving it in 1941. After the feast Göring drove out to Carinhall and vanished into the lakeside mausoleum for an hour.

> The climax [wrote correspondent Lochner to his daughter] was yet in store for me. When I arrived at the palace of the Minister-Präsident [Göring, the next day], I found, in the first place, that this attractive building had once again been rebuilt to suit Hermann's by no means cheap taste. . . . He has had a modern Wurlitzer organ built in so that he can have his own talkies at his home and have an organist play for the overture. . . .

Then Hermann himself turned up. "Gentlemen," he said, "I have asked you to come here in order that I may show you the gifts my people have given me."

They filled two rooms, including a Lenbach portrait of Bismarck from Hitler and a solid-silver schooner from the City of Hamburg, which Emmy had often ogled on school trips to the City Hall. Göring was unlikely to be troubled by the ethics of it all. He was forty-two, and the treasure-houses of the Reich were opening to him. The Reichsbank had given him the famous Breslau Castle dining service in Royal porcelain (Göring's office had the effrontery to ask later for two candelabra missing from the inventory). The Reich Board of Guilds had furnished an exquisite drawing room for the Görings. Czar Boris of Bulgaria had given a medal to Hermann and a sapphire bracelet to Emmy. Kings and emperors, ambassadors and ministers, the Labor Front and chambers of commerce—all had deemed it prudent to bestow gifts on him.

In Germany his popularity was zooming. "Göring," reflected Louis Lochner, "is a type of fellow whom one cannot be mad at. His vanity is so obvious and his love of pomp so naïve that one simply laughs, and lets it go at that." Göring had easily won over the ambassadors who found the more radical Nazis unpalatable: André François-Poncet, the papal nuncio, and Phipps all found him a good conversationalist and approachable in matters that went against the Nazi grain. The Polish ambassador, Lipski, and Göring were now as thick as thieves. (Göring, charged by Hitler to take special care of German-Polish affairs as from April 20, had invited Lipski to a shoot that month and once more hinted that Poland should join an alliance against the Soviet Union.) Roosevelt's urbane roving ambassador, William C. Bullitt, took a strong dislike to the general, however, calling him "quite the most unpleasant representative of a nation that I have ever laid eyes on."

Unofficial British visitors came to the same conclusion. Learning that the Prince of Wales—shortly to become King Edward VIII—had urged closer links between the British Legion and comparable German ex-servicemen's organizations, Göring cabled him from Berchtesgaden: "As a front-line soldier I thank Your Royal Highness from the bottom of my heart for the upright and chivalrous words . . . With humble duty to Your Royal Highness, Hermann Göring.'' He received the prince's ''warm thanks,'' but when a British Legion delegation did come to Nazi Germany that July, they were profoundly impressed by Adolf Hitler and not at all by Göring. Out at Carinhall he talked to them only about himself. ''He can be described,'' reported Captain Hawes, RN, who had been naval attaché in Berlin, ''as a mountain of egotism and pomposity.''

13
GETTING READY IN FOUR YEARS

B y the mid-thirties the authority of Hermann Göring was universally respected within the Reich. The gauleiters—Hitler's personal lieutenants throughout the Reich—and middle-ranking party officials saw him as a force to be reckoned with—as the "Man of Iron" (*der Eiserne*) upon whom their Führer relied. The people called him "Hermann," and were indifferent to the murderous aura about him. His Falstaffian corpulence, his gold braid, his stylish airs, enhanced his popularity. When the Reich adopted the swastika as its official flag, General Göring brought forth his own personal standard—what the British embassy loftily termed "an heraldic salad" with only the tiniest Nazi swastika visible in each corner, and the main field dominated by the Prussian eagle with wings spread and his own Pour le Mérite. The public loved it. "Out front," ran one popular jingle, "he's tinsel and medals aclatter. At bottom he's fatter and fatter and fatter."

There were, of course, some critics. There was the Protestant Vicar Schulze of Beiersdorf, who publicly scoffed at "this dandy" having his wedding solemnized by the "parson in chief" Müller. Foolishly, as it turned out, Göring had the vicar prosecuted. The defense called Martin Niemöller, who testified that Göring himself had called Müller the "parson in chief" in

December 1934, and found it hard to take him seriously; scorning Christian beliefs, moreover, Göring had told Niemöller, "This two-thousand-year-old superstition about Jesus of Nazareth—it's going to have to go!" Göring abandoned the case against the vicar, and decided to go for Niemöller instead.

His wedding to Emmy aroused a few snide remarks. Joseph Goebbels totted up the cost of the nuptials and brooded over evidence that she was "other than true Aryan." But Hermann demanded absolute respect for her and required that she be addressed as *Hohe Frau* (My Lady). He insisted on "ruthless prosecution" of every libel on her person. Justice Minister Franz Gürtner warned assize judges in a September 1935 circular that enemies of the state were systematically spreading "spiteful remarks about the prime minister's wife and untrue allegations about her non-Aryan origin and a previous marriage to a non-Aryan." Talking with Frick, minister of the interior, and Gürtner on November 15, Göring complained that one offender had got off with a five-month prison sentence. "In my view," he grumbled, "five years would have been more appropriate."

It does seem that he was covering something. Years later he confided to Milch that Emmy's past was not entirely flawless, and he mentioned certain photographs. The official genealogical brochure on Hermann Göring published in 1936 would reveal Carin's first marriage and divorce, but make no mention whatever of Emmy's. Salacious stories continued to circulate, not all of them untrue. "Since the abortive putsch in 1923 when he [Göring] was shot," Sir Eric Phipps informed London in February 1936, "he is, so I am told, unable to have children."

Göring accepted that this was true but put a good face on his incapacity, telling Madame François-Poncet philosophically that being childless was a godsend in troubled times. While a Goebbels must worry all along what might become of his children, he and Emmy had only themselves to care for.

Fueled by the hormone imbalances that his injury and the morphine had induced, his body had become bloated to a size that invited but defied caricature. Commissioning a homespun woolen garment in September 1942 for Göring's then-forthcoming fiftieth birthday, Heinrich Himmler would order the weavers to allow at least three times the normal weight of wool.

This manicured mountain of perfumed flab swept into Warsaw's cathedral for the state funeral of Marshal Pilsudski on May 17, 1935—"late," as Roosevelt's roving ambassador described the entrance, "as if he were a German tenor playing Siegfried."

> He is [added Bullitt] at least a yard across the bottom as the crow flies. . . . In an attempt to get his shoulders out as far as his hips he wears two inches of padding extending each one. . . . He must carry with him a personal beauty attendant, as his fingers, which are almost as thick as they are short, carry long, pointed, carefully

enameled nails and his pink complexion shows every sign of daily attention.

Bullitt suspected morphine from the way the general's eyes were "popping." Göring certainly dozed off during the funeral ceremony.

The death of Pilsudski was a setback to Hitler's plans, because when Göring now talked, after the funeral, with Polish Foreign Minister Józef Beck, he realized that all hope of doing a deal at Russia's expense was gone.

The basic cause was still Germany's comparative military weakness, and General Göring spelled this out at a secret Cabinet-level staff conference on his return to Berlin on May 20, 1935:

> Germany can not solve the Danzig problem at this moment. The limits of our support [for Danzig] are determined by the extents of our own vital interest: In the first instance, this is our restoration as a Great Power, and the completion of our rearmament is in turn a prerequisite for this.

His air force was still only an imperfect sword, one that both Hitler and he hesitated to lift from its scabbard. By the end of 1935 he would have on paper eighteen hundred planes, but few of these were of a type or quality that could be pitted against either the French or the Polish air forces. If anything, the Luftwaffe was useful only as a vehicle for Göring's personal advancement. In the summer of 1935 he dropped broad hints that he wanted the rank of Luftmarschall, but he drew a blank all around and had to wait until April 20, 1936, for his next promotion, to (four-star) Colonel General.

Even before the Luftwaffe squadrons started filling, his bluster became louder. In January 1936 he told Sir Eric Phipps that although Germany was perplexed by Britain's hostility, she did not want war. "If," he added, "our just demands prove in the course of time to be unobtainable by peaceful means, then, terrible as it is to contemplate, war seems inevitable." Among those demands he included Austria (he suggested a plebiscite be held among Austrians themselves); an end to the oppression of the German minority in Czechoslovakia (which thus figured for the first time on the Nazi strategic horizon); and "a colony." The French now ratified an alliance with Moscow, in violation of the Locarno Treaty, which also bound Hitler not to station troops in the Rhineland. On February 10, speaking again with Phipps, Göring pointed to France's violation. On March 7, Hitler reciprocated by sending his troops into the demilitarized German Rhineland. This act of temerity panicked his more craven generals and caused even Göring, as he admitted to Ivone Kirkpatrick, a senior official at the British embassy, moments of "intense anxiety." The operation was a brilliant coup, but it reinforced a feeling that had first gnawed at Göring during the Röhm purge—that his Führer was taking the curves too fast.

This was probably the last occasion on which his neighbors could have cheaply forestalled Hitler, but the bluff came off. "I don't think," Milch later wrote, "that either Hitler or Göring were fully aware of just how weak we were, particularly in the Luftwaffe." The air force had three squadrons (*Gruppen*) of fighters—I /JG2 commanded by Major Wieck at Döberitz; II/JG2 at Jüterbog under Major Raithel (operating the obsolete Arado 65 and Heinkel 51 planes respectively); and Bruno Loerzer's III /JG2, flying Arado 68 biplanes at Bernburg-an-der-Saale. Only one of these squadrons was actually operational, and its guns had not been calibrated. Göring ordered these ancient biplanes to be flown in a circus around the Rhineland airfields, painting fresh insignia on them between each showing to create an illusion of armadas.

Göring knew that a war of imperial conquest in the east would have to be prefaced by years of solid rearmament. Recognizing that imported raw materials like oil, rubber, and iron ore would be the strategic bottlenecks, he had signed a synthetic-gasoline contract with Dr. Carl Krauch of I.G. Farben as early as December 14, 1933, and in the spring of 1935 Hitler gave him control of both the gasoline and the synthetic-rubber production efforts. His profile as the Reich's leading political economist was further enhanced by the specific task that Hitler gave him in August 1935, to arbitrate between Darré and Schacht and the competing interests of agriculture and industry. In the spring of 1936 Göring adopted the title of Hitler's "fuel commissioner," and then went all out to become the Reich's economic overlord.

Ironically, both Blomberg and Schacht gave him the final boost into this impregnable position. On April 3, the defense minister invited Göring to become "inspector general of the German petroleum economy," and on the same date Schacht, anxious to harness Göring's prestige in the party, asked him to accept responsibility for the Reich's foreign-exchange reserves. The result was a secret decree, which Hitler signed the next day, appointing Göring "commissioner for foreign exchange and raw materials."

In this we can see the embryo of the future monolithic Reich agency known as the Four-Year Plan. Both Blomberg and Schacht had ingenuously seen the general as some kind of buxom, popular figurehead to adorn their own offices. But no sooner had Hitler signed that secret decree than the figurehead came alive, clambered on board, and seized the helm. Secret though the decree might be, Göring had it published and, to the chagrin of the other ministries concerned, he set up a new agency called "Prime Minister General Göring's Raw Materials and Foreign Currency Unit." It will be noted that he had subtly dropped the words "of Prussia" after "Prime Minister."

There is no doubt that if he had the choice, he would have elected to be remembered as the executor of Hitler's Four-Year Plan. Flattered by American financial interrogator Herbert Dubois in 1945, who told him that the plan was regarded as a "very interesting institution," Göring beamed.

"I have never been a businessman," he avowed nostalgically. "And this was something completely new to me. My job was to organize the German economy, and my energy was harnessed to get things started. Over the years I learned a lot. My main task was to safeguard the food supply . . . and to make Germany self-sufficient. The most important items were iron, petroleum, and rubber."

He was innocent of any formal training in economics, but he soon got the hang of things and shortly bragged to Hitler that Dr. Schacht's preserve was not the holy mystery he had made out. Schacht found his sacred economic theories overridden and ignored, and a wall of hostility arose between the two men. In the first of a series of "foreign-exchange" conferences called during May and June of 1936, Göring pushed and inveigled. Schacht, his vanity affronted, refused even to attend the first one, held on the morning of May 12, and forbade any of his departments to help the new "dictator." Schacht, however, found few allies, and he condescended to put in an appearance that afternoon at Göring's "Little Cabinet"—as the Prussian Council of Ministers was becoming known—where he brandished a new Führer directive, which, he claimed, superceded Göring's. But Schacht had to listen impassively (and silently) as his rival preached his new economic gospel—putting exports first to earn foreign currency, then projects designed to meet the Reich's raw-materials needs from its own native resources. The implication was obvious. Göring was hatching a siege economy for a future war, and Schacht did not like it.

The raw-materials bottlenecks would have to be tackled now. On May 26, Göring harangued the biggest names in industry—Flick, Thyssen, and Vögler among them—about the raw materials likely to prove scarce in wartime. He listed flax, jute, copper, metal scrap, and manganese among them, but identified particularly oil and rubber. "When war comes," he hammered into them, "we won't get a drop of oil from abroad." The same held true for rubber, so they had to expand synthetic-production capacity now. Using arguments of unmistakable bellicosity at a conference on the last day of June, he referred to two major tasks facing them, one being to feed the nation and the other to arm it for when it would be forced to "sally forth for freedom's last fight."

It must have been a novel, even distasteful, experience to be lectured by former Air Force Captain Hermann Göring on basic economics. But these industrialists had no choice. "The special powers given me by the Führer," he importantly explained, "have coerced me into this totally new field of endeavor. It has only recently dawned on me that this is vastly more important than those that the Führer has entrusted to me hitherto."

There were those in later years who called him lazy, and he hated the epithet. His diary would meticulously record the hours at which he rose, worked, relaxed, and retired to bed. While Schacht's civil servants went on summer furlough, Göring stayed in Berlin, called top-level conferences, and surrounded himself with his own handpicked economic specialists. He was unobtrusively usurping broad areas of Hitler's governmental functions. The Reich Cabinet now rarely met—when it did, on June 26, 1936, Martin Bormann specifically remarked on it in his diary. Göring was using his own Prussian Cabinet in its place, co-opting Himmler, Lammers, and other Reich ministers to meetings as he saw fit.

By July 1936 his staff was complete, handpicked from I.G. Farben, the Air Ministry, and his Prussian Ministry, or filched from existing government agencies regardless of party connection. He gave his cousin Herbert L. W. Göring the task of reviving Germany's quiescent trade relations with Russia. He selected the pragmatic Herbert Backe to take care of foodstuffs (*Reichsnährstand*), saying, ''I have the greatest faith in you.'' Erich Neumann would handle foreign exchange, Wilhelm Keppler raw materials, and Colonel Fritz Löb was temporarily shifted from the air staff to oversee the arms economy.

Göring's methods were innovative and effective. He stimulated coal production by tax incentives, then encouraged research on synthetic-coal products like gasoline and margarine. He provided cheap artificial fertilizers for farmers. He negotiated ten-year bilateral contracts with Romania and Yugoslavia, bartering his (already obsolescent) planes and weapons for their foodstuffs; he would negotiate similar bilateral deals with Spain, Turkey, and Finland for tungsten, chrome, and nickel.

The Four-Year Plan idea ripened throughout that summer of 1936. Hitler was summering as usual on the Obersalzberg, where the ''Berghof,'' his rebuilt villa, had just been handed back to him. On July 6, Göring told one of his economists, Wilhelm Keppler, that he planned to discuss still-controversial divisions of responsibility with Hitler. In particular, he wanted Hitler's sanction for a ''cautious but effective'' speech at the Nuremberg rally in September, warning the public to tighten belts, conserve foreign exchange, and stockpile raw materials. He put this idea to Hitler during the Führer's ten-day visit to the annual Wagner Music Festival at Bayreuth at the end of July.

There was one minor interlude during the music festival that had important consequences for the Luftwaffe. Two emissaries arrived at Bayreuth on July 25, bringing a letter from Spanish General Francisco Franco, appealing for planes to ferry his insurgent Moorish troops from North Africa to Spain to enable him to overthrow the far-left Republican government in Madrid. Hitler nodded, Göring concurred, and Milch—summoned secretly from Berlin the next day—was put in charge. By the end of the month he had already sent the first eighty-six Luftwaffe volunteers, thinly disguised as tourists, to crew the Junkers 52 transport planes.

Upon his return from Bayreuth to Berlin, Göring was host to America's most famous aviator, Charles Lindbergh. He invited the tousle-haired tourist to see anything he wanted and himself showed him the crown prince at

Potsdam, the resurrected Richthofen Geschwader at Döberitz, the dazzling Wedding Sword at Carinhall. He flattered him with a seat at the opening of the Berlin Olympics, then tantalized him with glimpses of Germany's coming bomber production at Dessau. ("We have nothing in America," Lindbergh wrote on August 6 to the U.S. air attaché, "to even compare with the Junkers factory." It had, of course, been carefully "dressed" for Lindbergh's benefit.) He lunched at Göring's palatial Berlin villa on July 28, and he left overwhelmed with admiration for the Germans, compared with whom, he said, the French were "decadent." Göring forwarded to Lindbergh an album of snapshots of the tour—their quality, Lindbergh found, was exceeded only by the thoroughness with which Göring's censors had excised all structural details.

That summer, at Hitler's command, Göring had called for written submissions from government and industry about ways of expanding their native production of steel, synthetic petroleum, rubber, and textiles. Göring took this file down to Hitler at the Berghof at the end of August, and here, he later testified, they strolled off together into the mountains to discuss the Reich's economic strategy. By the time they returned to the villa, they had jointly reached agreement—perhaps the last time in their lives that they would do so—and Hitler dictated a famous secret memorandum outlining the new economic plan. Its first part had strong echoes of *Mein Kampf*; its second was so closely attuned to Göring's own staff papers and his recent remarks in the Berlin conferences that Göring obviously had a hand in drafting it. This second part was subdivided into "Germany's Economic Situation" and "A Program for a Final Solution of Our Vital Needs." While it defined their long-range objective as expanding Germany's living space (*Lebensraum*), Göring had persuaded Hitler that the interim objective for the next years must be to stockpile raw materials as fast as the supply of foreign currency and the exploitation of their native resources would allow.

It was in this respect that the Hitler document came down so heavily against the "economic liberalism" preached by Schacht.

> Four precious years have passed [Hitler's memorandum began]. Without doubt we could by today already have been wholly independent of imported rubber and even iron ore. We are now producing seven or eight hundred thousand tons of our own gasoline each year; we could have been producing three million tons. We are manufacturing several thousand tons of our own rubber each year; it could have been seventy or eighty thousand tons. We are expanding our own iron-ore output from 2.5 to seven million tons, but we could be producing twenty, twenty-five, or even thirty million tons.

And so the document went on. Returning with it to Berlin, Göring summoned all the other ministers to a historic "Little Cabinet" meeting at midday on September 4, one that he himself declared to be "of greater significance than any that had preceded it." Gloating over Schacht's humiliation, he then read out the whole Hitler document.

> Germany [Hitler had dictated in it] is now and always has been the fulcrum of the West's defense against Bolshevist aggression. A victory by Bolshevism over Germany would lead not just to a new Versailles but to the final annihilation, nay extermination of the German people.

Now, he argued, they must subordinate all else to the expansion of Germany's armed forces. Only the conquest of Lebensraum would solve their shortage of foodstuffs and raw materials. "I therefore ordain as follows," the Hitler document proclaimed:

(i) the German army must be ready for action in four years;
(ii) the Germany economy must be ready for war in four years.

Characteristically, as he finished reading out the document, Göring added to his Little Cabinet orally what Hitler had not: The Führer, he said, was making him exclusively responsible for the new economic program.

There was no discussion, nor would there be in the future.

The rift between the pro-Göring and anti-Göring factions was wide open. The ministers who had witnessed the meeting immediately contacted those who had not. "Today," wrote Paul Körner triumphantly to the absent Herbert Backe, "we witnessed the most beautiful day in our economic history. Göring came back from the Obersalzberg bringing the latest guidelines for our work for the next years." Dr. Hermann Reischle phoned Darré in identical language—the minister, he exclaimed, had missed the most beautiful day of his life. "Göring," reported Reischle, "read out a devastating letter [sic] of the Führer's about 'economic liberalism.' Schacht just sat there, baffled and impotent."

The Four-Year Plan that Hitler formally announced at Nuremberg a few days later put Hermann Göring firmly in the economic saddle. Henceforth, industrialists and bankers alike would have to come to him with cap in hand—and not infrequently with open wallet too—since he would issue all the most lucrative government contracts from now on.

As the British diplomat Sir Robert Vansittart put it at the time, Göring waded into the new job "with the gusto of Smith Minor, suddenly possessed of unlimited tick [credit] at the school stores." Multinational corporations like C. & A. Brenninkmeyer, insurance firms like Allianz, industrial giants like Osram Electrics, Rheinmetall Armaments, and Junkers Airplanes hastened to sweeten him with bribes.

Philip Reemtsma, Germany's biggest tobacco manufacturer, was one such benefactor (and beneficiary). An ex-aviator lamed in a World War I flying accident, Reemtsma controlled 75 percent of the cigarette industry, with an annual turnover of 2 billion marks. He had first met Göring at a 1932 meeting of industrialists. These industrialists had begun deliberately withholding taxes on a significant scale, obviously with Göring's blessing. After Hitler came to power in 1933, Göring had agreed on a secret tax deal whereby all except Reemtsma should contribute to Göring's Art Fund; not wanting the Hitler Fund to profit from tobacco monies, the puritan Führer had readily agreed.

In return, Göring had helped Reemtsma in various ways. The SA had set up a rival cigarette concern in 1933; Göring settled the problem in 1934. Reemtsma himself was arraigned for perjury in 1934; Göring got him off the hook. In July 1942 transcripts show Göring urging Hitler to purchase "several billion Reemtsma cigarettes" as a productivity incentive; another transcript in August 1942 would reveal Göring recommending that governors of Nazi-occupied territories barter Reemtsma cigarettes in return for native Ukrainian peasant produce. Subsequently he passed on to Philip Reemtsma a hint that he should diversify into shipping, as Hitler planned to launch an antitobacco campaign after the war.

Reemtsma rewarded Göring in a manner that would certainly qualify as "passive bribery" under Sections 331 and 332 of the Reich Criminal Code: He paid a check for a quarter of a million marks every three months into Göring's bank accounts (the ledgers meticulously kept by Fraulein Grundtman show such payments from July 1937 right through to November 20, 1943 —"check for RM250,000 from Reemtsma of Hamburg-Altona, to be credited to the Art Fund''); over ten years, so Reemtsma and Körner candidly testified after it was all over, the firm coughed up nearly 15 million marks for Göring's "cultural and forestry activities." Wars came less cheaply— Philip Reemtsma would lose all three sons on Hitler's battlefields.

At the German Aviation Bank, Göring opened an account ("for needy aviators"), and this was kept in funds by the grateful aircraft industry. Years later Milch would ask aircraft-manufacturer Fritz Siebel outright about Göring's slice of his firm's takings. ("He turned bright red!" observed Milch with satisfaction.) Payments to Göring by industry would total 1,850,000 marks (around $600,000) in the one year from October 1940 alone. What he had he spent—mostly on Carinhall, which he intended to leave to the nation anyway. He possessed no hidden fortune. "I can await any revelations of your agents . . . with an untroubled mind," he smiled to American investigators; and then he teasingly inquired whether living conditions were better in Argentina or Chile.

* * *

Thus the law that formally appointed him Hitler's "commissioner for the Four-Year Plan" on October 18, 1936, gave him the key to the treasure-house. He controlled the Reich's entire foreign-exchange reserves. No corporation could purchase imports without his approval. Haranguing his Little Cabinet on the twenty-first, he uttered the bald statement that his Vollmacht (authority) was "unlimited." A week later he addressed a mass audience in the Sport Palace on the need to put guns before butter. "Too much fat," he roared into the microphones, and pointed at his own midriff, "means too big bellies."

On October 22, he circulated his decree setting up the Office of the Four-Year Plan. The appended organization chart filled six pages. As economic dictator in an authoritarian country he now enjoyed advantages that liberal economists could only dream of, and he began to succeed on a spectacular scale. His wiretappers gave him a winning edge. The rigid wage and price controls of the National Socialist economy did the rest. "Trust this man I have selected!" appealed Hitler, speaking to the leading industrialists on December 17. "He is the best man I have for the job."

Schacht blistered with anger. At the same conference he heard Göring advise the leading businessmen to go out and use any means, "fair or foul," to harvest foreign currency. Schacht protested sternly, but Göring was now above the law.

14
THE BRIDGE AT GUERNICA

Reporting that pompous wedding, the British ambassador had commented that Hermann Göring seemed to have reached the apogee of his vainglorious career. "I see for him and his megalomania," Phipps reported to London, "no higher goal, apart from the throne, unless it be . . . the scaffold."

The bride had had the same presentiments. When Hitler asked Emmy Göring if she still had any wish that fate or fortune could fulfill, she replied, "Yes, *mein Führer*—that my husband were just an actor."

But was not his life now an uninterrupted series of first nights, each more spectacular than the last? Each time the curtain lifted, or so it seemed, it was he who dominated the stage, clad in yet another costume. With Göring however, to continue the metaphor, there was one snag, the length of the run: No sooner had he earned his plaudits in one role than he was already reaching out for script and costume for the next. He did not consider that this betrayed any undue greed for power. Accused by an American in June 1945 of having been something of an egotist, he would reply, "The jobs were assigned to me, and I worked like a horse to get things done. I didn't ask for them."

Of course, he still hankered after Hitler's old title of Reich chancellor.

Still thwarted by Hitler and cheated of that rank, he decided to become Germany's greatest statesman since Bismarck anyway; and when his rivals' botched diplomacy finally resulted in war, Göring began reading for his most difficult role yet—the multiple role of Mightiest Warlord cum Most Honest Broker in All German History.

He was not lazy—this was a popular and hurtful misconception. He just could not be everywhere at once. Inevitably, as he discovered his hidden entrepreneurial skills, his devotion to the new air force declined. After the new Air Ministry Building opened in 1936, he rarely set foot in this imperious structure of concrete, glass, and marble. It was ruled by his stocky, rubicund, businesslike Staatssekretär, Erhard Milch. No lions roamed through Milch's purposefully furnished Berlin apartment, no jewels glittered on his fingers, but it was Milch who signed the orders and made the major decisions— which planes to build, where to erect the factories. Göring was content with the walk-on roles so long as they gave him adequate occasion to wear the full-dress uniform, buckle on the swords, and deliver great orations.

Occasionally Milch perambulated Göring around Rechlin Field to see the latest bomber or fighter prototypes, and it did not escape his watchful master's eye that Milch was the complete master of this domain. Göring began, that spring of 1936, to dismantle some of Milch's sub-empire. When General Wever was killed in a plane crash at Dresden on June 3, Göring overrode Milch's judgment to appoint Kesselring as the new chief of air staff, and he put his old Richthofen Squadron comrade Ernst Udet in charge of the all-important Technical Office as part of the same reshuffle. A balding, high-spirited stunt pilot, Udet was to become the Luftwaffe's nemesis; already heavily dependent on narcotics and alcohol, he was heading for the mental collapse that would kill him five years later. Milch soldiered on, although downright suspicious now of the morals of his master. It had not escaped him that a young nephew, Friedrich Karl Göring, born in 1908, had become a Luftwaffe officer despite examination failures; nor, as he had scrupulously noted in his diary in December 1935, that Göring was boasting that he had not paid the craftsmen who had built his Obersalzberg villa.

How Göring envied Benito Mussolini's marble-columned study at the Palazzo Venezia in Rome—the immense raised desk from behind which the Duce advanced with measured stride to meet him. On first seeing Schacht's poky office late in 1936, upon his resignation as minister of economics, Göring involuntarily cried out, "How can any man have great thoughts sitting in a cubbyhole like this?"

He had converted his Berlin villa into a Renaissance palazzo, knocking four already spacious rooms together to make an office even larger than Mussolini's, so that four sets of French windows opened onto the terrace and gardens outside. The ottomans were elephantine, the carpets were lavish, the hunting trophies that protruded from the walls were beyond compare. Each new visitor was bowled over in turn. The League of Nations high commissioner in Danzig, the venerable Professor Carl J. Burckhardt, entered the room late in May 1937 to protest about plans to introduce the anti-Jewish laws in Danzig and found the general reclining upon a Madame Recamier couch wearing a white velvet uniform loaded with decorations, his fingers bedecked with rings. At intervals a flunky brought in ice packs to apply to a pink-stockinged leg that had been kicked by a horse. Through the French windows Burckhardt could see an expressionless air-force sentry pacing the grounds, while a lion prowled the well-trimmed lawns.

Nicholas von Below, the slim air-force captain who marched in one month later (on June 16) to report formally as Hitler's new air-force adjutant, found Göring all but hidden behind the outrageously large framed photographs parading across the oaken desk. In this same room in November U.S. Ambassador Bullitt would find himself perched "like some sort of animated flea" on one of the outsized chairs—chairs so big, he reported to President Roosevelt a few days later, that Göring looked less than his size, "and, as you know, he strongly resembles the hind end of an elephant."

His domestic popularity was immense. Visited by Sir Robert Vansittart in August 1936 he suggested that, to prove his popularity, they drive together to the roughest location they could find. "I'll wager," he boasted, jabbing a pudgy finger at the diplomat, "that nothing happens to either of us."

"I have practically given up betting against certainties," replied Vansittart dryly.

Göring was said to pay three marks for the wittiest jokes about himself, but it took a foolhardy man to risk making one at his expense. After he was badly seasick during autumn maneuvers aboard the battle cruiser *Deutschland*, two navy lieutenants pronounced him "Reich feeder of the fishes" and presented the German Navy's traditional string vest to him. Göring told the fleet admiral to put both men under arrest. However, a motorist accused of dangerous driving apologized that Göring's car had been coming the other way and the general had forgotten to dip his decorations; he was acquitted. In 1944 captivity, a Focke-Wulf 190 fighter pilot would be heard asking if fellow prisoners knew about the latest medal, the Mammutkreuz—"It's to be awarded to Hermann Göring on our final victory. The Mammoth Cross of the Grand Cross, with diamonds, mounted on self-propelled gun carriage!"

By that time his predilection for diamonds was well known. "I want a pot of your finest diamonds," he once commanded his favorite jeweler. "You've got to play with trinkets," he told his goggling staff, "to learn how to trifle with men." Henceforth an adjutant had to carry the pot around on journeys in case Göring felt the sudden urge to play with them. It was the same way with daggers. At a public meeting in December 1936 Backe saw him surreptitiously running his thumb along the side of a favorite dagger while Darré, whom he could not abide, was speaking. His brother-in-law Eric von Rosen had given him a beauty, inscribed: "A knife from Eric to

Hermann.'' Count Eric also sent him a dagger specially made for him, with its crossguard and pommel encrusted with jewels, its hilt fluted with ivory, its scabbard richly engraved with hunting scenes (it is now a prized item in an American collection).

The pet lions were a carefully calculated part of this playful, primitive image. Once, while Italy's crème-de-la-crème sipped afternoon tea at Carinhall during the 1936 Olympics, he had bounced in with a full-grown lion frisking at his side. The Italian princesses Maria and Mafalda—the latter the wife of Prince Philipp of Hesse—shrieked; the Mussolini sons Vittorio and Bruno displayed pale-faced aplomb; Emmy clucked her tongue and shooed the beast outside.

The fighting in Spain intensified that winter as Russian, German, and Italian reinforcements and weapons poured in. ''The situation is very grim,'' said Göring in conference with his officers early in December 1936. ''Russia wants war, Britain is rearming.'' Germany, he said, had banked on getting four more years of peace, but she might find herself drawn in before then. ''In fact, we're in a war already,'' he pointed out, ''though not a shooting one.''

The first Luftwaffe operational squadrons had left Greifswald Air Base for Spain in December—Milch had taken the salute. Göring was now seriously worried about the slender strength of his air force. With Udet—not, it will be noticed, Milch—he toured the aircraft factories and delivered a pep talk to their bosses on February 20, 1937. That month Göring thoughtlessly scrapped Germany's only big bomber projects to make way for more smaller planes. ''The Führer,'' said Göring, when Milch found out in April, ''does not ask how big my bombers are but how many I have.''

''Göring,'' remarked Milch later, ''took only sporadic interest.''

During conferences, the general was seen to take copious notes. Some of these notebooks have been preserved, and while some (from 1938 to 1942, and one for 1943) do contain businesslike memoranda of meetings, many are filled just with his handwritten lists of gifts, donors, and recipients, ranging from the most important (''1. ego; 2. Emmy; 3. Lily [possibly Lily Martin, the widowed sister of Carin] . . .'') down to the cigars and gratuities for his foresters, flunkies, porters, and telephonists at the Reichstag. Such Göring notebooks often reveal his centimeter-precise measurements of the tapestries he coveted, and notes on furnishings for Carinhall:

> two mirrors for vestibule . . . elk-hide for chairs and writing desk
> . . . consider tapestry in Reichstag as curtain in front of movie
> screen, or for reception hall . . . locations and proper sequence
> for my letters of esteem (check library layout) . . . Have silver
> lamp made as per sample for writing desk . . . Look for big
> standard lamp for library . . . bust of self and bust of Carin . . .

To Göring the actor, such stage-setting was essential for his diplomatic tours de force. Against this lavish, egocentric setting he spoke with often startling frankness to foreign industrialists, visiting aristocrats, and hunting partners. While solemnly promising the Poles, as he assured Marshal Rydz-Smigly, visiting Warsaw on February 10, 1937, that Germany had no designs on the Corridor, and uttering similar guarantees to Mussolini about Austria, he made no bones in his conversations with the British about Hitler's ultimate goals. He had warned Vansittart in August 1936 that Germany would eventually give up her wooing of the British, and in October he had laid bare his "expansionist" strategies in conversation with Lady Maureen Stanley, who was visiting Berlin with Lord Londonderry. "You know, of course, what we are going to do," he had told her ladyship, with eyes twinkling. "First we shall overrun Czechoslovakia and then Danzig. And then we shall fight the Russians. What I can't understand is why you British should object?" In conversation with Mussolini in January 1937, the record shows, Göring grumbled about Britain's posture as "governess of the entire world," and he drew attention to Berlin's attempts to establish ties with Britain's conservative elements—"In which context it has to be borne in mind that the present British government [of Stanley Baldwin] is not conservative at all, but fundamentally leftward inclined." That amiable gentleman, the Englishman in the street, was basically pro-German, said Göring; but not the British Foreign Office, and he went on to lecture Mussolini about the pervasive influence of Jews and Freemasons throughout the British Empire.

The Spanish civil war divided Britain and Germany for the next two years. Aided by Russian, British, and French contingents, the left-wing Republicans lynched and tortured their opponents; aiding the Nationalist insurgents, the German and Italian "volunteers" machine-gunned and bombed Republican-held towns. There were horrors on both sides.

On April 26, 1937, nine German planes—three flights of three Junkers 52's—attacked the Basque town of Guernica to cut the road junction northwest of the town. "We badly need a success against the enemy personnel and equipment," Colonel von Richthofen, commanding the air-force contingent, wrote in his diary. "Vigón [the Spanish ground commander] agrees to push his troops forward to all roads south of Guernica. If we pull this off, we'll have the enemy in the bag." Tiny though the bomb load was—the planes carried only nine bombs of 250 kilos and 114 of fifty kilos—the little town was wrecked. "As our first Junkers arrived," wrote Richthofen in some puzzlement, "there was smoke everywhere. . . . nobody could see any roads or bridges or targets in the outskirts, so they just dumped their bombs on the center." Afterward, the mystery was partially explained, when townspeople showed him evidence that fleeing Asturian miners had liberally dynamited entire streets of buildings to halt the Nationalist advance. "The Reds," Richthofen recorded after touring the damaged town, "torched ministries, public buildings, and private houses simply by tossing gasoline cans into the ground floors.'' Most of Guernica's five thousand inhabitants had already left, but, the Luftwaffe colonel learned, ''a few were killed.'' This author carried out investigations in the town records that revealed that some ninety people had been killed, most of them in two incidents as bombs hit a primitive shelter and a mental hospital. The Communists' own newspaper published a list of the injured, totaling thirty-two names. Since ''Guernica''—symbolized by the Pablo Picasso painting—would ever after be chalked up as an atrocity against Göring's name, these figures are worth reporting.*

The propaganda echo of Guernica was immediate. Left-wing intellectuals around the world touted their versions of the air raid as typical Nazi *Schrecklichkeit*. Nowhere was the outrage louder than in Britain, where the opposition Labour party and the Communist party had begun whipping up feelings against Göring, claiming that he was angling for an invitation to the coronation of King George VI in May. Lord Londonderry did diffidently suggest Göring might come for the coronation, but the British ambassador, Phipps, warned the Foreign Office that there was ''quite a good risk of his being shot in England,'' and no invitation was ever issued. During February 1937 Communist party branches and ''left book-club study groups'' published resolutions insulting him, and one notoriously far-left Labour member of Parliament, Ellen Wilkinson, talked of his ''bloodstained boots.'' Göring felt deeply wounded by the campaign. ''The man in the street,'' he told Lord Lothian on May 4, referring to the less amiable German of that species, ''is now beginning to sense that Germany's real enemy is Great Britain.''

''Other countries have colonies,'' complained General Göring in the same private conversation, ''but Germany is to have nothing. The fact is that if a German hand so much as tries to pluck a feather from a goose, the Anglo-American boot appears and kicks our hand away.'' He reminded the British peer that his air force was now superior to Britain's RAF—and then dangled before him the very tempting prospect of a world-embracing Anglo-German alliance. ''It is Germany's primary interest,'' he explained, dismissing with a flabby wave of one hand the adjutant who insistently reminded him, after two hours' talking, that he was already late for lunch with the Führer, ''not to see any weakening of the British Empire. In fact,'' he added, mentioning for the first time an idea that he had obviously cleared with Hitler, ''I would go so far as to say that if the British Empire were gravely menaced, it would be to our interest to come to its support.''

Replacing Baldwin in May 1937, Britain's new prime minister, Neville Chamberlain, sincerely desired to improve relations with Germany. He replaced the loose-tongued, sarcastic Phipps as ambassador with Sir Nevile Henderson. Henderson had admired Göring ever since his *coup de théâtre*

---

*Picasso's art notebooks show that he had begun sketches for the painting—depicting in fact a bullfight—months before the air raid.

at the Belgrade funeral ceremonies, and he had a leaning towards the new Germany. He had recently crossed the Atlantic aboard Germany's majestic liner *Cap Arcona*, to brush up his spoken German. Once, the giant Zeppelin-built airship *Hindenburg* hovered overhead, exchanging greetings, until its 2,750-horsepower engines propelled it over the horizon. Both ships became symbols of the violence of world feeling against Hitler: Sabotaged by anti-Nazis, the airship would crumble in flames at Lakehurst, New Jersey, a few days later, killing thirty-five passengers and crew; and eight years later the *Cap Arcona* would be sunk by a single British airplane in the Baltic with the loss of seventy-three hundred civilian lives—five times as many as died aboard the *Titanic*.

The mutual attraction that ripened between Henderson and Göring was of the kind that does sometimes flourish between gentleman and gangster. Whatever his timetable, each would always make time to receive the other. Henderson found the general's questions shrewd, his humor irresistible, his frankness disarming. At their first meeting on May 24, 1937, Göring repeated what he had told Phipps and the former air minister Lord Lothian. "Germany can't even pick a flower," he grumbled, "without Britain saying *es ist verboten.*" He emphasized that the Führer was besotted with Britain—hence the naval agreement; and he himself, he added, had forbidden his Luftwaffe to designate Britain as an "enemy" in war games. (This was true.) When he mentioned the irksome Anglo-French alliance at a further meeting, on July 20, the ambassador responded with a critical allusion to the axis between Berlin and Rome. "That's just the point," sighed Göring. "If it weren't for your London-Paris axis, we in Germany would never have taken up with those Italian s.o.b.'s—we don't trust them an inch!"

In September he would confess to Henderson that he admired Sir Francis Drake precisely because he was a pirate. It was a pity, he added, that the British had now gone soft (or been "debrutalized," as he put it).

Henderson was bedazzled by this astute ex-aviator. In September 1937, in a letter to Foreign Secretary Anthony Eden, he would call Göring "the frankest and most sincere of these Nazi leaders with the exception of Hitler." Eden must have choked on his porridge at this line—he himself classed the Führer at that time as only marginally less frank and sincere than Machiavelli. Four years later, composing his memoirs in wartime retirement, Henderson would still confess to unrepentant admiration for Hermann Göring and everything that he had done for Germany.

The Four-Year Plan revolutionized Nazi Germany's economy. Resisting the temptation to set up a special ministry, Göring had used instead his own Prussian Ministry staff as a kind of matrix, to which he appointed extra civil servants—one thousand of them—and co-opted the Staatssekretär (roughly, deputy minister) from each Reich ministry to attend plan meetings. Iron ore was crucial to the plan's success.

Göring's seminal interest in iron ore probably originated in a meeting with local ironmaster Hermann Röchling in Saarbrücken in November 1935. Röchling had warned him not to rely on Swedish ores in any future war—and had startled Göring with the remark that there was enough iron ore, admittedly of low grade, in Germany to cover any wartime needs: They could produce around fourteen million tons of pig iron every year. Göring was skeptical, and the Ruhr steelmakers scornful. They pointed out that the German ores contained only 25 percent iron, compared with 60 percent in the Swedish and Lorraine ores; besides, the German ores were acidic and difficult to smelt.

For a year Göring had done nothing. At the Berlin conference on May 26, 1936, he had casually asked, "Is there anything to be said for increasing the output of iron ores from our own ore fields?" Put in charge of the Four-Year Plan, Göring had the authority to answer that question himself. Encouraged by coal-baron Paul Pleiger—who called the biggest steelmakers "scrap-metal merchants"—and by his own distant American cousin, Hermann Alexander Brassert, (of H. G. Brassert & Company, Chicago), who undertook to design for the new Hermann Göring Works blast furnaces capable of reducing these difficult native ores, Göring decided on a confrontation with the Ruhr steel industry. "I gave them one year in which to exploit the ores," he recalled. The Ruhr metallurgists scoffed at the idea; in one report to Göring, an expert described the native ores as "trash"—whereupon Göring compulsorily purchased the mining rights from Vögler's United Steel Works, paying a price that they could hardly refuse for "trash."

Throughout the spring of 1937, while his top secret plans for his own steelmaking empire were being laid, Göring fought a rearguard action against Hjalmar Schacht, the economics minister, who still put profitability before the nation's long-term strategic interests. Neither Schacht nor the steel industry had any inkling of Göring's plan to erect a steelworks until it was publicly announced on July 15, 1937. On the next day he issued the contract to H. G. Brassert & Company. He broke the news to the leading men of the steel industry at a meeting in Berlin one evening a week later, saying, "We're going to put up the biggest steelworks the world has ever known at Salzgitter." Talking of the steel bottleneck that was the limiting factor in all the rival nations' rearmament programs, Göring added, "I am going to show people that the Third Reich is better able to get around it than all these countries with their parliamentary governments."

The "Reichswerke AG für Erzbergbau und Eisenhütten Hermann Göring" (Incorporated Reich Works for Ore Mining and Iron Smelting, "Hermann Göring")—or the Hermann Göring Works, H.G.W., as it formally became one year later—rapidly developed into one of Europe's biggest industrial combines. The Ruhr industrialists who had partly financed the Nazi rise were now confronted by a powerful outsider who cheerfully threatened confiscation if need be to lay hands on the ore fields he required; the nine biggest steelmakers, united under the leadership of Krupp von Bohlen in the Steel Association (*Stahlverein*) of Düsseldorf, declared war on Göring; encouraged by Schacht, they signed a protest to the government. Schacht himself sent a twelve-page letter to Göring protesting the cost of the new steelworks. "In a totalitarian state," he argued, "it is wholly impossible to conduct a split-level economic policy." He appealed to Hitler, but the economically illiterate Führer left it to Göring to fight this battle. On August 22, Göring sent a stinging twenty-four-page reply to the minister, full of rhetoric but totally ignoring the arguments. He had brute force on his side, and was well aware of it. Replying to the Steel Association's protest in a telegram two days later, he accused them of barefaced "egotism," and of sabotaging the interests of the Reich. He hinted at prosecution. Schacht went on leave with his tail between his legs and eventually resigned.

The H.G.W. remained solely Göring's concern. It was not state controlled, no ministry supervised its rambling affairs. He appointed his stooge Pili Körner chairman of the board. As late as July 1944, the Ministry of Economics would complain that no agency could tell who was on H.G.W.'s board or how it ran its affairs. The answer was one word: autocratically. H.G.W. spread stealthy tentacles across Germany and Austria into the Balkans and southeastern Europe, swallowing strategically interesting companies in interlocking financial deals behind a veil of military secrecy, deals that would have made Göring a hard man to beat on Wall Street. H.G.W. took over iron-ore mines in the Palatinate belonging to Flick; bought up Austria's iron-ore fields in Styria, and eventually built a new steelworks at Linz to process these ores; erected entire cities at Salzgitter and Linz to house the workers; secured basic limestone and coal requirements by swallowing the Walhalla Kaliwerke AG at Regensburg and the Deutsche Kohlenzeche and by forcing Ruhr coal mining companies to sign long-term contracts for supplies. (H.G.W. would eventually control ten major coal mines.)

In Germany, H.G.W. then purchased 53 percent of the Rheinmetall Borsig Arms Company in the Ruhr, with affiliated companies in Essen (Eisen & Metallgesellschaft AG) and Duisburg (Hydraulisch GmbH); in Austria, 78 percent of the auto manufacturers Steyr-Daimler-Puch AG, 100 percent of Steyr Guss-Stahlwerke (which in turn controlled a Swiss arms factory), 51 percent of Maschine und Waggonbau AG at Simmering, 50 percent of the Paukersche Werke AG and the Fanto oil refinery. Ultimately H.G.W. would also purchase controlling stock in the First Danube Navigation Corporation (Ersten Donaudampfschiffahrt AG), thereby gaining important commercial rights and assets in Hungary and Romania. Austria, in fact, was the economic gateway to the Balkans, which was one more reason why Göring wanted to bring Austria under German control.

A few days after he signed the contract for Brassert to build the Hermann Göring Works, the new, enlarged Carinhall was handed over to Göring for permanent occupation. The Görings dispatched a fulsome telegram to Hitler at Berchtesgaden thanking him for the keys. "We know," this said, "that, as with everything else, we owe it to you that we are able to move into this beautiful house today." There was no other home like it. The footmen were liveried in forest-green plush, with sleeve cuffs reversed and coattails caught up behind in eighteenth-century fashion.

Their very first guest on July 20, 1937, was Ambassador Henderson. He challenged Göring—now that he was out here in his own domain—to come clean about Nazi Germany's ultimate ambitions.

"Germany," replied Göring, "has been placed by fate in the heart of Europe. She has to be militarily strong, and now that we have abandoned all idea of expanding in the west"—a renewed promise that Germany would not try to recoup Alsace and Lorraine—"we have to look to the east."

Henderson urged Göring to be patient. He was able, he assured the general, to appreciate the great qualities of Hitler's government. It had reduced unemployment in four years from six million to six hundred thousand and much of its social program was highly progressive. "I can not believe," he continued, "that Herr Hitler desires to risk all his work on the chance of war."

An encouraging smile spread across Göring's face. "You can set your mind at ease," he said. "There'll be no more surprises for several years."

There was one surprise for all Germany that autumn—Emmy Göring announced that she was pregnant. She boasted of it at a farewell luncheon for Mussolini at Carinhall on September 28. "Mrs. Göring," wrote Staatssekretär Milch in his diary, "is expecting a baby in eight months." (He stifled his astonishment, clearly recalling that Göring had told him that he was impotent.) Irreverent witticisms swept Berlin's nightclubs and cabarets. "The baby's to be called Hamlet if it's a b-b-boy," exclaimed Werner Finck, a stuttering comedian. "*Sein oder n-n-nicht sein!*" (To be or not to be—it translates equally in German as "His, or not his?") It was not the kind of wisecrack that Hermann Göring rewarded, and Finck was rehoused abruptly in the concentration camp at Esterwegen.

15

THE VERY PRIVATE KINGDOM

Only those who saw General Göring with his lions could sense the fondness that each felt for the other: So wrote his chief forester, Ulrich Scherping, in 1937. "And," he added, "these lions were not just cubs—the kind that society ladies might like to be photographed with in the Berlin Zoo. They were great hulking brutes. Many a voice was raised at his temerity in trifling with being slashed by tooth or claw."

There was an unsuspected empathy between this man, Hermann Göring, and the animal kingdom, and there was no phoniness about it. An animal can smell fear, but it also seems to sense the true animal lover. Scherping, an honest woodsman whose great-great-grandfather had served three kings of Prussia as a forester, knew the acuity of a wild animal's perception and marveled at the manner in which Göring controlled man and beast alike.

Of all Göring's works during that grim period known as the Third Reich only one has survived to this day: the enlightened Game Laws that he introduced. The animal world remained his own private kingdom. He was an impassioned huntsman—from a fraternity that has always deemed itself a cut above the rest. Hitler actually called the clannish hunting fraternity "that green Freemasonry." He detested huntsmen, but even he found it useful to indulge Göring's passion. Göring's hunting diaries—which are preserved—portray a cavalcade of foreign diplomats and martial gentlemen accepting his invitations to Prussia's hunting grounds. There he could meet as equals Czar Boris of Bulgaria, or the regent of Hungary, the kings of Greece and Romania, and the prince regent of Yugoslavia.

This was all to the good, but it went beyond that. With Göring, the huntsmen had the inside track. Senior air-force officers who were not good shots found the going difficult. Hunting was as indispensable an asset to promotion in the Luftwaffe as polo was in the British Army. And woe betide those who did not praise Göring's hunting hospitality or criticized his game. Invited to a shoot during the Olympics, the Swedish prince Gustaf Adolf shot a magnificent twenty-point stag but remarked loftily that he hoped to do better on his father-in-law's estate (he had married the German-born Sibylla). "Things didn't go so well between him and Hermann . . ." wrote Thomas von Kantzow in his diary. "Hermann won't be inviting him back to Carinhall in a hurry."

It had all begun rather unpromisingly. When he had become speaker of the Reichstag in 1932, Göring had declined the rather unprepossessing hunting ground assigned to him by the then-reigning establishment. He prophesied confidently that within a year he would be prime minister, with the pick of all Prussia's state forests at his disposal. In 1933 he found the hunting scene to be a microcosm of Germany itself—plagued by petty rivalries and self-interest. Each humble parish or great estate seemed to have its own hunting laws and taxes. Wildlife could be hunted down at will. Conservation and breeding of the dwindling species were impossible. In Germany, the eagle, bear, bison, and wild horse were almost extinct.

Göring had directed Scherping to set up a uniform nationwide hunting association (*Deutsche Jägerschaft*) to regulate the sport, restock the lakes, tend the forests, and protect the dying species. The association would levy taxes on huntsmen to pay for the upkeep of the forests and game parks. "I want a new hunting law for Prussia," he had briefed Scherping on that day, May 9, 1933, "one that can later serve for the entire Reich."

With one stroke of the pen he made it a criminal offense to kill an eagle, or hunt with poisons, artificial light, or the steel trap ("that medieval instrument of torture"). When the professional bodies bleated protests, Göring waved them augustly aside. His Prussian Game Law, passed on January 18, 1934, was envied far beyond Germany's frontiers. He insisted that the new game officials must be animal lovers, dedicated National Socialists, and unafraid of speaking their minds. In practice these desiderata proved unworkable. The best foresters were not always Nazis, and when it came to the test he did not encourage independent minds. In May 1937 Professor Burckhardt, sitting in that cavernous office in Berlin, witnessed him take a phone call from a forester asking for permission for local farmers to take their own action against a plague of wild boars. "One more word," bellowed

Göring, after listening with mounting anger, "and I'll blast a shotgun up your snout!" Turning to the Swiss diplomat he apologized. "That's how revolutions begin," he said, "letting people take the law into their own hands!"

Keen to pioneer new techniques, he established nature reserves on Darss, a Pomeranian peninsula, and at Rominten in East Prussia. His proudest achievement was the Schorf Heath, on Berlin's doorstep. It was here, on June 10, 1934, that he had inaugurated his new bison sanctuary—oblivious of the snickers of the Berlin diplomatic corps—with two pure bulls and seven hybrid cows. He introduced elk as well. Successions of Prussian kings had tried and failed to restore this noble, ungainly beast to the Schorf Heath; he consulted zoologists, foresters, biologists and—interestingly—experts on artificial insemination, and succeeded, though not without experiencing his own initial disappointments. Neither Swedish elk nor Canadian moose prospered, so he had finally brought in elk calves from East Prussia: seventeen in the fall of 1934, ten a year later, and eleven in 1936. His first native elks would calve in the Schorf Heath sanctuary in May 1937, by which time he had also reared forty-seven local bison.

The whole Schorf Heath experiment worked. From its Werbellin Lake Game Research Laboratory he reintroduced the rarer fauna into the heath, like night owl, wood grouse, heathcock, gray goose, raven, beaver, and otter. During 1936, 140,000 townsfolk forked out 20 pfennigs apiece to tour the wildlife sanctuary. It became a forerunner of the great national parks in other countries.

"For us," he would tell huntsmen assembled for their Saint-Hubert's Day festival that November, "the forest is God's cathedral."

There were those who found the rifle and the huntsman's knife an incongruous way of serving the Creator. But there was a scientific logic in what Göring called "conservation by rifle." Game populations had to be culled to avoid starvation or epidemics, and he and his fraternity pursued this pseudoreligious duty with grisly relish and high ritual.

This animal-loving side of Göring's nature produced strange contrasts. He was capable of unparalleled callousness toward the human species; yet history shows that he introduced a tough antivivisection law through Prussia, preceded by a broadcast warning that he would throw each and every violator into a concentration camp even before the law passed through all its stages of enactment. While in Britain defense scientists contented themselves with testing blast bombs on goats and chimpanzees, in 1942 Göring's high-altitude aviation experts would show no qualms in conducting lethal low-temperature and low-pressure experiments on human beings (criminals under sentence of death supplied by Himmler's concentration camps).

Both facets of Göring's character—the protector of the animal kingdom and the ruthless persecutor of his human enemies—occasionally intersected. At one and the same Reich Cabinet meeting on July 3, 1934, Hitler reported on the "shooting of forty-three traitors" in the Night of Long Knives that Göring's alter ego had managed, and then Göring celebrated the passage of his Reich Game Law. The law transferred control over all forestry and hunting to one wise man, Hermann Göring, who thus became the first Reich chief huntsman (*Reichsjägermeister*) in two hundred years. In 1937 the French chairman of the International Game Committee commended him for creating a new hunting law that "has earned the admiration of the entire world."

At that same Cabinet session, a gaunt Franz von Papen had flounced in and resigned as vice-chancellor.

A few days later Papen agreed to go as Hitler's special ambassador to Vienna. Within two years Papen procured a gentleman's agreement with Dr. Kurt Schuschnigg, who had succeeded Dollfuss as chancellor and foreign minister. Göring had only contempt for this "compromise" and took care not to dignify it with his presence when it was ceremonially signed on July 11, 1936. Over the next months he, and not Hitler, would become the mainspring behind Germany's campaign for union (*Anschluss*) with Austria. He made no bones about it. He felt that only international chicanery had thwarted Austria's own attempts to unite with Germany in 1919, 1922, and 1931. Years later he would write in despair to Emmy from his Nuremberg prison cell, "Even the Anschluss is a 'major crime' . . . What has become of our poor fatherland?"

In a way he was by inclination more Austrian than German. Nostalgia for his childhood years at Castle Mauterndorf, gratitude for his exile in Innsbruck after the 1923 putsch, a yearning for the hunting forests of Styria and Carinthia—all, coupled now with the economic imperialism of the Hermann Göring Works—generated a magnetic field that drew him into Austria. Both his sisters had now married Austrians—Olga had wed Dr. Friedrich Rigele and Paula had chosen Dr. Franz Ulrich Hueber, lawyers of Saalfelden and Salzburg, respectively. Dr. Arthur Seyss-Inquart, the mild-mannered Viennese Nazi who would briefly succeed Schuschnigg as chancellor, later confirmed that it was through Göring's two married sisters that the leading Austrian Nazis established links with him. It was Rigele who brought art dealer Dr. Kajetan Mühlmann to see Göring on the Obersalzberg at the time of the July 1936 agreement; a jovial, thin-faced man with a habit of rubbing his hands together, Mühlmann subsequently acted as a courier for the Austrian Nazis, visiting Göring at his mountain villa, or at Carinhall and the Air Ministry. Göring's younger brother Albert was also in Austria, working for the Tobis-Sascha Film Company. When the company asked Albert to persuade his big brother in Berlin to increase film imports from Austria, Hermann agreed—on condition that Albert introduce him unofficially to the Austrian deputy foreign minister, Dr. Guido Schmidt. Schmidt was a thirty-six-year-old Viennese, fervently and energetically patriotic. Meeting Göring for the first time on November 20, 1936, he tried to be firm, but it was not easy.

"So long as I have any say in it," he warned, "there will not be the slightest deviation in Austria's independence." Göring merely beamed, and Schmidt, relaxing, told colleagues back in Vienna that the German general had displayed a kind of Austrian *Gemütlichkeit*—"At least it was possible to talk with him," he said.

Recognizing Göring's pivotal position in the Nazi hierarchy, on January 29, 1937, Guido Schmidt took up his pen and initiated a year-long correspondence with him by formally inviting him to hunt in Austria. Göring replied with immediate flattery. ("You [are] the very best kind of German-Austrian," he assured the minister.) It seemed a good beginning to both of them.

Austria was never very far from his thoughts. When British newspaper correspondent G. Ward Price visited him on March 3, 1937, he touched upon the possibility that Chancellor Schuschnigg might stage a restoration of the Hapsburg monarchy to thwart the movement toward Anschluss. *"Dann werden die Kanonen sprechen!"* boomed Göring. "Then the cannon will speak!" He assured the Englishman that 80 percent of Austrians would vote for Anschluss with Germany in any free plebiscite. As for the rest of the political horizon, Göring predicted that Prague would make voluntary concessions over the Sudeten Germans. Germany, he added, had no quarrel with Britain over colonies, but Britain's shortsighted foreign policies were driving Hitler into the arms of his enemies. "Germany," promised Göring, his eyes wide with hurt innocence, "would give England every guarantee in the west that she required—covering the integrity of Belgium and Holland as well as France—but she must give us a free hand in Eastern Europe."

He reverted to the theme of British Empire interference when the benign, perennial Canadian prime minister William Mackenzie King came to see him on June 29, 1937. This liberal statesman was something of a mystic—he often heard celestial voices and consulted in equal measure the Holy Scriptures. Before strolling over to see Göring, his eye had lighted upon a verse of the Ninety-First Psalm: "The young lion and the dragon shalt Thou trample under feet." As he was shown into Göring's villa at ten-thirty, the startled Canadian saw a lion in the study, nuzzling General Göring's cheek as he sat, white-uniformed, at his desk. Their interview rambled on for ninety minutes, making the usual shambles of Göring's appointment card; Göring thanked Mackenzie King for a Canadian bison, then inquired whether Britain could prevent Canada from exporting wheat and raw materials to Germany. The Canadian tried to explain how the empire worked—how its very strength lay in the independence of its dominions. Göring, his mind roaming, asked whether Canada would blindly follow Britain in everything—"For instance," he pressed, "if the peoples of Germany and Austria wished to unite, and if Britain were to try to prevent them, would Canada back Britain?"

"What I think England is most concerned about," replied Mackenzie King, "is the danger of Germany taking some precipitate action that might set all of Europe aflame."

Göring reverted to his bullying of the Austrians. At a banquet with visiting Austrian industrialists a few days later, to celebrate the anniversary of Papen's "gentleman's agreement" with their country, he said with a leer that Anschluss was inevitable. He recalled to them how at Geneva in 1931 the casting vote of one obscure South American delegate had wrecked the first Customs Union proposal of their two governments. "We can't forever be dependent on the vote of one jungle savage," he lectured these pained visitors to Berlin. "So why don't we present the world with a fait accompli? Why not!"

The Austrian envoy, Stefan Tauschitz, picked up a telephone and angrily recommended his superiors in Vienna to cancel the rest of the official visit in protest. The Forschungsamt intercept reached Göring only minutes after he returned to his villa. He telephoned a startled Tauschitz to assure him that he had been misquoted. "I had the distinct impression," the incredulous diplomat would testify, "that Göring's office had listened in to my conversation." As for Göring, he was unrepentant and recalled years later the pleasure it had given him to "put the wind up those gentlemen."

That summer of 1937 Guido Schmidt of Austria hinted, again via the lawyer Friedrich Rigele, that he would welcome another meeting with Göring. Göring suggested Carinhall—"where we would be completely undisturbed"—and offered to send his private plane down to Vienna. (During August, he explained, he would be away cruising aboard his latest toy, the diesel yacht *Carin II*, which the Motor Manufacturers' Association had donated to him.) Schmidt, venturing literally into the lion's den, arrived at Carinhall on September 7, and stayed for several days.

Göring again found him amiable and boisterous—perhaps a type not often met in northern Germany. Schmidt killed a stag called Hermann.

"You've done me in, have you!" exclaimed Göring playfully.

"Wish I had," replied the Austrian minister.

"Not very nice of you," retorted Göring, and he had a lion brought in when they returned to Carinhall. The furry beast lay under the table, licking Guido Schmidt's feet.

"Next time," faltered the Austrian, "I shall bring an animal of my own, a lamb."

"Good," roared Göring. "And a black sheep too. Yourself and Dr. Schuschnigg!"

It was September and time for the annual party rally again. This time London instructed the British ambassador to attend, and Henderson saw for himself the spectacle of aggregate manpower as hundreds of thousands of brownshirted party automatons paraded at Nuremberg. Hitler arrived after dark, the arrival of the "messiah" announced by the simultaneous uplifting of three hundred searchlight beams to intersect thousands of feet up, leaving the hushed and darkened stadium inside what Sir Nevile called "a cathedral of ice." The thousands of standard-bearers marched up the main lanes carrying red or gold lights that formed five flowing rivers of color in the darkness. The dour Henderson involuntarily thrilled to this pageant as much as if it had been His Majesty's birthday parade.

General Göring joined Henderson in Nuremburg on the eleventh, mentioning oh-so-casually that he had just told Guido Schmidt that the sooner Austria bowed to the inevitable, the better. He assured Henderson once again that Germany's strategic objectives would astonish Britain by their moderation: first, Austria; after that, the oppressed Sudeten-German minority in Czechoslovakia; Poland would then come into line automatically. And this big Robin Hood lookalike with the polished, rouged complexion repeated to the ambassador what he had first said on his arrival in Berlin: "We have no desire to lay hands on anything at all that Britain possesses. We want to be friends with the British Empire. We are prepared to fight for its survival and would, if need be, lend half of our army for that purpose. All that we ask in return is that Britain guard our rear and that the British Navy keep our communications open, if we are attacked in the east."

When Henderson voiced a lame protest about the concentration camps, Göring produced an encyclopedia. "First used by the British," he read out, "in the South African war." Knowing that Sir Nevile was one more member of that international "green Freemasonry," he invited him to come and shoot a stag at Rominten, East Prussia, that October.

All along it had seemed likely to Göring that Italy would object most to any Austrian Anschluss with Germany. Mussolini had no desire to see Hitler's troops on his northern frontier. "It's intolerable," Göring had told one Austrian, banging his fist on the table, on November 20, 1936, "that Italy has to play policeman and keep us apart. I am going down to see Mussolini shortly," he added, "and I intend to tell him quite clearly that Anschluss is coming—like it or not!"

Göring visited Rome in January 1937, and told the Italian government that for six million Germans to live outside Germany's door was "against all morality." Mussolini, who had believed Göring was coming only to talk about Spain, was taken aback by Göring's unexpected approach on Austria. He left no doubt that Italy regarded the German-Austrian agreement of 1936 as inviolate. According to the Italian foreign minister Count Ciano, Göring undertook not to indulge in any surprises—"Whatever decision Germany makes on questions so vital to her as Austria, Danzig, or Memel will be preceded by consultations with Italy." Afterward, however, Göring told his friend the ambassador in Rome, Ulrich von Hassell, that Italy was going to have to accept that Austria was in the German sphere of interest. Following a brief vacation in Capri, Göring returned for a pointed talk with Mussolini on January 23, in which—as the transcript in Göring's papers shows—he adopted a more restrained position. He now merely asked Mussolini to prevail on Vienna to adhere to the 1936 agreement. "In Germany's name he [Göring] could reassure him—and he assumed the same held true for Italy—that there were to be no surprises over Austria." "Yes," triumphed Ciano afterward to the Austrian ambassador in Rome, "a highly inflated Göring arrived here . . . a rather more modest one left."

General Göring had not, however, given up over Austria. Before the Duce visited Berlin in September 1937, Göring commissioned an artist to paint on one wall of Carinhall a medieval-style fresco, a map of the Reich with each city designated by its "trademark"—and with the frontier between Germany and Austria erased. He paraded the Italian dictator past it several times but eventually had to direct his attention to the map. "That gave me an excuse," Göring recalled later, "to talk bluntly about the two countries uniting."

To Hitler, Austria was but a tedious foreplay to his own grandiose strategy. "We're going to tackle the Austria question first," he told his agriculture experts Darré and Backe on the last day of that month, September 1937, lifting one corner of the veil that concealed his innermost thoughts—to which Göring was probably long privy. "But our real future," Hitler continued, according to Darré, who recorded these words in his private diary, "lies on the Baltic and in the open spaces of Russia. Better to sacrifice another two million men in war, if this will give us the room to breathe."

In East Prussia, Germany's easternmost province, dawn came an hour earlier than in the west. Its hardy frontier breed had suffered in each war but anesthetized that suffering with a grog made of much rum and little water. They hunted across wildernesses dominated by the cry of rutting stags, beasts known to them by names like Matador or Chandelier, Robber Chieftain or Osiris—this latter would become the Neu-Sternberg preserve's "royal stag" of 1937. The very finest beasts (later called "Reichsmarschall stags") were reserved for Göring himself to stalk for days, then slay exultantly or, when raison d'état required, deliver to the "gun-guest of honor"—Hungarian regent Miklos Horthy or some Balkan king.

Of course, not every statesman succumbed to Göring's allures. The diplomatic archives record that after seeing Hitler, Britain's Great War leader David Lloyd George said gruffly, when told that Göring was awaiting the pleasure of his company at a shooting box in southern Germany, "I am going back to the Hoek [of Holland], and Göring can go to the devil!"

Göring was for all that a fine shot and true sportsman. He preferred the breathless pursuit of his quarry through moor and bog and fen, from tree to tree, to sitting passively in a blind. Up at 4:00 A.M., he would stalk for six or seven hours until the most stalwart accompanying forester would capitulate to his moaning stomach. Even then, back at the lodge, if word came that their quarry had been sighted, Göring would gallop back.

Somehow his game diary for 1936 and 1937 survived the war. Its entries, penciled in his broad and flowing hand, capture something of the carefree flavor of those years. Like a snapshot album, which shows us the world of the photographer as though through his own eyes, this scrappy diary suggests which elements of stalking each fine animal particularly commended themselves to the writer. To the nonhunting outsider, reading the endless details of the pursuit and kill, the huntsman seems to have been half-voyeur, half-Casanova, so obsessed with the intoxicating thrill of pursuit that the whole ritual became an end to itself.

SEPTEMBER 26, 1936: 11:30 A.M., arrival [at Rominten] from Gumbinnen by car with guests Emmy [Göring, her sister] Else, Scherping, Menthe, [Göring's adjutant Bernd] von Brauchitsch, Robert [valet] . . . Hetzelt [Göring's architect] hands over new building, "Emmy Hall" . . . 4:00 P.M., stalking 22-pointer, [shot it] clean through the heart at 300 to 330 yards; the stag broke cover baying, unaccompanied. Five P.M. bagged "Werner Junior," a 16-pointer . . . an old stag, thirteen or fourteen, but a royal one.

SEPTEMBER 27, 1936: Very fine weather, sun shining, brisk and cold. Guests arrive—[Reich Foreign Minister] von Neurath, [Franz] von Papen, Milch, Korner, Himmler* and Udet. 11:30 A.M. to 2:00 P.M., stalking a royal stag [in fact it was the stag "Der Grossmächtige von Schuiken," according to the Sèvres porcelain plate fired in his honor for the Göring collection] . . . after Scherping called me in. Stag sat on the edge of a marsh in full cry, then worked its way around us. I felled it with a bullet in the liver. . . . The stag collapsed after eighty paces, my second shot missed. . . . Gave the coup de grâce to recumbent stag. Strongest stag ever seen on this heath, strongest German or international royal stag . . . Canceled stalk this afternoon, turned it down.

4:30 P.M.: accompanied and guided von Neurath . . . He shot at a royal 16-pointer with particularly noble antlers. Looked for it afterward without any luck.

SEPTEMBER 28, 1936: Sunny and cold. Stags crying magnificently. Arrival of Lipski [Polish ambassador] . . . Afternoon, I shot Mar-

* Here and in the following entry "Himmler" was inexplicably rubbed out.

schombalis, royal 18-point stag with splendid royal left crown
. . . clean through the heart, killed outright.

Horn-blowing trial with Hungarian horn successful with young
stag-to-be. Other stags were shot today by Himmler, a royal 16-
pointer; Milch, a very powerful 14-pointer; von Papen, a powerful
18-pointer. Neurath's stag found dead. . . .

SEPTEMBER 29, 1936: Stalked 20-pointer at 5:00 A.M. in Jodupp
. . . Not a sound anywhere. Waited in vain . . . Midday a royal
14- or 16-pointer was reported in Budwertschen preserve . . .
Very heavy going. Stag was grazing, had four other animals and
several lesser stags with him. Lesser fry kept getting in our way.
Drove it step by step toward ravine. Stag not crying much. Other
stags picked up our wind, took off with harem. Deeper into the
underbrush. Lengthy wait, called off the chase . . . Lipski's stag
found.

SEPTEMBER 30, 1936: Fine sunshine, stag was crying well. Had
a harem, was drifting around same ravine as yesterday. We stalked
it from far side, the stag suddenly came back, was driving an
animal ahead of it. Dropped it at range of about 100 yards, shot
clean through the heart . . . about 30 yards from where I bagged
that royal 14-pointer in 1933.

Then the season was over. On October 1, Göring made a note upon the
virtual soundlessness of the heath, and delivered a speech of thanks to the
foresters at 4:00 P.M. that day. His own bag had been six stags, the killing
of each one accompanied by a primeval frission of masculine achievement
that those outside the fraternity would never comprehend.

The same game diary shows that he spent two days here at Rominten,
hunting wild boar, at the beginning of the new year, 1937, with a guest list
including Carin's widowed sister Lily Martin, Paula, Emmy, her sister and
niece and, more quaintly, "one lion." In mid-September 1937 he again
dallied here, this time with his full-time attendant, nurse Christa Gormanns,
his private staff, and Count Eric von Rosen. On October 3, 1937, Sir Nevile
Henderson joined them, with London's express permission. Göring took him
straight out to a tall blind that evening and the selected stag duly turned up
half a mile away. The honor of England being at stake, Henderson elected
to climb down and stalk to a forward position from which he felled the beast,
a "royal 12-pointer," with one shot. Göring could not refrain from remarking
how much it pleased him to see diplomats crawling on their bellies.

Over these two days, October 3 and 4, Göring once more confidentially
unveiled Hitler's program to Sir Nevile: Austria; the Sudeten German territories now forming part of Czechoslovakia; then the loose ends like Danzig,

Memel, and the Polish Corridor. On the morning of the fourth, Göring noted, "Thick fog, sun partly coming through. Discussion in the morning with Henderson." He again outlined to the Englishman his broad vision of a partnership between Britain and Germany—with Britain recognizing Nazi Germany's hegemony in the continent of Europe. He concluded his diary:

> Henderson this A.M. shot another fine stag, 14-pointer . . . 3:00 P.M., stalked alone in Jodupp. On bare ground to right of Wollner pasture watched a scene of activity just like rutting at its peak, about ten stags were there crying in full voice, several combats. Kept a right royal 20- or 22-pointer under observation for some time, only six years old but a magnificent future. He had a harem, but was beaten off by an older 14- or 16-pointer. A most engrossing spectacle.

Henderson would never forget those two days at Rominten. As dusk fell, the chief forester ceremonially called the bag. Göring thanked all the huntsmen, and they sounded the hallali (death of the stag) on their hunting horns. "In the starlit night in the depths of the great forest," wrote Henderson, "with the notes of the horns echoing back from the tall fir trees in the distances, the effect was extremely beautiful."

There was an intimacy, transcending all frontiers and enmities, between these hunting men; nor has it been without purpose to dwell upon it here. We shall see that as the final curtain descends upon the caged Hermann Göring, and he casts about him like an injured animal caught in "that medieval instrument of torture," a steel-jawed trap, for a friend to deliver the releasing coup de grâce, his eye lights upon an officer—and huntsman, like himself.

With proper panoply and flourish, with shouts of *Heil* and the roll of drums, with the rattle and slap of a guard of honor from his "Hermann Göring" Regiment presenting arms, Göring opened the International Hunting Exhibition in Berlin in November 1937. Once again money had been no object, and there were sections in the spacious galleries devoted to each country, to the history of hunting, and to the most famous paintings on this ancient lore.

Britain was well represented. Carl-Maria von Weber's opera about Marksmanship, *Der Freischütz* (*The Sharpshooter*), was staged on November 2, as an overture to the exhibition, and during the intermission Göring walked over to Sir Nevile Henderson and thanked him for the friendly reception just accorded to his top generals Milch, Stumpff, and Udet during their recent tour of RAF squadrons and establishments. "It is inconceivable," Göring beamed to the ambassador, "that there should ever be war between men who get on so well together and respect each other so much as the British and German airmen."

The exhibition was a box-office triumph. On some days forty thousand people thronged the halls, and Göring ordered the run extended to three weeks. For those three weeks he was in his element. He besported himself in his baroque hunting costume, he banqueted as Reich chief huntsman in Berlin Castle on November 3, he dined with the world's leading huntsmen on the fourth, he presided congenially over the Conseil Internationale de la Chasse on the fifth.

At 4:00 P.M. that day he mysteriously melted away from the festivities, to reappear at the Reich Chancellery, in full uniform, an hour or two later: Hitler had summoned a secret conference that was to go down in history. He had returned to the capital a few days before, brimming with dangerous ideas. Since his return von Below, had glimpsed him pacing the broad carpet in the glass-fronted winter garden sunk in thought, or speaking quietly with Rudolf Hess, or strolling up and down with Göring, sometimes for three hours or more.

Originally, the army had called for this conference on November 5 to resolve the conflicting demands for steel allocations. But Hitler had decided to bring home to the army's recalcitrant commander, Werner von Fritsch, that he had certain plans. As he told Göring shortly before the others arrived, it was time to "raise steam" in his generals.

After the others—War Minister Field Marshal von Blomberg, Foreign Minister von Neurath, and Navy Commander Admiral Erich Raeder—had assembled in the winter garden, Hitler motioned to a servant to draw the curtains across the glass doors and began, reading from notes, to "set out his thoughts on future strategic objectives" (as Blomberg dictated to one of his officers, Colonel Alfred Jodl, afterward).

Colonel Friedrich Hossbach, Blomberg's adjutant, shortly wrote out in longhand a full summary of Hitler's remarks. "There is only one possible way of solving Germany's problem," Hitler declared, "and that is to use force. There is no risk-free way of solving it." Nor could they afford to wait, he added, because in six years the balance of power would tilt against them again. They were going to fight for Lebensraum—but even before then he might order a lightning attack on Czechoslovakia if circumstances were propitious.

Hitler's speech met with a muted response. Göring's only recorded contribution was to suggest that they ought, therefore, to wind up their operations in Spain now.

At 8:30 P.M. the little intermezzo was over. Göring hurried back to the grand reception that he had organized for the visiting huntsmen of Europe at the Aviators' Building (the Haus der Flieger, which had previously been the Prussian Parliament). Here he playfully buttonholed Stefan Tauschitz, the Austrian minister in Berlin. "The Führer still owes us one breakfast treat," he boomed, "Austria!"

The next evening Guido Schmidt came to the "lion's den" again. Göring invited him out to Carinhall on the seventh and nonchalantly walked him past the map fresco, which Göring had left in place since Mussolini's visit. "It's such a fine map," he apologized to the Austrian, "and I didn't want to have to keep changing it. So I have had it drawn in keeping with the way that things are shaping anyway."

Hermann Göring's hunting exhibition acted as a honeypot to all the big bears of European field sports. On November 17, his brother-in-law Franz Hueber tipped him off that the head of Austrian security, Paul Revertera, was privately visiting the halls. He sent a chauffeur to fetch the visitor from the Hotel Eden at 5:00 P.M., and the well-tailored, gray-haired Austrian was piloted by an SS man through the marble labyrinth into Göring's villa soon after. Their two-hour conversation started in the safe preserves of the new hunting laws, but then Göring guided his guest out into more rugged terrain. He criticized the fortifications that Austria was now building on her frontier with Germany, and accused Vienna of violating the 1936 agreement. He said that "people" were pressing for a solution. "Our Seventh Army, they say, would go through Austria like butter." He advised the Austrian not to bank on Paris or London; France was exhausted, he claimed, and the British dominions would discourage any intervention by London. This left only Prague, he suggested, adding with a grin, "And we'd take her on too!"

Sweetening these inhospitable remarks, Göring flattered Revertera by saying that Austria had the better leader types and would therefore provide the Reich with a reservoir of fine commanders; and he also drew a benign picture of Austria as the future cultural center of the Reich. The Austrian official returned to the Hotel Eden aghast at the general's crude bluster.

A far more significant exhibition visitor came to see General Göring three days later. Lord Halifax, traveling to Berlin as "master of Middleton hounds" rather than as a British Cabinet member, toured the halls round-eyed, conferred with Hitler, and returned to Berlin on November 20 to meet Göring. Göring telephoned Hitler at Berchtesgaden to ask if he might speak frankly with the Englishman, and toward midday sent his most luxurious limousine down the new autobahn to bring Lord Halifax out to the Schorf Heath.

Summarizing their meeting in his diary, Lord Halifax admitted he was "immensely entertained." "Göring," he recorded, "met me on the way dressed in brown breeches and boots all in one, with green leather jerkin and fur-collared short coat on top. . . . Altogether a very picturesque and arresting figure, completed by green hat and large chamois tuft!" After paying the obligatory homage to Göring's elk and bison, he found himself being driven off to see the tree-planting operations in a shooting phaeton drawn by a pair of high-stepping Hanoverian chestnuts, then on to Carinhall itself—"a large house," wrote Halifax, "built between two lakes in pine woods, stone with deep thatched roof and latticed dormer windows out of it. It occupies three sides of a courtyard, with a colonnade across the end."

As Colonel General Göring, master of all these domains, led his guests through the long entrance gallery and rooms already filling with treasures, Carinhall began to work the familiar magic on this High Church Yorkshire viscount. His nostrils flared, picking up the mansion's pervasive, unmistakable atmosphere of aristocratic pretentions; it was like an alcoholic getting a whiff of his first tot of the day. His voyeur's eye missed no detail: the hunting trophies, the devotional garden doorframe carved somewhere in Bavaria depicting an Assumption of Our Lady, the great hall with its remote-controlled wall of glass overlooking the lake at one end, the dining room lined with a parchment that looked to Halifax's approving eye rather like mother-of-pearl.

> After luncheon [he noted in his diary], which included some of the rawest beef I have ever seen, Göring took me off with [chief interpreter Paul] Schmidt to talk. I repeated to him what I had said to Hitler, namely that we did not wish and had never wished to stand strictly on the present state of the world, but that we were concerned to see reasonable settlements reached.

"It would be a disaster," agreed Göring, "if the two finest races of the world were ever to be so mad as to fight." The British Empire was, he suggested, a great influence for peace—but Germany too was entitled to her 'special spheres of influence.' "

Afterward, Lord Halifax found himself wondering how many assassinations his host had commanded, "for good cause or bad." He had to confess that the general's personality was attractive—"like a great schoolboy, full of life and pride in all he was doing, showing off his forest and animals, and then talking high politics out of the setting of green jerkin and red dagger."

16

THE BLOMBERG-FRITSCH AFFAIR

In December 1937 Göring issued instructions—in line with Hitler's command at the winter-garden conference—for his air force to prepare a lightning operation primarily against Czechoslovakia.

The alarmed war minister, von Blomberg, circulated an urgent corrective on December 7: "I forbid any measure that might lead headquarters units or troops to conclude that war is likely before the end of 1938."

This message highlighted in its way one of the architectural defects that had developed in Hitler's military hierarchy—Göring's now wholly anomalous position, simultaneously straddling the three highest tiers of the German command structure. As air-force commander in chief, Göring was subordinate to the war minister Blomberg (whom Hitler had appointed field marshal on April 1, 1936, to underscore this), but equal to the army's commander in chief, Colonel General von Fritsch. As a Reich minister, however—of aviation—Göring was Blomberg's equal. And as the Fuhrer's chosen successor and adviser, he regarded himself as Blomberg's superior.

Blomberg was fifteen years older than Göring—he had passed through Lichterfelde when Göring was still an infant. Since 1933 he had grown closer to the Party—allowing army officers to accept the Nazi "blood medal"

(*Blutorden*) for their part in the 1923 putsch, for example—but not close enough. Several times since 1935 Karl Bodenschatz had overheard Göring and Hitler discuss the possibility that the top army generals might be plotting against the regime, and in the autumn of 1937 Göring asked Blomberg outright whether his generals would follow Hitler into a war.

It is clear that by December 1937 Göring had begun to indulge in fantasies of taking supreme command of the armed forces himself in place of Blomberg. The only other candidate would be General von Fritsch. At fifty-eight, Fritsch was not much younger than Blomberg, and Göring felt it unlikely that Hitler would feel comfortable with him. Promoted to colonel-general on April 20, 1936, Fritsch came from a puritan Protestant family. His upright bearing suggested he might even be wearing a lace-up corset. With a monocle screwed into his left eye to help his face remain sinister and motionless, he was an old-fashioned bachelor who loved horses and hated Jews with equal passion. "We are in the midst of three battles," he wrote to a baroness in 1938, "and the one against the Jews is the most difficult." For the time being, however, he had left the Berlin stage, vacationing in Egypt—unaware that Himmler (perhaps at Göring's instigation) was having him tailed by the Gestapo. Nor, as yet, did Blomberg provide Göring with an inch of leverage although (as Admiral Raeder later gathered from a chance remark) Fritsch had ordered that Blomberg be shadowed, and Himmler's Gestapo was later found to have concealed a microphone in Blomberg's office.

Göring could find no way to fault Blomberg until mid-December. Then, suddenly, the tip of a promising scandal began to surface in the War Ministry. The sixty-year-old widowed field marshal announced that he too was going on leave. Those who knew spread the word that he too was taking a twenty-four-year-old secretary with him. "The field marshal is inexplicably agitated," Colonel Jodl carefully recorded on the fifteenth, adding, "Apparently a personal matter; going away for eight days, destination unknown." His agitation was explicable: The secretary had just informed him (quite untruthfully) that she was pregnant by him (so the field marshal's family informed this author). Less than a week later Hitler ordered him to attend the state funeral of Ludendorff in Munich—to be held on December 22 in the shadow of the Feldherrnhalle where Hitler, Göring, and Ludendorff had confronted the blazing carbines of the Bavarian *Landespolizei* fourteen years before. As the ceremony ended, Blomberg walked across the snow-covered square to Hitler, asked to see him in private, and formally asked his permission to marry the girl; he added no more than that she was of "humble means"— a secretary in a government agency. To complete his folly, Blomberg approached Göring, of all people, a few days later and asked him to use his powers as head of the Four-Year Plan to see that an alleged "rival" for the young lady's attentions was spirited out of Germany. "It's an unusual request," growled Göring, "but I'll see what I can do."

On January 12, 1938, guests at Hermann Göring's forty-fifth birthday celebration were perplexed to see him rise from the table and depart. "I'm off to a wedding," he told Milch—and chuckled out loud as he said it.

Most of what has been written hitherto about what now became the Blomberg-Fritsch affair has been based on the narratives left by embittered adjutants like Friedrich Hossbach, Fritz Wiedemann, and Gerhard Engel. The availability of more reliable materials, like Milch's private diaries, Blomberg's own manuscripts, the verbatim Gestapo grilling of General von Fritsch, and the secret letters and manuscripts that he wrote in 1938 and 1939 (now in private hands in Moscow) enables us to dispense with these narratives.

Both Blomberg and Fritsch were relics of an older generation, representative of the generals who had never really swallowed the National Socialist revolution of 1933. The career generals under their command refused to accept that an air force created and directed by two former lieutenants, Göring and Milch, could be of any real value. Fritsch in particular resented the recent interpolation of a Wehrmacht high command under Blomberg as supreme commander. When he returned from his Egyptian vacation—he had taken only a young adjutant, Captain Joachim von Both, as companion—on January 2, Fritsch had done nothing to discourage mounting criticism of Blomberg by the army generals. Looking bronzed and fit, Fritsch was among the guests at the luncheon in honor of Göring's birthday on the twelfth, and he too must have wondered why Göring left early.

Any doubts that Göring may have entertained about Blomberg's chosen bride were dispelled as he attended the wedding, held behind closed doors of the great hall of the War Ministry that afternoon. As the girl came mincing in, heavily veiled, Göring and Hitler exchanged mute glances. She was slim and blonde, and her genre was quite unmistakable. Blindly content, Blomberg left to honeymoon in Capri. General von Fritsch's papers record a two-hour meeting with Hitler three days later, on January 15, at which the Führer "spoke in great agitation of his concern about the spreading of anarchist propaganda in the army." Fritsch asked for proof, but Hitler declined to show it. (Probably it was Forschungsamt evidence, which a general could not be shown.) Six days later, Hitler delivered a three-hour dissertation to hundreds of senior generals in Blomberg's ministry, lecturing them on history, race, and nation—and on Germany's need for Lebensraum, "which we are going to have to seize by force."

That same day, January 21, the bubble burst in Berlin. An anonymous caller, impersonating a general, telephoned the army high command and demanded to be put through to General von Fritsch. When this was refused, the caller shouted, "Tell the general that Field Marshal von Blomberg has married a whore!"

Hitler had left Berlin for the Obersalzberg; Blomberg had been called to his mother's funeral. The Brown Page reporting the anonymous phone call to Fritsch rocketed across Berlin into Göring's villa. Everything began happening at once. At 4:15 P.M. Count Wolf von Helldorf, Berlin's police chief, brought into the War Ministry a police index card and asked Blomberg's chief of staff, General Wilhelm Keitel, if he recognized the photo: Was this Blomberg's bride? Keitel replied uneasily that he had not yet set eyes on her—perhaps the police chief ought to try General Göring instead?

Late the next morning Helldorf drove up the autobahn to Carinhall. Perhaps the photograph came as no surprise to Göring. More than one person suspected that he might even have engineered Blomberg's meeting with this particular woman. (He denied it.) Others (Fritsch, Göring himself, and Keitel among them) suspected the SS had rigged it. "They exploited Blomberg's vulnerability to railroad him into this marriage," Fritsch recorded at the time. "The ink was hardly dry on the marriage papers when mountains of documents began to turn up about the Blomberg woman's past."

A couple of days later Keitel brought over to Göring the complete police file on her—a buff vice-squad folder with fingerprints, "mug shots," and pornographic photographs of the woman who had just married the field marshal with Hitler and Göring as witnesses. It was a Sunday, he recalled years later. "For three hours I sat at the table [overwhelmed] by the contents. It was not necessary to add anything." Göring appears to have done the decent thing, because as soon as Blomberg returned from the funeral he sent Bodenschatz over with "documents" to Milch, which Milch was to take over to Blomberg—"documents about F.B.," as Milch's diary records (probably referring to Frau Blomberg).

Göring was waiting on the steps of the Reich Chancellery as Hitler arrived back in Berlin. The buff folder was in his hands. Hossbach, Blomberg's ADC, also showed up, hoping to secure an immediate appointment for the field marshal with Hitler. Göring waylaid him, tapped the folder, and said, "It always falls to my lot to bring particularly unpleasant matters to the Führer's attention." He paced the floor like an angry lion, waiting for Hitler.

"What I have witnessed today," he snarled at Wiedemann, Hitler's ADC, waiting with him, "knocks the bottom out of the barrel!"

The prim, prudish Hitler winced as Göring showed him the file and photographs. As Göring hastened to point out, Blomberg had made fools of both of them, he had flouted the officers' code in marrying this woman, and he had brought ridicule on the Wehrmacht. Hitler sent Göring over to speak with Blomberg. The frosty interview lasted less than five minutes. Göring told the white-faced field marshal that the Führer insisted he resign.

Göring must already have been certain that Fritsch was out of the running. He hoped that Fritsch's opposition to Hitler's planned military adventures ruled Fritsch out. "What would your prime minister have done," he rhetorically asked Sir Nevile Henderson a few days later, "if the chief of the imperial general staff [the British equivalent to Fritsch] had come to him and not only demanded the resignation of the war minister but also expressed dissatisfaction with the government's foreign policy and other measures?"

Göring immediately began extensive canvassing to be awarded the War Ministry. He sent over Bodenschatz to brief Wiedemann; he briefed von Below himself. But Hitler hesitated to give him the supreme command. His own solution, which he would disclose to Blomberg a few days later, was to become supreme commander himself, making use of Blomberg's staff, the Wehrmachtsamt, for the time being.

Unaware that Hitler had decided to award himself the prize, Göring took furtive steps to disqualify the only other runner, General von Fritsch. He recalled that the general had apparently once been accused of a peccadillo and sent for the police file to refresh his memory. Two years earlier a young convicted blackmailer, one Otto Schmidt, had claimed that in November 1933 he had witnessed a male prostitute, one Sepp Weingärtner, engaged in a homosexual act with a man who identified himself as "General Fritsch"; Schmidt had extorted twenty-five hundred marks from the man afterward. Among other homosexual victims Schmidt had named were Walter Funk and other leading Nazis. The authorities had notified Hitler and Göring. Hitler had ordered the investigations discontinued, because the Rhineland crisis was brewing. But evidently the investigations continued nonetheless, because early in July 1936 Schmidt was turned over to the Gestapo for higher inter- rogation, and this time the chief of the Homosexual Crimes Squad, Josef Meisinger, showed the blackmailer a photograph of General von Fritsch. From the general's private papers we know that at the end of 1937—perhaps coincidentally, some days after Blomberg had invited a wide-eyed Göring to ship his rival out of Germany—the Gestapo not only suddenly resumed its interrogations of the blackmailer but also located and began to question the male prostitute involved, Weingärtner.

"I do not know," wrote Fritsch in his own hand a few days later, "from whom the actual initiative came, be it from Hitler, from Göring or Himmler. Whoever it was, the crown witness, who was currently serving time in the Papenburg camp, was immediately produced."

It seems upon deeper analysis unlikely that Göring had initiated the whole fiasco. For him to have started the move against Fritsch as early as December 1937 would imply that he had realized that the Blomberg fiancée was indeed "a whore," and that he had nonetheless allowed himself and Hitler to be made ridiculous by attending her wedding in January.

Overimpetuous this time, Göring jumped bum-deep into this juicy scandal—not suspecting that he would shortly sink in almost up to his neck. He brought the dossier on the "homosexual Fritsch" to Hitler's attention at the same time as that on the Blomberg bride. Hitler told him to question the blackmailer, Schmidt, in person.

Age thirty-one now, the felon was brought into the Göring villa. He had been sentenced to seven years on December 28, 1936, on multiple counts of blackmail, impersonating a police officer, and a variety of homosexual offenses. General Göring scrutinized him from behind his desk and decided that the dark-haired, sallow-featured man with penetrating dark eyes had the physiognomy of a criminal. He passed some photographs across the desk, and Schmidt easily picked out the one of Fritsch. Later, Göring would bluff the accused general, saying that the accomplice, Weingärtner, had also identified him from pictures; this was not true. Schmidt, however, seemed convincing enough. "It is quite possible," conceded Fritsch later, "and I shall do them the honor of so assuming, that both the Führer and Göring genuinely believed that the available evidence amply proved that I indulged in homosexual acts."

Such, at any rate, was the prelude to one of the most unlikely confrontations in the history of the German high command. Early on January 26, 1938, the Wehrmacht adjutant Hossbach tipped off Fritsch about the allegations. The general stormed around to the Chancellery and demanded to see Hitler. He was left to cool his heels until 8:30 P.M., when he was shown into the library where Hitler and Göring were awaiting him.

> The Führer [wrote Fritsch in his private papers] declared at once that I stood accused of homosexual activity. . . . If I confessed, he said, I should be required to go away on a long journey and that would be the end of it. Göring also spoke in this vein.

Greedy for a quick decision, Göring tried bluffing a confession out of Fritsch. There could be no doubt, he said. "This blackmailer has consistently spoken the truth in over a hundred other cases."

Unexpectedly, Fritsch denied the charges—but not angrily or heatedly, because he had been tipped off by Hossbach hours before. He was altogether too cool about it in Hitler's view. Hitler handed over the Otto Schmidt file for the general to read. Fritsch did as bidden, gaped at one particularly perverse allegation, and his monocle fell out.

"While I ran my eye over the document in understandable commotion," he wrote, "the blackmailer was brought in, a creature completely unknown to me. Acting astonished, he exclaimed—or so they said—'Yes, that's him!' "

This was the scene: a pale-faced Führer, an oversized air-force general beaming like a bemedaled Buddha, a scrawny blackmailer wearing an ill-fitting borrowed suit and pointing a quivering finger—and a Prussian baron and four-star general, standing ramrod stiff, with his monocle screwed firmly back in place. Göring broke the suspense, turning on his heel and stalking over to the dining room where Colonel Hossbach was waiting. "It was him!" he gasped melodramatically, lowering himself into a sofa. "It was him, it was him!" He produced a handkerchief, and mopped his brow.

Back in the library, General von Fritsch protested his innocence. "My word of honor," he recalled, with burning indignation, "was cast aside in favor of the allegation of a scoundrel with a criminal record . . . I returned home deeply shaken by the wounding attitude shown by the Führer and Göring.''

On Hitler's instructions, still protesting his innocence, the general was questioned by the Gestapo officers Werner Best and Franz Josef Huber the next day. Göring obtained the verbatim transcript and, with Himmler and Huber at his side, personally questioned not only Schmidt but Weingärtner too. Huber would never forget the incredulous contempt on Göring's face as he set eyes on the latter, the homosexual prostitute. Schmidt stuck to his story, but his pal was by no means so positive about Fritsch.

Shortly Göring had more cause for misgivings. He and the minister of justice jointly grilled Weingärtner alone, and the man again said that he ''could not swear'' that the army general had been his client.

Himmler's discomfiture was only beginning. At Gestapo headquarters Detective Franz Huber glimpsed on a colleague's desk a seized bankbook belonging to a certain cavalry captain, Achim von Frisch—and there were withdrawals in it that tallied exactly with the twenty-five hundred marks that Otto Schmidt claimed to have extorted from Fritsch. Huber warned his superiors, Heydrich and then Himmler: Neither told Hitler or Göring, nor did Göring have the moral courage to report his misgivings about Weingärtner, because in the meantime Hitler had bowed to army pressure and appointed a court of honor to try the Fritsch case, and—callously preempting its findings—he had already begun searching for a new commander in chief for the army.

Hitler dismissed without a second thought Göring's own greedy application to be given command of the army as well as the air force. His choice of successor eventually narrowed down to General Walther von Brauchitsch, father of one of Göring's adjutants. True, Brauchitsch was also involved in delicate matters: divorce negotiations revealing that he had spent years in an adulterous relationship. But he was the only army general who seemed to measure up to Hitler's requirements.

Over the last three days of January 1938 Göring negotiated with this general and his wife; she turned out to be demanding a large cash settlement before agreeing to a divorce. The cash was forked out by a philosophical Hitler, who had long ago learned that everything, from Carinhall to Eva Braun, had to be paid for. That obstacle out of the way, on the afternoon of February 3, 1938, he ordered Colonel General von Fritsch to resign.

Hitler camouflaged the whole nauseating scandal by a sweeping purge at the highest level. Dozens of generals learned literally from their morning *Völkischer Beobachter* that they had been axed. Over at the Foreign Ministry Neurath was replaced by the haughty Joachim von Ribbentrop, while the Ministry of Economics—currently though inconspicuously held by Göring himself—went to Walter Funk, who was indeed a well-known homosexual.

Hitler consoled Göring with Blomberg's old rank, field marshal—no mean consolation, of course, since he thus outranked every other officer in the Reich. For two hours on February 5, Hitler offered his own account of these last weeks, while his senior generals and admirals clustered in a semicircle around him and Göring. Göring had appeared carrying a field marshal's baton. (It was probably the only such baton to be fished out of a stinking bog of intrigue, the army's illustrious Erich von Manstein reflected.) Hitler spared no sordid detail of Fritsch's felonies before making the only announcement that really mattered—that he had appointed himself supreme commander of the Wehrmacht.

A few days later, brooding upon the circumstances of his dismissal, General von Fritsch would surmise, "Above all, somebody must have systematically and deliberately poisoned the Führer's confidence in me." He suspected Himmler, and even Blomberg. "For the last four years," he meditated, "he [Blomberg] has not been honest with me. But there must be some special reason—otherwise this lack of trust of the Führer and betrayal by Göring defy comprehension."

Field Marshal Hermann Göring—how grand that sounded!—would have to preside over the court of honor now convened to hear the Fritsch case. Raeder, Brauchitsch, and two legal assessors would assist him. But now his position was markedly different from two weeks earlier. No longer in the running for either Blomberg's or Fritsch's posts, he had no personal interest in the outcome other than a very urgent concern to protect his own reputation.

Fritsch had instructed an attorney well known to Göring to defend him, Count Rüdiger von der Goltz. By coincidence, Otto Schmidt had also claimed to have blackmailed this lawyer once. It soon turned out to have been a totally different lawyer, Herbert Goltz. This misidentification prompted the count to begin intensive house-to-house inquiries in the area around the scene of General von Fritsch's alleged homosexual encounter. On the second day of March he found what he had been looking for, a retired cavalry captain, Achim von Frisch. This officer not only admitted that it was he whom Schmidt had blackmailed, but even produced the actual receipt that the obliging blackmailer had given him for the twenty-five hundred marks. It was signed "Detective Kröger," the identity Schmidt had already admitted impersonating. It was an open-and-shut case.

The discovery threatened to put Göring, the general's arch accuser, in a hideous position. Count von der Goltz alerted Erich Neumann, the Staatssekretär in Göring's Four-Year Plan office. Neumann, seeing only the horrid implications for his chief's reputation, blurted out, "But this is ghastly!" Hitler, however, suspected immediately that this was just a clever cover-up by the army, and insisted that the court of honor go ahead. The Gestapo prevailed on Otto Schmidt to swear an affidavit that the Frisch episode was quite distinct from the Fritsch affair.

The court's first session thus threatened to become a day of reckoning for

Göring and Himmler rather than for the blameless general. Fritsch himself was in the clear. On March 7, General Stumpff, the chief of air staff, told Milch (as the Staatssekretär noted in his diary) ''all the latest about the innocence of Fritsch.'' And yet, when the day came and the court of honor opened, at 11:00 A.M. on March 10 in the Prussia Ministry Building, Göring seemed strangely unconcerned. He swaggered in, toting his new baton. Decked out in rows of hard-won medals, General von Fritsch came to attention before him. Admiral, general, and two judges took their seats next to Göring, and the hearing began.

Schmidt was led in, his features pale and pasty from the Gestapo dungeons. He stuck doggedly to his lying testimony. Göring was unwilling to give the general any quarter, even now.

> Göring [wrote Fritsch a few days afterward] denied my defense
> attorney's motion for the blackmailer to be transferred from Ge-
> stapo custody to that of the Ministry of the Interior so as to remove
> him from the baleful influence of the Gestapo. Himmler, he said,
> might take it as a sign of a lack of confidence.

Then, before the case could proceed, there was an unexpected development. Wearing the same grin as he had when slipping away from his birthday luncheon two months before, Göring abruptly rose to his feet, lifted his baton, and adjourned the hearing sine die.

Something had cropped up, he announced: something impinging upon the vital interests of the Reich.

17

THE WINTER BALL

itler had laid down the new pecking order in the Reich at his first diplomatic reception after the Blomberg-Fritsch scandal, on February 15, 1938. "First comes Generalfeldmarschall Göring," he ruled, "then Ribbentrop, and only then Hess and Neurath." To Göring the new rank sounded like a real mouthful. "Tell the troops," he instructed his valet, "to say just *Feldmarschall*!" Even that took some getting used to, and when Robert wakened him next morning Göring heard the words, "Good morning, *Herr Feldwebel*." That was a corporal.

Ribbentrop's appointment as foreign minister nettled Göring more than he allowed people to see. He had hoped he might get that post too, and he continued for a year to act as though he, rather than Ribbentrop, had been appointed. He was generous enough, however, to advise Sir Nevile Henderson not to assume that Ribbentrop was anti-British—"Not that it really matters what he thinks," he added. "There is only one person dictating foreign policy in Germany, and that is Hitler himself."

At first there had seemed no urgency about Austria. The Wehrmacht had made no preparations apart from Blomberg's directive (*Case Otto*), issued in June 1937, to cover the unlikely contingency that Vienna restored the Hapsburg monarchy in Austria: in which case Germany would invade immediately. In July Hitler and Göring had appointed economist Wilhelm Keppler as their agent in Vienna, bypassing both Neurath and Papen. By the end of 1937 Keppler was complaining frequently about the Austrian Nazis. "Those chronic hotheads down there," Göring would recall eight years later, "were always stirring things up." On Göring's instructions Dr. Arthur Seyss-Inquart, a leading Austrian Nazi, had begun talks with the Schuschnigg government about concessions for the still-banned Austrian Nazi organizations. On January 6, 1938, Keppler had reported that these talks had bogged down and that both Seyss-Inquart and the pro-German minister of national affairs, General Edmund von Glaide-Horstenau, were contemplating resignation. Göring directed a secretary at Carinhall to phone Keppler that the resignations were to be prevented at all costs and that Göring had sent for Joseph Leopold, leader of the Austrian Nazis, to give him a piece of his mind.

Göring's methods of putting pressure on the Schuschnigg government to come closer toward the Reich were more subtle. In mid-January he had invited the prime minister of Austria's neighbor, Yugoslavia, to Berlin and accorded him a reception more calculated to worry Vienna than to impress Belgrade: Göring had greeted Milan Stojadinović with the "Hermann Göring" Regiment at the station; staged two gala opera performances (with audiences in full ceremonial dress); provided tours of Krupps and the synthetic oil plants at Scholven-Buer—all of which the agitated Austrian envoy, Stefan Tauschitz, had reported in jealous detail to Vienna. On January 22, Göring had mentioned to the timid Austrian that Germany's perennial problem of how to pay for the iron ore and timber imported from Austria would be "solved" during the spring—by implication, permanently.

That was the day when Herman Göring was confronted with the dossier on the Blomberg bride. From then on the two crises—Austria and the Wehrmacht scandal—marched in step. Four days later (the day of the infamous confrontation between Otto Schmidt, the blackmailer, and General von Fritsch in Hitler's library) Hitler ordered a cable sent to Vienna, telling Papen that he was willing to meet Dr. Schuschnigg, the Austrian chancellor, in mid-February. It was no coincidence. The Führer, Keitel told his demoralized staff a few days later, intended to distract attention from the Wehrmacht scandal by something that would "make Europe catch its breath."

Göring disapproved of what Hitler was planning with Schuschnigg. It was going to be another time-wasting compromise, he knew it. When Dr. Schuschnigg met Hitler on the Obersalzberg on February 12, the newly created field marshal therefore deliberately stayed away and sent only Dr. Kajetan Mühlmann, his Austrian "art expert," to the Bavarian villa to keep him informed on what developed. Hitler tried the usual Nazi methods. He himself bragged to Göring afterward that he had fetched his two most "brutal-looking" generals, Hugo Sperrle and Walther von Reichenau, and talked loudly with them during the luncheon with Schuschnigg about the Luftwaffe and its latest bombs. Then he had told his Austrian guest to get rid of "those silly little barricades you have put up on our frontier," failing which he would have to send in German engineer battalions to do the job. During one intermission Schuschnigg heard him call imperiously for General Keitel—a hint that he was going to use armed force.

Schuschnigg made no difficulty about signing the new supplementary agreement that Hitler demanded. It gave Germany a greater influence on Austria's economy and domestic affairs (Seyss-Inquart, for example, would become minister of the interior in Vienna). Three days later, on February 15, the Austrian government formally ratified the "Berghof Agreement." At Hitler's Berlin reception for the diplomatic corps that evening, Göring shook hands particularly warmly with Tauschitz, the Austrian, and remarked, "A new epoch is beginning in German history."

This harmony was short-lived. British newspapers now suddenly screamed rape. On February 16, Göring sent for Sir Nevile Henderson to deliver the now-familiar homily on how much Germans resented this perpetual British interference in their "family affairs." Seldom do the archives reveal the hidden price of newspaper-circulation wars more dramatically than in this instance: Two days later Field Marshal Göring ordered his Luftwaffe to investigate the feasibility of conducting air operations against London and southern England after all.

For three more weeks Hitler clung to his Berghof Agreement with Austria. In his great Reichstag speech on February 20, he praised Schuschnigg for his statemanship, and bound Germany once more to the July 1936 accord with Austria. When word reached Göring via Keppler the next day about fresh outrages being planned by Captain Joseph Leopold, the Austrian Nazi rabble-rouser, he and Hitler sent for him and sacked him without notice. On March 8—the final evidence of Göring's state of mind on the very eve of what now happened—Göring dictated a letter to his protégé Guido Schmidt mentioning the "high hopes" he vested in the Berghof Agreement and offering belated congratulations on Schmidt's appointment as foreign minister in Vienna. This letter was found years later, still unsent, in Göring's desk. It was never sent because late on the ninth Dr. Schuschnigg astonished Berlin by announcing that he was calling a snap plebiscite in Austria in four days' time, designed to reassert his country's independence.

Hitler had told Major von Below that he half expected Schuschnigg, sooner or later, to take a false step. Now he had done just that. He "felt that the call of Providence had come," as he put it one month later. He phoned for Göring, and telegrams went out to bring back the missing generals. Uneasy at his own temerity, Schuschnigg meanwhile directed his military attaché in Rome to ask the Fascist government what it would do if the Germans marched into Austria. Mussolini's response was comforting—he was sure that the Germans would never do it. "Göring gave me his word!" he said plaintively.

This, then, was the matter of vital interest to the Reich that had suddenly "cropped up," obliging a wildly excited Field Marshal Göring, the next morning, to adjourn the court of honor against Fritsch sine die. Delighted that Ribbentrop was momentarily in London, he seized control in Berlin.

That morning, March 10, 1938, he found the Chancellery already teeming with ministers, generals, and brown-uniformed party officials. General Keitel had sent off for the *Case Otto* file. Hitler summoned General Ludwig Beck, the unenthusiastic chief of general staff, and directed him in a five-minute interview to have two army corps standing by to cross into Austria on Saturday the twelfth. At 5:00 P.M. Milch arrived back in Berlin and went straight into an operational conference with Göring and Stumpff. Ribbentrop's Staats-sekretär Baron von Weizsäcker suggested they cloak their invasion in a semblance of legality by getting an "appeal" from the Austrian government for German troops to come in and "restore order." Göring did not at first see the point of such a stunt—"We don't need it," he told Hitler. "We're going in anyway, come hell or high water!"

At the back of his mind were the five Italian divisions that Mussolini had mobilized once before on the Brenner frontier, in 1934, after the Nazis murdered his friend Dollfuss. "I wanted," Göring later explained, "to make things quite plain [to Mussolini] and discourage any intentions he might have." German troops pouring into Austria would not only deter the Italians from laying greedy hands on the eastern Tyrol, but they would prevent the Hungarians and Czechs from seizing other border provinces of Austria. By nine P.M. Göring had drafted a letter to Dr. Schuschnigg, calling on him to resign in favor of Seyss-Inquart, since he had violated the Berghof Agree-ment, and a suitable telegram for Berlin to receive from Seyss-Inquart. Göring sent the documents down to Seyss-Inquart in Vienna by courier that same night.

Friday March 11, 1938—D-Day minus one—found Göring "the busiest man in Berlin," as he unashamedly boasted during his trial. At 10:00 A.M. he called a further military conference with Brauchitsch, Beck, and Milch. He wedged his bulk into a phone booth in the Reich Chancellery and began dictating orders down the line to his agents seven hundred miles away in Vienna. He sent Keppler down with a list of Austrians he had selected to form Seyss-Inquart's first Cabinet. Among them were Ernst Kaltenbrunner, a soft-spoken thirty-four-year-old lawyer defaced by dueling scars, to control the secret police; Major Alexander Löhr, an Austrian Air-Force officer, for defense; the lawyer Hans Fischböck for trade and industry, and Paula Gö-ring's husband Franz Hueber to take over justice and foreign affairs.

Schuschnigg stalled for time. At 2:45, Seyss-Inquart phoned Göring from Vienna saying that the chancellor had agreed to postpone his plebiscite. It was not enough. After consulting Hitler, Göring phoned Seyss-Inquart back an hour later. "You must send off that prearranged telegram to the Führer,"

Göring demanded, and at 4:00 P.M. he phoned Seyss-Inquart again, this time to dictate an ultimatum to Schuschnigg to resign by 5:30.

Göring kept his patience only poorly. Several times during phone calls, Vienna cut him off. (In retrospect, it is a mystery why the Austrians did not sever the line completely.) The clock was ticking on toward the deadline he had appointed. "God knows who half the people rattling around in that embassy were," he said later. Once, he understood he was speaking with a Dombrowski—in fact, it was the Trieste-born Austrian Nazi Odilo Globocnig, later an SS mass-murderer, whom Seyss-Inquart had sent to the embassy to report that he was making only slow headway with the Austrian president Miklas, the constitutional obstacle to any Nazi takeover.

Göring extended the deadline by two hours. The formerly banned Austrian SA and SS units were now blatantly patrolling Vienna's streets in uniform. Göring told Globocnig to get rid of the country's newspaper chiefs: They were to be replaced, he said, by "our men." He spelled out who the new ministers were to be—"Justice, that's straightforward. You know who gets that."

> GLOBOCNIG: *Ja, ja!*
> GÖRING: Well, say the name.
> GLOBOCNIG: *Ja*, your brother-in-law, right?
> GÖRING: Right.

At five-thirty he received a call from the staff in Seyss-Inquart's chambers in Vienna's Herrengasse. He could hear the panic in their voices as they realized that he really was planning to invade. He shouted down the line to Seyss-Inquart that he was to march right back to the president's palace, taking the German military attaché General Wolfgang Muff with him this time. "If our demands are not accepted, our troops will invade tonight, and Austria's existence will be over! . . . Tell him we're not kidding now. If Miklas hasn't grasped that in four hours, then tell him he's got four minutes to grasp it now." He tossed the receiver back onto its cradle, and settled back to wait.

That evening he was staging his Winter Ball, and it was time to change into his ceremonial uniform. He found that the Austrian envoy and his military attaché had sent their excuses, but over one thousand other guests were already arriving at the ornate Aviators' Building. The air-force band oom-pahed and the beautiful people of Berlin waltzed around the floor—and all the time liveried footmen slipped in and out with messages and telegrams as the final orders went out to one hundred thousand troops and hundreds of air crews.

The big question mark was Italy. Dour-faced Italian diplomats cluttered the floor, stiff-lipped and saying nothing. Together Hitler and Göring had drafted a long letter during the day to Benito Mussolini, justifying their coming action in Austria. The complete typescript text, found years later in Göring's papers also made plain to the Duce that Germany intended to act against Czechoslovakia next. Göring had sent his friend Prince Philipp down to Italy with this new epistle to the Romans.

Göring waited at the Chancellery for word from Vienna and Rome. The seven-thirty deadline came and went. Just before eight Seyss-Inquart phoned again: Schuschnigg had merely "withdrawn," leaving everything in suspense. "Okay," replied Göring, "I'm going to order the invasion. . . . Tell those in charge that anybody resisting us will be turned over to our drumhead courts-martial. Is that clear?"

As they pensively trooped back to the conference room, Hitler slapped his thigh. "All right," he announced. "We go in!"

Hitler signed the executive order at eight-thirty. Back at the ball, an invisible tension, taut as a bandsman's drumskin, held the building as Göring returned to the floor. He took General Milch aside and murmured, "We go in at dawn."

It was not a secret that could be kept. In whispers and asides the news rippled across the floor. Göring reassured Massimo Magisrati that no German troops would advance south of Innsbruck; the diplomat's response was glacial. Then the surface tension eased, as droplets of good news arrived. At 8:48 P.M. Wilhelm Keppler phoned from Vienna—President Miklas was ordering Austrian troops not to resist. As the Prussian State Opera corps de ballet began to pirouette and whirl around the floor, Göring, sitting at the center table of the guests, tore a blank page from his program and penciled a note to Sir Nevile Henderson:

> As soon as the music is over I should like to talk to you, and will explain everything to you.

They met in his private room. The British ambassador said, "Even if Schuschnigg has acted with precipitate folly, that is no excuse for Germany to be a bully."

Two hours later Mussolini gave his assent to Hitler's action. He had told Prince Philipp frankly that he had written off Austria as soon as Schuschnigg had committed the plebiscite *"Dummheit."*

"I always knew we could bank on Mussolini," Hitler congratulated Göring. "This is the happiest moment of my life. Not for one second did I doubt the greatness of the Duce."

Encased on three sides by hostile German forces, Czechoslovakia realized that its future strategic position would be impossible. At 11:00 P.M. the Czech minister Vojtěch Mastný scurried over to Göring and presented his compliments. The field marshal rose to his feet and solemnly gave his word that Prague had no grounds for concern. Mastný passed this reassurance on to the Czech president, Dr. Édvard Beneš, who promised for his part not to mobilize Czech forces. "Good," said Göring, told of this at midnight. "I am now able to repeat my undertaking officially because the Führer has put me in supreme charge—he's going elsewhere for a short time."

Elsewhere was Austria. Learning at 2:30 A.M. that Heinrich Himmler had already flown there, Göring ordered one of his minions to phone urgent instructions to the exhausted Seyss-Inquart in Vienna: "He [Göring] wants you to take over their wiretapping agencies right away, okay?" Göring did not want Himmler getting his hands on these.

From first light onward three hundred Luftwaffe transport planes began ferrying troops into Austria. Acting head of state for the first time in his life, Göring remained in Berlin, relishing every moment of this brief taste of power. He phoned Mastný, this time to promise that no troops would come within ten miles of the Czech frontier. He sent for Tauschitz and mockingly remarked that he had missed him at last night's ball.

The Austrian envoy asked only, "Where is the Führer?"

"He's gone," roared Göring, laying it on thick and rotten. "He's gone where he's not been allowed to go for twenty years: to visit his parents' grave in Austria."

Göring's vague plan now was that President Miklas should step down, to allow Hitler to be voted in as president of Austria. At midday that Saturday—it was now March 12—he sent Milch down by plane with a special mission, to reassure the president that Germany would respect his pension rights if he retired. "With fourteen children to support," he had guffawed the day before, "you can't just do as you please!"

That Saturday evening he settled back at Carinhall and tuned in to the radio commentaries coming from all the world. He was unquestionably proud of what he had done for his Führer. Hitler was being given the Austrian equivalent of a ticker-tape parade as his automobile plowed slowly through cheering crowds into the first big town, Linz. Hysterical Austrians mobbed the car, strewing flowers in his path. "People are weeping and sobbing with joy," Göring related to one caller. "It's so unnerving that even our men can't hold back their tears. . . . Just one great outburst of joy from everybody, give or take a few panicky Jews and other guilt-stricken gentlemen."

Soon the airwaves carried the voice of Hitler himself, broadcasting from a balcony in Linz, while half a million Austrians packed into the square below. Göring heard Hitler, an orator like few others, tongue-tied with emotion.

Some hours later the phone rang, and it was Hitler calling, still choked with pent-up feelings. "Göring," he said, "you just can not imagine. I had completely forgotten how beautiful my country is."

"Yes," reported the field marshal, glowing, to Ribbentrop the next morning. "The Führer was just about all in when he spoke to me last night."

There were many Austrians, of course, who did not welcome the coming new order with garlands or exultation. An exodus of Austrian Communists began. As twenty thousand nationalists, exiled by Schuschnigg, poured back in, thirsting for revenge, twenty-five thousand Viennese Jews stampeded across the frontiers into Poland in the first twenty-four hours. "We could just leave the frontier open," Prince Philipp suggested on the phone to Göring. "We could get rid of the entire scum like that."

Göring agreed, then remembered his fiscal duties as chief of the Four-Year Plan: "But not those with any foreign currency. . . . The Jews can go, but their money they'll have to leave behind. It's all stolen anyway."

For forty minutes that Sunday morning he spoke on the cross-Channel phone to Ribbentrop, still in London. ("As you are aware," he began, rubbing the point in, "the Führer has put me in charge of running the government.") Since the new Reich foreign minister was about to fly back to Berlin anyway, it is obvious that their chat now was purely for the benefit of the wiretappers in London. Göring acted calm, cocksure, confident, and did not stint in his flattery of the British statesmen.

"I'm looking forward to seeing you," he told Ribbentrop, tongue in cheek. "The weather's wonderful here in Berlin. Blue skies! I'm sitting here wrapped in blankets on my balcony in the fresh air, sipping coffee. . . . The birds are twittering, and from time to time I can hear on the radio snatches of the immense excitement down there."

Ribbentrop responded that he had just held secret talks with the British prime minister ("Chamberlain," he said, "is absolutely honest in his desire for an understanding") and Lord Halifax.

> RIBBENTROP: I don't want to say too much on the phone but . . .
> I told Halifax that we too genuinely want an understanding. He remarked that he's just a teeny-weeny bit concerned about Czechoslovakia.
> GÖRING: Oh no, no. There's no question of that at all. . . . Yes, I'm convinced too that Halifax is a pretty intelligent man.

"Anybody who threatens us," he continued, "will find (in strict confidence) that he's up against fanatical resistance from both our countries."

A few hours later Ribbentrop arrived in person at Carinhall, having driven straight over from Tempelhof Airport. Together they listened to the welcome accorded to Hitler on his return to Linz from his parents' grave at Leonding. But the big shock was just about to come.

At about 9:00 P.M. the Forschungsamt, still tapping the Austrian legation's telephones, heard an official of the foreign ministry in Vienna, one Max Hoffinger, telephone Tauschitz, the Austrian chargé d'affaires, with news that the new Seyss-Inquart Cabinet had approved a suggestion by Hitler that the two countries agree to immediate Anschluss, an indissoluble union. Tauschitz telephoned this historic news to the Reich Foreign Ministry.

The Brown Page hit Göring like a trench mortar. Anschluss now—just like that? Ribbentrop telephoned Tauschitz direct to investigate, only to have the phone snatched out of his hand by Göring, indignantly bellowing, "What the hell is going on!"

Of the astonishment in their voices there can be no doubt. Tauschitz, testifying nine years later, vividly recalled it.

So this was how Germany and Austria came to be reunited, in the fifth year of Hitler's rule. Anxious for the safety of his protégé Guido Schmidt, Schuschnigg's foreign minister, the field marshal sent his personal plane down to Vienna to whisk him out of the Gestapo's clutches and bring him straight to Carinhall. He waved a jocular hand at his wall fresco. "Well, Schmidt," he said, "got your own wall map now?" In a two-hour conversation with the perspiring, nervous ex-minister on Monday morning, Göring promised him sanctuary if ever he needed it. Once, their talk was interrupted by the phone—it was Sir Nevile Henderson. Göring mischievously mentioned that he had Guido Schmidt right next to him—"I'm thinking of giving him a diplomatic post!"—and was gratified to hear an indignant gasp at the other hand. ("Talk of Judas!" the ambassador wrote, most unfairly, to London about Schmidt. "He has lost no time in coming for his thirty pieces of silver.")

To Austrian legation official Hans Schwarzenberg, who had driven Guido Schmidt out to Carinhall that morning, it was plain that Göring was baffled at the sudden twist that events in Austria had taken the day before. "We had all been of one mind with Hitler," the field marshal remarked as they rejoined their car, "that Austria should be allowed to retain her autonomy."

Göring shrugged. The people of Linz had knitted the rope, and Hitler had merely jerked it tight.

Years later, this letter from Göring's sister Paula was found tucked away in his desk, describing her feelings in the first days of post-Anschluss Austria:

Wels, March 15, 1938

My truly beloved brother!

For three days now I've been going about in a dream, I just can't believe this gigantic and wonderful event! I'm so deeply moved I can't do anything but sit for hours glued to the radio while the tears stream down and my eyes just won't dry! I would have dearly loved to write you on Friday night, but I couldn't even have held a pen! Bursting with gratitude, I booked a phone call on Saturday evening but it kept getting delayed by official flash connections [Blitzgesprächen], and then on Sunday at eleven P.M. I got your dear phone call, which made me so happy and for which I thank Emmy a thousand times—I was just sad not to hear your own dear voice so I could tell you all that was in my overflowing heart.

So now I have to throw my arms around your neck like this, in writing, and express our ardent and genuine thanks to our wonderful Führer and to you, my dearest brother, for this miracle that has saved us in the nick of time.

Dearest H'm, none of us can grasp even now that we Austrians belong at last to you, and that no frontier divides us anymore. The fantastic pace at which these things all happen—we can scarcely keep up with these wonderful times. What a pity you can't join the Führer's triumphal entry parade, because you've got to stand in for him [in Berlin]. But when you do come, there will be even more scenes of exultation. . . .

I must tell you that I have never found the death of Friedrich* so painful to bear as now. I just keep thinking, over and over, if only he could have lived to see this miracle. . . .

This nationwide exhilaration was shared by millions, many of whom would afterwards remember differently. Baron von Weizsäcker, later one of the more trenchant critics of Hitler's policies, found fit to comment in his diary on the Führer's ''remarkable knack of catching opportunity on the wing.''

Those words would apply equally well to the manner in which Göring now moved to consolidate his position in the wake of General von Fritsch's resignation.

The court of honor resumed, after this seven-day interlude, on March 17, 1938. Under the guidance of the tall, thin army prosecuting counsel, Colonel Biron, the homosexual blackmailer Otto Schmidt once more rehearsed his allegations. Then the defense case began. A dozen youngsters to whom the general had played host testified that he had never molested them in any way. With heavy irony, the general's counsel, Count von der Goltz, asked for Reich Minister Walter Funk and the other ''alleged homosexual'' victims to be called as witnesses. Göring denied the application, but he must have begun to ponder the effect of the general's virtually inevitable acquittal on his own reputation. ''Initially,'' wrote Fritsch at the time, ''I had the impression that Göring wanted a verdict of non liquet, not proven. . . . But under the weight of evidence, even Göring had to announce that nobody endowed with even the slightest intelligence could fail to be convinced of my innocence.''

His brilliant, assiduous attorney had located a young man to whom Otto Schmidt had once pointed out the house of an officer he had, as he coarsely

*Friedrich Rigele had died recently, leaving Göring's sister Olga a widow.

put it, "shaken down." Cross-examined about this phrase the next day, March 18, in a tense and expectant court, Schmidt fell squarely into the trap: He confirmed that he had been referring only to the accused, General von Fritsch. But the house had already been located, and it was that of the cavalry captain Achim von Frisch.

Göring's temper snapped. Now, in fact, it was *sauve qui peut*—this was his last chance to abandon the leaking man-o'-war that Himmler had launched against Fritsch weeks earlier. "How much longer," he thundered at Schmidt, "do you imagine you can keep on lying to the court?"

Schmidt's face betrayed no flicker of emotion. "So it was a lie," he said in his coarse Berlin accent.

"And why did you lie? If you tell the truth now, you have my word that no harm will come to you."

"This morning," explained Schmidt, "Kriminalrat Meisinger sent for me and said that if I didn't stick to the story, then—" and he jerked a thumb upward.

"What d'you mean—'then'?" persisted Göring, jerking his thumb too.

"—then it's the high jump for me!"

The verdict was Not Guilty. Göring left the podium and pumped the general's hand. Unmoved, Fritsch wrote: "Both during the examination of witnesses and in his oral findings, Göring was at pains to justify the conduct of the Gestapo."

He doubted that the Führer would rehabilitate him and restore him to the army command, and he confided to his attorney afterward that Göring's closing remarks would seem to indicate that it was unlikely. He himself blamed Himmler. During the two-day hearings it had come out that only three days after the fateful Blomberg wedding, a low-level Gestapo official, Kriminalkommissar Fehling, had impounded the all-important bankbook of Fritsch's "double," the cavalry captain Frisch (this was the book that Franz Huber had seen at Gestapo headquarters). Among Fritsch's papers, now in Moscow, is the draft of a letter he wrote challenging Himmler to a duel with pistols; but no army general was willing to act as his second, and the letter was never sent. Significantly, he never challenged Göring—he gave the field marshal the benefit of the doubt.

The whole affair left a bad odor, a guilty scent in Göring's nostrils. In July 1942 Himmler was still holding the blackmailer, Otto Schmidt, in the Sachsenhausen concentration camp. He had now been certified as a paranoid schizophrenic, and Himmler's medical experts declared him unfit to serve further time. "I request, dear Herr Reichsmarschall," Himmler wrote to Göring on the seventh—recalling, perhaps, that Göring had promised Schmidt his personal protection if he told the truth—"your agreement for recommending that consent be given for Schmidt's execution."

Göring picked up a mauve pencil. "He ought to have been shot *long* ago," he scrawled across the letter. But he retained the letter in his files.

Fritsch was for all practical purposes dead too. Hitler penned him a handsome letter of apology—but did not reinstate him. He would meet an ordinary soldier's death in 1939. Let us hear his voice for one last time, writing in his private papers: "In his oral findings Göring . . . spoke of my tragic fate, but added that there was no way of turning the clock back. What came through most clearly was his sentiment that they'd got rid of me, thank God, once and for all. Over and over," recorded this innocent victim of Göring's lust for power, "and with added emphasis, Göring kept talking of 'Colonel General von Fritsch, Retired.' "

PART 3
THE MEDIATOR

18
BLAME IT ON NAPOLEON

Afew days after the court of honor finally adjourned, George Ward Price, the British journalist, came out to see Göring at Carinhall. He had seen Hitler down at Linz, and had revealed in a drunken stupor to officials in Prague four evenings later that the Führer now intended to recover the Sudeten German territories from Czechoslovakia. This was not what Hermann Göring had promised the Czech minister, Mastný, at the air force Winter Ball, of course; but then Göring had also promised Otto Schmidt that nothing would happen to him.

Ward Price, the *Daily Mail*'s star foreign correspondent, had known Göring for five years. Jibes about the "Jewish bosses" in London, Paris, and Prague tripped naturally off his tongue—particularly when he had been drinking. It was March 23, 1938. The two grown men stood at the control panel of the miniature railway that Göring installed at Carinhall—complete with remote-controlled planes that released bombs—and as they manipulated the levers and shunted trains around the hundreds of feet of track, the field marshal began to talk. He talked of Britain's stupidity in obliging Germany to sign the Anti-Comintern Pact with Japan ("contrary to all our racial principles"). And then, as Ward Price reported afterward to Whitehall, Göring orated, "clasping his hands above his head in an emotional and enthusiastic manner," about National Socialist Germany's willingness to pledge her entire strength to the defense of British interests throughout the world. At one stage, Göring offered to invite three thousand British working-class men to tour Germany at his expense and see the truth for themselves.

The spring of 1938 had brought only a sense of frustration to Göring. He felt cheated of his ambitions, and he sensed a new ice age descending on relations with Britain. "Creeping over Britain," he would comment four months after the Anschluss, "we can see a certain—I won't say belligerence—a sense of the inevitability of war."

He tried hard to soften Hitler's attitude to Britain. When, at the crucial moment before the Anschluss, his code-breakers had deciphered French dispatches revealing that Britain was refusing to join forces with them against Germany, Göring had flown the two Brown Pages concerned—N83,709 and N83,722—down to Hitler in Vienna. ("That's why I want us to be a bit friendlier toward Britain," he forewarned Bodenschatz, who was accompanying Hitler, by phone. "So keep your eyes peeled for the Forschungsamt courier, and have him tell the Führer I want him to read those intercepts particularly. Make sure those two are on top, so that the Führer can see for himself how the great powers are lined up.")

On the day after Ward Price's visit, Göring set out on a whistle-stop tour of Austria, electioneering for the plebiscite that was to give Austrians and Germans alike a chance to approve the Anschluss. Before he left, he received a letter from Sir Nevile Henderson, acting on Queen Mary's behalf, asking him to intercede for certain Austrians and monarchists, and in particular for Baron Louis de Rothschild, the Jewish banker whom the Nazis had now detained as an economic hostage.

It was his first visit to Austria for many years. At Castle Mauterndorf he called on his godfather's aged widow, Lily von Epenstein. In a string of orations he appealed to the Austrian voters' endemic nationalism and anti-Semitism, and he promised social reforms, power stations, and superhighways—Hitler would turn the first shovel of earth for the new Salzburg autobahn three days before polling day. On that day, April 10, 1938, the vote went so overwhelmingly in Hitler's favor—with 99.08 percent of the forty-nine million voters between the North Sea and the Alps openly affirming their faith in him—that a British government official sadly commented that their ambassador in Vienna had obviously totally deceived them about the mood in Austria.

At Carinhall, Göring was filling a bookcase with morocco-bound albums portraying his growing industrial empire. At Linz in Austria the Hermann Göring Works began erecting a steel mill to exploit the Styrian iron-ore reserves. On January 1, 1939, H.G.W. would purchase 70 percent of the Vienna-based Alpine Montan Corporation, controlling strings of iron-ore mines, ironworks, and heavy engineering firms. It is worth noting that Göring privately authorized that proper severance payments and pensions should be paid for the three outgoing Jewish directors and eight Jewish employees who were discharged, and that these were paid until 1945. He also found a job for Arthur Schuschnigg, brother of the arrested chancellor, at the Kaiser-Friedrich Museum in Berlin, remarking to Mühlmann, his art adviser, at the time, "I suppose your party bigwigs in Vienna will scream bloody murder at me again." On Hitler's suggestion Göring would also appoint Guido Schmidt as an expert on the Balkan market to the board of H.G.W. in July 1939. "There goes your blasted friend Göring again," lamented Kaltenbrunner to Mühlmann, "taking another black sheep under his wing."

To recover the Sudeten territories from Czechoslovakia, Hitler proposed to use political and military blackmail, and if those failed, naked force. On April 21, he secretly briefed General Keitel to draft *Case Green*, a high command (OKW) directive for the rapid invasion of Czechoslovakia, to be justified by some outrage like the attempted assassination of the German envoy in Prague (an unwitting career diplomat named Ernst Eisenlöhr). If, as seems likely, the intention was to stage-manage such an "incident," this would explain why Göring dropped repeated hints over the coming months about the consequences of "the slightest provocation by Prague," and there are signs in the *Green* planning files that he was closely consulted on the military preparations.

He had no personal animus toward Czechoslovakia. In April 1937, when Mastný had come to promise Czech government cooperation in tracking down a terrorist gang rumored to be after his blood, Göring had mentioned that it would be "idiotic" (*blödsinnig*) to attack Czechoslovakia. He had not tampered at all with Czechoslovakia's frontiers on the big fresco that he installed in his study that September—as Mastný had not failed to notice. And, of course, he had solemnly promised Mastný at the air-force Winter Ball on March 11, 1938, that Czechoslovakia had nothing to fear.

Somehow, Hitler won him over. To make him more receptive, Hitler again secretly nominated Göring, in his political testament dated April 23, as the next Führer. And when Hitler departed for his great state visit to Rome on May 2, he again left Göring in Berlin as acting head of state. There was therefore a dual track emerging in Göring's character. He was peaceably inclined, but his greed for the ultimate office kept him aboard Hitler's accelerating military juggernaut. He adopted Hitler's language as his own. On May 3, as the king of Sweden passed through Berlin, we find Field Marshal Göring gossiping grandly with him, as one head of state to another, about "pushing the Czechs back to Russia, where they belong."

Hitler returned to Berlin, and all Europe awaited his next move. On May 21, Czech gendarmes shot dead two Sudeten German farmers. The jumpy British press abused Hitler, accusing him of moving his troops. For once he was not guilty. Humiliated by his own momentary military impotence, on May 24 he concluded from the Fleet Street clamor for the first time that the

British might well figure among his enemies after all in some future war. He summoned his high command to a briefing in Berlin four days later.

Shortly before he addressed these generals, he broke it to Göring that he was going ahead with *Green* in the fall—that a purely political settlement was no longer acceptable. Göring clutched at straws. He argued that the army generals had made barely any progress on the vital West Wall, the line of bunkers defending Germany's frontier against France. Hitler was unmoved. "We'll deal with Czechoslovakia using these old generals," he said mockingly, "then we've got four or five years."

Göring's awe of Hitler was absolute, and this was his gravest impediment. "I try so hard," he once admitted to Hjalmar Schacht, "but every time I stand before the Führer, my heart drops into the seat of my pants." His heart wallowing around those nether regions now, he buttonholed Hitler's personal adjutant just before Hitler's conference of May 28 began. "Wiedemann," he pleaded, "does the Führer really imagine the French won't do anything if we light into the Czechs? Doesn't he read the Forschungsamt intercepts I send over?

Hitler paid no heed to Göring's misgivings. "It is my unshakable resolve," he said to the generals, "that Czechoslovakia shall vanish from the map of Europe."

He gave them until September to be ready.

And then one day late that spring, five days after the Hitler conference, one of the telephones on his desk rang. "Congratulations!"—he recognized Emmy's voice—"from tiny Edda and me!"

A father at forty-five, the field marshal jumped into his sports car and hurtled over to the West Sanatorium clutching a bouquet of roses, while diplomatic Berlin heaved a sigh of relief: Göring, the ambassadors hoped, the complete family man, must now become a man of peace and conciliator in the councils of war.

Emmy settled into motherhood. "Hermann likes women who are fat," she told Sir Nevile Henderson, and comfortably complied.

Troubled by his heart, Hermann himself made token forays in the opposite direction. Along with the other amusements at Carinhall (which included a dentist's chair to "bore" his guests) he had installed an Elizabeth Arden reducing machine, and for the benefit of the visiting duchess of Windsor he forced himself between its rollers in full-dress uniform. The duke gave him a signed portrait photograph, which Göring later displayed next to the Führer's; he had had the latter specially enlarged and framed by his master silversmith, Professor Herbert Zeitner.

He had all the happiness that money could buy and more money than was proper to buy it. Tax declarations found in his files show that in fiscal 1936 he had paid only 2,832 marks tax on his 28,160-mark salary as air minister, and only 190 marks on his 15,795 marks pay as prime minister of Prussia.

But his emoluments from other sources were already substantial—enough for him to fork out 120,000 marks (about $40,000 1936 dollars) for an ancient Greek gold bangle and smuggle it out of Italy in the ambassador's diplomatic bag ("I am delighted," wrote the ambassador, Ulrich von Hassell, to Göring, sending him this Christmas "gift" on December 23, 1937, "that it has been won for Germany. Of course, there must be no mention of which country it comes from"); Göring's fortune was also large enough for him to contemplate buying two or three ancient towers in Italy, including the Castello di Barbarossa, which his friend the Swedish author Axel Munthe offered him on "God's own island," Capri.

Most of all he liked to cruise in his—or more strictly, Emmy's—yacht, *Carin II*, a pleasure that cost both the Prussian purse and his benefactors dear. The AEG company had to pay thirty thousand marks for the electrical machinery alone, while Prussia had to bear the cost of demolishing and rebuilding the bridges over the rivers and inlets around Carinhall, since the boat's superstructure was too high.

In June 1938 he cruised up to the North Sea pleasure island of Sylt, where Emmy was nursing Edda at "Min Lütten," the dunes cottage she had bought out of her earnings as a film actress. Early in July he cruised up to Copenhagen to see *Hamlet* at Castle Elsinore, meet Crown Prince Fredrik, and above all to purchase twenty-one dozen *skrubbar*—Danish pastries—at the Christian Bach bakery. He had fallen for them while visiting Denmark in 1919. "Göring," recalled pastry-cook Hermansson, "drove up in three cars. The girls in the shop had to pack the pastries into cardboard boxes and carry them in a shuttle service out to the cars." His reducing efforts had evidently been short-lived. On the following Sunday the Danish townsfolk crowded into the bakery—everybody wanted to sample the Göring *skrubbar*. "Later," said Hermansson, "he ordered more pastries and *kranskaka* [a ring-shaped cake], which we had to send him by train."

His favorite cruising routes took *Carin II* along the inland waterways from Berlin into the Elbe and down the canals to the Rhine. Proud, contented Germans lined the banks and waved as their chubby field marshal chugged past. Arrayed in a white uniform, he sprawled in a deck chair and lapped up applause and sunshine while the boat's loudspeakers boomed gaudy songs like "Blame It on Napoleon." At dusk they made fast at some village quay and he settled down to a beer and a game of skat at a pfennig a point. The very idea of losing was unthinkable, and his adjutants sat with faces bleached at the thought of accidentally winning. Game over, the field marshal would stuff a pajama pocket with bonbons scooped up from a jar and retire to his lavish, mahogany-paneled bedroom.

At 6:00 A.M. his valet, Robert, often found him up on deck, swathed in blankets and contemplating the rising sun. Göring would motion to the valet to switch on the phonograph down below, and then the chosen riverside village would be awakened by an entire Wagner opera blaring from the boat's loudspeakers. When, toward midday, the final golden chords had enveloped the countryside, Göring would send for Robert. "Again!" he might command; or, more mercifully, "Let it run through again as far as 'Behold the golden pommel's gleam in the sun's bright rays.'"

"I wouldn't have your job for a thousand marks a month!" whispered the chief adjutant, Major Conrath, to the valet once. Robert showed him a glittering new air-force dagger, and asked him to get Göring's name engraved on the hilt.

The major was a pessimist. "Nobody'll give you anything for it," he sniffed, "—afterward!"

These summer weeks of 1938, which should have been golden-hued after the birth of his daughter, Edda, were overclouded for Göring by Hitler's planning against Czechoslovakia. President Beneš was proving less tractable than Schuschnigg—he relied on his country's Maginot-style frontier fortifications, and on his alliance with France. Britain, however, though treaty-bound to help the French, was not eager to assist Beneš. "There can be no doubt that Britain doesn't want war," Göring assured his aircraft industrialists in a secret speech at Carinhall on July 8. "Nor does France, for that matter. With America," he added, "you can't be certain."

The aircraft manufacturers in his audience, including the big names like Claude Dornier, Ernst Heinkel, Willi Messerschmitt, and the directors of Hugo Junkers, heard him again predict a Czech "provocation."

> Don't any of you gentlemen imagine that if Germany yet again fights and loses a war, you'll be able to crawl away and say, 'I never did want this war—I was always dead against it and the system—I never had any truck with them.' They'll just laugh you down. You are Germans, and they won't care two hoots whether you were part of it or not.

To encourage them, he dropped a broad hint about Germany's bright future if and when they won: "Germany will be the greatest power on earth. The world's markets will belong to Germany . . . But we must venture something for this. We have to make the initial investment." He assured his listeners at this Carinhall conference that he conferred at least once a week with General Udet, his chief technical officer. "Nothing important is ordered—nothing whatever—without first being discussed down to the very last detail and approved by me." He reminded them of the new generation of aircraft engines coming along, including the air-cooled radial BMW engine and the Junkers Jumo 211, but pleaded for forward thinking by these aviation experts:

> I still don't have [complained Göring] a strato-bomber capable of flying at eighty [thousand] or one hundred thousand feet . . .

I still miss the rocket engines that would enable us to fly at that attitude. And I still see no sign at all of a bomber that can carry five tons of bombs to New York and get back. How happy I'd be to get such a bomber and ram some of their arrogance right back down their throats.

As that summer wore on, he lazed in the sunshine, strolled around the forest glades, coddled the infant Edda, devoured adventure books, and leafed through the newspapers. They carried photographs of him accepting yet another sword, handmade by Paul Müller of Solingen, four feet long with its cross guard encrusted with twenty-five rubies and gold lettering emblazoned on the blade: TO THE HONORARY MASTER OF THE GERMAN CRAFTSMEN, FIELD MARSHAL HERMANN GÖRING. "With this sword," he said, raising the heavy weapon in both hands, "I shall smite all the enemies of Germany!"

He wondered who they would ultimately be. Would Hitler really order *Case Green*? What would Italy do this time? On July 9 he entertained the Italian chief of staff, General Alberto Pariani, at Carinhall. He boasted about his air force and claimed that Britain and France had no intention of helping the Czechs. Pariani disagreed, and warned the field marshal that Germany must finish Czechoslovakia with one thrust.

"We must hang together," Göring cautioned him, "for better or for worse."

That summer's entries in Göring's thick, leather-bound diary—lettered in gilt, "*Besprechungen*" ("Conferences")—reflected his energy in mobilizing the aircraft industry for war. The diary opened with a July 11, 1938, conference on securing the requisite manpower, including women, for the aircraft factories, training new apprentices and converting unskilled workers into specialists. On the same day he conferred with a building contractor about proposals to use Reich autobahns for aircraft runways and hangars, and he discussed the construction of new air-raid shelters and underground factories, while the same diary reveals him on the fifteenth and sixteenth in secret talks with Four-Year Plan agents, Neuhausen and Bernhardt, on ways of extending Nazi influence in Yugoslavia and Spain, and on obtaining foodstuffs and raw materials from Spain in return for arms deliveries to General Franco. ("Caution," Göring noted, "because of Nonintervention.")

The Luftwaffe's plans for *Green* were now complete. Four hundred fighters, six hundred bombers, and two hundred dive-bombers and ground-attack planes would operate against Czechoslovakia, while 250 Junkers 52 transports would drop paratroops into the heart of the fortifications. Simultaneously General Helmuth Felmy's Second Air Fleet (*Luftflotte*) would stand by to operate from airfields in northwestern Germany against Britain as soon as *Green* was over.

As fall approached, Göring became restive. He had a lot more to lose in a war than his Führer. On July 14, he approved Milch's suggestion that a British fighter squadron be invited over to Germany for a friendly visit to the Luftwaffe. Using Wiedemann's girl friend, Princess Stephanie von Hohenlohe, he had inquiries made in London whether he himself might fly over to see Lord Halifax. On July 18, the latter, now foreign secretary, received Wiedemann in secret in London and provided the one assurance that the field marshal had asked for, that he would not be exposed to public insult. But then, when Wiedemann reported this outcome to Hitler the next day on the Obersalzberg, Hitler said that it was "out of the question" for Göring to go to London now.

Hitler had begun waging an ultramodern war of nerves on Prague—what he called in a secret speech in August "whetting the blade." Göring played an active part in this, and his Forschungsamt closely monitored its results.

This psychological warfare reached its climax when the French air-force commander, General Joseph Vuillemin, visited Germany in mid-August 1938. Göring allowed him to see the beer gardens, swimming pools, and saunas that he had provided for aircraft-industry workers; as Vuillemin's gaping aides counted the brand-new Me 109 fighter planes lined up on Döberitz Airfield—twenty-seven—a four-engine Focke-Wulf Condor touched down. At Oranienburg, where only cows had grazed twelve months earlier, an Ernst Heinkel factory was now producing seventy He 111 bombers a month— more than the entire French aircraft industry in a year. In a remarkable new hedgehopping Fieseler Storch, Ernst Udet flew the French Commander in Chief at a lazy eighty miles an hour over the local concentration camp (Vuillemin noted that it was visibly "well attended"—"très habité.") As the Storch fluttered down onto an airfield, it rocked in the slipstream of the new record-breaking He 100 zooming a few feet overhead at full throttle. It was purely a laboratory-test vehicle, but Milch blandly asked about "production plans," and Udet grinned and said, "The second mass-production line is just starting and the third in three weeks' time."

And so the amiable bullying went on. At Messerschmitt's Augsburg works airfield a twin-engined Me 110 heavy fighter prototype, jacked up in the butts, blasted away with a twenty-millimeter cannon, and another was looped and stunted with one engine shut down. At Junkers' Magdeburg plant officials bragged that the 1,250-horsepower Jumo 211 would replace the standard 210 from November (it would still not be in squadron service five years later).

In his final report General Vuillemin warned Paris that the German Air Force was one of "truly devastating power," and this undoubtedly helped the vacillating French to make up their minds when the time came.

Whatever his own misgivings, Göring cooperated with the OKW on the tactical planning of *Green* and heaped criticism on the army generals and their plans. He insisted that the all-important "provocation" be timed to ensure the right flying weather for his air force. On August 23, he summoned his commanding generals to Carinhall, and two days later his air staff issued a directive for *Enlarged Case Green*, confronting the possibility that other countries would come to Czechoslovakia's aid. According to the diary of Hitler's SS adjutant Max Wünsche, Göring spent five hours alone with Hitler on the Obersalzberg on the last day of that month.

Although we have no record of their conversation, there was one curious incident that suggests that Göring was now a very worried man. His chief economic adviser, Helmut Wohlthat, sent a secret courier to Switzerland to rendezvous in Basel with Edgar Mowrer of the *Chicago Daily News* and ask him to put a very oddly worded question to his friends in the U.S. State Department on behalf of someone "very highly placed indeed" in Berlin: If war broke out, this question read, and if the Nazi regime collapsed, would Washington intervene with London to prevent France dictating "another and even more draconian Versailles Treaty" to a defeated Germany? The "very highly placed" Berlin gentleman, Wohlthat's message explained, "had decided that at the present juncture he must ask himself where his duty lies."

In London the Foreign Office officials were amazed. They noted that this was the first feeler to have come clearly from Göring.

Of course, Göring's "feeler" may just have been an advanced ploy in psychological warfare. But he took a conciliatory line with Sir Nevile Henderson too. Hitler, he said on September 8 at Nuremberg, attending the party rally, had asked him to inform the British government that if they allowed him to settle the Sudeten problem, they would be surprised and gratified at the moderation of his other suggestions. Later that day he drove the ambassador out of the drum-thumping, belligerent Nuremberg rally arena to the peace and quiet of Castle Veldenstein, and here he again raised the possibility of a Czech "incident"—for example, the assassination of the Sudeten German leader Konrad Henlein. He followed this with the intriguing suggestion: "Chamberlain and Hitler ought to meet."

Chamberlain had in fact been planning to meet the Führer. Early on the fourteenth, Henderson phoned Göring—who had withdrawn from Nuremberg to Carinhall suffering from blood poisoning—and asked for his help in bypassing Ribbentrop to secure an invitation from Hitler to the elderly British prime minister. "Of course!" exclaimed Göring, and phoned Hitler, down at Berchtesgaden, at once. Chamberlain met Hitler the next day. They made some headway and agreed to meet again a week later. Bodenschatz brought a record of the Berghof meeting up to Carinhall on the sixteenth.

On the morning of the seventeenth, Sir Nevile Henderson came out to Carinhall and found Göring, still unwell, studying the record of the meeting. In an hour-long talk the ambassador gave voice to his fears that Ribbentrop, closeted alone with Hitler on their mountaintop, might rush the Führer into some precipitate military action before Chamberlain came for the second meeting. Göring put his mind at rest on this score but continued with some of his toughest language yet. "If," he told Henderson, "Britain means to make war on Germany, one thing is certain. Before the war is over, there

will be very few Czechs alive, and little of London left standing either."
He hastened, however, to add, "There is no cause for anxiety unless something *catastrophic* happens," and he repeated the suspect word several times during the hour.

As Henderson left, Colonel Ulrich Kessler came in. He had been in London, deputizing for the absent air attaché during the recent crisis. Göring had plans to appoint him chief of staff of Luftflotte 2, the air-force command that would confront Britain in time of war. But word had reached the field marshal that Kessler had panicked in London—that during the 1936 "Rhineland crisis" he had ordered all the air attaché's papers burned and had persuaded the army attaché, Lieutenant Colonel Bechtolsheim, to do the same.

Kessler uncomfortably tried to justify his decision. "I was sure then that the British would fight."

"You are wrong," said Göring. "Henderson had just left me. He tried to work on my tear glands. I told him that if there's a war, Britain will be smashed."

Since Kessler stuck to his guns, Göring angrily paced the room producing arguments pointing to a German victory. "We have powerful allies. Poland and Italy will be with us."

As Kessler continued to express strong doubts, Göring's face became doleful. "I've got to demand one thing, that the chief of staff of the Luftflotte confronting Britain has faith that we can smash Britain if she declares war."

Kessler pointed to the problems of fighting a sea power, and the likelihood that the United States would join in.

"The United States will not poke its nose into European affairs," said Göring flatly. "And Britain will be impotent once her fleet is sunk. I agree our puny German Navy can't do this, but our air force can. Where there's a will there's a way!"

As the general left, Göring made a note that the general had an inferiority complex, and he ordered his future appointment canceled.

Göring had no intention of allowing anything "catastrophic" to happen. In faraway Godesberg on the Rhine, Hitler was preparing to meet Mr. Chamberlain again, but in East Prussia the stags were in full cry, a symphony to Göring's ear. The rutting was almost over and he would wait no longer. By special train he set out with Körner, Udet, and Loerzer for the Alt Sternberg Hunting Ground. His chief foresters, sent on ahead, met him with news that they had seen "royal" stags, including one that came so regularly to the same meadow, where he sat on his haunches and bayed, that they called him "the Fountain Statue."

The mustachioed Czar Boris of Bulgaria joined them, and for three days they waited for this stag each dawn and twilight; but it was not until the final evening that the Fountain Statue, a magnificent beast with towering, powerful antlers, strutted out of the undergrowth onto the broad meadow to join his herd. At a range of three hundred yards Göring dropped him with a shot through the heart.

There was one peculiar incident on September 22, still unexplained. At ten-thirty that morning the Forschungsamt intercepted a message from Prague to Mastný in Berlin reporting that Eisenlöhr's legation there was being stormed by a Czech mob. Göring actually prepared to bomb Prague, but twenty minutes later the intercept was formally withdrawn. Had somebody triggered a fake "incident" too soon, or were the Germans testing the machinery, or was it more psychological warfare, designed to intensify the war of nerves?

Late the next day Göring's party traveled on to Rominten in East Prussia. The rutting here was just beginning, bringing the excited hunters to their own sweaty climax of anticipation. Throughout the afternoon of the twenty-fourth, as Hitler and Chamberlain still locked horns at Godesberg, Göring stalked the legendary stag the Prince. Nobody knew how big he really was, but many claimed to have seen him. But then, as though he knew that the Reich master huntsman himself had come for him, the Prince strolled proudly forth—and cheekily sat down just as Göring took aim. When finally, after Göring had been waiting for hours, the stag cantilevered himself to his feet, a smaller animal trotted right into the line of fire. Göring loosed off one shot nonetheless, and the Prince's reign was over. It was the biggest beast the field marshal had ever killed, with twenty-two points (worth 221.70 on the then-fashionable Nadler Scale).

All this masked the distant clatter of foreign armies girding for war. In England gas masks were issued, slit trenches dug. For one more day Göring lingered at Rominten, where he felled three more stags, all of the "Reich master huntsman" category (rating over 195 points on the scale).

Before leaving these eastern territories, he watched several aurochs, or European bison, being turned loose into the Rominten Heath. The aurochs was a shy though noble animal that had all but vanished from Europe centuries before. Göring had nurtured these specimens in the Berlin Zoo and now they stood there, proud Reich master huntsman and timid aurochs, both species by rights extinct. They blinked at each other for some time; then the shaggy, inoffensive animals shambled off into the unfamiliar landscape while their master joined his train to revert to his own habitat, the councils of war and industry in Berlin.

The news there was disconcerting. At Godesberg, Hitler had learned from the Forschungsamt intercepts that Czech President Beneš was not going to honor any obligations, and issued an ultimatum. The intercepts fairly sizzled with obscene Czech references to the wimpish British government. Göring handed the whole red-hot sheaf of Brown Pages to the carnationed British ambassador Henderson, hoping thus to hammer a wedge between the British and the Czechs.

Göring now knew what Hitler probably did not, that his air force was

totally inadequate for war with Britain. On his triumphant return from East
Prussia, he was handed a shocking report dated September 22, written by
General Felmy, who chaired the air force's "Special Staff Britain." Felmy
warned that none of their bombers or fighters could operate meaningfully
over Britain. True, existing bombers might carry half a ton each, but they
would arrive over London unescorted by any fighters.

> Given our present means [General Felmy concluded] we can hope
> at best for a nuisance effect. Whether this will diminish the British
> will to fight depends in part on imponderable and unpredictable
> factors . . . A war of annihilation against Britain appears to be
> out of the question.

Panic seized the field marshal. He reached for a colored pencil, and where
Felmy had warned, "Our training has hitherto disregarded the requirements
of operating far out to sea," he scrawled in the margin, "See to it immediately!" Next to Felmy's list of possible British targets, Göring wrote,
"Work these up with priority!" "I don't believe," Göring wrote, "that I
asked for a memorandum casting doubts on our prospects and underlining
our weaknesses—I am fully aware of them myself."

Searching for a solution, he ordered his generals to Carinhall on the twenty-
seventh and told them to mass-produce the still untested Junkers 88 high-
speed bomber. It was the last word in bombers, with self-sealing tanks,
variable-pitch propellers, and retractable undercarriage. A prototype had broken all records in April 1938. He refused to heed the sober warnings uttered
by Milch that the fully loaded military version would probably not fly faster
than 180 miles per hour, with a range more like nine hundred than thirteen
hundred miles.

He had no choice, because he had found on his return to Berlin that Hitler
had issued a public ultimatum to Czechoslovakia, set to expire at 2:00 P.M.
on September 28.

Fortunately for Göring a "thaw" suddenly set in.

From Göring's vantage point as he scanned the Brown Pages of the Forschungsamt intercepts, the ice could already be heard cracking. First the
French, then the British, embassy was overheard that morning discussing
fresh proposals they had been instructed to offer Hitler. Even now there were
some among Hitler's advisers who wanted events brought to a head. Göring
regarded the foreign minister Ribbentrop as their leader, and he had given
him a severe scolding already at Nuremberg on account of his belligerent
posturing. The Brown Pages were a distinct relief to Göring. At 10:00 A.M.
Sir Nevile Henderson telephoned him direct, complaining that his French
colleague François-Poncet was getting no reply to his request for an audience
with the Führer.

"Don't say another word," said Göring. "I'll go right to him."

Hitler still agreed with Ribbentrop, however, and Göring had to argue with him all that morning. Hitler called him an "old woman." While Göring and the former foreign minister Neurath tried to apply the brakes, Ribbentrop's foot had jammed on the gas pedal.

At 11:00 A.M.—three hours before Hitler's ultimatum was due to expire —Mussolini telephoned his Berlin embassy: The British had sent him a message, and he wanted time to consider—would Hitler prolong the ultimatum by twenty-four hours?

The Forschungsamt brought advance notice of this plea. Ribbentrop pouted. Göring, acutely aware of the weakness of his air force against Britain, accused him of actually wanting war.

Hitler silenced them both. "Nobody wants war!" he snapped, perhaps the only clue he ever let slip that he was only bluffing all along.

He rapidly abandoned *Green*. By lunchtime a Four-Power conference had been arranged for the next day in Munich. Hitler told Göring he had realized that the German people were not ready for war, and he had serious doubts about Mussolini's steadfastness.

The rest is history. At Munich Hitler and Mussolini met Chamberlain and the stocky, balding French prime minister, Edouard Daladier, at the party's headquarters, the Brown House. Göring squired the Frenchman around and sat in on the first session, since Hitler was counting on the Luftwaffe as the factor most likely to concentrate his opponents' minds. Agreement—the historic, infamous Munich Agreement—was finally reached twelve hours later at 2:30 A.M. Half an hour after that Göring tumbled into Emmy's hotel bedroom, his face beaming. "We've pulled it off," he said. "It's peace."

The agreement restored to Germany the former Sudeten German territories of Czechoslovakia, which incidentally contained her most formidable frontier defenses. Czechoslovakia was now therefore virtually defenseless. But the Munich episode left a sour taste in Hitler's mouth. Behind Göring's back he accused him of cowardice. "The next time," he snarled, "I shall act so quickly that there will be no time for any old women to object."

Meanwhile Göring accompanied the Italian foreign minister, Count Galeazzo Ciano, to the railroad station. Their interpreter, an air-force lieutenant, saw the field marshal tug at Ciano's sleeve. "Now," he said, "there's going to be a rearmament the likes of which the world has never seen."

19
SUNSHINE GIRL AND CRYSTAL NIGHT

A princess might have envied the infant Edda Göring her beauty as a child. Her parents called her "Sunshine." Her forehead and her eyes betrayed a trace of her father's arrogance. Millions of picture postcards were sold of him enfolding her in his arms. Reich Bishop Müller officiated at her christening on November 4, 1938, and Hitler himself acted as godfather. The wiser men of Germany came bearing gifts. Milch gave one Lucas Cranach, the burghers of Cologne another. A million Luftwaffe officers and men subscribed to build a very special doll's house for her in an orchard at Carinhall—a miniature Sans Souci Palace with kitchens, drawing rooms, and dolls to scale. Her fourth birthday would see her wearing a Hussar's red uniform manufactured by the State Theater's costume workshops; her fifth, learning the piano; her sixth, meeting an orphan plucked at random out of a trainload of grimy evacuees being shipped eastward from the blazing Ruhr.

The war's privations would pass her by. For the last wartime Christmas, in 1944, Emmy would give her six pink nightdresses made of heavy bridal silk provided by the Reich Chancellery. By that time the refugees were streaming past Carinhall in the other direction.

The religious christening irked the party as much as the Göring church wedding had. (Rudolf Hess, also a first-time father, opted for the party's own pagan "naming ceremony" six days later.) Martin Bormann, Hess's powerful chief of staff, found out that Göring's nanny was not a party member. Emmy confessed sweetly, "I am not either!" To protect her from further reproof, Hitler would give her a golden party membership badge as a Christmas gift, engraved with a low number—744,606—borrowed from a member who had passed on to a place where, no doubt, party membership no longer counted.

A few days after the christening Göring took the sleeper back to Berlin. As the train passed through Halle, an adjutant shook him awake and raised the blind. The clouds were lit by a distant conflagration. He thought no more about it until driving through Berlin to his ministry—he found his car slithering across broken glass, and there were smoldering ruins where Jewish stores and synagogues had been. It was the first he knew of the nationwide pogrom organized by Dr. Joseph Goebbels.

Göring had fallen out with the "little doctor" over Goebbels's unconventional life-style. During October Magda Goebbels had come over to Carinhall to weep on Emmy's shoulder about the "devil incarnate" whom she had married. She admitted that she was herself entangled with her husband's handsome secretary, Karl Hanke, but everybody in Berlin knew that Goebbels was shamelessly coercing young actresses for sexual favors. The latest was the elegant Czech actress Lida Baarova. Göring authorized a security wiretap on her phone, and ruthlessly broadcast the scandal around Nazi high society. The Gestapo joined the hue-and-cry. "There are literally dozens of cases," Heinrich Himmler, no paragon of virtue himself, chuckled to Alfred Rosenberg. "The women are standing in line to swear affidavits on how he coerced them. I've turned over the choicest statements to the Führer."

Goebbels justified himself to Göring by saying that his wife was "frigid as an iceberg." Pacing up and down his study, puffing a Virginia cigarette, Göring solemnly listened then sent the couple down to see Hitler. The Führer patched things up.

The pogrom of November 9 was Goebbels misguided way of saying thank you.

Göring had no time at all for pogroms. Since the Nazis had come to power, his speeches had betrayed a dutiful anti-Semitism that met the mood of the moment in Central Europe. Ethnic imbalances have always provided ammunition for nationalists, and nowhere more so than in Germany. In 1933 its half million Jews made up less than one percent of the population, but they crowded the more lucrative and influential professions. Berlin's 160,000 Jews provided 27 percent of the doctors, 48 percent of the attorneys, and fifty-six percent of the notaries. Vienna had even more. "Vienna," declared

Göring, speaking there on March 26, 1938, "can no longer rightfully be called a German city. Where there are three hundred thousand Jews, you cannot speak of a German city."

He made liberal use of Nazi solecisms about the Jews. Telephoning Ribbentrop after the Anschluss, the FA heard him say, "The fact is that apart from the Jews clogging up Vienna, there's nobody at all who's against us." Why should a Hermann Göring use different language when even the British ambassador was warning of "Jewish troublemaking" and lobbying in favor of a preventive war against Hitler?

The Göring attitude toward Jews was beset by inconsistencies. He dealt with them when purchasing fine artifacts and precious stones; through his valet, Robert, he would purchase in Paris a recording of Offenbach's *Tales of Hoffmann*, although Offenbach's works were proscribed in Nazi Germany. The Nuremberg Laws on race, drafted by the Ministry of the Interior in September 1935, came as a surprise to him. ("I am still wondering," he would say in an overheard May 1945 conversation, "where they could have originated.") He moderated where he could. When the fervent Nazi gauleiter of Danzig, Albert Forster, wanted to introduce the laws there in 1937, it was Göring who prevented it. He shielded individual Jews, like Arthur Imhausen, the Jewish co-inventor of synthetic edible fats. "At my suggestion," he wrote to the Ruhr chemist on June 23, 1937, "in view of your services, the Führer has authorized your recognition as a full Aryan." He allowed Gustav Gründgens the (homosexual) artistic director of his Prussian State Theater, to hire actors with Jewish wives, and he encouraged Emmy to intervene with the authorities on behalf of Jewish stage colleagues (until a personal letter came from Hitler urging her to desist).

While the doctrinaire Nazis fought the Jews at every level of their existence, Göring fought only certain Jews, and on a much narrower front. The economic factor underlay all his directives against them. On May 15, 1936, soon after being appointed "currency dictator," he had remarked, "Scandinavian importers want German motor vehicles but are being put off by bad representation of our interests, mostly by Jews." "It's a fallacy," he argued on the same occasion, "to believe that Jews are going to work exceptionally hard to please us. There are exceptions, but these just prove the rule."

In this economic battle he would be quite ruthless. A few days after the November 1938 pogrom he referred to an earlier conference "at which we discussed this problem for the first time and took the decision to Aryanize the German economy, to throw the Jews out of our business life and into the debtors' register." The concept had been sound, he said, but he complained that the execution had been only mediocre.

All that would change during 1938. As chief of the Four-Year Plan he gave warning in his Vienna speech of March 26 that Jewish businesses were to be compulsorily purchased and sold off to non-Jews—"systematically and carefully, legally but inexorably."

The remaining Jews in Austria fought back with all they had. One teamed up with two streetwise English clergymen and sold back-dated christening certificates to two thousand wealthy Viennese Jews before the three were caught. Göring then issued regulations making it impossible to camouflage Jewish-owned businesses in this way. On June 24, issuing a circular on the "Exclusion of Jews from the German Economy," Martin Bormann welcomed the new impetus that Göring was bringing to the campaign, and called it "the beginning of a definitive solution."

> All over the world [said Göring, addressing aircraft manufacturers at Carinhall on July 8, 1938] the Jew is agitating for war. And it's clear why: Anti-Semitism is turning up in every country today, a logical consequence of the growing Jewish stranglehold on them.
>
> The Jew sees only one salvation, namely if he can set the whole world on fire. And mark my words when I say the Jews are praying for war—because it's the same Jews who control the bulk of the world's press and can exploit its psychological effects.

Göring's little-publicized campaign to hound the Jews out of German business life was as carefully planned as any battle that his paratroopers would later fight over Corinth or Crete. His targets were the big multinational corporations, some of which had set up complicated interlocking banking and holding corporations designed to conceal their ownership from the Reich and other anti-Semitic countries in which they operated in Central Europe. He made no distinction between Jews who were Germans and those who had adopted different nationalities "just so as to save their skins." "In Austria and the Sudeten territories," he would say, "all of a sudden there's a host of them who're becoming Englishmen, or Americans, or what have you. It won't cut any ice with us."

Under his chief economic adviser, Helmuth Wohlthat, he raised a team of official bloodhounds specially trained to sniff out these corporations and strip off their Aryan camouflage so that he could expropriate them in the name of the Reich. This extraordinary battle can be illustrated by one example, the ruthless liquidation of the two mining conglomerates built up in Central and Eastern Europe by the feuding brothers Julius and Ignaz Petschek. In 1934 Ignaz had bequeathed a fortune of two hundred million Reichsmarks to his four sons—all of whom were nominally Czechs. The sons had immediately begun to divest their empires, salt away their fortunes, and appoint "front men" of unchallengeable German blood for their operations inside the Reich. The assets were concealed so cunningly that Wohlthat confessed to "insoluble difficulties" when Göring gave him the job to "de-Semitize" (*entjuden*) both Petschek empires in the spring of 1938.

Göring suggested he mop up the smaller empire, Julius Petschek's, first.

That job was done by July 1938 and the (partly American) stockholders were paid off in full. Then he blew the whistle for the major offensive against the heirs of Ignaz Petschek, who controlled Germany's lignite-brickette production through three syndicates. For months Wohlthat directed his attack on this commercial battlefield, aided by intelligence from the Gestapo and Forschungsamt. The multimillionaire Petscheks clung to their property with a recklessness bordering on bravado; just before Munich they vanished and surfaced in London, now claiming British citizenship and, incidentally, over £750,000 of the £6 million British government fund set up to aid Czech refugees. Nothing, not even Göring's personal "promise of safe-conduct," persuaded them to return to Germany for questioning.

In the Petscheks' now-abandoned German offices, Göring and Wohlthat found a grinning band of front men—Germans, English, and Swiss bankers. Foreign holding companies surfaced from the financial swamp and claimed title to the Petschek fortune. It seemed that the Petscheks had thought of everything, but now Göring took the radical decision that brought victory after all. He deemed the apex corporation of the Petschek conglomerate, a certain holding company named "German Coal Trading, Inc.," to be a Jewish business within the meaning of the Reich Citizenship Act of June 14, 1938, which decreed: "A business shall be deemed Jewish if under predominantly Jewish influence." This caved in the Petschek defenses, because Göring had established that this innocently named corporation was in fact the Petscheks' Konzernbank, or corporate bank. One after the other, the remaining firms in the Petschek empire were proclaimed Jewish and turned over to the Reich trustees for disposal.

Simultaneously Göring unraveled the financial problem of buying out the Petscheks. The non-German stockholders were paid off in full when the lignite deposits were sold in December 1939; as a bonus for Göring the Reichswerke Hermann Göring bought the deposits to exchange for urgently needed coal mines in Westphalia. Meanwhile, as the Germans had occupied the Czech territories, Göring's agents had confiscated crates filled with corporate Petschek records just before they could be freighted to neutral Switzerland. A detailed audit showed that the family had defrauded the Reich of eighty million Reichsmarks in taxes. The penalties and tax arrears would far outweigh the 100 million Reichsmarks due to the German "front men," so the battle was over. In May 1940 Wohlthat and his team would report to Göring that this was the "biggest single tax-fraud and currency-violation case" in German history.

Göring pondered upon "the Jewish problem" most evenings as he motored up the autobahn from Berlin to Carinhall. He tried to put it out of his mind as he passed the SS guardhouse and entered his own domain, with its herds of bison and moose and Carin's lake. But as he chewed contentedly on his long-stemmed pipe and watched Emmy nurse their infant daughter by the roaring fire, those moose reminded him of the problem again. "We'll give the Jews a forest of their own," he cruelly jested when Goebbels asked in November for an ordinance banning Jews from public parks, "and [Undersecretary] Alpers will see to it that all the animals that look like Jews—the moose has that same hook nose—are put in there and allowed to apply for naturalization."

Nobody wanted Europe's Jews. When Jews who had emigrated from Poland began to flood back there in alarm, their own Warsaw government passed a law designed to keep them out. A furious Polish Jew stormed the German embassy in Paris and pumped bullets into the ambassador's deputy, an impulsive action that was the beginning of the Jews' long journey into darkness, because a vengeful speech by Goebbels triggered a pogrom throughout Germany and Austria—a dusk of agonizing screams, of arson, and of shattered shop windows that would go down in history as "Crystal Night."

Unquestionably, Göring approved of punishing the whole Jewish community in some way for the diplomat's murder. "The swine will think twice," he said, "before they inflict a second murder on us." But the unthinking and needlessly destructive mode of revenge that Goebbels had selected outraged him. As his limousine made its way through the shards in Berlin the next morning, November 10, he got fighting mad and called a terse meeting of the Nazi party leaders at the Air Ministry Building. Walther Darré heard Göring call the pogrom "a bloody outrage." The field marshal lectured them all on their "lack of discipline." He reserved his most pained language for Dr. Joseph Goebbels. "I buy most of my works of art from Jewish dealers," he cried.

Goebbels rushed yelping to the Führer's lunch table but found little sympathy. Hitler had spent the night in Munich issuing orders to stop the outrages and sending out his adjutants to protect Jewish businesses like Bernheimer's, the antique dealers. Himmler was also furious with Goebbels for having made free with the local SS units to stage the pogrom. Over at the Chancellery that afternoon, November 10, Göring waded into Goebbels. "This is going to cost us a bloody fortune abroad," he shouted, "and I'm the one who's got to earn it all!"

Hitler did not take sides but expressed concern to Göring over the undisciplined approach to "the Jewish problem" and ordered him to draw up stringent laws immediately. Later that day he telephoned Göring to make the point: "All the key measures must be in one central hand." Lest he be misunderstood, he instructed Bormann to send Göring a letter emphasizing that the Führer wanted a uniform attack on the whole problem.

On Hitler's instructions, Göring called a Cabinet-level conference on November 12. "I am sick and tired of these demonstrations," he bellowed. "They don't harm the Jews but they do end up hurting me, because I am the one who has to hold the economy together."

Most of Crystal Night's appalling results were now in. Nazi-directed mobs had wrecked seventy-five hundred Jewish stores and a hundred synagogues, often setting fire to neighboring non-Jewish property. A single Berlin jeweler's like Margraf's had been looted of 1,700,000 Reichsmarks ($375,000) of stock. The total loss—provisionally assessed at 25 million Reichsmarks ($5.6 million)—would fall squarely on the (non-Jewish) German insurance market. Meanwhile the government would lose all tax revenue from the seventy-five hundred wrecked stores. It was a massive "own goal" that Goebbels, the Nazi "minister for public enlightenment," had scored. "It seems," snapped Göring at the conference, "that our own public could do with some enlightenment!"

The chief of the Insurance Companies' Association, Eduard Hilgard, assessed the glass damage alone at 6 million Reichsmarks. He confirmed that the major loss would fall on non-Jews, since the Jewish businessmen mainly just rented their stores.

> GÖRING: "That's just what we were saying."
> GOEBBELS: "Then the Jew must pay for the damage."
> GÖRING: "That's not the point. We haven't got the raw materials. It's all foreign plate glass [a Belgian monopoly], and it's going to cost a fortune in hard currency! It's enough to drive you up the wall!"

While Göring had some expectation of picking up foreign currency if the German insurers had reinsured abroad, his hope that they might even refuse to pay out on claims submitted by Jews was frustrated.

> HILGARD: "If we refuse to honor clear and binding obligations, it would be a blot on the honor of the German insurance market."
> GÖRING: "But not if I intervene with a statutory order!"
> HILGARD: "I was about to come to that."
> HEYDRICH: "You could cough up on the insurance all right, and then we could confiscate it at the point of payout. That way you save face."

Hilgard was still uneasy and thought that would "not be a good thing" in the long run.

"I beg your pardon!" exclaimed Göring. "If you're legally obliged to pay out six millions and all at once an angel descends from on high, in the form of my somewhat corpulent self, and tells you that you're let off paying a million of that—the hell you can't say it's a good thing!"

The verbatim record of this discussion provides an unsavory picture of Hermann Göring. Told that even the looted merchandise was often German-owned and sold by the Jews only on a commission basis, Göring wailed, "I wish you'd done in two hundred Jews and not destroyed such assets."

"Thirty-five," corrected Reinhard Heydrich, the ice-cool head of the Gestapo. "It's thirty-five dead."

The upshot was two laws, co-signed by Göring, purporting to eliminate Jews from the economy and to levy a collective fine on the Jewish community of one billion Reichsmarks for the diplomat's murder. There is little doubt that Hitler and Göring had jointly hit on this cynical idea as one way of bridging Germany's growing currency deficit. As Göring frankly explained at a meeting of the Reich Defense Council on November 18, 1938, this penalty and the sale of Jewish businesses provided an "interim remedy" for the budgetary shortfall.

There remained some loose ends after the pogrom. He signed a fistful of decrees over the coming weeks providing the legal framework that Hitler had been demanding for an orderly, regularized solution of "the Jewish problem."

Undoubtedly his purpose was to prevent any recurrence of such pogroms. In his eyes Heydrich was the real villain, after Goebbels. "The rest of them," his sister Ilse Göring told a friend, quoting Hermann, "are tolerable. Himmler himself is quite unimportant and basically harmless."

Heydrich had a clever legal mind and had thought the whole "Jewish problem" logically through. "The problem [is]," he had explained at the November 12 meeting, "not how to get the rich Jews out but the Jewish mob." He foresaw a ten-year plague of rootless, unemployed Jews in the Reich and demanded that they wear distinguishing badges.

"My dear Heydrich," said Göring, "you're not going to get anywhere without the large-scale erection of ghettos in the cities."

In some instances he moderated the anti-Jewish ordinances. At the end of November he ordered the release of any World War I combat veterans found among the twenty thousand Jews detained during the "reprisal action" after the diplomat's murder. To avoid excesses, in mid-December 1938 he issued a circular stating, "To ensure uniformity in dealing with the Jewish problem, which is of vital concern for our overall economic interests, I request that all regulations and other important directives bearing upon it be submitted to me for sanction before being issued."

Irritated by the continuing arbitrary actions by officials against Jews, he secured clear guidelines from Hitler later that month. "I have sought the Führer's pleasure on these matters," Göring announced, "and in the future this, his will, is to be considered the sole guiding principle." In the future, no Jews were to be deprived of protected tenancies (that is, tenancies from which they could not legally be evicted); Hitler merely suggested that they be brought under one roof. The expropriation of Jewish-owned housing was to be halted. "Most pressing," defined Göring, "is the Aryanization of factories and businesses, agricultural real estate and forests." While Jews were no longer to use railroad sleeping cars or dining cars, a petty discrimination for which Goebbels had agitated in November, Göring ruled out the introduction of "Jews Only" compartments or any total ban on using public transport. Finally he said, Hitler had ordained that Jewish civil servants would not forfeit their pensions.

In one respect Hitler, Göring, Ribbentrop, and Himmler all saw eye to eye. All three saw Jewish emigration—to Tanganyika, to Madagascar, or to Palestine, as the only realistic solution. On January 24, 1939, Göring set up within the Ministry of the Interior a Central Reich Office for Jewish Emigration, and ordered Heydrich to organize a suitable Jewish agency to process applications, raise funds for the poorer Jews, and agree on destinations. Göring insisted on being kept informed. "My decision," he ruled, "is to be obtained before taking any fundamental actions."

With Göring's inauguration of this central office, the expulsion of Jews from the German-controlled area of Europe gained momentum. Two thirds thus escaped before the war obliged Heinrich Müller, of the Gestapo, to order a halt on October 23, 1939: Three hundred thousand Jews had left Germany, 130,000 Austria, and 30,000 Bohemia and Moravia; seventy thousand of these had found their way to Palestine.

Emigration was only one possibility that Göring foresaw. "The second is as follows," he said in November 1938, selecting his words with uncharacteristic care. "If at any foreseeable time in the future the German Reich finds itself in a foreign political conflict, then it is self-evident that we in Germany will address ourselves first and foremost to effecting a grand settling of scores against the Jews."

20
LOSING WEIGHT

When he turned forty-six on January 12, 1939, the gift that would please him the most was a scale model of the sprawling Hermann Göring Works. He was not interested in war—he wanted to exploit the economic potential of southeastern Europe. Politically he was increasingly at odds with Hitler. As he heard the Führer unveil his plans for world domination in a series of secret speeches that January and February 1939, he would feel the gulf between them growing wider. In the coming year Göring would repeatedly appear on the side of the moderates. But he was cautious even then, not wanting to forfeit his hard-earned status as Hitler's principal lieutenant.

Little was left of their earlier intimacy. Leaving Germany for San Francisco in February 1939, Hitler's adjutant Fritz Wiedemann would reflect that in recent months he had seen Goebbels, Hess, Bormann, and other Nazi notables among the late-night guests at Hitler's table, "but rarely Göring."

From the field marshal's diary it is evident, however, that he continued to have "his pudgy fingers in every pie," as his later prosecutors at Nuremberg would put it.

Considering his later reputation for indolence, his 1938 diary entries are often of a surprising intricacy and length. October 3, three days after the sellout of Czechoslovakia by the great powers at Munich, both the Czech and French diplomats were beating a path to his door, anxious to mend the fences damaged during the crisis:

> Ambassador [André] François-Poncet, October 3. Comes directly from Paris, where he had long talks with [Prime Minister] Daladier and [Foreign Minister] Bonnet. Powerful inclination there to arrange a deal with Germany in a new and lasting way. Daladier has great confidence in the Führer. Swing of opinion among French public, but the left-wing parties are intriguing against Daladier, etc. [Wants] entente [with Germany] similar to that with Britain: no war, consultations first! That would be decisive.
> This would strengthen Daladier's hand and he would be able after elections to get rid of the "People's Front" and [French] alliance with Moscow.
> Strike while the iron's hot!

Thus read Göring's diary entry for that day. The Frenchman assured him that the Paris-Prague alliance was finished. French public opinion, he said, even showed a wide understanding now for Germany's colonial aspirations.

> Never [said François-Poncet, according to Göring's diary] was public opinion in Europe so disposed to turn over a new leaf. Germany has now definitely established herself as a Continental power of the first rank. Only the left-wing parties do not want to recognize this.

Later that day, at Henderson's request, Göring received the cringing, frightened Czech minister, Vojtěch Mastný, in Berlin:

> Mastný, October 3. Very downcast. Says he was not listened to . . . that Beneš [was] completely besotted with the League of Nations, et cetera. A rude awakening for the *Tschechei* to realization that everything possible must be tried to set things right and agree [on] a common policy with us. Beneš will resign . . . [Dr. Emil] Hácha, who was always in favor of a compromise with us, is the coming man. . . .

On the seventh and eighth, Göring toured the "captured" Czech frontier fortifications. He had no military interest in the rest of the country (*Tschechei*), and tried to persuade Hitler that its economy was so dependent now on Germany's that it would fall into their hands like a ripe fruit. Prague recognized this harsh truth and sent its envoy Mastný back to assure Göring that they would follow Hitler's policies slavishly at home and abroad. In particular, they promised, they would "seriously tackle the Jewish problem." Göring once again scrawled a lengthy note in his diary:

> Minister Mastný, October 11. [Offers] most emphatic assurance that the new *Tschechei* will realign her foreign policies; closest friendship with Germany. Assurance that internally the coming regime will lean to the extreme right. Liquidation of communism. Fate and life of *Tschechei* are in Germany's hands. He pleads that the country not be reduced to penury . . . Nation realizes that a 180-degree about-face is necessary. It is only possible, however, with Germany's help.

Göring was in the dark as to Hitler's next moves. It is plain that he did not expect a general war until 1942 at the earliest. Meanwhile he tried to exploit the post-Munich turmoil in southeastern Europe. Göring's diary shows him in furtive conferences with Czech, Slovak, Romanian, and other politicians. His own strategy was directed at establishing a German empire in the east with Poland's help after Germany had first subverted the rest of the now-hyphenated Czecho-Slovakia, Romania, and the Ukraine by economic warfare and covert means. Göring was the inspiration behind this "Grand Solution," as Ribbentrop revealed to the Swiss Professor Burckhardt (on December 17); if Poland would agree to this imperialist design, she would be promised new territories in the east to compensate for returning the former German territories around Posnan and Thorn to the Reich. "The Führer," Ribbentrop explained confidentially, "is inclined to favor this solution, but he hasn't finally made up his mind." The subversive operations that Göring was envisaging in the east are alluded to in a diary entry of October 13, after a discussion with Arthur Rosenberg, the party's chief intellectual. "Confidential office in Berlin for refugees from all parts of Russia," this stated, in part. "All German government departments agree, but Rosenberg is against it. The suggestion comes from the high command (OKW)."

Four days later the same diary showed the field marshal in secret cabal with separatist politicians from Slovakia. "One of them looked like a Gypsy," he recalled in 1946, trying to play down the significance of the meeting. The Nazis intended to use Slovak separatism rather as a road builder uses a stick of dynamite to crumble a rock barring his path. "A Tschechei without Slovakia is even more at our tender mercies," he wrote in an official note on this meeting. And, with his Grand Solution at the forefront of his thoughts, he added, "Very important to get air bases in Slovakia for our air force to operate against the east." The internal politics of Slovakia were hopelessly entangled, as his diary shows: The Slovaks warned him that their Jewish citizens were hoping that Hungary would annex parts of their country. Göring assured the Slovak visitors that throwing in their lot with Germany was the only sure way of keeping the Hungarians at bay.

Still tinkering with his Grand Solution, on October 21 he invited the Polish ambassador out to Carinhall. His diary shows that he again hinted at a deal with Poland. Józef Lipski, who confirmed the date from his own diary, was later astonished to hear that Göring had kept such a detailed record.

> Lipski, October 21. Discussion of Poland's intentions. [We must] maintain contact, avoid misunderstandings. Obstacle is the Carpatho-Ukraine [the eastern tip of Czecho-Slovakia, bordering on Poland, Romania, and Hungary]. Poland interested but not as a territorial matter. Poland is afraid that Communist troubles might take root there. The region inclines toward Hungary. Should be a bridge for settlement of the Greater Ukraine issue. There was and is a Communist center established there for subverting the Balkans and Poland. Such a hotbed of Ukrainian intransigence is very disturbing for Poland; it might exacerbate the Ukrainian problem in Poland. Poland's wish is therefore that this region go to Hungary, so that it can be brought under control.

It is worth quoting such diary entries if only because they show both the extraordinary complexities induced by Europe's ill-fitting frontiers in the winter of 1938/39 and the far-flung interests of Field Marshal Göring. "I protested," he records on one page, "about the treatment of Germans in Poland [and insisted on a] strict warning from Warsaw that Germans are to be well treated." And on another page he shows his economic interest in the German film industry as an export earner. "Great shortfall in Italy," he writes. "Political considerations there, as Italian film industry would otherwise collapse. It's costing us foreign currency. . . . Losses in France through joint film venture. . . . Poland—nothing doing. Yugoslavia refusal. . . . Balkans must be conquered. In the north we are definitely catching up."

Simultaneously with the consolidation of Germany's political gains after Munich, the diary shows Göring acting to force the pace of rearmament. On October 14, he summoned arms industrialists to the Air Ministry. "The Führer," he revealed to them, "has directed me to execute a gigantic program beside which all our achievements hitherto pale into insignificance." Specifically, Hitler had ordered an immediate fivefold increase in the air force. Discussing priorities with the OKW's General Keitel at Carinhall six days later, Göring said that food supplies must come first, followed by exports —but then, "Major expansion of air force for attack, including reserves."

The target now under discussion was Britain, and Milch's own notes for October 26 portray Göring discussing with Udet and him a bizarre plan to set up a private air-force navy under Kessler, officially to be designated "commander of security ships." It would operate fast patrol boats of upward of one thousand tons armed with flak guns and torpedo tubes, capable of circling two or three times around the British Isles and, in Göring's words, "faster than any warship."

On Hitler's instructions he had revived the old Reich Defense Council, a body consisting of every minister and Staatssekretär plus Bormann, Heydrich, the commanders in chief, and their chiefs of staff. Chairing its first session at the Air Ministry on November 18, Göring delivered a three-hour opening address on the need to triple Germany's overall arms level, and on the attendant problems: lack of production capacity, manpower, and foreign currency.

As the new year, 1939, began, Göring was noticeably unwell. By January his normally cherubic features were gaunt and drawn, and on the doctors' advice he was trying to lose weight.

By the time that Sir Nevile Henderson saw him on February 18, he had shed forty pounds and hoped to reduce even more.

Something of the old Hermann Göring still remained, however, because when Henderson told him of his new G.C.M.G. (Grand Cross of the Order of St. Michael and St. George), tears of envy came into the field marshal's eyes; indeed, as Henderson dwelt innocently upon the tantalizing details of the splendid ermine-lined robes and insignia, Göring murmured in response, "Such orders are never bestowed on foreigners—are they?"

This powerful awe of the British and their empire led Göring into conflict with Foreign Minister Joachim von Ribbentrop. Göring had persistently meddled in foreign diplomacy. Between Göring and Ribbentrop's predecessor, the sedate and gentlemanly Baron von Neurath, there had been a profound mutual respect: Neurath had indulged Göring's flights of diplomatic activity—but not Ribbentrop. Now Göring had to rely on the Forschungsamt's Brown Pages to find out what Ribbentrop was up to. Forgetting that he himself had greeted the pope in 1933 with the Nazi salute, he told Hitler that Ribbentrop had done the same with King Edward VIII when presenting his credentials in 1936. "*Mein Führer*," he persisted, when Hitler seemed undismayed, "suppose Moscow sent a goodwill ambassador to you and he came and greeted you with"—and he raised his clenched fist in salute—"Long live the Communist revolution!"

"I understand," remarked Nevile Henderson, jousting playfully, on February 18, "that Ribbentrop has now gathered all the threads of foreign policy into his own hands."

Göring rewarded him with a scowl. "There are certain countries such as Poland and Yugoslavia," he insisted, "which remain my preserve. Besides, the foreign minister has instructions from the Führer to keep me informed at all times."

The two men, now firm friends, reverted to the old theme of the "warmongers" in London and Berlin. Henderson agreed that "the intelligentsia and London opinion" wanted a preventive war against Nazi Germany. Göring retorted wearily that nobody in Berlin except for a few fools wanted war of any kind. "Tyrants who go against the will of the people," he boomed, "come to a sticky end."

Surprising the ambassador, he revealed that he had decided to leave Germany in March for a long rest. "People can make what mistakes they like while I am away—I shall not care."

For a few more days he fulfilled engagements in Berlin. On February 24, looking already substantially slimmer than at Munich, he granted an interview to four British financial experts at his villa. They sat in a line in enormous chairs in front of a high writing desk on a dais, behind which sat the field marshal at some distance. "It was not," reported one of them to Whitehall, "an easy position for a friendly chat." Challenged about the war rumors flooding foreign newspapers, Göring dismissed them as nonsense. "I have never seen any memorandum, plan, or proposal about this so-called Ukraine business," he said. "It simply does not figure in our calculations."

His imagination was already on the sunlit shores of the Mediterranean. He took leave of Hitler later that day, reviewed an Air Force Day parade on March 1, then left with Emmy for the tiny Italian principality of San Remo. He took "Pili" Körner and his "court biographer," Erich Gritzbach, with him. For a few days he lazed around, soaking up sunshine and sea air. Photographers snapped the Görings buying violets like a happy honeymoon couple, but the idyll did not last.

Late on the tenth his chief intelligence officer, Colonel Beppo Schmid, arrived from Berlin with a sealed envelope.* Göring tore it open and sat down heavily. "Something's up in Berlin," he exclaimed. "No sooner do I leave than something goes awry. I've got to hurry back and straighten things out."

At this the colonel revealed that the Führer had dictated an oral postscript—on no account was Göring to leave San Remo before German troops entered Czechoslovakia, so as not to arouse worldwide suspicions.

Göring choked on this. He knew that Hitler's only purpose was to prevent the "old woman" from interfering again.

He sent Schmid back to Berlin with a letter begging Hitler not to invade Czechoslovakia. Fretting, he then decided to ignore Hitler's prohibition, told Emmy to leave everything unpacked at the hotel, and set out by slow train northward to Berlin. Milch met him at the station late on March 14—with word that it was too late: Keitel had already reported the Wehrmacht ready to invade Czechoslovakia at 6:00 A.M. The good news, however, was that once more the British government was just shrugging its shoulders. For-

---

*A similar message had gone to General Milch, vacationing in Switzerland: "The Czecho-Slovak state is breaking up. Wehrmacht intervention may become necessary within the next few days."

schungsamt intercept N112,097 showed Chamberlain instructing Ambassador Henderson that His Majesty's government had "no desire to interfere unnecessarily in matters with which other governments may be more directly involved."

Göring swallowed his distaste and abetted Hitler's plan. The elderly Czech president Hácha arrived in Berlin that night. In the early-hours conference, at which Hitler demanded absolute Czech submission to his will, it was Göring who threatened the frail president, declaring that his bombers would appear over the streets of Prague at dawn otherwise. "The bombs," he added menacingly, "will serve as a salutary warning to Britain and France too." Hácha signed on the dotted line at 4:00 A.M. This was fortunate for Göring, as the 7th Airborne Division selected for the actual invasion was grounded by snow at Schönwalde Air Base. With Göring looming over him like a bronzed Zeppelin in air-force uniform, Hácha crumpled and shouted the requisite orders over the phone to Prague, instructing his troops not to open fire on the Germans.

The invasion operation began at 6:00 A.M. While Hitler drove in person into Prague, Field Marshal Göring stayed in Berlin, once again acting as head of state. He phoned the Hungarian ambassador about rumors that the Hungarians were about to march into Slovakia; he promised that if the Poles put as much as one foot over the Czech frontier, Germany would evict them; he listened sympathetically when the Polish ambassador complained about Ribbentrop's inaccessibility at this vital hour; he fielded the British ambassador's belated outrage over Hitler's action and professed well-feigned surprise that Britain should get worked up over "such a trifle." When Hitler returned, Göring took the entire Reich Cabinet to the station to welcome him.

He did not alter his private opinion that the invasion had been unnecessary and a mistake. On November 28, he had directed General Udet to buy up all the machine tools that he could from Prague, and added the recommendation that the Reich buy shares in Czech factories—so he had evidently had no inkling then of Hitler's move. Now he told Udet to go into Czechoslovakia, inspect their industry, and take what he needed. That done, he left Berlin as suddenly as he had arrived, at midday on March 21. He took the train back to San Remo on the Italian Riviera. "You will stay behind," he told General Milch, "as my 'Lookout Number One.' "

The Nazi occupation of Czechoslovakia would provide Hitler with the industrial capacity and gold that he needed for his final armament effort. The Czech industrialists and businessmen were eager to deal with their new masters. The Hermann Göring Works would buy control of the big arms firms like Škoda, Brno Weapons, Poldi Ironworks, and Witkowitz Steel. (Göring would install his brother Albert, the "black sheep," as Škoda's export director.) H.G.W. would in time become the biggest industrial combine in Europe. Warning that Hermann Göring had thereby acquired sufficient clout to exercise "a great deal of influence" over the major German firms in New York, the FBI's director J. Edgar Hoover would write to President Hoover early in 1940, "[He] has enough wealth to make him very dangerous."

21
OUT OF FAVOR

After Prague, Göring was left in the dark, and he felt the humiliation deeply. Arriving back at San Remo to resume his interrupted vacation on March 22, 1939, he learned that Ribbentrop had browbeaten Lithuania into returning the little territory of Memel (population: 150,000) to the Reich. Göring telegraphed dutiful congratulations to Hitler at once.

He cabled off more congratulations on April 2, the day after Hitler launched the mighty new battleship *Tirpitz* at Wilhelmshaven. It was one of the major ceremonial events of the Nazi spring of '39, and it is noteworthy that even now Göring stayed away. On April 7, the Görings and hangers-on boarded the Hamburg-Amerika liner *Monserrat* at Naples and set out across the sparkling Mediterranean to North Africa. Multitudes of Arabs darkened the quays as they sailed into Tripoli escorted by two Italian destroyers. There were flags and placards everywhere, because Fascist officials had ordered every household in Libya to hang out the one and paste up the other.

Göring had a genuine weakness for Italo Balbo, the bearded governor-general of the colony. Invited to cruise in *Carin II* eight months earlier, Balbo had bestowed on him a star fashioned from black and white diamonds; Göring declared their friendship undying, and would cry genuine tears when the Italian was shot down by his own flak in Libya in 1940. For three days now he marveled at the ancient Roman excavations at Leptis Magna, visited more modern establishments at Homs and Misurata, and exposed acres of his famous boyish grin to Arabs and Italians. He took in a military parade at Bu Ghueran and battleships at Tripoli, then watched "desert battles" at Cascina Grassi enacted across stretches of camel thorn and desert scrub that would see grim fighting three years later. Before leaving for Italy on April 12 his party visited the "Jewish troglodytes" in their caves at Garian.

Trying to upstage Ribbentrop, he arranged to meet the Italian leaders in Rome in mid-April. Count Ciano had last glimpsed him five months earlier in Vienna, wearing an Al Capone-style suit of gray, with a cravat passed through a big ruby ring, matching rubies on his fingers, and a Nazi eagle studded with diamonds in his buttonhole. More somberly attired now, Göring delivered a restrained speech in Rome promising that the Italian and German peoples would march shoulder by shoulder in their common struggle. Meeting Mussolini on the fifteenth, he lied blandly in the same cause of improving relations with Italy, assuring the Duce that Hitler had telephoned instructions to express his "extraordinary pleasure" at the recent Italian invasion of Albania (in fact, Hitler was furious). He himself, Göring pointed out, had been at San Remo when the decision was taken to invade Czechoslovakia —but Hitler had of course kept him "fully informed," another lie. Confidentially discussing with the Italian dictator Germany's preparedness for war, Göring explained that his air force's re-equipping with the Junkers 88 bomber was not yet complete, but Britain's own position in the air was unlikely to improve before 1942. Meanwhile he hoped to persuade Britain to reverse her anti-German policies.

After Rome the Görings returned to Germany. Hitler would soon be fifty, and Hermann did not want to miss the spectacular birthday parade. His train arrived back in Berlin at 6:00 P.M. on April 18. Press photographers snapped him striding along the platform looking brown and fit, in a light summer coat and soft felt hat, and jauntily swinging a gold-knobbed walking cane.

A real shock awaited Göring at dinner with Hitler that evening. Hitler told him that he intended to recover the free city of Danzig by military action if Poland refused to come to terms. (The ancient German city had been placed under a German-Polish condominium after the war.) It was the first that Göring had heard of Hitler's April 1 directive to prepare *Case White*, covering a possible war with Poland. The secrecy was Ribbentrop's revenge: Göring had not bothered to inform him of his "state visit" to Rome—indeed, he had blandly ignored the queries that Ribbentrop had telegraphed to Libya.

The news about Danzig flabbergasted Göring. Poland was his preserve. "What am I to understand by this?" he gasped.

"I prepared the other situations skillfully," was Hitler's measured retort. "This one will be no different."

Word of this rebuff reached the British ambassador. Henderson learned that the field marshal had returned from Italy with "counsels of moderation" but that Hitler had scolded him about being so *weibisch*, such an "old woman."

Europe seemed to be heading for another war. At 10:00 A.M. on the morning of his fiftieth birthday, April 20, Hitler called his commanders in chief into his study and sobered them with a brief, blunt discourse on the need to seize the initiative. His first half-century, he said, was now over. "I am at the summit of my powers," he added, without emotion. "So I have decided to strike now, while we still possess the arms lead that we do." As the Reich capital shook to the thud and blare of the five-hour military parade that day, Göring decided not to stay in Berlin one day longer than necessary. Göring's aide Karl Bodenschatz hinted to the French air attaché that Göring's health was "beyond repair" and that Ribbentrop had completely eclipsed him.

For two more weeks Göring performed official functions, such as laying a wreath on Baron von Richthofen's tomb on April 21. On the twenty-fifth he instructed Milch to take up the staff talks with Italy and was briefed by his new chief of air staff, the young Colonel Jeschonnek, on the planning for *White*. Then, on May 3, 1939, he absconded to San Remo yet again.

Göring's esteem was at its lowest ebb. A few days later he suffered his most humiliating reverse and again saw Ribbentrop as being behind it. He had instructed his Four-Year Plan agent in Spain, Johannes Bernhard, to arrange a meeting between Göring and the now-victorious General Franco but had forbidden him to notify the German ambassador about it, citing its "military character." Initially Franco agreed to the meeting, but then postponed it for "political reasons." Göring declared that he would come anyway, and days of excruciating haggling began. Ribbentrop, alerted by the ever-garrulous Bodenschatz on May 1, instructed his ambassador to intervene. Franco still refused, but on May 9, Göring received a telegram notifying him that the new dictator had after all agreed to see him at Saragossa. Göring objected to the location. He demanded that Franco meet him near Valencia, boarded the Hamburg-Amerika liner *Huascaran* on the tenth, and weighed anchor for Valencia escorted by four destroyers, with the intention of proceeding thus to Hamburg after the meeting.

The little armada dropped anchor off Castellón to news that Franco adamantly refused to come to Valencia. Hitler signaled, forbidding Göring to go ashore. Thwarted and outraged, the field marshal stalked the liner's decks, as Beppo Schmid later testified, using the obvious and by now much-overworked simile, "snarling like a caged lion."

Suspecting that Ribbentrop was behind this humiliation, Göring ordered the liner's course reversed to Livorno, Italy, and charged back overland to Berlin. Here, he was handed a stinging six-page rebuke dictated by the foreign minister on May 16, expressing "profound concern" at Göring's unauthorized "state visit" to Rome and his appalling Spanish diplomatic fiasco.

"Doing things in this way," Ribbentrop lectured, "only serves to create in foreign minds an impression of disorder and disunity in German government agencies."

Göring seethed and sought out Alfred Rosenberg.

"Ribbentrop has made only one friend here," complained Göring, referring to Hitler himself, "otherwise nothing but enemies. He writes me smart-ass letters expressing his 'profound concern.' I've a good mind to show them to the Führer." (In fact, Ribbentrop had already taken that precaution himself.)

"As thick as two planks," agreed Rosenberg. "But with all the arrogance to get his own way."

"He sure took us in with his 'contacts,' " Göring groused. "When we got a closer look at his French counts and British lords they all turned out to have made their fortunes in champagne, whiskey, and cognac. And now this idiot thinks he's got to act the Iron Chancellor everywhere." He mused for a while, then added, "The one good thing is that fools like him destroy themselves in the long run anyway."

On May 21, 1939, the Italian foreign minister Count Ciano arrived in Berlin to sign a military alliance. Göring had not been consulted, but Ribbentrop invited him to stand behind him as photographers filmed the signing ceremony.

"Do you think I'm crazy?" snapped Göring. "I don't even know what is being signed."

"Just imagine," he recalled, still fuming, in November 1945, when it no longer really mattered. "With the newsreels and all that he wanted me— the second man in the Reich—to stand approvingly behind him. The gall of the man! I told him that if I did pose for them, I would sit down and he could stand behind me!"

His humiliation was complete when he saw the fabulous decoration that he coveted, the diamond-studded Collar of the Annunziata, bestowed at the Italian embassy upon his smirking rival. He took it as a deliberate slight and raised hell at every level up to the king of Italy, being mollified only by the award, twelve months later, of the identical Collar in consolation.

Still sulking, he ducked out of official appointments in Berlin. He appeared in full uniform at the formal opening of the Air Defense Academy at Wannsee on the morning of May 23 but sent his deputy General Milch to attend an important secret address by Hitler in the Reich Chancellery that afternoon. "From four to eight-thirty P.M.," wrote Milch in his diary, "Führer [talks to] commanders in chief, great plans. I stand in for Göring, fetched at last moment by Bodenschatz." Hitler's chief adjutant Rudolf Schmundt later compiled a record suggesting that Göring was present; he was not, but learning of Hitler's address he redoubled his efforts that summer to head off the coming war.

British intervention was more than likely—that he knew. Germany's offer of friendship to the British Empire had been deliberately ignored. To Sir Nevile Henderson on May 27, 1939, Göring spoke with tears in his injured eyes about the silence with which Britain's press and Parliament had blanketed this offer. By his reply, the ambassador showed that the two countries had drifted helplessly apart since Hitler's invasion of Czechoslovakia: His Majesty's government, he intoned, would not shrink from declaring war if Germany once more resorted to force.

At Carinhall later that day Göring showed him colored sketches of some tapestries that he was buying from William Randolph Hearst, the American newspaper magnate. The tapestries portrayed a bevy of toothsome ladies identified by names like Mercy and Purity. "I can't see one called Patience," Henderson dryly observed.

Göring had no more authority than a circus ringmaster that summer—a master of ceremonies. When the slim, slightly built Prince Paul of Yugoslavia paid his first state visit to Berlin early in June, Hitler permitted the field marshal to stage a thundering air display across the city's rooftops and to entertain the royal couple at Carinhall, but it was clear to Henderson, who was among the invited guests, that Göring no longer had the special responsibility for Yugoslavia (and Poland) about which he had bragged four months before.

"I wish I could see how to put a stop to the present situation," Henderson ventured to Göring. "It's getting very dangerous. We British don't want war. You may think we do, but we don't. But we shall certainly go to war if you attack the Poles." He added, "If Herr Hitler could now give us an indication that he's prepared to abandon the policy of coups and aggression, Mr. Chamberlain might give a not-unfriendly reply."

Göring shrugged. He spelled out once more Germany's "final demands," and reminded Henderson that there existed an influential clique in London who wanted "war at any price."

While not denying it, Henderson countered with Ribbentrop's name.

"People can say what they like," replied Göring, thrown onto the defensive. "But when a decision is called for, none of us counts for more than the gravel on which we are standing. It is the Führer alone who makes the decisions."

Henderson climbed into his limousine.

"Do you think that I want war?" appealed Göring, waving a hand toward the luxuries of Carinhall. "I was against war last September, as you know. And I would be again."

His influence on foreign affairs was diminishing each day. Foreign Minister von Ribbentrop boasted to the Italian ambassador in June 1939 that he had buried the hatchet with Göring—on condition that the latter stopped meddling in diplomacy. Göring kept a baleful eye on him nonetheless through the wiretaps on foreign embassies, and he opened private lines of communication to Prime Minister Chamberlain.

* * *

Many European businessmen shared his uneasiness, among them Axel Wenner-Gren, the fifty-eight-year-old millionaire boss of the Swedish Electrolux corporation. Eric von Rosen had introduced him to Göring at Nuremberg in September 1936; during a friendly conversation the general had made a better impression than the Swedish visitor expected, although Göring expressed some resentment at the anti-Nazi temper of the Swedish newspapers. On May 9, 1939, Frederick Szarvasy, president of the Anglo-Federal Banking Corporation in London, told Wenner-Gren of recent remarks by Field Marshal Göring that he had felt compelled to convey to Neville Chamberlain; the banker had suggested that the Swede should visit Göring again to ascertain if there could even now be a basis for agreement between Britain and Germany.

Wenner-Gren had turned up at Carinhall on May 25. Göring began their three-hour talk by boasting of Germany's advances since 1936. The Swede responded, "What a pity that such progress only seems to lead to war—which might well end in a new German catastrophe!"

"We don't want war," retorted Göring. "Only the warmongers in London are pushing toward that. If I could sit down and talk matters over alone with Chamberlain, I feel sure a basis could be found for an understanding." Unlike Ribbentrop, Goebbels, and Himmler, he added, he wanted peace with Britain; he spoke of a twenty-five-year peace treaty with Britain. The snag was that he insisted that the world first satisfy Hitler's "final territorial demands."

The Swede asked if he might tell all this to the British government.

Göring looked at him for a moment, then said, "Well, if I were sure that the British Foreign Office was not to be involved, it might be worthwhile for you to see Mr. Chamberlain."

In London, Wenner-Gren spoke with top Conservative party officials like David Margesson and with the prime minister himself on June 6. Chamberlain pointed out that Göring's plan involved "all *give* on our side and all *take* on his." Moreover, the guarantees that he offered were no different from those that Hitler had so recently been breaking. "If," Mr. Chamberlain continued, "I were to propose even discussing the colonial question with Herr Hitler in the present atmosphere, I should be swept out of office without a month's delay." He invited Wenner-Gren to repeat all this to Göring. "I take him," he added, "to be a man with whom one can speak frankly."

By the ninth, Wenner-Gren had reported back to Göring in person; in a letter to Margesson on June 10, he described how he had pointed out that "under prevailing conditions a discussion [with Chamberlain] could not lead to results but that Mr. Chamberlain would gladly consent to an exchange of views in regard to all of the vital questions when more time had passed after the Czecho-Slovakian occupation, or at any time if Germany would be able to show in a drastic and convincing way her desire and real will to an understanding."

The Nazis, Wenner-Gren advised Göring, must do something "really
dramatic" to restore Britain's faith in them. "A mere discussion," he warned,
"would be fruitless."

Back in Stockholm, Wenner-Gren drew up a seventeen-page letter to
Göring outlining a peace program based on a twenty-year peace treaty. This
document reiterated that only deeds could prove that the Nazis had turned
over a new leaf. They should call their next party rally a "rally for peace,"
they should end racial persecution, release both the former Austrian chancellor Schuschnigg and Pastor Niemöller from the concentration camps, and
close all those camps down.

Göring acknowledged this by telegram on July 1:

I confirm with thanks the receipt of your highly interesting letter.
Will study the matter. Sincerely, Göring.

He read Wenner-Gren's proposals closely and did not relish them at all.

Göring reluctantly began forward planning. On June 21, he inquired of
General Udet, "Can the Volkswagen plant turn out warplane engines if
hostilities eventuate?" Two days later, chairing the second session of the
Reich Defense Council, he directed the attention of this "key Reich body"
to the current bottlenecks of coal output, transportation, and manpower. "The
German transport system," he warned them, "is not ready for war. You
cannot regard our three operations during 1938 and 1939 as real mobiliza-
tions." He instructed them to improve the transport system now, in case of
"an unexpected call, at short notice" for a military confrontation.

Battling to restore his own esteem in Hitler's eyes, he conferred on June
27 with Udet about plans for a spectacular display of top-secret Luftwaffe
equipment at Rechlin research station. "Show everything achieved up to
now," he jotted down in his diary after the conference with Udet: "Charts
displaying industry's expansion, 1,000 fighters, 1,000 bombers."

The glittering display of ultramodern Luftwaffe weaponry was staged on
July 3. It was to prove the origin of many wrong conclusions drawn by Hitler
about his air force's lead in both quantity and quality. The aircraft and guns
he was shown were the most advanced in the world, but still a long way
from mass production. Göring showed Hitler the rocket-propelled Heinkel
176 fighter, an experimental plane with an astonishing rate of climb, first
test-flown at Peenemünde only a few days earlier. Ernst Heinkel had also
brought along his He 178, the world's first jet-propelled fighter. "Field
marshal," test pilot Erich Warsitz disclaimed, "in a few years you won't
see many propeller-driven planes in the skies!"

"An optimist!" roared Göring to Udet, and ordered a twenty-thousand-
mark bonus paid to the pilot. "From the *Sonderfonds*," he added. "You
know, the special fund."

The Rechlin display was something Göring would never forget. "Once," he would recall four years later, "before the war, at Rechlin, they put on such a demonstration for me that I can only say this now: What bunglers our finest magicians are in comparison! We're still waiting for the things they conjured up there before my very eyes—and worse still, the Führer's."

The evidence is that in July 1939 Göring was hoping there would be no war. He opened up another direct channel to London, using his economist Helmuth Wohlthat this time to establish contact with Neville Chamberlain's men.

Wohlthat had conducted talks in London early in June about the Czech gold deposits there and the financing of Jewish immigration. On June 6, as Wenner-Gren was seeing Chamberlain, Wohlthat was putting to Sir Horace Wilson and Sir Joseph Ball (both close secret advisers of Chamberlain) his ideas for economic cooperation based on Britain recognizing Germany's interest in southern and southeastern Europe.

During July, Helmuth Wohlthat, sent to London for a further clandestine meeting with Chamberlain's advisers, talked with Sir Horace Wilson. The latter, as both Wohlthat and the German ambassador recorded, dangled before the German emissary the prospect of a generous British economic-aid package in return for concessions by Hitler to peace. Two days later Robert Hudson, secretary to the Department of Overseas Trade, told Wohlthat that both Britain and America would help Hitler if he showed a willingness to disarm; Hudson breezily added that he thought Germany could have her old colonies back on trust as well, and agreed that all this might be secretly conveyed to Göring.

Wohlthat did so on July 21, but simultaneously the anti-German faction in the British Foreign Office leaked details to the press. On July 23, the *Daily Telegraph* printed a report that Britain had offered Nazi Germany a "billion pound credit" in an attempt to buy off Hitler. Göring had no option but to dismiss the Wohlthat-Hudson proposals as "utter rubbish," and did so in conversation with another Swedish businessman on July 22.

But beneath that brazen exterior and the glowing, rouged complexion, the field marshal's heart still pumped with terror at the idea of open conflict. Once that summer he growled at Joseph Goebbels, the poisonous minister of propaganda, "We haven't slaved for six years with such success, just to risk losing the lot in a war."

22
HOPING FOR ANOTHER MUNICH

F ar into the war a soft-spoken Swedish machine-tool manufacturer, Birger Dahlerus, would act as the secret, unofficial link between Göring and Neville Chamberlain. His presence in London was kept top secret, and great anguish was felt there in 1942 when it was realized that he had compiled a fifty-four-page dossier revealing how the Foreign Office had "bungled the negotiations" and even rejected what he called "a reasonable settlement" in 1939. The Dahlerus dossier virtually shifted the war guilt onto Britain and Poland; in the wrong hands, warned the Foreign Office, the file would have a "devastating effect," and it assembled rebuttal in case the Swedes ever leaked it. In October 1944 the Foreign Office decided to blackmail Dahlerus into silence by threatening to put his exports on the blockade blacklist.

The dossier began on July 5, 1939. Dahlerus had recently toured Britain's industrial midlands and met many British businessmen. Visiting Göring at Carinhall that day, he talked of the impatience of the average Englishman with Nazi Germany; some of the businessmen had urged him to get Göring to start negotiations "before the killing started." Dahlerus suggested that Göring might meet these influential Englishmen on neutral territory, to explore the possibility of summit talks between Britain and Germany.

Göring nodded. Dahlerus busily put the idea to three English company directors visiting Berlin, Messrs A. Holden, Stanley Rawson, and Charles Spencer. They welcomed the initiative, but now Göring got cold feet. When Dahlerus came out to Carinhall again on July 8, Göring merely suggested they meet again in Hamburg in two weeks' time; but he did send Dahlerus to ask fellow Swede Axel Wenner-Gren whether he would lend his luxury yacht *Southern Cross* for the conference. On July 19, he received a discouraging reply from Wenner-Gren: Mr. Chamberlain, he said, had confided to him that the revelation of any high-level secret conference might well bring down his government; in his letter Chamberlain had, however, agreed that Field Marshal Göring did appear to be out of step with Hitler.

The mere thought of this sent shudders down Göring's spine, and over the next months he seldom tired of protesting that he would "never, never" go behind Hitler's back.

For a few days he lazed along the waterways in *Carin II*, ostensibly inspecting them on behalf of the Four-Year Plan. Dahlerus did not give up. Visiting London, he obtained Foreign Office approval for the proposed informal Anglo-German meeting. Late on July 22, he came to Göring's luxury suite at the Hotel Atlantic in Hamburg and tackled the field marshal again. Although involved in costuming himself in his whitest uniform preparatory to addressing a mass rally, Göring talked to him for two hours, then agreed to meet seven selected English businessmen. He anxiously stressed that he proposed to ask Hitler's permission for the meeting.

Carin II conveyed him onward through choppy seas to the island of Sylt. At Westerland he conferred on July 25 with his generals, ordering them to crank up the newly acquired Czech factories for war production. "Now that we've got them," Körner heard him protest, "none of you *Scheisskerle* has the faintest idea of what to do with them!" Significantly, he ordered an immediate halt to warplane exports. "Germany," he said, "must now come first." By way of explanation he added, "The political situation has changed quite a lot." On the following day he underlined this by receiving Colonel Beppo Schmid for a secret intelligence report on *Blue*, Britain, which seemed a probable consequence of war against *White*, Poland. "Contrary to his usual custom," recalled Schmid afterward, "Göring listened for several hours and expressed complete agreement."

On Friday, August 4, Göring began another weekend cruise on the *Carin II*. He was still ambivalent about the prospects of war. Nervous and apprehensive, he kept asking Beppo Schmid the one question that the intelligence officer felt least qualified to answer: "What will the British *do*?"

Göring had informed only his closest colleagues—Körner, Bodenschatz, and Görnnert—about the coming top-secret meeting with the seven English businessmen. He and Dahlerus had selected the remote farmhouse belonging to the Swede's wife at Sönkenissen-Coog, on the west coast of Schleswig-Holstein in Germany's far north. On the pretext of joining Emmy and Edda at their beach house on the island of Sylt, he halted his train on August 7, 1939, at Bredstedt, the last station before the narrow rail causeway to the island. It was at Bredstedt that he was to meet Dahlerus. The local police had taken unprecedented precautions—with the inevitable result that gaping multitudes lined the station platforms, and the local newspaper *Friesenkurier* printed a vivid report of the scene in its afternoon edition. Wearing a stylish hat specially selected from his wardrobe for the occasion and smoking a Havana cigar, Göring stepped furtively out and climbed into a car with the Swede and drove off in a slow procession with his security escort through the dense crowds to the Dahlerus farmhouse nearby. A Swedish flag fluttered from its flagpole to offer a pretense of neutrality.

Dahlerus introduced the seven Englishmen to Field Marshal Göring— Brian Mountain, Sir Robert Renwick, Charles MacLaren, and T. Mensforth had come over with Holden, Spencer, and Rawson for this unique meeting. After three hours (during which he incidentally claimed that Nazi Germany would be synthesizing 12 million tons of gasoline in 1942) they all ate lunch. He proposed a toast to peace, but his visitors still left the farmhouse mildly uneasy—the impression that Spencer took away was that Göring "expected to take part in very important conferences with Herr Hitler on about August 15." How Spencer arrived at this (remarkably accurate) prediction his report, now in British Foreign Office files, does not disclose.

He was due to see Hitler on the fourteenth. On August 12, he revealed, telephoning Dahlerus, that he had instructed the Nazi press to go easy on Britain.

The days passed, and there was no response from London. He planted his bulk on the beach at Kampen and soaked up the sun, protected from the North Sea winds by a sandcastle and shielded from the less illustrious tourists by notices warning of the perils of unauthorized photography. He hoped he had not gone too far with these illicit feelers.

There was one move in this deadly game of chess that would put Poland in a hopeless position—if Stalin would agree to sign a pact with Hitler. The Soviets, like the Germans, had several unresolved issues with Poland. Ever since January, Hitler had been putting out feelers to Moscow. Göring probably knew of this, because he spoke to Beppo Schmid at San Remo in March of restoring Germany's trading relations with the Soviet Union, he had discussed the merits of such a deal when visiting Mussolini in April, and he had then begun dropping dark hints to the British and French embassies in May. "Germany and Russia," he had somewhat ominously observed to Henderson in June, "will not always remain on unfriendly terms." He had issued further such warnings that summer of 1939: "It is still open for us to negotiate with Russia," he told Dahlerus and the English businessmen on August 7. "We still have many friends in Russia."

Even so, his heart was not in this kind of political blackmail. At Carinhall five days later he commented to Lord Runciman's son Leslie on the undignified spectacle, as all the Great Powers were now pandering to Russia. He threw himself back in his chair and exclaimed, "Oh, if only my English were really good. I would come across [to Britain] and make them see these things! If there were war between us now, the real victor would be Stalin."

Stalin played into their hands. London's ponderous negotiations for their own pact with Moscow stalled and on August 12 he agreed to receive a German negotiator. Thus encouraged, two days later Hitler briefed Göring and the other two commanders in chief that he had decided to attack Poland in less than two weeks' time. Britain, he assured them, would not intervene. The next day, on August 15, he started the *White* time clock ticking, denoting the twenty-fifth as zero hour. Göring told his generals. "At eleven o'clock," noted Milch, summoned to the Obersalzberg, "G. informs us of the intention. G. is *nervös* [on edge]."

Encouraged by Göring, Ribbentrop had called Stalin, offering to visit the Kremlin himself. Time weighed heavily as Göring waited for London's reply, through Dahlerus, and Hitler waited for Moscow's. Once, on the twenty-first, Göring went to see Hitler. Together with Himmler and Brauchitsch they reviewed the tricky military "overture" to *White*—a bold strike by dive-bombers and special assault forces to seize the mile-long Dirschau Bridge across the River Vistula.

Then the phone rang again. It was Hitler, jubilant. "Stalin has agreed," he said.

Overnight Göring's edginess vanished. Now, surely, Britain would never interfere. Poland's fate was sealed. "Each time you see the Führer," he sighed to Beppo Schmid after visiting the Berghof, "you come away a new man. He's a genius!"

At noon on August 22, Hitler invited his fifty top generals and admirals to come to a "tea party"—in plain clothes. They converged on Berchtesgaden from every quarter of the Reich—fifty scar-faced, monocled gentlemen with unmistakably military comportment—and drove up the mountain lanes to the Berghof. A summer thunderstorm was rumbling slowly along the valleys, crowding out the August sun. Unpublished candid snapshots by Hitler's air-force adjutant, Nicolaus von Below, show Göring lolling near one door, his ample lower half clad in gray silk stockings and matching knickerbockers, the upper in a white blouse and sleeveless green leather hunting jerkin; his leather belt sagged under the weight of a golden dagger. "Field marshal," shouted General Erich von Manstein, no friend of such uniformed foppery, "Are you the bouncer?"

Hitler spread out a sheaf of notes on the grand piano. In his ninety-minute speech he made clear his resolve, as Manstein wrote in his pocket diary, to "settle Poland's hash." Dramatically, he declared that Ribbentrop was departing for Moscow to sign the Nazi-Soviet pact. "Now," he triumphed, "I have Poland where I want her!"

After lunch he told them why Germany had no cause for apprehension: The Luftwaffe had 390,000 men, compared with Britain's 130,000 and France's 72,000. The enemy might blockade Germany, but they surely would not fight. "I have only one fear," he bragged, according to the reliable notes that Vice-Admiral Wilhelm Canaris took, "that at the last moment some *Schweinhund* may offer to mediate." As he concluded ("I have done my duty, now you do yours!"), Hermann Göring waddled importantly forward, mounted a step, and turned to face his Führer. "The Wehrmacht," he promised, "will do its duty."

Even so, Göring's heart fluttered when he thought that real war might come. Lord Halifax, the British foreign secretary, recorded in his diary a message from Göring, transmitted through "C," the head of the British secret service, indicating that he would like to come in secret to see the prime minister. Preparations were made to give the staff at Chamberlain's country house the day off, but when Göring broached to Hitler for the first time confidential details of the lines that he had begun stringing into Whitehall, he was disappointed by the response. "*Ja, Gott!*" exclaimed Hitler. "You won't get anywhere. The English do not want to go along with us." A new message went to the British secret service regretting that Hitler did not think the proposed flight would be "immediately useful."

The field marshal did not give up hope entirely. Early on August 23, his Berlin staff phoned the Obersalzberg to say that that the Swede, Dahlerus, was on the other line from Stockholm, badgering them for a decision about the "Four-Power summit conference" idea. At 10:23 A.M. Göring had his secretary call Stockholm back to tell Dahlerus, "The situation has deteriorated." He asked Dahlerus to come to Berlin to meet his "Norwegian friend" (i.e., Göring himself) the next afternoon. Meanwhile Göring flew up to Berlin and called a ministerial meeting in the seclusion of Carinhall, where he informed the Reich ministers, in Hitler's name, of the grim decision that had been reached at Berchtesgaden. "It's been decided," recorded Darré in his diary that afternoon, August 23: "War with Poland!" "You must keep this top secret," the field marshal instructed.

"On [August 23]," wrote Darré's Staatssekretär, Herbert Backe, a few days later,

> We were summoned to Carinhall. Göring . . . informed us in strictest secrecy that it had been resolved to attack Poland. Asked about our war preparations. . . . We managed to stave off bread-and potato-rationing for the first four weeks thanks to our good stockpiles. . . . To maintain surprise Göring very solemnly insisted on absolute secrecy. The mood of the gentlemen present was one of optimism.

"There won't be a world war," Göring assured them. "It's a risk worth taking."

The newspaper headlines that morning were full of the newly completed Nazi-Soviet Pact. Now, surely Britain and France would think twice about interfering. As Birger Dahlerus arrived at one-thirty that afternoon, workmen were draping camouflage netting over Carinhall.

There can be no doubt of the Swede's motives, but Göring's were now very open to speculation. He knew that Hitler planned to invade Poland at dawn in three days' time. Was he merely using Dahlerus to poison the opposing alliance?

Göring suggested that London send over a top general like Sir Edmund Ironside to talk with him. Later that day he drove Dahlerus to Berlin in his two-seater sports car, and repeated the offer that he had made so often, of German military aid to defend the British Empire. He felt confident that he could "persuade" Hitler to limit his claim to Danzig and the Polish Corridor. Meeting the Polish ambassador an hour later, he argued that their differences were only minor. "The main obstacle," he said smoothly, "is your proposed alliance with Britain."

Over at Hitler's Chancellery he found Ribbentrop back from Moscow, gleeful about his diplomatic triumph. The Nazi-Soviet Pact was signed and sealed—and Poland was delivered: In a secret addendum to the pact Stalin undertook to invade Poland soon after Hitler, and that was not all.

Göring was clearly shocked. At 11:20 P.M. he phoned Dahlerus in his hotel suite. "The agreement with Russia," he disclosed, using guarded language, "will have far-reaching consequences. These are of a considerably more comprehensive nature than the published communiqué shows." Still hoping to trump Ribbentrop's ace, he asked the Swedish businessman to fly to London at once and repeat this to Mr. Chamberlain.

By August 25, 1939, the slow burning fuse had almost reached the powder keg. "Efforts," recorded von Weizsäcker, Ribbentrop's Staatssekretär, "are still being made to split the British from the Poles." At 1:30 P.M. Hitler hinted to Ambassador Henderson that he would not take it amiss if Britain waged a "phony war." The Forschungsamt heard the ambassador phone the Foreign Office: "Hitler's just trying to drive a wedge between Britain and Poland," he said. The wiretappers also overheard Mussolini telephoning Berlin from Rome; his response seemed satisfactory, and at 3:02 P.M. Hitler issued the order for *White*, the invasion of Poland, to begin at dawn. All phone links with London and Paris were abruptly severed.

Almost at once everything fell apart. At five o'clock the Forschungsamt detected Count Ciano, the Italian foreign minister, dictating a formal note warning that his country would *not* fight. At five-thirty the French ambassador delivered to Hitler due warning that France *would*. At 6:00 P.M. the press agencies reported worse: Britain had just ratified her alliance with Poland. So the Moscow Pact had not deterred either London or Paris at all.

Whitefaced with anger, Hitler ordered General Keitel, chief of the high command, "STOP EVERYTHING!" and telephoned Field Marshal Göring for advice.

"Is this just temporary?" asked Göring.

"Yes," admitted Hitler. "Just four or five days until we can eliminate British intervention."

"Do you think four or five days will make any difference?"

Göring must have contemplated the fiasco with mixed feelings. He rushed over to the Chancellery. His rival, Ribbentrop, had fled. "Führer pretty broken up," recorded General Franz Halder, concealing his own relief. "Slender hope of maneuvering Britain into accepting terms that Poles will reject." He rounded off this diary entry with the cryptic phrase: "Göring—compromise."

This was indeed Göring's advice now. At 10:20 P.M. Bodenschatz whispered to him that Dahlerus was on the line from London. Göring took the phone. "I'm at the Reich Chancellery with the Führer at this very moment," he shouted into the mouthpiece. "The war orders are just being written out."

"What's gone wrong?" he heard Dahlerus gasp.

"The Führer regards London's ratification of the Polish alliance as a slap in the face."

It was not the only reason, but Göring was doing all he could now to halt the madness that he and Hitler had themselves wrought. He returned to Carinhall and embraced his sister Olga. "Everybody wants war," he said. "Everybody except me—the soldier and field marshal!"

Dawn came. The immense military machine that Hitler had ordered set in motion the previous afternoon had halted, teetering on the very brink. Airports were closed, all overflights forbidden. Göring set out early from Carinhall that day, August 26, 1939, and drove into Berlin. Since the planned Reichstag meeting had been canceled at the last moment, he had chosen to wear a casual ensemble in pure white, with a black cravat passed through a ring embellished with rubies, diamonds, and sapphires.

At midday a courier brought a red envelope to his office with the latest FA intercept—of an immense list of ludicrous Italian raw-material demands being phoned through by Ciano from Rome. The list, Italy's price for joining *White*, included millions of tons of coal and steel, impossible quantities of molybdenum, tungsten, zirconium, and titanium, and 150 flak batteries as well. By the time that Ambassador Bernardo Attolico, a balding, small-headed Italian blinking through pebble-glass lenses, had brought the message over to Hitler, some embassy wag had added the words ". . . to be delivered *before* hostilities" to the text.

Göring goggled, but Hitler remained unmoved.

"Two can play that game," he said, and dictated a reply promising the Italians everything, including entire flak *battalions* too.

"That's out of the question!" remonstrated Göring.

"I'm not bothered about actually *making* the deliveries," Hitler soothed him. "Just depriving Italy of any excuse to wriggle out."

Göring joined his special train near Carinhall, and an adjutant shortly brought Birger Dahlerus aboard. The Swede had just flown back from London. "We're heading for my headquarters," explained Göring, and they puffed off in the darkness toward "Kurfürst," a bunker site among the beech groves that had once been a royal hunting ground near Potsdam.

Dahlerus launched into a self-important two-hour narrative of his day's confabulations in Whitehall, and eventually revealed that he had brought a personal letter from Lord Halifax, the foreign secretary, to Göring.

The field marshal gasped and snatched it rudely out of his hand. ("Did he think I'd plonk my ass on it first and leave it till next day?" Göring later said.) The British statesman's courtly, platitudinous epistle was not much compared with the bloody parchment that Ribbentrop had brought back from the Kremlin, but Göring decided to rush it over to Hitler despite the lateness of the hour.

Gaping midnight crowds lined the Wilhelm Strasse as he arrived. The Reich Chancellery's iron gates were open, the building itself was lit like Coney Island. After hearing Göring, Hitler sent for Dahlerus—it was by now twenty minutes after midnight—and subjected him to an emotional speech, ending with the words, "However many years the enemy holds out, the German people will always hold out one year longer." He repeated his offer of an alliance with Britain, provided she help Germany over Danzig and the Polish Corridor; Göring tore a page out of an atlas and outlined the areas in pencil to Dahlerus, as Hitler spelled out an even more tantalizing promise for the bemused businessman to carry straight back to London. "Germany," Hitler dictated, "would not support any nation—not even Italy, Japan, or Russia—which commenced hostilities against the British Empire."

Out at Kurfürst, the Luftwaffe headquarters, Göring called a further Little Cabinet meeting later that day, August 27.

> Göring informs us [recorded Staatssekretär Herbert Backe] that Italy wouldn't play ball and that's why the attack [on Poland] was called off. Says that Mussolini has written a frantic letter to the Führer: "Factors beyond our control make it impossible for us to fulfil our treaty obligation;" says the king refused to sign his mobilization order. Göring speaks warmly of Mussolini and his plight, but adds that a *real* man would have toppled the monarchy.

At one stage during the day, Dahlerus telephoned from No. 10 Downing Street to ask whether Henderson might delay his return to Berlin, with Britain's formal reply to Hitler's "offer," until the twenty-eighth. Later

Göring dictated to him the route his plane must take to avoid being shot down over Germany.

Dahlerus was back in Göring's Berlin villa a few minutes after midnight. This time he had brought a document drafted by another high Foreign Office official. It spoke of Britain's anxiety for a "settlement" with Hitler, but upheld the guarantee to Poland. It was vague and diplomatically phrased, but Göring proclaimed himself satisfied and took it over to Hitler. He phoned the hotel in sparkling mood at 1:30 A.M. "The Führer," he told the Swede, "agrees with every point but he wants to know, is Britain proposing that this settlement culminate in a treaty, or in an alliance? The Führer would prefer the latter."

Sunshine broke out in Dahlerus's heart. The wiretappers heard him phoning the British embassy jubilantly at 2:00 A.M. "We had a message early from Dahlerus," wrote Lord Halifax in his diary, "saying that he thought things were satisfactory and hoped 'nothing foolish' would be done by either end to upset them."

By five-thirty that morning, August 28, 1939, Dahlerus and staff at the British embassy had composed a telegram advising London on how to phrase the reply that Henderson was to carry back to Berlin. Göring's wiretappers followed closely. Dressed in a green gown clasped at the waist with a jewel-studded buckle, he welcomed the Swede back at Kurfürst at 7:00 A.M. "You look like you had a good night's sleep," he said with a broad grin. (He knew precisely where Dahlerus had been all night and even showed him the FA's nocturnal crop of Brown Pages.) Göring again undertook that if Chamberlain reached agreement with Hitler, Germany would "withhold assistance from any power that attempted to attack . . . Great Britain, even if it should be Italy, Russia, or Japan"—Hitler's own allies.

Göring was cocksure, and so was Hitler now. That morning they re-timetabled *White* to begin on September 1. Army liaison officer Colonel Nicolaus von Vormann found the Führer in dazzling spirits. "He's confident," recorded the colonel, "that we can manipulate Britain so that we have only Poland to contend with."

Later that day Henderson returned with Britain's reply. It did not say much. Retiring to the conservatory with Hitler and Himmler, Göring urged them with perceptible nervousness, "Let's stop trying to break the bank."

"It's the only game I've ever played," retorted Hitler, "—breaking banks."

Hitler's restless optimism infected the building. "The Führer," wrote one colonel in the Abwehr, "has told Ribbentrop, Himmler, Bodenschatz, etc., 'Tonight I'm going to hatch something diabolical for the Poles—something they'll choke on!'" Baron von Weizsäcker, sensing the buoyant new mood, attributed it to Dahlerus and his "rose-tinted" views. Göring commanded an adjutant to telephone the hotel to express Germany's thanks to the indefatigable Swede.

The emotional high continued the next morning. Dahlerus found it at Göring's—Bodenschatz pumped his hand, and Göring acclaimed him with the words, "The Führer insists that you are to be given the highest distinction that the Reich can bestow."

Later that day Hitler handed to Henderson his new terms. They were diabolical indeed—generous beyond belief, but coupled with the demand that a Polish "plenipotentiary" arrive in Berlin to negotiate on the very next day, the thirtieth.

"This," said Henderson, choking, "sounds like an ultimatum!"

At 8:28 P.M. the FA's wiretappers heard the British embassy staff dictating the new terms to London, then Henderson phoning the Polish ambassador Lipski to spur Warsaw into action. Later still they heard the Foreign Office warning that it would be near impossible to get a Pole to Berlin in time. Göring asked Dahlerus to carry the "generous" new German terms in person to Chamberlain, and underlined the salient points in red. "With 1,800,000 troops—not to mention the Soviet divisions—confronting Poland," he warned, "anything may happen."

Leaving Carinhall that morning, August 30, 1939, Göring still hoped that he had eliminated the British. He told Emmy, "I think we've pulled it off."

Under his admiring gaze Hitler dictated a final "offer to Poland," which would, they agreed, surely sunder the enemy alliance. Couched in sixteen points, the new offer was a document of suffocating reasonableness; it banked on Poland's stubbornness and pride.

At midday Dahlerus phoned from Downing Street in London.

"The Führer is drafting his proposals now," Göring assured him.

At one-fifteen Dahlerus phoned again. Lord Halifax, the foreign secretary, wanted Göring to realize that Hitler's proposals must not be a *Diktat*. Göring chuckled broadly. "They are a basis for discussion. They are fabulous. It is, however, *essential* that a Pole come here and get them."

Later the Swede phoned on Chamberlain's behalf to inquire why a Pole must come to Berlin. Göring explained flatly that the Reich Chancellor, Herr Hitler, had his residence there. Halifax found this attitude less reassuring, and later that afternoon the FA overheard his London officials warning Henderson by phone about the Nazis' diplomatic tactics. "They really can't expect to pull it off again," said the disembodied voice from London, "by summoning people, handing over documents, and getting them to sign on the dotted line. Those days are over."

Bewildered by events, the innocent Dahlerus—totally out of his depth in this maelstrom of high diplomacy—flew back from London to Berlin. He boarded Göring's command train at 11:00 P.M. The field marshal told him that at that moment Ribbentrop was putting the sixteen-point proposals to Henderson; at Kurfürst, Göring asked him to phone the British embassy to obtain their first reactions. A senior official there revealed that Ribbentrop had merely "gabbled through" the long document in German, had declared it *überholt* (out of date) since no Pole had arrived, and tossed it on to the table, where it remained unread.

Göring froze. It was vital that London learn and digest the Sixteen Points. He directed Dahlerus to dictate the document over the phone to the British embassy. Shortly, his wiretappers heard Henderson repeating the text to Lipski and suggesting that Poland and Germany bring together "their two field marshals," Göring and Rydz-Smigly.

Lipski went back to bed. He ignored the document, as Hitler and Göring had hoped he would.

It was August 31, the last day of the Old World. Tempers were fraying. Henderson was old and terminally ill—a diplomat and gentleman surrounded by knaves and reporting to fools.

Shortly after 8:00 A.M. the wiretappers heard Warsaw instructing Lipski "not to enter into any concrete negotiations"; then Henderson warning the Polish embassy that there were only a few hours left; then Henderson repeating this to the Foreign Office in London, while adding uneasily that it might all be a Nazi bluff.

Unaccustomed to these lethal poker games, the weak-kneed in Berlin diplomatic circles were losing their nerve. At about 10:00 A.M. former ambassador to Rome Ulrich von Hassell pleaded with Olga Göring to get her brother to listen to him; she phoned Hermann, and he could hear that she was crying. Von Hassell begged the field marshal to intervene for peace. "Weizsäcker has just spoken to me. He says that Ribbentrop will be the gravedigger of the Third Reich." To rub it in, he added, "Carinhall will go up in flames!" Hassell reported that he had learned from Henderson how Ribbentrop had described the Sixteen Points as *überholt*.

"They are only *überholt*," thundered Göring, "if and when no Polish negotiator comes."

"I'll tell Henderson—!"

"—but one must come at once."

Göring persuaded Lipski to see Dahlerus. The Pole seemed past caring. "A revolution will take place within a week in Germany," Lipski confidently predicted. "And we are strong enough to take on Germany."

The FA heard Dahlerus phoning No. 10 Downing Street about this at midday. Although the Sixteen Points were "extremely liberal," waffled the Swede, Ambassador Lipski was rejecting them out of hand. "My government will not budge," Lipski had said.

Just before 1:00 P.M. the OKW teleprinters issued the executive order for *White* to the commanders in chief. Göring received it out at Kurfürst. He summoned an immediate Ministerial Defense Council (a body set up by Hitler by special decree on the thirtieth). He was convinced that he had eliminated the risk of British intervention. "[Martin] Bormann optimistic," recorded Staatssekretär Herbert Backe after this secret session.

Göring says things look good. The Poles wanted to play for time,
we are inflexible. Decision in twenty-four or forty-eight hours.
[He] mentions publication of something or other [the Sixteen
Points] that may just keep Britain out. . . . Poland will be defeated. Unfortunately we have forfeited the element of surprise
and this will cost us a few hundred thousand more [casual-
ties]. . . . Big danger is to the Ruhr [industrial region in western
Germany]. Since the new frontier will be shorter, massive demobilization is probable after Poland's defeat—and then relent-
less armament against Britain.

Toward 1:00 P.M. Göring returned to Berlin and found tempers running high
among Ribbentrop's less bellicose juniors. "Are we obliged," Staatssekretär
von Weizsäcker heatedly asked the field marshal, "to watch the Third Reich
being destroyed just to please some mentally defective adviser of the Führer?
Ribbentrop will be the first to hang, but others will follow!"

At 1:00 P.M. a dispatch rider arrived at Göring's official villa in Berlin,
picked his way around the crates being hurriedly packed with priceless objects
at Fräulein Grundtmann's direction in case of air raids, and handed him a
red folder. It contained an intercept of Warsaw's latest instructions to Lipski,
given at 12:45 P.M.: The ambassador was to tell Ribbentrop only that Warsaw
would reply (to London) "in due course." Göring scrawled a copy of the
intercept for Dahlerus. Later that afternoon he invited the British ambassador
over for tea. Henderson threw a bleak look at the packing crates and workmen
and deduced from the mere fact that Göring could afford time to gossip that
the die had now been cast. That evening the wiretaps showed a gulf yawning
in the enemy front. Henderson had angrily exclaimed to his French colleague
that Lipski had disdained to see the Sixteen Points, even when he visited
Ribbentrop at seven. "It's a farce, the whole thing!"

Göring roared with delighted laughter. Later still, the FA sent further good
tidings out to Kurfürst: The British and French ambassadors had been heard
slamming the phone down on each other.

It was now September 1, 1939. Shortly before 5:00 A.M. Hitler's armies
engulfed the Polish frontier. Simulating anger, Göring reported to Dahlerus
at eight o'clock that the Poles had demolished the Dirschau Bridge (in fact,
the Nazi "first strike" there had failed) and had seized a German radio station
at Gleiwitz (in fact these "Poles" were SS men in Polish uniforms). He still
had a faint hope that Britain and France would hesitate to wade in. Throwing
a cape around his shoulders, he climbed into his two-seater sports car and
drove into Berlin.

At the Reichstag Building he took Rosenberg aside. "I fought like a lion
last night," he disclosed, "to get the decision postponed twenty-four hours
to allow time for the Sixteen Points to sink in. But Ribbentrop saw the Führer

talking tough with Henderson, so the peabrain thought he had to talk even tougher.''

Wearing soldier's field-gray tunic, Hitler climbed the podium of the Reichstag assembly hall and announced that he had invaded Poland. ''If anything should befall me in this struggle,'' he announced, ''then my successor shall be party-member Göring.''

Too jaded to be much elated at this public endorsement, Göring phoned Dahlerus afterward and brought him around to discuss with a tired but dispassionate Führer the vanishing prospect of getting Britain to a conference table. Hitler was intransigent. ''I am resolved to march on,'' he snarled, ''and to smash Poland's intriguing and obstructionism once and for all.''

Afterward the FA heard Dahlerus phoning London, but Sir Alexander Cadogan, the permanent undersecretary at the Foreign Office, was taking an unexpectedly hard line: Hitler, he insisted, must withdraw all his troops from Poland.

When the Little Cabinet now met out at Kurfürst, Göring told them for the first time about Dahlerus.

Still neither Britain nor France had either declared war or moved. Continuing to scheme, Göring sent Dahlerus to the British embassy once more, to talk about a ''cease-fire.'' Britain, however, insisted on withdrawal first, and late on September 2, Chamberlain's Cabinet decided to issue an ultimatum. Twenty-four minutes after midnight on the third, Göring's late-night shift of wire-tappers heard Henderson receiving corresponding instructions from London—he was to demand an audience with Ribbentrop at 9:00 A.M.

Seven hours later the Forschungsamt heard a British embassy official saying, ''Henderson's going over now, to ask for a reply by eleven. If that's not forthcoming, then it will all be over.''

On tenterhooks, Göring phoned the foreign ministry a few minutes later, at nine-fifteen. Ribbentrop coldly confirmed that he had received a British ultimatum; it was due to expire at eleven. Perspiration trickled down the fat field marshal's brow as he replaced the receiver. Their calculations were going badly wrong. ''Never in world history,'' he gasped to Dahlerus, ''has a victorious army been required to withdraw *before* negotiations begin!''

The Swede suggested that Göring himself fly to London. Fired by this dramatic idea, Göring phoned Bodenschatz at the Chancellery. ''I won't commit myself,'' he promised, ''until I hear London's attitude.''

Ensconced in Göring's specially built railway train, Dahlerus put the call through to London from a phone booth next to the kitchen. Whitehall said they would think it over. Göring could hear the Swede shouting hoarsely that he had done his ''damndest,'' and allowed himself a wan smile as Dahlerus parroted his own remarks to the Foreign Office official, shouting that a victorious army had never in history been required to withdraw before negotiations.

It was ten-fifteen. In his imagination Göring was already in London, feted as the savior of world peace.

He ordered Görnnert to have two Storch light planes standing by, and to get two Junkers 52 airliners warmed up at Staaken Airfield. He told Robert to press a dinner jacket. He instructed his detectives to put on their best suits. At 10:50, however, Dahlerus was still cajoling the Foreign Office. "I think I can talk the field marshal into flying," he was saying.

At the other end of the line there was a brief, unheard consultation with Lord Halifax, then a stiff and formal rebuff: His Majesty's government was still waiting for a "definite reply" to the ultimatum.

Ten, twenty, thirty minutes passed. For a while Hermann Göring brooded in the sunshine, slouching at a trestle table set up beneath the beech trees. At 11:30 A.M. Staatssekretär Körner sidled over with a note—Mr. Chamberlain had just broadcast on the radio, declaring war on Germany. General Albert Kesselring, whose Luftflotte was spearheading the attack on Poland, saw Göring telephone Ribbentrop, purple with rage. "Now you've got your %!¶§% war!" he screamed at his foe. "You are alone to blame!"

Shortly, the phone rang again. Görnnert answered: It was Hitler himself. Bodenschatz had just told him of Field Marshal Göring's planned jaunt to London.

"Give me the field marshal!"

Göring clutched the receiver, the blood draining from his taut lips. *"Jawohl, mein Führer! Jawohl, mein Führer! Jawohl, mein Führer!"*

"Görnnert," he sniffed, carefully replacing the receiver, "get Schulz and the car."

Wilhelm Schulz, age thirty-one, was his chauffeur. At 11:45 A.M. Göring set off to the Chancellery in Berlin.

PART 4
THE PREDATOR

23
DOCTOR READY TO BECOME BOSS

During the coming war Göring's popularity with the German public remained largely intact—often shaken, but never entirely shattered. He could visit the most heartrending scenes of air-raid devastation and be cheered by the common people. After touring the Ruhr in October 1943, he would say, baffled by his own popularity, "I would have expected them at least to throw some rotten eggs at me." The public readily forgave him his vain boast that if ever an enemy bomber reached Germany they could call him "Mr. Meier." The people did not even begrudge him his extravagant life-style; it was only at the very highest level that his sybaritic indulgences lost him friends. After Göring froze him out as minister of agriculture, Darré would write in his diary (on December 28, 1939) harsh comments about the field marshal's hedonistic existence at Carinhall. "It seems to me," opined the minister, "that Göring is succumbing more and more to a luxury-loving Caesar complex and is losing contact with reality."

The feud with Ribbentrop, of course, continued. Göring got his own back in petty ways. "Among other things," recalled Beppo Schmid years later, "Göring ordered his chauffeur always to cut in on Ribbentrop's limousine, to ensure that he, Göring, always had second place in Hitler's motor cavalcades.''

His relationship with Hitler meanwhile underwent grave changes as he alternated between opportunistic loyalty and despairing infatuation. Prince Paul had confided to Dahlerus one remark by Hitler: "I am not a lonely man—I have the best friend in the world, I have Göring!" Hearst-group journalist Karl von Wiegand confidentially testified to the FBI in 1940 that the clue to Göring's complex character lay in his determination not to forfeit the succession to the Führer. "That," he suggested, "is why Göring is so subservient. He takes abuses that no other man would take. He knows that Hitler has the power to eliminate him just by the scratch of a pen."

Something of the old camaraderie was revived during *White* and *Yellow* (invasion of France, Belgium, and Holland) thanks to the achievements of the Luftwaffe; but it would slip with each subsequent reverse, reaching a low point at Stalingrad (January 1943) from which it never recovered. With the exception of two specific episodes, the air attacks on Warsaw and Belgrade, Göring fought a more chivalrous war than his enemies, as befitted the last commander of the Richthofen Squadron. He employed the tactical air force with moderation during the 1939 Polish campaign; although the contemporary British and French propaganda claimed differently, the captured secret dispatches of the French air attaché in Warsaw, later published by the Nazis, documented this unexpected restraint. On Hitler's orders, in the first days of the war Göring issued orders that sharply limited the operations of his crews—forbidding them to use poison gas, to attack civilian targets, or to sink Red Cross ships, and flatly embargoing London as a bombing target.

This misplaced sentimentality accented his "farewell conversation" with Dahlerus at Kurfürst on September 4, 1939. "Whatever happens," the field marshal said, with a ponderous attempt at sincerity, "the efforts of the German government as well as myself will be directed to waging war in the most humane manner possible." Germany, he emphasized, would take no initiative whatever against either Britain or France.

He gave the same assurances to the British ambassador later that day. "And what if a bomb should hit my own person accidentally?" inquired Henderson.

"Then," replied Göring, slapping him on the back, "I shall send a special plane to drop a wreath at your funeral."

He probably meant it, too. He was still living amid the fantasies of the Richthofen era, when chivalrous aviators did that sort of thing.

Field Marshal Göring had planned to open his assault on Britain with an immediate surprise attack on the British Fleet anchored at Scapa Flow, its base in the north Scottish isles. Hitler forbade it. Each side still hoped to restore the peace, and the British also remained initially inactive, as did the

French. The Deutsche Reichsbahn's crack "Rheingold" express train shuttled unscathed the length of the French front each day, from Amsterdam to Basel.

For all his bombast and bellicose utterances, Göring detested the senseless destruction of war, as he was about to demonstrate, and this increased the mutual contempt between him and the career soldiers like Manstein, Rommel, and Halder.

While Hitler toured the front, Göring remained in Berlin. When Hitler returned, Göring transferred his own "headquarters" to the state hunting lodge at Rominten in East Prussia. He invited the crown prince to join him hunting stags there, but received the frosty answer that the prince would accept only when hostilities were over. Once, when Ribbentrop was away negotiating the future Nazi-Soviet demarcation line in Poland, Göring telephoned Hitler's command train to plead for the inclusion of the Bialystok forests in the German zone because of their valuable timber. "He says timber," scoffed Hitler, "and means big game." A photograph taken on September 29 showed the field marshal inspecting front-line units in a rain-soaked leather coat, while Kesselring looked on. By that time Göring had dictated to Beppo Schmid the ultimatum ordering Warsaw to surrender, and when this was refused he ordered the saturation bombardment that brought the Polish war to an end. Hitler rewarded him with the unique Grand Cross decoration to the Iron Cross.

During those first few weeks Göring's Ministerial Defense Council restored a semblance of Cabinet government to the Reich. "The Defense Council," wrote Schwerin von Krosigk, the fifty-two-year-old Oxford-educated minister of finance, "sat several times a week and he co-opted onto it any outside ministers he needed. I regularly attended these first sessions. At its meetings Göring not only allowed but actively insisted on a completely frank discussion of the matters on the agenda. So at long last we had what we had been urging for years." But, wrote this minister, their pleasure was short-lived. Hitler returned to Berlin after the victory parade in Warsaw, and Hans Lammers, the senior civil servant who had headed the now-defunct Reich Cabinet, took charge again. Turning down Göring's request for a Defense Council session to discuss amendments to the penal code, Lammers indicated that Hitler would now be resuming regular Cabinet meetings. Probably it was a maneuver by Lammers to regain his own lost authority; the damage to the political direction of the war was permanent, because Hitler never convened the Cabinet again. "Moreover," lamented Krosigk later, "when Hitler shifted his headquarters back out of Berlin again, Göring never resumed the customs he had adopted during those first weeks of the war."

The earlier meetings of the Defense Council are portrayed in the private records kept by participants like Goebbels, Darré, Backe, and the OKW armaments specialist, Georg Thomas. "Göring," noted Darré on September 4, the day after Britain and France had declared war, "looked fresh and every inch a soldier. What a guy! Hess sends his stooge as usual; what a zero, he can't stand up to Göring. Thus the dwindling party is gradually frozen out."

"Britain," ruminated Göring at this session, "has nothing to gain in this war. But we might inherit the British Empire."

At their council's session on the sixth, Goebbels objected to Göring's plan to print the party emblem on food-ration cards, arguing that it would hardly advance the party's popularity. "I'm afraid, dear Dr. Goebbels," retorted Darré, "that this is not a war that can be won by popularity." Göring nodded vigorously.

Thomas's files show the Defense Council allocating oil and steel between the U-boat, Ju 88, explosives, and ammunition production programs. "The Führer," Thomas heard Göring say on September 11, in one of the few indications that Hitler consulted him on the harsh Nazi occupation policies, "intends to establish great Reich domains in Poland, and to endow particularly deserving [German] personages with farms and large estates." Hinting at the bloody purges just beginning in Poland, Göring claimed that the Polish clergy were directing a protracted guerrilla warfare against the Nazi invaders.

After this meeting, Darré noted with some disbelief the field marshal's optimism that Hitler would yet make a deal with Britain. "All the indications are," commented the minister in his diary, "that the Führer is facing a war lasting years."

By the end of the year 1939 the Defense Council had fallen into disuse. "Why does Adolf Hitler just let domestic affairs drift?" complained Darré in his private chronicle on December 4. "We ministers can't get through to him anymore. . . . In civil matters he deals with Göring alone now."

Astonishingly—because they are not even hinted at in British official histories—Hermann Göring maintained his secret channels of communication to British Prime Minister Neville Chamberlain during these nervous months of what was later called the "phony war." He also entered into a round of talks with emissaries of President Franklin D. Roosevelt through contacts established by Dr. Joachim Hertslet, the Four-Year Plan's agent in Mexico. Göring talked in Berlin with the influential Swedish banker Marcus Wallenberg, and urged him to press the British to accept the German peace plan; and he sent his anglophile friend, Prince Max Egon zu Hohenlohe-Langenburg, to initiate secret talks with British diplomats in Switzerland.

The most startling feature of Göring's diplomatic activities that winter of 1939/40 was that he hinted to the British that he was willing to take over the real power in Germany from Hitler, and that he would halt the persecution of Jews and pull out of the "non-German" parts of Poland; Hitler would be shunted off into "some sort of presidential role."

His peace offensive began on September 8. On that day he phoned Dahlerus in Stockholm with the triumphant news that two-thirds of the Polish Army was now surrounded. He repeated that his Luftwaffe would refrain from bombing Britain first—"In fact," he volunteered, "Germany will wait for Britain to act first in everything else too." Addressing Berlin munitions workers on the following day, he stated explicitly that Germany was still willing to make what he called "an honest peace."

Simultaneously he directed Hertslet—who was currently visiting Berlin —to send a message in code to a high-level contact in the United States, William Rhodes Davis. The telegram, dated September 8, was addressed to Davis in New York: ALL WELL NOW, WAR IN EAST SUCCESS. Three days later a second code message followed: NECESSARY FOR DAVIS TO COME SEPTEMBER 26 ROME TO MEET DOCTOR. DOCTOR READY TO BE BOSS HERE. (The FBI, who decoded these messages, had already identified "Doctor" as Göring from other items.) On the fifteenth, Davis was allowed an audience with Roosevelt (as the presidential diary shows). Three days after that, Göring directed Hertslet to cable a further code message to Davis, evidently hinting at a Göring-controlled Reich government: CAN ASSURE ABSOLUTE APPEASE-MENT AFTER POLAND WAR IF NEW COMBINATION HERE IS ASSISTED BY NEU-TRAL U.S.A. GOVERNMENT.

In Washington the labor-union boss John L. Lewis, a close friend of Davis, showed this extraordinary message to President Roosevelt. Davis reported by code to Berlin the next day, September 19: CONTENTS YOUR CABLE DIS-CUSSED WITH FRANKLIN D. ROOSEVELT WHO IN PERFECT AGREEMENT . . . THIS SIDE READY PROVIDING FLEXIBILITY WITH YOU. The upshot was a further American code message to Hertslet in Berlin, for Hermann Göring, on the twentieth, announcing that Davis had now left for Europe. (Ten days later he would actually be in Berlin, negotiating with the field marshal.) Sadly for history, nothing came of Göring's remarkable initiatives.

Equally circumspectly, though with even less success, Göring pursued his other contacts with London throughout September 1939. When two RAF airmen were shot down in Germany he phoned Dahlerus on the tenth, and sent their letters to London with a personal message to say that they were alive and well. (The indignant Foreign Office requested the Swedes not to forward any more such letters, since the Red Cross was the proper channel.)

After the Soviet Union sprang its armies on eastern Poland on September 17, Göring telephoned Dahlerus in Sweden. "What are you going to do about it?" he asked.

"I am remaining *here*," Dahlerus replied emphatically; but he related this renewed approach to the British legation the next day. "The field marshal is willing to do all he can to arrange a truce," he said, "provided he gets the credit." If Göring could meet somebody like General Ironside on neutral ground, this would give him the necessary leverage to persuade Hitler. Arriving back in Berlin on the twenty-first, however, Dahlerus had to tell Göring that the British were refusing to state terms—it was for him to find out first what Göring had to offer, they said. Three days later Dahlerus met Sir George

Ogilvie-Forbes at the British legation in Oslo, but the diplomat merely suggested dryly that perhaps Göring ought to reflect upon the treatment the Soviet Army was meting out to his "shooting pals" in Poland.

Göring took the search for peace seriously. He sent Prince von Hohenlohe to a secret Swiss rendezvous with Colonel Malcolm Christie of the British secret service, with instructions to hint that if a properly authorized Englishman—he now suggested Vansittart—should arrive there with British terms, then he, Göring, would be ready to act against the Führer.

He was painfully aware that once again time was running out. On September 26, Hitler revealed to him and the other commanders in chief his intention of invading France as soon as possible. Göring brought Dahlerus to see Hitler the same day, then sent the Swede straight to London with details of the German offer. For three days, from the twenty-eighth to the thirtieth, the Swede was closely questioned by Cadogan, Halifax, and then Chamberlain in person. (Birger Dahlerus, curiously, concealed from the British that Hitler himself was behind the offer: Perhaps Hitler did not want to lose face.) The British position remained unchanged. They would not, they said, trust the word of Germany's "present leaders"; and they wanted guarantees about the future.

Göring quaked as each day passed, lest Hitler order *Yellow*—the assault on France—to begin. The Luftwaffe's easy baptism by fire in Poland had not concealed from him the inherent unreadiness of his air force for serious war. Above all, the all-important Ju 88 standard bomber was still not in mass production.

Accordingly, when William R. Davis, the American oilman, arrived from Washington with his curious message from Roosevelt, Göring paid close attention to him. He sent Wohlthat to hear Davis out first, on October 1. Davis suggested that Roosevelt hoped to appear in his coming presidential-election campaign as the "angel of peace"; he had undertaken, in conversation with him, to restore Germany to her 1914 frontiers and colonies, and to grant economic aid as well. Göring discussed this alleged proposal with Hitler, then handed to the American emissary a *signed* list of Germany's peace terms, to disclose only to Roosevelt. Orally, he added that the Reich was willing to restore independent governments to Poland and Czechoslovakia. Davis departed, carrying this portentous document to Washington: It has since vanished, but he told the *Des Moines Register* on the last day of 1940 that he handed it to the State Department. (On August 1, 1941, he died of a heart attack, allegedly commissioned by "Intrepid," the head of the British secret service in North America.)

Meanwhile Birger Dahlerus returned to Berlin, saw Göring and the Führer on October 3, and subsequently informed Lord Halifax by telegram that he now had more specific German suggestions for the British government to hear. London did not reply. On October 9, Göring again took Dahlerus to see Hitler. The Swede concentrated on the awkward problems presented by

Poland's frontiers, disarmament, and the need for a change in Germany's foreign policy. Hitler hesitated, but after two further meetings with Göring and the Swedish businessman on the tenth, he agreed to discuss the Polish question at a later "peace conference." They sent Dahlerus off to The Hague to await an invitation to London; he carried a letter of authority, again signed by Göring, and memorized the list of proposals—a summit conference to discuss Poland, disarmament, colonies, and population transfers, after an initial mini-summit of senior officials like Göring and Ironside. Germany would undertake to build an *Ostwall* along the River Vistula in Poland to restrain the Soviet Army (her own allies). In the private letter to Dahlerus, Göring reiterated that Hitler profoundly believed that if the war continued, millions of people would be killed to no purpose, since the same problems as now would have to be faced sooner or later.

All of this intense diplomatic activity by Göring failed. In a BBC broadcast on October 12, Prime Minister Chamberlain rejected the German offer. "Now," rasped Hitler to Göring, Udet, and Milch—as the latter recorded that day in his diary, "you must produce bombs. The war goes on." At nine-thirty that same evening Göring phoned Dahlerus, still waiting at The Hague to travel on to London. The Reich government, he said, would not be replying to Chamberlain's broadcast. "It was a declaration of war," he said.

Even so, in the utmost secrecy the Anglo-German dialogue went on. On October 12, Göring had a further two-hour conversation with Dahlerus, back in Berlin. Again they agreed there should be an informal mini-summit of senior officials to thrash out a basis for an armistice. While spurning this approach, the British made plain in their response that they *would* negotiate with a Hitler government provided they received plausible guarantees against further aggression. Lord Halifax coldly indicated that they would expect major internal changes.

On October 19, 1939, Göring hinted in an interview with James D. Mooney, president of General Motors, Berlin, that Germany was willing to restore a degree of independence to Poland and Czechoslovakia. "If we could only reach an agreement with the British today," said Göring temptingly, "we'd dump the Russians and the Japs overboard tomorrow." According to Mooney's own notes the field marshal asked him "on behalf of our government" to go over to London and "find out what this war is all about." "We have read Chamberlain's recent speeches," Göring added, "and we can't figure out whether he really wants to fight or not."

In London Vansittart's brother was European manager of General Motors. But after listening to the inquiry that Göring had made, even he could only give his friend Mooney the oral response that London could not trust the present Nazi leadership. The field marshal himself should *act*, said Vansittart.

Yellow was now drawing closer, and Göring knew it. On October 22, Hitler fixed a date three weeks later for attack. On the twenty-fifth, Göring had two further urgent sessions with Birger Dahlerus. The Swede agreed once more—"at the field marshal's request, which was repeated several times"—to endeavor to resolve the impasse. Göring now promised that if London sent plenipotentiaries he would submit concrete *written* proposals, particularly on Poland. "The Führer," he warned, however, "is not likely to make any concessions at present on the *Tschechei*." Dahlerus left that evening for The Hague in neutral Holland, and waited once again.

Although the head of the secret service dictated a note to Chamberlain the next day reading, "We should be extremely chary over placing any reliance on Göring," the Foreign Office did not entirely dismiss the notion of dealing with him. Anticipating "possible developments," their squeamish Central Department vetoed one "most offensive" leaflet that would have called the German public's attention to the field marshal's drug problem, his corpulence, and his "impulsive, vain, jovial, and coarse nature." "He is the one," noted one Foreign Office official, "[whom] we should try not to offend more than is necessary."

Göring's balancing act was common knowledge in conservative military circles. Colonel Helmuth Groscurth of the *Abwehr* took note in his diary on November 4 that Göring was opposed to *Yellow*. Hitler obstinately pressed ahead with his own preparations, admonishing his generals assembled on the twenty-third that time was running out for Germany. "To hope for a compromise," he told them candidly, "is infantile."

As winter set in, the few remaining clandestine channels between London and Berlin slowly froze over.

Göring had always understood the purpose of the Nazi-Soviet alliance—it was a pact with Beelzebub to drive out Satan. Hitler had had to calm the fears of the more obtuse members of his party on two or three occasions. "In history," he lectured the top party officials on October 21, acording to Darré's diary, "the victor is always right! Thus, in this war I have only the dictates of my own conscience to follow. . . . Ice-cool, I shall resort to actions that will probably violate every valid law of nations. What we need is space. And I hope to acquire the space we need in the east."

According to Colonel Beppo Schmid, Hitler had convinced Göring of the vital importance of satisfying every political and economic demand that the Soviets made meanwhile. Germany relied on Soviet deliveries of oil, rare metals, and foodstuffs. The Trans-Siberian Railroad was the one blockade-proof route for the rubber and other supplies coming from the Far East. As head of the Four-Year Plan, Göring had no option but to comply, although he already bore the more irksome side effects of the Nazi-Soviet pact, like the permanent attachment to his staff of a swarthy little Russian liaison officer, Colonel Skornyakov, with greater fortitude than courtesy (he referred to him openly as "that bastard son of a vodkaholic").

The field marshal was shocked as the extent of the Soviet trade demands became known that December of 1939. They included not only German machine tools, weapons, and blueprints, but entire warships like the brand-new cruiser *Lützow*. Ambassador Karl Ritter, who had conducted the trade talks in Moscow, reported to Göring in mid-December:

> Ambassador Ritter, December 14 [as Göring jotted in his diary].
> Russian negotiations, promises: 900,000 tons of petroleum, 100,000
> cotton, 10,000 flax, 1,000,000 wheat. Eighty million marks of
> timber; huge quantities of manganese.
>   Our demands: butter, scrap metal, iron ore, flax, oil plants,
> and oil cake.

The trade talks were continued in Germany, and each item on the Soviet "shopping list" staggered Göring more than the last:

> Negotiations in Berlin. Russian requests:
>   1. Industrial item. Three hundred million marks of machinery
> (of which 60 million in machine tools, very awkward).
>   2. Material for armaments: 700 or 800 millions. Navy: cruiser
> *Lützow*, small craft. Blueprints for big ships. Army: heavy artil-
> lery, medium artillery. Air [force]: 300 millions' worth of aircraft
> and sundries, latest blueprints.
>   Open items: major industrial investments, totaling 1 billion?

From a reading of these straightforward entries in Göring's notebooks it is hard to visualize him as a warlord who also consulted the dark forces of the occult. He trusted clairvoyants, and Beppo Schmid saw him swinging a diviner's pendulum across a map, trying to guess why the British and French were still not assailing Germany. He was as artless and primitive as he was ambitious and shrewd. He often boasted that he was completely ignorant of how a radio set worked, and routinely insisted that the Americans might know how to turn out excellent razor blades and refrigerators but could never mass-produce anything as advanced as warplanes or armored fighting vehicles. Hermann Göring would willingly pay millions of marks to a scientist who claimed to have invented an anti-aircraft death ray. (The man had misplaced the decimal point: The effective range turned out to be three centimeters!) And in his understandable anxiety to ensure that bad weather thwarted Hitler's plan to launch an early *Yellow*, Göring paid more millions to a rainmaker, whose "scientific apparatus" turned out to be a very ordinary radio set gutted of all its circuitry but the outside knobs.

    In those months of the "phony war," Göring's squadrons remained almost idle apart from anti-shipping operations against the British. Drugged by its easy triumphs in Poland, the Luftwaffe was resting on its laurels. Operational analysis was unknown. It was enough for a Luftwaffe pilot simply to claim to have sunk the carrier *Ark Royal*. Winston Churchill, first lord of the British

Admiralty, denied it, and months later Göring would still be asking Dahlerus to make discreet inquiries in London about the carrier.

He had become inordinately fat again, and according to his staff physician, Dr. Ramon von Ondarza, his circulation was poor and his blood pressure irregular; his pulse rate sometimes went up to 220. Ondarza diagnosed a heart-muscle weakness and instructed Göring to take things easy. He did so at Carinhall, where he felt safe from his rivals and at peace with the world. Twice more during that December of 1939 he put out furtive feelers to London—once through Count Eric von Rosen and then through Major Tryggve Gran, a Norwegian Air Force officer. Both men were, of course, neutrals.

Out of sight here at Carinhall, he did as he pleased. The only man whom he allowed to share his Jacuzzi was Ernst Udet. "Those two little fat frogs," Milch was once heard saying, perhaps a trifle enviously, to incredulous fellow prisoners after the war, "used to sit there naked in a sort of swimming pool."

Ensconced with family circle and friends in his basement movie theater he would watch forbidden films like *Gone With the Wind*. A director of the Ufa Movie Corporation revealed wryly that the private theater had cost them over one hundred thousand marks to equip; Göring had cheerfully returned their invoice, unpaid, with his thanks to Ufa for their "magnificent present."

After consulting with Göring on January 10, 1940, Hitler had fixed *Yellow* to begin one week later. But on the day of their consultation an air-force courier plane of Luftflotte 2 crash-landed on neutral Belgian territory. In breach of all security regulations it was carrying the Nazis' top-secret plans for *Yellow*. On the next afternoon the two staff officers assured Göring's air attaché in Brussels that they had managed to burn the documents in a stove. But that night the Brussels newspapers claimed that a Belgian officer had been able to salvage the flaming papers virtually intact.

Göring needed little imagination to know how Hitler would react. Von Hassell glimpsed him "beside himself" with fright. Göring tossed a file of papers into a stove to see how fast they burned, and roasted his hands quite badly trying to snatch them out. At Emmy's suggestion he consulted a clairvoyant, and this sage gentleman reassured him that the secret dossier had been totally consumed by the flames. Göring happily reported this to Hitler. The whole episode did permanent damage to Göring's prestige: Although he himself was spared, Hitler ordered him to dismiss the Luftflotte 2 commander, Felmy, and his chief of staff.

Already jittery because of the repeated delays, Hitler decided to recast *Yellow* along unorthodox lines. Pure opportunist that he was, he speculated that if the enemy *had* obtained the charred documents, they might be misled into believing that this was still the Nazi plan of attack.

Four days after Göring's glum birthday celebration, therefore, on January 16, 1940, Hitler ordered the offensive postponed until the spring, and restructured to ensure total secrecy and surprise.

24

YELLOW AND THE TRAITORS

Years later, awaiting the end in his cell at Nuremberg, Hermann Göring would philosophize about the little accidents of fate that affect human lives. In 1919 he had been waiting at a bus stop, en route to his initiation as a Freemason: a toothsome blonde had crossed his path, and he had stalked off after her instead. As a Freemason he would have been disqualified from joining Hitler's Nazi party. But for that blonde, he reflected, he might not be languishing in that prison cell in 1945.

So it was with that plane's crash-landing in Belgium in January 1940. It nearly ended his career: that he stayed in office, and therefore had to pay the penalties that duly accrued, was probably a chance by-product of a little known service that he was able to perform in revealing an ongoing treason being perpetrated at the highest levels of the Nazi high command. On January 13, Göring secretly visited Hitler with the Forschungsamt dossier containing intercepted Italian and Belgian telegrams passing between Rome, the Vatican, and Brussels. The intercepts showed that an unidentified traitor in Berlin had repeatedly passed each of Hitler's deadlines on *Yellow* to foreign diplomats. The FA intercepts showed the Italian military attaché Colonel Efisio Marras tipping off Count Ciano, and Ciano warning Brussels and The Hague. Further intercepts showed that the traitor was updating the Belgian and Dutch military attachés each time Hitler amended the *Yellow* deadline, on January 14, 15, and 17—sometimes within hours of the decision. Furious at this leak, Hitler briefed Göring and army commander in chief von Brauchitsch on the twentieth. "I am convinced that we shall win this war," he told them, "but we are going to lose it if we cannot learn to keep our secrets."

The only concession that Hitler had made to Göring's air-force requirements in these weeks was to include Belgium and Holland in *Yellow*. He was reluctant to carry the war into neutral territory, and as recently as January 15 he refused Göring permission to attack shipping in the Downs, squeamishly pointing out that there might be neutrals among them. But Jeschonnek, the young chief of air staff, had persuaded Hitler that he could not reach Britain without the Dutch and Belgian airfields, so *Yellow* was extended.

In the interim Field Marshal Göring maneuvered to restore his prestige, mainly by undermining the other commanders in chief. "Raeder has got a fine navy. What a pity he's a churchgoer!" he remarked somewhat hypocritically to Hitler. Sensing Hitler's hostility to the clerical influences, Göring had dispensed with all the air force's chaplains a few weeks earlier.

He expected a high standard of personal conduct and brooked no laxity. Writing in May 1946 the air force's judge-advocate general Baron Christian von Hammerstein would ascribe to him a ruthless determination to maintain discipline. Airmen guilty of drunken crimes of violence were inevitably courtmartialed, and rapists could expect short shrift. Hammerstein listed cases in which Göring had substituted a death sentence on a rapist where originally a lesser sentence had been handed down; in the case of one Russian rape victim, Göring ordered the felon to be hanged in her home village. When a drunken party official who had joined the air force as a first lieutenant, Otto von Hirschfeld, shot several Polish convicts to death in December 1939, Göring demanded the death sentence as a matter of course. Hitler refused even to confirm the verdict. Hans Lammers, chief of the Reich Chancellery, came to Carinhall on January 4 to discuss with Göring both this case and the increasing evidence of other atrocities in Nazi-occupied Poland—"In particular," noted Lammers, "about the manner and scale of the deportations, expulsions, and executions." Göring agreed that these scandals were "rapidly becoming a danger" for the whole Reich. Lammers's file shows that the field marshal immediately sent for Himmler to rebuke him. Göring was no less shocked by the barbarous Polish atrocities committed against their ethnic German minority. He told his sister Olga in February 1940 of one captive German farmer, Hermann Treskow, whom the Poles had shot when a bleeding foot prevented him from marching any farther. Treskow's widow begged Göring to stop the Nazi atrocities.

One episode that spring illustrated his compassion. Late one night as three young airmen returned to barracks drunk and carousing, an army officer stopped them and laboriously checked their I.D.s. Anxious to get back in before Lights Out, they snatched their paybooks back and fled. Their Luftwaffe general, Wolfram von Richthofen (VIII Air Corps) turned them over to army commander Walther von Reichenau, and a firing squad put all three to death for mutinous behavior. Field Marshal Göring, angered by the whole episode, sent for both generals and issued a humiliating reprimand. "The right to confirm sentences is your most priceless jewel as field commanders," he said. "It embraces not only a duty to maintain discipline, but the duty to care for the men entrusted to your command. You, Richthofen, deserted three airmen in their hour of need." For years afterward, recalled Baron von Hammerstein, Göring could not put the death of those airmen out of his mind.

He now controlled the world's most powerful air force, and was conscious that all Europe trembled at the prospect of *Yellow*; but he still hoped for an early end to hostilities. Lufthansa chairman Dr. Emil-Georg von Stauss, a non-Nazi whose opinions Göring valued, persuaded him to receive the Lutheran bishop of Oslo, Dr. Eivind Berggrav, on January 21, 1940. The bishop found him initially standoffish, until he mentioned that he had just been to Britain and had not found the British nurturing any real hatred of Germany so much as a calm determination to see the thing through.

"The Führer," interjected Göring, "is quite convinced that Britain's only war aim is to smash Germany."

The bishop shook his head. "If you are right," pondered Göring, "then there's no point whatever in this fight. But we've tried negotiating with the British. They won't meet unless we agree to preconditions."

Those conditions, which the bishop had outlined—the restoration of sovereignty to the Poles and Czechs—were, the field marshal added, quite unacceptable. "Poland and Czechoslovakia—those are our bargaining counters."

"Which would you rather have," challenged the bishop. "Peace, or victory?"

"Peace, no doubt about it!" That was Göring's spontaneous answer; then he chuckled and added, "I should very much like to have victory first."

Under the lash of Dr. Goebbels's propaganda, the German people now came to regard Britain as their born enemy. "It is necessary," Göring had told the Norwegian bishop, "to give the British a knock hard enough to stop them from trying to act as our schoolmaster. The Führer is to be trusted when he says that our interests lie in the east." Baffled by England's obstinacy, he posed the rhetorical question "Do the British think that we want to destroy their empire?"

The German war economy was entering a bottleneck. Hitler had told Göring that he wanted all-out arms production now, believing that he could end the war in 1940 if he could throw a heavy enough punch at France. Göring willingly repeated this argument to Georg Thomas on January 30, and in a letter to Economics Minister Walter Funk four days later. Thus Hitler and Göring kept the economy tuned to Blitzkrieg warfare throughout the coming months—gearing it for armament in intimidating breadth, rather than in the depth that would give stamina for a long, hard struggle. Göring called several command conferences that winter at Carinhall, and made a show of attending to all the minutiae that *Yellow* would involve—how to avoid friction over the local womenfolk, whether Dutch fuel could be used in the high-performance Me 109 fighter, and how to overcome the ammunition and bomb shortages, given the coal and steel shortages that the bitterly cold winter was causing. "Transport is *the* problem," he told his generals.

Assuming that the Nazis would capture the raw materials of Belgium, Holland, and northern France it seemed logical to plunder Germany's own resources meanwhile. On February 9, he invited the arms experts out to Carinhall to investigate ways of cranking up arms output in time for *Yellow*. Göring made fateful decisions about his country's long-term projects. "Whatever is not crucial to *this* war," he dictated, "is to be held over."

Three days later—self-importantly describing himself now as "prime minister" (omitting the words, "of Prussia")—Göring discussed with his generals, with the gauleiters of the newly annexed eastern provinces, and SS Chief Heinrich Himmler (attending in his new capacity as "Reich commissioner for the Strengthening of Germandom") the best ways of exploiting occupied Czechoslovakia and Poland. He proclaimed that they must become the new granaries of the Reich; they must be stripped of church bells and other scrap metals, as well as old rubber and leather. He told Hans Frank, the governor-general of rump Poland (the "General-Gouvernement") that his domain would have to fend for itself.

It seems that Göring was aware of Hitler's geographical solution of the "Jewish problem"—bulldozing all of Europe's Jews as far eastward as possible. "The General-Gouvernement," he reminded Frank at this meeting, "is going to have to accommodate this orderly exodus of Jews from Germany and from our new eastern provinces." But he did direct that there were to be no further trainloads of Jews shipped into Poland without his approval, and on March 24, 1940, he would issue a specific prohibition in these terms: "I hereby forbid further such deportations unless I have given my consent and the governor-general [Hans Frank] is in agreement. I will not tolerate the excuse that subordinate agencies have permitted such 'emigrations.' "

In Berlin on March 2, Göring was given the detailed operations plan for the Nazi attack on Norway. Angry at not having been consulted, he forbade the subordination of any of his air-force units to this new theater's commander. Göring decided to put his deputy, the rough-tongued General Milch, in command of air operations in Norway when the time came. He kept up his attack on the army's Norway plan. On March 5, at a Reich Chancellery conference, he dismissed it as unworkable. Hitler solved the dispute simply: He excluded the field marshal from all the remaining planning conferences that month.

Late that month the Forschungsamt intercepted a crucial Finnish diplomatic telegram, sent from Paris to Helsinki, revealing that Winston Churchill had disclosed in secret French talks that a British expeditionary force was poised to invade Norway. Shocked into emergency activity, on April 2 Hitler ordered Göring and navy chief Raeder to land German troops in Norway seven days later. That same night the first three steamships sailed for Narvik, in Norway's far north, laden with concealed infantry and their arms and ammunition.

Germany invaded Norway and Denmark on April 9, 1940.

In southern Norway Göring was able to demonstrate conclusively the role of air power. Göring's paratroops captured airfields and within minutes the first transport planes were debouching troops onto them. His planes landed on frozen Norwegian lakes and unloaded guns and equipment. His fighters and bombers strafed the British expeditionary force without mercy. On April 19, Hitler would direct Göring to destroy any Norwegian villages occupied by the British—''without regard for the civilian population.''

At Narvik in northern Norway General Eduard Dietl's force was heavily outnumbered and cut off from supplies. Germany hoped to persuade Sweden to allow the transit of supplies across their territory, and on April 15 Dahlerus arrived in Berlin bringing Vice-Admiral Fabian Tamm, commander of the Swedish navy, for talks. At the Air Ministry Göring subjected the delegation to an hour-long diatribe. ''While Göring was speaking,'' recalled one of them, Gunnar Hägglöf, ''I noticed that he wore on the middle finger of his left hand an enormous red gemstone, which gleamed in the light.'' Tamm warned that Sweden had every intention of defending her frontiers.

''Against the British too?'' challenged Göring.

''Against everybody who tries to force their way across Sweden's frontiers,'' the admiral responded.

As the days passed, there were grave crises in Norway for the German invaders. The theater commander, General Nikolaus von Falkenhorst, lost his nerve. Göring despatched relays of his own trusted observers up to see Milch in Oslo. The crises passed, however and by the end of April most of Norway was under Nazi rule. Hitler directed Göring to have his entire air force ready for *Yellow*. On May 4, Göring sent his private aircraft up to fetch Milch back to Germany. He intended to leave Milch in charge of Berlin, while he directed *Yellow* air operations from the front line himself.

The Swedish government was still refusing to allow even nonmilitary German supplies up to General Dietl in embattled Narvik. Göring telephoned Dahlerus to fly down from Stockholm to Berlin on May 6. Dahlerus offered to negotiate an armistice at Narvik, placing the region under neutral Swedish supervision until the war was over.

* * *

Operations in Norway had restored the field marshal's esteem, not least in his own eyes. Colonel von Waldau surprised him practicing Napoleonic gestures in front of a mirror in his train. But to mock his elephantine vanity would be to overlook his air force's contribution to both Norway and *Yellow*, the coming campaign in Western Europe. In a string of secret conferences since November 1939 Göring had plotted and planned the all-important surprise air attack against the Dutch and Belgian fortifications that would open the offensive. There is no indication in the archives that Göring had either legal or military qualms about the campaign.

Göring demanded several consecutive days of perfect flying weather. For three or four more days, waiting for that weather, Hitler postponed zero hour, and the Forschungsamt wiretappers could hear the bafflement and confusion that the repeated delays engendered among the still-unidentified traitors in Berlin. On May 6, a voice calling from Luxembourg was heard to ask Berlin, ''Are they coming or aren't they?'' In Holland, all leave was canceled, telephone links cut, and guards of strategic bridges doubled. On May 7, the FA intercepted a sinister telegram from the Belgian envoy at the Vatican reporting that an unnamed German traitor* had arrived from Berlin on April 29 and informed the ''scoundrels in the Vatican'' (as Göring always termed them) of Hitler's latest *Yellow* deadline.

Hitler and Göring were on hot coals. They were losing the element of surprise. On May 8, the weather was still too uncertain to begin.

25

VICTORY IN THE WEST

Placing Göring briefly in command in Berlin, Adolf Hitler departed for the new western front on May 9, 1940. As the next dawn's clear spring sun lifted on the eastern horizon, nearly 4,000 Nazi warplanes—including 1,482 bombers and 248 twin-engined and 1,016 single-engined fighter planes—scythed unannounced into France and across the neutral Low Countries, hammering the enemy's air defenses and providing close battlefield support for the advancing tanks and infantry.

Dressed in summer whites and sporting some of his most optimistic rings, Field Marshal Hermann Göring set out in his special train from Carinhall to join his generals at Kurfürst, the air staff's permanent headquarters just outside Berlin. Waiting with the other exuberant Luftwaffe generals there, Milch wrote in his pocket diary, "Afternoon, the field marshal arrives in train. Huge victories, great [enemy] losses! Eben Emael [the most important Belgian fortress] captured by air force."

For five days the air-force commander would live aboard his train at Kurfürst while his generals fawned on him. His new special train, code-named *Asia*, was adorned with velvet upholstery, tapestries, rich paneling, and an outsized bath that would not have been out of place in his other mansions in Berlin and Carinhall. Since the Nazi party was above all a *motoring* party, the train boasted of not only the usual two freight cars bristling with flak guns, but also a string of flat tops on which he had ordered an assortment of his finest automobiles to be loaded, including command cars built by Buick and La Salle, two Ford Mercuries, a Citroën, a Ford pickup, and two other Mercedes vehicles (a six-wheeled cross-country car and a shooting brake). This train also provided a fully equipped darkroom for Sonderführer Eitel Lange, his personal photographer; a mobile hospital with six beds, and an operating theater; and Göring's personal barber shop, whose surviving inventory shows that he was not accustomed to travel without hand mirrors, compacts and powder puffs, perfume atomizers with rubber bulbs, jars of cream, bottles of hair cologne, and sun lamps.

From the comfort and safety of this train he followed the triumphs of the German armies. Each day General Milch climbed aboard with darkroom-damp aerial photographs that he had personally taken of the fighting at Dinant and Charleville. On May 11, 1940, he told Göring that they had already obliterated a thousand enemy planes. At Sedan, France, the German troops threw a bridgehead across the River Meuse, and Bruno Loerzer's II Air Corps was giving good support to General Heinz Guderian's armor as it rammed into France. Göring rushed the euphoric reports to Hitler's headquarters with a swiftness that the army could not match. His name was written there in letters of gold. The Luftwaffe's operations had gone without a hitch. Later interrogators would find it hard to stop Hermann Göring talking endlessly of these glorious exploits of May 1940. He prattled happily about one Dutch Army lieutenant who called up his supreme commander, General Winkel-mann, to ask permission to blow the vital bridge over the Albert Canal. "There are paratroops coming down all around!" The general had refused, stating that blowing the bridge would cut off two of his divisions. "No paratroops," he exclaimed, "would dare to drop so far behind our lines." Minutes later the lieutenant had phoned him again: "General," he said, "I am about to be taken prisoner."

Air supremacy was once again decisive, as it had proven in Norway. Göring's air force had displayed its now-familiar power on May 14 against Rotterdam: Thirty-six bombers were dispatched to silence a Dutch artillery position in the old port city. Soon after they took off, the Dutch fortress commander capitulated, and Göring's paratroop general, Student, fired red signal flares to halt the bombing attack. One wave, however, missed the flares and completed its bombing run. The resulting fires got out of hand and ravaged the old city, killing nine hundred people.

Göring was unrepentant. "I'll tell you what happened," he said heatedly under interrogation. "The fire brigades were so scared to death that they refused to move out and do anything about the fires. You can ask the bur-gomaster of Rotterdam about that and he will tell you the same thing. All those stories of 'thousands of dead' "—Churchill had repeatedly talked of

By the end of World War I Hermann Göring was one of Germany's top-scoring fighter aces. NATIONAL ARCHIVES

Hermann Göring (far right) with fellow fighter pilots. He had already earned his Iron Cross, but still lacked the coveted Pour le Mérite. COLLECTIONS OF THE LIBRARY OF CONGRESS

At war's end, Lieutenant Hermann Göring, lean and handsome, proudly displayed the "Blue Max," the Pour le Mérite medal, at his throat. NATIONAL ARCHIVES

Hermann Göring (center) photographed with other fighter pilots, all holders of the Pour le Mérite, 1917 COLLECTIONS OF THE LIBRARY OF CONGRESS

Hermann Göring with his mother (far left), and sisters Paula and Olga at Bad Tölz COLLECTIONS OF THE LIBRARY OF CONGRESS

Soulful and mystically inclined, Carin von Fock became Göring's first wife in 1923 NATIONAL ARCHIVES

*A youthful Göring, seen with his bride, Carin, during their painful,
penurious stay in Italy in 1923*   GERD HEIDEMANN

At St. Mark's Square in Venice, 1924, Göring is snapped with Carin by a street photographer. His smile betrays a shadow of the worries already besetting him. GERMAN FEDERAL ARCHIVES

Prince August-Wilhelm ("Auwi"), the Hohenzollern pretender to the German imperial throne, was one of the many aristocrats persuaded by Göring to join the Nazi party. NATIONAL ARCHIVES

Hermann Göring attending to his toilette, with an array of bottles and sprays that would have done a vaudeville actor proud COLLECTIONS OF THE LIBRARY OF CONGRESS

In 1934 Göring was appointed Reich chief huntsman. His game laws were a model for those enforced throughout Europe today. Satirical journal Simplicissimus *portrayed the animal world saluting him for having prohibited vivisection in the Reich.* AUTHOR'S COLLECTION

On the vast Schorf Heath estate Göring established a bison sanctuary, which he toured with bemused diplomats on June 10, 1934.
NATIONAL ARCHIVES

June 20, 1934: Göring's dream comes true, and his first wife, Carin, is reburied in a stone crypt on the Carinhall estate while a bareheaded Führer and the Reich's top dignitaries pay homage to her.
NATIONAL ARCHIVES

The eve of the Night of the Long Knives, June 28, 1934; a grim-faced Hitler and (partially obscured) Göring attend the wedding of Nazi Gauleiter Josef Terboven.
NATIONAL ARCHIVES

In 1934 all was harmony with Hitler's commanders as he rebuilt the German armed forces. Flanked by (left to right) Raeder, Göring, Fritsch, and Blomberg, Hitler reviewed the Armed Forces Day parade. In 1938 Blomberg and Fritsch, victims of two sordid scandals, quit, leaving Hitler and Göring with absolute power.
NATIONAL ARCHIVES

After the Röhm massacre, Göring's rivals for power had been eliminated. Officially Prime Minister of Prussia (seen here addressing the Prussian Parliament), he soon dropped the words "of Prussia."
NATIONAL ARCHIVES

The sumptuous 1935 wedding of Hermann Göring to Emmy Sonnemann put an end to two years of scandal and rumor.   GERD HEIDEMANN

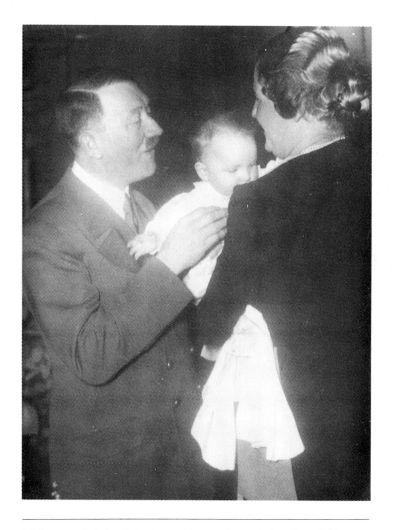

*Hitler attended the christening of Emmy Göring's daughter, Edda;
later he called Emmy a "rotten influence" on her husband.*

Edda Göring presents her father with flowers, while Göring's chief aide, General Karl Bodenschatz (at right), looks on. Edda's near-miraculous birth in June 1938 changed Göring's life, making him malleable and understanding. NATIONAL ARCHIVES

Invited on annual hunting trips to Poland, Göring tried hard to persuade the Poles to join with Germany in an invasion of Russia.

In November 1937 Göring, as Reich chief huntsman, opened the biggest game exhibition that Europe had seen in half a century. NATIONAL ARCHIVES

Göring inspects one of the exhibits. NATIONAL ARCHIVES

Entering Vienna in April 1938 after the Anschluss, Hermann Göring, clutching his new field marshal's baton, found that he was genuinely popular. VOAK COLLECTION, HOFFMANN ARCHIVES, VIENNA

On April 20, 1939, his fiftieth birthday, Hitler secretly told his three commanders-in-chief to expect war soon, probably that year. Photo shows (left to right) Field Marshal Walther von Brauchitsch (army), Reichmarschall Hermann Göring (air force), and Grand Admiral Erich Raeder (navy). NATIONAL ARCHIVES

Göring returning from Rome in April 1939, shown here leaving the Anhalter station in Berlin VOAK COLLECTION, HOFFMANN ARCHIVES, VIENNA

A rare candid snapshot of Hitler—taken by Adjutant von Below—at the famous secret meeting at the Berghof, August 22, 1939: Visible among the plainclothed generals are (left to right) Göring, Manstein, and Brauchitsch. STANLEY S. HUBBARD COLLECTION

Göring designed the interior of Carinhall to resemble a Swedish hunting lodge. GERD HEIDEMANN

Lions recognized an animal lover in Göring, and respected him; Göring's guests were less at ease when the lions frisked around them. GERD HEIDEMANN

An upper floor at Carinhall was devoted to Hermann Göring's model railway layout. Model planes on wires could "bomb" the trains.
GERD HEIDEMANN

Swedish businessman Birger Dahlerus (here testifying at Nuremberg in March 1946) acted as Göring's secret courier to the enemy powers from 1939 to 1941. NATIONAL ARCHIVES

Göring's motor yacht Carin II, *was a gift of the German automobile industry.*   GERD HEIDEMANN

In the occupied countries, Hermann Göring was able to satisfy his lust for priceless works of art at will, purchasing seized Jewish collections at knockdown prices; in Italy, he had to use more legal methods.
NATIONAL ARCHIVES

In November 1941 General Ernst Udet (in top hat, center, carrying a wreath to Richthofen's tomb) committed suicide. He left the German Air Force's production in chaos, but Göring was really to blame.
NATIONAL ARCHIVES

General Ernst Udet, a skillful caricaturist, portrayed himself wrestling with aircraft production schedules. MILCH ARCHIVES

At Fischhorn Castle, an American soldier snapped a sad picture of Emmy and Edda Göring at the moment the Reichsmarschall was driven off into captivity. KEITH WILSON COLLECTION

In his Nuremberg prison cell, November 23, 1945, Göring pens a postcard to his wife. For months he wondered why there were no replies. NATIONAL ARCHIVES

On the table of his cell—deliberately flimsy to thwart suicide attempts —the Reichsmarschall displayed his precious photographs of Edda and Emmy, and of his mother and father, the colonial governor of German South West Africa (Namibia). NATIONAL ARCHIVES

Colonel Burton C. Andrus, U.S. Cavalry, had the thankless task of governing Nuremburg prison during the war crimes trial. Here he is seen helmeted and in uniform at the far left. NATIONAL ARCHIVES

In the dock at Nuremberg, Göring found himself seated next to Rudolph Hess, Hitler's "truant" deputy. SIGNAL CORPS PHOTO

Prison fare at Nuremberg was a plate of soup. The surroundings were less luxurious than Göring had been accustomed to.

Searching for the U.S. prison officer who might help him to escape the gallows, Göring's eyes lighted on Lieutenant Jack G. Wheelis, a Texan, and a huntsman like himself. NATIONAL ARCHIVES

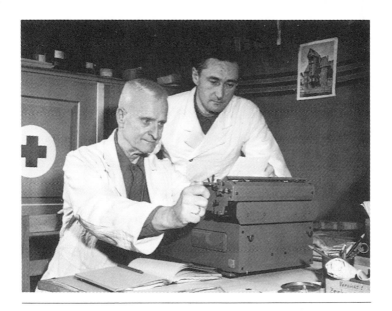

The German physician at Nuremburg prison, Dr. Ludwig Pflucker (seated) shook hands with the Reichsmarschall as they parted for the last time. ("Because, the last time, it was difficult for a doctor not to shake hands. . . .") NATIONAL ARCHIVES

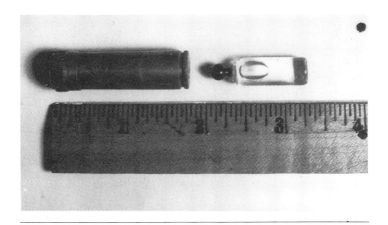

This brass bullet and the glass cyanide ampule it contained are identical to those used by Göring to escape his punishment.
MILTON SILVERMAN

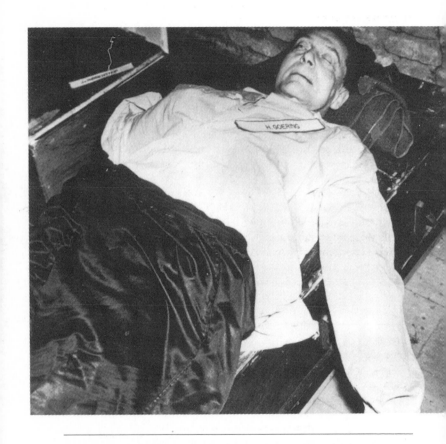

Göring dies—with one eye open, and one eye winking shut. He cheated the hangman, and only he knew how. U.S. ARMY PHOTO

"thirty thousand" killed at Rotterdam, to justify his own strategic air offensive—"are pure invention."

Late on May 15, 1940, Hermann Göring ordered *Asia* hauled across Germany to the western front.

Hitched to the train now were the extra carriages for his own own "little general staff," a unit that would prove a source of irritation to Jeschonnek's air staff housed in its own command train, *Robinson*. Göring had surrounded himself with a number of smarmy young adjutants, overpromoted and handsome but unencumbered with either the training or the experience of the staff officers serving under Jeschonnek. Supervising this young private staff of cartographers and teleprinter and radio operators was the chief adjutant, Major Bernd von Brauchitsch (son of the German Army's Commander in Chief). He briefed Göring on the daily operations. As the tide eventually turned against Germany, he would unashamedly color his reports too, to favor and reassure his chief.

Göring's extra-long command train reached its assigned halt at 11:00 A.M. on May 16, close to a tunnel in western Germany's mountainous Eiffel country. A special wooden platform had been erected alongside the track to enable the portly field marshal to dismount—though he rarely did so. He and his closer cronies partook of free wine and caviar at the long table in the No. 1 dining car, while the lesser fry ate (and paid for) their meals in the less comfortably appointed No. 2. Since extra carriages had been coupled on for Brauchitsch's young team, the train's toilet outlets no longer coincided with the sewer inlets beneath. Such being the prerogatives of absolute power, Göring claimed for himself the only one that still functioned properly and ordered all other lavatories sealed.

Once Göring ordered Fritz Görnnert, his train's commandant, to sound a dummy air-raid alert. The results were farcical. The locomotive engineer sent it plunging into the tunnel, ripping out all the communication cables from their railside sockets. Trailing cables and wires, the train hurtled through the sheltering tunnel and emerged, still accelerating, from the far end. Göring's handsome adjutants pulled every emergency handle in sight, while the field marshal screamed, red-faced, "Has the fellow gone stark-raving mad?"

He soon forgave Görnnert as the victory reports poured in. With the Nazi breakthrough at Sedan on May 16, France was already doomed. Three days later Göring sent for the Swedish consul general in Paris and suggested that he invite the French to sue for peace. "We are ready," he assured the Swede, "to grant reasonable conditions." He basked in Hitler's praise. Once he ordered his chief of air staff to bomb the airfields around Paris. "Jeschonnek," he boomed grandly, "let my air force darken the skies!" On May 23, he handed out the first eight Knight's Crosses to his airborne troops. On that day the British expeditionary force began its humiliating retreat to the English Channel ports, abandoning their Belgian and French allies. Göring picked up the phone and bragged to Hitler that his bombers would set those ports ablaze, then wipe out the enemy troops trapped in northern France. VIII Air Corps commander Richthofen noted Göring's orders in his diary: "Destroy the British in the pocket."

Hitler indulged his air-force commander, ordering his tank forces on May 24 to hold back. "The air-force," wrote General Franz Halder, chief of the general staff, in his diary that evening, "is to finish off the encircled army!" "Our air-force," Göring announced, beaming, to his deputy, "is to mop up the British. I've persuaded the Führer to hold the army back." The halt order was controversial, but it made sense to the generals at the time: There was a belief that the campaign was all but over; there was no question of "going easy" on the British. "The Führer wants us to give them a lesson they'll never forget," Göring told Milch.

As his squadrons geared up for this task, Göring shifted his train *Asia* forward once more, to Polch, then flew off in a Junkers 52 to gloat over the destruction at Rotterdam. Taking just Loerzer and Udet with him he continued by road to Amsterdam, treasure city of the world of art and antiques. His growing lust for costly baubles temporarily satisfied with well-timed purchases, he flew in a Storch light plane back to Hitler's headquarters to report on the "mopping up" at Dunkirk. "Only fishing boats are coming over for the British," he scoffed. "Let's hope that the Tommies can swim!"

As he left France on May 30 and returned to Potsdam, he was unaware that three hundred thousand British and French troops were slipping away from the beaches of Dunkirk. Three hundred German bombers stood impotently by, grounded by ten-tenths cloud. Milch broke the bad news about the completed evacuation to Göring when *Asia* returned to France on June 5. "I saw six or seven dead Negroes," Milch told him, "and perhaps twenty or thirty other dead. The rest have got clean away. They abandoned their equipment and fled." He suggested that they throw airborne troops straight over to seize a beachhead and capture airfields in southern England, just as they had in Norway.

Göring dismissed the idea. "It can't be done," he said. He had only one airborne division, he would later explain. "If I had had four, I would have gone straight over to Britain."

The worst of the fighting in France over, he resumed his direction of the war economy, summoning Cabinet-style meetings aboard his train. Looking not unlike Prince Danilo in *The Merry Widow*, he appeared afterward in his dining car resplendent in white uniform, sash, and sparkling brooches, his belly held in by a belt inlaid with jeweled golden plates. First Lieutenant Göring, his nephew, went off on scavenging expeditions across occupied France. From a clothing store at Rheims he "liberated" a truckload of shirts, stockings, and other booty, which was duly parceled out among the officers on the field marshal's staff with a note, "A gift of field Marshal Göring." His charisma was undeniable. One Luftwaffe officer said that for all his fancy uniforms Göring was still a *Kamerad*. "First-rate guy," agreed another. "Pity he's so fat." "He's got a pot belly," said another officer, a lieutenant whom Göring had recently decorated, "he looks a bit unhealthy, carries a knobbed cane and an outsize pistol, and wears brown boots and a white cap—a bit ridiculous, to tell the truth." One squadron commander heard Göring tell fighter pilots not to panic if they *heard* a Spitfire coming up behind. "I wanted the ground to open and swallow me up!" said the squadron commander. "*Donnerwetter*, the ignorance! In a plane's cockpit you can't even hear your *own* machine guns."

Attempting to stay informed, Göring called conferences right down to squadron-commander level. "Hermann," reported one pilot to comrades shot down over Britain, "listens to men like [Major Werner] Mölders and [Colonel Adolf] Galland in preference to any of his generals. He had one meal with us and kept asking, 'What do *you* think, major?' And people tell him, too: 'First, broadcasting should cease at dusk; second, only experienced men as squadron commanders, not men who've never seen combat; third, don't send home all our best men as instructors.' "

Once he ordered a forester from Carinhall to bring a deer down to France for him to shoot. Donning hunting costume, he sallied forth, leaving Milch, Jeschonnek, and other staff members to hold the situation conference without him. Milch finished not only the conference without him, but dinner and dessert as well. Göring returned in a foul temper, having fallen asleep on his stand and missed the deer when it appeared. Finding both conference and dinner over, he spluttered angrily, then brightened. "Right," he snapped to an aide. "Take down this order. Staff conference in ten minutes followed by dinner. All officers are to attend and eat dinner as usual."

Hermann Göring believed the war virtually over. The French had asked for an armistice. "All this planning," asserted Udet, downgrading the He 177 four-engined bomber project after he returned to Berlin, "is garbage."

Göring had begun one of his major wartime pursuits, beefing up his art collection from the galleries of the defeated nations. On the expensive notepaper of the Amstel Hotel, Amsterdam, he penned a "list of pictures delivered to Carinhall on June 10, 1940"—nineteen priceless Flemish paintings by Rubens and other Old Masters from the Königs collection and seven more bought from other sources including several works by Rembrandt, Pieter Breughel the Elder, and Göring's favorite, Lucas Cranach the Elder.

When, one week later, on June 18, Milch warned Göring in a report written on the basis of his front-line inspections that the Ju 88 was not meeting its specifications as a bomber, Göring turned a deaf ear. Final victory seemed just around the corner to him as he took his generals to the pompous armistice ceremony at Compiègne on June 23. "The town of Compiègne is still smoldering," wrote Lieutenant General Hoffmann von Waldau in his diary:

> Barely any population left, houses sliced open to display their
> shattered contents, stray dogs roaming the streets. Huge applause
> from the soldiers, Labor Front, and auxiliary services. Our "Her-
> mann" really is immensely popular. Drive through the fine forest
> and broad avenues to the dining car of [Marshal] Foch. [The car
> of France's famous World War I commander was a static exhibit
> in the forest.] An avenue leads to a large clearing surrounded by
> pine trees; the dining car is at its center.
>   At 3:20 P.M. the French appear . . . Their airman displays a
> studied nonchalance. After the Preamble has been read, the Führer
> departs. It was an uplifting hour.

Hitler's commanders followed him in a carefully prescribed order, with
Göring immediately behind, then Ribbentrop, Hess, and Raeder. Squeezing
his bulk behind the long dining table in *Asia* afterward, Göring declared
happily, "You know, even as a boy I always knew that one day I should
become a *Feldherr* [warlord]!"

Through a man whom Beppo Schmid would identify in his papers simply
as a "third party," Göring learned that Hitler was proposing only to *simulate*
invasion preparations against Britain under the code name *Sea Lion*, a "gigantic bluff" to bring the British into line. This suited the field marshal down
to the ground. He did not want to invade Britain; talking in private with
Milch, he dismissed the notion of an invasion as superfluous. Schmid was
not surprised when the air staff made no call for the targeting preparations
that a real invasion operation would have required. On June 22, Waldau
recorded that regrouping had begun, but after attending a command conference called by Göring on the following day he recorded, "Nothing of military
significance [is planned] before [Hitler's] Reichstag speech"—which would
not be for two or three weeks.

On June 25, Jeschonnek frankly told the major liaising between the air
staff and the high command (OKW), Baron Sigismund von Falkenstein,
"There isn't going to *be* any *Sea Lion*. And I haven't got time to bother
about it." Expanding this remark in a postscript that day to Waldau about
the air force's possible role in an invasion, Falkenstein wrote that Jeschonnek
had refused any comment "since in his opinion the Führer has not the slightest
intention of crossing the [English] Channel."

Hitler and Göring both believed that air attacks on Britain's shipping
lifeline would suffice to force Churchill to see things their way. Göring
ordered his squadrons to begin small-scale raids on British ports and
harbors—but attacks on inland towns were explicitly forbidden.

Göring himself had been drawn back to Amsterdam to run a greedy eye
over the amazing art collection of a bankrupt Dutch dealer, J. Goudstikker.
His absence on these curious shopping expeditions was a relief for the air

force. On June 27, his chief of operations, Waldau, commented in his private diary, "Field marshal is away on his travels, a blessing for us." Two days later he returned in *Asia* to Berlin, and here he would stay until early September—which testified to his complete lack of interest in the "phony" *Sea Lion* operation. Idling out at Carinhall, he drooled over his new art acquisitions, and considered which of his generals to ennoble at the end of the war. He rewarded his friend Ernst Udet immediately with the Knight's Cross on July 5, although Udet's desk job as director of air armament had involved hardly any heroism at all.

Hitler told Göring that he was planning to make a magnanimous peace offer to Britain in his major Reichstag speech. The field marshal warned that the British would insist on a total withdrawal from Norway, Poland, and the west—though they *might* allow Germany to retain Alsace-Lorraine and the Polish Corridor. Hitler quieted Göring with the disclosure that he was going to promote him at the same Reichstag session to "Reichsmarschall," or six-star general. There had only been one other in German history, Prince Eugen of Savoy. Göring swelled with pride and began poring over suitable fabrics for the new uniform immediately—a color that would establish that he was Reichsmarschall of all three services, and not just of the Luftwaffe. He finally plumped for a soft pearl gray. Valet Robert murmured that it was a woman's fabric. "If *I* wear it," hissed Göring, "then it's for men."

Before delivering his speech on July 19, Hitler once again displayed his real contempt for Göring's authority by refusing to let him see his speech in advance. He delivered his peace offer to the British in such clumsy terms that Göring realized at once, as he told interrogators later, that "the fat was in the fire."

As Reichsmarschall, however, he was the highest-ranking officer in Europe, indeed the world. Göring hurried home and tried on the new uniform before a mirror, then paraded it for Hitler's benefit in the Chancellery. Hitler handed him the parchment title deed as Reichsmarschall in a specially designed casket encrusted with diamonds and emeralds that Göring would later describe as the most precious gift he had ever received from the Führer. "Göring," wrote General von Richthofen, visiting Carinhall on July 21, "was radiant, full of the Führer's acclamation of him, full of his house, of his paintings, of his daughter—in short, full of everything."

The new Reichsmarschall had invited the generals over to Carinhall on that day to hear his plans for the next weeks of the air war against Britain. For most of those entering his large study it was their first glimpse of their commander's accumulating wealth. A detailed inventory of this room's contents, compiled a few weeks earlier, survives: four long marble-topped tables, two green leather-topped tables, six smaller round tables; an outsize desk and chairs, with their green leather upholstery embossed with the Göring crest—a mailed fist clutching at a ring. Six chandeliers illuminated the room, two of baroque pewter style, two of gilt (gifts from the city of Aachen), and two of silver and crystal (gifts of the Reich Handicrafts Association on his most recent birthday). Fourteen wood carvings, including three medieval Madonnas (one donated by the publisher Brockhaus at Christmas) stood in niches between the twenty-two paintings that Göring's experts had selected for him—some of them literally beyond price, like Leonardo da Vinci's "Leda," while others were dictated by a sense of history, like Lenbach's 1888 portrait of Bismarck, and Knirr's painting of the Führer.

This naked display of wealth had its purpose, of course. It was an implicit statement by Göring that his piratical authority was absolute—and an unspoken promise that similar riches awaited all those who followed him.

Looking around this sumptuous chamber, Göring made out the faces of Kesselring, Sperrle, and Milch—all three had been promoted to field marshal. He told them that the *Endkampf* against Britain would begin in about one week, since Britain was refusing to throw in the sponge. Meanwhile he directed them to attack Britain's merchant shipping, promising to follow with "violent attacks" (he did not say on what) "to unsettle the whole country." Ten days later Hitler told his army generals that he intended to await the results of the first ten days of this "intensified air warfare." His purpose was to bully Britain into accepting his peace offer. In secret, Göring resumed his clandestine contacts with London, inviting, on July 24, the Dutch airline director Albert Plesman to Carinhall to act as an intermediary.

But the air war did not produce the results Hitler had expected. He himself had applied such irksome restrictions to it—forbidding attacks by night or on civilian targets, and upholding a total embargo on bombing London— that Göring was prevented from unfolding his real air power against the enemy. It was a strategic error, particular since the fine summer months were already upon them. He now had about 230 twin-engined Me 110's available, but they were proving too cumbersome for combat: he had some 760 Me 109's, but these could not reach London with enough fuel for combat. The British Air Force was, moreover, showing unwelcome signs of resilience. With each day that passed it was recovering, yet Hitler was still pussyfooting. Directing Göring on August 1 to "eliminate the British Air Force in combat," he still expressly forbade "terror air raids."

With a feeling of hopelessness Göring called his field marshals back to Carinhall on August 6 and outlined the details of *Eagle Day*—the opening strike of a three-day grand slam against the British airfields and radar stations, designed to force the remaining British squadrons up into lethal air combat. Several days passed while he awaited the right three days, and when he launched *Eagle Day* on the thirteenth, if went off half-cocked. As the weather worsened that day, Kesselring recalled his force, Luftflotte 2, and the next two days would see only halfhearted skirmishing. On the fourteenth, Göring heard Hitler say while briefing the newly promoted field marshals at the Chancellery that *Sea Lion*, the invasion, was purely a threat—"a last resort, if other pressures [on Britain] fail." Later that day the Reichsmarschall angrily summoned Milch and the two other Luftwaffe field marshals out to Carinhall to express his displeasure at the air offensive's failure.

Air-crew morale was spiraling downward like an He 111 bomber with its tailplane shot away. The Luftwaffe was now fighting a determined enemy in his own skies. The Me 110 was being mauled. The Ju 88 was defective. Mass fire raids on London were still denied them. Repeating Hitler's words to the Luftwaffe that day, August 15, Göring's face adopted the familiar "angry lion" look. Milch noted Hitler's bombing embargoes in his green leather diary: "Still not cities in general, and in particular not London."

At Carinhall Göring continued to sweat that summer out. Down at Berchtesgaden Hitler began to seek scapegoats. Göring anxiously offered to blast the British into submission, but on August 24 the high command again stated Hitler's absolute prohibition on terror raids on London. Two nights later, however, Churchill took the initiative, ordering the first raids on the center of Berlin. Three nights later the RAF bombers returned to Berlin, killing eight people. Outraged, Hitler directed the Reichsmarschall to stand by to retaliate against London at the end of the month. He hated the decision even now, and on the fourth the high command recorded that the Führer was still forbidding raids on London, although half a dozen British raids on Berlin had by now occurred. When two days later Hitler finally lifted the year-long embargo, it was Göring who hesitated, aware that the first bombs on London would crush once and for all his hopes of peace. Beppo Schmid observed Göring's reluctance, as did the hard-bitten General von Richthofen, who wrote on September 6, "This afternoon the decision comes to raid London. Let's hope the Reichmarschall stands firm. I've got my doubts on that score."

Göring departed unhappily for Holland, announcing that he was taking personal command of the Battle of Britain. On the seventh, his train moved on to La Boissière le Déluge, a little rail station near the Channel coast. Flanked by Field Marshal Kesselring (Luftflotte 2) and General Loerzer (II Air Corps) he stood that afternoon on the cliffs, swelling with newfound pride as his bombers thundered overhead to raid London for the first time. That night 380 Londoners were killed—it was the beginning of a murderous new form of air war, for which Hitler and Churchill would bear equal responsibility.

Provoked by the August 1940 raids on Berlin, Hitler and Göring had thus trashed the meticulous staff planning in Schmid's target-dossier *Blue*. They had done so at the very instant when the Luftwaffe had almost gained supremacy by gouging out the radar stations on which Britain's fighter defenses depended. As the Battle of Britain underwent this fateful metamorphosis from a chivalrous dueling in the skies to a brutal exchanging of bombing raids, Göring again lost interest. Once, seated in *Asia*'s dining car, he asked General Jeschonnek, one of the foremost advocates of this terror bombing, "Do you think that Germany would cave in if Berlin was wiped out?"

"Of course not!" retorted Jeschonnek stoutly, then smiled thinly as he realized what he had said. "British morale," he then suggested, "is more brittle than our own."

"That's where you are wrong," said Göring.

By the end of September 1940 his bombers had killed seven thousand Londoners, but he saw no sign of a political collapse. As the glamor of command-train life faded, he moved to Paris, took over a floor at the Ritz, had an especially large bath installed, wolfed down caviar, and began to live in a fantasy world of his own. Once his signals officer had to put him through on the phone, using "command flash" priority, to Emmy and Edda at Carinhall. "Can you hear, Emmy?" he shouted, seated on his hotel bed in a green silk kimono. "I'm standing on Cap Gris Nez at this very moment, while my magnificent airplanes are thundering overhead to England!"

Clanking with brand-new medals, his commanders watched his antics with more amusement than anger. Burdened on September 12 with the Golden Flying Badge with Diamonds, Richthofen mused sardonically in his diary, "One gets to look more and more like an ox in the Whit [Sunday] Parade."

Aware that his air force was meeting its match in the skies over southern England, Göring was mentally and physically drained. He returned briefly to Berlin early that October, but did not enjoy it as the sirens now often wailed there, forcing four million Berliners to seek shelter—many of them muttering incantations about "Meier the Broom": To his earlier promise to change his name to Meier, Göring had foolishly added another, to eat a broomstick, if one enemy bomber should reach the Reich capital. On October 3, he had to preside over a ministerial conference on providing flak defenses and air-raid shelters for the city. Two days later he saw Hitler briefly—the Führer directed him not to concern himself with food shortages in France and Belgium, but to treat the "Nordic" countries Norway, Denmark, and Holland well "for political reasons"—and then returned unenthusiastically to France. The diary of the later-famous Hermann Göring Regiment records that his train *Asia* arrived back at headquarters at 8:00 P.M. on October 10, 1940.

While losing the initiative in the Battle of Britain, Hitler had taken the first steps to seize an historic initiative in the east. He was preparing for the coming Nazi assault on the Soviet Union. Göring had remained at Carinhall while Hitler and his army generals brooded over these momentous decisions in Bavaria, and he had not been consulted. At the August 14 Chancellery conference he had not paid much attention to Hitler's apparent afterthought, that he would attack the Russians if they deviated from their present pro-Nazi policies or if they turned against Finland or Romania. Those "ifs" probably occluded Göring's perception of danger; besides, Hitler undertook not to make up his mind until May 1941 which way to turn next—whether against Britain or the Soviet Union. Talking to munitions expert Georg

Thomas that day, Göring mentioned that they would not have to keep up their war supplies to Russia in perpetuity. "From the next spring," he predicted, according to the notes that Thomas took, "we'll have no further interest in meeting Russian requirements in their entirety." There is some evidence that the obese and indolent Reichsmarschall was uneasy even then about what the army might be up to. On August 21, the high command's diary registered that the air force would decline to create a large ground organization for *Eastern Buildup* (*Aufbau Ost*), the translucent code name under which the army was currently concealing its planning against Russia, if left in "ignorance of the 'broader intentions.' " Perhaps Göring was assured that the buildup was purely defensive in nature. After seeing him on the twenty-ninth, arms chief Thomas told his department heads that Hitler's main concern was to prevent any further Russian inroads into Western Europe.

The Reichsmarschall would remain in France until early November 1940, unaware of the planning in Berlin. He forayed occasionally into Paris, where he loitered at the Casino de Paris or banqueted at Maxim's with General Friedrich Karl von Hanesse, the corrupt air-force commandant of Paris. Tiring of the Reichsmarschall's company, General von Waldau penciled into his diary on October 22 that he had decided to "put some distance" between himself and the "Big Chief." "It isn't conducive to hard work," he added, "to have to keep somebody company and eat big meals all the time."

Five days later Göring took *Asia* and *Robinson* around the French coastal railroad network, inspecting German Air Force units and "invasion forces" at Le Havre before trundling on in stiflingly hot autumn weather to a tunnel west of Deauville, the fashionable seaside resort where Richthofen had established VIII Air Corps headquarters. Unloading a limousine, Göring drove languidly around the airfields of Normandy, between fields and orchards where the peasants were already harvesting the apples and grapes. He wished he were in East Prussia, and the wish became master of the man: He needed rest and recuperation; his heart was troubling him. In a letter to his brother-in-law Count Eric von Rosen he referred to his "exhaustion." On the last day of October, attending a well-fed commanders' conference on winter training at Deauville, the Reichsmarschall mentioned casually that he intended to go on leave "for a month or two."

He began the long return journey across Europe in stages, arriving back at La Boissière in pouring rain on November 3. He decided to pause for a day or two in Paris, and on the fourth he was at the Ritz again. Here in the capital of Occupied France he was a different man altogether: no longer commander in chief of a now-struggling air force, but Hermann Göring the noted art connoisseur. Indeed, the contents of the captured treasure-houses of France's fleeing Jews were about to be spread at his feet.

26

THE ART DEALER

Göring returned to his sybaritic life-
style at Carinhall. Occasionally
he undertook fresh forays into the
newly occupied territories, returning each time with art treasures loaded
aboard his train. Postwar interrogators would criticize his taste, referring to
his collection of florid nudes and vulgar altarpieces, to his avarice and vanity.
But this negative judgment did less than justice to his real shrewdness as a
collector. By the end of World War II he would have built up, often by only
marginally legal means, a collection worth hundreds of millions of dollars,
and it was not merely Germanic art. As art expert Denys Sutton commented
in one November 1945 report: "Is it surprising that a taste for female nudes
and a desire for unlimited acquisition predominate in Göring's character?
Are these characteristics not shared by other large-scale figures?" He recalled
that banker J. P. Morgan and newspaperman William Randolph Hearst had
a similar appetite for works of art, while the monarchs Rudolf II and Henry
VIII dearly loved paintings of the nude. "I am the first to agree that Göring
was a ruffian," Sutton lectured U.S. intelligence officers, "but from the
facts produced, could it not be argued that he was one better than his colleagues at the top of the Nazi party?"

In the last half of 1940 Göring plunged into art dealings with a zest that left ripples that would not subside for half a century. Connoisseurs and governments still fight greedy battles over the canvas and plaster and marble and bronze that he acquired. He bought many works quite legally, like Peter-Paul Rubens' "Venus and Adonis" which he had "paid through the nose for" at a Paris dealer's. All were seized in 1945. In December of that year an internal memorandum of the Monuments, Fine Arts & Archives branch of the U.S. Control Commission for Germany defined that "looted objects" would even be understood to include "those extracted under duress against some form of remuneration and even those bought from French, Belgian, and Dutch art dealers . . . Thus a picture bought by, or on behalf of, Göring from a Paris dealer will be restituted, when discovered, to the French Government, it being considered as part of the artistic patrimony of France." In 1945, this legal *léger-de-main* was used to confiscate the Reichsmarschall's entire collection including the paintings that he had inherited.

Toward the end of the war, more than one French or Dutch or Belgian dealer had declined to give him a bill of sale—"hoping," as one American officer later surmised, "that they could eventually reclaim the objects *and* keep the purchase money." The moral code of the art dealers was, Göring once said, on a par with that of the horse trader.

In 1944 he valued his Carinhall art collection at fifty million marks. Raising the money to buy it was no problem for the chief of the Four-Year Plan. "I was the last court of appeal," he recalled disarmingly in 1945. "[I] always took enough money along on the train—I had a private train—I would give an order to the Reichsbank and they would get the money. I had to okay the order myself." One day he intended to bequeath the collection to the German people, or so he assured Hitler. In any case, no enemy captor could take away from him the blissful hours that he had spend creating it, and we shall see Hermann Göring obsessed with expanding his art collection even at moments of his country's most desperate military crises.

He had begun his "shopping expeditions" in Amsterdam in the summer of 1940. His personal agent in this Dutch city of canals was Alois Miedl, a thirty-seven year old Bavarian merchant whom the Görings had known for many years. Olga had often stayed with the Miedls in Munich or Amsterdam. It did not bother Hermann that Miedl's wife, Fodora, was a Jew. In 1940 it was Miedl who had introduced him to the extraordinary Goudstikker transaction by which the Reichsmarschall would acquire a fortune in paintings at little ultimate expense. Goudstikker, a wealthy Dutch Jew, had owned a moated castle, Nyenrode, and an art dealership valued at six million guilders. His collection included thirteen hundred modern artworks and Old Masters, including works by Paul Gauguin, Cranach, and Tintoretto (Jacopo Robusti).

Some months before Hitler attacked Holland in May 1940, Goudstikker transferred everything to a dummy corporation, verbally gave power of attorney to a non-Jewish friend, and fled. However, Goudstikker's friend died. Then Goudstikker's ship was torpedoed and he drowned. Then the Dutch banks foreclosed. Goudstikker's widow, a former Austrian *chanteuse* living in New York, asked an Amsterdam attorney to wind up the estate. Given the war circumstances, the appraisers now valued it at only 1.5 million guilders. When Miedl brought it to the attention of Göring's adjutant Erich Gritzbach, however, the purchase price had somehow risen to 2.5 million. None of them could lay their hands on the cash like that, so Miedl brought the Goudstikker dossier in to the guileless Göring, cadging a loan of 2 million guilders, as he said, "to make up the 3.5 million purchase price." Göring greedily agreed—provided that he was given the pick of the art collection.

A Mr. Aa ten Broek signed the sale contract on behalf of Goudstikker's widow on July 1, 1940. The 2.5 million guilders was paid in securities selected by her attorney. For his 2 million, Göring got "all removable objects"; he kept the best, Hitler took fifty-three of the rest for the Führer Building in Munich, and Miedl eventually bought back those that were left over for 1.7 million guilders.

It is difficult to see even now who was cheating whom. Goudstikker's widow got the price she asked, the banks were repaid, the paintings and business legally changed hands. Only later did Göring learn that Miedl had hornswoggled him—that he had advanced the whole purchase price himself with Miedl contributing virtually nothing. "I [had] thereupon," Göring grieved later still, "twice paid out large sums of money to Miedl." Miedl had covered his tracks well. "I once tried," recalled Seyss-Inquart, then Nazi governor of Holland, "to probe into it with police help. But the Reichsmarschall . . . blocked all further investigations." Originally Göring bragged of his "big art killing" to his envious generals. Later, he admitted, he saw it in an "altogether different light."

After the war, the Dutch government claimed the restitution of the entire Goudstikker collection as "looted property." (Mrs. Goudstikker, of course, kept the purchase money in New York.)

By the summer of 1940 Nazi art experts were scouring occupied Western Europe primarily for Göring's benefit. Walter Hofer, whose visiting card proclaimed him to be "curator of the Reichsmarschall's art collections," acted as his principal adviser. The biggest search operation was conducted by his friend Alfred Rosenberg. Hitler had assigned to Rosenberg the job of securing the "ownerless" treasures abandoned by fleeing Jews—forfeited by them in lieu of the compulsory refugee tax.

Göring very rapidly got wind of the Rosenberg operation. Dr. Harold Turner—civilian head of the military occupation authority in Paris, and a Göring-appointed *Staatsrat*—asked the Reichsmarschall to decide the future of the seized collections. Göring thus got first wind of the best bargains and often had them loaded aboard a boxcar attached to *Asia* before Hitler's "art professors" Hans Posse and Karl Haberstock got a look at them. In fact Göring held all the aces: His Four-Year Plan currency agents had the power to open French safe deposits. An Inspector Dufour of the French Sûreté and a Mademoiselle Lucie Botton, formerly employed by Seligmanns, the art dealers, led the agents straight to Jewish caches that often concealed paintings and jewels as well as currency. Göring provided Rosenberg's staff with armed guards, Luftwaffe truck transport, and specialists like art historian Bruno Lohse, released from air-force duties for the purpose.

The Reichsmarschall was the only Nazi with the time to conduct "shopping expeditions" in Paris. The first trip in September 1940 was to "get the feel of the art market," as he later explained.

Minister of Justice Raphaël Alibert protested on October 21 to the head of the military occupation, General Alfred Streccius, about Göring's behavior. His remonstrances fell on deaf ears. Rosenberg wanted the art collections merely photographed and catalogued, and then held at the Führer's pleasure as a bargaining counter for future peace negotiations. Göring merely *wanted* them, and he could come up with hard currency faster than any other source.

On November 5, tiring already of the Battle of Britain, he arrived in Paris again. Groveling French officials received him at the famed Louvre Museum, where Professor Marcel Aubert thanked him on behalf of all his French colleagues for having ordered his bombers to spare their historic monuments during *Yellow*. Touring the galleries afterward, Göring took a fancy to three hunting sculptures, including the Diane de Fontainebleau. He ordered Rudier's, the Auguste Rodin foundry, to cast copies in bronze for him.

That afternoon he visited the beautiful Jeu de Paume gallery at the entrance to the Louvre. Here, Rosenberg's first treasure haul—302 items culled from the collection of the fugitive Lazare Wildenstein—was on display to a privileged few. Göring selected four of them and indicated in lordly fashion that he would take them to Germany. When Rosenberg's officials chafed at this, the Reichsmarschall that same day issued a directive defining their job as being merely to catalog and crate the objects selected for his art collection (and Hitler's) and ship them off to Germany immediately "with Luftwaffe assistance." The remainder were to be auctioned off to dealers and museums. "The monetary proceeds," Göring stipulated in this document, appeasing his own pricking conscience, "shall be assigned to the French State in benefit of the French dependents of war victims."

Through this Nazi treasure-house installed in the Jeu de Paume would be sluiced over the coming four years the confiscated art fortunes of the Hamburger brothers, Isaac, Jean, and Hermann; of Sarah Rosenstein, Madame P. Heilbronn, Dr. Wassermann, and many others. By and large the Nazis left the non-Jewish art collections in France untouched. To provide a spurious aura of legality, a timid French professor, Jacques Beltrand, was required to appraise the values of the items. Beltrand, president of the Société des Peintres-Graveurs Français, set the values absurdly low. Göring's files reveal the professor valuing two paintings by Henri Matisse and portraits by Amadeo

Modigliani and Pierre Auguste Renoir at a total of one hundred thousand francs (about five hundred dollars); two Picassos at thirty-five thousand francs; and "Galante Scène" by Antoine Watteau at thirty thousand francs.

Bragging that his task force's haul of art treasures in Paris, Brussels, and Amsterdam already topped 500 million marks, Rosenberg appealed for further operating funds. "I shall ask Reichsmarschall Göring," he wrote to the Nazi party's treasurer on November 14, "to refund this money to you . . . [He] has visited the depot in Paris several times and is evidently very satisfied with the rich pickings." The party bleated in reply that, strictly speaking, the funds had been provided for Rosenberg to research into Jewish and Masonic affairs. On November 18, Hitler intervened with a formal order seeming to override Göring's directive of the fifth. Göring did not yield one inch. "As far as the confiscated art works are concerned," he argued, pleading his own case in a letter written from Rominten on November 21, "let me highlight my own success over a considerable period in recovering concealed Jewish art treasures. I have resorted to bribery and hiring French detectives and police officials to winkle these treasures out of their (often devilishly clever) hiding places."

Asia would arrive in Paris with only a few hours' warning, and the Reichsmarschall would demand to see the latest haul at the Jeu de Paume. With a carload of detectives following a hundred yards behind him, he cruised through the bazaars of Paris. It was a rare spectacle—the highest-ranking soldier in Europe trafficking with "the shadiest collaborationist art dealers, disreputable lawyers, quasi-dealers [and] expert valuers," as they were tersely characterized in an August 1945 report—"All the riffraff of the international art market."

He would invade Cartier's, exclaiming delightedly at the "cheapness" of their diamonds (exchange rates strongly favored the Reichsmark). He would pick up a bag of cash from General Hanesse, his sleazy air-force commandant in Paris. He liked to pay in cash, and he was furious when he couldn't. In Ghent, Belgium, he saw a giant ring on display and then found he had not enough cash with him. "When I drive around this part of the world," he thundered at his three adjutants Gritzbach, Teske, and Ondarza, "I insist that each of you carry at least twenty thousand marks." He was not short of takers. "In Paris," he would tell American questioners five summers later, "the people ran after me to sell." His mail bulged with offers. "If I went to Holland, or Paris, or Rome," he told one Nuremberg investigator, "I would always find a stack of letters awaiting me . . . Letters from private people, from princes and princesses." Baron Meeus begged Göring's agents in Brussels to buy his interesting Dutch Old Masters. A New York dealer wrote, offering portraits from the thirteenth-century school of Fontainebleau. A certain Pierre Laisis ("expert in antiquities") invited him to buy twelve stone capitals inscribed with the letter *N*, and assured the Reichsmarschall that their previous owner was Napoleon himself.

There is contemporary evidence of this eagerness to sell. "Just watch their eyes light up when they hear they're dealing with a German," Göring said with a snort in August 1942. "They triple the price, and *quintuple* it if it's the Reichsmarschall buying. I wanted to buy a tapestry. They were asking two million francs. They tell the lady the purchaser wants to see the tapestry . . . So she has to come too, and finds out she's coming to the Reichsmarschall. By the time she arrives, the price has rocketed to three million." (Göring sued the vendor in the French courts to enforce the original price.)

"Göring," reported the OSS in 1945, "fought shy of crude, undisguised looting; but he wanted the works of art and so he took them, always managing to find a way of giving at least the appearance of honesty." Questioned on how Göring bought the magnificent Emil Renders collection of Flemish primitives for twelve million Belgian francs, Miedl insisted that the vendor had sold willingly (and Hofer's files bear him out). One advantage was that Göring often paid well over the going price, as Hitler's art agent Karl Haberstock told one Reichsminister with a knowing smirk.

Though they usually conformed to the laws of an otherwise lawless age, Göring's methods were often unbecoming. Visiting Paris late in 1940 he called at the Quai d'Orléans home of an Englishmen, Don Wilkinson, whose wife had been interned. "My dear Marshall Göring," this Englishman wrote him a year later, enclosing a snapshot of a painting:

> Do you recall this, our favourite portrait? It is that of one of Germany's noblest women, Juliana von Stolberg [1506–1580, mother of William of Orange] which hangs in our small living room and has become one of our family circle.
>
> When here, you turned this portrait towards the light admiringly. Noting your interest, someone behind you asked rather too eagerly, "Is it for sale?"
>
> Do you remember how you let the picture swing softly back against the wall and, going to the window, gazed out over the Seine? Then, your impatience passed, you quietly turned back to me and, referring to the possible liberation of my wife, said simply in English, "I will see what I can do."

Unsurprisingly, Wilkinson's wife was freed from custody, and he told her of Göring's visit. "We both agreed," the Englishman wrote to him, "that we wanted you to have 'Juliana' always, to thank you for what you so modestly did for [us]."

The Reichsmarschall's unsavory business tactics rubbed off on his already streetwise agents. On September 26, 1941, Hofer would apologize in a letter that he had bought only one picture for him at Hans Lange's latest auction because of their runaway prices, but bragged that he had snapped up for 3.78 million francs some bargains from the Jeu de Paume depot, including seven Camille Corots, three Honoré Daumiers, four Claude Monets, five Renoirs, a Vincent van Gogh, an Henri de Toulouse-Lautrec, and assorted sketches and watercolors, all from the collection of "the Jew Paul Rosenberg" and all "eminently suitable for swapping." Since Beltrand had valued them *above* their original asking price, Hofer had insisted on paying the latter. Currency agents, he further reported to Göring, had impounded Georges Braque's personal art collection at Bordeaux, but here there was a snag: Braque was not a Jew, so they would have to release his collection. "I have dealt with him in person about his Cranach of a girl," wrote Hofer, knowing of Göring's weakness for this painter. "And I have hinted that the collection may be restituted to him more quickly if he agrees to part with the Cranach to us!!!" Nazi agents had also discovered in Paris a Rubens and an Anthony Van Dyck. "I am having inquiries made whether the owner is a Jew," Hofer notified Göring. "Meanwhile the paintings remain in the bank's safekeeping."

By October 20, 1942, no fewer than 596 paintings, sculptures, tapestries, and articles of furniture would have found their way from the Jeu de Paume into Göring's possession.

Italy rivaled France and Holland as the sources of Göring's fabulous art collection. In October 1938 General Italo Balbo had transported to Carinhall an antique marble copy of the Venus of Praxiteles, excavated at Leptis Magna near Tripoli. As Mussolini's own military misfortunes began, at the end of 1940, he became eager to ingratiate himself with the Germans. In January 1941 Hofer arranged for him to give to Göring eight large Vipiteno paintings for his birthday. "I can imagine how surprised and pleased Hermann must have been," wrote Frau Hofer, congratulating her husband on the deal. "Without you he would never have got those paintings. What kind of lunch did you get [from Göring]? It was Hot-Pot Sunday. I'm surprised that Goebbels was there too—they must have buried the hatchet."

To evade customs duties, his agents routinely underdeclared the values, with the connivance of Mussolini himself. In November 1941 the export office at Rome was shown a manifest of thirty-four sealed crates of art bound for Carinhall, allegedly worth a mere two hundred thousand lire (or roughly $1,000 in 1941). In fact, the crates contained two Canaletto landscapes, works by Spanish, Venetian, and Florentine masters, furniture, and a marble relief of the Madonna and Child; the fifteen largest of these items had been purchased by Hofer from a Florentine antiquary on May 29 and October 20, 1941, for 12.5 million lire. In July 1942 this kind of customs fraud would be repeated with sixty-seven crates packed with antique sculptures and bas-reliefs.

To his harassed secretary Gisela Limberger would fall the job of keeping track and creating inventories of her boss's objects d'art and of the palaces and villas where they were currently displayed or stored. But the fate of the Paul Rosenberg collection shows the kind of problem she faced. Wanting to send his wife to safety in Switzerland, Miedl had asked Göring for funds: Göring allowed Miedl to transfer the Van Gogh and Cézanne paintings out to Switzerland instead. Hofer's papers show that Göring formally sold the paintings to Miedl for 750,000 marks on March 31, 1942. On April 15 Fräulein Grundtmann paid Miedl's check into Göring's art fund. The ex-Rosenberg pictures reached Berne by diplomatic courier later that summer.

Fräulein Limberger's task was further complicated by the Reichsmarschall's exchange transactions, like the one employed to acquire seven paintings from the Renders collection together with one mysterious "Vermeer." Paintings by Jan Vermeer Van Delft were highly sought after. Göring had previously handled only one, "The Man with the Hat." In 1942 another was offered to him, and Bruno Lohse's files show that Fräulein Limberger told him on July 18 to travel to Holland and Monaco, with another art expert, to examine it. Back through Hofer came word that the painting was authentic. Then a third "Vermeer" surfaced, slightly damaged. When Göring still hesitated to meet the very stiff price, the dealers piled on pressure—showing him by comparison a color photograph of a "Vermeer" with a biblical theme, "The Road to Emmaus," which, after Hofer's wife, a professional restorer, had cleaned it, showed the same bluish yellow, characteristic of the true Vermeer, as the one on offer to Göring. Soon afterward, Miedl cabled Göring urgent word that the noted Dutch Rijksmuseum had now bought the damaged one. Thus reassured, Göring clinched the deal, trading no fewer than 112 lesser works including 54 milked from the Goudstikker collection, in return for the coveted "Vermeer."

Years later, with less than six weeks to live, he learned that the one he had acquired was a forgery, one of seven skillfully concocted since 1937 by the master forger Hans Van Meegeren (including, incidentally, the "Emmaus" shown to Göring as a comparison). "They told me," recalled the pained Hermann Göring, "that there was a second painting that the Rijksmuseum in Amsterdam had acquired. So I thought that mine must be genuine. You say it isn't? I regard it as genuine," he stoutly persisted, even when told the embarrassing truth. "It would be a colossal fraud otherwise, because I paid most of all for that one!" The Americans, relishing his discomfiture, revealed to him now that that forger was one of Hofer's friends. "They set you up," the Americans told him, then congratulated him ironically on the fact that there were only two such fakes in his collection—the "Vermeer" and a "Rembrandt." "That was a Hofer too," sighed Göring. "And I paid a very stiff price for the Rembrandt, and in Swiss francs too." "Yes," he added, becoming visibly pensive. "I gave Hofer pretty much *plein pouvoir*." He added, "I think my own experience shows that you've got to be damned careful when you associate with art dealers. They're in a class by themselves—I noticed that myself toward the end."

As works of art were acquired by the Reichsmarschall, purchased, borrowed, loaned out, traded, transferred to air-raid shelters, and finally shipped across Europe before advancing enemy armies, Fräulein Limberger's cataloguing task became hopelessly entangled. Ultimately her inventories grew to be so voluminous that she compiled lists of them, and these alone would fill several pages at the time that the Americans took charge of them in 1945. In their final interrogations, conducted when Göring had not long to live, they tried to get him to reveal where he had buried some of the missing objects, including the bronze replicas of well-known statues, the marble sculptures, and the priceless Venus of Praxiteles.

Göring teased his interrogators, revealing only that a Major Frankenberg had been in charge of burying his heavier treasures at Carinhall. "By the way," he remarked, "we interred some good wine with those things there." "Where he buried the stuff," he added, smiling sardonically, "the Russians now are. . . . I hope after the Russians leave, I shall be able to show it to you."

27
THE BIG DECISION

Reichsmarschall Göring called his deputy, Milch, out to Carinhall on November 14, 1940, handed over command of the Luftwaffe, and departed for Rominten in East Prussia. Here he would stay, barely thirty miles from the Soviet demarcation line, until his forty-eighth birthday lured him back to Berlin in January 1941.

By November 1940 he had learned of Hitler's half-formed intent of attacking the Soviet Union in the coming spring. That he opposed this decision was confirmed by all Göring's personal aides. Karl Bodenschatz, talking in British captivity (he believed without being overheard), was later adamant about this: "I could tell you," he related to fellow generals, "of many moments in the Hitler-Göring saga where it was all or nothing."

For instance [continued Bodenschatz] their first god-almighty clash was over whether to attack Russia. Göring fought that one tooth and nail. But he was just a loyal henchman and ultimately there was nothing else he could do. The Führer just said, "I command it!"

This capitulation was typical of the Hitler-Göring relationship. Although Major von Below, Hitler's air-force adjutant, had noticed an estrangement during the Battle of Britain, he observed that Hitler continued to consult his air-force chief on any major initiative for three more years. Not that he felt bound to heed Göring's advice: As Ribbentrop would write in August 1945, once Hitler had made up his mind, nobody—"not even Göring with his overbearing influence"—could change it for him.

Göring hated the developing Nazi plan to attack Russia. In vain he canvassed his own strategy, for a concerted action by German, Italian, and Spanish forces to seize the British Empire's fortress at Gibraltar and capture the Suez Canal, thus sealing off the Mediterranean. After that he proposed they occupy the Balkans and North Africa. Hitler would not listen, and invited the Soviet foreign minister, Vyacheslav Molotov, to Berlin for one final parley before making up his mind. Göring and Ribbentrop entertained the Soviet potentate at the Kaiserhof Hotel on November 12, but the price that the stocky little Russian shortly stated for further Soviet collaboration took Ribbentrop's breath away: The U.S.S.R. now demanded Finland, Romania, and Bulgaria, control of the Dardanelles Straits—and more, because when British bombers arrived over Berlin after dark that night, Molotov confidentially stated to Ribbentrop in the air-raid shelter beneath the Reich Chancellery a demand that made the Nazi leaders tumble out of their seats, as Göring later put it. Moscow now insisted on being awarded naval bases on the North Sea outlets of the *Baltic*. "I told them," Ribbentrop haughtily assured the Reichsmarschall, "that there could be no talk of that."

By the next day, November 13, Hitler's decision had hardened. The high command's diary shows that Russia was among the three topics that he discussed with Göring. One was raising an airborne corps, a second was whether or not to capture Cap Verde, the Canaries, and the Azores, and the third was the mounting of an assault on Gibraltar under General von Richthofen's command, prior to an "eastern campaign" that might begin thereafter on May 1, 1941.

It must be said that Göring's motives for opposing Hitler's Russian campaign were economic rather than moral. Nazi Germany was dependent on Soviet deliveries of grain and oil, and on the Trans-Siberian Railroad. He urged Hitler to concede all of Molotov's demands except for the outrageous claims in the western Baltic, pointing out slyly that these Soviet advances would bring Moscow into open and direct conflict with London. The Wehrmacht, he argued, could hardly march all the way to Vladivostok. Besides, Hitler himself had argued in his *Mein Kampf* against fighting a war on two fronts. "There is only one front," Hitler retorted stolidly. "That is in the east." Göring disagreed, but Hitler steamrollered his arguments aside. "Listen," Bodenschatz heard him say. "I'll only need your bombers in the east for three or four weeks. Then you'll get them back. When we've finished off Russia, the army will be cut back to thirty Panzer divisions and twenty mechanized divisions, and the remaining manpower will be packed into your air force. It's going to be tripled, quadrupled. . . ."

Göring allowed himself to be persuaded. Over the next few weeks he parroted the Führer's arguments to Pili Körner, he revealed to Fighter Commander Adolf Galland that the Luftwaffe was to attack Russia shortly, but that "in ten weeks" that campaign would be over and Britain's turn would come. When General Thomas reminded him of Stalin's growing industrial base beyond the Ural mountains, he replied, "My air force will smash that too. My airborne troops will seize the Trans-Siberian Railroad and restore our links to the Far East." "He got me to help him," recalled the Reichsmarschall, describing Hitler's persuasiveness with a thin smile in August 1945, and added, "as always."

Four years later Bodenschatz would suggest that men like Göring had become "infected" with their own life-style. "He has Carinhall," the general, Göring's longtime friend, observed. "And that's the cancer within him."

On November 14, 1940—the night that he handed over power to Milch—the air force that Göring built fire-bombed the British industrial city of Coventry, pathfinding by the new electronic beams. Perhaps, if the Luftwaffe's high command had not been so geographically far flung, the subsequent autumn and winter air offensive might have been really dangerous for Britain. But Göring was sulking at Rominten in East Prussia. He had fetched the young chief of air staff, Hans Jeschonnek, to his side. Kesselring, Sperrle, and Stumpff were at their widely dispersed Luftflotte headquarters, and Milch was deputizing for the Reichsmarschall at la Boissière. "There's a lot that needs doing," cursed Jeschonnek's deputy Hoffmann von Waldau in a private diary entry on November 16, "and for want of the Reichsmarschall we have to act on our own."

It seemed a bizarre way to run a modern air force. Milch, Waldau, and Galland found themselves getting orders dictated by phone from Göring's nurse, Christa Gormanns, canceling night raids on one town and ordering attacks on others. The Reichsmarschall's health was clearly indifferent. From one of Fräulein Limberger's gift lists it seems that at one time or another he retained nine different doctors and physicians to minister to him. His heart was playing up, and licentious living had debased the human tissues. His exhaustion is clear from a long letter that he sent to Count Eric von Rosen by a princely courier (Victor, prince zu Wied) on November 21, a week after his departure for East Prussia:

> I am currently taking several weeks' convalescent leave as I was at the very end of my tether. I'm spending it with Emmy and

> Edda here at my hunting lodge at Rominten, getting away from
> everything that's going on and summoning up strength for the
> year to come.

Göring's letter also leveled a thinly veiled warning at the Swedes, whose newspapers were reporting Berlin's air-raid damage in grotesquely exaggerated language. "Coventry," he gloated, "has been completely and literally razed to the ground. London has suffered immense damage, and entire districts look like they've been hit by an earthquake." By November 1, he claimed, his Luftwaffe had dropped 15,872 tons of bombs on London; but the British had succeeded in dropping only 31 tons on Berlin. Criticizing Stockholm's "bourgeois press," he added, "If Sweden believes that the freedom of her press is more important than her own future, so be it. But Sweden must not be surprised later on if, one day, Germany draws the appropriate conclusions."

In a paragraph marked "Confidential" he dropped a hint about Russia that he asked Count von Rosen to pass on to Finland: "Your Finnish friends," he wrote, "can rest assured about the future—even after Molotov's visit to us." He had sent an agent to Field Marshal Mannerheim several weeks earlier about this, and the same agent would visit him again, in a few days' time. Meanwhile Göring said that he welcomed the signs that the Finns had been shrewd enough to abandon their former policies and move closer to the German line.

Göring allowed little to disturb his East Prussian vacation. Once, he languidly directed Jeschonnek to phone orders through to Milch to bomb Liverpool and Manchester at once, whatever the moon, and to deliver "a heavy blow at London" in between.

On December 3, Milch and Waldau brought out to Rominten the plans that they had drafted on Hitler's instructions for a Luftwaffe Air Corps to be moved to southern Italy to help extricate Mussolini from his own military quagmires in North Africa and Greece. Göring still loathed the Italians in general and Mussolini in particular. "If I were a Frenchman," he had sneered when Mussolini belatedly entered the war in June, "I should spit on the ground every time I saw an Italian." But every Italian setback now just boosted British morale, so Göring had to approve the rescue plan.

"Wet autumn day," wrote General von Waldau in his diary. "A very nice heart-to-heart with the Reichsmarschall, most of it in the shooting brake that conveyed us to the feeding place of the world-record stag, Matador."

For a while the raids on Britain continued—against London, Birmingham, Liverpool, and Sheffield. Over Christmas, however, Hitler, of all people, ordered a festive lull in the mutual killing match. The British, not to be outdone, did the same. From his East Prussian retreat Göring was inspired by the Christmas spirit to send bank books to the children of airmen killed in action, each with a deposit of one thousand marks from his own bulging account. By the end of that year Hitler had issued the formal directive for *Barbarossa*, a possible attack on the Soviet Union. Göring's task would be to force a "brisk conclusion" in the east.

As a military band serenaded the Reichsmarschall's hunting lodge, the New Year arrived at Rominten. The first days were clear but cold at $-20°$ Celsius. Göring's red-leather pocket diary for 1941 has survived, with daily notes neatly entered in blue or green crayon, tabulating his activities for each moment of his day. Typical pages record him rising at eight-thirty, playing twice for an hour with Edda, conferring with foresters, taking his latest guests on sleigh rides, inspecting pedigreed Trakehn horses, drinking coffee, and supervising Fräulein Limberger's filing work before taking in a late movie in his private cinema or playing a hand of bridge. Sometimes he went skiing through the forests with Paula or hunted wild boar with Olga. It was left to his physician, Dr. von Ondarza, to brief him on the war—the night raids against the British Isles and the harassing attacks by General Geissler's X Air Corps against the British naval base of Malta.

He savored the approach of his birthday like a small boy, reviewing the arrangements with Görnnert two days beforehand but still managing to express surprise at all the gifts. The Italian ambassador, the smirking and obsequious Dino Alfieri, displayed to him Mussolini's own gift—the early fifteenth-century altar from Sterzing in the South Tyrol. Built by the Swabian master Hans Multscher, it consisted of eight great paintings and wood carvings.

The birthday itself passed almost flawlessly. The Hermann Göring Regiment paraded in drifting snow. A luncheon was provided by Horcher's, Göring's favorite gourmet restaurant. Afterward, the Prussian State Theater staged the comedy *Cherries for Rome* in the Air Ministry's largest hall. One mystery did, however, mar the day. The diamond-studded cigarette box that Emmy had given him vanished from the gift-laden tables. "Six P.M.," Göring entered grimly in his diary. "Investigation into the theft of Emmy's present." Arrayed in a red silk dressing gown and furry slippers, he elbowed through the piles of packages, his face trancelike, looking for the missing trinket. He changed into a pure white uniform for dinner, but his smooth, glossy complexion was flushed with anger at the theft, and when Emmy announced that she had telephoned a clairvoyant friend, a doctor in Kassel—"He says it's still in the building!"—Göring just harrumphed.

His diary outlined the events of the next day, January 13, 1941: At 12:30 P.M., "Conference with Körner, Neumann, and Backe on nutrition." (Backe's diary shows that he warned of a food crisis looming in Europe.) 1:30 P.M., "Detective finds stolen cigarette case!" (A Horcher waiter had evidently stuffed it down a sofa.) "2:00 P.M., lunch with guests. 3:00 P.M., packed my birthday presents. 3:30 P.M., rested in bed." At five o'clock his air-force advisers Jeschonnek, Milch, and Bodenschatz came to "report on conference with the Führer, operational matters," joined an hour later by General Udet.

Milch summed up this secret conference in one word in his own notebook: "*Ost*" [East]. And Jeschonnek informed his staff at La Boissière that Hitler had resolved to "sever the head of the danger menacing us in the east."

Göring still hankered after peace with Britain. On January 14, the Swedish Count Bonde, who had visited Lord Halifax quite recently, was brought in. Göring was crestfallen to learn that Bonde had brought no particular message from the British. "We have offered Britain peace twice," said Göring wistfully. "If I send any message now, they will take it as a sign of weakness." He resumed his art pursuits. The diary glimpses him at Carinhall on the eighteenth, haggling with his art agents Miedl and Hofer. He swam and sauna'd often, but his health had worsened perceptibly, and after addressing air-force officers on the nineteenth he suffered a midnight heart attack. Clearly it was not his first, since his diary treats it almost routinely. Professor Siebert took an electrocardiogram, and on the twenty-second Göring was fit enough to meet Kesselring, Jeschonnek, and other generals again.

The coming war with Russia overshadowed all else. His differences with Hitler over forward strategy became more marked as the shaping of *Barbarossa* now began. For some weeks Göring found that he was getting phone calls discouraging him from attending Hitler's daily war conference, the *Führerlage*. "I don't know what's up," Emmy heard her husband remark. "The Führer stops me going over. Something's going on." The diary confirms this. Between November 14 and mid-March he met Hitler only four times, and they telephoned each other only rarely—e.g., on January 16, when he reported that X Air Corps had sunk the British cruisers *Southampton* and *York* and the aircraft carrier *Illustrious*.

General Kurt Student, the Parachute Division's commander, came out to Carinhall with Jeschonnek on January 24 and stayed aboard Göring's train when it left for Berchtesgaden. As they talked that evening, Student found the Reichsmarschall bitterly opposed to *Barbarossa*. Arriving at Berchtesgaden, Göring tackled Hitler at midday, lunched with him, and stayed with him alone until 8:00 P.M. They were probably arguing, because General Student would recall four years later that Hitler left afterward "sunk deep in thought." According to Student, Göring was already thinking he had succeeded—"Thank God, no war with Russia!"—when Hitler phoned two days later: "Göring," he said, "I have changed my mind. We shall attack in the east."

By that time Hermann Göring was back in Berlin, immersed in three days of Cabinet-level conferences on raw materials and the coming campaign in the Balkans. On January 28, 1941, he was again summoned to the Führer's presence, this time in the Reich Chancellery. On the following day the Reichsmarschall revealed in a three-hour conference with his arms experts and economics advisers, according to Körner's later testimony, that war with Russia was definite. He asked each of those seated around the table for his view. Fritz Todt, Friedrich Syrup, Erich Neumann, Georg Thomas, Carl Krauch, and Fritz Fromm all declared that such a war was "economically unthinkable," citing precisely the same raw-material considerations that had vexed Göring. The exception was Herbert Backe. Backe, born in Russia himself, pointed out pensively that the conquest of the Ukraine would solve Germany's chronic grain shortages. Unconvinced, unhappy too, Göring directed Thomas to set up a special economic unit to study the problem.

Visibly agitated, he took Emmy for a walk afterward and confided to her that Hitler had decided to invade Russia. Emmy was about to leave for Bad Gastein to take the cure for her rheumatism. This, Emmy later testified, was the only political conversation that she ever had with her husband the Reichsmarschall. How unlike Carin she was! "Is that why the Führer wouldn't see you for weeks?" she asked. Göring laughed out loud. "You may not be a very political animal," he said, "but you've got your head screwed on." He now told her that Hitler had confirmed it himself. "I refused to see you, Göring, because I knew you would do all you could to talk me out of it."

Disconsolate at his failure, the Reichsmarschall left for Holland on January 30, 1941—the party's anniversary—taking his sisters and a one-hundred member staff. He parked his train and strolled around the art dealers at The Hague and Amsterdam with Miedl and Hofer, dealing indiscriminately with Jew and Gentile as he traded guilders and Reichsmarks for gilt and canvas. Arriving back at La Boissière, the air staff's forward headquarters, on the first day of February amid snow and slush, he resumed operational command from Milch but stayed in bed with a headache until, brightening, he recalled Alfred Rosenberg and his haul of "ownerless" Jewish treasures. He executed an art raid on Paris that would exceed anything else to date, last for three days, from February 4 to February 6, and demonstrate his ruthlessness as he pursued the barely legal enrichment of his art hoard.

His thieving friend General Hanesse collected him from the Gare du Nord. Hanesse had housed his offices in the gallery of Roger & Gallet, at 62 rue du Faubourg Saint-Honoré; this was just down the street from the opulent former residence of the Rothschilds, which Hanesse had converted into a Luftwaffe hostel complete with priceless Persian carpets and crested plates and cutlery. Göring liked that: He had developed something of a taste for fine tapestries and carpets himself.

Here in Paris, Göring and Hanesse lunched with Submarine Commander Günther Prien, who had sunk the British battleship *Royal Oak*, then strolled around fine jewelers like Perugia, Magnet, and Hermès. He jotted the one word *shopping* in his diary, and that said it all. The same little notebook shows that he was visited after tea by Dr. Hermann Bunjes, the German Army's "art-protection officer," and Colonel Kurt von Behr, an unpleasant, bullying official whose high-ranking Red Cross uniform concealed his true rank, that of a *Feldführer* in Rosenberg's task force in Paris.

> Reichsmarschall Göring [stated Bunjes in his subsequent report]
> took the opportunity to hand to Feldführer von Behr a file of
> photographs of the works of art that the Führer wishes to acquire
> from the Jewish art treasures secured by the Rosenberg task force.

Bunjes also reported that the French government had lodged the first of a
series of formal protests about Rosenberg's operation. Göring airily dismissed
it. "I shall take this up with the Führer," he promised. "As for the Rosenberg
task force, my orders are to stand."

The spectacular all-nude Folies Bergères was doing business as never
before now that the Wehrmacht was in town. That evening, February 4,
1941, Göring invited art agents Angerer and Hofer—who had spent the day
with the French collaborators leading them to still more concealed Jewish
art hoards—to see the revue. His headache had evidently gone. Rising early
the next day, he again conferred with the two men, then consulted Staffelt's
currency snoopers before setting off to the Jeu de Paume. As he swept up
the steps, flanked by Angerer, Hofer, and General Hanesse, he found his
way temporarily barred by two German officials, clearly determined to prevent him from shipping any more pictures out of France. One was Count
Franz Wolff Metternich, a haughty aristocrat and director of the army's Fine
Arts Commission in Paris; the other, a top German civil servant. The Reichsmarschall thrust them angrily aside, and motioned Bunjes to follow him
inside. ("I was shouted down by him in the most uncouth manner," testified
Metternich in a manuscript later. "He sent me packing.") Even Bunjes
became uneasy as he guided the Reichsmarschall around this Aladdin's Cave
of looted treasures, and he again drew attention to the "legal uncertainties."
Not only had the French officially protested, he pointed out, but the Nazi
military governor General Carl-Heinrich von Stülpnagel had issued a different
ruling on the disposal of confiscated Jewish treasures.

Göring bristled. "My orders are final," he said. "You are to do as I say."
His directives were very blunt and to the point. Bunjes was to load the items
that he, Göring, had earmarked for himself and the Führer into two boxcars
attached to his special train. They would accompany him to Berlin. Bunjes
described all these transactions unhappily in his subsequent report. To Göring, he gasped that the lawyers might take a different view. "My dear
Bunjes," roared Göring, clapping him on the shoulder, "let me worry about
that! I am the highest legal authority in the land." He scrawled these instructions on a scrap of paper:

> 1. All the pictures marked H are for the Führer;
> 2. All the pictures marked G are for me, plus the unmarked
> crate AH;
> 3. All the special black crates (Rothschild) are earmarked for
> the Führer. Nurse Christa has the keys to them!

My things—the pictures, furniture, silver, tapestries—are to go to my rooms.

Later that day he inspected the Palais Rothschild, bought a sixteenth-century stone table and two granite lions on the Quai Voltaire, and purchased more stone figures at the Galerie Gouvert. And that evening, inspired by word that his Luftwaffe pilots had shot down eighteen planes, he took a party to the city's other nude revue, the Bal Tabarin, and dinner at Maxim's. His raid was nearly over. After buying up some diamonds at Cartier's and inspecting progress at the Rudier foundry, he set out the next morning, February 6, for La Boissière, his train laden with plunder. He was like a small boy returning from a party, but clutching the spoils of war.

28
WARNING BRITAIN
ABOUT *BARBAROSSA*

Throughout the spring of 1941 Hitler's planned conquest of eastern territories cast its nightmarish shadow over his principal lieutenant. Along every ministerial corridor in Berlin could be heard the echo as *Barbarossa* approached with ponderous tread, and none dared stand up to the Führer long enough to talk him and his eager army out of it. The coming operation intruded on Hermann Göring's contentment as he cruised the galleries of Amsterdam, as he unpacked the crates of artworks at Carinhall, and as he briefed his agents to scout the treasure-filled bazaars of Switzerland and Italy, of France and the Low Countries, for anything that he might have missed himself. But for Hitler's *Barbarossa* plan, Göring would have had few cares: His air force was operating with merciless precision against its English targets; his own wife and infant daughter were safe at Rominten in East Prussia; and out there the stags and wild boar awaited with ill-concealed impatience the arrival of the quaintly clad Reich master huntsman.

But the nightmare remained. And one fact, as the actual day approached, would demonstrate the depths of his despair at Hitler's deliberate opening of a second front. Hermann Göring would leak to the British both the fact and the actual date of _Barbarossa_—an extraordinary act bordering on treason, of which Hitler was surely not aware.

The German Army high command backed Hitler solidly in his historic intent, and Göring could not count on the support of Grand Admiral Raeder, either. Relations with the navy's commander in chief were strained. Raeder's warships were having to operate virtually without air reconnaissance. Moreover, when Raeder now complained to Hitler on February 4—as Göring vacationed in Paris—that the British bombers had begun raiding the North German coast with impunity, Hitler agreed that the navy should take over control of the Luftwaffe's KG40, one of Göring's proudest squadrons. Göring exploded with fury and summoned the nearest admiral, U-boat Commander Karl Dönitz, from his Paris headquarters to La Boissière. Over coffee he heaped upon the admiral remarks that Dönitz described in his report as "distinctly unfriendly." "You can be sure of one thing," Göring snapped. "As long as I live, or until I resign, your Grand Admiral Raeder will never get a fleet air arm." Pointing out that he, Göring, was "the second man in the state," he threatened that even if Dönitz should somehow get his hands on KG40 he would not be likely to find replacements for its long-range planes. "I need FW 200's too," he shouted. "And it'll serve you right!"

After leaving France on February 9, 1941, Göring found that he still needed to soothe his tattered nerves by cruising around more art galleries for a couple of days, those at The Hague and Amsterdam. With his sisters and the latest loot from the Jeu de Paume loaded safely aboard, his train took him back to Berlin. Here, on February 11, he made one of his last attempts to talk Hitler out of attacking Russia, asking Schnurre, the German diplomat handling the renewal of the Soviet trade agreement, to put to him the serious economic disadvantages of fighting Nazi Germany's principal supplier of both grain and petroleum.

Without waiting for the result, Göring left for East Prussia and spent the next days hunting stags, stalking elk, and sleigh-riding.

In the second half of February 1941 he began to accept _Barbarossa_ as a necessary evil. Riding his train south to Bavaria on February 18, he thoughtfully discussed Germany's alternative petroleum supplies with a Dr. Fischer, his principal expert on Romanian oil. Soon after, Göring began actually to advocate the benefits of capturing the Soviet oil fields. His diary shows that on February 19 he lunched at Hitler's Berghof and spent the next six hours in private conclave with Hitler and General Jeschonnek, the chief of air staff. Hitler robustly stated that if anybody else talked to him about the economic drawbacks of _Barbarossa_, he was going to block his ears. "If Russia is on the point of attacking Germany," he reasoned with the Reichsmarschall, "then economics don't come into it."

Still uncomfortable, Göring reminded him of Napoleon's defeat in Russia.

Hitler would not heed him, and Göring, characteristically, saw no choice but to fall into line. When the Reich minister of finance, Count Schwerin von Krosigk, wrote to him pleading against *Barbarossa*, Göring instructed Paul Körner to reply orally that the planned campaign was preventive, and hence necessary. On February 22, the Reichsmarschall wrote two eloquent, perhaps even fatalistic, words in his diary. "East: deadlines."

The change in his posture was apparent when he discussed the long-term economic effects of *Barbarossa* with General Thomas of the OKW on the twenty-sixth. He agreed that there was little point in occupying just the Ukraine. "At all costs," said Göring, "we must get the petroleum fields around Baku too."

> He shares the Führer's opinion [noted Thomas immediately afterward] that when the German troops march into Russia the whole Bolshevik state will collapse and that in consequence we have no cause to anticipate the large-scale destruction of supplies or demolition of railroads that I fear.

"What matters most," said Göring, "is to finish off the Bolshevik leaders, fast, first, and foremost."

Visiting Vienna on March 5, he casually asked the visiting right-wing dictator of Romania, General Ion Antonescu, whether his country could increase its petroleum output—"Since our other oil supplier [Russia] might one day drop out." He asked equally casually, "How many of your Romanians live on Russian soil?" and when Antonescu told him, the Reichsmarschall made a silent scooping gesture with one hand.

To dupe the British into believing they were next on his menu, Hitler sent the gaudy Luftwaffe commander back to the west for two weeks later that month. Göring bore this banishment with fortitude, happily hobnobbing with his shady art-dealer acquaintances in The Hague and Amsterdam—where Nathan Katz, the Jew who had sold him three paintings, including Van Dyck's "Family Portrait" (for eighty thousand dollars), was now wangling exit visas to Switzerland—and in Paris, where he made further raids on the Jeu de Paume on the eleventh and twelfth.

Göring no longer tried to talk Hitler out of *Barbarossa*. On March 19, 1941, as his train had returned from The Hague to Berlin, General Thomas had come aboard to brief him on the organization for *Barbarossa* and on the strategic stockpiling of fuel and rubber. Six days later Göring talked for an hour with Birger Dahlerus and, according to the Swede's wife, told him for the first time of the coming campaign in Russia. When Field Marshal Milch came out to lunch at Carinhall the next day, spluttering protests that *Barbarossa* was bound to drag on into the coming winter, Göring calmed him down. "Russia," he said, "will collapse like a house of cards." Hitler himself had assured him so—"The Führer is a unique leader, a gift of God. The rest of us can only fall in behind."

When the new Japanese ambassador, General Hiroshi Oshima, paid a courtesy visit that day, Göring dropped a broad hint to him about *Barbarossa* too. "First we shall defeat Britain," he boasted, following the official deception strategy, "and next the Soviets." Over a banquet thrown two days later by Hitler for the Japanese foreign minister, Göring talked briefly with Goebbels on the awesome event that was to follow the "long-prepared assault on Greece" (due at the end of the first week in April, as an urgent measure of assistance to Mussolini).

> The big project [noted Goebbels, after discussing *Barbarossa* with Göring] is coming later: against "R." It is being very carefully camouflaged and only a handful of people know about it. It will begin with extensive troop movements to the west. We shall divert suspicion to all sorts of places. . . . A mock invasion of England is in preparation. . . .

Not entirely capable of suppressing his own apprehensions, Goebbels noted that the campaign had "parallels with Napoleon," and that these had momentarily troubled the Reichsmarschall too.

Hitler's plan to aid Mussolini in Greece was dramatically complicated by a pro-British coup in Yugoslavia on March 27. He was enjoying a farewell tête-à-tête with Dahlerus at midday when he received the sudden summons from Hitler to attend, along with Ribbentrop and the other commanders in chief, a briefing at the Reich Chancellery. Göring noted merely, "1:00–3:00 P.M., Führer briefing (Yugoslavia)." Hitler was in an ominously buoyant mood, because he had made one of his sudden snap decisions: He announced that he had resolved to "smash Yugoslavia" immediately, at the same time as invading Greece. Equipped with Hitler's simple order, the air force and army swiftly pulled together the additional forces that a Yugoslav campaign would require. After a late lunch, Göring had a two-hour conference with Udet, Waldau, Schmid, and Quartermaster General von Seidel. General von Waldau noted in his own diary: "In the afternoon I am summoned to see the Reichsmarschall at the Führer's official residence. The Yugoslav putsch has created a new situation in the Balkans. The decision is made to mount a military operation as rapidly as possible.

Göring reported back to the Führer at 7:30 P.M. The Luftwaffe's task would be to destroy the Yugoslav and Greek ground organization, after flattening Belgrade itself by saturation bombing. Waldau worked far into the night switching air-force squadrons from the west to the southeast: the KG51 bomber wing would move to Wiener-Neustadt; the bombers of KG2, the dive bombers of Stuka 77, the fighters of JG54 would leapfrog across Europe to new bases in the same region. "What is politically absolutely essential," commented Waldau after conferring with Göring, "is for the punch to be hurled at Yugoslavia with merciless force and for the military smash (*Zerschlagung*) to follow like lightning." Göring's diary shows him galvanized into action over the next days, recording appointments with Austrian-born General Alexander Löhr (commanding Luftflotte 4, Vienna), with Franz Neuhausen, who was handling the economic exploitation of the Balkans, and with a kaleidoscopic cast of other generals, ambassadors, art agents, goldsmiths, air-force lawyers, sculptors, and test pilots (one of whom, Hanna Reitsch, he accompanied to receive her Iron Cross from Hitler on March 28). The name of Professor Siebert again figures in the diary, because Göring's cardiovascular system was still causing alarm.

On March 30, three days after the Belgrade coup, Göring attended a three-hour secret speech by Hitler to his generals in the Chancellery's paneled Cabinet Room. Trying to explain why Britain was stubbornly fighting on, Hitler accused "the warmonger Winston Churchill and the Jews around him," and he blamed the Italians and their "accursed military incompetence." But, he argued, Germany must defeat the Soviet Union first, and he mentioned particularly the growing strength of the Russian Air Force. According to the notes taken by the chief of general staff, Franz Halder, Hitler expressed approval during this speech of their plan to liquidate the Soviet political commissars found among Russian prisoners. Hitler explained to his high-ranking secret audience that *Barbarossa* would see two conflicting ideologies locked in mortal combat—"We must abandon the notion of soldierly camaraderie. The Communist," he said, "has not an ounce of comradeship in him." He directed, "Communists and GPU [Soviet secret police] men are criminals and are to be dealt with as such."

None of this gave Hermann Göring any sleepless nights. Innocent of any feelings of guilt, he joined Emmy briefly at Bad Gastein, then took his train on to Austria on April 4. He would remain there languidly directing air-force operations from a tourist hotel on the Semmering until the Balkan campaign ended three weeks later. It opened with a vicious VIII Air Corps raid by three hundred bombers on Belgrade at 7:20 A.M. on the sixth (the Yugoslavs claimed that the raid left seventeen thousand dead). Hitler had, however, forbidden Göring to bomb Athens, and during the remaining fighting there was little for Göring's squadrons to do other than harry the transport ships that eventually evacuated the British expeditionary force.

On the Semmering he walked and swam, trying to strengthen his heart, but the mountain air was heavy with the sleet and drizzle of early spring. For company he took Pili Körner and Milch, or Udet and Jeschonnek, but these Luftwaffe generals were vain and immiscible. Jeschonnek, his chief of air staff, was sensitive, withdrawn, and unimaginative—the very opposite of the flamboyant and corrupt Reichsmarschall. Every two or three days Göring drove over to Hitler's command train, which was halted between two tunnels at Mönnichkirchen. He reported that his bombers had again raided Coventry, Glasgow, Bristol, and Liverpool. On April 9, the British retaliated against Berlin. Göring's State Opera was gutted. The British newspapers boasted that three thousand Berliners had died in the fires (the true figure was eleven). Göring retaliated with a violent attack on London a week later.

A few days after the London raid an air-force technical mission returned from Moscow. The air-force experts brought disturbing news of the Soviet Union's industrial mobilization. They had been allowed to tour half a dozen huge factories manufacturing equipment from ball bearings and special alloys to warplanes and aero-engines. Over dinner on the eighth, Soviet aircraft designer Mikoyan had blustered, "You have now seen the mighty technology of this Soviet nation. We shall bravely shatter any aggression, no matter where it comes from!" Colonel Dietrich Schwenke, head of the Luftwaffe mission, warned Göring that just one aircraft engine plant at Kuibyshev was bigger than all of the six biggest German factories together.

Göring dismissed Schwenke's report as defeatist. But Hitler became very pensive when told, and afterward mentioned Schwenke's report as having clinched the decision for him.

At the beginning of May 1941, with the Balkan campaign all but over, Göring traveled to Paris, taking his art curator Walter Hofer with him. Establishing a pretext for the trip, Göring entered in his diary for the second, "Major conference on full-moon attack [on London] by Second and Third Luftflotte," with "many participants." (The attack would take place on the night of May 10–11.)

His diary, as he arrived in Paris, shows that nothing had diminished his acquisitive zeal:

> May 1, 1941, Paris.   Spring sunshine.
>   8:00, rose; 9:00, newspapers.
> 10:20 arrive at Paris Gare de l'Est station.
> 11:00 briefing by Hanesse and [the general's adjutant, Major]
> Drees
> 11:15 [art dealer] Bernheim and Hofer
> 12:00 [Feldführer] von Behr.

Behr, chief of Rosenberg's Paris task force, persuaded him to sign this important document:

> THE REICHSMARSCHALL OF   Headquarters, May 1, 1941
> THE GREATER GERMAN REICH
>   The struggle against Jews, Freemasons, and the diverse ideo-
> logical and hostile forces allied with them is an urgent duty for
> National Socialism during this war.
>   I therefore welcome Reichsleiter Rosenberg's decision to set

up task forces in all occupied territories with the mission of securing all research material and cultural assets of the above-
designated groups and transporting them to Germany.

The Göring document ordered all party, government, and military agencies
to afford Feldführer von Behr "every conceivable support and assistance."
He resumed his diary:

> 12:15 P.M., Angerer (long talk!)
> 1:45 Staffelt [head of Currency Protection Unit]
> 2:00 war briefing by [chief adjutant Major von] Brauchitsch
> 2:30 lunch at Cremaillère
> 3:45 Bernheim at Grand Hotel
> 4:15 Jeu de Paume (paintings)
> 5:30 Napoleon's crypt at Invalides Cathedral
> 6:00 return to Palais and read
> 7:30 report by [Hitler's air-force adjutant Major Nicolaus] von
> Below
> 9:25 situation [conference with] chief of air staff
> 10:00 dinner with guests at Maxim's, back at 11:00.

The next two days passed in the same sort of whirl—conferences with fighter
aces Werner Mölders and Adolf Galland, sumptuous meals at Maxim's, erotic
evenings at the Bal Tabarin, "shopping for furniture for Veldenstein," another finger-licking trip to the Jeu de Paume, and then back to his train—
but not before he had negotiated with Bernheim the purchase of the priceless
"Bagatelle Ceiling." ("The Russians have it," he would say sardonically
when asked by the Americans what had happened to this fabulous painted
ceiling in 1945.)

He had to be back in Berlin for Hitler's grandiloquent, triumphant, sarcastic
speech to the Reichstag on the Balkan campaign. His train pulled in at 4:00
P.M. on May 4, he spoke with Hitler privately a few minutes later, and took
his seat on the dais behind the Führer and his deputy, Rudolf Hess, at six.
Nothing in the latter's demeanor betrayed that he was planning a spectacular
adventure a few days later. The next day Göring inspected architect Albert
Speer's latest dazzling models for the reconstruction of Berlin—an immense
monument to Hitler's thousand-year Reich, with triumphal arch, broad ceremonial boulevards, and a great domed assembly hall. "I have the same
admiration for your architectural ability," he flattered the young Nazi architect, "as I have for the Führer's political and military talents!"

His heart still molesting him, he went on brief leave to Bad Gastein,
rejoining Emmy, before returning on May 9 to Veldenstein Castle in Franconia, to discuss plans for its interior renovation.

* * *

Hermann Göring had again left Milch in charge of the air force. On Saturday May 10, 1941, it flew the moonlight attack on London—its most severe attack so far, causing immense damage to the city and wrecking the Parliament Building. On Sunday Dr. von Ondarza brought the first reports to the castle. The Reichsmarschall had just settled down for lunch after that when the telephone rang—a command-flash call (*Führungs-Blitz-Gespräch*) from Hitler on the Obersalzberg. Göring recognized Bodenschatz's voice first: "The Führer wants to see you!" Since Göring had just spent two hours alone with Hitler in Munich on Friday, he involuntarily groaned. Hitler's gruff voice replaced the general's: "Göring! You are to come down here. *At once*!"

Panic replaced puzzlement. Göring fled to his special train, but it was 7:00 P.M. by the time it reached Munich, and it took two more hours to drive on to the Berghof. There he saw Martin Bormann, Hess's chief of staff, hovering around grinning unpleasantly, and a white-faced Joachim von Ribbentrop. Walther Hewel, Ribbentrop's ambassador on the Führer's staff, wrote in his diary: "Göring gets here after supper at nine P.M. From what Bodenschatz told me he's also very agitated. Long discussion downstairs in the hall between F., foreign minister, Göring, Bormann. Very heated, a lot of speculation."

Hitler thrust several pages of paper into Göring's hands. "Reichsminister Hess has flown to England!" he burst out. "He left this letter." In the document Hess declared himself willing to risk his life to make peace with Britain and end the bloodshed. Göring was contemptuous. He dismissed Hess as insane. ("Do you think," he would ask rhetorically in October 1945, "Hitler would really have sent the third man in the Reich on such a lone mission to Britain without the slightest preparation? . . . If he really wanted to deal with the British, there were reliable semidiplomatic channels through neutral countries. My own connections with Britain were such that I could have arranged it within forty-eight hours.")

The next day, Monday, May 12, Göring returned with General Udet to discuss with Hitler the vital question whether Hess could have handled the difficult Messerschmitt 110 aircraft alone and landed in Scotland. Might he not have disappeared silently into the North Sea? Ribbentrop, however, was terrified that Britain might announce Hess's arrival at any moment—and that might blow the already strained Axis alliance wide open. All that afternoon Hitler and Göring debated this dilemma.

"A very disturbed day," wrote Hewel. "Investigations into Hess's flight . . . Neither Göring nor Udet believes Hess capable of pulling off the difficult flight to Glasgow. . . . But the Führer thinks Hess has the skill. We make announcement at eight P.M."

Soon after Göring returned to his train, down at Berchtesgaden, the BBC broadcast from London that Rudolf Hess had landed in Scotland. At 9:00 P.M. Göring telephoned Hitler with the news. His own investigations began.

Bodenschatz found out that Hess had made complex, level-headed flight plans, including the use of a blind-navigation radio beam. Bodenschatz was not surprised by the deputy Führer's flight. "Hess," he would say in captivity, "was the exception. He had *nothing*—no castles, just a simple apartment. He could bring himself to part with his possessions."

The next morning, May 13, Göring tackled Professor Messerschmitt. "I see that anybody can fly at your airfield, despite the regulations," he thundered at the aircraft designer.

"Hess," retorted the aircraft designer, "was not just anybody. He was one of the most important ministers."

"Well, you knew Hess was crazy!"

From all over the Reich the gauleiters and ministers were assembling at the Berghof that afternoon to hear Hitler's report on the background to the Hess affair. Göring drove up there at three-thirty and spent an hour alone with Hitler first, discussing who would succeed Hess as "party minister." There was no talk of reviving the hollow title of deputy Führer. The Reichsmarschall spoke bluntly against promoting Martin Bormann to the job. Hitler assured him he was thinking of Bormann more in terms of becoming party treasurer.

"You're way out if you think Bormann will be satisfied with that," retorted Göring.

"Bormann's ambitions," said Hitler, "are a matter of indifference to me."

Hitler went down into the hall followed by a grim-faced Göring, and directed Bormann to read out the letters that Hess had left behind. The sixty or seventy Nazi leaders clustered round in a silent semicircle. Hans Frank had not seen Hitler so grief-stricken since the suicide of his niece Geli, ten years before. It was obvious that Hess's venture had taken him by surprise.

Pausing only briefly at the showrooms of United Handicrafts (Vereinigte Werkstätten) in Munich to select more furniture for his castle, Göring resumed his interrupted vacation at Veldenstein. A few days later his morning newspaper told him that Hitler had opted for Bormann after all, appointing him "director of the party chancellery." This hundredfold increase in the powers and status of Hess's ruthless red-neck chief of staff was a real setback for Göring. He had never got on well with Bormann. "Bormann," he would subsequently lament, "was a glutton for hard work and thus he consolidated his position . . . He matched his daily routine to the Führer's. He was always on hand when the Führer needed him." Bormann was far more radical in his anti-clerical and anti-Jewish campaign than Göring. From now on, a chance lunchtime remark by Hitler would be converted instantly by Bormann into a written Führer decree. Clean-living and not susceptible to bribery, he loathed the Reichsmarschall and the style of life that he led. As the troubles of the air force began to multiply, Bormann undertook a personal vendetta against its commander that Göring would reciprocate beyond the grave.

"Do you think Bormann is dead?" he would be asked in October 1945.

"If I had any say in it," he spat out, tossing both hands in the air, "I hope he's frying in hell."

In the air force his own prestige was still high. Even in enemy hands his officers showed by their private remarks that they admired him. "Hermann," said one officer in June 1941, "is definitely the man who rakes in the most money in Germany. But there's not a man who begrudges it, because he really earns it!" They admired his even-handedness. "There was this unit on the West Wall," said one Messerschmitt 109F pilot shot down over Malta. "Some officers with only two sorties to their name already had the Iron Cross Second Class while rookies with ten sorties had nothing. Then Hermann paid them a visit . . . he had some Iron Crosses brought in at once and dished them out to these men himself. The CO was sacked—boy did Hermann have a temper! Driving off, his car got stuck in the mud. In front of all the men he tipped the generals out and made them push it free."

Air-force morale was high, and this carried it through its bloodier episodes, like the parachute assault on Crete on May 20. Göring prided himself on having planned this coup, but it stood under an ill omen. He and Brauchitsch had refused to agree whether the airborne division should come under air-force or army control, which left only General Student's one parachute division for the assault. What was far worse was that through the Luftwaffe's insecure machine ciphers the British learned the precise hour and dropping zones of the paratroops, and four thousand were killed in the first assault wave. "We had the impression," said General Rudolf Meister, "and I don't think I'm mistaken, that the British knew the exact time and the morning on which we were coming, because full preparations had been made." Despite this, the air force never investigated the possibility that their ciphers had been broken. There is indirect evidence that Göring knew that *some* ciphers were insecure, because in June British code-breakers heard him issuing to his bomber forces target priorities for a "new blitz" against British cities—which was, in fact, just part of the high command's strategic deception plan prior to *Barbarossa*. On June 8, Göring phoned Milch to order him to tour Field Marshal Hugo Sperrle's dwindling Luftflotte 3 in the west; this was part of the same grand deception, designed to conceal the fact that Kesselring's Luftflotte 2, with twenty-five hundred warplanes, had already been transferred to the eastern front.

During May 1941 Göring had committed the air force to one other minor theater of war. After an Arab rebellion against the British forces in oil-rich Iraq, he had despatched a small force of Messerschmitt planes under General Felmy to aid the rebels. But it was too little and too late, as Göring explained to Hitler and Foreign Minister Ribbentrop on the last day of May. "They don't know anything about aviation out there, and airlifting fuel would have been pointless and costly."

Thus he glossed over his own inadequacies while emphasizing those of his colleagues. Unfeeling and scheming to maintain position, Göring used the sinking of Germany's newest battleship, *Bismarck*, four days before, with the loss of twenty-three hundred sailors, to generate bad feeling against Admiral Raeder. His own prestige was high. On May 31, he was able to deliver a victory report on Crete to Hitler (although the Luftwaffe had lost 150 Junkers 52 transport planes in the assault).

> Air force is overextended [wrote Hewel after Göring's visit to the Berghof]. Had no respite since this war began. Based on Crete, a determined struggle will now begin against the British Fleet and Tobruk [the main obstacle to Rommel's advance across Libya] . . . Göring and F. use harsh language about *Bismarck* and the navy.

By now they had received secret reports of a speech that Stalin had delivered at a Kremlin banquet one month before, announcing his intention of invading Western Europe sooner or later. Göring had to admit that once again Hitler was proving to be right. Hitler planned in three weeks' time to launch the mightiest onslaught in history on Russia, and for this he would approach almost every one of Russia's western neighbors for assistance. Only the Swedes would not be invited—"Their ruling class is basically pro-British," Hitler explained to Julius Schnurre in mid-May. "Even the Reichsmarschall has been cured of his infatuation for Sweden."

Göring spent five hours with him and Jeschonnek on June 1. The new campaign was going to be some party, and it was time to start sending out invitations. On June 2, Hitler dropped a broad hint to Mussolini. On the third, after again consulting all afternoon with Göring, he tipped off the Japanese ambassador. The RSVPs trickled in: Hungary and Romania, eager to assist; the Finns, glad to join in. A few days later the high command sent out invitations to forty of Hitler's top commanders to attend a meeting at the Berlin Chancellery on the fourteenth. Almost at the same time, Birger Dahlerus received in Stockholm what he described immediately, on June 9, to the British envoy there as "a rather cryptic message . . . which seems to indicate Germany will attack Russia by about June 15." The message, Dahlerus said, had been telephoned to him by a mutual acquaintance who had just arrived in Stockholm from Berlin. From American files it is plain that Dahlerus had also notified the American legation—"Dahlerus . . . had it first hand from Göring that Germany meant to attack Russia almost at once."

The historic briefing session began at 11:00 A.M. Göring wrote in his diary, "Führer briefing. Rehearse attack on Russia with high command (OKW), War Dept., Admiralty, all army groups, Luftflotten and staffs present." After lunch, the "discussions continued." Hitler explained more or less convincingly why Germany had no option but to strike at Russia. Deputy Chief of Staff von Waldau recorded a summary in his diary:

Hitler's after-luncheon speech. The main enemy is still Britain. Britain will fight on as long as the fight has any purpose. . . . But Britain's fight only makes sense as long as they can hope that American aid will take effect and that they may find support on the Continent. This explains why they have high hopes that the Russians will intervene. . . . We want this conflict with Russia to come early, however. Indeed, it is absolutely essential, if we are not to forfeit the favorable conditions that now prevail.

"The bulk of the Russian forces," continued Waldau's note, "are standing on the frontier, so we have a good chance of defeating them right there." At 6:00 P.M., Göring briefed Hitler alone on the Luftwaffe's plans. He would commit twenty-seven hundred warplanes on the first day. Reconnaissance pictures showed four thousand Soviet planes just across the demarcation line, and radio intelligence had located a thousand more. Göring's own attitude was hard to divine—Waldau remarked on his "meager interest," and when the Reichsmarschall assembled his Luftflotte, air zone (Luftgau), and corps commanders at Carinhall the next day, Milch too thought him "depressed." After a long stroll around the garden at Carinhall, that evening Göring returned to Berlin, talked for over an hour with his art dealers Behr, Lohse, and Hofer, and boarded his train. At eight-thirty it moved off, and as though materializing from thin air, the mysterious Swede, Dahlerus, entered his private cabin.

Five days later the Polish prime minister, an exile in London, met American ambassador Tony Biddle. Biddle reported his conversation that same day in a letter to President Roosevelt: The Pole had revealed that Göring had now told a close Swedish friend that "he might expect Germany to launch an attack against Russia on Sunday June 22."

29
SIGNING HIS OWN
DEATH WARRANT

"At last a proper war!" exclaimed General Jeschonnek as the German armies uncoiled into Russia on June 22, 1941. The chief of air staff had good cause for satisfaction. The Luftwaffe enjoyed total technological supremacy on the eastern front. Milch's diary records 1,800 Russian warplanes destroyed on that first Sunday, 800 on Monday, 557 on Tuesday, 351 on Wednesday, and 300 on the fifth day, June 26.

Nobody expected the war to last more than a few weeks longer, and jostling for power and position had already begun. Alarmed by Bormann's elevation to the full dignity of Reich minister two weeks earlier, Göring arrived at the Wolf's Lair, the new Führer headquarters, on the twenty-eighth. He wanted reassurances from Hitler, and got them. On the next day Hitler signed a secret decree confirming Göring as his exclusive successor in the event of his own death, and as his "deputy in all offices." This by no means eliminated the rivals. Himmler also had ambitions, but as SS Obergruppenführer Gottlob Berger, one of his principal aides, commented, Göring was still the more powerful of the two. "However," added Berger, under interrogation in May 1945, "Himmler had a thing or two on Göring even then." The SS chief at The Hague, Wilhelm von Rauter, had discovered, for instance, that the

Reichsmarschall was quietly buying up uncut diamonds from Jews in Amsterdam; Himmler began filling dossiers with data like this. His Gestapo chief, Reinhard Heydrich, also had ambitions. He coveted Göring's Currency Protection Unit because of its mouth-watering harvest of seized foreign currency, but he trod very warily. "Heydrich," Göring would smugly comment later, "was much too clever to pick a fight with me." Heydrich preferred to keep Göring's power intact—so that he might pursue his own evil causes under its gaudy, all-embracing cloak.

Göring established his headquarters east at Rostken, just south of Lake Spirding in East Prussia, and parked his luxurious train *Asia* here, about an hour's drive from the Wolf's Lair. Jeschonnek had established the air staff's mobile headquarters, *Robinson*, at the neighboring Lake Goldap. The humid climate that summer affected Göring's health. There were almost daily checkups by his cardiologist, Professor Heinrich Zahler. Zahler's name figures in Göring's diary on July 20, 22, 23, 24, 26 ("bed rest, headaches"), 27 ("stomach upset, headaches"), and on August 23 ("heart palpitations"), 24, and 25, and again in September—on the twenty-third the Reichsmarschall would record, "heart pains, bad night." Determined to hang on to life long enough to enjoy the fruits of power, Göring began a strenuous program of daily swims, walks, horseback-riding, and even an occasional game of tennis. He telephoned Emmy and Edda daily, arranged occasional flying visits to them; but not once that summer did he visit a front-line Luftwaffe unit. He was bored with the war. When General Hans-Jürgen Stumpff (commanding Luftflotte 5 in Norway) came to see him, Göring interrupted the briefing: "Enough! Now let's take a look around Carinhall!" Stumpff noticed that he kept nodding off.

By mid-July 1941 it was clear that Hitler had launched *Barbarossa* none too soon, and had in fact underestimated the Russian strength. As they marched East, the Germans discovered that the Russians had massed twelve thousand tanks and eight thousand warplanes for strategic plans of their own. "The Red Army's equipment staggers us," wrote Jeschonnek's deputy on July 15. "In their Lemberg [Lvov] salient alone, sixty-three huge airfields, each with two runways and still incomplete, bear witness to Russian attack preparations."

On the following day, July 16, Hitler called his ministers together to discuss how to consolidate Nazi rule in these new territories. Göring wrote in his diary, "7:30 A.M., rose. Party cloudy, sultry." He spent an hour on dispatches and swimming, was briefed at 11:00 by Jeschonnek, and met Milch and Udet at midday, before setting out for the Wolf's Lair at 1:30 P.M. "3:15 p.m., conference with Führer: Rosenberg, Milch, Lammers." (Hitler had appointed Rosenberg minister with overall responsibility for the new eastern territories.)

Both Otto Bräutigam, Rosenberg's ADC, and Bormann wrote full accounts

of the day's historic talks: "At 3:00 P.M.," wrote Bräutigam in his diary,
"the Reichsmarschall appeared and the proceedings began." " 'Let there
be no doubt in *our* minds,' " Bormann quoted Hitler as saying, " 'that we
shall never depart from these territories. Never again shall there be any
military power west of the Urals, even if we have to fight one hundred years
to prevent it.' " There remained only to apportion responsibility for these
conquered eastern territories between the Four-Year Plan (Göring), the party
(Bormann), and the police executive (Himmler). "Toward 6:00 P.M.,"
continued Bräutigam's diary, "they took a coffee break. During this the
Reichsmarschall thanked the Führer for the high honor he had accorded to
fighter-ace Lieutenant Colonel [Werner] Mölders (the Diamonds to the Oak
Leaves of the Knight's Cross). The Reichsmarschall was accordingly in high
spirits. The Führer heaped scorn on the Swedes for their meager contribution
to the struggle against Bolshevism. The Reichsmarschall also termed the
Swedes 'decadent.' "

"As you know," continued Hitler, turning to Göring, "I had serious
misgivings about this campaign . . . I don't know if I would have made the
same decision, if I had been aware of the overall strength of the Soviet Army
and particularly of its gigantic tank forces. Then again, it's become clear
that it was high time to attack the problem. Next year might already have
been too late."

They reached a final settlement on the division of territories. At 8:30 P.M.
Rosenberg took his aide, Bräutigam, aside and told him the details:

> We have reached compromises [wrote the aide] with the Reichs-
> marschall, who is to control the economy of the occupied terri-
> tories with his Economic Operations Staff East, and with the
> Reichsführer SS [Himmler] who fully intends to direct the op-
> erations of his SS police units from Berlin.

To exploit the Caucasus oil fields Göring had set up a commercial monopoly,
but the retreating Russian troops had destroyed the wells and removed all
the rigs and drilling machinery. Thomas reported to Göring on July 17, then
recorded, "Reichsmarschall wants rapid investigation of ways of increasing
German fuel imports from (a) Romania (b) the Caucasus."

The Soviets were still far from collapse. Hitler ordered the Luftwaffe to
execute "terror raids" on Moscow. Göring called in Jeschonnek on July 18
and 19, and his bomber and fighter experts Galland and Werner Baumbach
on the twentieth to discuss the raids. "The signs are multiplying," intelligence chief Canaris told his Abwehr staff that day, however, "that this war
will not bring about the internal collapse of Bolshevism that we had anticipated, so much as its invigoration." Göring evidently felt the same misgivings, as he had a four-hour talk alone with the mysterious Swede, Dahlerus,
that same day, and invited Canaris for a similar secret talk five days later.

The air force meanwhile bombed Moscow on July 21 and 22; Stalin showed no signs of yielding.

At the end of July Emmy Göring came back from Bavaria to meet her husband in Berlin. The Reich capital was dampened by summer rains. Late the following afternoon, July 31, as the drizzle cleared, Göring called in briefly at his ministry. Here, at 6:15 P.M., he had a visitor—Gestapo Chief Reinhard Heydrich wanted the favor of the Reichsmarschall's signature on a document. The SS officer had drafted it himself, he had even *typed* Göring's letterhead. Göring obliged the young Obergruppenführer, then hurried off to the station a few minutes later to meet Emmy, unaware that he had just signed the document that would be used to condemn him to the gallows five years later: a paper empowering Heydrich to ''make all necessary preparations . . . for an overall unraveling (*Lösung*) of the Jewish problem within Germany's sphere of influence in Europe.''

He was tired of the war, and awarded himself several weeks' leave at Carinhall. His mind strayed far from the battlefields. Judge-Advocate General von Hammerstein briefed him on August 1 on court-martial cases in Crete, and described the sprawling Palace of Minos. Göring interrupted with his familiar scooping gesture. ''That's coming to Carinhall too,'' he bragged.

''Do you know how big the palace is?'' gasped Hammerstein.

''Have you any idea,'' countered Göring, ''how big Carinhall's going to be?''

Several times he was awakened by air-raid alerts, and the Russians actually raided Berlin on August 7, an impertinence that caused Göring to summon General Hubert Weise, the Luftwaffe's commander in chief center, to discuss their air defenses in the east. His diary two days later records two visits by Sepp Angerer, who unrolled a dozen Italian tapestries for his approval. Göring purchased six, including a battle scene and two Renaissance works richly embroidered with gold and silver thread. Two of the larger Gothic tapestries were, Angerer reported, jointly owned by a Princess Rospiljosi with her English sister and American brother—the tapestry expert suggested persuading Mussolini to sequestrate the Englishwoman's share, while a future war with the United States would enable Italy to seize the brother's share too. Göring approved. He did not hesitate to exploit Mussolini, as his papers show. After the Fascist dictator visited his train at Rostken on the twenty-sixth, he was able to acquire the tapestry.

In mid-August Göring left Carinhall to vacation in Bavaria. He rummaged around art galleries in Munich, then took his train on to Paris ostensibly for an air-force conference at the Quai d'Orsay but in fact in order to cast covetous eyes once more over the Jeu de Paume and the diamonds at Cartiers. A naval signals unit billeted in a château in the Bois de Boulogne had just found a strong room concealing another Rothschild cache, of eighteenth- and nineteenth-century Dutch and French paintings. Göring grasped these treasures too, and returned contentedly to the sweltering heat of Berlin.

* * *

There is good reason to dwell upon Göring's shopping mania. Like the crude attack of dysentery that now smote Hitler himself, it is the kind of petty factor that History ignores at its peril: During Göring's three-week absence from East Prussia a strategic controversy had developed between Hitler and the general staff—Hitler had always demanded a diverging, two-pronged attack with pincer arms extending toward Leningrad and the Caucasus, while the army had inclined to a frontal assault on Moscow. Now that the general staff found the Russian armies massing in front of the capital, all their inclinations were to ignore Hitler. Hitler forbade any advance on Moscow until Leningrad had fallen. The battle slowed. "The seasons are drawing on," wrote General von Waldau, incensed, on August 14. "At the beginning of October the war will choke on its own mud."

The army held out for Moscow. Weak and nauseous from dysentery, Hitler took three days to dictate a reply, rejecting the army's arguments. Returning to Hitler's headquarters for the first time on the nineteenth, Göring protested at the way that Field Marshal von Brauchitsch had "watered down" the Führer's brilliant strategies. He accused Brauchitsch of double-crossing Hitler, of going behind his back.

They pulled no punches in their altercations. Brauchitsch suffered a mild heart attack, but showed up for afternoon tea with Göring aboard his train *Asia*. Göring suffered too—his diary shows that his heart thumped so much that he called in his doctor, Ondarza, again that evening. Neither fish nor fowl, the German autumn offensive faltered and eventually failed.

The metal-toothed paratroop general Bernhard Ramcke arrived with his commander, Kurt Student, one afternoon to receive the Knight's Cross at Göring's hands. "They had built this big jetty on the edge of the lake," recalled Ramcke, "a big wooden platform. His train stood next to it." A photographer snapped pictures while the Reichsmarschall posed, looking commandingly across the lake. Erich Koch, the gauleiter of East Prussia and one of Göring's former protégés, stepped forward, clutching a map. "Now, Herr Reichsmarschall," he said, "About these new domains. These forests"—he tapped the map—"always belonged to East Prussia before."

"Of course," said the Reichsmarschall with a vague gesture. "Of course." Koch pointed to the Bialowieźa hunting ground.

"Of course," said Göring, "East Prussia gets that too."

The scene was characteristic of Göring in his later years. His vagueness upset many Luftwaffe generals outside his own clique. Attending what he called a "dumb briefing conference" on September 3, Richthofen asked for "clear and concise orders" but noted in his diary that night, "[The] RM can't grasp most of it. He just passes things on to Bodenschatz to bring up for his next chat with the Führer." To avoid hearing awkward truths, Göring canceled their subsequent appointment. "In the evening," wrote the bullet-skulled VIII Air Corps commander, "there were some Oak Leaves fighter-pilots there and the Reichsmarschall devoted himself exclusively to them." The contrast with the ("magnificently clear-headed") Führer maddened Richthofen.

> *September 4*: I coach Field Marshal Kesselring, who is here today with all the other Luftflotte and corps commanders. He shares my views . . . The only war they believe in here is the fantasy version painstakingly cobbled together each week for the news-reels. No wonder, as [Göring] never visits the front!

The weather worsened, as Waldau had predicted. On the seventh and eighth, Göring registered thunderstorms and hail. In lordly style, he continued to haunt the hunting grounds, eliciting from Waldau on the ninth further signs of edginess. "It's a real drag working at Rominten—a round trip of eighty miles each day . . . There's no comparing our existence with that of the troops."

On the ninth the rain began bucketing down along the whole front. It was the heaviest downpour since 1874. The highways became morasses. "We are heading for a winter campaign," wrote General von Waldau. "The real test has begun."

Throughout that summer of 1941 Hermann Göring had ducked the ugliest problem confronting him. It stared him in the face—the fact that Ernst Udet, whom he himself had appointed GL—director of air armament—two years earlier, had failed to increase aircraft output since war began. Udet, Göring's once-handsome comrade from the old Richthofen Squadron—produced apologetic graphs that established apparent crippling shortages of raw materials and manpower. Göring trusted him. "If they plonk graphs in front of me," he would say three years later, sadder and considerably wiser, "then I know from the start that I am about to be swindled. And if they are planning a really big fraud, they draw them in three colors. I've been lied to," he added, "duped, cheated, and robbed blind by the GL."

In March and April, as Udet's surviving agendas show, he regularly postponed the discussion of items like "supply situation" and "increased fighter output." He was no longer normal. He was flooding his system with alcohol and mind-numbing narcotics, there was a constant ringing in his ears, his brain blared with all the symptoms of persecution mania. While Milch slogged on in Berlin, Göring took Udet around Carinhall on the last afternoon in August. Now he too saw that Udet was mortally depressed and persuaded the reluctant general to enter the central air-force clinic immediately.

Udet discharged himself from the clinic prematurely, on September 16, and arrived out at the Sternberg hunting ground in East Prussia. For a week Göring's diary showed them going on boat or carriage jaunts, taking coffee, hunting with Scherping, Galland, Jeschonnek, or Milch.

By now the shortages of air-force equipment were slowing down Luftwaffe operations on every front. By enforcing multiple sorties, Luftflotte 4 alone was flying sixteen hundred sorties a day in the east, but the global tasks confronting the air force were expanding. The British bombing of northern Italy was affecting morale there, and British-held Malta was a constant annoyance to the supply lines to General Erwin Rommel's armies, fighting in North Africa. Göring called a frank inter-Axis conference with the Italian chief of air staff, General Francesco Pricolo, at Rominten on October 2, but the Reichsmarschall's diary suggests that the Rommel supply convoys were less significant to him than the "exchange of gifts and medals" at 2:25 P.M., and "deer stalking" at 6:00. "It would have been practical," he unhelpfully lectured the Italians, "if your Duce had declared war by seizing Malta!" On his advice Hitler now had to sanction the transfer of Luftflotte 2 (Kesselring) and II Air Corps (Loerzer) from the Russian front to Italy.

That day, the army offensive against Moscow resumed, but Göring remained at Rominten. Two days later a Romanian air-force general—Göring did not catch his name—came "with the most illustrious decorations for me."

The offensive made colossal strides. The German armies, aided by their allies, trapped seventy-five Soviet divisions at Vyazma and Bryansk. Millions of Russian prisoners began the long march into captivity. "We have finally and without any exaggeration won the war!" triumphed General Jodl on the eighth. Göring too believed that it was game, set, and match. He went to Berlin for a heart checkup and a new suit. He phoned Emmy every day. Immense battles were now raging on the Russian front, but on October 12 the Reichsmarschall inscribed in his diary, "Strolled around the house [Carinhall] with Emmy and [Fräulein] Limberger inspecting the new art treasures." With total lack of emotion he entered the news that his nineteen-year-old nephew Peter had been killed as a fighter-pilot in France.

Victory seemed within their grasp. On October 15, the air staff issued a map of their proposed new air zone, *Luftgau Moskau*. But Göring returned to Rominten the next day to find the weather once more deteriorating. "Our wildest dreams," wrote deputy chief of air staff von Waldau that same day, "have been washed out by rain and snow. . . . Everything is bogged down in a bottomless quagmire. The temperature drops to $-8°C$ [11°F], eight inches of snow falls and then it rains on top of that."

Even in the warmer southern Ukraine ice and snow grounded the Luftwaffe's squadrons. Interservice bickering broke out anew. General von Richthofen, frustrated, wrote on October 23, "I know that the Russians are through . . . but the fatigue and disarray of our [army] commands right down to regimental level are horrendous." Tempers frayed. That day, Vice-Admiral Canaris visited the Wolf's Lair, Hitler's headquarters, to report on Abwehr plans to seize the Caucasus oil fields. When he mentioned that he would be seeing Göring the next day, Field Marshal Keitel (chief of the OKW) flew off the handle. "The Reichsmarschall," he shrieked, "is the

uncrowned chief of the OKW as it is! He goes behind my back all the time."
Bursting into tears, according to Canaris's diary, Keitel predicted, "Any
proposals or successes you tell him about, Göring will turn them to his own
advantage—he'll report them to the Führer as though they were his own,
without so much as mentioning me as chief of the OKW!"

Canaris arrived at Rominten on the twenty-fourth, but it is plain from the
archives that Göring's mind was once again focused elsewhere. That day he
was poring over yet more paintings—a Stefan Lochner and Cranach's "Ad-
oration of the Three Kings"—and a 1550 Flemish tapestry that several Swiss
dealers had brought to him.

Nobody at any Luftwaffe headquarters believed that the Russians could
hold out much longer. "General Jeschonnek," wrote Richthofen to General
Rudolf Meister at air-staff headquarters on October 26, "is assuming we
shall be staying here until about November 6." But that day came and went,
and the snow that began drifting down onto East Prussia, enveloping both
Göring's train at Rostken and the Wolf's Lair at Rastenburg, no longer melted
away.

He had spent the last half of October 1941 and the first half of November
on these freezing, fog-enveloped moors, grilling generals about flak production and radar production, receiving the medal-bearing Slovak leaders
Tiso and Tuka, and entertaining his family and in-laws (the relatives of both
wives), although Emmy herself had made her excuses and migrated to the
warmer climes of southern Germany. He had seen Udet only twice, he
realized—the last time on November 1. Göring had returned to Berlin and
forgotten the general completely in the press of events—renewed sessions
with his cardiologist, and a conference on ways of injecting one million
Russian prisoners into Germany's labor-starved war industries. One evening
as he was meeting Emmy at the Anhalter Station, the air-raid sirens forced
them to shelter in the Kroll Opera's bunker until nearly 5:00 A.M. (Four
hundred RAF planes were raiding Mannheim and Berlin.)

At midday on November 17, his personnel chief telephoned to say that
Udet was dead. Lying on his bed, the general had phoned his mistress that
morning, cried, "They're after me!" and had shot himself while still holding
the phone so she could hear. In the suicide's room Körner found empty
cognac bottles and crazed farewell messages scrawled across a wall. "Man
of Iron," said one, using Göring's nickname from earlier times, "you deserted me!"

Grim-faced, Göring drove straight over to Hitler and stayed with him
five hours. Hitler's verdict was harsh. "He took the easy way out," he
would remark a year later. Göring was more understanding. "When he
saw the chaos," said Göring in 1943, "[Udet] did something which one
obviously cannot endorse but which I understand better today than I did at
the time."

To hush up the suicide, Göring told his doctor, Ondarza, to have the Air Ministry issue this communiqué:

> While testing a new weapon on November 17, 1941, the director of air armament Colonel General Udet suffered such a grave accident that he died of his injuries . . . The Führer has ordered a state funeral.

Every air-force building in the Reich flew its flags at half-mast on the day of Udet's funeral. Every holder of the Knight's Cross attended, as well as the fighter aces Walter Oesau, Günther Lützow, Hans Hahn, and Gordon Mac Gollob. They filled the front rows in the great hall of the ministry, with the party, government, and diplomatic notables arrayed behind them. "The last to appear," described bomber commander Werner Baumbach, "was the Reichsmarschall, wearing red-brown boots, light-gray uniform and smart gold braid." After the strains of Ludwig von Beethoven's *Eroica* had died away, Göring clanked up to the dais in his golden spurs and spoke with a voice breaking with emotion. "I can only say I have lost my best friend," he said.

"A *tour de force* by actor Hermann Göring," observed Baumbach cynically.

Hitler appointed Milch as the new GL—a sound decision, because by June 1944 the aircraft industry would be manufacturing fifteen times as many planes. Göring's indulgence of his unstable, happy-go-lucky World War I companion had cost Germany dear.

A second disaster compounded the Udet tragedy. Returning to the eastern front, Mölders, general of fighters, crashed at Breslau. After that funeral Göring motioned to Galland with his baton and appointed him Mölder's successor.

He took Galland with him as his special train conveyed him once more in state and style across Germany to France. On the first day of December he tackled the aged French collaborationist leader Marshal Pétain, remarking to Galland that he expected to be through in twenty minutes. But three hours passed before he emerged, ruffled, pink-faced, and angry. He told Mussolini two months later that Pétain, acting as though France had won the war, had tried to hand him a document setting out *French* conditions on further collaboration, and when he had declined to accept it, the Frenchman had leaned forward and tucked it into his pocket.

Far away, on the snow-gripped Russian front, Field Marshal Fedor von Bock had begun to bludgeon his army group's way into Moscow, despite the sub-Napoleonic temperatures. The high command hoped that they might yet pull it off—they had, after all, already killed 1.4 million Russian troops and taken 3.6 million prisoners. The Nazi spearheads were only twelve miles from the center of Moscow. The Soviet capital's streets were mined, the remaining population was reported to be buying German dictionaries. Göring's diary shows that he spent this week accompanied by art experts Behr, Hofer, and Robert Bernheim, trawling through the Jeu de Paume and private galleries in Paris; Rosenberg's files reveal that a shipment of works of art was dispatched to Carinhall on December 2. Then Göring went on to try his fortune in Antwerp, The Hague, and Amsterdam with his sister Olga and his sisters-in-law Ilse and Else.

He could hardly hear it from here in the conquered western territories, but the whole eastern front was creaking like an iceberg about to break up. General Heinz Guderian, whose frozen Second Panzer Army was struggling forward south of Moscow, found his ill-equipped tank crews dying of cold. The infantry were poorly clad and ill-equipped too. "The Luftwaffe," he fumed in a letter to his wife, "is methodically commanded. But we in the army have to put up with horrifying bungling." On December 5, at −35°C, with tank turrets frozen solid, guns jamming, and explosives only fizzling in the sub-zero temperatures, Guderian had to stop his assault.

With this, the nightmare began. Stalin unleashed a counteroffensive, with the magnificent T-34 tanks appearing en masse. The German reverse threatened to become a rout. Hitler dismissed pot-bellied army generals, flew out to investigate on the spot. "If you think about it," reflected Air Corps Commander Richthofen in his diary, "there's got to be a catastrophe."

Still Göring whiled away the hours in France, visiting Emmy's Paris couturier, raiding Cartier's (with General Hanesse's adjutant clutching the necessary funds), and taking Ilse to see her son Peter's fresh grave. His only official duties were a visit with Galland to 26 Fighter Wing, where he was shown the new Focke-Wulf 109 fighter plane. On the sixth he turned up with Loerzer among the Jewish bazaars of Amsterdam—the Jews were noticeably fewer—and noted "visits to art dealers and shopping" in his diary before boarding *Asia* for the overnight trip back to Berlin. Just after noon the next day he telephoned Hitler from a wayside halt in the Rhineland.

It was probably only now that he learned that the Japanese had attacked Pearl Harbor. At the Reichstag session on December 11, Hitler declared war on the United States. Once again he had not consulted Göring. Three years later, addressing the air staff in November 1944, Göring would imply that he had always taken the risk of war with America seriously.

> The Americans had years to observe the war and to recognize that victory depends first and foremost on having a powerful air force. It was clear to me—and to you gentlemen as well—that here was a country with consummate technical skills, with immense material wealth and manpower at their fingertips, and able to work unmolested day and night without having to unscrew a single lightbulb. . . . The moment that this power factor America came in I recognized that it was now a matter of "all hands on deck" for us.

At San Remo in March 1939 he had gone so far as to assure Beppo Schmid, "The only thing they are good at is making automobiles—but not planes!" Even in January 1942 he would emptily assure Mussolini, "America is all talk and no action." But his very next words revealed that he was becoming uneasy. "If the war lasts much longer," he told the Duce, "we must assume that the Axis is going to feel something of the planes being produced by America."

As the eastern front began to cave in, several army generals developed urgent reasons for retreat. Brauchitsch panicked too, and did nothing to halt the rout. Göring returned from Carinhall to Rominten on December 17, and when Richthofen came to see him the air corps commander painted a picture that was deliberately somber—to bring home to him that "this is really war," as he explained in his diary that night.

> Reichsmarschall [he recorded] keeps trying to inject rosier hues
> . . . When I tell him that this is far better judged from up front
> than from here, in the rear, he flies into a rage. Tell him he
> shouldn't have asked if he only wanted to hear what's sweet and
> nice. He gapes, pulls himself together. At subsequent "gala war
> conference" I am once more the well-tolerated visitor from the
> front.
>   Drive over to Goldap with Jeschonnek in Reichsmarschall's
> automobile. I am once more attacked for whining . . . Railcar to
> Führer's headquarters. As I am seriously annoyed and remain
> icily aloof [Göring offers] handsome apology after three minutes.
> I then bask in an unusually intensive "gracious sun."

A pragmatic and useful commander, Richthofen suggested that Göring should make available spare Luftwaffe troops for infantry combat—telling them "they must fight, win, or die where they stand." He pleaded with Hitler in the same vein—the army must not even think of retreat. Hitler must issue a personal appeal to each soldier to stand fast. "The Reichsmarschall and I," recorded Richthofen, "were very persuasive. Führer swears loudly about the army commanders responsible for much of this mess." Between them, Göring and Richthofen that day persuaded Hitler to issue the famous orders that now halted the rout.

Göring's diary shows that he was drained by this immense human drama on the eastern front, and fled south and west as fast as he was able. He had intended going to Berlin, but he ordered a thousand-mile detour via Berchtesgaden (to see Emmy) instead. "Curious outcome of all our deliberations on the gravity of the situation!" observed Richthofen, furious at this dereliction.

Hitler evidently thought the same, and took a firmer hand than ever. On December 19, he retired the army's bumbling commander in chief, and took over the army himself. On the next day, issuing orders over Göring's head, he directed the Luftwaffe squadrons to destroy every vestige of dwelling space that the advancing Russians might use.

Heedless of the bad feeling that his absence aroused, the Reichsmarschall made only two more brief visits to the Wolf's Lair that winter, on December 22 and 27. Otherwise, surrounded by his female relatives and friends, he stayed at Carinhall, drooling over his art treasures and buying more. "For days now the Reichsmarschall has vanished," recorded General von Waldau with unmistakable asperity on Christmas Eve. "*He* gets to spend Christmas at home." But in a way Waldau was glad to be shivering at *Robinson*, the air staff's forward headquarters. "It is important to set an example in little things," he reminded himself in his diary. "We are going to have to get used to harder times."

PART 5
THE BANKRUPT

30

THE "INSTRUCTION"
TO HEYDRICH

That winter of 1941/42 Hermann
Göring heard rumors of mass killings in the east.

Given his control of the Forschungsamt and the Four-Year Plan, it would
be surprising if he had not heard earlier. Pathetic transports of Jews deported
from the west had clogged the railroad lines into Poland and eastern Europe,
and his papers would show him several times that spring discussing "transport
bottlenecks in Upper Silesia" with Hitler.

History now teaches that a significant proportion of those deported—
particularly those too young or infirm to work—were being brutally disposed
of on arrival. The surviving documents provide no proof that these killings
were systematic; they yield no explicit orders from "above," and the mas-
sacres themselves were carried out by the local Nazis (by no means all of
them German) upon whom the deported Jews had been dumped. That they
were ad hoc extermination operations is suggested by such exasperated outbursts as that of Governor-General Hans Frank at a Cracow conference on
December 16, 1941: "I have started negotiations with the aim of sweeping
them [further] to the east. In January there is to be a big conference in Berlin
on this problem . . . under SS Obergruppenführer Heydrich [the "Wannsee

Conference" of January 20, 1942]. At any rate a big Jewish exodus will begin. . . . But what's to become of the Jews? Do you imagine they're going to be housed in neat estates in the Baltic provinces? In Berlin they tell us: What's bugging you—we've got no use for them either, liquidate them yourselves!"

It is doubtful that "Berlin" meant Hitler, let alone Göring: The Führer was at the Wolf's Lair, directing the historic rearguard action against the Russian winter offensive, while the Reichsmarschall's presence in the capital was equally rare. His attention was already focused on a two-week jaunt to Italy at the end of January. No, "Berlin" more likely meant the party—or Himmler, Heydrich, and the SS.

On the last day of July 1941 Göring had signed that relatively innocuous *Auftrag* (instruction) at Heydrich's request. In full, it read:

> Amplifying the task assigned to you by [my] decree of January 24, 1939, of solving the Jewish problem as rapidly and as conveniently as possible by emigration or evacuation, I herewith instruct you to make all necessary preparations in an organizational, logistical, and material context for an overall unraveling (*Lösung*) of the Jewish problem within Germany's sphere of influence in Europe.
>
> Where this will impinge upon the purviews of other government departments, these are to be consulted.
>
> I further instruct you to lay before me shortly a comprehensive draft of the organizational, logistical, and material advance preparations for carrying out the desired final solution of the Jewish problem.

Göring had no reason to believe that he had signed anything but a routine administrative directive expanding Heydrich's existing powers to the more recently occupied eastern territories. It is worth bearing in mind as his defense counsel argued in his final plea for clemency on October 4, 1946, that while Göring had undoubtedly initiated the economic sanctions against the Jews, it remained unproven that he had even known of their "biological extermination." His earlier decree to Heydrich had been dated January 24, 1939, at a time when nobody was contemplating extermination as a "solution." Moreover the ominous phrase "final solution" would become synonymous with extermination only later, and even then only in Himmler's intimate circle.

History cannot, however, exonerate Göring from blame. Anxious not to be toppled from his post as heir-apparent—one stroke of the pen would have sufficed—he was careful not to probe too deeply into Himmler's methods.

Thirty miles from Carinhall, recalled Dr. von Ondarza, was the Oranienburg concentration camp. "Göring never once set foot in one," said Ondarza. "He just didn't have the guts. It was characteristic of him," Göring's aide added, "that when the going got rough he just scuttled off to Paris or Italy." No, Göring carefully eschewed any criticism of the SS. "Whoever attacked Himmler," he would explain evasively in May 1945, when taxed with these atrocities, "was eliminated. Besides, he lied to me." Prudence replaced propriety in Göring's demeanor: In August 1942 Himmler wrote to the Air Ministry soliciting assistance with unspecified low-pressure and low-temperature experiments on condemned prisoners at the Dachau concentration camp. Neither Göring nor his Staatssekretär inquired into what kind of experiments were involved. "I *did* tell Göring," Milch confided to his private diary four years later. "Göring was against any collaboration but insisted on a very polite tone toward Himmler."

In fact, Göring went out of his way to cultivate the Reichsführer's friendship. The records show Himmler writing to Chief Forester Scherping on September 12, 1942, thanking him for Göring's invitation to shoot a "very fine Rominten stag." When Herbert Göring—by now manager of the Berlin office of United Steel—incurred Hermann's wrath in 1943, the Reichsmarschall would write asking Himmler to strip Herbert of his rank as honorary SS Obersturmbannführer, and invite Hitler to pass a law depriving "unworthy" people of their famous names. And when Göring's brother Albert (who picturesquely insisted under American interrogation, "I am the *real* brother of Hermann Göring!") reported rumors from a Dr. Max Winkler about the machine-gunning of Jews in Poland, the Reichsmarschall ingenuously forwarded the letter to the SS to attend to.

In the winter of 1941–42 he did send a senior Forschungsamt official, Ernst-Friedrich Scholer, to investigate a rumor of atrocities in the Ukraine. Scholer returned with snapshots of men pointing rifles downward into large pits. In such disturbing instances, Göring regularly allowed himself to be fobbed off, as he related three years later.

I heard, for example, that a large load of Jews left for Poland during the winter and that some of them froze to death in their vehicles. I heard of these things mostly from the ranks of my employees and from the people. When I made inquiries, I was told that such things would not happen again—it was claimed that the trains had been misrouted.

Then there was some talk about *Vernichtungstruppen* [destruction squads]. What I was told was this—that there were many diseased people in these camps, and that many died of epidemics. These squads had the job of taking the corpses to a crematorium where they would be cremated.

* * *

Göring's role as evidenced in the archival documentation is clear. Since November 1938 official Nazi policy had been to extrude the Jewish community from Greater Germany. In January 1939, as chief of the Four-Year Plan, Göring had put Reinhard Heydrich in charge. By mid-1940 some two hundred thousand Jews had emigrated, often under the most harrowing and humiliating circumstances. Since few countries were willing to accept them, the idea had emerged in Berlin of resettling all of Europe's Jews eventually in Madagascar, a large French colonial island where no neighbors could molest them, and where they could not intrude upon their neighbors, either. But Hitler's vast military victories in 1939 and 1940 had brought three million more Jews under the Nazi aegis and, writing on June 24, 1940, to Foreign Minister Ribbentrop, Heydrich had suggested adopting what he termed "a geographical (*territoriale*) final solution" instead—shipping the millions of Jews overland eastward out of Europe, rather than overseas to Madagascar. Twelve months later *Barbarossa* provided the necessary territories, and Göring naïvely endorsed the Auftrag that Heydrich had drafted that rainy evening in Berlin. It was a document that Lord Halifax would have described as "platitudinous," but the SS Obergruppenführer made liberal use of it. Issuing invitations to the interdepartmental conference to be held—as Hans Frank had urged—in Berlin's leafy Wannsee suburb, Heydrich had prefaced each letter with the words, "On July 31, 1941, the Reichsmarschall of the Greater German Reich instructed me—" etc., and he attached a photocopy of the document with Göring's signature.

In the entire files of Göring's Stabsamt and other bureaus there is no evidence that Göring knew of Heydrich's ultimate intentions. At the Wannsee conference on January 20, 1942, he would be represented by the sharp-witted, hard-working Staatssekretär Erich Neumann, of the Four-Year Plan, but the actual proceedings were more obscure than might be supposed from the conference's subsequent notoriety. "Gruppenführer Heydrich told the conference," reported Ribbentrop's representative, the arrestingly named Martin Luther, "that Reichsmarschall Göring's Auftrag to him had been issued at the Führer's behest and that the Führer had now approved evacuating the Jews to the east instead of emigration as a solution." What was actually happening in "the east" was never discussed at the meeting.

The ministries had only to assent to measures specifically within their own ambit. On January 24, Fritz Görnnert of Göring's Stabsamt notified the SS, "The Reichsmarschall has no objections to the proposal by [Heydrich] to put signs on Jewish dwellings." Heydrich himself was studiously vague about his ulterior aims. Asking the SS personnel office to take cognizance of the Göring Auftrag, he added merely, "Preparatory measures have been put in hand." Writing to Luther about the same Göring document in February, he asked him to delay producing the draft proposals that the Reichsmarschall had called for until further discussions. In any case, Heydrich would be assassinated a few weeks later, before any such document could be drafted.

The documentary record shows that the initiative for specific atrocities came from Nazi officials in the field. Even Hitler's own role is thrown into question by recently discovered documents, and verbatim conference transcripts show Göring to have been aware of the Führer's less rigid attitude. Two days after visiting Hitler on July 4, 1942, he presided over the first session of the new Reich Research Council. Here Göring expressed anger that although the Führer had expressly forbidden it, Jewish scientists were being taken off vital research:

> I've just briefed the Führer about this. We have exploited one Jew in Vienna for two years, and another in the field of photography, because they've got things we need of the utmost value to us at this time. It would be madness to say, "He'll have to go! Of course he's a great researcher, a fantastic brain, but he's got a Jewish wife and can't be at the university, and so on."
>
> The Führer has made similar exceptions all the way down to operetta level.

A month later Göring could have heard Rosenberg telling the assembled gauleiters this, according to the stenographic record: "The solution of the Jewish problem continues apace . . . It can only be solved by rigorous and ruthless force. [*Storms of applause.*] We ought not to rest content with Jews being shipped from one state to another, leaving Jewish ghettos here and there. Our aim must be the old one: the Jewish problem in Europe and in Germany will not be solved until there is not one Jew left on the European continent. [*Lively applause.*]"

Such harsh words were not, of course, uttered in a vacuum. The whole trend was toward illegal and brutal modes of war—toward innocenticide on a grand scale. Violent air raids had resumed. The partisan warfare developing in Russia was barbarous beyond belief. Millions were starving too. At the same conference Göring evidently asked what food the Jews in Riga were getting, because the local Nazi official there, Reich Commissar Hinrich Lohse, corrected him: "Only a small fraction of the Jews [of Riga] still live." He continued, no less ambiguously, "Tens of thousands are gone."

"All cruelty," protested Hermann Göring, first confronted with evidence of the Nazis' atrocities, "was abhorrent to me. I can name many people whom I have helped, even Communists and Jews. My wife was so kind—I really have to be grateful for that. I often thought, if only the Führer had a sensible wife who would have said to him, 'Here's a case where you can do some good, and here's another, and this one—' That would have been better for everyone. It was very depressing for me.''

Göring's policy on the Jewish relocation program after Hitler's invasion of Poland is only rarely glimpsed in the archives. His brother Albert had asked him over dinner once during those months, and Hermann had replied that he favored awarding a large area of Poland (with Warsaw as its capital) to the Jews, who would be collected there from all over Germany, Austria, and Czechoslovakia—a huge, autonomous ghetto. No other Final Solution ultimately evolving in the east is even hinted at in the thousands of pages of Görnnert's files as Göring's office chief, let alone in the Air Ministry or Four-Year Plan files. Görnnert's files reflect the Reichsmarschall, albeit often cautiously, investigating every instance of Nazi heavyhandedness reported to him. He forwarded the grosser cases of excess to Philipp Bouhler for review. Bouhler's staff, however, usually rejected the complaints. In one case, when the Ministry of the Interior classified Baroness Elisabeth von Stengl as a Jew, Göring's staff redirected her indignant protest to the bureau. In vain—she was "relocated" (*umgesiedelt*). Göring again protested on her behalf, which drew a reply from Adolf Eichmann himself, dated October 7, 1942: "As her manner appeared to have become intolerable," it coldly explained, "the instruction was issued for her to be relocated as soon as possible to the Old Age Ghetto at Theresienstadt, regardless of her case pending at the Reich Genealogical Bureau (*Reichssippenamt*)." (The Baroness, born June 6, 1900, was only forty-two.)

Göring appears not to have suspected the character of Theresienstadt, as a showpiece "clearing station" through which elderly Jews passed on their final journey to "the east." On May 22, 1942, the Gestapo's chief (Heinrich Müller himself) had written him about a Jew, Hans Martin Manasse, and his wife, Rosa Cohn. Görnnert replied on June 17, "May I draw your attention to the Reichsmarschall's handwritten comments and request a brief word from you before any further steps are taken re Manasse/Cohn to enable the Reichsmarschall to pronounce finally on this case." On September 17, Görnnert brought Müller's decision to Göring, who directed his aide to notify the Gestapo official "that the Reichsmarschall requests that this couple should be deported together to Theresienstadt (*Judenstadt*)." The Reichsmarschall, Görnnert continued, had notified Himmler, and he added, "The deportation to Theresienstadt is to be carried out as soon as possible and the Jewish couple are to be enabled to stay there as long as this town is made available for this. The Reichsmarschall asks to be informed as soon as they have been deported." Göring appears to have known of Auschwitz only as the gigantic new synthetic rubber plant built there by Albert Speer. At a central-planning session on July 2, 1943, Pili Körner would mention the current plans to expand Auschwitz's output to twenty-eight thousand tons of rubber.

There is one clue that by 1942 Göring had learned of Hitler's systematic "mercy killing" of the population of Germany's mental institutions, because on May 6, he instructed Görnnert to write a letter in these terms to Heydrich: "The Reichsmarschall desires that the high command be required to order that—adopting Obergruppenführer Heydrich's own proposal—Wehrmacht soldiers who are in the future committed to institutions for the mentally ill shall be placed in institutions exclusively reserved for soldiers, so that the said institution attains the character of a military hospital."

Besides Philipp Bouhler, who ran the euthanasia "mercy killing" operation, it was Martin Bormann who forced through these less merciful campaigns. "Bormann," testified Göring, squirming under American interrogation in September 1945, "would make everything three times as bad, in order to please [Hitler] . . . Bormann used to walk around with his pockets stuffed with notepaper. He used to take down everything the Führer said, even if it was never intended to be taken seriously." By March 1942 Göring would be fighting tooth and nail to keep Bormann out of his own operations. Across one document on economic policy that Dr. Robert Ley submitted to Hitler —through Bormann—Göring scrawled, "This is an area where decisions until now have been solely in my hands. I recently mentioned to the Führer that unless I am informed and in agreement then no 'Führer decisions' are to be requested on any domain of mine except by me in person."

But the fanatics no longer heeded Hitler either. "Reichsminister Lammers," recorded the Staatssekretär to the minister of justice in the spring of 1942, "told me the Führer has repeatedly declared to him he wants to see the solution of the Jewish problem postponed until after the war." But the "solution" had already begun, and Göring, as Hitler's surviving successor, would be called to account for it.

31
THE THOUSAND-BOMBER RAID

As 1942 began Hitler's armies in Russia were in crisis. From the Crimea and Kharkov northward to Kursk, Moscow, and Leningrad, the starving, ill-equipped, and frozen German troops could barely withstand the furious onslaught. Hitler changed his army generals all along the front, but he had only praise for the Luftwaffe commanders like the hard-bitten General von Richthofen.

Göring willingly joined in his Führer's lashing of the army generals. Meeting Hitler in sub-zero temperatures at the Wolf's Lair on January 2, 1942, he marveled at the way the dictator halted the army's stampede and consolidated the crumbling front lines. "I have rarely seen such greatness," he told Mussolini, visiting Italy later that month.

In the last days of the old year, Lieutenant General Hans von Sponeck, acting against orders, had abandoned the peninsula of Kerch in the Crimea. The Reichsmarschall took it upon himself to punish Sponeck, which aroused indignation when he told his staff about it at Rominten the next day. "You can't dish out orders from on high," observed Luftwaffe operations chief Hoffmann von Waldau afterward, "and then make somebody else carry the can when things go wrong." Göring disagreed, and convened a court-martial at Hitler's headquarters. He did not have things all his own way, even then.

"The Reichsmarschall," Heinrich Himmler would later recall, "had the utmost difficulty in getting his fellow judges—all [army] generals—to agree to sentence this coward to death." In this instance even Hitler felt Göring had gone too far, and commuted the death sentence to fortress arrest.

Göring's merciless stance—more Catholic, it seemed, than the pope—strengthened Waldau's resolve to get out. "For three years," he wrote privately on January 3, "I have held down this job with almost total self-denial. I have labored to the best of my conscience and ability. I have gladly borne the burden that meticulous devotion to duty and permanent mental servitude have thrust upon me, but in the long run that burden, coupled with the knowledge that I bear the ultimate responsibility for events without the slightest means of influencing them, entitles me to the view that three years is enough."

Göring continued his vendetta against the army. Meeting Hitler again on the ninth, he criticized the army's feeble winter preparations. He had had to turn over three million sets of winter clothing to the army. Warning that the war was going to last into yet another winter, Göring recommended stockpiling fur hats and goggles now. "Göring told me," Hitler told his staff, impressed, "that when he goes hunting he always takes heat packs with him like the ones we've been finding on Soviet soldiers."

As the war's problems became more intractable, Göring took refuge in trivia and minor postwar problems. British code-breakers intercepted his instruction, passed to troops on the Russian front, that all air-force personnel summoned to his or the Führer's presence "must be free of lice." His leather-bound diary shows him at Carinhall on January 23, 1942, discussing with Nazi labor leader Robert Ley plans for postwar pensions that would embrace even the lowest income groups, and a "suggestion for a luncheon where party veterans can meet and talk to me." Another diary note, "Assistance for evacuees," reflects, however, the one nightmare that would not go away with the dawn: the RAF's bombing offensive. Nor did it escape his attention that when he now left East Prussia for Berlin, one after another, sixteen locomotives pulling his train broke down in the cold. For his next conference with Hitler he dictated this reminder: "Responsibility for provision of sufficient locomotives in good time for winter 1942–43, capable of trouble-free operation at temperatures below -40°C."

Hitler sent him down to see Benito Mussolini and reassure him about Germany's will to fight on. After taking explicit instructions from Hitler on what to say in Rome, Göring departed aboard *Asia* taking valet, nurse, doctor, and a multitude of staff officers, including his nephew Lieutenant Göring, Görnnert, and Bodenschatz with him. The hapless Hoffmann von Waldau, scandalized by this new extravagance, cynically recorded that Göring made "considerable preparations, mainly of a sartorial nature" for the jaunt. He added, "How I hate to go swanning off at times like these!" Waldau's tender gaze was spared the more scandalous displays of opulence. Becoming restless once during the journey Göring sent for the pot of diamonds, tipped them out and counted them, then paraded them across the table, mixed them up, and calmed down completely.

In Rome the Reichsmarschall made no attempt to consult with Italy's foreign minister, Ciano (who learned of this diamonds-fetish episode)—"In fact," wrote Ciano in his diary, "ever since we bestowed that [diamond] Collar on von Ribbentrop, [Göring] has adopted an aloof air toward me." "We are having a hard time," Göring had whispered to Mussolini at the station, alluding to the army's difficulties in Russia. Meeting again more formally, he blamed this crisis on the sub-Napoleonic temperatures. "Such difficulties will not recur," he promised. "Whatever happens in the coming year, the Führer will halt and take up winter quarters in good time."

As for North Africa, the main problem was that of supplies. Göring loftily suggested that Italian submarines transport forty thousand tons of supplies a month to Rommel. The "bloated and overbearing" Reichsmarschall got on Ciano's nerves. Dining at the Excelsior on February 4, Göring talked to Ciano only of his rings and jewelry. Accompanying him to the station, Ciano—who appears to have known about such things—reflected that Göring's full-length sable coat was what a high-grade call girl might wear to the opera.

A serious challenge to the Reichsmarschall's authority confronted him soon after his return to East Prussia. On Sunday morning, February 9, the munitions minister, Fritz Todt, perished in a plane crash at the Wolf's Lair. With barely a flicker of grief, Göring hastened over to demand Todt's ministry for himself, only to learn that Hitler had already selected his thirty-six-year-old chief architect, Albert Speer, for the job. In terms of blind ambition and pathological zest for intrigue, Göring had now met his match. When Milch brought Speer to him, Göring blandly emphasized that his new job was merely the production of *army* munitions. Milch, he continued, would make a better munitions minister and would shortly call a big conference of arms industrialists at the Air Ministry. "The Ministry of Munitions," he reminded Speer some weeks later, "was set up at my own suggestion purely to offset the shortcomings of the Army Weapons Office." Todt had agreed not to trespass on the Reichsmarschall's Four-Year Plan, and now Göring invited Speer to sign a similar agreement. Realizing immediately what Göring was up to, Speer raced back to the Wolf's Lair and persuaded Hitler to endorse him personally as the new minister. Hitler complied in a two-hour speech delivered to the arms industrialists in the Reich Cabinet room—Göring was informed that his own presence was not necessary.

For years afterward, Göring seethed over his humiliation at Speer's hands. No slouch in the art of power politics, Speer initially flattered and fawned upon Göring, inviting Göring to appoint him as "general plenipotentiary for arms production in the Four-Year Plan" (to enable him to draw upon Göring's still considerable residual authority). He also won Keitel's arms chief, the stiff-necked, bureaucratic General Georg Thomas, to the idea of creating "a small body of men gathered around the Reichsmarschall to direct central planning policy." Sitting on this new central-planning body, Speer and Milch would allocate all raw materials. It effectively spelled the end of the Four-Year Plan. That agency now became a hollow shell, represented in Central Planning only by the witless Pili Körner. The Plan retained control only over manpower allocation, through Labor Commissioner Fritz Sauckel, and here Göring freely interfered. When Sauckel, searching for two million more workers, drew attention to the untapped reserves of female labor in the Reich, Göring objected: Some women, he averred, were born to work, while others were not. It was like plough horse and racehorse. "Reichsmarschall Göring," Himmler was informed, "also says that ladies who are the bearers of our culture should not be exposed to the silly talk and insolence of the simpler womenfolk." Oblivious of Germany's crucial manpower shortages, Göring would allow his own private office and personal staff to grow to 104 people in September 1942.

Again visiting Paris during March 1942, Göring bought half a dozen paintings, a terra-cotta figurine of Madame du Barry as Diana, and a vase. He toured the Left Bank dealers. Hofer totted up the purchases and handed the list to Fräulein Limberger aboard Göring's train on March 15.

During his absence abroad, Milch had drawn up tables showing that Germany was now producing 850 airplanes per month, of which only 314 were fighters. The air staff's current requirement was 360 fighters—itself a ludicrously low figure. "Herr Reichsmarschall," Milch said, tackling Göring at Rominten on March 21, "if you were to say *thirty-six hundred* fighters, then I should be bound to state that against America and Britain combined that figure is still too few!"

"I shouldn't know what to do with more than three hundred sixty," retorted General Jeschonnek, baffled.

Milch suggested they double the figure to 720. Göring paused, agonizing as ever whenever a firm decision was called for. Outside, the temperature was 26 degrees below freezing. In mid-discussion, so the minutes record, "the Reichsmarschall went for a sleigh ride at 5:25 P.M. Conference resumed at 6:55 P.M. . . ." He told Milch to go ahead. Two years later Milch would be manufacturing three thousand fighter planes a month.

As though on the devil's cue, a few days later the British fire-bombing of Europe's ancient cities began in mortal earnest. RAF Bomber Command now had orders to attack the population centers rather than the Nazi factories. Earlier in March 1942 they had bombed Paris, killing eight hundred Frenchmen. Hitler's first instinct had been to demand reprisals against London—"That's what counts," he raged at Göring. "The maximum shock and terror—not the economic damage inflicted." By March 21, however, he had changed his mind, and when Göring inquired after the reason, Jeschonnek could only explain, "The Führer doesn't want to provoke attack on Germany's cities so long as the British keep to their present small scale and we aren't able to deliver annihilating blows in the west."

The German hesitation went unrewarded. One night a week later, 230 British bombers burned the heart out of medieval Lübeck, killing three hundred people. On the morning of that raid, March 28, Göring had again met his sleazy art "curator" Walter Hofer at Carinhall. The day's typed agenda was crowded with items remote from the terrors of mass fire raids— the acquisition of paintings of Stefan Lochner, Italian art treasures from Count Contini, Alois Miedl, and his three Cézanne watercolors and a Cézanne landscape, and notes about "two little figurines from Brussels," and "[Emil] Renders still has some sculptures." The day's agenda also mentions the Dutch Jew Nathan Katz (whom Göring was smuggling across to Switzerland with his wife and children in return for valuable paintings deposited with the Swiss consul at The Hague) and Katz's paintings by Van Gogh and Van Dyck.

While the cities of Hitler's new empire began to burn, the Reichsmarschall indulged his caprices. He regarded himself as above and beyond the law. When Milch celebrated his fiftieth birthday at the end of March 1942, Göring gave him a valuable tapestry and ordered the media to give prominence to "photographs portraying the Reichsmarschall and Field Marshal Milch." Milch was tactless enough to ask, "Where was the tapestry snitched?" Adopting the double standard that comes so easily to those in power, Göring was ruthless in campaigning against corruption among others. He forbade Professor Messerschmitt to set aside scarce aluminum for postwar ventures; he prohibited Daimler-Benz from manufacturing twelve-cylinder limousines for other Nazi leaders. But Görnnert's files bear witness to the substantial orders that Göring placed for personal radio sets, refrigerators, and deep freezers—all virtually unobtainable in wartime Germany—for his family and benefactors. SS Gruppenführer Otto Ohlendorf learned of the priceless trinkets showered on Göring by Felix Schüler, head of the Reich Association (*Reichsgruppe*) of Handicrafts; when the Ministry of Economics opened an investigation, Göring's office impounded its dossier.

"Göring," Hitler chided him that March, worried about the top soldier's image, "do you think it looks good to be photographed with a pipe? What would you say to a statue with a cigar in your mouth?" More caustic comments were sometimes heard from the public at large. The Gestapo reported that cinema audiences also grumbled about Göring's chunky cigars at a time when by contrast, they themselves were fobbed off with noxious tobacco substitutes like lime-blossom leaves. The newsreel audiences remarked too upon his uniforms—always spotless white at a time when they could not buy soap powder—and criticized his obesity at a time when "the Russians were having to eat grass." On April 2, one SS Gruppenführer complained to Himmler that Emmy Göring had invited eighty generals' wives to coffee, "and the table fairly groaned under the weight of delicacies."

He was able to entertain so lavishly in part because of a colossal black-market operation allegedly designed to procure consumer goods for blitz victims. Through the Four-Year Plan's senior economists Friedrich Gramsch and Kurt Kadgien he had already plundered the west's gold, foreign currency, and jewels. Now he set up an External Agency West (*Aussenstelle West*) to bulk-buy artifacts, wine, and foodstuffs—for his own use and disposition— throughout the occupied west. His senior purchasing agent here was Colonel J. Veltjens, a Richthofen Squadron veteran possessed of the right bucca-neering spirit.

It is plain that Göring had a large stake in several business enterprises. He had a pecuniary interest in the near-worthless "vitamin pills" dispensed by the billion to the German armed forces by Hitler's doctor Theo Morell, because when the Luftwaffe's chief surgeon, Professor Erich Hippke, pro-tested that the pills were useless, Morell complained in a letter to Göring dated July 31, and the Reichsmarschall sacked the professor without a hear-ing. Questioned whether he had a stake in Otto Horcher's famous, leather-walled gourmet restaurant in Berlin, he would deny it ("I am not that versatile!"), but the archives show that he had ordered Horcher's key staff to be exempted from the military draft, had tripled the gas allocation to Horcher vehicles, and had exempted the restaurant from Goebbels's "total war" decrees. Learning that Otto Horcher knew how to lay hands on seventy thousand bottles of port wine for the air force, Göring sanctioned the deal "provided that a small quantity is diverted for his personal use" and "ten thousand bottles are set aside for Horcher's."

After the fire raid on Lübeck Hitler reversed his decision about retaliation, and ordered Göring to carry out "terror attacks" on British cities other than London—like the ancient and beautiful towns of Bath and Exeter—until the British lost what he called their "appetite for terror." Göring complied. The British responded by setting fire to Rostock on the Baltic. Unhappy at this rising tide of barbarism, on April 19 the Reichsmarschall nonetheless lectured his Luftflotte commanders at Rominten about the need to show no quarter to the Soviets: "The Russian," he said, "is an enemy of barbarous methods. They ought not to be initiated by us, but we've got to show a sterner face." As the war slithered down its toboggan route of terror and counter-terror, Göring for the most part took refuge from taking responsibility for atrocities in the excuse of "superior orders."

In Paris it was spring. On May 14, the Reichsmarschall once more climbed aboard *Asia* with assorted Görings and Sonnemanns and headed back to France. But each visit now left him angrier than the last. "The people there are eating off the fat of the land," he would grumble, speaking to gauleiters three months later. "It's a disgrace. I've seen villages where armies of them parade around with their long baguette loaves under their arms . . . and with baskets of oranges and fresh dates from North Africa." Dining at Maxim's in Paris the Reichsmarschall found himself surrounded by bloated French tricksters and wealthy black marketeers. "They're richer than ever," he fumed in the same speech, "because they charge us lunatic prices."

Train journeys like these brought home to him the gradual collapse of the wartime railroad system. French express trains still ran daily between Brussels and Paris, but the German railroads did not unload freight on Sundays or at night; fully laden trains choked the eastbound lines as Hitler's armies wound up for his spring offensive into Russia, and there were 165,000 empty freight cars waiting to return. The immense distances now covered effectively halved the available rolling stock. The result was a gradual breakdown of the railroad system that was starving the arms industry of coal and steel.

Reluctant to harm Reich Transport Minister Julius Dorpmüller—a personal friend and benefactor—Göring persuaded Hitler that the minister's sixty-five-year-old Staatssekretär, Wilhelm Kleinmann, was to blame for the railway chaos. Acting on Göring's advice, on May 24 Hitler told Speer and Milch to take charge of the transport system. Addressing these two men, he significantly reaffirmed his own esteem for Göring—"That's why I have appointed my best man," said Hitler, "who is somewhat younger than myself, as my successor."

Göring needed this kind of reassurance. He suspected that the Führer had begun to go behind his back. Hitler had spent several hours eating alone with Göring's subordinate, General von Richthofen, on May 21, discussing the Crimean campaign. He had even scoffed at the hunting fraternity. "I wonder why," mocked Hitler, "our soldiers don't hang up the jawbones of dead Russians in their rooms!" A few days later Richthofen dictated this smug note into his diary: "Göring has bawled out Jeschonnek [chief of air staff] because I was with the Führer!"

Far worse was to come for Göring. Late on May 30, 1942, as he was entertaining Speer and Milch, the new "transport overlords," at Veldenstein Castle, the phone rang. It was the Nazi gauleiter of Cologne, Josef Grohé. A violent British air raid had begun, he screamed. After a further exchange during which Göring claimed that it could only be a small-scale attack the guests heard him bellow, "Are you calling me a liar?" and slam the phone down. The phone rang again, and Göring snatched it. This time he fell silent—and it was obvious who was calling now. Hitler, telephoning from his special train in East Prussia, told him the gauleiter was talking of "hundreds" of British bombers attacking. There had never been a British raid in such numbers before. But Göring assured him that the gauleiter's figures were wrong—seventy planes, at most, had attacked. As daybreak came, he learned that his defenses had shot down forty bombers. It looked like a big victory, even though five hundred people had died in the raid. But the wire services brought the sensational news that Churchill had solemnly announced in London that over one thousand bombers had taken part. White-faced, Göring bleated that this was just a lie. Jeschonnek nervously agreed, but Hitler refused to be deceived. "It is out of the question," he told his own staff, "that only seventy or eighty bombers attacked [Cologne]. I never capitulate to an unpleasant truth. I must see clearly if I am to draw the proper conclusions."

This first thousand-bomber raid marked a perceptible watershed in their relations. "The British have learned it all from us," the Reichsmarschall lamented months later. "That's the most depressing thing about it. Except for their electronic warfare they have learned it all from us—the how and the why of delivering concentrated air raids. They have cribbed the lot. They were botching things up so beautifully to start with!"

32

THE ROAD TO STALINGRAD

"Hitler had told me," Göring reminisced later, "that he proposed to consider the Russian war at an end when his armies were established on the Volga. Thereafter he would contain the Russians by occasional punitive expeditions while turning the bulk of his forces against the west."

Early that summer of 1942 the Germans seemed on the point of realizing these aims, as Göring's pilots pounded the far-flung enemies of the Reich from Leningrad and Voronezh to Tobruk, as they bombed towns in southern England and freighters of Allied convoys in the Arctic bound for North Russia.

Göring's stock soared with the successes of the Luftwaffe, and he often ate with Hitler at the Wolf's Lair. A lunch guest that July 4 found the calmness that the Reichsmarschall radiated "impressive," and remarked upon his "good-naturedness" and his "air of honest, unconditional loyalty." When their table conversation turned to procuring vegetable oils from North Africa, Göring affably launched into a discourse on how he was stockpiling food by worldwide black-market operations—"often without letting his right hand know what his left hand was up to."

This allusion to oil procurement was a first hint of problems to come. The shortage of refined aviation spirit was already setting back Luftwaffe training and operations. Russian petroleum reserves, estimated at two thousand million tons, would provide the only long-term solution to Hitler's needs. According to the figures shown to Göring, the Baku Field—beyond the Caucasus Mountains—had reserves of 613 million tons, followed by Maykop with 137 million, and Groznyy with 120 million. But there was a snag: The retreating Russians had comprehensively sabotaged the wells, and the German invaders lacked the expertise and drilling equipment to restore production. They would need at least 120 rigs, and Göring now found that he had not set aside enough steel to make them.

On July 10, he called in the oil experts to discuss how to bring Maykop back into production once this field was captured. "Are we clear," he asked, "how we are going to tackle the demolitions? My own hope is that in the circumstances they will have had no time to carry out demolitions, because the wells are kept pumping until the last minute."

The experts dispelled his optimism. "I think," said one, "that once they've been prepared, demolitions are feasible in a very few hours."

At Kherson in the Ukraine the Germans were reassembling a refinery seized and dismantled in France. This would be able to produce four hundred thousand tons a year, but it would take until May 1943 to erect. "Does it have to take so long?" asked Göring.

"The Russians have wrecked everything," was the explanation. "So we have to rebuild from scratch."

"Getting oil wells working in winter," one expert lectured him, "is exceptionally tough."

"That's not the point," rasped Göring. "Even if it's tough, it's still got to be done."

As the armies hammered their way southward and southeastward into Russia, Göring reviewed his art collections yet again. The Dutch art dealer Hubert Menten offered him Adriaen Ysenbrant's "Madonna and Child"; Göring paid him thirty thousand Swiss francs for it. Deals in less valuable currencies ran less smoothly. After buying a series of Flemish tapestries depicting the life of the emperor Charlemagne for 4 million French francs from the Galerie Charpentier in Paris, Göring learned that the delighted vendors had only recently purchased them for one tenth of that price. The furious Reichsmarschall resorted to the usual offices of Dr. Helmuth Knochen, chief of the Paris Gestapo, but recovered only eight hundred thousand francs.

The most lurid example of his Byzantine purchasing methods came when he learned of two magnificent Flemish hunting tapestries in the Château de Bort, near Limoges. Owned jointly by the Marquis de Sèze and his estranged wife, each was thirty feet long and over fifteen feet high, woven over four hundred years before but with colors as fresh as yesterday. "If my uncle sees those," Lieutenant Göring had gasped, "they'll be packed up and taken away!'' Sure enough, in September 1942 Göring sent two French art agents, Messrs. Violet and Bourdaniat, to photograph them, ostensibly for an art catalog. The agents casually mentioned to the estranged Madame de Sèze the tempting sum of 20 million francs, but she said the tapestries were not for sale. Even under occupation law, Göring had to tread very carefully. Her husband agreed—if suitably bribed—to persuade her, provided Marshal Pétain himself would sign the export license. Madame de Sèze, however, fought back: She persuaded the French Administration des Beaux-Arts to list the tapestries as historic monuments. When the agents appeared at the château with Göring's cash, she announced triumphantly that she had given the tapestries to the nation. Göring instructed his General Hanesse to threaten Prime Minister Pierre Laval with massive retaliation, but Beaux-Arts now spirited the treasures away to Aubusson for "restoration," and the Laval government, refusing to be strong-armed, formally accepted the "gift" by decree of June 26—indignant, as Hanesse's adjutant Major Drees recorded that day, that Göring had larded 20 million francs around in bribes to French officials in addition to his original 20 million-franc offer. "In the absence of further instructions," reported Drees in a revealing message, "I shall refrain from making a song and dance with the French government, to avoid any of this coming to the ears of the German embassy here." Using top-secret Luftwaffe communication channels, Göring instructed him to tell Pétain that he was "incensed" by the tapestry affair and regarded the whole maneuver as a "swindle" by certain civil servants: "Surely the Government is able to refuse the gift and recognize the sale. I am just asking for my rights. In Germany something like this would be impossible: The state has enough authority to deal with such a case."

Laval capitulated. His chief of police seized the tapestries, and in August they would be shipped to Carinhall. Afrika Corps commander General von Thoma happened to witness their arrival, accompanied by an unidentified Luftwaffe major, probably Drees himself. "I've just flown in with the Junkers," Thoma heard the major announce. "And at last we've got those damned tapestries."

The gods of war did not stand aside while Göring indulged his muses. In June 1942 his defenses shot down their first British Mosquito bomber. Its fuselage was made of wood, which made it both fast and virtually invisible to radar. Göring angrily recalled that back in 1940 he too had ordered the manufacture of wooden planes (though "suggested" would probably be more accurate). Udet's staff had vetoed the production of "such garbage." Göring's investigators were unanimous, however, that he, Göring, could not escape the blame entirely—and he still preferred jaunts to Paris, Amsterdam, and Florence to listening to bad news at the ministry. "According to both the figures you supply and those we are getting from Britain," he jeered to Milch on June 29, "the British are making more bombers and more fighters than we are!'' (The conference minutes add that he himself considered this ''out of the question.'') The truth was there, written in the skies, but he averted his gaze to more pleasurable horizons. His air force was overextended on every front, but he would not believe it. At the end of July the high command's General Walter Warlimont would return from North Africa with a bleak picture of Rommel's troops fighting against crushing enemy air superiority. ''Do you hear that, Göring?'' said Hitler, with an unpleasant edge to his voice. ''Saturation bombing in the desert now!''

Hitler shifted his headquarters to Vinnitsa in the Ukraine in mid-July 1942. Göring settled at Kalinovka, about half an hour's drive away. The countryside was devastated and idle, there were airplane wrecks on the local airfield, and the surrounding peasantry were desperately poor. Göring made only one sortie into the conquered Ukrainian countryside, venturing forth into a local town. He sent a servant off with two cigar boxes to trade with the peasants, and a woman gave him a dozen fresh eggs for each of them. ''The boxes were quite empty,'' laughed Göring delightedly later, ''but they were pretty to look at. The woman was enthralled, she'd never had anything so beautiful in her life.''

It was not only Hitler's temper that Göring now had to allay. Public anger in the Reich was aroused by the continual air raids and food shortages. On August 5, the gauleiters stated their complaints to him in the lavishly furnished ''Hermann Göring Room'' of the Air Ministry. The next day Göring counterattacked, blaming the food shortages on the slackness of the gauleiters of the newly occupied territories. ''Our troops,'' he complained, ''have already occupied the incomparably fertile lands between the Don and the Caucasus . . . and yet the German people are still going hungry.'' In Western Europe the rich crops were being harvested, yet nothing had been delivered by Holland, Belgium, or France to Germany. ''Gentlemen,'' he complained to the gauleiters, ''these people all hate our guts and you won't win one of them over with your namby-pamby methods. They're charming to us right now because they've got no choice. But if the British once get in there, just watch the French show their true face! The same Frenchman who keeps inviting you to lunch now will very rapidly show you that the Frenchman is a German-hater.'' ''I'm fed up to here,'' he said a few moments later, slicing his hand across his thick neck. ''We win victory after victory. Where's the profit from these victories?''

He suggested one typically cynical way of procuring consumer-goods from the occupied territories. ''We must first buy up all that pink junk and those frightful alabaster things and trashy jewelry in Venice—there's not a country on earth that can match Italy for kitsch. . . . . The [Ukrainian] peasants won't part with anything for money, but they do barter. . . . For face powder you can get butter or anything you want. So let's buy up kitsch. Let's open kitsch factories!''

What was happening behind the eastern front now was no joking matter.

The summer offensive was no longer making such rapid progress, and the high Caucasus Mountains were looming ahead of Field Marshal Wilhelm List's army group. Months earlier, Göring had asked secretly for data on the Caucasus. His staff had supplied eight library books including Karl Egger's *Conquest of the Caucasus*, the journal of the Austrian Alpine Association, and a pocket guide to the U.S.S.R. He had read the books by June 25 and returned them, satisfied that he was now an expert on the Caucasus. When the army's chief of staff, Franz Halder, now reminded Hitler of this mountain barrier, Göring swept his bejeweled, sausagelike fingers across the map and declared, "The Caucasus? It's no different really from Berlin's Grünewald."

Out of the forests and marshes behind the advancing German armies there now rose hordes of Soviet partisans. Göring suggested releasing convicted poachers and smugglers into special units of desperadoes to combat partisans with their own irregular methods—they could "burn and ravish," as he put it, in their assigned operational zones. To this suggestion he then added the idea of conscripting Dutchmen willy-nilly into two antipartisan regiments. When a police general at his conference on August 6 remarked that previous attempts at recruiting the Dutch had failed, Göring rounded on him angrily. "Then shanghai them! Dump them in the partisan territories, and don't give them any guns until they get there! 'Root, hog—or die!' " Gauleiter Lohse stated that the partisans were appearing in military formations equipped with better weapons than the police units.

> GÖRING: You'd make a great fiction writer, Mr. Lohse—
> LOHSE: They're reports from the police and Wehrmacht!
> GÖRING:—If they're from our Wehrmacht then I'd say, *best-selling* fiction. . . . If ten partisans turn up with muskets, then the Wehrmacht afterward talks about whole divisions of them!

In the far south General von Richthofen decided that Stalin's armies were beaten, and dictated this observation into his diary. Beppo Schmid, Göring's Chief Intelligence officer, assessed the Soviet air strength at less than one thousand planes. But Theo Rowehl's reconnaissance squadron brought back photographs of thousands of planes concealed on airfields up to six hundred miles behind the enemy lines. Schmid decided that the planes were dummies; he decided too that on balance it would be prudent to withhold the more awkward photographs from the air staff. Jeschonnek was worried enough about the future. Schmid overhead him telling his staff, "If we haven't won by December, then there's no chance."

As General von Hoth's Fourth Panzer Army slowed to a virtual standstill outside Stalingrad that August, Göring's criticisms of the army generals became more trenchant. Armed by Richthofen with specific details, he accused the generals of cowardice and of exaggerating the Soviet strength. On August 27, Richthofen's operations officer, Colonel Karl-Heinz Schulz, came to report on the defeatism and feeble leadership of the Sixth Army's commander, Friedrich Paulus, and his corps commanders. Göring passed these complaints on to Hitler. There could be no talk of "strong enemy forces," he insisted—"Reconnoitering northward," he continued, "my air force had its work cut out to find any enemy troops at all, in wide-open terrain."

Hitler was in no mood to listen to the army's defense against Göring's allegations. The sweltering, mosquito-laden climate of Vinnitsa contributed to the ill temper. Oppressed by fear that the British bomber squadrons would soon start to devastate Munich, Vienna, Linz, and Nuremberg, he instructed Göring to start building flak towers in those cities at once. Göring told his staff of Hitler's gloomy prognosis on September 1, and added a prediction of his own: "We'll probably get these [raids] once our troops are standing south of the Caucasus." But that triumphant moment suddenly seemed more distant than ever; Field Marshal List arrived at Hitler's headquarters with maps showing that he could make no further progress through the tortuous, narrow mountain passes. Feeling cheated and betrayed, Hitler flew into a tantrum, refused to shake hands with one general and erupted like a volcano over another. Göring fled from the headquarters before the glowing lava engulfed him too. Milch, who arrived at midday, noted afterward: "Row over List, Göring already left." The Reichsmarschall sent off for twenty more books on the Caucasus.

But the real fulcrum of the fighting now became Stalingrad, not the Caucasus. The city was a grimy, sprawling sea of houses and factories straddling the Volga River. Each side realized that Stalingrad was the key to the Russian campaign. On September 10, Richthofen wrote, exasperated, "The throttling of Stalingrad gets slower and slower." From his base headquarters at a fighter airfield only ten miles from the city he phoned Göring on the thirteenth to demand that one single army commander take over that sector—and he did not mean Paulus, whom he regarded as "worthy but uninspiring."

The Americans had now begun raiding German targets with their famous B-17 Flying Fortress squadrons. The bomber flew fast and high. It was heavily armored and equipped with eleven heavy machine guns. A gloomy overcast settled on Göring's fighter commanders.

Göring concealed the bad news from the German public. "If Mr. Churchill brags," he thundered to a Berlin audience on October 4, "that he is going to have thousand-bomber jaunts over Germany every night, let me just reply this: He won't be making any at all." He dismissed the American bomber threat equally cheerily. "In the American language," he scoffed, "one word is spelled in capital letters: Bluff!"

But one of the formidable B-17's had now been shot down—it had drifted out of formation—and when Milch came out to see Göring at Kalinovka a week after the speech, he brought the dossier on it. The field marshal solemnly warned against underestimating this plane.

"How come they tell me one thing," Göring challenged, uneasily alluding to the air staff, "and you another? Whom do I believe?"

His experts had now spotted what looked like turbochargers on photographs of an American B-24 Liberator bomber. That meant that they might soon be flying into German airspace at thirty thousand feet. Göring shrugged it off. "The Reichsmarschall," Milch reported to his staff in Berlin a few days later, "told me that there is no cause for anxiety about the American planes and that four-engined though they be, we can can contemplate the future with equanimity. I told him that I do not agree—I think the Flying Fortress and B-24 are remarkable planes."

Facing allegations of the hoarding of labor in his bloated Luftwaffe, in September 1942 Göring was ordered by Hitler to release two hundred thousand of his troops to the depleted army. It was a bitter blow. He offered to set up twenty Luftwaffe "field divisions" instead, and Hitler relented.

It was a controversial decision, even in the air force. General von Richthofen feared (rightly, as it turned out) that the Luftwaffe divisions would prove "a colossal blunder," and noted this belief in his diary after flying over to see the Reichsmarschall on October 15, bringing photographs of the ravages of Stalingrad:

> [Göring] curses List, Kleist, and Ruoff [the army's commanders in the Caucasus] dreadfully. I stoutly defend the latter two, but there's no reasoning with the Reichsmarschall. Drags me off with Jeschonnek to make an unannounced call on the Führer and lets fly there [against the army generals].

Helmuth Greiner, the high command chronicler, wrote in his own private diary that day, "The witch hunt by the air-force brass against the army goes on. Ghastly ass-licking." Back aboard the train Asia Richthofen tried to curry favor with Göring over dinner. "I praise his really very good [Berlin] speech. He swallows the flattery hook, line, and sinker. Hints at an early field marshal's baton for me. . . . I protest at having to lug a baton around."

As the exhausted German infantry slogged into Stalingrad and the rumors of a huge Red Army counteroffensive multiplied, Göring left for a week in Rome. The German diplomats there did not relish his coming, and the chortling German ambassador phoned the Palazzo Venezia on October 19 that Göring had been suddenly stricken with dysentery, and was "unable to leave his throne even for ten minutes." When Göring finally limped in to the palace four days later, Mussolini harped on Rommel's oil crisis and the troublesome British base on Malta. Four days after their meeting, the British launched their triumphant offensive against Rommel at Alamein. On November 2, British code-breakers heard Göring's headquarters frantically diverting bomber squadrons from Norway to the Mediterranean. Richthofen's Luftflotte 4—

already pushed to its limits by the Stalingrad fighting—was ordered to detach night fighters to Greece.

Disobeying Hitler's orders ("Victory or death!"), Rommel pulled his armies back to a line that he had secretly prepared at Fuka. Göring, sensing another army debacle, ordered Field Marshal Kesselring to fly to Africa. Kesselring, who was the high command's commander in chief south, returned to Rome late on November 5 and phoned the Reichsmarschall.*

GÖRING: What is the situation?

KESSELRING: It is such that the Führer will approve all the measures we have proposed. Down here a situation developed that flatly contradicted the orders of the Führer. The line that is now crucial is the one at Fuka.

GÖRING: Is it well organized?

KESSELRING: No, but it does offer considerable advantages, so I feel that if it is manned by the necessary forces, it will afford at least temporarily a viable resistance.

Worse was to follow. The Germans sighted an Allied invasion convoy approaching through the Straits of Gibraltar. Göring directed Kesselring that evening to order heroic sacrifices to halt the convoy.

GÖRING: According to our calculations the convoy will be within our air-force range in forty or fifty hours. Everything must be ready by then.

KESSELRING: Herr Reichsmarschall, what if the convoy should attempt a landing in Africa?

GÖRING: I am convinced that it will try to land in Corsica, in Sardinia, or at Derna or Tripoli.

KESSELRING: More likely one of the ports of North Africa.

GÖRING: Yes but not French North Africa. . . . If the convoy could be given a severe thrashing, the countries in Africa will get a very different picture of the situation and this would reduce the effect of the defeat [at Alamein]. Therefore the Führer has asked me to tell you that this convoy battle is first and foremost. If the convoy should be beaten, decimated, destroyed, dispersed, then [Rommel's] defeat will have no more importance than a tactical breakthrough—which in fact it is for the time being.

Tomorrow you are to deliver an appeal to your troops stating that their actions, their capacity for sacrifice, their courage, their stamina will redound to the glory of the German Air Force. Tell them that I expect every German airman to do his utmost, even

*Italian intelligence wiretapped this and the subsequent conversation with Göring.

the supreme sacrifice. The convoy is to be attacked without pause, day and night, wave after wave.

When the airmen load their bombs, tell them their job is to attack the aircraft carriers so that the planes can't land or take off. Next, hit the troop transports: matériel without men is worthless.

No other operations are to take place beside those against this convoy. It is the most important convoy. It is Number One. You are to direct the operations against it in person.

KESSELRING: Yes, sir.

GÖRING: I wish you all the best and am with you constantly in my thoughts.

British code-breakers heard Kesselring issue the order precisely as Göring had specified, but nothing could halt the great Allied invasion (Operation *Torch*). On November 8, the British and American forces landed in French North Africa (precisely where Göring had not expected them). Reacting swiftly, Hitler ordered a new bridgehead established in Tunis. Meeting their Italian allies in Munich the next day, Göring silently accompanied Hitler to the Führer Building, then told Count Ciano candidly that this invasion of North Africa was the first real point the Allies had scored in this war.

With the final collapse of List's Caucasus offensive the Stalingrad catastrophe began. Hitler was faced with doleful decisions. On October 29, British code-breakers had already heard Göring instructing Richthofen's Luftflotte 4 to destroy the coveted oil installations at Groznyy. A week later he ordered Baku bombed as well.

As the focus of military events shifted back to Stalingrad, the Nazi leaders were widely dispersed. Hitler was in Bavaria, the air-force and army staffs were in East Prussia, and Göring in Berlin. The Reichsmarschall was fulfilling mundane duties there—appointing professors in his capacity as prime minister of Prussia, recruiting experts to the new Reich Research Council, supervising guided-missile developments, and selecting Nazi "commissioners" (*Beauftragte*) for high-frequency physics and nuclear-physics research. And he refused to accept that the Four-Year Plan was dead. "For the sake of historical truth," he admonished Albert Speer in a letter on November 5, "I should like to make it absolutely plain that I have not relaxed my grip on the essentials of the Four-Year Plan for one instant. A glance at the dates of the conferences and sessions, at their minutes, at the decrees, laws, and ordinances that I have issued throughout this war, should satisfy you immediately that I continue to shape the crucial affairs of the Four-Year Plan despite my preoccupation with the air force."

He was still in Berlin two weeks later as the Red Army counteroffensive at Stalingrad began, across the River Don. On the next day, November 20, the Russians established a second breach in the German lines. Göring, telephoned about these developments by Hitler, was not especially concerned. Nothing shows that he realized that an immense Soviet pincer movement was beginning, and about to encircle the Sixth Army in Stalingrad, trapping twenty German divisions, two Romanian, and the air force's own 9th Flak Division. He remained at Carinhall. It was in Göring's absence, therefore, that the young chief of air staff Hans Jeschonnek, who had arrived that day in Berchtesgaden bringing a skeleton air staff from East Prussia, made the fateful offer to Hitler: Jeschonnek assured Hitler that the Luftwaffe could airlift enough supplies into Stalingrad, using transport planes and bombers, even if the Sixth Army was encircled there.

At 3:25 P.M. on November 21, Hitler thus signaled to that army's commander, General Paulus, ordering him to stand firm "despite the danger of temporary encirclement." Paulus was to hold open the rail link as long as possible; an airlift would follow. Hitler told Colonel Eckhard Christian to get Göring on the line, then took the instrument from him. Still in Berlin, the Reichsmarschall agreed that the air force would do what it could.

The Stalingrad airlift—or rather, its failure—would ever after be linked with Göring's name. Yet for once he was not entirely culpable. Exonerating him three months later, Hitler would admit to Richthofen that he had promised the airlift to Paulus "without the Reichsmarschall's knowledge."

At the time of Hitler's phone call, the afternoon of November 21, Göring was presiding over an oil conference in Berlin. German troops had occupied the Maykop oil field that summer, only to find that the Russians had shut in the wells and dropped unremovable hundred-pound steel "mushrooms" down each borehole. Göring was frustrated to find his men so tantalizingly near to the vast oil reserves. "I'm fed up!" he exclaimed. "Months have passed since we captured the first oil wells, yet we still aren't getting any benefit." The steel mushrooms baffled him. "Can't you just drill them out with something like a gigantic corkscrew?"

The experts shook their heads. The Russians had, moreover, unhelpfully left behind faked "oil-field charts." Göring blamed the delays on the high command, who had been running the operation without any reference to him. "Before we even went into Russia," he raged, "it was made quite clear that the entire economic setup would come under me, right up to the front-line troops. I didn't just have that odd eastern organization, what's its name, at my service." (*"Wirtschaftsstab Ost,"* murmured Körner helpfully.) "It is scandalous of this Mr. Thomas," the Reichsmarschall ranted on, referring to Georg Thomas of the high command. "He knew full well that the Führer had signed this. . . . Now I am beginning to see it all more clearly. . . . Let me make myself clear. If the Russians can manage, then so can we. Otherwise, we shall have to resort to Russian methods too."

His experts hastened to soothe him. "Herr Reichsmarschall," pleaded one, "we'll manage somehow, bank on it."

"If there's no oil flowing by next spring and we have to send oil down to our armored divisions, then God help the lot of you. Because let me say this, I am *plein*—up to my back teeth!"

The high command had put a General Homburg in charge of the Petroleum Brigade. Göring challenged the experts: "That's what this general is there for. He must push the button. He's got to tell the army commanders, Do you want the oil next year or don't you!"

"But he can't do it if he's sitting two hundred miles away from Maykop," pointed out another expert.

Göring seized on that. "Where!?"

"At Pyatigorsk, two hundred miles from Maykop."

Göring of course had his desk considerably farther from the oil fields than that. But he knew what it meant if they failed to find oil soon: He would need scapegoats.

That day he ordered all his phone conversations logged in a register, showing the location and time of each call.

If the record book had survived, it would have answered several outstanding questions about the worsening Stalingrad crisis. By now Richthofen was cautioning everybody who would listen that the Luftwaffe lacked the lift to sustain the Sixth Army. He phoned Göring in Berlin, he signaled to General Karl Zeitzler, Halder's successor, in East Prussia, he warned the army group commander, Maximilian von Weichs, on the Don front. Ex-Lufthansa chief Field Marshal Milch, however, was evidently among those who assured Göring that the airlift was practicable. As the Reichsmarschall's white-jacketed dining-car attendants served dinner off silver salvers in *Asia* that night, Göring summoned his quartermaster staff and ordered every available transport plane mobilized for the airlift, including his own courier flight.

Later that night his train set off for Bavaria.

Trusting in Hermann Göring, his "faithful Paladin," at midnight Hitler again signaled to Paulus in Stalingrad, ordering him to stand fast.

Nineteen hours later the Sixth Army commander replied: His army, he announced, was now cut off by the Russians; his food and ammunition were already low; and he had fuel for six days.

Asia reached Berchtesgaden at about the same time as this signal, late on November 22, 1942. The train was hauling its now-familiar rolling stock, including flat tops laden with cars—the Reichsmarschall's personal armored Mercedes, an armored coupé, a 5.4-liter Mercedes, a 3.4-liter Mercedes, a Ford Mercury, a 1.7-liter Mercedes, and assorted baggage trucks and motorbikes. Surrounded by a sizable retinue that included valet Robert, nurse Christa, and heart-specialist Professor Heinrich Zahler, Göring was impatient to continue the journey that night: He had several long-standing appointments with art dealers in Paris that he did not want to miss.

Visiting Hitler on the mist-shrouded Obersalzberg, he barely discussed either Stalingrad or the 250,000 men trapped there. "Hitler," he explained guiltily to Pili Körner a few days later, "already had [Jeschonnek's airlift] plan before I set eyes on it. I could only say, Mein Führer, you have the figures. If these figures are right, then I am at your disposal."

But the figures were not right at all. Jeschonnek only now realized that the standard "250-kilo" airlift container on which he had based them in fact held far less than that load—its name derived solely from the 250-kilo bomb position it occupied on the bomb racks. Göring winced when the general confessed this to him, but forbade him to tell Hitler. "I cannot do this to the Führer—not now!" he said. Telephoning Hitler himself, he repeated that the Luftwaffe airlift would go ahead, and he invited him to phone Milch if he still harbored any doubts.

For Hitler the fatal decision was the product of political pride. He had committed himself publicly to capturing the city, and he could not go back on that pledge. Later, Göring mentioned operational factors that influenced him. There was, he said, no reason to believe that the army's main front line would fall back as far and as fast as it did, and it was the increasing distances that ultimately thwarted the airlift.

Down in the Berchtesgaden valley that night, November 22–23, 1942, Göring's train *Asia* slid off toward Paris.

At 10:00 P.M. Hitler's train also departed, in the other direction—returning to East Prussia. He would arrive at the Wolf's Lair twenty-four hours later. At 5:40 A.M. on November 24 he sent yet another grim signal to the embattled General Paulus at Stalingrad: The Sixth Army, this stated, was to stand fast. "Airlift operation by one hundred more Junkers is starting up."

33
FALL FROM GRACE

A quarter of a million of Hitler's troops were encircled in Stalingrad; they would become Stalin's hostages, and very few would ever be seen alive again. Göring would soon suspect that, given the simultaneous failure to prevent the Allied landings in northwest Africa, only a deal with Stalin would offer Nazi Germany any chance of survival. But, as he admitted to interrogators three years later, whenever he tried to speak frankly to Hitler, his heart sank to the seat of his pants.

At first he did not realize the scale of the Stalingrad tragedy, but that did not make his personal movements any less scandalous or unforgivable.

He arrived in Paris on November 23, 1942, and on the next day—even as Field Marshal von Manstein was signaling to Paulus, "We shall hack you free!''—Göring continued his Paris spree with a visit to the Jeu de Paume. It was to be his last visit to this treasure-house. He was in an ill humor, which he worked off by abusing Hanesse loudly as they toured the little gallery. Archival documents dated that day number among them valuations by Göring's tame assessor, Professor Beltrand, on fifty-eight items, including Van Goghs, a Corot, and (at ten thousand francs) Utrillo's "Suburban Street," which latter the Reichsmarschall proposed to exchange for Jodocus de Momper's "The Rock Chapel." Further documents surviving from this jaunt included a bill of lading typed by the Rosenberg task force and headed: "The following items were loaded aboard the Reichsmarschall's special train today"—listing seventy-seven crates of confiscated, bartered, or privately purchased paintings, tapestries, floor- and wall-coverings, and other bric-à-brac, including a carved oak-and-pewter washstand, seven fragments of an ancient sarcophagus, bronze and marble statuary, and silver plate. A further Rosenberg list dated this same November 24, 1942, described thirteen priceless carpets and silk rugs that he had bought. Among the other items loaded aboard *Asia* on the twenty-fifth were five Scipio tapestries, purchased for 2.8 million francs, a Salomon Koninck portrait of an old man in a red beret, and a Cranach for which he had forked out fifty thousand Swiss francs. Stalingrad, it seems, had been forgotten.

The Utrillo purchase illuminated the unsavory demimonde into which his passion for art dealings had propeled him. Seeking high protectors, the Paris dealer Allan Löbl, an Austro-Hungarian Jew, offered Göring the priceless art library of the Kleinberger Gallery as a gift. Not wanting to obligate himself to a Jew by accepting a *gift*, Göring instructed Bruno Lohse to give Löbl the Utrillo in *exchange*. Suspecting that his charmed existence might not last forever, Löbl then suggested that he and his brother Manon Löbl should act as stool pigeons for Göring in Paris. On June 15, 1943, Lohse would suggest to the Reichsmarschall that he formally request the Gestapo to continue to make "the Jewish brothers Löbl" available as informers. Göring approved, but Fräulein Limberger noted the caveat he uttered thus: "Lohse must see he doesn't do it in any way that might link the Reichsmarschall's name with Jews! If possible, do it clandestinely."

By late November 24, 1942, it would have become plain to Göring, were he not in Paris, that his air force had bitten off more than it could chew at Stalingrad. In theory, five or six transport squadrons could airlift five hundred tons of supplies a day. But given the worsening weather conditions, the lift would in practice call for 12 to 15 squadrons, or between 630 and 795 Junkers 52 transport planes. Göring had lost hundreds of them at Crete. They had only 750 Ju 52's left, and Hitler had recently committed most of these to the supply of Rommel's armies in Africa. Richthofen had predicted this all along, but what could he now do to discourage the airlift? "I urge Jeschonnek and Zeitzler to *tell* the Führer my view, and to harness the Reichsmarschall," he dictated to his diary on November 25, "but he's in Paris."*

---

*This diary entry, and the Rosenberg documents cited above, render most suspect the General Gerhard Engel "diary" published by Professor Martin Broszat's Institute of Contemporary History in Munich, which has Engel "witnessing" a row between Hitler and Göring at East Prussia this same day!

By the time Göring arrived back in East Prussia, the Stalingrad situation was beyond repair. Tempers flared. "Manstein," recorded Richthofen on November 27, "[is] desperate about the decisions taken at top level."

Incredibly, Hitler's staff were less concerned with Stalingrad than with North Africa. At 3:20 P.M. on November 28—to everybody's astonishment— Field Marshal Rommel appeared in person at Hitler's headquarters and demanded his permission to abandon Libya altogether, pulling back to a new line at Gabès in Tunisia, where he proposed to fight a completely new campaign. Icily contemptuous, Hitler asked Rommel which front he did propose to hold. If North Africa were lost, he pointed out, Italy would probably defect. Writing in his own diary that night, Rommel dictated, "Five P.M., conference with Führer in presence of Reichsmarschall. Talked until eight. Führer is flatly against giving up the African theater. . . . The Italians must be put under pressure to make a really serious effort to ferry supplies to Africa."

Hitler packed Göring and Rommel off by train to Rome that same night, with orders to tackle Mussolini. The Reichsmarschall grudgingly packed his bags, hoisted himself aboard *Asia* and set off with the desert commander for Italy. Rommel's wife, Lucie, who joined the train at Munich, would recall later with distaste that Göring chatted only about his art acquisitions and his gems throughout the journey. But Rommel humored him, and used the two-day train journey to work on him: By early on the thirtieth, as their train puffed into the Italian capital, Rommel was recording that Göring now fully endorsed his Gabès plan. Exuding optimism, Göring ordered twenty of the powerful new eighty-eight-millimeter flak guns rushed to Rommel's forces, and he phoned Milch to come down immediately to Rome to step up Italian aircraft production.

Then, however, he received Field Marshal Kesselring. Kesselring pointed out that retreating to Gabès would bring the enemy air force within close range of the Axis bridgehead harbors in Tunisia. Accepting the logic of this, Göring now declared that Rommel must on no account abandon Tripoli.

He was driven across Rome to see Mussolini that evening. In a three-hour wrangle with him, the thin and pale-skinned Duce made plain that he too had favored the Gabès plan; but he could not ignore Kesselring's arguments.

Hearing this, Rommel plunged into a depression. At a joint session the next morning, December 1, he heard Göring repeat that Tripoli must be held. The Reichsmarschall's optimism now bordered on the insufferable. For once, he bragged, the Axis had the edge. "For the first time we are not far removed from the field of battle. A mere panther's spring! Therefore, we have every chance of rushing troops and matériel into Tunisia." He promised to pack four first-class divisions into the new Tunis bridgehead—the 10th Panzer and those bearing the names of Hitler, Göring, and Deutschland. "We must try to push the enemy back toward Oran, and then head for Morocco," he said.

He proposed laying two immense minefields across the narrow Straits of Sicily, with a safe channel to sluice their transport ships through to North Africa. Germany would supply the necessary mines. "I realize that this is a vast undertaking," he conceded, "but we should think along such lines." Answering the angry comments of the Italian Fleet commander, Admiral Raffaelo Riccardi, and German Admiral Eberhard Weichold, the Reichsmarschall jeered, "The navy's prejudices and opinions are out of date."

He cabled Hitler afterward, reporting that the Italians agreed that Rommel's next line should be at Buerat and speaking of Rommel's loss of nerve. He handled the field marshal so tactlessly over lunch that Milch, arriving from Berlin as it ended, found Rommel upstairs weeping with rage at Göring.

After that Göring traveled in arrogant luxury aboard *Asia* down to Naples, where he talked with the dockhands and inspected port defenses. Disregarding Rome completely, he ordered the youthful local Fascist chieftain to take charge of the transport ships to Africa. "Göring," wrote the indignant Ciano on the fifth, "continues to preside over meetings to which he invites civilians, [Guido] Buffarini [Fascist minister of the interior], technical ministers, and so forth. . . . Yesterday, when Göring arrived at the supreme command's headquarters, he was received in the courtyard by our military chiefs!" Ciano put it around that Göring evidently saw himself as a future *Reichsprotektor* of Italy.

On December 11, 1942, the Reichsmarschall reported back at the Führer's headquarters. "[Göring] says," Hitler reported to his staff the next day, "that Rommel has completely lost his nerve."

In private Göring told Hitler that Mussolini was advising them to call off their now-pointless war against Russia. A few days later the despondent Italian foreign minister Ciano and Marshal Ugo Cavallero, chief of the supreme command, came to East Prussia to repeat this advice. Göring and Ribbentrop nodded approval, but Hitler responded with an encouraging catalog of his victories since 1938. The matter was not mentioned again.

His airlift to Stalingrad struggled lamely on. A typical day was December 19: His planes flew only seventy tons into the "fortress." Göring scoffed during Hitler's main war conference that day that the food situation probably was not as bad as General Paulus made out. From the front line a thousand miles away Field Marshal von Manstein sarcastically suggested that the Reichsmarschall himself take over. "Let the 'confident' commander," he declared, "take charge of the sector that he's so confident about!"

On the thirtieth, Richthofen telephoned Carinhall. The distant Reichsmarschall replied with what Richthofen referred to only as "words of fire." "I would have preferred more forces," observed the Luftflotte commander.

* * *

Göring's own diary opened in 1943 to reveal him still at Carinhall, seeing the New Year in. He made only occasional forays into Berlin. He proudly watched little Edda at ballet school, listened to Rosita Serrano sing, went for drives in the snow, hunted wild boar; he canceled a conference with Galland and Dietrich Pelz, his bomber commander, and in general refused to see what was bearing down on Germany's skies. On January 4, Milch and his technical chief Colonel Wolfgang Vorwald brought out to Carinhall the red top-secret volume of enemy production statistics: Britain, the United States, and Canada, this showed, had been producing 1,378 bombers and 1,959 fighters per month during 1942, while German industry had averaged only 349 and 247 respectively. "Milch," thundered the Reichsmarschall, comfortably seated behind his great desk, "have you joined the dreamers too? Do you really believe all this?"

The next day Milch confessed to his staff, "The Reichsmarschall doesn't quite see eye to eye with me on these figures."

"Even if they *are* making these numbers," he quoted Göring as saying, "they're no use whatever to their forces in Africa if they can't back them up with the necessary shipping space."

In a few days' time Göring would complete his half-century. Late on January 6, 1943, he left for East Prussia, spent seven hours the next day with Hitler, jotted into his diary a jumble of notes on discussions with Speer, Rosenberg, Bormann, and Milch; then waddled back to Carinhall. The preparations for his fiftieth birthday helped to deaden the ever-fainter cries coming from Stalingrad, and the hollering from North Africa. He had one talk with Kesselring about "the case of Rommel," but his birthday overshadowed all else. Pandering to his eager mood, the Italians awarded him the first Gold Star of the Roman Eagle at their embassy. The Berlin theaters were closed, but he ordered one reopened and bused his staff in from Carinhall to hear music by Handel and an aria from a Glück opera ("O that I were never born"), followed by scenes from *A Midsummer Night's Dream* and a play by Kleist. Two of the actors had Jewish wives, but Göring had extended to them his personal protection.

The birthday gifts might seem to have borne witness to the enduring strength of his political position in Germany. Mussolini had sent a golden sword originally destined for General Franco. (As Ciano observed, "Times have changed.") Ciano himself gave him the Star of San Maurizio (once earmarked for King Zog of Albania, but also reassigned.) Three leading German businessmen gave a twenty-four-hundred piece Sévres porcelain service of a hunting design. Kurt Schmitt, the Allianz Insurance Company's chief, had swiftly complied when Gritzbach of Göring's staff phoned to suggest giving three medieval statues at seventeen thousand marks apiece. Paul Pleiger had given one million marks (one hundred thousand from H.G.W., the rest from a political fund controlled by the Reich coal owners' lobby).

Hitler had sent a personal handwritten letter dated January 11, 1943; it was among Göring's most prized papers in 1945, but was looted and is now lost, as is the solid-gold jewel-encrusted cassette handcrafted by Hitler's favorite designer, Gerdi Troost, and handed by Keitel to Göring to house his white parchment authority as Reichsmarschall.

Hitler had ordered public celebration, but Göring saw through the phony acclamations and later described this birthday as the final watershed in his fortunes. Overwhelmed by depression, he retired to bed, entering in his diary on the thirteenth the words "ill" and "bed rest because of heart palpitations," and on the fourteenth, again, "Bed rest all day, ill! (Heart)." Professor Zahler was sent for.*

In part the heart problems were a consequence of his massive obesity; in part the malaise was probably psychological. He could see his authority being openly dismantled. On January 13, Hitler created a "Commission of Three" (*Dreierausschuss*) to control manpower. Göring was excluded. On the four-teenth, bypassing Göring, Hitler sent for Staatssekretär Milch and instructed him to take over—even at this eleventh hour—the vital Stalingrad airlift.

On the night of January 16–17, the RAF attacked Berlin using new "block-buster" bombs. After inspecting the damage, Göring lunched at Hitler's headquarters on the eighteenth. Hitler showed him the latest hysterical signals from Paulus about the airlift. Göring phoned them through to Milch, now at the front line. "The most frightful signals are coming from the fortress," Göring complained.

In fact Göring had provided the planes he promised, but the squadron commanders were letting him down. They had done nothing to keep the waiting air crews warm, the crews themselves were ignorant of standard cold-start procedures, and morale was rock-bottom. Of 140 Junkers 52 trans-ports, only 15 were operational on the day Milch arrived; of 140 Heinkel 111's only 41, of 20 FW 200's only 1. Of these planes only seven Junkers and eleven Heinkels were actually scheduled to make the round trip that day. Milch at once sacked the incompetent generals, organized new landing grounds, parachuted radio beacons and flare-path equipment into the fortress. But as the weeks passed, the airfields in Stalingrad were lost, and the front line retreated so far that the Heinkels could no longer make the return flight.

Hitler ordered Milch to fly the highly esteemed Panzer general Hans Hube out of the fortress. "Why not kill an air-force general or two!" Hube told him, pointing out that there was not one Luftwaffe general now left inside Stalingrad. Hitler passed the scathing remark on to Göring. "Isn't it re-markable," sneered Göring to Milch, "how anybody who goes to the front immediately loses his clear view of the front!" Richthofen, listening on the

---

*Göring was now taking Cardiazol, Pentamethylene-Tetrazol, manufactured by Knoll of Lud-wigshafen, a heart stimulant of relatively short-lived effect. Back in November 1941 Göring's staff had ordered from Siemens a portable electrocardiograph for Professor Zahler, and Görnnert had endorsed the order as "very urgent."

other earpiece, looked around for "a wall to run up," as he admitted in his diary. When Göring, calming down, phoned again on the twentieth, Milch said that both he and Manstein regarded the Sixth Army's plight as hopeless.

Impotent to help the Sixth Army, Göring now haunted Hitler's headquarters. Milch wrote in his diary on January 23, "Telephoned Führer's headquarters until 2:00 or 3:00 A.M. Göring sends endless telegrams." Displaying a frenzy born of belated guilt, Göring spent five hours with Hitler that day, phoned him twice on the twenty-fifth (about a new crisis developing at Voronezh), and personally attended Hitler's main conferences on the twenty-sixth and twenty-seventh.

Milch now had trainloads of transport gliders, ground crew, preheating equipment, and mass-produced airlift containers bearing down on the Stalingrad front; a squadron of the new Me 109G fighter planes was also on its way. But the Army Department rang with vicious criticism of the Luftwaffe. The army spokesman General Kurt Dittmar described in his diary the sense of bitterness at what they saw as Göring's "unfulfilled promises" of an airlift, and Hitler made no secret of his disgust at the fiasco of the vaunted He 177 long-range bomber in the airlift.

On January 27, 1943, unescorted American B-17 bombers delivered their first daring daylight raid on German territory, attacking Wilhelmshaven Naval Base. A more direct affront to Göring's pride followed on the thirtieth. It was the tenth anniversary of the Nazi "seizure of power." Göring was due to broadcast at 11:00 A.M. over every German radio station; but with sublime indifference to his feelings the RAF sent Mosquito bombers scudding right across Germany to Berlin, to drive him underground at that precise hour.

Hitler had directed him on the nineteenth to tend specifically to the air defenses of Leipzig, Dresden, Weimar, and Kassel. On the twentieth Göring had told the night-fighter commander, General Hans Kammhuber, to extend their night defenses to the north of Berlin and into southern Germany, he had ordered every fighter-squadron commander to come to Carinhall at the end of the month. (The British code-breakers intercepted this signal.) Colonel Adolf Galland was among the commanders who lunched and conferred with the worried Reichsmarschall now, discussing ways of defeating this two-fisted Allied bomber menace. Galland described his plans to strengthen the day-fighter forces; his deputy, Colonel Lützow, spoke about the expanding radar-tracking network. For the first time Galland referred to the Reich's coming jet planes like the Me 262 and the Me 163 rocket-powered interceptor. Worse was to come: Luftwaffe experts discovered revolutionary new electronic equipment in an RAF bomber shot down that very night, January 30–31, near Rotterdam—an on-board radar screen designed to give a picture of the terrain and cities beneath regardless of darkness and cloud cover.

The Stalingrad drama ended. Sixteen army generals, including Paulus, chose Soviet captivity to death and glory on the battlefield. The army's General Erwin Jaenecke, flown injured out of Stalingrad on one of the last planes, urged Hitler to punish the guilty men—"Even," he spat out, "if that means the Reichsmarschall himself!" But Göring was not to be seen. His diary shows that he spent much of the next week at Emmy's hospital bedside—she had been operated on by Professor Gohrbandt for sinus problems on February 1—and he manifested no urgent desire to face his Führer. Hitler vented his rage on Jeschonnek instead—then clapped the unhappy general on the shoulder after the conference and reassured him, "It wasn't *you* I meant!" "I alone bear responsibility for Stalingrad," he frankly admitted to Field Marshal von Manstein on February 6—but then devalued that acceptance of the blame by adding, "I could pin the blame onto Göring . . . but he is my designated successor. So I can not."

Reassured by General Bodenschatz that Hitler was not disposed to blame him, Göring slunk back in to the Wolf's Lair later in February. Hitler avoided puncturing his pride. Göring's posture at this time is described in an insightful entry of Richthofen's diary—the Luftflotte 4 commander had arrived at Rominten on the tenth, to find Göring just setting out to hunt wild boar. They dined alone together, and commiserated about the soldier's hard lot. "As you know," said Göring, carving juicy chunks off a leg of veal served to him as a third course, "the only luxury I allow myself is to have fresh flowers sent in from time to time." He admitted having approved of the Stalingrad airlift, but only because he expected the encirclement to be temporary. Then the Italian Army had collapsed, and this had triggered the catastrophe.

Richthofen ventured the remark that Göring ought to have risked going in person to the Stalingrad battlefront. "If you can't trust in your own lucky star," he said, "then you have no right to believe in your destiny in larger things. None of our army commanders is a Caesar or an Alexander," he continued. "But they all know their job and do their duty. They just need to be given tasks they understand." He praised Manstein in particular.

The next morning, February 11, they went to see Hitler. Richthofen repeated his comments. "If I didn't straitjacket my commanders," Hitler told Richthofen tersely, "they would all be fighting on German soil by now."

Göring nodded tame approval. He did attempt one diffident interpolation, but Hitler deftly deflected the conversation to the Old Burg Theater in Vienna. "Now that," chortled Hitler, aware of Göring's pride in his Prussian State Theater, "was *really* art, of a kind you don't find too often nowadays."

Assembling all the Luftwaffe's top generals at Rominten for three days of confidential consultations ("to go over everything, issue guidelines, and deliver a pep talk for the coming months," as he put it in his diary) Göring was frank about the gravity of the crisis that now faced Nazi Germany. General Karl Koller, chief of staff of Luftflotte 3, took this shorthand note:

We've suffered the gravest possible setback in the east [said Göring]. Irrelevant who's to blame. . . . After thirty-six of our allies' divisions on either flank simply vanished, ran away, our whole overextended front was bound to collapse. . . . We have lost regions of paramount importance for our nutrition, and moreover everything left behind represents a horrendous loss to our own food supplies. We abandoned 157,000 tons of harvested and stockpiled oil seeds of immense importance for our supply of fats. Besides, the enemy successes have naturally given a huge boost to their morale. Africa is a complete write-off, Suez is now beyond our reach, and the enemy is drawing very close to us in the south. Plus their invasion of North Africa. . .

What might the enemy do next? They may land in Sardinia, that won't cause any problems; possibly Sicily. The main danger is to Portugal, intelligence on this is hardening. . . . In charge of Spain is a weakling [Franco] who has the worst possible counsel: cowardice! . . . And add to this the very real danger that the enemy may turn against Brittany and Normandy. There is also the possibility that he may undertake an invasion of Norway, not on a large scale but in regimental strength, possibly using ski troops; American troops are standing by in Scotland and they might be airlifted to Norway.

Extraordinary armaments potential of the Americans, danger of poison-gas warfare: The Americans are in favor, because of course nothing can happen in their own country; the British are probably set against it but won't be able to get their way with the United States, which is interested only in swallowing the British Empire and tossing Europe to the Bolsheviks. Britain is playing a game nobody can understand any longer. She's bound to go under—the game she's playing—even if she is on the victorious side.

We have these allies: one who fights magnificently [Japan], fights like a German, but is far away . . . A second ally [Italy] who is absolutely useless; not one of its divisions is worth anything at all; an entire army [the Italian Eighth Army] that ran away and was going to be sent into the partisan area has now reported that it does not feel a match for the bandits. They weren't even able to pacify the Balkans, although the enemy there only has muskets and not one piece of artillery.

All this shows how grim the situation is. To underline our ultimate war aim I can only repeat what the Führer said in his speech. At the end of this war there will only be the survivors and the dead: It is madness to believe there can be a salvation if Bolshevism triumphs! . . . We cannot say how much use the

European nations will be. Spain perhaps; France, torn inside out, won't help, she will rise against us when it comes to the crunch; the same goes for Norway. We have not one of the nations we have occupied on our side. Italy's weakness is undeniable, its military strength is zero. Domestically, defeatism rules supreme, just a few Fascists are holding the whole thing together, nobody else is working, let alone fighting. The awful thing is that the Duce can not even trust his own son-in-law [Ciano] and had to sack him. . . .

The next biggest danger is southern Russia. Stalingrad: the question was whether or not to pull out. At first there was no reason to, we were entitled to the view that our troops were strong enough there to hold on until relieved. . . . If the men had fought harder, particularly in Stalingrad itself, we should still have the city today and it would not have been captured. Paulus was too weak, he didn't turn Stalingrad into a proper fortress. Thousands of Russian civilians were fed along with his troops. He should have sacrificed them ruthlessly so that his soldiers had enough to survive, and that goes for the hopelessly injured—they shouldn't have been dragged along but allowed to fade away. The Paulus army just relied on the Luftwaffe and expected miracles from it . . . And then this army's chief of staff General [Arthur] Schmidt has the gall to say, "The Luftwaffe has committed the biggest treachery in history because it could not manage to supply the Paulus army." The army lost its airfields—how on earth was a mass airlift supposed to be possible after that?

That spring Hans Thomsen, the new Nazi ambassador to Sweden, visited Göring. He found the Reichsmarschall wearing his golden dagger, leather jerkin, and puffy silk sleeves. After driving Thomsen around his Carinhall estate, Göring changed into an arresting kimono of violet-colored silk for dinner. A diamond-studded brooch graced his neck, a bejeweled belt his paunch.

At about the same time Göring admitted to Ribbentrop's Staatssekretär, Ernst von Weizsäcker, that he was worried about the future. "It's not quite clear to me how we are going to end this war," he said.

34

JET-PROPELLED

Göring's air force had airlifted into Stalingrad 8,350 tons of supplies, a daily average of 116 tons. But he had lost 266 Junkers 52 transports, 165 Heinkel 111 bombers, and 42 Junkers 86 bombers—virtually an entire air corps. "I always believed in the strategic use of air power," he would tell renowned American aviation philosopher Alexander Seversky a few days after the war ended. "My beautiful bomber fleet was exhausted in transporting munitions and supplies to the army at Stalingrad. I was always against the Russian campaign."

Shown the new aircraft-production program by Milch when he received him for the first time in five weeks on February 22, 1943, he bleated the complaint that it seemed to show nothing new even for 1946.

Milch pointedly reminded him that their only four-engined bomber project had been killed off as long ago as 1937. The field marshal felt that Göring's eyes looked perhaps more glazed than usual this day.

Depressed by the austerity of Berlin, Göring retired to his villa on the Obersalzberg. Pili Körner begged Emmy to talk him into approaching Hitler about seeking an honorable peace with one enemy or the other while he still could. It is unlikely that Göring ever did, but during February the pressure did grow on him to revive the Little Cabinet of the first war weeks—the Reich Defense Committee. Milch took it up with Speer; Speer got Goebbels's backing for the idea, and came down to the mountainside villa on the last day of February. Göring talked with him for several hours. The minister was fascinated by the apparently rouged cheeks and lacquered fingernails of the Reichsmarschall. Before bringing Goebbels back with him the next afternoon, Speer warned the propaganda minister that Göring was "rather resigned." Göring was wearing what Goebbels dryly described as "a somewhat baroque costume, which would look rather grotesque if one did not know him so well." Both ministers tried to restore the Reichsmarschall's waning self-confidence; he turned down the Little Cabinet idea. "I gained the impression," wrote Milch in his memoirs, "he was afraid of Hitler."

That night, March 1–2, the British weakened his bargaining position still further by blitzing Berlin. The raid gashed the Air Ministry, started six hundred fires, wrecked twenty thousand buildings, and killed seven hundred Berliners. Hitler ordered massive retaliation against London, but only a dozen planes even found the empire's sprawling capital. "When is the Reichsmarschall coming back?" asked Hitler irritably of his staff at midday on the fifth. (Stenographers recorded his words.) "This can't go on! We'll never cut the British down to size like this!"

Göring, however, had fled to Rome, to see Mussolini and—no doubt, incidentally—his art-dealer friends. From the letter that the Fascist dictator wrote to Hitler a few days later, it is clear that the Italians were again begging Nazi Germany to make peace with Stalin on whatever terms they could get.

The papers of Walter Hofer reveal how Göring comforted himself after the meeting with Mussolini. Visiting the country estate of art dealer Eugenio Ventura in Florence on March 8, he decided to acquire various objets d'art, including four Italian and Tyrolean paintings and triptychs, and four wood carvings of garlands. Greedy to lay hands on them, he instructed his staff to load them aboard his train immediately. "It's getting late already," he remarked suavely, "so I'd better take the things with me right away."

In exchange, he offered nine nineteenth-century works confiscated in France, including three Monets and works by Sisley, Cézanne, Degas, Renoir, and Van Gogh, which Hofer had removed to Florence in December for "restoration."

Further crates were loaded aboard, of objects bought from Count Contini, including a sixteenth-century walnut bench, a table, a large medicine cabinet, a prayer stool, and religious and hunting sculptures, a marble "Aphrodite After the Bath" purchased from Iandolo in Rome, and ten items bought from Grassi in Florence, including a bust of the Emperor Hadrian. Lost in the familiar art collector's trance, Göring had put the war behind him.

Scathing about the absentee Reichsmarschall, Hitler discussed the new violent RAF raids with Goebbels and Speer at the Wolf's Lair. That afternoon, March 8, 1943, he described Göring as being oblivious of the war in the air, and totally misinformed by his ex-Richthofen Squadron cronies like Bodenschatz. ''While I brood day and night on how to stop these air raids,'' an adjutant heard him say, ''the Reichsmarschall leads his carefree life.''

That night the RAF dropped eight hundred tons of bombs on medieval Nuremberg. Hitler had Bodenschatz fetched out of bed and raged at him.

Twenty-four hours later Munich was the British bombers' target. The fear of German retaliation was evidently no deterrent at all. Hitler blamed this on Göring's portly friend Field Marshal Hugo Sperrle, who had set up his Luftflotte 3 headquarters in a French château. ''He has about as much interest in bombing Britain as in wolfing down a gourmet dinner,'' said Hitler, and ordered Göring back from Italy.

To his adjutant Jeschonnek remarked emptily that perhaps he ought to commit suicide—then Göring might mend his ways. The remark revealed how much the general was being pulverized between these heaving millstones of the high command. Later that spring the adjutant managed to wrest a revolver out of Jeschonnek's hand—he heard the general muttering about wanting to be buried in East Prussia on the shores of Lake Goldap.

He arrived back at the Wolf's Lair at 4:00 P.M. on March 11, 1943, chatted for a while with Rommel, who had relinquished command of his army in Tunisia the previous day, and slunk in to see Hitler at 9:30.

Hitler gave Göring one more chance to redeem himself.

Göring put pressure on to his plane manufacturers. Assembling them for a ninety-minute tirade at Carinhall a week later, he ladled vitriol over them—the Professors Messerschmitt, Heinkel, and Dornier—for Germany's ''total failure'' in aviation technology. ''I have been deceived,'' he roared, ''on a scale to which I was hitherto accustomed only in the variety acts of magicians and conjurers.'' ''There are some things, which were reported to me before the war as completely ready, but which are *still* not even ready today!'' To which remark he significantly added, ''I am not talking of the eastern theater at all. When I speak of the 'enemy' now, I am referring only to the enemy in the west.''

''The most modest requirement,'' he shrieked at Messerschmitt, ''is that your aircraft must take off and land without their pilots risking every bone in their body.'' He glared at Heinkel: ''I was promised a heavy bomber. The Heinkel 177. After calamity upon calamity they tell me, 'If only the plane didn't have to *dive*, it would be the finest bird in the world—it could go into service at once. At once!' I declare at once, 'It doesn't *have* to dive!' But now that it's been tried in operations there have been catastrophic losses, none caused by enemy action. So, Mr. Heinkel, what do you say today! And how many will go up in flames? Half of them! . . . How *amused* we all were about the enemy's backwardness, their 'plodding four-engined crates,' and so on. Gentlemen, I'd be delighted if you'd just copy one of their four-engined crates, double-quick! Then at least I'd have a plane to brag about!''

So he raged on. (The transcript covered one hundred pages.) ''That's what gets under my skin," he said at one stage. "They can drop their bombs through cloud cover into a pickle barrel in a railroad station, but our gentlemen 'can't quite find London.' " His admiration of the British electronic equipment was limitless. "I have long been aware," he said, "that there is nothing the British do not have. Whatever equipment *we* have, the enemy can jam it without so much as a by-your-leave. We accept all this as though it were God's will, and when I get steamed up about it, the story is we haven't got the workers. . . . Gentlemen, it isn't manpower you're short of, it's brainpower." The British H2S radar set—first recovered from the RAF bomber at Rotterdam—was a fine example. It filled half a dozen steel cabinets. No German bomber was big enough to carry them. "That's because they have built those 'old four-engined crates,' " he mimicked. "Aircraft so big you could lay out a dance floor in them!"

He rounded on General Wolfgang Martini, the shy and academic chief of Luftwaffe signals. "I refuse to be led a song and dance like this," he declared. "The enemy can actually see whether he is over a city or not, right through the clouds. We cannot jam him. You tell me that we also have something, and in the same breath you add, 'But it can all be jammed by the enemy!' "

Later that month Göring retreated to Berchtesgaden, and tried to clear his mind. The catastrophic air raids on Berlin and the Ruhr were increasing in violence, and now the American bombers were joining in. The Reich had lost fifteen thousand dead in air raids. On April 4, American daylight raids killed 229 Frenchmen in Paris and 221 Italians in Naples; on the fifth, the U.S. bomber squadrons killed 2,130 Belgian civilians in Antwerp. Telephoning Goebbels in Berlin on the sixth—fully aware that the Forschungsamt would courier reports of his scathing language to Göring—Milch heaped obloquy on the Reichsmarschall's name.

Intervening in Luftwaffe operations, Hitler ordered fighter squadrons switched to the Russian front. "It's out of the question," Göring ranted over the phone to Jeschonnek. "It's about time you learned to stand up to the Führer." Swamped in the east, run out of Africa, almost nonexistent in the west, his air force struggled to survive. Troubled by the Reich's growing food shortage and threats of cuts in the meat ration, Göring took refuge in bed. His diary shows April 1943 ending with visits from Hitler's surgeon Karl Brandt and his own doctor Ondarza, who helpfully prescribed still more bed rest.

Göring still found time for less martial pursuits—he inquired of Fräulein Limberger "whether the amethysts were ready," he ordered designer shoes from Perugia for little Edda's birthday, and drove down to Munich with Emmy to buy expensive china. Richthofen turned up once on the Obersalzberg, and noted in his diary on April 26 that he feared that Stalingrad and the latest North Africa débacle had "put the skids" under Göring for good.

In Tunisia 250,000 more German troops went into enemy captivity. Göring now took refuge in his childhood castle at Veldenstein, and here he would stay until the end of May 1943. Milch came down on the thirteenth to tender what he circumspectly entered in his notes only as "general advice on the overall situation." That situation now seemed totally intractable. Just ten enemy planes droning high overhead on the next day drove twenty-five *million* Germans into their shelters. On the sixteenth, RAF bombers using special rotating bombs collapsed the massive Eder and Möhne dams, drowning 1,217 people in the ensuing flood disasters. General Dittmar recorded three days later that the high command was stunned at the Reichsmarschall's failure even to show his face in the stricken Ruhr cities now.

Göring lingered behind his medieval battlements at Veldenstein. He snoozed in the sunshine, went for drives in the surrounding forests. Scarcely anybody came to consult with him—the Göring diary glimpses only Beppo Schmid fetching his Knight's Cross, General Hube arriving from Italy to report, General Kastner coming to brief him on the dams. While the heartless nocturnal carnage continued, Göring followed events at a safe distance, talking to Bodenschatz, shouting over the phone to Jeschonnek ("Send photos of Ladoga, Leningrad, and Novorossisk to the Führer!"). His air force, meanwhile, was barely denting London. KG2 and KG6 raised only seventy or eighty bombers to attack London, Norwich, Hastings, and Bournemouth. On one night, May 23–24, the British effortlessly dropped over two thousand tons of bombs on Dortmund in the Ruhr.

The Reichsmarschall lay low, humiliated and angry.

"My people tell me, 'We're not sure we can find London at night,' " he mimicked, months later. "But their guys fly over to a dam that's socked in with fog, and whack right into it."

Just at this lowest ebb in his fortunes, Göring had a visitor who brought hope. Colonel Adolf Galland, the young, cigar-chomping general of fighters, came on the twenty-fifth to talk about that Messerschmitt 262 jet fighter— the first operational jet fighter in the world. He had test-flown it three days before. "The bird flies," he said. "It flies like there's an angel pushing."

The Me 262 was a clear 130 miles per hour faster than the Me 109G, the fastest German conventional fighter. "If the enemy sticks to the piston engine," wrote Galland in the report he handed to Göring, "the Me 262 is going to give us an unimaginable lead."

Even as Göring took in these words, Milch came on the phone from Berlin. It would, he said, be quite feasible to slot the jet straight into the mass-production program. "I want your permission," asked Milch, "to drop the Me 209 and turn out every 262 we can, as a matter of urgency."

Göring panicked. He hated decisions. He threw a glance at Colonel Galland, listening on the second earpiece. "Well?"

Galland nodded.

"Agreed!" said Göring.

"Dump the Me 209, replace with Me 262," recorded Milch in his pocket diary.

35
EXIT JESCHONNEK

On the night that Colonel Galland saw Göring about the Me 262, RAF Bomber Command thumped two thousand tons of bombs into Düsseldorf, capital city of the Ruhr. Two days later the RAF's wooden Mosquitoes bombed the Zeiss precision optical works at Jena. "Jena," roared Göring, "is right in the heart of Germany! What cheek, that's all I can say: and what contempt for our own fighter forces!" Two nights later still, the RAF left 2,450 dead and 118,000 homeless in the little Ruhr valley town of Wuppertal.

As the towns and cities crumpled in ruins, Göring vacationed at his mountain villa above Berchtesgaden, inferring that provided he did not bomb Churchill, the latter, being a gentleman, would not bomb him. That spring of 1943 he met only infrequently with his Führer, now recuperating himself from the winter's ordeals only a few hundred yards up the Obersalzberg hillside and brooding upon Citadel, his coming great tank offensive at Kursk.

A surviving handwritten notebook kept by Göring in those months reveals how extensively his horizon was clouded by the war in the air—by the thundering squadrons of B-17's, Lancasters, and Mosquitoes. The breaching of the Ruhr dams had shaken him badly, and he cast around for revenge. "Bigger barrage balloons," he wrote. Later he added, "Very hard for me to know of all our important objectives. Führer must decide new defense priorities," and he made the note: "All Reich agencies and party districts must report immediately their most vital air-defense targets."

He turned his mind to possible ways of hitting back. "Scottish dams. Heavy raids [on] Russia, nuisance raids on the Urals." A later entry shows that he felt that General Robert Ritter von Greim's Luftflotte 6 was only "bespattering" the Russian targets with its haphazard attacks; he decided to place two or three Geschwader (wings) of near-obsolete He 111's under one air-corps command on the eastern front to execute heavy night raids on Kuibyshev, Moscow, and the more distant Soviet arsenals. "Handfuls of planes won't even dent these gigantic plants," he observed. "But if one or two hundred bombers batter them, time after time, then we'll get somewhere!"

In the same notebook he wrote reminders to commission Professor Kurt Tank to design a wooden bomber like the Mosquito, and to ask for volunteers for anti-Mosquito operations, and "a particularly dashing officer" to command them—he jotted down shortly the names of two suitable candidates: "Graf and Ihlefeld—job, tackling the Mosquitoes." He also crowded the pages with notes about missile attacks on warships, flak for the Ruhr and U-boat yards, and setting up a long-range strategic bombing force equipped with the new Heinkel 177 and Junkers 290 four-engine bombers, adopting the Americans' "tight squadron formation" tactics. "How come the British," he wrote, "can operate their bombers by day, with or without fighters, while we are hard pushed to operate at night? We need new fighter tactics against the big fighter-escorted bomber formations," he reflected. "Pelz and Storp," he entered hopefully on June 1, "have a few surprises up their sleeve, like intruding [German bombers] into the returning British bomber stream [and] long-range night fighting."

That day he had signed the Me 262 jet fighter into mass production. He recorded in his other pocket diary notes for briefing Hitler on the Luftwaffe, "My intentions." The air force should, in short, become the main weapon against the Atlantic convoys. "The British will then have to mount colossal operations against us in the Atlantic." Submarines could finish off the scattered merchantmen. He intended to overhaul the Luftwaffe's incompetent organization in France, and noted criticisms of the luxurious command posts installed by the Luftwaffe in various French châteaux. "It is just not possible," he wrote, "for everybody to have their own command apparatus. I'm going to set up defense districts with one person in charge of the day fighters, night fighters, flak artillery, and all signals units. . . . And one common radio frequency for the whole country."

In further random jottings that June Göring foreshadowed his later allegations of cowardice. Formulating his opinions on his fighter pilots, he listed the four determining factors as "Technology—numbers—morale—officers.""Basically," he more realistically assessed, "our wafer-thin resources are to blame. We don't concentrate anywhere. We are inferior. So we are pushed back all along the line. Air power holds the key—as witness the efforts of our enemies.''

Pelz, now a major-general, had suffered grievous losses in restarting the blitz on Britain. In March 1943 alone, KG 2, based in Holland, had lost twenty-six crews. Over the following months Göring was obliged to limit operations to only two squadrons of FW 190's and Me 410's carrying out high-speed nuisance attacks by full moon on targets like Hull, Norwich, Ipswich, Chelmsford, Portsmouth, Plymouth, and Cardiff. The ''Kammhuber Line,'' Göring's ponderous, extravagant night-fighter defense organization, mean-while proved incapable of halting the concentrated British bomber tactics. Terrifying conflagrations ravaged the German cities. On June 11, the RAF again dropped two thousand tons of bombs on Düsseldorf. Thousands more civilians were killed in a second fire raid on little Wuppertal. Still Hitler and Göring hankered after ways of hitting back at Britain, when their air force could not even do damage now to Russia.

One of Göring's lengthier diary entries that June shows that he was not entirely insensible to advice:

> Our air force in Russia is fresh and keen! Willing to fight but weak in manpower, technical staff, and planes, because rein-forcements don't keep pace. They feel that they're being used like a fire brigade everywhere, that they can't stage mass raids of their own and that they don't get much chance to relax—just dogsbodies to the army!! Tossed this way and that—this army one day, that the next, and then back again. Particularly damaging how the Geschwader get split up: This freezes out the Geschwader commodores, although they're very important people. Three squadrons may be operating from the same base, but each belongs to a different Geschwader . . .
>
> The troops want a reasonable degree of forward planning and not just these fire-brigade duties.

Hitler was planning ahead. While he plotted Citadel, his final tank offensive at Kursk, Göring lingered on at his nearby mountain villa, sitting in his white uniform in the sunshine or strolling with Emmy. The news from the Ruhr did not encourage him to attend Hitler's daily conferences at the Berghof.

One afternoon, however, June 18, Ulrich Diesing came—Göring's bright new young technical officer. Diesing brought tidings of a revolutionary new Luftwaffe missile that promised to be a means of hitting back at the British after all—a small, steel-skinned robot plane that would carry a one-ton warhead over two hundred or three hundred miles. A Luftwaffe unit at Peenemünde, on the Baltic, had tested fifty already, and thirty-five of these prototypes had functioned perfectly. Field Marshal Milch was planning, said Ulrich, to mass produce five thousand a month. Greedy for revenge, Göring added a zero to the figure on the document: *fifty* thousand; and ordered construction work to begin immediately on the first one hundred catapult-launching sites along the French coast. "The enemy air force will be obliged to attack these launching sites," predicted Milch in a letter to Göring a few days later, "and our fighter planes and flak will have wonderful opportunities to inflict annihilating damage on them." Göring began to savor the moment when he could not only launch these flying bombs against London but against General Dwight D. Eisenhower's supply ports in North Africa and—from the decks of U-boats cruising off the American coast—even against the skyscrapers of New York too.

All this lay some time in the future. Meanwhile a number of urgent personnel problems had to be faced. Smoldering over Göring's insensitive recourse to his own "little air staff" of Brauchitsch, Diesing, and Ondarza, the chief of air staff, Hans Jeschonnek, reported "sick"—or so his deputy General Rudolf Meister told Göring on June 21, 1943. Probably the illness was more psychological than real, because the cure that Göring contemplated was giving Jeschonnek command of a Luftflotte (the Fourth) and sending Richthofen up to *Robinson*, the Luftwaffe's forward headquarters, to supplant him. Had Göring not always accused Jeschonnek of being too pliable at the Wolf's Lair? "You just stand at attention to the Führer, with your thumbs on your pant seams!" he had jeered. The job switch looked like the ideal solution, but Göring hesitated to appoint such a forceful, blunt-spoken character as Richthofen to Hitler's conference table. So the decision was postponed, not once but several times.

Göring's own stock was too low at present. People in the Ruhr were bitter that he did not show his face there. "This," wrote Goebbels after seeing Hitler on June 22, "is why Göring's failure oppresses [Hitler] so much: because he's the only man capable of taking over if anything should happen to him."

Summoned to the Führer's presence the next day, Göring penciled into his notebook reminders that betray an apprehensive state of mind:

> Situation in the south! In the southeast! In the north! My own position as commander in chief. Jeschonnek (on leave)—Milch (Udet) controversy. My own activities (stenographic record, produce my appointment diary). Influencing subordinates, consulting with them. Troops' confidence in me.
>
> Worst will be over this autumn. Inspection visits by me. Examples, Vienna airplane-engine works!
>
> *My present task*: Overhauling the air force. Clear technological objectives. Revive flagging spirits.

"Please," he intended to tell Hitler, "make use of Bodenschatz for any wishes, complaints, or orders." This was not good enough for Hitler. Perhaps at Martin Bormann's suggestion—because the latter entered it in his diary —Hitler called in all the aircraft designers four days later and, telling them not to breathe a word of this to Göring, grilled them about the chaos in the industry.

Göring had more immediate preoccupations. Operating one thousand bombers most nights now, the RAF was executing ruthless saturation raids on every Ruhr city, dumping two thousand tons of bombs on Krefeld, 1,640 tons on Mülheim and Oberhausen, 1,300 tons on Gelsenkirchen. When the American bombers now joined in by day, wrecking the vital Nazi oil refinery at Hüls on June 22, Milch reminded Göring in an alarmed letter that half of their entire synthetic-fuel capacity was concentrated in the Ruhr, within easy bombing range. Milch urged that the Führer be prevailed on to divert June's entire fighter production to the air defense of the Reich. As if this were not enough, Göring's experts now sent a two-page report advising that the British could at any time poison the radar defenses with showers of aluminium foil; there was, warned the unfortunate signals chief Martini, as yet·no antidote. Frightened of giving the enemy even a hint about this awful device, Göring halted all German research into the "antidote" that Martini mentioned.

Instead, he continued to search for unorthodox solutions to the problems of air defense. On the day that Hitler secretly hosted his meeting with the aircraft designers, Göring was holding a discussion with his top bomber experts, the buccaneering majors Werner Baumbach and Hajo Herrmann. Herrmann had recently taken a single-seater plane up to observe RAF night-bombing techniques for himself—the dazzling spectacle of cascading pyrotechnic flares. He had not needed radar at all. The enemy bombers were clearly silhouetted against clouds lit by the fires, flares, flashes, and flak from beneath. His proposal was to throw hundreds of single-seater fighter planes at the British, crewed by *day*-fighter and even bomber pilots.

Again Göring followed closely, as his handwritten notes show:

> *Free-lance single-engined night fighting*! Major Herrmann. Combat over target area using searchlights. New tactics in conjunction with flak. In the Ruhr often a hundred [bombers are held] in searchlights—forty during the big raid on Berlin.
>
> Our present system does not permit night fighters to mass at [bomber] point of penetration [of Kammhuber Line]. Use 200-centimeter [searchlight] with Mars radar to guide fighters. Enemy will be sighted even in haze as the 200 is radar-controlled. . . . Best thing is to shoot down the Illuminators [RAF Pathfinders] and then send in our own Illuminators.

Göring authorized the major to begin trials. Milch backed the bold scheme, in a letter. "Given the right weather," he wrote on June 29, "we can expect substantial successess." Major Hermann transferred his experimental unit to the Ruhr, and waited for the next RAF attack.

The Allies were about to invade southern Europe, perhaps Sicily. The Reichsmarschall had summoned Kesselring to Berchtesgaden late in May to discuss defense measures. The field marshal warned that the German Air Force there was exhausted. "We are not capable of defending Sicily against a determined assault," wrote Göring in his diary. "Italian Air Force completely useless. . . . Transport network catastrophic, no low-loaders for tanks."

Göring's immediate solution was to transfer Richthofen—now a field marshal—from Luftflotte 4 on Manstein's front in Russia to Luftflotte 2 in Italy until the invasion crisis there was over. He called Richthofen to see him on the Obersalzberg on June 11.

> Reichsmarschall pretty critical of Kesselring's direction of the
> battle [recorded the Luftflotte commander in his diary] but em-
> phasizes that there is still the same old trust between them (or so
> he says). . . . I have to point out that the net result for me is less
> pleasant. I haven't the faintest idea whether I can run the war
> any differently and stress that any new arrangement in the south
> is bound to take time.

Citadel, Hitler's ground-shaking final attempt to regain the strategic initiative in the east, was about to begin. Spring vacation in Bavaria over, Göring followed him back to East Prussia and sat in on the speech that Hitler delivered on the first day of July to his Citadel commanders. He promised that they would have sixteen hundred tanks, but they knew that the Russians had three thousand. The room was icy and unheated, and Hitler found it difficult to rouse enthusiasm. Several generals allowed their gaze to wander. General Otto von Knobelsdorff recalled two years later that the Reichsmarschall looked "goofier" (*mehr verblödet*) than ever. "Hermann [Göring]," he told fellow prisoners, "sat next to [Hitler], wilting more and more from one quarter-hour to the next, until his face looked downright sheepish. He kept stuffing himself with pills and then perked up again for a while." Manstein picked a fight with Göring, demanding the immediate return of the irreplaceable Richthofen at least for the duration of Citadel. Göring jealously refused.

Still seething, he summoned all his own field marshals to the hunting lodge at Rominten for the next two days. He thus set eyes on Milch for the first time since May. The field marshal had had the thankless duty of touring the cratered Ruhr cities. He brandished a recommendation for quadrupling the day-fighter force "until we ram the American victories down their throats." "You don't imagine I read the trash you write!" shouted Göring, humiliating

Milch in front of all the others. The commander in chief, flak, General Walter von Axthelm, got the same short shrift. "You bloody fools fired so little," the Reichsmarschall shouted across the room at him, "that those swine [the Americans] have destroyed Hüls!"

Profoundly mistrustful of Kesselring's ability to interpret the signs in Italy correctly, Göring asked Richthofen to come to Rominten on July 3. The field marshal found the hunting lodge thronged with thirty or forty generals.

> I was promptly called in [wrote Richthofen upon his return to Luftwaffe headquarters, Rome] and set out the purely military position. . . . Lunch was to have been followed by a big conference, but instead of this the Reichsmarschall took me out into the country alone and asked me what's going on down here. . . . Nothing I have found out about the military setup and morale surprised him.
>
> Reichsmarschall is petrified I may sneak back to the eastern front. While agreeing to serve where duty calls, I admit I would prefer to resume command of Luftflotte 4, though I accept that if I am to keep my eye on things I must stay down here, reluctant though I am . . . I have no freedom of action here as the whole Luftflotte [2] still pays homage to [Kesselring] so long as he is here.

Over at the Wolf's Lair, Jeschonnek pleaded with Richthofen to get him the Luftflotte 4 command. The next day, July 4, while Jeschonnek flew out to Luftflotte 4 to get the feel of Citadel, Richthofen sat around Rominten. "They're at the trough all day long here," he observed caustically. He tagged along that afternoon to the Wolf's Lair with Göring, who conferred à deux with Hitler. Hitler firmly squelched the idea of exchanging Jeschonnek for Richthofen, and reverted to the major war problems. "No time to raise the less immediate issues," recorded Richthofen, disappointed, "as major problems overshadowed all else." However, he did add this: "Führer and Reichsmarschall are hugely optimistic about the future of the war," and there were reasons for this cautious optimism. During the night Major Herrmann's experimental flight had shot down a dozen RAF bombers over Cologne. "You just have to hang around their flare clusters," Herrmann reported on July 6. He voiced the opinion that a proper force of such "free-lance" night fighters could destroy eighty bombers a night.

The defense of the Reich began to dominate Göring's signals, as the British intercepts reveal. "The Reichsmarschall," said one, sent in July to every fighter squadron, "has laid down for the purpose of awarding decorations the following ratio for aircraft shot down by day: destroying one four-engined bomber equals destroying three twin-engined bombers." An angry signal to Colonel Galland expressed astonishment at his protracted sojourn in sunny

Italy: "The Reichsmarschall expects you to return as soon as possible."
Further intercepts revealed to the Allies unwelcome news that "twenty more
Me 109's are re-equipping at Erding with 21 cm"—the formidable Nebelwerfer air-to-air rocket—and that the bomber Geschwader KG 100 was
equipping one squadron of Do 217's with the rocket-propelled Hs 293 anti-
convoy missile and another squadron with the wire-controlled Fritz X, an
armor-piercing bomb for attacking heavy warships. That month, July 1943,
Göring's factories produced one thousand fighter planes for the first time.
The post-Udet era was beginning.

Citadel, the biggest, bloodiest tank battle in history, began in Russia on July
6, 1943. The initial euphoria was soon forgotten as news came on the ninth
that the Allies had invaded Sicily. In East Prussia the Reichsmarschall clung
to the long-distance telephone, roasting his generals in Rome. "Long talk
with Reichsmarschall this evening," wrote Richthofen on the tenth. "He
seems frightfully agitated." The next day: "Angry phone call from the
Reichsmarschall this evening . . . I calmed him down. Swears furiously at
our fighter pilots, who are not, in fact, to blame this time. Soothed him with
our own bomber successes. All our bombers out attacking shipping south of
Syracuse [in Sicily] tonight."

On July 13, Hitler decided to abandon Citadel. Göring told Milch that day
that reinforcing Richthofen would now have top priority. Hitler sent air-force
officers Below and Bodenschatz down to Italy to report. "Bodenschatz,"
wrote Richthofen after lunching with the general, "informs me of fundamental decisions on the prosecution of the war in the east and in the Mediterranean. And," he added gloomily, "they don't appear to have been taken
at all voluntarily."

The political importance was that if Sicily was overrun, Italy would probably defect from the alliance, bringing British and American troops—not
to mention their bomber squadrons currently based in North Africa—to
the very frontiers of the Reich. Hitler conferred with Rommel about this on
the eighteenth. "In the east," recorded Rommel, "the Russians are on the
attack. . . . The Führer," he added, "is probably going down to meet the
Duce."

Göring accompanied Hitler, the latter literally bent double by agonies of
apprehension, aboard his Focke-Wulf 200 for the long flight to Italy. Hitler's
porcine physician Morell told Göring that his patient had had little sleep
despite injections of various morphine substitutes.

> In the [FW 200] Condor [recorded Morell] Reichsmarschall Gör-
> ing ventured to give me a few last-minute tips. "You must give
> him Euflat," he said.* "That once helped me a lot." "Yes, two

*Göring got the names wrong initially but Dr. von Ondarza corrected him. Euflat was a proprietary

tablets three times a day: I'm doing it already." "But you've got
to keep doing it over a long period. I took them for eighteen
months. And then you must give him Luizym too!"
    "We're already doing that!"

As Hitler met Mussolini in northern Italy, news came that the Allies were
raining bombs on Rome. He parted from Mussolini convinced that the
Italians—for all their protestations to the contrary—were on the brink of
defecting.

    "I can only keep saying," Milch told Göring a few days earlier, "1943
is going to be a year of clenched teeth—but in 1944 things are going to
change dramatically. And we're going to see the first of these changes this
autumn."

    Hitler wanted those changes now. "You can only smash terror with ter-
ror," he snarled at Göring and his generals on July 23, 1943. "You've got
to strike back! Anything else is nonsense." Scornful of Göring's latest plans
for small-scale intruder raids against RAF airfields, Hitler snorted, "You
can count yourself lucky if you find *London*!" "The British will stop," he
shouted, still fuming, at his staff two days later, "only when it's their cities
that are being wrecked. I won't have a monkey made out of me, and that's
what I tell the Reichsmarschall. I don't mince my language with him."

    Shaken by this downturn in their personal relations, Göring hurried to
Rechlin in *Asia* on the twenty-fourth, and watched with Milch as the fourth
prototype of the Me 262 streaked majestically past. The howl of the twin
Jumo 004 jet engines—a sound that not many people in the world had heard
until then—gave the two Luftwaffe chiefs newfound confidence.

    That night the RAF began Operation Gomorrah, a macabrely named at-
tempt at literally wiping out an entire city with its population. Cascading
tons of aluminum foil to blind the German radar defenses—precisely the
electronic trick that Göring had feared and forbidden his own forces—the
RAF smashed Hamburg hard, killing fifteen hundred civilians for the loss
of only twelve bombers.

    "One single suburb," gasped Hitler at midday on July 25, "has lost eight
hundred dead!" Turning to an air-staff officer he again declared, "The British
will stop only when their own cities are being wrecked." Forthwith he signed
a decree to Speer to mass-produce the army's A-4 long-range rocket to
bombard London.

    Although this change of priorities looked like yet another erosion of Gör-
ing's role, Hitler still needed Göring—the "Iron Man," as he liked to be
called—badly. That evening he phoned Göring: There were reports that
Marshal Pietro Badoglio, "our deadliest enemy," had seized power in Italy.

indigestion tablet commonly prescribed against a bloated abdomen. Luizym is a proprietary enzyme
tablet to help break down cellulose and carbohydrates in the stomach.—David Irving, *Adolf Hitler:
The Medical Diaries* (London & New York, 1983).

The stenographers recorded only Hitler's end of the phone dialogue, but even the Reichsmarschall was evidently incredulous.

> HITLER: Hello, Göring . . . Did you get the news?
> Well, there's still no direct confirmation but hardly any doubt about it—the Duce has quit. Badoglio's stepped into his shoes. . . .
> It's a *fact*, Göring, beyond shadow of doubt. What's that? I don't know, we're trying to find out.

Göring suggested they wind up the eastern front altogether. Hitler interrupted him:

> That's utter nonsense. *That* goes on, and how! They'd better believe it, that's going on!
> I just wanted you to know. You'd all better get over here as fast as you can. . . .
> What? I don't know. I'll tell you later. But assume that it *is* correct.

Arriving at the Wolf's Lair the next morning, the Reichsmarschall found a rare Cabinet-level meeting in progress with Hitler and Grand Admiral Dönitz, the new commander in chief of the navy, as well as Ribbentrop, Speer, Goebbels, and Bormann. Grim but composed, Hitler told them he was convinced, despite the new Badoglio regime's assurances, that Italy was plotting to surrender. Accordingly he planned to switch the crack SS *Leibstandarte* "Adolf Hitler" Division immediately from Russia to Italy. He would evacuate Sicily forthwith—"just like Dunkirk," he said—and allow these seventy thousand crack troops of the "Hermann Göring" Panzer Division and the 1st Paratroop Division to leave behind their heavy weapons if necessary. "They can deal with the Italians with their small arms if need be," he added contemptuously. He would also switch the 2nd Paratroop Division from southern France into Italy. When ready, he would pounce on Rome, arrest the government and king, and "take out" the Vatican too—"Lancing the whole abscess," as he put it.

At the evening war conference thirty-five men crowded around the map table. Göring was silent, and it was Rommel who urged caution. Far better, he argued, to lay the plans with care. "As soon as we act," Göring agreed, "our opponents will scream for help and protection!"

"But it will still take them a finite time to get ready to invade," replied Hitler, referring to the Allies. "First of all they'll be caught completely flatfooted—as usual!"

He prevailed upon Göring to send his paratroop commander Student down to Richthofen carrying a pouch of secret directives for the seizure of Rome. Richthofen was horrified. He recorded that Student was an "absolute idiot" with no notion of the likely consequences. He told Student not to bother with Göring's orders, as he was flying straight up to get them rescinded.

> Saw Reichsmarschall at once [Richthofen wrote, after arriving in East Prussia]. He's staying at the Führer's. Sketched out situation in Rome to him. The people up here have a completely different view, can't believe that Fascism has vanished without trace and maintain that the new regime is on the point of doing a peace deal. I hold out against this view.

Göring took him into Hitler's nine o'clock conference that evening. Rommel was now thirsting for action against the hated Italians. Richthofen stuck doggedly to his guns. They must plan meticulously first. Leaving at eleven-thirty, he subjected Göring to an hour's badgering. "The same thing over and over," wrote the field marshal later. "Did what I could to make him less certain that there are any Fascists extant whatever."

That night a fresh disaster befell Hamburg that had few parallels in history. The British bombers struck again, and nothing could prevent them from dropping thousands of tons of fire bombs. They uncaged in this ancient Hanseatic port an awful new phenomenon of war, the "fire storm." The artificial hurricane whipped out the window panes, tore off roofs, and cat-apulted people, trees, and even railway cars into the heart of the infernal flames. The fires flashed through whole streets in seconds, generating blast-furnace temperatures that melted glass, glazed bricks, and reduced every organic and animate object to ashes, after mercifully poisoning them first with invisible gases.

Göring's blood ran cold as he read the first teleprinter messages. He sent Bodenschatz to Hamburg. Gauleiter Karl Kaufmann told him that twenty-six thousand bodies had already been counted—mostly those of women and children. (The night's final death toll would exceed forty-eight thousand.) In Berlin, Speer and Milch were heard soberly proclaiming that Germany had "finally lost the war." Toward midday on the twenty-eighth Göring had his adjutant Brauchitsch phone Milch: "The Reichsmarschall notifies the field marshal that the main effort is to be focused forthwith on the defense of the Reich."

The next morning they met in Berlin, then Göring and Milch took to Hitler a formal proposal for the introduction of a refined version of Herrmann's "free-lance" night-fighting system—guiding entire squadrons of fighters into the RAF "bomber stream," which ironically could now be located the more easily by its own cascades of aluminium foil. During the following night, in the third British attack of the Operation Gomorrah series, Herrmann's pilots brought down eighteen of the twenty-eight bombers destroyed. In its own small way it seemed like a turning point in the air war.

All Germany waited for the next fire storm. "Things can't go on like this," an SS Obergruppenführer wrote to Himmler on July 30. "Someone's got to speak to the German people. They won't listen to the Reichsmarschall now. Not just because of the obvious supremacy of the enemy air force, but because he has failed to go into the blitzed areas and talk with the people." On August 2, Hamburg was again the RAF target. Milch sent a frantic telegram to Göring, demanding that fighter squadrons be brought back from Russia and even Italy. "It's not the front line that is battered and fighting for life," this telegram said. "It is the fatherland that is under grave attack, and fighting a desperate battle."

Göring cast Hans Jeschonnek, chief of the air staff, as the scapegoat for Hamburg. Jeschonnek crumpled. Beppo Schmid saw it happening, and so did Kurt Student, whom Göring fetched back from Italy to plot ways of liberating Mussolini as soon as his whereabouts could be found. The destruction at Hamburg propelled Jeschonnek into a terminal, three-week-long bout of depression. He had recently lost his father, and his brother and brother-in-law had been killed in action. His frail efforts to escape from the stifling atmosphere of *Robinson* and the Wolf's Lair had been thwarted. As recently as the end of July he had told General von Seidel that he was being given a Luftflotte, but Göring quailed at the idea, and Hitler talked him out of it. After an "all-field-marshal" luncheon with Hitler on July 28, as Richthofen recorded, Göring had touched on possible replacements for Jeschonnek—"I agree a reshuffle is necessary," Richthofen delicately recorded afterward, "but who? He names [Günther] Korten and myself. I recoil in horror, but have to admit I don't think Korten is up to much." Göring, however, abandoned all idea of replacing Jeschonnek. On August 5, Major Werner Leuchtenberg, Jeschonnek's adjutant, broke it to Field Marshal Richthofen in Rome that the Reichsmarschall had used "distinctly pejorative" language about him and had warned his staff, "We've got to make damn sure that the Führer never gets to hear of Richthofen's views!"

Jeschonnek phoned Seidel that same day. "It's all off," he said gloomily. "I've got to stay put."

At the Wolf's Lair the jostling for position began, with Göring reduced to the role of occasional onlooker. He hung around East Prussia until mid-August 1943, observing the comings and goings of the new strongmen. The balance of power there was tilting against him. To Göring it was clear that Hitler was opting for the proponents of brute force. Bormann regularly attended Hitler's main conferences. So did Himmler, who now became minister of the interior. "From now on," Göring would recall, "Bormann had Himmler to contend with as well: because as far as the succession was concerned, Himmler came right after me."

Hitler promised Rommel that he would soon be marching into Italy to restore the Fascist regime. Down in Rome, Richthofen wrote uneasily: "[I] definitely hope I can superimpose my appreciation of the situation here upon any decisions they take up there"—meaning at the Wolf's Lair.

All that summer, in the shimmering heat of Central Europe, the Allied bombers continued to blast away at the Reich. On the thirteenth, American bombers flew all the way up from North Africa to wreck the Messerschmitt works at Wiener Neustadt. Hitler heaped calumnies on the wilting chief of air staff for four hours afterward. "Why doesn't the Führer say all that to the Reichsmarschall?" whined Jeschonnek. "Why me?"

The answer was that Göring had traveled down to the Obersalzberg, to escape the glare of his fellow ministers and the lash of Hitler's sarcastic tongue. Holing up in Bavaria, he sought solace in his old interests. He phoned Professor Ludwig Peiner about four paintings on offer, "The Four Seasons." Peiner told him with regret that Speer had laid hands on one of them already ("Autumn," a nude lady with a bowl of fruit.) Göring directed Gisela Limberger to see that the professor nominated his two best pupils to escape the draft and paint a new "Autumn" to fill the gap. On the following day, August 17, the Americans pattern-bombed Messerschmitt's works at Regensburg and the ball-bearing factories at Schweinfurt before flying on down to North Africa. Four hundred Messerschmitt workers were killed. Given the chaotic structure of the air-defense command, this further humiliation was not surprising. The defenses were controlled by Jeschonnek in East Prussia, by Göring in Bavaria, by General Weise in Berlin, and by XII Fighter Corps at Arnhem. Even the 4th Fighter Division at Metz, in France, had a finger in the pie. "It was," recalled Dr. von Ondarza, "a wonderful summer's evening." It was also the first time that the American bombers had penetrated so deep into Germany.

> Hitler [said Ondarza] took it out on Göring mercilessly by phone, and Göring then put through a very, very long phone call to Jeschonnek. I didn't listen myself, but the SS sentries standing outside the open window said he was ranting and raging frightfully.

A bright moon came up that night. In a mental turmoil Jeschonnek punted out into the middle of Lake Goldap with Leuchtenberg, to watch the evening flight of wild duck. Later he broached a bottle of champagne to toast his daughter's birthday. At 11:00 P.M. word came that RAF Mosquitoes were setting out flares and target markers over Berlin, the chilling heralds of a mass attack. All fifty of Herrmann's "free-lance" fighters were ordered to Berlin. Göring, alerted by phone, directed the Berlin flak to lower its ceiling of fire to eighteen thousand feet. At 11:35 P.M. Metz ordered, "All night fighters to *Bear* [Berlin]." But Berlin was only the decoy. The only planes over the city were the Mosquitoes, Herrmann's men, and some twin-engined nightfighters on whom these trigger happy free-lancers now opened fire. For two hours the slam-bang barrage went on over Berlin.

At 6:00 A.M. the next morning Luftwaffe headquarters learned that the night's real RAF target had been Peenemünde, the top-secret army-missile establishment where the A-4 long-range rocket was being built and tested. It was in flames, and seven hundred rocket scientists and engineers were dead. Jeschonnek was awakened with this awful news at Goldap at 8:00 A.M. Hitler phoned soon after from the Wolf's Lair. "You know what to do!" he snapped. Jeschonnek did—there was precedent enough.

Later that morning a teleprinter message arrived on the Obersalzberg from General Meister. It informed Göring that Jeschonnek had shot himself dead. Betraying no emotions, Göring notified Richthofen in Rome. The laconic telegram merely said that Jeschonnek had died suddenly of a "stomach hemorrhage." Equally stone-faced, Richthofen dictated his own diary comment: "Lost a good comrade and friend. Who will succeed him?"

Göring, of course, had to fly up to East Prussia immediately. Major von Below, Hitler's air-force adjutant, and Meister met him at Rastenburg Airfield. "Jeschonnek promised me he would never do this," said Göring helplessly.

At air-force headquarters Jeschonnek's mortal remains were lying in his little wooden hut. Göring went in alone, and emerged shaking his head. "Some saint!" he sniffed. He ordered Meister to open the general's safe. It contained two envelopes addressed to von Below. The major scanned their content briefly, said simply that they were private, and made no effort to hand them over.

The safe also contained a ten-page memorandum dictated by Jeschonnek to his secretary, Lotte Kersten. Göring read it, his face reddening, then exclaimed, "I forbid staff officers to write down their personal opinions!" (The document recommended that Göring appoint a capable deputy commander in chief.) "Look at this," he cried, brandishing the sheets of paper at Meister. "The man was working against me all along!"

Meister shook his head. "General Jeschonnek was loyal to you to the very end."

Two revealing notes were also found in the desk. One read, "I can't work anymore with the Reichsmarschall! Long live the Führer!" The other cursed the glossy officers of Göring's little air staff. "Diesing and Brauchitsch," it stipulated, "are not to attend my funeral."

As it happened, Kesselring was the only field marshal to attend. Richthofen decided, on balance, not to face the Reichsmarschall right now. Göring admitted to Ondarza that the memorandum had shaken him. "He had no option but to shoot himself," he murmured. "He blamed me and the Luftwaffe for everything." "I am endlessly sorry," he admitted to Pili Körner. "How he must have struggled with himself! I never really knew him before I read that document."

He submitted Jeschonnek's staff to cross-examination. Leuchtenberg told him straight out that Jeschonnek had lost faith in him. Göring adopted an expression of pained innocence. The major reminded him of certain violent episodes aboard Göring's train. Infuriated, Göring pounded across the room with clenched fists.

"*Herr Reichsmarschall!*" screamed the junior officer, alarmed. "Pull yourself together!"

Göring skidded to a halt, and slumped into a chair.

"How many of you," he roared eventually to the high-ranking officers who had watched this scene, "would have had the courage to tell me what this young man has today!"

He placed both hands on the major's shoulders.

"I'd like you on the air staff. Have a word with Loerzer about it."

He had appointed his crony Loerzer—disgraced by the fiascos in Italy—as chief of personnel. A few days later Leuchtenberg found himself posted to the remotest corner of the eastern front, attached to I Air Corps in the Crimea.

36
SCHWEINFURT

For the rest of 1943 the tide of the war in the air would ebb and flow dramatically. Aided by new tactics and electronic equipment, Göring's pilots would have temporarily crippled the RAF's night-bombing offensive by the winter of 1943/44; but simultaneously the Americans began throwing precision raids by day deeper into Germany.

For the defense of the Reich Göring had stationed 8,876 of the formidable 88-millimeter flak guns and nearly 25,000 light flak guns. The flak gunners had claimed by the end of September 1943 no less than 12,774 enemy planes, the fighter pilots 48,268 more. Over one hundred thousand German civilians had been killed by the Allied bombing, however, and there was an air of desperation in the streets. In mid-September a glider pilot who had survived Eben Emael and Crete volunteered to form a suicide squadron of men willing to hurl old Junkers 88 bombers packed with high explosives into the midst of American bomber formations (and bail out if they could at the last moment). General Günther Korten, Jeschonnek's successor, put the idea to Göring; the Reichsmarschall shared his reservations.

Göring's own popularity remained undiminished. "Göring swears like a trooper," said one admiring Dornier navigator, shot down in February 1944.

"No doubt about it, though, Hermann is very popular, particularly in Berlin." At Hitler's headquarters his arrival was greeted each time with less enthusiasm. On October 27, 1943, as Hitler's distant armies in Russia began to fall back, he reminded the Reichsmarschall that the defense of Western Europe was of paramount importance: because there he could not afford to lose one inch of territory.

The Luftwaffe had lost the initiative, with little prospect of regaining it until the new mass-produced jet airplanes entered service. Thus Göring became the most plausible scapegoat for each Nazi defeat. Speer felt safe in expressing pronounced hostility. On November 8, Rommel too would tell anybody who would listen at the high command that Göring had been to blame for his defeat at El Alamein in 1942—"He just refused to believe the British had air supremacy." On November 20, Milch noted that he had "poured out his heart" to SS Reichsführer Himmler about the Reichsmarschall.

Perspiring freely, the Reichsmarschall had no option but to swallow the insults that Hitler hurled at him, often in front of junior officers. "The Führer's estrangement from me grew," he recalled two years later, speaking with George Shuster. "I could see his impatience when I briefed him. He often cut me off in midsentence, and began to intervene more and more in Luftwaffe affairs."

"Do you think there's a squadron left in your air force with the guts to fly to Moscow?" Hitler would challenge. Ordering him to intervene in Leningrad, he would sneer—"Always assuming that you still have bombers able to fly that far!" Luftwaffe liaison officer Karl Bodenschatz, no more eager than Göring to sweat it out round the clock at the Wolf's Lair, rented overnight rooms at the Park Hotel at Königsberg, and took to fleeing there by Storch each night until Göring found him out. "Your job is to be with the Führer," he snapped.

The Korten era began at 2:00 P.M. on August 20, 1943, when Göring introduced him to Hitler as Jeschonnek's successor as chief of air staff. Over the eleven months until his untimely death in July 1944 General Günther Korten would give the air force a new sense of strategic purpose. Backed by his new deputy, the ponderous, Bavarian-born Lieutenant General Karl Koller, Korten pulled fighter squadrons out of Russia and Italy and transferred them to the defense of the Reich. General Rudolf Meister was given command of the new IV Air Corps, which would bomb the seven main power stations along the Upper Volga, in Moscow, and in Leningrad, on which Soviet tank and aircraft-engine production depended.

The nights were soon long enough for the British to reach Berlin again. The first RAF raid on August 23 killed 765 people. Hitler wanted to strike back, but he knew that reprisals were going to have to wait. Meanwhile British code-breakers heard Korten ordering Luftflotte 4 on August 26 to transfer elements of KG51 bomber wing to Illesheim for conversion to the new Me 410 with the death-dealing 21-cm Nebelwerfer rocket. Fighter planes were now equipped with the excellent SN2-Lichtenstein cockpit radar, the infrared detector Spanner, and Naxos-Z, a device that homed onto the enemy bombers' H2S on-board radar. Beppo Schmid, now commanding the XII Fighter Corps, had set up a countrywide network to track these radar emissions. To confuse the bombers' radar operators, Göring's engineers had moored reflectors on thousands of lakes and erected jamming transmitters code-named *Roderich* up and down the country; decoy sites as big as cities were torched in the path of the invading aircraft. Each night Göring's controllers fed the fighter squadrons into the bomber stream, led by "shadowers" equipped with sophisticated tracking gear and homing beacons. Each night the single- and twin-engined fighters jousted with the marauding bombers over the guttering cities. Sometimes one controller at Arnhem was directing 250 fighter pilots by running radio commentary.

The RAF fought back with all that deviltry that had won the British a great empire. Planes laden with advanced electronic gear cruised amid the bombers, monitoring, jamming, interfering. Fake fighter "controllers" sent Göring's pilots to the wrong end of Germany or, more devilishly, warned of worsening weather, panicking them into landing prematurely.

Uncertainty about Italy lay like a pall across the Wolf's Lair. When Marshal Badoglio demanded that Germany supply no less than 1.7 million tons of grain, whereas the little-lamented Mussolini had made do with less than 300,000 tons (of which 200,000 tons were returned each time from the somewhat later Italian harvest), it became clear that Badoglio was just searching for a pretext to get out of the war. Göring's agriculture expert Herbert Backe, who visited him at Rominten at the end of August, shared this view.

Backe pleaded with Göring to prevent further retreats in Russia, as Germany was now largely dependent on food imports from there. "If we are really going to fall back on the lines now being sketched in," Backe noted on the last day of August, "I'll have to chuck in the sponge." The Reichsmarschall evidently recognized this too, and promised to mention this "higher up," i.e., to Hitler.

> During the meal [Backe wrote in a letter] I sat on the Reichsmarschall's right, with an Oak Leaves holder, the dive-bomber pilot Lieutenant Kupfer on his left. Kupfer spoke with welcome bluntness to him. He said we still don't know how to build defenses in depth, and that we are too gentlemanly to force the civilian population to do it like the enemy does every day. Hence the so-called "breakthroughs" that aren't anything of the sort because there was nothing in front of them and the Soviets were just groping forward into empty space. He had harsh words for the feeble army commanders up front, and compared them with the SS units: Where an army division fled in panic, a single

company of the SS Totenkopf had held the whole line. In fact,
only the SS is still worth much in air-force eyes.

That night the British hurled a second major attack at Berlin. This time they
lost forty-seven heavy bombers, most of them to Major Herrmann's non–
radar-controlled "free lancers." The British were now in serious difficulties.
Trying again to wipe out Berlin, they killed 346 people on September 3, but
lost 22 more bombers. In the three raids only twenty-seven planes had come
within three miles of the aiming point. The miles of craters tailing back
across the countryside were vivid evidence of lowering bomber morale. The
British called off the attack on Berlin.

Marshal Badoglio announced on September 8, 1943, that he had signed a
secret armistice with Eisenhower. Göring was not surprised at all. At the
same time the Allies landed at Salerno in southern Italy. Hotly contested by
the Luftwaffe, the beachhead became an Allied bloodbath as II Air Corps'
rocket-firing fighters raked the landing craft and troops. Richthofen's bombers
and torpedo planes damaged an Allied battleship and three cruisers, not to
mention the Italian battleship *Roma*—sunk by an Hs 293 missile—and several
other Italian warships destroyed by KG 100 as they scurried for the safe
haven of British-controlled ports.

That day Hitler told Göring that he had already marched Rommel into
northern Italy, while Student was disarming the Italian forces around Rome.
By his well-placed mistrust of the Italians Hitler had saved Germany's sizable
forces in southern Italy from betrayal to the enemy. On the afternoon of the
tenth the Reichsmarschall was among the admiring Nazi leaders who crowded
around Hitler as he broadcast to Germany and the world, uttering the grim
assurance that "within three months" the Reich would arise anew and go
on to final victory.

A few days later the paratroops rescued the imprisoned Fascist leader
Mussolini in a daring coup, and flew him to Hitler's headquarters. What
little admiration that had remained for the Duce was dispelled as Rommel's
troops made astonishing discoveries of strategic materials that the Italians
had squirreled secretly away, and as Kesselring uncovered hundreds of brand-
new Italian fighter planes. "The Italians and the Duce," Göring lectured
Hitler triumphantly, expectorating an anger that had built up over twenty
years, "have been carrying on deliberate sabotage for years. They simply
hid all these materials and the planes. The Duce was plain dumb. He ought
to be shot right now." As Hitler's war conference ended, Göring took Rommel aside. "Act like lightning against the Italians," he advised. "Above
all, don't wait until the Duce's back in office!"

"They had bigger stocks of copper than we do!" shouted Göring to Milch
a few days later. "But the most astonishing thing is the fuel oil. Hidden in
two tunnels we found enough to keep their entire navy operational for a year!

The swine tucked it away, barrel upon barrel, and then came whining to me for more. 'We would dearly love to fly, but we haven't the fuel!' I gave them another thousand tons. And now we find they have sixty-five thousand tons tucked away!''*

Vengeful and angry, Hitler ordered Göring to bomb an Italian city like Brindisi or Taranto before the Allies had time to organize air defenses. "We've got to show the Italian public," rasped Göring, passing on Hitler's logic to his generals, "and some of the neutrals and our other indolent allies, that even if you chuck in the sponge you're not out of the war!" Told that Italian Air Force officers, before turning their equipment over to the Germans, had riddled the aircraft engines with machine-gun fire and ripped up the parachutes, Göring ordered the culprits hunted down. "I would have them hanged on the airfield," he said, "and leave the bodies dangling for three days."

Yes, Hermann Göring had loathed the Italians ever since 1924.

"You have no idea," he would tell U.S. General Carl F. Spaatz on May 10, 1945, "what a bad time we had in Italy. If they had only been our enemies instead of our allies, we might have won the war."

"As commander in chief of the air force," said Göring that October, 1943, "people hold me responsible, and rightly so." For a few days that month the war in the air seemed to have taken an uglier turn. Spaatz's bombers attacking the German coastal port of Emden on the second were clearly monitored carrying radar, so they too could bomb through ten-tenths cloud. The Luftwaffe seemed increasingly impotent. By day Galland's fighter squadrons seemed paralyzed by fear. "Göring's fighters have arrived," the people took to saying. "So the raid must be over!" The Luftwaffe sent a mere twenty-two long-range night fighters to harass RAF bases one night. Hitler was infuriated. "I far prefer," he said, telephoning Göring, "to keep bombing their cities, whatever you say."

On October 4, although the skies were sunny and agents had actually told the Germans what the target was—Frankfurt-Heddernheim— Galland's pilots barely intervened. Frankfurt was badly mauled. Hitler phoned Göring derisively at nine-thirty that evening. Göring found out subsequently that the 5th Fighter Division had been "grounded by bad weather." "The German public doesn't care two hoots about your fighter losses," he snapped at Galland. "Go to Frankfurt and ask what impression your fighter losses that day left on them. They'll tell you, 'You're out of your mind—look at our *thousands* of dead!' " He added, "For the sake of our Luftwaffe prestige, there can't be a second Frankfurt. Perhaps you can take it. *I* can't!"

Summoned to Hitler's presence the next day and cursed for ninety minutes, Göring showed off the new production program, number 224. It featured the

*Rommel had discovered thirty-eight thousand barrels in the tunnels at La Spezia; the Germans also seized 123 million liters of gasoline.

262 jet for the first time, but Hitler's eagle eye detected what Göring's had not—that bomber production virtually vanished in the spring of 1944 although he was calling for a strike force by May 1944 capable of defeating the expected Allied invasion in the west.

Göring transmitted Hitler's anger vocally to his staff. "I was told I just had to hold tight for a year," he raged, "and then everything would come out right in mid-1944. But that's not true. This month the program shows 410 bombers, and next October only 266. . . . What on earth is the field marshal [Milch] thinking of? I want an end to this swindling, once and for all," he shouted, losing his temper. "This is worse than under Udet. Where's the 'production increase'?" He learned only now that the He 177 would have no rear gun turret at all. Göring suddenly snapped. Face glistening, he ordered the arrest of Udet's erstwhile chief engineer Reidenbach by the Gestapo, along with his "fellow bunglers." "There's to be no court-martial . . . If they're at fault they'll be executed. Just watch—if we announce in a week's time that the former heads of development and planning and the chief of staff of air armament have all been shot—that'll make the whole herd of swine sit up and take notice!" His staff listened in bemused silence. Göring reddened. "The field marshal is always talking about shooting people," he screamed. "When *I* say it, it will be done without mercy. I am not all mouth!"

Shaken by the increasing daring of the American raids, Göring flew down to the Obersalzberg—although he was now understandably reluctant to commit his valuable person to the unfriendly skies. As his Focke-Wulf 200 droned south for four hours, his colorful imagination came into play as vividly as though he were once again on the battlements of Veldenstein. Now he imagined himself an American air gunner, trapped in a Flying Fortress while hundreds of Nazi fighter planes zeroed in and hammered away relentlessly from every quarter. After an hour he realized that *his ammunition belts were empty*. Around him (in his imaginary scenario) the other guns were jammed or the gunners were dead or dying. By the time his plane landed near the Obersalzberg, he knew how to defeat the Americans: attack and attack and attack. "There's not one squadron that could take that," he told Galland and the generals at his villa on the seventh.

Galland blinked skeptically and lit a cigar.

"How long can you fire—from every buttonhole?" persisted Göring.

"Seven minutes," replied the fighter force commander.

"Right," said Göring, and did the calculation for him. "That means you can make three sorties to engage the enemy during each four-hour raid—if you really wade into them!"

Galland hesitated to commit himself.

"Three times," said Göring flatly. "I insist!"

Thus he became the architect of the Luftwaffe's biggest victory over the American bombers one week later.

For three days, meanwhile, on October 7, 8, and 9, 1943, he held a technical inquisition. His tongue had lost none of its edge. "Our Luftwaffe," he would brood to his generals on the eighth, "is at the bottom of an abyss. It has lost the confidence of the public and the armed forces. . . . The people are saying that our fighters chicken out and trail along behind while the big enemy squadrons fly unmolested over our cities for hours on end in 'Nuremberg party rally' style. Yes, that's the catchphrase now."

Milch defended the fighter pilots. To Göring, however, these youngsters were just "pussyfoots." "They just have to close the enemy to four hundred yards instead of a thousand; they just have to bring down eighty instead of twenty. Then their low spirits will be gone, and I will doff my hat to them. But as for taking potshots at two thousand yards, my attitude is this: *Götz von Berlichingen* [Lick my ass]!"

As he was speaking the next day, October 9, a message was handed in to him. Despite a colossal air battle over northern Germany involving German fighters from all over Central Europe, the American bombers had wrecked 90 percent of the Focke-Wulf assembly plant at Marienburg in East Prussia. "Things can't go on like this much longer," announced Göring. "Orders must go to Minister Speer at once to build six underground factories for fighter planes."

The Americans had lost twenty-eight bombers that day. They took revenge by attacking Münster on October 10, and lost thirty more. At midday on the fourteenth, Göring called a conference of aircraft-industry bosses at Berchtesgaden. They were two acrimonious hours, with Professor Messerschmitt's utopian Me 264 New York bomber high on the agenda. "If only," said Göring wistfully, "we could manage that—dropping a few bombs over there [on the United States] and forcing the blackout on them too!" More rational minds argued, however, that working on the 264 would delay the Me 262 jet, which Hitler had now rediscovered as the cure to all his strategic problems. "I do need that [New York] bomber," agreed Göring with a sigh, "but the fighter is more important."

At that very moment an historic air battle had begun. It was the day that the U.S. Air Force nearly fell out of the sky. Their target was once more the ball-bearing factories at Schweinfurt. Word reached Göring of the drama as he drove back up the lanes to his Obersalzberg villa. As the American escort fighters withdrew, Galland's squadrons closed in, hurling bombs, rockets, machine-gun, and cannon fire at the three hundred heavy bombers. This time, as Göring had ordered, the fighters were landing all over southern Germany to refuel, rearm, and take off again. With big gaps already torn in their tight formations, the lead bombers of the U.S. First Air Division hit Schweinfurt at 2:40 P.M. At 2:57 P.M., 160 German fighters thundered in simultaneously to attack the withdrawing bombers. For only 14 losses that day Galland would claim to have destroyed 121 of the Americans. Proud and happy at this very real victory, Göring telephoned Hitler at 9:00 P.M.

As bad luck would have it, his rival and enemy Albert Speer was sitting next to Hitler at the precise moment that phone call came through. Putting down his knife and fork, the young minister slipped out to phone one of the ball-bearing factories. The foreman told him that the whole town was devastated. Speer hurried back to report this to Hitler in his own triumphant way. Speer's report at least temporarily diminished the impact of Göring's. In fact, not one tank or plane was lost to the Nazi production in consequence of this raid. The Americans made no further attempt to penetrate deep into the Reich until they obtained proper long-range fighter cover in early 1944.

After Schweinfurt, Göring decided it was safe to go out and tour the ravaged cities of the Rhineland. He had already decided to inspect the fighter, flak, and radar organizations. Surprisingly, wherever his bulletproof limousine halted—whether in Cologne, Wuppertal, Krefeld, or Bochum—he was mobbed by cheering civilians. He took in all the unfamiliar sights of the blitz—people reopening stores amid the rubble; messages chalked on broken walls from relatives seeking next of kin; signboards pointing to shelters; and broad arrows indicating safe escape routes if the whole city should catch fire. True, when Göring appeared, there were ironic shouts of "Call me Meier!" but there were mothers holding out babies to him as well. "I'm human too," he said a few days later, "and I would have understood it if these people who had just ruins all around them—just rubble to the left and right of them—upon seeing a brass hat go by (and the one responsible for the whole mess at that, or at least responsible for their defense)—might, well, not exactly toss rotten eggs at me, but at least throw the odd scowl or shout 'You fat old lump!' " He turned to the generals who had witnessed these scenes with him. "You saw how the people all streamed over to me. What a welcome! I could have cried. And in the fifth year of the war at that! That's when I knew," he continued, "that provided we, their leaders, don't perpetrate any really serious blunders, we can't lose this war!"

In a similarly optimistic vein he addressed bomber pilots of the hard hit KG2 on an air base in Holland. "How he cursed the Dutch," recalled one listener, radio operator Corporal Schürgers, shot down soon after:

> He said, "I noticed this morning as I was driving here through Holland, how the mob of women was loafing around with rucksacks and picnicking in the woods of a Sunday morning, instead of working for a living like any decent German woman. *She* is standing at a lathe right now, while these lazy beggars gallivant around and gape at me as I drive past."
>
> "Gentlemen," says he, "I'll soon put a stop to that. I want all Dutchmen who are too idle to work locked up."

Up speaks old Sperrle. "Well, Herr Reichsmarschall, that's easier said than done. We've got to show respect—"

"To hell with respect in wartime," says he. "Do you think the Russians would have their own soldiers laboring on an airfield or something? Let's show them who's boss around here!"

"In Holland," continued another NCO, a Dornier observer, "Hermann told us that the evacuees from the Ruhr are coming to Holland. The Dutch will have to live in encampments."

Göring spent the night of October 22–23 at the main fighter-control center at Arnhem. That night's RAF attack unfurled with all the cunning of a poker game—with feints and decoy runs, with the main bomber stream and Mosquitoes darting about Germany tossing out aluminium foil and false flares. As the fighter controller began broadcasting the running commentary, a German émigré began transmitting false directions from Dover countermanding his. Göring intervened several times, warning the pilots, "*Achtung!* Those orders were fake!" An unholy confusion resulted. By midnight the city of Kassel—home of the Fieseler Aircraft Works, where the Luftwaffe flying bomb was being mass-produced, was ablaze. Six thousand citizens would perish in this second fire storm in Germany.

Addressing fighter pilots the next morning in a hangar at Arnhem's Deelen Airbase, Göring angrily accused them of being "leery"—"In fact, a lot of you are *very* leery." He scornfully recalled their boast that they would make a meal of the "four-engine jobs" if they came close. "Well," he said, "they've come close. But so far, no meal!" "Bear one thing in mind: The German public is suffering terribly, day and night, from the enemy bombing terror. By night, they can understand in part, because they realize it isn't all that easy to tackle a bomber in the dark. What they don't grasp is why you can't do it by day—in brilliant weather—and they say so in countless letters to me. After seeing how you fight, they tell me I obviously just recalled *cripples* to take over the air defense. If I now make your losses public, and tell them, 'Wait—we have three airmen dead and eight or even twelve are missing,' they're going to tell me: 'We thought they were soldiers! They know war isn't child's play!' " Glowering at the rows of pilots, Göring thundered, "I can assure you of one thing. I will not have cowards in my air force. I will root them out."

On October 27, 1943, Hitler called a top-level conference on whether or not to pull out of the Crimea. Göring repeated the arguments to his own staff the next day.

GÖRING: In Russia, in the vast outfield that we have won, we can *operieren* [make tactical withdrawals]. But we must have the firm resolve to have so many troops under arms by a given time—

spring [1944] at the latest—that we can kick the Russians out all over again. Whether the Russians are at Krivoy Rog or one hundred miles closer to us or not—that is not vital.

What *is* vital is to be able . . . to prevent any second front emerging in the west at the same time.

And this is where our air force is of crucial importance. The Führer made this quite clear yesterday, in the presence of Dönitz. The Führer said, ''The jet fighter with bombs will be vital, because at the given moment it will scream at top speed along the [invasion] beaches and hurl its bombs into the massive buildup that is bound to be there.''

I thought to myself, ''I don't know if we'll have the jets by then.''

He had informed Hitler that he had just run into Messerschmitt at Neuburg Airfield, and that the professor had warned him the Me 262 was running three months late because he needed four thousand more workers. Hitler ''almost had a stroke,'' said Göring.

Arriving at Messerschmitt's now-tattered Regensburg factory on November 2, 1943, Milch challenged Göring with what he regarded as the vital question—how the Reich was to be defended in the spring when the Americans began returning with long-range fighter escorts.

''Even if every single German city is razed to the ground,'' barked Göring, ''the German nation will survive! . . . It lived long before there were cities. Even if we have to live in caves! But if the Bolsheviks pour in, life comes to an end for us.'' Resorting to a rhetoric that masked the really prophetic quality of his words, he continued that he saw in fact two cardinal dangers: the first, ''When we are told one fine day that the Soviets have Army Group So-And-So in Silesia, and another in East Prussia—that there's one on the river Vistula and another advancing up the Oder.'' The second danger was Britain and her air force, the RAF. ''That's why I still need a bomber force—for defense. I've got to be able to bomb them. For two years they haven't been bombed. But,'' he exclaimed, ''the moment the British try to land in France and establish their second front, I'm not going to leave a single fighter plane to defend the Reich: That same day everything that can fly will be sent across [to France].

''If the British once get a foothold on the Continent,'' he explained, ''that would be fatal for us. If they bomb our cities for those two or three days, that is bad but not fatal.''

37

THE BLIND LEADING
THE BLIND

Göring would admit to the gauleiters in November 1943 that the
Luftwaffe could never regain su-
periority in numbers. The enemy's thousand-bomber raids were now a com-
monplace. "Just a year ago," wrote Herbert Backe sarcastically afterward,
"he was talking of [the Americans] as a race of razor-blade and button
manufacturers. It's hair-raising. But," added the Staatssekretär, "he has
declared that he will publicly pronounce retribution the moment we can attack
the [British] Isles with one hundred planes."

Understandably Göring vested his hopes in the new jet. "I don't want to
come up with the 262 half a year too late," he had remarked nervously in
mid-October. A modest preproduction series was now planned—one Me 262
in January 1944, eight in February, forty in March, and sixty a month after
that. Real mass production would not begin until November 1944.

Displaying the kind of energy that only occasionally spurred him now,
the Reichsmarschall toured the jet-aircraft plants in November 1943. At
Regensburg, on November 2, Professor Messerschmitt showed him the sixth
Me 262 prototype to be built and a new, top-secret rocket-powered interceptor, the Me 163. Overimpressed as usual whenever he saw a new plane,

Göring spoke of attaining supersonic flight, and announced that Hitler wanted the Me 262 primarily for a bomber role against the Allied invasion forces.

"But Herr Reichsmarschall!" beamed the professor, eager to deceive. "We have always provided for two bomb racks in the plane . . . One 500-kilo, or two 250-kilo bombs!"

Göring believed him, and asked how long it would take to install the bomb-release gear.

"Two weeks," answered Messerschmitt without batting an eyelash.

Visiting Dessau on the fourth, Göring inspected the Junkers production lines tooling up for the Jumo 004-B jet engine, and saw the prototype of the near-supersonic swept-wing Ju 287 jet bomber too. His last stop was at Brandenburg, where the Arado Company had now assembled five prototypes of Professor Blume's Arado 234 jet bomber. It had a top speed of 500 mph and a range of a thousand miles. There were plans to manufacture one thousand by mid-1945.

Thus things would look up for the Reich if the war lasted long enough, and Göring no doubt emphasized this when he reported to Hitler on the sixth. Generals Zeitzler and Korten had just briefed Hitler on their respective "revenge" weapons—the A-4 rocket and the Fi-103 flying bomb. The catapult sites and launching bunkers in France would be completed by mid-December. Hitler began to talk of delivering what he called a "New Year's present" to the British.

At Dessau the Reichsmarschall had advised Junkers to find underground floor space as soon as possible for production. "What has been damaged by fire," he told them, "is beyond repair." Speaking to the assembled gauleiters in Munich on November 8, he asked their help in locating suitable tunnels and caves. He also promised them that the He 177 bomber—in which he had still not lost faith—would one day carry to London six tons of Trialen, an explosive twice as powerful as anything the RAF had developed. "There are, thank God," he added, "lots of extraordinarily important targets along the east coast that we shall tackle first. It is better to wipe out a town of one hundred thousand people entirely by a terror raid, than to make a dent in a giant city."

His fighter planes were now also much more heavily armed than a year earlier, and he was imbuing a spirit of self-sacrifice in the pilots. On the same November 8, Colonel Galland was heard issuing this order, number 2159, to his squadron commanders, creating an elite shock troop within the fighter force: "The Reichsmarschall has ordered the setting up of a *Sturm Staffel* [storm unit]. It is to scatter the enemy bombers using heavily armored fighters in level, close-formation attack, pressed home to point blank range."

The intercepted signal specifically left it to each pilot whether to destroy the enemy by shooting him down at minimum range "or by ramming." "Once initiated, the attack by storm units will," Galland continued, quoting

Göring's order, "be carried right into the heart of the enemy without regard for losses." Galland asked for volunteers—"pilots who are absolutely determined to take their opponent down with them rather than land without a victory."

RAF Bomber Command had promised to win the war by obliterating Berlin. On November 22, 1943, they began their attempt, launching a raid that killed fifteen hundred Berliners, inflicted serious damage on the ministries and factories, and totally wrecked Göring's "pet," his Forschungsamt. On the following morning he invited Korten, Milch, and their bleary-eyed production experts out to Carinhall to discuss routine problems of jet-aircraft production and the shortage of skilled industrial manpower. Milch pleaded with him to draw Hitler's attention to the army's reserves of manpower— the field marshal claimed that of 8.3 million German soldiers now on the eastern front only 260,000 were actually *fighting*. "Two million soldiers," he insisted, "could be moved into the front line proper in three weeks." But visiting Hitler on the twenty-fourth, Göring was cowed into adopting precisely the opposite line: According to Admiral Dönitz's record, Göring declared himself convinced that a large number of new front-line soldiers could be obtained from the Luftwaffe's rear areas, never mentioning the army's.

That night the RAF returned to Berlin, killing twelve hundred civilians and devastating the Chancellery, the famous Kaiserhof Hotel, and the entire government district. Göring had forbidden the flak to open fire since 193 German fighters were scrambled, but on this occasion the fighters arrived too late to destroy more than a few attackers.

To restore his Luftwaffe's sagging prestige, Göring ordered an impromptu display of its newest equipment for Hitler. He directed his engineers to assemble everything possible—including the Hs 293 and Fritz antishipping missiles, the radars, jets, and the flying bomb at Insterburg airbase, which was a short train journey from the Wolf's Lair—on November 26. With the same recklessness that he kept accusing his engineers of, Göring even ordered prototypes of planes not yet in production to be shown, like the Junkers 388 bombers, an updated Ju 88 powered by two double-row radial BMW 801's. "It doesn't actually have to fly," he had pleaded to them on the twenty-third. "Just so the Führer can see it!"

As a public-relations exercise, the display was a disaster for Göring.

Plucking the program out of Milch's hand, the Reichsmarschall read out the specifications as he conducted Hitler past the rank of parked planes and missiles. Abreast of the stubby, squat Fi-103 flying bomb Hitler asked when it would be ready. Kröger, a Luftwaffe staff engineer from Peenemünde, volunteered, "By the end of March 1944." Hitler's face darkened, and Göring, who knew that Hitler was thinking of New Year's Eve, winced.

At the Me 262 jet fighter, Hitler again paused. "I'm not interested in this plane as a fighter," he commented. "Does it carry bombs?"

Messerschmitt bounded forward, saluted, and announced that the 262 could carry one ton.

Hitler announced, "I order this plane built as a bomber!"

He took only Milch onto the roof of the control tower to watch the 262 fly past. "The Reichsmarschall," he said, "is too fat to get up through the trapdoor."

Göring returned to the hunting lodge at Rominten. At Carinhall, gangs of laborers had completed installing twenty-millimeter flak positions and bunkers across the surrounding Schorf Heath. Scores of soldiers were sweeping the leaves of autumn off the estate's asphalt roads, in case the Reichsmarschall returned. But although he had two well-equipped air-raid shelters at Carinhall—one for family and one for staff—Göring decided to remain in East Prussia, far from the howl of the sirens and the blast of the bombs.

On the night of the Insterburg display the RAF sent 450 planes to Berlin and 178 on a diversionary raid to Stuttgart.

Hitler ordered Göring to exact violent retribution against London. The Reichsmarschall called Koller and Pelz aboard his train and directed them to scrape together every available Ju 188, Ju 88, Me 410, and He 177 for Operation Capricorn—planning to saturate the city's air defenses by sending in first 300 bombers, then 200 of them returning that same night, and 150 more the following morning. Pelz suggested sending the ten He 177's to drop two 2500-kilo bombs each, filled with Trialen, on Parliament.

Göring greedily approved. "Just imagine the effect," he chuckled, "of twenty Bix Maxes thumping down with this super explosive in them!"

On December 3, he issued the formal order for a general new blitz on Britain's industrial centers and ports, and directed that the German bombers were, like the British, to carry 70 percent incendiary loads and the biggest blast bombs available. Leaving written instructions with Field Marshal Milch that the Me 262 was "only to be regarded as a jet *bomber*" as Hitler had ordained, Göring departed for Paris on the sixth, to supervise Capricorn the Blitz on London.

In Paris, surrounded by the familiar cosmopolitan sights and aromas, he reverted to his old haunts and habits. He had been trying for some time to prise out of the Musée de Cluny a fabulous example of German goldsmiths' craft—the Basel altar known as the Antependium of Emperor Otto II. He proposed a swap, acquired title to the three objects offered in exchange, and on December 11, 1943, had the magnificent, ornate Antepedium brought around to the Quai d'Orsay. But the French had now grown crafty: They sensed which way the war was turning, and wanted to make a *gift* of it in recognition of the Reichsmarschall's "services in protecting the national treasures." A gift, in their view, could be subsequently recovered. Outsmarted, Göring gave up this particular quest. Deciding to examine the altar anyway, he knelt artlessly down to scrutinize the pedestal's workmanship.

The museum directors chuckled silently at the image of the paunchy, be-medaled Reichsmarschall groveling before their ancient altar.

Capricorn was delayed, first by weather, then by equipment shortages. Wanting to spend Christmas with his family, Göring returned to Carinhall.

The British night raids on Berlin had not diminished. On typical nights high-powered British transmitters flooded the fighter-controller's radio chan-nels with bell sounds and snatches of Adolf Hitler's speeches. On December 16, Hitler instructed Göring to speed up the Me 262 bomber—although Hitler was thinking now less of reprisals than of the coming Allied invasion. "With every month," he confided to his staff two days later still, "the probability grows that we'll get at least one squadron of jet planes. The vital thing is to rain bombs down on the enemy the moment they invade. . . . Even if there's only one plane up, they'll have to take cover and they'll lose hour after hour! Within half a day we'll be bringing up our reserves. Even if they're pinned down on the beach only six or eight hours, you can figure what that'll mean for them.''

That Christmas his troops in Italy presented Göring with something of a cuckoo's egg. His aides Brauchitsch, Gritzbach, and Hofer unpacked from sixteen crates at Carinhall some of the rarest art treasures Göring had ever seen—a prebirthday surprise from the paratroops in Italy. Even Göring be-came uneasy at theft on such a grand scale. His inquiries revealed that the Italians had evacuated 187 such crates from Naples galleries to the moun-taintop abbey at Monte Cassino. With the connivance of the new Nazi "Art Protection Commission" in Rome, the Hermann Göring Division had offered to transport them to the Vatican—but only 172 crates would eventually arrive there (on January 4). The contents of the other sixteen now lay spread out for the Reichsmarschall's delectation—lifesize bronze statues of Hermes Resting, a female dancer, an Apollo from Pompeii, two stags from the Herculaneum, antique gold and silver, and a stack of paintings too: two Titians ("Danse" and "Portrait of Lavinia"), a Claude Lorrain landscape, a Raphael, a Tiepolo, a Palma Vecchio, and Pieter Breughel the Elder's famous painting of "The Blind Leading the Blind." His barely used con-science sorely troubled, Göring put them on "temporary" display at Carinhall and asked Hitler for a ruling on this booty. Hitler told him to remove them immediately to the safety of the flak bunker at *Kurfürst*, air-force headquarters outside Berlin.

Ironically it was thus Göring and Hitler who rescued these famous treasures for posterity. American officers afterward solemnly accused the Reichsmar-schall of having "stolen" the Monte Cassino treasures: In view of the de-predations visited by their strategic bombers upon the historic abbey just a few weeks later, in February 1944, they were, however, in no position to press their point.

* * *

The year 1944 would see the final ruination of Germany's most beautiful cities, but also the beginning of a painful Luftwaffe revival, with the jet-propelled aircraft leading the way. On January 3, 1944, Hitler told Göring that he attached top priority now to the new U-boat types XXI and XXIII, and to these jet planes. "If I get them in time," he reiterated, "I can ward off the invasion." It had become an obsession for him. From *Asia* that evening, Göring sent a telegram to Milch to ask whether they could scrap even more aircraft types to boost the jet's production. With Heinrich Himmler's help he now planned to put mass-production lines for both the 262 and its Jumo 004 jet engine underground, in a cavernous factory beneath the Harz Mountains. There was no time to be lost: On the seventh, British newspapers revealed that they too were working on jet propulsion.

Göring's fifty-first birthday, a few days later, was a shadow of its predecessors.

Any last vestiges of festive mood were spoiled by a demanding inquiry from Hitler about the heavy Me 410 fighter armed with the fifty-millimeter cannon, one of the planes displayed to him at Insterburg. "Again and again," Göring testily cabled to Milch that day, "the Führer inquires how many of these planes are in operation. Since I unfortunately have to tell the Führer that virtually no such planes are in operation, and that only two or three have been equipped with the cannon, the Führer has begun to look upon such displays in the same light as the famous Rechlin one [of July 1939]."

On January 20, 1944, the RAF dropped twenty-four hundred tons of bombs on Berlin, an extraordinary effort considering the range, and considering the Luftwaffe's difficulties one year earlier in lifting just one hundred tons over the short range to Stalingrad. On the following night Göring launched the much-delayed Operation Capricorn. He believed that three hundred or four hundred bombers had attacked London, but the British mockingly put the number arriving at about thirty. "You've got agents," snorted Hitler at General Korten. "Find out!" Göring fled to Carinhall, preferring the thunder of the raids on Berlin to the hidden tones of menace in Hitler's voice.

That winter the paratroop general Bernard Ramcke came to see the Reichsmarschall in this, his natural habitat. For Ramcke it was an unforgettable experience.

Brauchitsch apologized that Göring was sleeping late after a five-hour dispute with Milch the day before. Upon awakening, Göring had a posse of art dealers to haggle with. It was 7:00 P.M. by the time Ramcke strutted into the lavishly appointed, sixty-foot-long library lined with priceless furniture and precious books. "Lieutenant General Ramcke," he announced, saluting. "Commander of the Second Paratroop Division, reporting fit and at your service." (He had broken an arm.) His steel front teeth glinted in the pink light.

Göring was sitting in a finely crafted armchair reading a red leather-bound book with gold lettering. He rose to his feet, the sleeves of his gold-brocaded robe of green silk plush uncoiling down his arms. Ramcke took note of the silk plush—it looked familiar—and of the lacquered slippers, the golden belt, hem, and tassels, and noticed the well-permed hair and well-oiled rosy features. ("A cloud of the finest Oriental aromas wafted from his outsize cheekbones toward me," chuckled Ramcke afterward, relating the episode to fellow generals.) "Well, Ramcke," said Göring, nonchalantly laying aside the book. "How have you been getting on?"

The emeralds in his gold and platinum rings matched the silk robe, noticed Ramcke. As he began chiding Göring for never visiting one of his paratroop units—let alone seeing the men jump—Edda came gamboling in. "Papa, Papa! My pearl necklace broke all over the floor, and look, Papa, I found them all!"

The Reichsmarschall gathered the child up in his arms. "Oh, your lovely necklace!"

He began threading it for her. A kiss was planted on her. "And now one for Papa!"

Ramcke, tiring of the display of domesticity, realized where he had seen the robe's green silk plush before—on a new lampshade in his own home. Down in Italy Bruno Loerzer's headquarters had been at Taormina, and the locals had produced textile goods as tourist souvenirs. Ramcke had bought a lampshade, and Göring evidently this robe.

By night the fighter squadrons turned the war in the air Göring's way, and decisively.

On February 19–20 the RAF dispatched 816 bombers to Leipzig. Schmid's experts plotted the bomber stream's radar emissions perfectly. Although the defense radar was again jammed and voice communications swamped by the familiar bell sounds and Hitler speeches, the weather was fine enough to detect the enemy route changes, and 294 German fighters made contact, bringing down 78 of the RAF planes. No bomber force could sustain this loss rate for long.

By day it was a different story. On the morning of February 20, one thousand American bombers opened "Big Week"—the attempt to throttle Göring's air force once and for all. Over the next five days they set down ten thousand tons of bombs accurately on every important target of Göring's aircraft industry.

For an instant it appeared that the Luftwaffe was defeated. The week-long offensive left thousands of Göring's skilled aircraft workers in mass graves and the gutted, useless skeletons of hundreds of half-built planes on wrecked production lines. But Göring gave Field Marshal Milch permission to set up an interministerial, troubleshooting Fighter Staff (*Jägerstab*), and even agreed to allow it to be placed under the control of Karl-Otto Saur, Speer's loud-mouthed, dynamic right-hand man. That way, Albert Speer could no longer evade final responsibility for the Reich's air defenses. The Speer ministry rose to the challenge and released the vitally needed raw materials and machine tools; aircraft production began to pick up again.

On February 24, Göring packed his suitcase aboard *Asia* and told his staff he was taking three weeks leave at Veldenstein Castle.

The next day the new fighter staff met for the first time—at Speer's ministry. It was a further significant abdication of power by Göring to his rivals.

38

IMMINENT DANGER WEST

While the new fighter staff—Milch, Saur, and their principal lieutenants—toured the ravaged aircraft factories in a special train in the days after the fires and carnage of Big Week, Hermann Göring and his "little air staff" relaxed in their Franconian castle at Veldenstein. A seventy-two-hour week was introduced throughout the aircraft industry. Driven—whether by the desire for victory or the thirst for revenge—the men, working often in factory buildings stripped of roofs and windows, achieved a production miracle. Their factory delegates came with Milch and Saur to the castle to report to Göring and his chief of staff Günther Korten on March 4, 1944. Göring passed on to them the word that the Führer was ordering work begun at once on two big bomb-proof aircraft factories. Milch noted maliciously in his pocket diary afterward, "He was lacquering his fingernails!"

That same day the American bombers made their deepest daylight thrust into Germany yet, to targets near Berlin. On the seventh, after they bombed Berlin itself, Hitler assigned top priority to aircraft production—putting Göring's factories even above those producing the tanks and submarines on which victory must ultimately depend. On the eighth, Milch and Galland stood outside the 1st Fighter Division operations room at Döberitz watching the glittering procession of hundreds of American bombers high above the capital yet again—"An extraordinary picture with their condensation trails," Milch entered thoughtfully in his pocket notebook.

Despite these raids, morale in Berlin remained high. The Japanese ambassador cabled to Tokyo that he had seen people crowding the streets to watch the spectacle "with scarcely any signs of cringing on their faces." He attributed this "excellent morale" to the Nazi party's prompt relief measures like the "Göring Relief Train" (which distributed the food and black-market luxuries bought by Colonel Veltjens in the occupied west.) The Allies' saturation-bombing raids were in short, producing, an unintended result—people felt that they had no alternative but to fight on to the bitter end.

This trend was reflected in the ascendancy of radicals like Himmler and Bormann. Himmler came to Veldenstein for the afternoon on March 9, to report to the Reichsmarschall on the use of slave labor. He had already supplied thirty-six thousand convicts to Göring, and promised over fifty thousand more for the mass-production lines, as well as one hundred thousand additional convicts to labor on the underground and bunker excavations.

Later that month Hitler arrived in Bavaria. Fearing an increase in Bormann's influence—the Obersalzberg was Bormann's domain—Göring moved from Veldenstein to his villa, to be closer to Hitler's. He did not attend many conferences, however, while Bormann and Himmler rarely missed them. On March 25, Himmler reported to the Führer that eighty RAF airmen had tunneled their way out of a prison camp in Silesia and that millions of man-hours would be wasted in hunting them down. Hitler ordered Himmler to take control of any airmen who were recaptured, and Göring later heard disquieting rumors that they had been shot by the SS for "resisting arrest." "With what were they supposed to have offered resistance?" he indignantly asked an interrogator years later. His only orders at the time were for the commandant, a Colonel von Lindeiner, to be court-martialed for negligence: Stalag Luft III, like other camps, had been equipped with the most sensitive cathode-ray display devices to detect tunneling sounds.

Göring's prestige was in steep decline. After General Gerd von Schwerin reported to Hitler from the Russian front that spring, General Schmundt accompanied him out to his car and laughed out loud at the mention of Göring's name. "Nobody," he said, "takes the Reichsmarschall seriously anymore!"

Göring had quiet hopes of recovering his political authority by defeating the Allied invasion in the west. He had issued his first order to prepare for the invasion on July 23, 1943; further orders had followed on December 6 and 15, followed on February 27, 1944, by the basic directive for defeating what he code-named *Imminent Danger West*. His fighter forces were now largely concentrated in the Reich: Here, he had eleven squadrons of single-engined and seven of twin-engined day fighters, and twenty-six squadrons of night fighters. His plan was to reinforce Luftflotte 3, in France, from these squadrons defending the Reich the moment an invasion operation began. While certain units like ZG26, ZG76, and the "bad-weather squadrons" of JG300 and JG301 would remain with Luftflotte Reich, he would rush nineteen fighter squadrons (the entire I Air Corps) to France along with a number of bomber squadrons and reconnaissance flights; eight of the fighter squadrons would be converted there to fighter-bombers and placed under II Air Corps (General Buelowius) as a ground-attack command. That was the plan, and Göring hammered it in with a number of orders that spring. "Invasion, invasion, invasion," one captured Ju 188 pilot was heard whispering to another in April. "You'd better believe it. That is going to be the clincher!" He recited two orders issued by Göring to be read out on the invasion front—one assigning specific altitudes to bomber squadrons for daylight formation attacks on the Allied invasion fleet, and the other saying verbatim: "This invasion *must* be defeated even if there's no German Air Force left at the end of it. . . . What Eisenhower asks of his troops I expect from my Luftwaffe, but more so."

Even before this exhortation, the fanatical Nazi woman aviator Hanna Reitsch had begun dreaming of a suicide force to attack the Allied invasion fleet—"piloted," as she put it under interrogation, "by healthy young men who believe that through their deaths thousands of soldiers and civilians can be saved." She was thinking in terms of one thousand volunteers. She took the project to Hitler on February 28, 1944, at the Berghof. Hitler scoffed at the idea of a kamikaze force. "It is not in keeping with the German character," he told her, but authorized her to develop the plan. Himmler welcomed it as a useful employment for condemned criminals. A suitable explosive chariot was selected—initially Reitsch picked the still-experimental Me 328 flying bomb: The pilot would guide it into the sea just short of the target; its two-thousand-pound warhead would explode beneath the hull. An aviation doctor at Rechlin was asked to investigate how close to suicide man could go and still function logically.

At the top Luftwaffe level Hanna Reitsch found little enthusiasm, however. Korten was lukewarm, and instructed Colonel Heigl of KG200, the special weapons Geschwader, to take the project up. Göring showed no enthusiasm at all for the scheme. "We needed strong leadership," Reitsch later said, criticizing the spirit with which the Reichsmarschall had imbued the Luftwaffe. "Leadership, tempered with an idealism to match our own."

Such thinking was not German exclusively. There was also fanaticism among the stoical British bomber crews, who kept doggedly coming back for more despite punishing losses. A Junkers 88 attacked an RAF heavy bomber over Stuttgart on March 15, raking it from underneath with a long burst from its "sloping music" (*schräge Musik*), a cannon set at an angle in the Junkers' roof. "We pulled up and opened fire," the sergeant-navigator Kugler said ruefully later. "We raked them from stem to stern. . . . They were dropping and on fire, but their rear gunner still opened fire on us! He was going down in flames, but he killed my radio operator and 'coachman'; missed me, but my plane was on fire and I had to bail out.''

Two weeks later, on the night of March 30–31, Göring scored his biggest defense victory of the war. The RAF bombers' night target was Nuremberg. Despite deafening jamming and clever feint operations, the fighters had no difficulty in sighting their prey as the eight hundred bombers scraped condensation trails across the clear moonlit sky, betraying their general position once more by their radar emissions. Schmid fed a total of 246 fighters of the 1st, 2nd, 3rd, and 7th Fighter Divisions into the bomber stream. ''From south of Bonn onward,'' his war diary grimly records, ''the bomber stream's route was marked by crashes.'' The fighters claimed to have destroyed 107 heavy bombers that night; the RAF's own records concede the loss of 94 over Germany, and a dozen more that crashed after limping back to Britain. After this catastrophe the RAF virtually called off their night offensive for six months.

A few hours later Milch was on the phone from Berlin with the March 1944 production figures.

''Tell him I got them already from Saur,'' said Göring at the Obersalzberg. Despite the crippling losses of Big Week, their factories had manufactured more planes that month than ever before—turning out 1,670 new fighter aircraft and repairing 530 more. It was in its way a victory over the Americans as satisfactory as the one just inflicted on the British.

As April 1944 began, Albert Speer was convalescing—or as some cynics put it, malingering—in the Tyrol. Walking on the mountainside with Speer's forceful deputy Karl-Otto Saur on the seventh, Hitler revealed his production strategy for the coming year. They could reconquer the Soviet Union and win the war only by increasing tank production. ''But the prerequisite for that,'' he said, ''is the one hundred percent fulfillment of the air-force program, to clear the skies over Germany this year.'' He said the same to Göring himself six days later. ''I need tanks and assault guns in deadly earnest. But first of all we've got to have a fighter umbrella over the Reich. That is the alpha and the omega of it all.''

Hitler considered that Speer had let him down badly. He had begun building a bunker for Me 262 jet production near Landsberg, but progress was slow. Now he told Göring to get on with the job, with or without Speer.

The next day Göring sent for Xavier Dorsch, chief of the Todt Organization that had built the autobahns before the war. Dorsch was on Speer's payroll, and loyally explained that Speer would not allow the OT to operate inside the Reich territories now. However, he did send for his own blueprints for bombproof aircraft factories, and Göring took the civil engineer up to see Hitler that evening. The Führer told them both to go ahead, regardless of what Speer might say. Walking on the seventeenth with Göring, on the sunny slopes of the Obersalzberg, Hitler told him that he would brook no further delay—he had to have a multistory underground factory to manufacture five hundred 262s per month, working around the clock. "First and foremost," Hitler explained, wearily spelling it out to the Reichsmarschall yet again, "I've got to be able to put a fighter 'dome' over anything I can't get under cover immediately. If I've got two thousand fighters on hand in the Reich, then the raids are going to cost the enemy too much . . . This 'cheese dome' of fighter planes constantly overhead—that's our top priority."

Göring passed this unchallengeable wisdom on two days later to Milch, Korten, Saur, Dorsch, and his own ubiquitous "little air staff." Blaming Speer for the delays, Göring recalled that he had asked for such a bombproof factory eight months before—"We could have had it long ago already."

Speer learned of this. From his place of "convalescence" he sent a long, paranoid letter to Hitler accusing everybody of plotting against him. Hitler ignored him, issued a formal decree to Dorsch to get on with the job, and ordered Göring to call a conference of civil engineers—"And do it without Herr Speer," he said, "so it is tackled with some gusto!"

Words like these were music to Göring's ears as he fought to maintain position on the slippery power slopes of the Obersalzberg. Fate had so far been exceptionally kind to him. He congratulated himself that the Allied strategic air forces had still not realized the real Achilles' heel of the Reich—the synthetic-oil plants. "I have heard," he speculated on April 19, "that the enemy isn't attacking them because he wants them for his own use. He thinks it's enough to pulverize our airplanes."

He was under no illusions about the coming of the Allied invasion. Against the opinion of most of the army generals, he and Hitler agreed that the invasion was likely to hit Normandy or the Cherbourg Peninsula. On April 25, his bombers executed their first attack on the invasion forces assembling at Portsmouth and Southampton. The returning planes reported sighting 264 probable tank-landing craft—enough to lift three divisions—and enough shipping for six more divisions dispersed along the south coast. The Luftwaffe photographs also revealed the prefabricated "Mulberry Harbor" caissons, each 68 meters by 20 meters, identified as "jetties for major landings." Coverage of the entire British coastline confirmed to Göring that this was the *only* invasion force. He transferred two of his best divisions, the 91st Airborne and the 5th Paratroop, to the Cherbourg Peninsula.

Another month had passed. Late on April 30, Saur phoned. They had now produced 1,859 new fighter planes and repaired 654. But on May 12, the Luftwaffe's terminal nightmare began. The Americans suddenly opened an offensive against the Reich's synthetic-oil refineries. The next day Allied code-breakers heard Göring ordering flak defenses switched from the already denuded Russian front and the aircraft factories at Oschersleben and Wiener Neustadt to the synthetic-oil plants. It was clear proof that the Germans were giving the defense of their oil a priority "even above the defense of aircraft manufacture," and the British code-breakers remarked upon it.

In the weeks before the invasion Göring was confronted with a moral issue that was to turn up again at his subsequent trial. Individual American fighter planes had begun machine-gunning trains and even civilians in the fields. The public responded with indiscriminate lynchings of crashed Allied airmen. More than one *German* pilot had to fight off peasants wielding pitchforks and shotguns in the resulting confusion. Shouts of "I am a German aviator!" were greeted more often than not with: "So, the *Schweinhund* even speaks German!" Göring had to issue *Deutsche Wehrmacht* brassards to his pilots. The high command deliberated on whether to sanction this lynch-mob justice. Göring wanted the Allied malfeasants dead, but favored the old-fashioned firing squad, preferably held "at once" and "in the locality of the action," as his staff were told on May 15. The problem would be to identify the actual culprits, as he pointed out to Hitler. After this discussion General Korten recorded that Hitler had decided that *in special cases* enemy aviators might be executed on the spot, e.g., for machine-gunning parachuting German airmen or public transport or individual civilians. Göring would later tell historian George Shuster that he had always instructed his officers to adhere to the Geneva Convention.

At one Hitler conference his aide Major Herbert Büchs saw the Reichsmarschall refuse the Führer's angry demand to be given the name of a Luftwaffe officer who had rescued an Allied airman from a lynch mob in Munich. A few weeks later, discussing the problem with Ribbentrop and Himmler, Göring again argued against lynch law, as is plain from his remarks on June 19: "We have to do all we can to stop members of the public acting against enemy airmen *not* involved in such acts. My view is that such acts can always be dealt with by the courts, since these are *murders*, which the enemy has forbidden his aviators to commit." There the matter would rest for the time being.

The respite on the Obersalzberg clearly did him good. But day after day, as Göring waited in his mountain villa for news of the invasion, the U.S. Fifteenth Air Force flew overhead from Italy making its way into Germany, while the U.S. Eighth Air Force flew southward by day from England and the RAF passed overhead by night en route to bomb targets in Hungary and Austria.

May 1944 was almost over, yet still the Allied invasion had not come. Göring, however, was satisfied that he had done all he could to prepare for it. On the twenty-fourth, his pilots procured magnificent photographic cover of Bournemouth, Poole, Portland, and Weymouth: These southwestern English ports were now crammed with invasion craft, confirming once more that Normandy, rather than the area around Calais, was the invasion target.

The Allies were beginning their final push toward Rome. On May 23, Korten brought Richthofen in to report on the Italian theater. "Reichsmarschall," wrote the field marshal later, "was very sensible. Gets the point of everything. Knows most of it, but unable to make decisions without the Führer. . . . Reichsmarschall looking good, and really sensible. . . . Reichsmarschall is optimistic."

The day began with an aircraft production conference held in the SS barracks on the Obersalzberg, chaired by Göring. Richthofen, who attended, was struck by the contrast between the Air Ministry veterans like Milch and the upcoming radicals clustered around the new "fighter-aircraft dictator," Saur. "Milch and his people were still in their old rut," wrote Richthofen in his diary afterward. "I said so to the Reichsmarschall afterward, and he basically agrees and wants changes."

"From the moment that America's entry into this war became inevitable," said Göring, according to the shorthand transcript, "it should have been clear to all of us that one day the enemy's numerical superiority would be colossal." The Allies had produced an armada of heavy bombers with devastating effect. The Germans had none even worth manufacturing now. General Korten warned that if Saur cut production of the remaining bomber types to 284 per month, the air force could not maintain more than twenty-four bomber squadrons. Göring paused, agonized, and left the crucial decision to the afternoon's session with Hitler himself.

It began at 3:00 P.M. As usual, Hitler's famous villa was outlandishly cold. He gazed absently across the valley while Milch began reading out the future aircraft-production figures until the field marshal reached the 262, listed under *fighters*. "I thought that was coming as a bomber!" Hitler barked, interrupting sharply.

The otl·rs exchanged uncomfortable glances. Milch had made the decision to build th ·m only as jet fighters, it turned out. "Is there anybody at all," snapped Hitler, "who obeys my orders?" He reminded them that at the Insterburg display he had ordered the 262 built only as a high-speed bomber—with its one ton of armorplate and armament replaced by bomb gear instead.

Milch could not remain silent. "Mein Führer," he exclaimed. "The smallest infant can see that this is a fighter, not a bomber aircraft!"

The next morning Göring confronted his generals—Korten, Koller, and Galland—with this new situation. They all agreed glumly that there was one obvious design problem: the one ton of armorplate was all *forward* of the jet's center of gravity, while any bomb gear would necessarily be *on* it. It was a major redesign that Hitler now called for.

"You gentlemen all seem to be deaf," said Göring. "I have kept repeating the Führer's perfectly clear order, again and again. He doesn't give a hoot for the Me 262 as a fighter. He just wants it initially as a fighter-bomber, a *Jadbomber*."

Asked when the plane could be operational as a bomber, Petersen made a wild guess. "Around three months," he said.

Göring thumped his fist on the table. The invasion was not going to wait for the 262. "You gentlemen dare to do what no civilian would ever dare —quite simply, to disregard orders! The most ill-disciplined bunch in Germany: our Wehrmacht, and our officer corps."

Hitler persisted over the coming weeks that the Me 262 was to be produced purely as a bomber. Perspiration glistening on his brow, Göring swore on his own life to comply. On May 27, 1944, he cabled to his generals, "The Führer has ordered the Me 262 to be operated exclusively as a high-speed bomber. There is until further notice no question of it as a fighter plane." Two days later he told General Galland that "to avoid misunderstandings" he was removing the 262 from Galland's jet-fighter specialist (Colonel Gordon Mac Gollob) and transferring it to Colonel Marienfeld as general of bombers.

Four days after this conference Göring saw Hitler strolling down the hill. He had come to pay his respects to little Edda on her sixth birthday. The child's mother detected a trace of irony in the "Frau Reichsmarschall" with which Hitler addressed her as he kissed her hand.

39
TOTAL SACRIFICE

"He would be awakened at nine," testified Göring, describing Hitler's life-style to interrogators, "read the newspapers, and then sleep some more. Then came the war conference. Ordinarily this lasted for three or four hours, during which he would get terribly excited." The news that excited Hitler one June 1944 morning was this: At 8:00 A.M. on the sixth, II Air Corps had signaled, "Enemy landed with strong forces between Dieppe and Cherbourg." It was the long-awaited Allied invasion at last.

Prodding the map unrolled across the marble table in the Berghof, Hitler announced triumphantly to Göring, "They're landing *here* and *here*—just where we expected!"

Göring beamed. For eleven months he had planned for this moment. Victory in Normandy would restore the Luftwaffe's diminished prestige for good. But what he had failed to bargain for was that the high command, befuddled by treason and complacency, would be so undecided that they could not rule during the first twenty-four hours whether this Normandy invasion was real or a feint.

Not until late on the seventh would the high command authorize Göring to start transferring the eight hundred fighter planes from the Reich to France.

Thus, for the air force the invasion battle was virtually lost before it began. Against the 10,585 sorties flown by Allied planes on the sixth, the Luftwaffe could muster only eighty Normandy-based fighter planes. Some units did make a fitful start from Germany. At 2:30 P.M. the first and second fighter squadrons of Jagd Geschwader 1 signaled that they were on their way with thirty-one and thirty-two FW 190's respectively; the third squadron reported, rather less ardently, that it would take off "when the thunderstorm now over the airfield has passed." The example of another unit, the third squadron of JG54, may stand for all the rest: Of twenty-two FW 190's setting out that evening from Cologne, only two arrived at the right destination—Villacoublay Airfield—and only one was serviceable the next day.

The papers of Karl Koller, Korten's deputy, show that by late on June 8, Buelowius had only five ground-attack planes and ninety-five fighters operational in Normandy. Allied code-breakers heard the Luftwaffe specify the airfields that seven new squadrons were to arrive at; within one hour those airfields were in Allied target dossiers. By the ninth, fifteen fighter squadrons (though still not the nineteen originally promised) had arrived with 475 Me 109's and FW 190's, of which total 290 were serviceable; but their airfields were moonscapes of bomb craters, and their ground organization nonexistent.

Richthofen's diary, however, reveals that optimism initially prevailed on the Obersalzberg. Koller's papers contain the upbeat message that Göring sent congratulating his staff on their brilliant work before the invasion. But the nectar of triumph soured even as it passed his lips. The BBC scoffed that the Germans had been caught with their pants down. Göring himself used a different sartorial metaphor. "The Reichsmarschall," his humorless office signaled all echelons on June 10, 1944, "has established that during enemy operations and the state of emergency men of the Luftwaffe have been sleeping with their clothes off." This signal too, was intercepted and deciphered by the British. This cipher weakness would prove crucial to the thwarting of Göring's anti-invasion operations in Normandy. On the seventh, for example, the British deciphered his orders to three fighter-bomber squadrons thus:

1. Concentrate attack on tank assemblies at Periers-sur-le-Dam. . .
2. Time of attack 17:00 hrs.
3. Fighter cover by simultaneous operation of elements of II Fighter Corps.

As things went awry in France, Göring recalled Hanna Reitsch and her suicide squadron. He found it had made little real progress. Production of the special Me 328 glider-chariot at Gotha was only fitful, so the unit was converting to the Fi 103 flying bomb, modified to include a pilot's cockpit; since several test pilots had been killed, Colonel Heigl of KG200 proposed using souped-up FW 190 fighter bombers instead: each could carry as much as a 1,800- or 1,400-kilo armor-piercing bomb (since it would not, of course, need any fuel for a return flight). Koller's record for June 9 confirms that Heigl's squadron had thirty-nine volunteers standing by to carry out what was coyly referred to as this "total operation" (*Totaleinsatz*) in fourteen days' time. Himmler, however, intervened to ask Hitler to forbid the premature mission and, on June 18, Koller noted that the Reichsmarschall also wanted "another talk with the Führer" about it. Incongruously, the supposedly life-weary glider pilots were unenthusiastic about converting to the dangerous, death-laden FW 190. When Lieutenant Colonel Werner Baumbach shortly replaced Heigl at KG200, the FW 190 plan was quietly shelved. Writing to Hitler on July 28, Speer would oppose wasting the brave men on the invasion ships —far more profitable, he would argue, to use them against the Soviet power stations instead. The suicide squadron became a hot potato. It was handed back to Hanna Reitsch, then to the scar-faced SS Colonel Otto Skorzeny. They forwarded it to Galland; he passed it to Göring, during a train journey from Rominten to Berlin; and the Reichsmarschall passed the buck to his lethargic crony, the chief of personnel Bruno Loerzer. This was his own sure way of ensuring that nothing got done.

There was an inherent fallacy, but only Galland seems to have spotted it. "I told my men," he recalled a year later, "that if you're going close enough to ram [a bomber] anyway, you can shoot them down *and* have a fifty-fifty chance of coming down alive."

On the first day of the Allied invasion Hitler had ordered Göring to launch the flying-bomb reprisal attack on London. After six days of rushed prepa-rations and a humiliating premature effort ending in fiasco, the pilotless missile attack on London was resumed in earnest on the fifteenth: 244 flying bombs were catapulted and an Me 410 pilot reported huge fires sweeping the British capital. Suddenly Göring was persona grata at the Berghof again.

Within a few weeks these missiles were destroying thirty thousand homes a day in South London. More important, they were diverting a colossal bombing effort away from German cities. In the twelve months up to the end of August 1944, the missile sites would attract 117,964 tons of Allied bombs.

That month the Luftwaffe scored another notable success. Earlier, Koller had requested permission to bring over their small strategic bomber force, IV Air Corps, from the eastern front for mining operations off the invasion beaches. Göring had refused. "Four Air Corps," he had replied on June 18, 1944, "is our last major reserve in the east. We have to bargain for a major [Soviet] offensive in the east." Unexpectedly, it was the Americans who had cause to regret Göring's obstinacy. On June 21, overconfident and care-less in anticipation of victory, they sent 114 Flying Fortresses to destroy a synthetic-oil plant at Ruhland, south of Berlin. An He 177 of General von Greim's Luftflotte 6 trailed the American bombers as they continued on to the Ukraine, and from their direction and from captured documents Luftwaffe commanders could predict that the force would be landing at Poltava. Göring ordered IV Air Corps to raid the Poltava Airfield that same night. Two hundred Luftwaffe bombers gate-crashed the Russian welcoming party, blasted them and the boozy Americans with 110 tons of fragmentation bombs, and returned to base in eastern Poland without loss. They left behind raging fires at Poltava as 450,000 gallons of aviation fuel blew up, silhouetting the blazing wrecks of forty-three B-17's and fifteen P-51 Mustangs as well as scores of Russian aircraft. "Those were wonderful times," reminisced Göring to Spaatz when they were all over.

Talking with Koller on June 24, Hitler was astonished to learn that the four-engined version of the He 177 would not appear in squadron service until 1946. But he was not shattered by the news. "What counts in our present situation," he said two days later still, "is to turn out fighters and still more fighters. Plus high-speed bombers. We've got to have that air umbrella over our home base and infantry, even if this means doing without a strategic air force for years."

His own sense of vertigo increasing with each slip in his prestige, Göring now told his generals that it was the "will of the Führer" that no more bombers be manufactured—even if it meant the end of minelaying and IV Air Corps. Anybody disobeying him, he threatened, would be swiftly expedited to the Land of the Dead.

On the eastern front, Army Group Center now collapsed. Again treachery had played its part. The air o. the Obersalzberg was vibrant with insult and intrigue. On June 24, Colonel Helmuth Stieff, one of the anti-Hitler plotters, witnessed Göring loudly cursing General Zeitzler and accusing the army of cowardice. The army hit back. When Hitler asked General Heinz Guderian's chief of staff on the twenty-eighth if he had noticed any Luftwaffe presence in France, the colonel replied that yes, he had once seen two fighter planes between Paris and Chartres.

A vicious circle was setting in. Fuel stocks were vanishing. New engines could not be test-run, pilots could not be trained, refineries could not be protected. With the repeated destruction of the refineries in Romania, Hungary, and Germany, the Luftwaffe's fuel supplies had slumped from a barely adequate 175,000 tons in April to only 35,000 tons in July. A signal intercepted on July 9 would show Göring ordering even the pettiest economies in fuel.

There is evidence that he now gave up France for lost. He ordered his art treasures there swiftly evacuated to the Reich, including the seven-ton marble copy of the winged goddess Nike of Samothrace—the air staff's last birthday gift to him. ("As the chief sculptor has had a bad nervous breakdown after an air raid," Dr. Bunjes had written from Paris on July 7, "I shan't be able

to send him to Germany for another three weeks to assemble the parts. This sculptor can then also retouch the Diana as the Reichsmarschall desires.'')
Rommel's troops were still containing the Allied beachhead in Normandy, but Göring did not expect them to do so much longer. In mid-July he had an urgent consignment shipped from France, including forty crates of ''porcelain and liquors'' for himself and Loerzer.

Strategically speaking, Hitler too had seen the truth but was drawing more positive conclusions. "Everything depends on our fighter program now," Hitler explained to Korten and Koller, revealing his interim strategic thinking. "We must keep this program strictly secret and conserve our strength meanwhile. The enemy will be astonished when the balance of air power begins to tilt against them four months from now."

With the Red Army now pouring through Poland toward the German frontiers, Hitler demonstratively returned to East Prussia on July 14, 1944. Soon, the Russian spearheads were only forty miles from Rominten.

Göring opted for Carinhall. Here, he received visitors in plain clothes— if plain is the word for silk pantaloons, red slippers, diamond-studded belt, green silk shirt, and violet-hued stockings that were an ill match for his peroxided hair and seemingly rouged cheeks. This chameleon existence was shattered a few days later, July 20. It was a stifling morning in East Prussia. The windows were open at the Wolf's Lair, where Göring, not far from Hitler's bunker, was grumpily discussing with Colonel Friedrich Kless, Greim's chief of staff, the reasons that Luftflotte 6 still felt unable to send its few He 177's to bomb Soviet power stations as far away as the Urals. "Our private discussion took place," Kless now recalls, "in a very heated atmosphere. Suddenly an alarm was telephoned to Göring. An attempt had been made on Hitler's life a few hundred yards away." The call came from Hitler's adjutant. Colonel von Below's voice sounded odd and shaken. He shouted that a bomb had gone off under the Führer's conference table—the Führer was alive, but the Luftwaffe generals Bodenschatz and Korten were both injured (the latter fatally, as it turned out). After going with Hitler to the local railroad station to meet Mussolini, whom he could not abide, Göring went over to the bomb-shattered conference hut. He marveled how Hitler could have survived the blast that ripped the heavy oaken table apart. "Today," he would tell his men the next day, "I believe more than ever that an Almighty Providence will favor us with victory."

A kind of euphoria anesthetized both Göring and Hitler. He heard Hitler assure Mussolini that fighter production would soon top five thousand, and that twelve hundred of the "new jet fighters" were going to mop up the enemy in Normandy. Their less euphoric henchmen spent the afternoon bitching and backbiting. "I am still foreign minister," Ribbentrop was heard to snap at the Reichsmarschall, who flourished his heavy baton in mock menace at him, "and my name is *von* Ribbentrop!"

Some of the instigators of the attempt to kill the Führer, notably the army's ex-chief of staff General Ludwig Beck, whom Göring had always regarded as a wimpish "drawing-room general," were shot by firing squad that same evening. "The whole creeping poison," the Reichsmarschall told his men afterward, "has come from this generals' clique, and I am convinced that with the elimination of these [flabby pricks] a roar of approval will go through the ranks of the entire Wehrmacht." The subsequent blood purge went further than Göring felt obligatory, however. "Just as in the Röhm putsch," he told historian Shuster, "more people were shot than necessary."

In a secret speech to air-staff officers some months later he called the assassination attempt "the greatest catastrophe we have ever suffered."

> GÖRING: Ignoring for the moment every other consequence, just let me mention one, gentlemen: In what light has the world until now viewed the Prussian officer? And how will he be seen henceforth?
>
> If in South America this *caballero* liquidates that *camarilla* and two months later vice versa, then they do it with drawn pistols and aplomb—with a lot of gunplay. . . . Even among these gentlemen there is some honor and chivalry. Not even in South America is it the custom for a comrade to tuck a bomb under his boss's feet.

The army plotters had intended to win over the air force *after* getting rid of Hitler. Despite their failure to kill him, late on July 20, they did make a lame approach to Stumpff's Luftflotte Reich at Berlin-Wannsee. But by that time Göring had already issued a signal to all inspectorates, Geschwader, squadrons, and flights reading (as the British code-breakers deciphered it): "All Luftwaffe units in Reich territory are subordinated to Colonel General Stumpff. Orders of army regional commands (*Wehrkreiskommandos*) are not to be obeyed."

Göring refused to allow Himmler to investigate any possible Luftwaffe involvement. "No officer of my Luftwaffe," he flatly declared, "would have a hand in such a thing." The only air-force officer involved, in fact, was Lieutenant Colonel Caesar von Hofacker, but he was attached to the army's general staff in Paris. Hofacker had initiated the air force's inspector of reconnaissance, General von Barsewisch, into the broader conspiracy; and Barsewisch had thereupon tipped off General Guderian; and Guderian had thereupon tactfully stayed away from the Wolf's Lair until the dust literally settled. According both to Gestapo chief investigator Georg Kiessel and to Rudolf Diels, the Reichsmarschall's misfit "half-brother," Herbert Göring, had actually attended plotting sessions with Carl Goerdeler, the conspiracy's civilian head; and of course, as history now knows, Göring's former Prussian finance minister Johannes Popitz was in it up to his neck.

It certainly seems incredible that Göring's Forschungsamt, which had moved by now to Breslau, had remained unaware of the conspiratorial ferment, given the plot's vast ramifications. ("Who would have thought," commented Heydrich's father-in-law in a letter, "that an entire clique of generals right next to the Führer could have practiced treachery unobserved!") Was Göring's absence from the hut more than fortuitous? "When I saw the room yesterday in which the contemptible assassination was attempted," he said, "I marveled that any man came out alive. The lethal device exploded violently barely a yard from the Führer . . . yet by a miracle the Führer was unscathed. By chance I was not present myself, but arrived half an hour later." However, Göring certainly had been present at the Hitler conference five days earlier when the same plotters had first hoped to set off their bomb. Nor had they at any time seriously considered recruiting him. Even his friend Count von Helldorf, the turncoat police president of Berlin, had dismissed the idea as ludicrous. "It was hoped at one time to include Göring," recalled Helldorf's son two weeks later, in British captivity, "but my father, after several visits to Carinhall, was opposed to this on the grounds that there was no evidence that he [Göring] would be sympathetic to the plotters and that in any event his physical condition—the consequence of addiction to drugs—would make him a doubtful asset."

The Reichsmarschall was fortunate enough to figure only on their hit lists. In their draft press communiqué, which the Gestapo seized from a hotel safe, Goerdeler had written, "The completely corrupt Göring—the 'Reichsmarschall' who can't grovel deep enough to his so-called 'Führer'—has the impertinence to tell us that the structure and responsibilities of the general staff are all wrong. . . ."

Thus he escaped both bomb and purge. However it would not have escaped Göring's attention that when Hitler broadcast to the world late on the twentieth, to prove he had survived, he invited Grand Admiral Karl Dönitz to speak next, *before* the Reichsmarschall.

For reasons of power politics Göring decided that the division bearing his name, the Hermann Göring Division, must become the savior of East Prussia. He had recalled it from Italy, and it was now assigned to defend the Rominten Heath. In a fighting speech on July 21, 1944, to his Escort Regiment—its elite unit—he made plain his belief that a blessed Providence had intervened to save Hitler. He assured them that the new bazooka (*Panzerfaust*) issued to them made each man superior to a Russian tank. "You should see what a rabble the Russian infantry is!" he encouraged them. "For brave men even tanks hold no fears, because now a staunch man can defend himself even at close quarters against tanks." But he also said, "Any soldier who throws away his arms, even a pistol, in order to retreat faster, puts himself beyond the pale of honor and obligation: each and every one of you, whether NCO or soldier, has the duty to shoot cowards like that on the spot."

> GÖRING: Just as the British and Americans in Italy now speak of
> your division with awe, the Russians must learn to fear you
> too. . . . Comrades, you must make this pledge: You may give
> ground in Russia—that is not decisive—but never in Germany.
> Not one German woman or German child must fall into their
> bestial hands. And if fate should be against us, if the Russians
> should come into this province, then that must only be possible
> when no soldiers of the Hermann Göring Division are left alive.

The total subservience of this superstitious, God-fearing man to Hitler had
been reborn by the bomb blast. On the following day one of Hitler's stenographers wrote in his diary:

> Before today's midday conference the Reichsmarschall addressed
> a brief speech to the Führer and proposed that as a visible token
> of the Wehrmacht's gratitude for his miraculous escape the Hitler
> salute be introduced immediately throughout the armed forces.
> The Führer signed this document, whereupon all those present
> spontaneously saluted.

It was Goebbels, not Göring, whom Hitler now appointed his plenipotentiary
for total war. On the train back to Berlin the little propaganda minister poured
out his heart about their enfeebled Reichsmarschall to bomber ace Werner
Baumbach. Baumbach decided to join forces in the campaign against Göring.

Mortified by Hitler's new snub to him, the Reichsmarschall withdrew from
the Wolf's Lair to Rominten, and for the next five weeks he would ignore
every hint that he should return.

At first his "illness" appears to have been just a pretext. He was not too
ill to receive Herbert Backe for lunch at Rominten one day (although he did
introduce Ondarza to the Staatssekretär as "the doctor who is treating me").
They went for a coach ride through the sunlit woods, and Backe told him
he was finished with Reichminister Darré. "The Führer," Göring warned
him, "won't let a minister go while there's a war on."

This was Göring's protection too. Hitler might show gross disrespect for
him, referring to him behind his back as "what's his name," but he would
be loath to let him go. Powerful bonds of party history still linked their
destinies.

After Korten's painful death, the appointment of a successor showed neither
Göring nor Loerzer in a favorable light. Karl Koller, the stubborn Bavarian
general now running the Luftwaffe from Goldap, was the obvious man to
take over as chief of air staff. On July 24, however, Göring summoned
instead the mild-mannered and academic chief of flying training Lieutenant

General Werner Kreipe from Berlin to Rominten. There followed what Kreipe called in his personal diary a "long monologue about the bad situation."

> Göring [asked] was I aware that Korten had wanted *me* to take over as chief of air staff from October 1?
> I said I was, and touched upon Koller—he was, after all, my superior at Luftflotte 3, and he's going to feel hurt if he's passed over. . . . Göring said he can't get on with the Bavarian.
> Lunched with him and Loerzer, then strolled with Loerzer who . . . made some spiteful comments about Milch. Back to Reichsmarschall, who's running a temperature and swallowing pills the whole time.

Göring appointed Kreipe and told him to rebuild the fighter force, establish "blitz-bomber" squadrons in Normandy, and expand the paratroop force. Kreipe was a puzzling choice. He had all the general-staff qualities that both Hitler and Göring detested. Knowing nothing, and caring even less, about Nazi Germany's coming world monopoly in jet-aircraft operations and in surface- and air-to-air missiles, the general was a dyed-in-the-wool pessimist. That evening Kreipe lugubriously moaned to a friend, Göring's former war diarist Werner Beumelburg, that the best they could hope for was to stave off defeat until December, and that Germany could never regain air supremacy even over a reduced Reich bounded by the Rhine and Vistula rivers.

Since Göring hesitated to introduce Kreipe to Hitler for several weeks, the luckless General Koller continued to officiate at the Wolf's Lair. The Reichsmarschall emerged briefly for Korten's funeral at the Battle of Tannenberg Monument on July 28, then vanished again. "Göring," wrote Kreipe, "delivers a very fine eulogy. Koller gives me the cold shoulder. Göring crumples at the end and flies home sick to Carinhall." Hurt and mistrustful, Koller misinterpreted the sudden exit. "The Reichsmarschall didn't talk to me," he noted angrily in his own papers, "although I am still acting chief, and need several decisions from him."

On the last day of the month, now confined to bed, Göring again received General Kreipe:

> Göring has an abscess in his throat and can't speak. He whispers to Brauchitsch, who repeats everything out loud to me (odd situation). I'm to go to East Prussia and start work at once. When I ask if Koller's been notified, he says no. . . . Göring hands me a note saying he wants to introduce me to Führer himself as soon as he's better. Until then I am to let Koller or Christian deputize for me at Führer conferences.

"The present state of play," wrote Koller that same day, disgusted with what was happening, "is that L [Loerzer] and RM [the Reichsmarschall] are at Carinhall, while I am holding the fort at Goldap and directing the Luftwaffe alone with a skeleton staff. RM can't be spoken to—is ill—mustn't be disturbed."

In four days, it seemed likely, the Russians might well be in East Prussia, so at Rominten elite troops of the Escort Regiment prepared to torch Göring's beloved hunting lodge. The headstone of Jeschonnek's grave was removed and buried. On August 4, Koller moved *Robinson*, the Luftwaffe's forward headquarters, to an open stretch of railroad at Bartenstein.

The eastern onslaught was held off, but now the western front suddenly collapsed as Rommel's ring of armor around the beachhead was pierced at Avranches.

Göring's staff still declared him sick. When Carin's young nephew Count Carl Gustav von Rosen flew in from Stockholm, he was not even allowed to phone Göring, let alone see him. Mystified, the Swede told his friends that the Reichsmarschall must be under house arrest. This was not so: not yet, at least. At the Wolf's Lair his enemies were still biding their time.

40
WITCH HUNT

By the late summer of 1944 Hermann Göring's air force was in worsening disarray. In August 1944, British code-breakers intercepted Luftwaffe orders limiting reconnaissance operations over Egypt and Cyprus to one flight per month, banning courier flights over the Reich during morning hours because of Allied fighter harassment, and forbidding ground crews to leave fuel in parked planes "to avoid losses."

As his star sank toward the horizon, Göring's circle of friends shrank. He remained loyal to Philipp Bouhler, who was himself in semidisgrace, and considered appointing him or even Bruno Loerzer to replace Milch, whom he had dismissed in June, as Staatssekretär; but Hitler flatly rejected them both as unsuitable. Fritz Sauckel was the only gauleiter toward whom Göring still felt any warmth. Friendship with Göring was no longer enough to avoid Gestapo arrest. Franz Neuhausen was arrested for misappropriating labor and transport to build a private estate near Belgrade and for smuggling foreign currency into Hungary and gold into Switzerland; Göring managed to secure his release but could not prevent his being exiled. Martin Bormann gathered evidence against Luftwaffe generals wherever he could. Party officials whispered scandalous allegations about General von Pohl, Göring's representative in Italy, and Pohl's female dietician; Party officials alleged too that his officers spent hours swimming or sunbathing with their secretaries.

In France Göring's ground troops fought well—the badly mauled 16th Luftwaffe Field Division made a heroic defense of northern Caën, while the 88's emplaced by III Flak Corps did a lot to halt General Bernard Montgomery's advance at Falaise. But even at that murderous climax in France, Göring was more concerned about extricating his last treasures to safety. On August 13, he ordered Alfred Rosenberg to evacuate all the works of art from the Nazi repositories in Paris and ship them back to the Reich "without delay."

The collapse in France was utter and complete. Luftwaffe officers, taking their cue from Göring, loaded trucks with fancy women, chaises longues, and other booty, and headed for the German frontier, stampeding into the Reich past disenchanted party officials, women, and children slaving to dig antitank defenses. As Göring's troops poured into Germany, the people said that the WL prefix on Luftwaffe number plates stood for "We're Leaving!" Hundreds of brand-new radar sets fell into American hands in Paris.

Himmler and Bormann reported all this to their Führer. Weeping with rage, Göring pleaded with Hitler to let him deal with the sinners. He began telephoning his chief judge advocate to demand, "I want death sentences! Where are they!" He realized it was hypocrisy and hated it. "So long as we were winning," he would remark ironically a few weeks later, "nobody got worked up if our units took over the finest châteaux in France or caroused or womanized. But now the times are rougher, everybody's glaring at us. . . . Yes, when we were winning, people told me straight out I ought to fly whorehouses out to the men."

While Pohl in Italy and the Luftwaffe in France brazenly used precious truck transport and gasoline to loot and pillage, Allied code-breakers could hear II Fighter Corps in France advising its squadrons to "get hold of horse-drawn vehicles" if they could; and in Germany, since each Me 262 used up 200 liters of J-2 fuel taxiing for five minutes, the squadrons were forced to use oxen to pull the jet planes around the airfields to save fuel.

Sensing his powers of intercession waning, in August 1944 Göring speeded up the escape of his remaining Jewish business friends. A year before, in The Hague, the Gestapo had detained art dealer Kurt Walter Bachstitz, a Jew. Bachstitz had the good fortune to be married to Walter Hofer's (non-Jewish) sister. Hofer wrote to SS Brigadeführer Harster, the Gestapo chief in Holland, "The Reichsmarschall wants Bachstitz permitted to emigrate, and the case held over until I report to him on the matter." Göring instructed that the case be dropped. "Bachstitz," he ruled, "is to be left alone." In September 1943 the dealer divorced his wife and transferred his property to her, thereby protecting it from seizure. And now, on August 14, 1944, he was escorted by Göring's private detective to Basel, Switzerland, leaving behind, of course, valuable paintings to express his gratitude to Hermann Göring.

In the Reichsmarschall's absence Koller had continued to sweat out Hitler's tantrums at the Wolf's Lair. "At every conference the Führer rants on for hours about the Luftwaffe," Koller wrote on August 8, 1944, in a shorthand note that verged on the hysterical. "He levels the meanest accusations about our meager aircraft figures, our technical blunders, our noncompletion of the replenishment squadrons in the Reich, the Me 262, and so on. The Führer says that he is given figures that turn out to be wrong. How can I know what the Reichsmarschall and General Korten were telling him—how can I help the mistakes made from 1939 to 1942!"

Since Göring was still acting "sick," Kreipe attended his first Hitler conference on August 11. "The Führer has become very stooped," he observed in his diary. "Cotton wool in his ears. He trembles violently, you can only shake hands with him gently." Hitler blamed the air-force "collapse" on Udet, Jeschonnek, and Milch. They had made premature promises on which he had based fateful strategic decisions. He asked Kreipe to ensure that "truth and clarity" once more supervened.

Significantly, Kreipe paid courtesy visits to Himmler and Bormann before returning to Bartenstein.

Bormann continued to load Göring's dossier with telegrams from party officials substantiating the Reichsmarschall's ineptitude and laziness. "Everybody curses the air force," recorded Kreipe unhappily on the fifteenth. "The Führer orders the gauleiters' reports investigated."

On the next day Kreipe noted that the Reichsmarschall was "still acting sick," and went to see him at Carinhall three mornings later. They haggled for four hours. Lunching with Bouhler and Körner that day, Kreipe found the Reichsmarschall more approachable—Emmy's feminine charm was keeping up his morale. "Hermann must take better care of himself," she chided the general.

Hitler did not agree. "How much longer," he asked Kreipe on the twentieth, "is Göring's illness likely to last?"

The fighting evacuation of France continued, but the Me 262 was still not ready for combat. "Boundless reproaches against the air force," wrote Kreipe after Hitler's conference on August 22, 1944. The next day Hitler apologized to him. "It wasn't *you* I was getting at!" he said, unconsciously repeating almost verbatim his remarks to Jeschonnek the year before.

Four evenings later Hermann Göring, wheezing and pale-faced, ventured back into the Wolf's Lair. He reemerged smugly after three hours. Hitler, he said, had not even raised the subject of the Me 262.

Kreipe was not so fortunate when he asked Hitler on the thirtieth to lift the veto on the Me 262 as a fighter. After ten minutes the Führer shouted him down. "None of you," he snapped, "has the faintest idea how to use the Me 262. I forbid any further discussion of it."

The next evening Kreipe phoned Göring to report that France had now caved in. The strategic effects would be disastrous. The Luftwaffe would forfeit its radar outfield, while the enemy would obtain bases for beam transmitters for precision-bombing raids on synthetic-rubber plants and the smaller towns like Bonn. But everybody blamed the Luftwaffe. "The general grumbling about Göring's setup," wrote Martin Bormann privately, "is attaining quite unparliamentary forms of expression." On September 3, word reached the Reichsmarschall that Hitler was again complaining about his prolonged absence, and threatening to wind up the air force altogether.

Göring hurried over on the fifth, and Kreipe, who went with him, wrote this record of their joint confrontation with Hitler:

> Just abuse of the Luftwaffe—it does nothing, it has gone down over the years, he has been constantly deceived over both production and performance figures. Total failure in France, the ground organization and signals troops just took to their heels . . . instead of joining the army in battle.
> Then back to discussion of Me 262 operations. Same old arguments . . . Then, in modified form, he developed his idea of manufacturing no more planes apart from the Me 262 and tripling the Flak artillery.

"Sat for a long time afterward with Göring," the general's diary continued, "who purred with contentment, congratulated me, and said we'd killed off the idea of dissolving the air force."

Hanging around the air-staff headquarters, Göring tired easily: He was tired of this war, in fact, but not yet tired of life itself. Once his personal assistant Fritz Görnnert ventured to remark, "Herr Reichsmarschall—it ought to be possible to make Adolf Hitler disappear. Not liquidate him, just spirit him away to the Zugspitze Mountain and lock him away. Then a big state funeral, and Hitler is 'dead'!"

Göring changed the subject.

On September 16 he learned from Kreipe that Hitler was devising an extraordinary counteroffensive against the British and American armies "from out of the Ardennes." "In bad weather," Hitler had said pointedly, "the enemy air force won't be flying *either*!" He intended to punch three armies through the weakest part of the Allied line and seize Antwerp. He would thus "Dunkirk" the British Army for a second time; Roosevelt would be defeated in the election; Germany would have won the war. His target date for this was November 1, 1944.

It was perhaps foolish for Göring now to have left the Wolf's Lair for his own domains at Carinhall, because it gave his rivals a clear field of fire. Hitler even regarded the Battle of Arnhem that began on September 17 as a major Luftwaffe defeat, although Göring had operated 650 planes against the Allied armadas of troop transports and gliders both that day and the next, shooting down hundreds of them.

"New reports about fresh landings in Holland," noted Kreipe after Hitler's conference on the eighteenth.

> Führer rages about Luftwaffe's failure. Wants immediate infor-
> mation which fighter forces were scrambled in Holland. Führer
> violently abuses me. . . . Says the air force is incompetent, cow-
> ardly, and letting him down. He has further reports of air-force
> units streaming back across the Rhine. . . .
> I ask for concrete details.
> Führer replies, "I refuse to talk with you further. I want to
> speak to the Reichsmarschall tomorrow. No doubt you are capable
> of arranging that?"

Kreipe had by now shifted the air-staff headquarters to the rear, a forest location at Rosengarten in East Prussia. When Göring now arrived here at *Robinson VII*, Kreipe warned him that the witch hunt was against *him*, the Reichsmarschall, alone. Göring just laughed.

The laughter faded after they went over together to the Wolf's Lair on the nineteenth. The mood was icy, and Hitler asked to see Göring alone. He instructed him to disband the air staff and its academy and get rid of Kreipe—a scheming, cold-blooded general staff officer, "defeatist and unreliable."

When Göring emerged hours later, "broken up and dismayed," Kreipe challenged him. "Now do you believe me? The whole vendetta is against *you*."

"The Führer," Göring retorted stiffly, "has again expressed complete confidence in me."

Told of Hitler's *Diktat* about the air staff, Kreipe shrewdly rejoined that this would give great comfort to the Allies, since dissolving the general staff had been one of the original dictates of Versailles. Back at Rosengarten that night Kreipe was notified formally by SS Gruppenführer Hermann Fegelein that he was not to set foot in the Wolf's Lair ever again.

Fegelein, Himmler's liaison officer to Hitler, had married Eva Braun's sister, Gretl; his influence was rising. "Together with Fegelein," Göring would growl to interrogators, "Bormann kept dishing up to Hitler the most unfortunate reports about the air force. Bormann naturally saw them as a magnificent opportunity to incite the Führer against me." The dossier kept by the indefatigable Bormann posed a real threat. "Never once," Göring would tell a Soviet interrogator, "not even at the height of my powers, did I have the influence that Bormann enjoyed in those last years. We called him the Little Secretary, the Big Intriguer—and the Filthy Swine!"

Göring knew that the man Hitler secretly hankered after to be the head of his air force was General von Greim—the oldest living fighter pilot, the first airman ever to take him up in a plane. He had sent for Greim after Arnhem, and the general arrived, on September 21, at Rosengarten where he was intercepted by an order from Hitler to go straight over to see him first. At the Wolf's Lair the Führer lectured the Luftflotte 6 commander on Göring's manifold "sins" and offered him the post of "deputy commander in chief."

Swallowing this fresh humiliation, Göring asked Greim to draw up proposals, but found his anger hard to suppress. "Greim," recalled Hanna Reitsch, the general's mistress, "met with a terrific outburst from him."

Like Kreipe's in July, Greim's first act now was to discuss his future position with Himmler, Bormann, and Fegelein.

The growing estrangement from Göring tore at Hitler's physical well-being, already fragile from his bomb-blast injuries. Stricken with jaundice and bedridden for two weeks, he blamed it on his anger at the Reichsmarschall, and began to press for courts-martial of Luftwaffe officers. Göring hastened to comply. On September 22, Luftflotte 3 was heard signaling, "The Reichsmarschall . . . has empowered Luftflotte Reich to set up instant courts-martial to try offenders on the spot, and where cowardice is proved to shoot them in front of the assembled personnel."

The possibility of delivering a fighter grand slam was drawing closer. Hermann Göring summoned squadron commanders to Luftflotte Reich headquarters and promised, "From now on things are going to be different." He revealed that large numbers of fighter planes were becoming available. Luftflotte Reich commander General Stumpff rendered what Kreipe—still acting as chief of air staff—cynically terms in his diary "a Byzantine pledge of loyalty." It was swiftly rewarded when Göring donated a house to him that same day. Kreipe—who had to make do with a more humble silver-framed photograph of Göring—came out to Carinhall on October 3:

> Von Greim had seen the Reichsmarschall before me. Göring was seething. Afterward, I was called in alone. Göring was completely shattered, said people were trying to get rid of him, Greim was a traitor. Says he is and will remain commander in chief. For him, Greim is finished. He's to return to his Luftflotte at once.

Kreipe reiterated his warning that the whole witch hunt was directed against the Reichsmarschall.

The Red Army now began its final assault on East Prussia. Hitler demonstratively remained at the Wolf's Lair not far from the battle zone. He was confident that if Nazi Germany could only hold on, the new submarines, missiles, tanks, and jet planes would arrive in time to restore supremacy. Swift and invulnerable, the Ar 234 jet was effortlessly photographing the Allied supply beaches and battlefields in the west. And now the much-vaunted, much-criticized jet-bomber squadrons were screaming into action against the Allies too. Operated by KG51, the first Me 262 jet bombers were punishing their troop concentrations around Nijmegen. In relaxation of Hitler's rigid veto, an experimental jet-fighter squadron with the first fifty Me 262 jet fighters would begin operations in mid-October from bases at Achmer and Hesepe. Altogether Göring now had around thirty-seven hundred fighter planes, but all these operations were severely curtailed by dwindling fuel, deficient training, and lowering morale.

Nowhere was morale lower than in the much-maligned air staff. On October 9, Brauchitsch brought to Carinhall a gloomy memorandum that General Kreipe had written on "Air Warfare in 1945," morbidly depicting a Reich hopelessly encircled by superior air forces. Göring sent for Kreipe on the twelfth and tossed the document on to the table. "It's defeatist!" he screamed. "It smacks of slide rule and general staff. I'm sorely disappointed in you. Now you too are stabbing me in the back! You've lost faith in victory. Aren't you aware that the Führer has forbidden the general staff ever to assess our overall situation? If I didn't hold you in such esteem I'd have to show this drivel to the Führer, and that would be the end of you."

He tore the paper in two, and threw the halves across the table. Kreipe's usefulness had come to an end, but whom could the Reichsmarschall now appoint as chief of air staff?

Still squirming at the name of Koller, he sent for General Kurt Pflugbeil, commanding Luftflotte 1 on the Baltic coast. Pflugbeil was untainted by general-staff training. Even so, he turned down the job.

Kreipe suggested the name of General Meister. "Meister," growled Göring, "is the same type as you. I don't intend getting any more black marks from the Führer."

With Göring's fighter defenses hamstrung by fuel shortages, the RAF now joined in the daylight raiding. On October 14, while one thousand American heavies attended to Cologne, a thousand more RAF bombers attacked Duisburg (and the same number returned to Duisburg that night). Confronted now with further "disgraceful failures" by air-force units on the ground, Göring announced that "in headlong flight, cowardly individuals—sometimes even entire units—have turned over undamaged weapons to the enemy." He again reminded every soldier of his duty to apprehend such cowards. "Executions," he ordered, dropping a broad hint, "do not require prior authorization from me."

It was a sorry departure from the avuncular and compassionate Hermann Göring who had ruthlessly carpeted generals like Richthofen and Reichenau in 1940 for arbitrary use of their powers of life and death over their men.

On October 16, 1944, the Third White Russian Front attacked East Prussia—a gigantic force of thirty-five rifle divisions and two armored corps. The province was defended by nine German divisions and a brigade of cavalry. Göring returned to East Prussia and turned up at Rosengarten wearing the clay-brown uniform of the "Hermann Göring" Panzer Corps, which was to defend this region. He ventured briefly over to the Wolf's Lair—now very much the domain of Bormann and Himmler—that day, then went hunting on Rominten Heath for one last time. Afterward, he signed some documents that General Kreipe brought over. "Very friendly reception," observed the latter after a stroll with the Reichsmarschall. "He commiserates with me, remarks for the first time that he now intends to stay on here permanently —he has to keep an eye on what Himmler and Bormann are up to. Himmler, he says, has just asked for air squadrons for the SS!"

Göring feared Himmler more than Bormann now. He knew that if Hitler died, Bormann would probably try to arrest him before he could be sworn in as legal successor; he intended to grab Bormann first and put him on trial. With Himmler, however, he would have to tread more softly. "I couldn't just have him liquidated," he reflected later to George Shuster. "He had the whole police force under him (while Bormann just drew on the Führer's authority). I would have had to undermine Himmler's position bit by bit."

On October 22, the first battle for East Prussia had been won—a significant German victory. The Hermann Göring Corps had counterattacked and thrown the Russians out of Gumbinnen and Goldap. There was terrible evidence of the Russian presence everywhere. Kreipe himself saw the scenes at Nemmendorf and recorded in his diary afterward, "Women shot and children nailed to barndoors." He ordered photographs taken for posterity.

On the twenty-third, Göring attended Hitler's conference, then went forward past long columns of panic-stricken East Prussians fleeing westward. Göring accompanied a regimental commander whose men were engaging Russian tanks at Trakehnen.

Still dissatisfied with his fighter-squadron commanders, he harangued them for three hours at Luftflotte Reich headquarters on the twenty-sixth. One FW 190 pilot recalled later that much of what he said was true, "But the rot [of doubt] had already set in." He adopted an unfortunate tone, mingling truculent remarks about the fighter pilots' "cowardice" with bluster: "If you don't shoot down five hundred B-17's the next time," he said, "you're all transferring to the infantry!" At one stage he dramatically ripped his medals off and slammed them down, declaring that he would put them on again only when his pilots starting shooting down planes. "That really nettled Galland," said one Heinkel pilot. "They *all* took off their Knight's Crosses then." Much of the sermon was vintage Göring—he forbade any aviator to abort a mission because of defective "water thermometers" or "speedometers." Adding insult to injury, he also ordered excerpts of his speech broadcast by loudspeaker at every fighter airfield.

Göring returned to East Prussia after that, fearing Bormann's vendetta more than Stalin's military rabble.

Hitler had meanwhile sent yet again for General von Greim. Torn between sentiment and pragmatism, he once more abandoned the idea of dispossessing the Reichsmarschall, however. "I think that Hitler still felt too close to Göring from the years of struggle," his air-force adjutant von Below said afterward. Bormann, thwarted once again, poured out his irritation in a letter on the last day of October. "People refer," he wrote, "to the constant failure of the Luftwaffe high command ever since Stalingrad and North Africa."

A few days later Kreipe's tenure of office was over. In a farewell conversation with him on November 2, Göring candidly referred to the general's somber memorandum, and advised him never again to commit such dark thoughts to paper. "I am sure," he prophesied, "that there is going to be a 'Nibelungen' struggle, but we shall fight it out—on the Vistula, on the Oder, and on the Wesel." Since these latter rivers were in the heart of Germany, it was not a joyous prospect.

Kreipe pleaded with him to persuade Hitler to revert to diplomacy.

After a long silence Göring responded, "That I cannot do, because then the Führer would lose faith in himself." "Since 1938," he added, taking both of Kreipe's hands in his in a parting gesture, "I have felt that the Führer does not discuss everything with me. Ribbentrop's appointment [on February 4, 1938] took me by surprise, and I have been excluded from several important political decisions since then."

Even as Hermann Göring, his broad chest still voluntarily shorn of medals, was coming under assault at the Wolf's Lair, the resurgent German fighter force was spreading profound alarm among the Western Allies. On October 21, 1944, General Carl F. Spaatz, commander of the strategic air forces in Europe, warned General Omar Bradley that maintaining air supremacy was going to cost the lives of at least forty thousand more Allied airmen. "Our daylight bombing is going to become very expensive." On November 2, nearly 700 of his bombers escorted by 750 fighter planes attacked the Leuna synthetic-oil plant. General Galland raised a record seven hundred fighter sorties against them, and the new Me 262's shot down three bombers without loss.

Ultimately Hitler overruled Göring and forced him to appoint Karl Koller as chief of air staff. For five hours Göring wrangled with the Bavarian general on November 5. After their third meeting that day Koller entered this account in his shorthand diary:

> RM describes his entire life, his work, and achievements in rebuilding the German Air Force. Spoke in utter dejection about the campaign being waged against him from every side—the army, SS, and party. Says he is fed up to the back teeth and the war situation doesn't interest him anymore; wishes he were dead. He'd join the paratroop army and fight with them in the front line but the Führer won't let him go, has told him that only he can rebuild the air force yet again.

Koller reminded him of the insults he had heaped on the air staff; but he took the job, under the proviso that he could speak his mind. "Reichsmarschall said that of course I could, and took my hands in both of his, beaming with happiness." "How long will this last?" noted Koller in a wise afterthought.

Two days after that, Göring was visiting Bodenschatz at the flak bunker hospital in Berlin. To Reichsminister Walter Darré, lying in a neighboring bed, Göring looked oddly naked without his medals, but "very well and self-satisfied" nonetheless. "You should have seen him eight weeks ago," the nurses told Darré. "Pale as death he looked then. We thought he wasn't going to last more than a few weeks."

Through party channels still more criticism reached Hitler—this time from Lieutenant Colonel von Klosinski, the party's NSFO (indoctrination officer) in the air force. Göring seethed, but asked Klosinski to Carinhall and invited him to take charge of purging the air force of its superannuated generals and colonels.

Klosinski balked at the job. "Herr Reichsmarschall," he lectured Göring. "You shut yourself away here at Carinhall. . . . You must get rid of the more unsavory officers of your entourage, like Brauchitsch and Loerzer." "Before Dunkirk," the colonel continued remorselessly, "I myself once heard you say Bruno is my laziest general!"

"I need somebody I can drink a bottle of cognac with in the evenings," said Göring truculently.

To the chagrin of Galland and the fighter force he now invited Pelz, the former bomber commander, to move into Carinhall with him. On November 10, he asked Pelz to take the chair at a "Luftwaffe Parliament" held at Berlin's Gatow Air Staff Academy with thirty or more top-scoring fighter and bomber aces. Göring told them that Hitler had commanded him to rebuild the air force, and their job was to comment and advise without fear or favor on whatever topic they liked, except, naturally, his own illustrious person and the Me 262. The meeting broke up in chaos as the feuding bomber officers like Pelz, Herrmann, and Baumbach tore into the fighter commanders Schmid, Trautloft, and Galland; and all of them rounded savagely on the Nazi fanatics like Klosinski, Staub, and Gollob.

Baumbach reported to Göring at Carinhall, and handed over the shorthand transcript. Asked about personnel changes, Baumbach said that they all felt that Loerzer, Brauchitsch, and Diesing should go. Brauchitsch heard this and bristled. Göring soothed his ruffled feelings by decorating him with the Air Leader's Gold Medal with Diamonds immediately afterward.

With unbridled hypocrisy Göring issued on November 10 an order severely criticizing Luftwaffe commanders in east and west. "Fortresses have been abandoned without order, troops abandoned without cause," he began. Then, as though his own frantic salvaging of works of art from Paris were forgotten, he continued, "Private goods have been brought to safety, air-force dumps destroyed in panic." He added, "I have already pronounced exemplary punishments.'' A few days later RAF Lancaster bombers capsized the German Navy's last great battleship, *Tirpitz*, in Norway. The Luftwaffe could do nothing to prevent it.

On that same day, however, Galland reported a huge force of fighter planes now standing by with both fuel and crews for the first grand-slam attack on the next clear day that the entire American bomber force invaded central Germany. Three thousand fighter planes would operate, and five hundred would take off for a second sortie to grapple with any surviving bombers on their return. He promised to destroy five hundred of the enemy bombers in the ensuing battle as the Reichsmarschall had demanded.

Hitler, however, was now minded to execute a grand slam of his own, the Ardennes Offensive. On November 20, he left East Prussia for the last time, abandoning the bombproof bunkers, security compounds, and minefields of the Wolf's Lair, and returned to Berlin. Here, Bormann secretly reopened his Göring dossier.

41
ZERO HOUR FOR HERMANN

Reichsmarschall Göring now again commanded a fighter force to be reckoned with. Occasionally the fighters had gone aloft—on November 26, General Galland had sent up 550 planes, destroying 25 American bombers over Hanover—but then Hitler ordered a halt. "Suddenly," recalled Göring a few months later, "the order came from the Führer that I was to use this air force for the offensive, rotating its front to north-south."

The "offensive" was to be Hitler's supreme, final gamble in the Ardennes. The thunderous launch of what became known as the Rundstedt Offensive at dawn on December 16 took the Allies by surprise, while the bad weather gave Göring local air supremacy over the battlefield for the first time. He had committed twenty-four hundred planes to this historic battle, and strutted proudly back into Hitler's forward headquarters, the Eagle's Nest, able to look the other commanders in the eye for the first time in months. For a week he had no reason to dodge the war conferences. He was his Führer's *enfant gâté*. For six days the record even shows Göring invited to tea with the Führer. But then the skies cleared, the enemy air forces came out again, and Göring hurried back to his family at Carinhall.

Like a true Christmas-card setting, the romantic Swedish-style mansion there was canopied in foot-thick snow, with a thin frozen mist drifting in and out of the surrounding conifers. The forest's surviving bison, stags, and reindeer grazed quietly, cocking their ears from time to time at the unfamiliar rumble coming from the east. Emmy greeted her returning warrior husband warmly. Baskets of presents stood ready, locked in the large hall, to distribute to staff and friends—Loerzer, Körner, Bouhler, and now Pelz were still in residence—and Hermann Göring had never been parsimonious with his wealth. Two furniture vans had arrived, bringing the household contents of Rominten Lodge, and Emmy distributed the furniture among her bombed-out friends of the Prussian State Theater. She too was a Christmas person. Every Yuletide she listed one thousand needy families for Hermann to send money to, and sat down with her sister Else and Heli Bouhler packing toys and writing cards to put in each gift parcel.

Not many soldiers could enjoy Christmas of 1944 with their families like this. After a flying visit back to Hitler's headquarters on December 25, just to inquire how the Ardennes fighting was going, Göring returned to Carinhall for the rest of his self-granted leave. The cloying odor of self-indulgence and corruption would cling to Carinhall until the end.

Seeking a new scapegoat for the failure of the air defenses, Göring had picked on General Galland, the colorful general of fighters, and began to freeze him out of his staff conferences. He made insulting remarks in the young general's absence; adopting a turn of phrase oddly reminiscent of his own controversial record in World War I, he spoke of generals who had "lied for each other's medals." By this time Galland's following among the lower ranks had dwindled. "That Galland," muttered one corporal after entering British captivity in February 1945, "is perfumed like a whore. I last saw him in November [1944]. . . . He may have been a good fighter-pilot, but you've got to have some talent for organization and technical ability too. He used to show up wearing boots, a general's stripes, and knicker-bockers: a real sight." Officers had more time for Galland, but higher up still his life-style had caused offense to Göring and the prudish Hitler. Even Allied interrogators would find his moral precepts peculiar—Galland had ordered his pilots not to marry, and himself lived with several women simultaneously, explaining that he "had to set an example to his men."

Galland in turn had little time for the Reichsmarschall. He had refused to pander to him—which was a mistake—and his eyes had been opened by Göring's sizable black-market operations in the west. Before returning to the Eagle's Nest, the Reichsmarschall ordered him to Carinhall and informed him, in the course of a two-hour monologue, that he was to be dismissed for employing the "wrong fighter tactics" and for insubordination. Until a successor could be found, he would be sent on leave.

His tail now between his legs, Galland drove back to Berlin. His dismissal was barely noticed, coinciding as it did with Göring's most spectacular operation yet—Operation Bodenplatte, the Luftwaffe's mass attack on the

Allied air forces. Speculating on the chance of catching the enemy aviators with their pants down, Göring had authorized a swoop on their airbases in the Low Countries at first light on New Year's Day 1945. Reconnaissance planes had brought back tempting photographs of their quarry—for example, of 149 P-47 fighters and 8 heavy bombers neatly parked at Saint Trond in Belgium, literally begging to be attacked. Göring brought in every available pilot, including instructors, pupils, and even veteran Geschwader commodores like Major Michalski, who would personally lead the fifty-five Me 109-G14's and FW 190-A8's of his Jagdgeschwader 4, and Lieutenant Colonel Herbert Ihlefeld of JG1.

Again the code-breakers did not realize what Göring was up to—even though at 6:30 P.M. on New Year's Eve his 3rd Fighter Division had been heard forecasting fine weather at zero hour and at 11:30 P.M. instructing the four Geschwader of fighter planes, "Zero hour for Hermann 0820 hrs."

At 9:15 A.M.—with zero hour delayed an hour by ground fog—Bodenplatte began, with the hundreds of FW 190's and Me 109's suddenly screaming across the Allied lines, firing rockets and cannon, and bombing every targeted airfield simultaneously. It was a more spectacular triumph than Poltava. The devastation caused, particularly to the British-occupied airfields in Belgium, was colossal though never officially admitted at the time. Göring claimed to have used twenty-three hundred planes, which may well have been true. Photographic reconnaissance planes brought back pictures of nine of the many airfields targeted, showing on these alone 389 Allied warplanes definitely destroyed and 117 damaged. But as the day wore on, it became clear that his own fighters had taken an unexpected hammering. "What we did not allow for," said Göring later, not without a degree of perverse pride, "was the intense concentration of [Allied] anti-aircraft guns set up against our V-1 [flying bombs]." Probably two-thirds of his own losses of about 227 planes were caused by his own trigger-happy flak gunners. (The German naval flak in Holland alone admitted having shot down twenty German fighter planes.) Both Göring and Koller defended the operation at Hitler's main conference, commenting that at least it had given his fighter crews a chance to take off. But Hitler forbade any repetition—he wanted the air battles to be in German skies, where his revenge-hungry public could see them.

Göring attended every conference at the Eagle's Nest until January 10, but they were increasingly joyless occasions. As Hitler's Ardennes gamble faltered and finally failed, his attitude toward Göring congealed to ice. With evident malice Martin Bormann wrote in his diary on the fifth, "Reichsmarschall summoned to the Führer on account of the air-war situation." Attending these conferences, Field Marshal Gerd von Rundstedt noticed that Hitler allowed him to sit, but always obliged the Reichsmarschall to stand.

"Things got so crazy," confessed Göring to American historian Shuster, "that I said to myself: Let's hope it's all over quickly so I can get out of this lunatic asylum." He barricaded himself in his special train, read cheap detective novels—sometimes devouring the same pulp book three times over—and smoked his favorite cigars, very slowly. "Three quarters of my shattered nerves are due—not to the war," he shouted to Bodenschatz, deaf ever since the bomb blast, "but to the Führer! I've been under massive attack for a whole year now." On January 11, having served his penance long enough, he fled the Eagle's Nest and returned to the uxorious comforts of Carinhall.

Indignant at the Bodenplatte casualties, and egged on by Koller and Greim, three fighter aces formed a deputation, with Oak Leaves-holder Günther Lützow at their head, to protest to the Reichsmarschall his exclusion of Galland. Göring listened soberly, then summoned all the Geschwader commodores to the sumptuous Aviators' Building in Berlin. Lützow again headed the deputation; he had tabulated their complaints, which included the undue influence of former bomber commanders like Pelz and Herrmann, the misuse of the Me 262, the Reichsmarschall's slurs on his fighter pilots, and his humiliation of Galland. Göring, his knuckles turning white with anger, shouted that this was a "mutiny without parallel in history," and threatened them all with the firing squad. Two days later he pronounced the banishment of Lützow to Italy; Galland was placed under house arrest, forbidden to return to Berlin.

Göring spent his last wartime birthday skulking at Carinhall, surrounded by his camarilla, and entertaining at luncheon the few remaining Axis attachés still accredited to Berlin. The Japanese attaché's report to Tokyo portrays a Göring in a chastened, introspective mood, candidly admitting that he himself had believed that for large enemy bomber formations to operate over Germany for any length of time was "a complete impossibility."

Without appreciating it yet, however, he was already regaining air supremacy for Germany. A week earlier, on January 5, 1945, the U.S. Air Force generals Carl F. Spaatz and Jimmy Doolittle had frankly warned Eisenhower that they were going to have to attack the jet-fighter production very soon. They estimated that ten thousand tons of well-aimed bombs might set the Me 262 back by three months. Eisenhower agreed, and on this very day, January 12, Spaatz issued a new directive establishing the German jet aircraft as the "principal objective for attack." If Hitler could prolong the war beyond the summer, Spaatz warned, he would have "jets of such superior performance and such numbers as to challenge our aerial supremacy over not only Germany but all of Western Europe."

The Soviet winter offensive that began that same day was going to be hard to stop. To halt the masses of tanks and infantry, Göring transferred twenty squadrons of single-engined fighters from the Reich defenses. Hitler left the Eagle's Nest and returned to Berlin. Göring showed his face only briefly in the Chancellery, then hurried back to Carinhall. As the Russian tank columns plowed on, literally flattening the refugee columns into the bloodstained snows, Göring found something of his old ruthlessness. On January 16, he announced a string of death sentences against junior officers and NCOs: for bolting under enemy mortar fire, for abandoning a flak battery, for putting on plain clothes and hiding with the French, for swapping gasoline for liquor. He ordered the Luftwaffe's General Waber shot for using military trucks in the Balkans, as Göring announced with well-simulated indignation, to transport "extraordinary quantities" of consumer goods back to Bavaria and Breslau: forty-one thousand cigarettes, a thousand bottles of champagne and spirits, and sixty kilograms of coffee had been found in Waber's houses there. "From one private house in Serbia he stole valuable works of art," Göring's announcement continued, itemizing: "A watercolor, a carpet, and two vases."

Over the next days it seemed that nothing would halt the Soviet invasion before Berlin. At night he heard the windows rattling to the gunfire and rumble of the tank engines. "Emmy," he said, padding into her bedroom, "there's nothing left between us and the Russians." Had the Nazis held on to the West Wall and the Vistula line, a compromise might have been possible—but not now. "People still won't see," his personal detectives heard him exclaim, "that we've lost the war!"

Hitler, however, believed that after the summer the new jets and U-boats would change the whole picture. Bormann and other fanatics backed him, and so did Grand Admiral Dönitz and Himmler. Göring now reluctantly agreed to give Galland's vacant office to Colonel Gordon Mac Gollob. ("I don't know him myself," said Hitler, "but the Reichsführer SS speaks highly of him.") That Göring was not behind Gollob's appointment was plain from the cold language of his Reichsmarschall Order of January 23, commending the new man to the Luftwaffe. "What matters," he suggested, "is neither the organization nor the man, only the aim that is common to us all—regaining mastery of Germany's air space."

Under house arrest in the Harz Mountains General Galland learned that the increasingly influential Colonel Gollob was building up a dossier on him—on his private use of Luftwaffe cars, his gambling, and his philandering. Galland lost his nerve as his private staff were called in for questioning about his alleged defeatism and disloyalty, and he talked of shooting himself like Udet and Jeschonnek. Acting through Hitler's adjutant von Below, Milch and Speer forced the Gestapo to drop the witch hunt to avoid yet another suicide scandal. Milch threatened to reveal to the Führer what he knew against Göring. "Just one percent of it," the stocky field marshal assured Colonel von Below, "will suffice to bring him a court-martial!"

The solution that Göring hereupon devised for the Galland problem was an uncharacteristically neat one: He summoned the general once more to Carinhall, ordered him to form an elite fighter squadron using only Me 262 jets, and to take the other "mutineers" like Steinhoff with him. In effect, given the crushing American daylight-fighter supremacy, Göring was making these fighter aces walk the plank. Galland's appointment to command this esoteric jet-fighter squadron, Jagdverband 44, was entered in the Luftwaffe war diary early in February 1945.

The evacuation of Silesia was almost over. Shortly these ancient, blood-soaked marchlands would become part of Poland. Asked by Hitler on January 27 about rumors that the British and American airmen held at the Sagan camp were going to be abandoned to the advancing Soviet Army, Göring heatedly blamed Himmler for his lack of foresight and pointed out, "They'll be getting ten thousand aviators." He suggested loading the prisoners aboard cattle trucks if need be. "Take off their pants and boots so they can't escape in the snow."

"Shoot them if they try to escape," added Hitler, approvingly.

Ten million refugees were now stampeding westward before the Russians across field and farm and frozen sea and waterway. The River Oder, last line of defense before Berlin, was still iced over. Some enemy tanks did get across, and on the night of January 29, one Russian monster clanked past Carinhall. The next afternoon Göring told all the women and children to leave Carinhall for the south. They mustered in the foggy, frosty courtyard. He lifted Edda and kissed her good-bye. Emmy arranged for her friends to join the Göring train west of Berlin and carried them down to Bavaria as well. Göring telephoned the Obersalzberg all day long until she picked up the phone and confirmed that they had arrived safely at the villa—still a peacetime idyll with warm baths and servants.

There was one unwanted family problem at this time. Heinrich Müller, chief of the Gestapo, had ordered Albert Göring's arrest for still more anti-Nazi misdemeanors. Invited in 1944 to a dinner in Bucharest with the ambassador Manfred Killinger, he had refused to "sit down with a murderer" (Killinger was the assassin of Socialist leader Walther von Rathenau). More recently, Albert had provided funds for Viennese Jews who had emigrated to Trieste. ("If you want to give money to Jews," the Reichsmarschall had lectured his younger brother, "that's your own affair. But be more careful —you're causing me endless difficulties.") Now he had to lean on the Gestapo again. "This is absolutely the last time I can help you," he told Albert after his release.

The jokes about Göring now had a more vinegary flavor. As one ancient German city after another paid the price of Göring's defeat, the British heard one captured Panzer Regiment's colonel wisecracking to his comrades that Göring was known as "Tengelmann," like the big chain store—"one in every city." Few of those cities had escaped destruction. The Reich capital itself, though scarred by thousand-bomber raids, was still alive and functioning, but Hitler held his conferences in the Chancellery's bunker—a subterranean labyrinth of tunnels and cramped cells, lavishly carpeted and walled with priceless paintings rescued from above-ground galleries.

Here, on February 2, 1945, he ordered Göring to move 123 heavy flak batteries from the cities into an antitank line along the frozen Oder: Holding the Russians here was more vital now than defending the ruins of ancient cities.

The next morning nine hundred American bombers launched a "terror raid" on Berlin. Huge new holes gaped in the Chancellery's façade. "During this morning's heavy raid on Berlin," recorded the Luftwaffe war diary, "the Reichsmarschall asks the chief of operations [General Christian] why not one of our own fighters was scrambled." The answer was that every available fighter was out counterattacking the Russians on the Oder. Göring decided to go out there too. With Emmy and the child gone, something of the old soldier stirred in his blood. After a hot bath and breakfast he now took to driving the sixty miles out to the front line and speaking with Skorzeny and the other officers defending the Frankfurt-on-Oder bridgehead. To this huntsman and forest spirit, the freezing plains were a welcome relief from the fetid, airless atmosphere of Hitler's bunker. ("He [Hitler] would scream about the uselessness of the Luftwaffe with such contempt and viciousness," recalled Göring later, "that I actually went red and squirmed. I preferred to go to the front to avoid these scenes.") Once, or so he would later claim, his car came under fire; and another time, sensing himself outflanked in the darkness by Russian tanks, Göring palmed a lethal cyanide capsule that Philipp Bouhler had obtained for him. The press ignored Göring's front-line visits, while those made by Admiral Dönitz were widely acclaimed. Hitler sneered at what he called Göring's "ridiculous excursions." "He *ordered* me to attend his war conferences," recalled Göring, "as though to say, 'Stand there and take it, damn you!' "

By February 6, his air force had emplaced 327 heavy flak batteries along the eastern front. Evidently none too sanguine about the battle's outcome, on the seventh the Reichsmarschall quietly called in Walter Hofer and chief architect Hetzelt to discuss evacuating the Carinhall treasures to Veldenstein—where to distribute the various items around the structure of this Franconian castle, and what modifications would be necessary to house the sculptures, paintings, tapestries, and furniture in its towers, tunnels, keeps, and stables.

The Russians launched a dangerous attack from their bridgehead at Steinau on the Oder. That day, February 8, Göring was—briefly—glimpsed down in Hitler's bunker with Field Marshal von Richthofen, now retired and terminally ill. That day too the American bombers were wrecking his synthetic-oil plant at Pölitz. With stocks of only six thousand tons of aviation fuel left, the air force would get only four hundred more tons in February. Inevitably, flying operations virtually halted.

Each time the Reichsmarschall eased his bulk into Hitler's bunker wearing the familiar uniform of soft, pearl-gray cloth, the diehard Nazis swooned with rage. Goebbels protested to Hitler. "Medal-jangling asses and vain, perfumed dandies don't belong in the high command," he wrote. "They must be eliminated."

Hitler agreed. "I am glad," he remarked, "that his wife at least has moved down to the Obersalzberg. She was the rotten influence on him."

Göring gloomily wrote his last will and testament on February 12, and drove in to Berlin for the afternoon conference. A thaw was breaking up the ice along the Oder, so the immediate danger there was lessening. But his fighter defenses were virtually immobilized by the lack of fuel.

Late on the thirteenth, radar reported enemy bombers penetrating deep into Germany behind a screen of electronic jamming. The night's real target was Dresden, Germany's "Florence of the Elbe."

One of Europe's most beautiful historic cities, Dresden had no air-raid shelters, and its streets were crowded with a million refugees from the east when the first three hundred RAF heavy bombers unloaded their fire bombs at 10:15 P.M. Three hours later, with the city's heart already a raging inferno visible 200 miles away, 529 more Lancaster bombers completed the destruction. Dresden, reported the Luftwaffe war diary, was "critically damaged, its inner city virtually destroyed, with immense casualties." On the following midday, the record book continued, twelve hundred American bombers attacked with "grave terror effect." Dresden had been engulfed during the night by a fire storm. The horrific scenes were without parallel in history— far worse than in Hamburg, Kassel, or Berlin. All telegraph lines were down, and British code-breakers heard Heinrich Himmler radioing to SS Obergruppenführer Ludolf von Alvensleben, the Dresden police chief, a message that showed how little Berlin was aware of the true horror. "I have received your report. The attacks were obviously very severe, yet every first air raid always gives the impression that the town has been completely destroyed. Take all necessary steps at once. . . . All the best." Göring, sensing disaster, sent Bodenschatz to report. The general returned to Carinhall ashen-faced, with word that fifty-one thousand dead had already been counted in Dresden. The death toll of that night's massacre would rise to over one hundred thousand.

As troops began to cremate Dresden's air-raid victims on makeshift pyres, five hundred at a time, Hitler swore revenge. His scientists had perfected the nerve gases tarin and sabun, which would have penetrated any Allied gas mask. Hitherto he had forbidden their use, as violating the Geneva Convention. Now he pondered whether it was not time to fight dirty too. Goebbels cackled approval, but Göring, Ribbentrop, and Dönitz were united in opposing any such late departure from the conventions and rules of war.

For Göring the setbacks now came thick and fast. One February morning French men and women agents were loaded aboard one of the Luftwaffe's two remaining captured B-17's in the high-security enclosure of Stuttgart's Echterdingen Airbase. Two billion French francs were stowed in the khaki-colored Flying Fortress with them. Their mission—the sabotage of France's entire economy. At ten-thirty all other flying operations were halted—"on orders from the Reichsmarschall"—while the plane took off, its obligatory tiny swastika barely visible on its tailplane. At three hundred feet the plane exploded. "One of those idiot bitches blew herself up," said a Heinkel pilot who witnessed the drama. "Eighteen dead! The next day the place was crawling with generals. . . . Hermann was furious. He got one hell of a cigar from the Führer for that one!"

Bad luck completed the disaster that poor security had begun. On March 2, the Luftwaffe lost its only other B-17: The plane had managed to set down its cargo and nine agents behind Allied lines. As it returned, an Allied night fighter shot it down, mistaking it for a German FW 200.

On the day after this incident Goebbels urged Hitler to replace the Reichsmarschall. Hitler had to reply that the air force had not produced one suitable successor. He also refused to force Göring to appoint an efficient Staatssekretär—"He'd freeze him out the moment he was appointed," Hitler said. "The Reichsmarschall can't abide strong personalities around him!"

Listening to the guns along the Oder, Göring dreamed that even now Hitler might stand down and allow him, the Reichsmarschall, to steer Germany into a negotiated peace. He admitted to Görnnert that this seemed unlikely, but he cautiously ventilated the subject of a deal to Hitler. "Frederick the Great," Hitler admonished him, "never struck bargains." He related to Goebbels on the eleventh that Göring had recommended they generate what he called "a new atmosphere" toward the enemy. "I told him," said Hitler, "he'd do better to occupy himself with generating a new atmosphere in the *air*." He could see the Reichsmarschall was completely shattered by his retort. "I just couldn't take it any longer," admitted Göring four months later. "I finally worked myself up into a state of nerves."

Hitler instructed him to lay the wreath at that year's Heroes Memorial Day. This was probably how he planned to employ Göring in the future—as a figurehead once more, while real men ran the war in the air. He engaged Himmler's ruthless engineer chief, SS Gruppenführer Hans Kammler, to take over the Me 262 deliveries to the squadrons.

On March 13, 1945, Göring sent his train to southern Germany loaded with a second cargo of art treasures from Carinhall—739 paintings, 60 pieces of sculpture, and 50 tapestries. He also turned over the seventeen priceless paintings and eleven crates of other relics "rescued from Monte Cassino" to the party Chancellery for separate shipment south, in a truck that left Berlin late on the fourteenth. It was loaded, as Martin Bormann was careful to notify his staff in Bavaria, with "the most valuable paintings from the

Reichsmarschall,'' and arrived at its destination, a disused mineshaft at Alt Aussee in Austria, two days later.

Göring now remained at Carinhall, although the walls were bare and the bookshelves empty. He descended into Hitler's bunker only infrequently. On March 18, a thousand American bombers again blasted Berlin, escorted by seven hundred fighter planes. Galland sent twenty-eight of his Me 262's into action against them. Hitler had now ordered every captured bomber aviator turned over to the Gestapo for liquidation. "Listen," shouted Göring to his chief of air staff, "has that man gone stark raving mad?"

Not caring what impression he made, Göring wheedled out of his Führer permission to travel down to Berchtesgaden briefly to "inspect the flak." More probably he wanted to check that his trainload of art had arrived safely at Veldenstein. He was living in a deranged world of his own. Hearing of the starvation among the refugees, he ordered one of his rare Schorf Heath bison shot and the carcass distributed to them. Choking upon a newspaper report of this, Goebbels recalled Marie Antoinette and her haughty advice to her own paupered subjects. His field offices reported an "unbridled hatred" of the Reichsmarschall—"Not a trace remains," rejoiced Goebbels, "of his former popularity."

In Göring's absence there emerged a crippling indecisiveness about certain secret Luftwaffe projects. Back in February, acting on the advice of Speer and Baumbach, Hitler had agreed to go ahead with Project Mistletoe, which the air force had long been planning: 120 piggy-backed planes—Ju 88's coupled with Me 109's—were standing by in East Prussia to bomb the principal Soviet power stations at last. Göring too approved, and the fuel was set aside. But in mid-March Hitler decided to hurl these planes at the bridges across the Oder and Neisse rivers the moment the major Russian offensive began. Then he changed his mind—he would use twenty-six of them against the bridges across the Vistula, in the Russians' rear. General Koller objected that the project had originally been designed to wipe out Stalin's power supplies, and that the remaining Mistletoes would not suffice for this project. Hitler hesitated, and was lost—torn between the immediate tactical needs of battle and his long-term strategic objectives: between inevitable defeat, and possible ultimate victory. "Imagine," he told Koller on March 26, "if the enemy had bombed all our power stations simultaneously! I'll forego the Vistula bridges—we can deal with them later."

"Ribbentrop," Hitler told his foreign minister, who was also anxious to end the war by diplomacy, "we're going to win this one by a nose." He mentioned the jet planes—in March 1945 Himmler's underground factory at Nordhausen would in fact assemble five hundred Me 262's and in April twice as many. The first Type XXI submarines were about to enter service —capable of cruising to Japan underwater and at high speed. By late 1945 bombproof underground refineries would be turning out three hundred thousand tons of synthetic gasoline per month. "If only," he remarked to Goebbels on March 21, "Göring had done more to rush the jets into service!" And he added bitterly, "He's just gone down to the Obersalzberg again with two trains, to see his wife."

Göring returned to Berlin keener on peacemaking than ever. When top civil servant Hans Lammers visited the Chancellery for the last time on March 27, he found the Führer very upset about the Reichsmarschall "attempting to start negotiations with the Allies." Emmy Göring certainly dropped hints to Görnnert, who stayed behind with the train, that her husband was thinking of contacting the Americans, and Göring confided to Speer that he was sure that the Americans knew he was on their side. One day five American airmen parachuted into the Schorf Heath, and Göring ordered their captain brought to Carinhall. Perhaps he was thinking ahead, to ways of establishing links to the Americans. But this officer had only been a movie director in Hollywood, and Göring lost interest in him.

General Koller's diary establishes how concerned Göring was to end the bloodshed now that Germany appeared to have lost. "Nobody tells us anything," Koller complained to Göring on March 28. "We badly need directives from top level."

> The Reichsmarschall agreed. He too is in the dark. F. [Führer] tells him nothing, won't permit the slightest political step. For instance, a British diplomat tried to enter into talks with us in Sweden, but this was flatly forbidden by Hitler.
>
> F. has prohibited Reichsmarschall to use his own extensive contacts. . . . F. has also rejected every opening that the foreign minister has reported to him.

Hitler ordered Göring to attend every war conference at 4:00 P.M., but he dealt preferentially with SS Gruppenführer Kammler. "Göring," wrote Goebbels on April 3, "has to listen day after day without being able to offer the slightest excuse."

Under pressure from every side, Göring made the decision to authorize Luftwaffe suicide missions. Volunteer pilots would ram the Luftwaffe's few remaining Me 109's into Allied bombers. In mid-March British code-breakers had already intercepted the message that Göring ordered all Geschwader commodores to read out secretly to pilots who had completed fighter training:

> The fateful struggle for the Reich, our people, and our native soil is at its climax. Virtually the whole world is fighting against us and is resolved to destroy us and, in blind hatred, to exterminate us. With our last and utmost strength we are standing up to this menacing onslaught. Now as never before in the history of the German fatherland we are threatened with final annihilation from

which there can be no revival. This danger can be arrested only
by the utmost preparedness of the supreme German warrior spirit.

Therefore, I turn to you at this decisive moment. By consciously
staking your own lives, save the nation from extinction! *I summon
you for an operation from which you will have only the slenderest
chance of returning*. Those of you who respond will be sent back
at once for pilot training. Comrades, you will take the place of
honor beside your most glorious Luftwaffe warriors. In the hour
of supreme danger, you will give the whole German people hope
of victory, and set an example for all time. GÖRING.

The first mission, code-named *Werewolf*, ran into pragmatic objections.
General Koller pointed out that if the Me 109's were used up on this, all
reconnaissance and conventional-fighter operations would collapse until
Focke-Wulf's new Ta 152 and the Me 262 became available in large
numbers. But Hitler gave the go-ahead. Several hundred volunteers were
given ten days of ideological training at Stendal, and on April 4, General
Pelz, whose IX Air Corps would control the mission, reported all ready for
Werewolf. "For psychological reasons," Pelz told the Luftwaffe high command, "we should not delay too long with the actual operation." Three days
later *Werewolf* was executed—one of the most desperate Luftwaffe operations
of the war. The Luftwaffe war diary confirms that 180 suicide crews took
part, escorted into battle by their less-exalted comrades from JG7 and the
first squadron of KG54(J). Astonished Allied radio monitors heard patriotic
marches flooding the fighter-control wavelength and a female choir singing
the German national anthem, while anonymous voices exhorted these 180
pilots to die—now—for the Führer and for Germany. Seventy of them did.

Such was the heroism of which Göring's young airmen were capable even
on the threshold of national defeat. But there were also acts of a different
hue. On March 30, Messerschmitt ferry-pilot Henry Fay picked up a brand
new Me 262 jet to fly to Neuburg Airbase on the Danube. He deserted to
the Americans and handed the top-secret plane over in return for a promise
of immediate release to his mother. Fay also revealed to the Americans where
the Me 262 and its fuel were manufactured, and described its most vulnerable
points. "Aim for the engines," he recommended, "as they catch fire easily."

At 5:00 A.M. on April 16, 1945, the final Soviet push across the Oder began.
Sixty more suicide pilots crash-bombed their planes onto the Oder bridges
in a desperate attempt to save Berlin.

But the decay of defeat had already reached the highest levels in the capital.
Learning that even Speer had disobeyed orders to destroy bridges within
Berlin, Hitler challenged him to say whether he still believed in victory.

"I cannot say that I do," the minister replied. But he agreed without
enthusiasm that he still *wished* that the war could be won.

"I thank you for saying the best you could," replied Hitler. "But I can say only this"—and Göring, watching, saw the perspiration standing out on his brow—"We must hold on until the last hour! No matter how much Donner and Blitzen! I know we shall come through."

Göring intended to come through. He was packed and ready to go. He was leaving one thousand air-force troops to guard his Carinhall estate. Demolition charges laced the beautiful structure. The art treasures too bulky to evacuate were being buried by troops of the Hermann Göring Panzer Corps and their position marked on a map—Houdon's "Bather," Pigalle's "Madame de Pompadour," and the famous Venus given to him by Italy. A costly fountain and two Cladion caryatids were carried out into the heath and hidden.

On April 19, he signed letters directing the August-Thyssen Bank to cable half a million marks to his personal account at the Bayerische Hypotheken und Wechsel Bank in Berchtesgaden, and closing out the old Deutsche Bank account that he had opened in Berlin's Schöneberg suburb when he first arrived there with Carin in 1928.

As midnight approached, he stationed his portly person outside Hitler's bunker and waited to go in, to present his birthday wishes. Many happy returns hardly seemed appropriate—he inquired whether he might be able to serve the Reich better at a distance from Berlin, Berchtesgaden perhaps?

Hitler merely nodded toward the door.

Göring took that as yes, but to his dismay Hitler phoned soon after to say that he would expect the Reichsmarschall at the midday conference as usual.

It was not a restful night, what with the Russian troops so close by. The next morning Göring plodded off through the pine woods to the mausoleum by the lake, to say farewell to Carin—the wife to whom he owed his personal salvation. As he eased his bulk down the narrow, moss-covered stone steps, he could hear the rippling sound of Russian artillery lobbing shells into the eastern outskirts of Berlin. He knelt briefly, then straightened and left the cold granite tomb where once he had planned to join her.

He drove along the deserted autobahn into the city, taking only his doctor Ramon von Ondarza with him. At the noon conference he found twenty senior officers standing shoulder to shoulder around the cramped briefing table. Hitler announced that he was splitting up the high command—Admiral Dönitz would command in the north and Göring in the south until such time as he himself arrived from Berlin. As he signed the orders, his right hand trembled violently.

Not keen to be trapped like a rat in Berlin, General Koller pointed out in his thick Bavarian brogue that nobody should bank on being able to fly out, and that the Russians might cut off Berlin at any moment. The bunker room emptied rapidly.

Göring lingered behind. "*Mein Führer*," he ventured. "I presume you have no objection to my leaving for the Obersalzberg right away?"

"Do what you want," said Hitler curtly. "But then Koller stays here."

It was an ignominious parting for two men who had been each other's fortune and misfortune for over twenty years. But even Koller found it hard to condemn Göring for turning his back on the clique around Hitler. He had not a single friend there now—there remained just ambitious men who had fought tooth and claw for power, while millions of ordinary citizens had perished.

It must have been now that a curious private discussion took place between Göring and Himmler. Göring touched on it only once in later months, saying it was the last time he saw Himmler (and Hitler's secretary Gerda Christian specifically recalled seeing Himmler and Göring talking this day). For "two or three hours," Göring recalled, they talked on the delicate topic of how to make contact with the enemy. Himmler smugly revealed that the Swedish Count Folke Bernadotte had recently visited him, and was actually returning for a further meeting that evening at Hohenlychen, the SS clinic. "You know," boasted Himmler, "he must be the man sent by Eisenhower to negotiate."

Göring felt sick. "I can't believe that," he said woodenly. "Don't take offense, but I doubt that they'll find *you* acceptable as a negotiating partner."

"Sorry to contradict," smiled Himmler. "But I have incontrovertible proof that I am considered abroad to be the only person capable of maintaining order."

At this, Göring shut up. Perhaps Himmler knew more than he. As they parted, the Reichsführer asked him rather too insistently whether he, Göring, would appoint him chancellor in the event that anything now happened to the Führer. Göring mumbled that that would not be possible since constitutionally both offices were now combined.

"Herr Reichsmarschall," persisted Himmler delicately. "If anything should prevent you from succeeding the Führer—say you are eliminated (*ausgeschaltet*)—can I have the job?"

Göring gulped. Eliminated? He recalled that after the July 1944 bomb plot Popitz had testified under interrogation that Himmler was planning to replace Göring in the line of succession, and that upon reading this he had asked permission to interrogate the condemned man himself: But the Gestapo hangman had got to Popitz first. "My dear Himmler," he replied uneasily. "We shall have to wait and see. That will depend upon circumstances. I can't see for the life of me what might prevent me from taking up the office."

Darkness fell on the Reich capital. RAF Mosquito bombers had begun pummeling Berlin. On an impulse Göring decided to visit the air-raid shelters—although he would have been better advised to depart before the one remaining road to the south was overrun.

It is clear that he wanted to test his own popularity. Wisecracking his way from one bunker to another, he said farewell to the stoical Berliners. Word spread ahead, and messengers came from other shelters—the people there wanted to see "Herr Meier," the Reichsmarschall, too. He doubted they would have greeted the Reichsführer SS like this. After that, in his own words later, "We headed for the hills."

It was 2:20 A.M. before he and Ondarza arrived out at Kurfürst. His own armor-plated limousine, chauffeured by the trusty Wilhelm Schulz, was followed out of the courtyard by four more, laden with staff, detectives, and Philipp Bouhler. In Göring's own limousine traveled his manservant Robert and nurse Christa, who had custody of his medicine cabinet. Throughout the night the convoy drove south between the closing jaws of the Russian and American armies. Once, around Jüterbog, he glanced back. The skyline was rimmed by a fiery haze lit by the flicker of artillery. Relief at escaping eclipsed all other emotions. Tomorrow he would be on the Obersalzberg: From there he intended to extend formal peace feelers to Eisenhower and Churchill. He would end the war parleying and dealing, just as he had begun it, and he would not allow Herr Himmler to preempt him.

The route passed through Pilsen in Czechoslovakia. The Air Ministry had been evacuated here, but he made no attempt to contact it, merely pausing at a mobile flak unit to refuel before driving on.

He arrived on the Obersalzberg at 11:00 A.M. The villa was crowded— Edda, Emmy, her sister, nephews, and nieces. Since Hermann's sister Paula was here too—the Russians were sweeping across Austria—he was surrounded by the females of his family. Here, he was at peace. No 88's barked into the tranquil mountain skies, no searchlights fingered the horizon, when phones jangled they did so only distantly.

Dismissing from his mind even the six railroad cars with Hofer and the art collection down at Berchtesgaden, Hermann Göring tucked himself into his bed and fell into a long and dreamless sleep.

PART 6
THE SURROGATE

42

INTO THE CAGE

Often it is only in adversity that a man rises above his superficial character. For Reichsmarschall Hermann Göring, now age fifty-two, that adversity began with his delivery into American hands on Tuesday evening, May 7, 1945. He possessed at that moment the same lethal elixir that many of his comrades now chose; he had concealed about his personal effects at least three brass capsules that Philipp ("Ango") Bouhler had given him—each fashioned from a nine-millimeter cartridge case about one and a half inches (35mm) long, and each containing a glass phial of hydrocyanic acid.

But he did not mean to swallow poison yet. He was acutely aware that his illustrious name was now the butt of derision. Meaner contemporaries might prostrate themselves before their captors, but he would stand his ground, fight one last defiant round, and die in honor.

As the little convoys of American and German cars met, the darkening valleys around echoed with the crackle and thunder of exploding ammunition as German troops destroyed their remaining stocks. Brigadier General Robert I. Stack, assistant commander of the 36th U.S. Infantry Division, motioned Göring toward his car. To the young Luftwaffe troops who clustered around, the American general's aide announced, "Your Reichsmarschall is kaput!"

Stack suggested that they spend the night at Fischhorn Castle near Zell am See before returning to the American lines.

As they drove up to the gaunt stone building, Göring glimpsed a G.I. and an SS officer standing guard on opposite sides of the gateway. Rather alarmingly, the castle still housed the staff of an SS cavalry division.* "Guard me well," he said, turning to his captors, but a Luftwaffe major noticed that his face was wreathed in smiles. Emmy and Heli Bouhler fell into each other's arms as they stepped out of the cars.

"When do I get to meet Eisenhower?" asked Göring.

Stack answered evasively.

Later, Göring returned to the matter. He turned to the interpreter. "Ask General Stack," he said, "whether I should wear a pistol or my ceremonial dagger when I appear before Eisenhower."

"I don't care two hoots," retorted the general.

Göring flushed, and went up to the room allocated to him to take a bath before dinner. He put on his pearl-gray uniform and a dozen medals, and posed impatiently for photographers, standing in front of the Lone Star flag of Texas. Before retiring from the dinner table, he asked whether he might retain four submachine guns for his protection. After talking it over with the castle's SS commander, Standartenführer [Colonel] Waldemar Fegelein, the American allowed him this comfort.

"I've formed a good impression of Stack," Göring told Emmy privately. "Perhaps I can still do something to help Germany."

She automatically lowered the window blinds before switching on the lights. "The war's over," Göring benignly reminded her, and withdrew into his room. She had asked for a separate room for herself and little Edda— she wanted her husband to be alone to compose his thoughts for the next day's historic meetings. She could hear the floorboards creak as he paced up and down in carpet slippers, imagining his dialogue with General Eisenhower the next day.

They parted in the castle courtyard the next morning. He had chosen a plain air-force uniform with forage cap—a ring or two and bejeweled cufflinks being the day's only concession to foppery. "It's not farewell," he reassured her as he climbed into the flashy twelve-cylinder Maybach for the drive through the lines to Stack's headquarters. "Things are looking good."

She gave him a meaningful look. "Do you still have what Ango gave you?"

He nodded, barely perceptibly, not taking his eyes off the matching blue set of luggage as it was stowed into the American cars. They parted. It would be eighteen months before he saw either wife or daughter again.

---

*In its basement an SS officer had concealed a tin trunk containing the private diaries of Hitler's mistress Eva Braun and bundles of the hundreds of letters that she and Adolf had exchanged. Found by an American CIC officer a few months later, these documents are now sadly missing.

The Texas Division had its headquarters in the five-star Grand Hotel at Kitzbühl. G.I.'s and reporters mobbed the little convoy as it arrived. The division commander, Major General John E. Dahlquist, saluted Göring, shook hands, and invited him to share his lunch of chicken, potatoes, and peas eaten out of a mess tin. Afterwards, the Reichsmarschall—for such was still his rank—went out onto the hotel balcony so that the American and German troops milling around the Maybach could take snapshots. One report even said he had a champagne glass in his hand.

Dahlquist asked his opinion of the other Nazi leaders. Still angry at the Führer's all too recent death sentence on him, Göring described Hitler as narrow-minded and ignorant, adding that Ribbentrop was a scoundrel and Hess an eccentric. Dahlquist perceived an underlying irritation at his captors' tardiness in bringing him together with Eisenhower.

As the days wore on, such a meeting seemed increasingly unlikely. A tiny Piper Cub flew him on May 10 across to U.S. Seventh Army headquarters at Augsburg. His composure was unshaken until Lieutenant General Alexander M. Patch asked him why Nazi Germany had not overrun Spain and Gibraltar in 1940, thus bottling up the British Fleet in the Mediterranean. "That was always my advice!" screamed Göring. "Always, always, always! And it was never, never taken."

At 5:00 P.M. he was brought face to face with his principal American adversary, General Spaatz, commanding general of the U.S. strategic air forces. Göring saluted, and Spaatz gave the correct salute in response (nor did he have the slightest misgivings about doing so, as he told Colonel Lindbergh five days later). Bruce Hopper, Spaatz's chief historian, took in the heavy silver ring on the Reichsmarschall's third finger, the clear blue eyes, the ruddy but not unpleasant features, the outsize thighs, and the tan-colored boots. Göring responded to questions with a good humor that belied his growing concern.

"In the Battle of Britain," asked Spaatz, "why did you maintain such rigid formations of fighters and bombers?"

"It was necessary to escort the bombers because their firepower was low (not like your bombers)."

"Was the Junkers 88 designed for the Battle of Britain?"

"We had nothing else," explained Göring. "I was not in favor of engaging in the Battle of Britain at that time. It was too early."

He asked Spaatz if a bottle of whiskey could be produced, and General Patch rather grudgingly obliged. Spaatz asked the Luftwaffe chief whether the jet airplane ever really had a chance of winning the war.

"Yes," said Göring, "I am convinced—if only we had had four or five months more. Our underground installations were practically ready. The factory in the Harz had a capacity of a thousand to twelve hundred jet airplanes a month. Now with five to six thousand jets, the outcome would have been very different!"

Lieutenant General Hoyt Vandenberg, of the Ninth Air Force, chipped in, "But could you have trained sufficient jet pilots given your shortage of oil?"

"Oh, yes," replied Göring. "We would have had underground oil plants producing a sufficient quantity for the jets. The pilot's conversion to the jets was very easy. Output of jet pilots was always a month ahead of jet-aircraft production."

Spaatz leaned forward. He inquired intently which had contributed more to the defeat of Nazi Germany—precision bombing or area bombing? It was a question of patriotic importance, and Göring knew it. "Your precision bombing," he flattered Spaatz, "because that was decisive. A ruined industry was difficult to replace. . . . I myself planned to carry out only precision bombing at the beginning. I wanted to lay a barrier of contact mines around Britain and seal off her ports, but again I was forced to do otherwise by political *Diktat*."

Recalling this unusual dialogue years later in an oral interview, Brigadier General Glenn O. Barcus remembered that Spaatz asked Göring whether he had any recommendations as to the improvement of American airpower. "Göring kind of smiled, and said, 'I should be telling *you* about how to use air power!' " The verbatim record in Spaatz's papers shows that he asked, "If you had to design the Luftwaffe again, what would be the first airplane you would develop?" "The jet fighter," said Göring, "and then the jet bomber. The problem of speed has been solved. It is now a question of fuel. The jet fighter consumes too much. The Me 264 jet bomber, designed to fly to America and back, awaited only the final solution of this problem."

"Did you have a three-inch gun for the jet?" asked Spaatz.

"The fifty-five-millimeter cannon, which is only now going into production, would have made a great difference in the jet. While waiting for that, we were using the fifty-five-millimeter rocket. You might find some jet airplanes around Germany equipped with [55mm] antitank guns. Don't blame me for such monstrosities. This was done on the explicit orders of the Führer. Hitler knew nothing about the air . . . absolutely nothing. He even considered the Me 262 to be a bomber, and he insisted it should be called a bomber!"

After this talk they took him into the kitchen of the camp office, and stripped him of all his medals and insignia except for his Reichsmarschall's epaulets. On the following day, May 11, 1945, he was taken out of the back door of the two-story suburban house in Augsburg to meet fifty Allied newspapermen. Gripping a pair of matching gray suede gloves, he slumped into an easy chair and mopped at his brow as the shutters clicked. After five minutes they allowed him to move into the thin shade of a willow tree. The questioning resumed. Heaping blame for the first time in public on Martin Bormann, he insisted that it must have been Bormann and not Hitler who had nominated Dönitz as the new Führer. "Hitler," rasped Göring, "did not leave a thing in writing saying that Dönitz was to take his place!"

He publicly revealed that he had opposed Hitler's attack on Russia. "I pointed out to him," said Göring, "his own words in *Mein Kampf* concerning a two-front war. . . . But Hitler believed that by the year's end he could bring Russia to her knees." He revealed to the newspapermen his unhappiest moment of the war. "The greatest surprise of the war to us was the long-range fighter bomber that could take off from England, attack Berlin, and return to its home base. I realized," he added disarmingly, "that the war was lost shortly after the [June 1944] invasion of France and the subsequent breakthrough."

Asked inevitably about the Nazi extermination camps, Göring was dismissive. "I was never so close to Hitler as to have him express himself to me on this subject," he said. He was sure that these atrocity reports were "merely propaganda. Hitler," he concluded, recalling that trembling right hand signing the documents, "had something wrong with his brain the last time I saw him."

Göring was removed to the Seventh Army's interrogation center at the Villa Pagenstecher in Wiesbaden and he was held here for a week. "Göring tried hard to make a case for himself," wrote one of the Intelligence officers after interviewing him, "and despite rumors to the contrary is far from being mentally deranged. In fact he must be considered a very 'shrewd customer,' a great actor and professional liar who most likely made some mental reservations, trying to keep what he might consider a few aces up his sleeve in order to have some bargaining power if and when the need arises." "If you know my speeches," Göring said at one point, "you will admit that in none of them have I attacked foreign statesmen in person." With the utmost sincerity he even claimed never to have signed a man's death warrant, or sent anybody to a concentration camp—"*never, never, never*. Unless of course," he remarked as an afterthought, "it was a question of military necessity and expediency!"

He still sidestepped all knowledge of atrocities in the camps. "I always thought that they were places where people were put to useful work," he said. Shown grim pictures taken at Dachau, he pondered overnight and came up with this answer: "Those pictures that you showed me yesterday must depict things that happened in the final few days. . . . Himmler must have suddenly derived a fiendish pleasure from such things." He redoubled his efforts to disclaim any responsibility. He reminded his interrogators that the atrocity stories spread after World War I had turned out to be untrue.

Hidden microphones heard him discuss at length with Hans Lammers the "fraudulent" claim by Dönitz to be the new head of government. "You know about it," Göring reminded Lammer, "only through Dönitz's broadcast. Anybody might turn up tomorrow and declare, 'I received a radio signal after Dönitz got his—now *I* am head of state!' But *I* have written proof." Lammers listened intently. "Yes," he agreed, "that's clear. He'll have to produce documentary proof."

The two men reexamined the decrees signed by Hitler in 1934 and 1941, then reconsidered the last signal Bormann had transmitted from the bunker: "*In the place of Reichsmarschall Göring, the Führer appoints you, Grand Admiral, as his successor.*" "Is there anything," shouted Göring, "more fantastic than this fraud committed by Bormann? . . . Well, I must say those damn crooks have pulled a fast one. It beats everything. . . . I always knew that if anything happened to the Führer, my life would be in the gravest danger for the next forty-eight hours. After that I would have been sworn in and it would have taken legal effect. Whatever happened, I would have arrested Bormann in forty-eight hours—and he knew it, too!—and sacked Ribbentrop. Those two were the thorns in my flesh."

Talking with interrogators again, he willingly blamed Hitler but denied that they had seriously planned to use chemical warfare or nerve gas. "None of your gas masks would have afforded any protection," he added. "This gas was so dangerous that I would not permit another demonstration. I knew that the gas would have had to be transported to the rear when the Americans came, and the result of an air attack on the train might have been cata-strophic. . . . We knew we were the more advanced in chemical warfare and that we had the more deadly gases." Talking of the fire storms in Hamburg and Dresden, he dabbed at his eyes. "It was terrible," he said. "The people of Dresden could not believe that you would bomb their city, because they thought that Dresden was too well known as a cultural center." Then he changed the subject. "The people," he boasted to chief interrogator Major Paul Kubala, "never called me anything but Hermann! Just Hermann! Never anything but Hermann! To be called by one's first name—*that* is the height of popularity."

His evacuated Carinhall art collection had now been found. The special train had carried on from Veldenstein to Berchtesgaden on April 13. Göring's troops had carried the most spectacular items into a secret cavern walled into a tunnel beneath his staff quarters on the Unsterstein Mountain. As the French Moroccan troops invaded Berchtesgaden, Hofer and Göring's secretary Fräu-lein Limberger fled the train. "Jewel cases were opened," said Göring later, "and the gems taken, the settings were scattered all around."

After the French came the Americans, the famous 101st Airborne Division. Questioning Göring's household staff, Lieutenant Raymond F. Newkirk heard the first rumors of the walled-up cavern. The tunnel's engineer was located, and he led Newkirk to the second level of a series of underground tunnels. A platoon of U.S. Army engineers broke into the hidden room. It took four days to empty the cavern. It was very damp, and the priceless contents were protected from the water dripping from the ceiling only by costly tapestries that had been hastily flung over them. The paintings were stacked up outside—works by Rubens, Rembrandt, Van Dyck, Boucher, and Botticelli. There was the "Infanta Margareta" by Velázquez, which Göring had bought from a seized Rothschild collection in 1941; and there was a "Rembrandt" head of an old man with marvelous nuances of gray, which Göring had bought from a Paris dealer in 1940.*

Göring never let his blue luggage out of his sight. Occasionally he checked his magnificently crafted toilet case with all the colognes, hand cream, and talcum powder to make sure that nothing was missing.

"Where are your private jewels?" he was asked by one interrogator.

"I would like to know that myself," was his wan reply.

On May 14, his valet Robert had been sent back to Fischhorn Castle to collect a Rothschild painting. Göring handed it over to Major Kubala and the French liaison officer, Captain Albert Zoller, on the fifteenth—a fifteenth-century painting called "The Madonna of Memling." His bejeweled Reichsmarschall's baton was at that very moment in a parcel being mailed home by a G.I.; intercepted by U.S. Customs, it is now on display at West Point. His 1935 Wedding Sword, stolen by an American platoon sergeant, dwells in a bank safe in Indiana—its value enhanced by the legends about its owner, as though it were Siegfried's sword itself.

Göring had several conversations with the Frenchman Zoller. "Little things," he philosophized, "can have big results. All our cities were devastated, one after the other, and those damned aluminum strips were to blame!"

Several more times the hidden microphones overheard him talking to Lammers about what he would have done if Hitler had died earlier. "I told some gauleiters who were close to me," he remarked on May 19, "about a year and a half ago . . . that if Fate ever destined me to succeed Hitler, I would place a supreme court above me. I told myself that no man ought to assume the responsibility of being answerable to nobody. A dictatorship," he wheezed, "must never come again. It does not work. We see it now. In the beginning everything is wonderful, but then it all gets out of hand."

He complained several times about the humiliating treatment by the Americans. "It is usual," he told Major Kubala, "for a marshal to have a house of his own to live in." Kubala reported that Göring was claiming to have asked Eisenhower for safe-conduct when he "gave himself up," and was indignant now to find himself a prisoner of war. "He is worried," added Kubala on May 23, "about his private possessions."

Göring kept a huntsman's weather eye open for officers whom he could use. He blatantly flattered the Americans. "Without the American Air Force," he assured Lieutenant Colonel Eric M. Warburg, a former Hamburg banker who had served in the Prussian artillery in World War I, "the war would still be going on—but assuredly not on German soil!" He pitted his brains particularly against "Major Evans,"—in real life the Wall Street financier Ernst Englander. Englander was motivated by a thirst for revenge. "I should like to see those boys hang and sweat," he wrote in one private letter at this

---

*The "Rembrandt" was a fake.

time, "rather than to make themselves out as heroes and martyrs." For several days they sparred. "I found it easier," Englander wrote, "to deal with them by getting reasonably chummy, and as a result Göring asked me to do a favor and see his wife for him."

A tattered snapshot of Emmy and Edda was Göring's most cherished possession. On the back he now penned these words to Emmy: "Major Evans has my confidence. Hermann Göring." To remunerate the officer he also gave him a portrait, signed to "Major Evans, in grateful memory, Hermann Göring." Englander thanked him effusively. It did not escape the prisoner that some American officers would do almost anything in return for a personal souvenir.

On May 20, 1945, they flew him in a small six-seater plane—he had to enter through the cargo hatch—to Luxembourg. With him went a written report from Major Kubala, warning against regarding the captive as a comical figure. Göring was cool and calculating, and "able to grasp the fundamental issues under discussion quickly. He is certainly not a man to be underrated."

They held him in Luxembourg for three months. It was plain that there was to be a major trial. Among the fifty fellow Nazis interned here in the Grand Hotel of the little spa town of Mondorf-les-Bains he found Hans Frank, his wrists still bandaged from a suicide attempt, as well as Bohle, Brandt, Daluege, Darré, Frick, Funk, Jodl, Keitel, Ley, Ribbentrop, Rosenberg, and Streicher. He registered with quiet satisfaction that Dönitz, his rival as "Hitler's successor," had also been unceremoniously dumped here too. They agreed on an uneasy truce. "I have always been the second man in the state," Göring told the admiral's adjutant Walther Lüdde-Neurath. "And you can be quite certain that if we're for the high jump, mine will be the first head into the noose!"

There was little luxury about his fourth-floor room. To prevent suicides, the Americans had removed all power supplies and light bulbs and had replaced sixteen hundred window panes with Perspex sheets. After General Greim, his successor as commander in chief, swallowed poison on May 24, the Americans suddenly seized Göring's luggage, to his dismay, and a triumphant G.I. immediately found the brass cyanide cartridge that he had concealed in a tin of American coffee. The Americans now looked no further.

This unusual hotel was commanded by Burton C. Andrus, a pompous and unimaginative colonel in the U.S. Cavalry who moved about majestically, his plump figure impeccably garbed in a uniform and highly polished helmet. Andrus had not been anxious for the job. He knew, as he told his family a year later, that this was one job where he could not win: Like a tightrope walker crossing Niagara Falls, he knew that if he slipped it would be his neck; while if he didn't, the box-office receipts went to the stockholders. Göring gave him sleepless nights to the end of his life. Minutes before Colonel

Andrus died, years later, he stumbled out of bed, wide-eyed and staring, moaning: "I've got to get to Göring's cell—he's killing himself!"

The hatred was mutual between the two men. Göring called him the "fire chief" because of that helmet, and squirmed to think that this man had sequestered all his treasures, including, according to the inventory in the Andrus papers:

> one gold Luftwaffe badge; one gold Luftwaffe badge with diamonds; one desk watch; one traveling clock by Movado; *one large personal toilet case*,* one gold cigarette case, inlaid with amethyst and monogrammed by Prince Paul of Yugoslavia; one silver pill box; one gold and velvet cigar case; one square watch by Cartier, set with diamonds; one gold chain, gold pencil, and cutter; three keys; one emerald ring; one diamond ring; one ruby ring; four semi-precious buttons; one small eagle with diamond clips; one diamond Luftwaffe brooch; four cufflinks with semi-precious stones; one gold pin (evergreen twig); one pearl stickpin; one gold stickpin with swastika of diamond chips; one watch fob (platinum, onyx stones, diamond, inlaid Luftwaffe insignia); one personal seal (in silver); one small watch set with artificial diamonds; one medal Pour le Mérite; one Iron Cross 1st Class, 1914; one Gross Kreuz; one gold cigarette-lighter, one wrist watch; two old Norse collar buckles; one brass compass; *one fountain pen inscribed "Hermann Göring"*; one silver cigar-cutter; one brooch; one silver watch; one set of lapis lazuli cuff buttons; one silver box, heart-shaped; one platinum Iron Cross; one gilded pencil; *one large Swiss wristwatch*; 81,268 Reichsmarks.

It is worth noting what became of this personal treasure trove. The "toilet case" italicized above was back in his possession at the end, nobody knows how. After Göring's death, Emmy signed a receipt—still in Andrus's private papers—for 750 Reichsmarks, two large suitcases, one hatbox, one fitted bag, and other listed items that did not include any of the medals inventoried earlier, nor the fountain pen or large Swiss wristwatch italicized above. Evidently he had given these away. The latter items, pen and wristwatch, were later seen in the possession of the widow of Jack Wheelis, the U.S. Army second lieutenant whom he had befriended before his death, as will be seen.

Andrus was a meticulous keeper of records. He was committed to keeping these men alive, and his security measures here at Mondorf did not improve

---

*Italics here and below are the author's.

their mood. He allowed them no knives, and meals were eaten off plain brown glazed crockery with a blunt spoon.

"I used to feed my dogs better than this," growled Göring.

"Then you fed them better than your own soldiers," shouted a German kitchen hand—a remark that convinced Colonel Andrus, as he later testified to an army board of inquiry, that he could rely on these Germans not to give illegal succor to his captives.

Göring plunged into a deepening gloom. He began to worry incessantly: about the fate of Emmy and little Edda, and about how to get into his blue leather cases.

43
FAT STUFF

"The cause for which Göring stood," the Seventh Army interrogation center had reported on May 23, 1945, "is lost. But the canny Hermann even now thinks only what he can do to salvage some of his personal fortune, and to create an advantageous position for himself. He condemns the once-beloved Führer without hesitation. Up to now he has not made a plea in favor of his former henchmen, alive or dead. Yet behind his spirited and often witty conversation is a constant watchfulness for the opportunity to place himself in a favorable light."

Göring's treatment at Mondorf had undoubtedly shaken him. His valet Robert had been taken away from him. His room was barely furnished and unlit. Of his toilet articles he had been left only a sponge, soap, and toothbrush—nothing else, not even a comb. He wrote to protest to Eisenhower at this illegal treatment. "I cannot believe that Your Excellency wishes and knows about the humiliating effect this treatment has upon me." He requested permission to return briefly by plane to his family so that he could at least make the most essential arrangements for them and take proper leave of them. He received no reply.

To while away that time, Admiral Hans von Friedeburg's adjutant taught the fifty imprisoned men how to play Battleships. Göring sank Dönitz's warships with as much gusto as if they had been real, but he did not like to lose, and once the admiral protested, "Hermann's cheating! If he doesn't like where my shells are falling, he marks them in on different squares!"

Given a medical examination, Göring weighed in at 264 pounds, which was very fat indeed. (He would weigh only 186 pounds at the end.) His height was five foot ten, he was perspiring profusely, short of breath but not acutely ill. His pulse was 84, but full of extra contractions (systoles). "His skin," reported the medic, "is moist, pale, and sallow except his face, which is flushed. There is a marked irregular tremor of both hands and he appears to be extremely nervous or excited." They found no diseases, and remarked that he was well developed "but extremely obese, flaccid, and generally in very poor physical condition." Göring told the doctors that over the past few months he had suffered increasingly frequent heart attacks "manifested by pericardial distress, dyspnoea, profuse perspiration, and nervousness."

The Americans had found two thousand mysterious white pills in his possession. He told them he took twenty each day, night and morning. "My surgeon," explained Andrus helplessly to Supreme Headquarters, Allied Expeditionary Force (SHAEF) on May 23, "reports that if we suddenly remove this [medication] from him he will become totally demented." SHAEF replied that their only concern was that the prisoner remain coherent for some time to come. "There are a number of things we wish to ask him," they notified Andrus, referring probably to Europe's missing art treasures, "before we finally lose interest in what happens to him."

Colonel Andrus directed his prison surgeon, Captain (M.C.) Clint L. Miller, to reduce the dosage of these pills as rapidly as possible without killing Göring or driving him insane. Nine of the pills had meanwhile been sent to Washington, D.C., for analysis. "It was found," reported the FBI in a letter signed by J. Edgar Hoover himself, "that the tablets contain 10 mg or 1/16 grain of the narcotic dihydro-codeine." Dr. Nathan B. Eddy of the National Institutes of Health described this as "not approaching morphine in its effects or degree of addiction," being only about one-fifth as strong as morphine, but Eddy warned that any abrupt withdrawal would evoke the same severe symptoms.

The interrogations of "Fat Stuff," as the Americans here called him, were less friendly than at Augsburg. Major Hiram Gans, a SHAEF financial expert, tried to throw light on the truculent Reichsmarschall's monetary dealings. "Does your wife have an insurance policy?"

"No."

"Did you leave anything for your child?"

"She gets something at the age of twenty. You can have that too!"

"We're not kidding! These are things that you robbed from everyone else, and we are going to see that they are restored."

Göring corrected him. In his view he had acquired his art collection quite legally.

"Most of these things were bought, yes," conceded Gans, who had evidently done his homework. "But at a price fixed by you!"

Subtly playing on underlying American fears, Göring spoke of the seductive Russian propaganda methods and reminded Gans that once before Germany and Russia had collaborated for a century. "At first," he continued, referring to most recent history, "the Germans were very afraid of the Russians. . . . Immediately after the collapse, the Russians did a skillful job over the radio: they proclaimed that Germany must not be partitioned again, and they started to reopen the German theaters. In this zone you have adopted the opposite approach."

The Americans found it hard to undermine his morale although he was now deeply concerned about Emmy and Edda. On June 25 Lieutenant Herbert Dubois took over the grilling. "Do you know that Hitler, Himmler, and Goebbels are dead? . . . You are the last great Nazi. How did you manage to survive? Why haven't you died?"

"It was an accident," responded Göring. Dubois discomfited him by asking about the billion Reichsmark fine that he had levied on the Jewish community in November 1938. "Is a German field marshal never ashamed?" he challenged.

At first the Reichsmarschall was evasive—"I don't have to answer that question under the Geneva Convention"—but he immediately afterward softened enough to utter one of his rare expressions of personal remorse. "I regret it. You have to take the times into account."

On May 10, 1945, Dr. Robert Kempner, a former Prussian civil servant who had emigrated to Pennsylvania, wrote to the Pentagon pointing out that during Göring's jurisdiction over police matters in 1933 many people had been tortured and killed. "Such cases," Kempner continued, "were brought to his personal attention. At that time bribery was one of the chief means of obtaining release from concentration camps. The money, jewelry, or gold cigarette cases were turned over to his fiancée, now Mrs. Emmy Sonnemann Göring, who has also been captured." Little of this was true, but to break down Göring's "staged self-assurance" Kempner pleaded for Göring to be brought to the United States for interrogation on his morphine addiction, on Emmy's "former intimate friendship with a Jewish theatrical man" and Hermann's "relationship to the late Austrian Jewish landowner Baron Hermann von Epenstein." The suggestion was disregarded. Instead Kempner, himself a Jew, would be taken onto the prosecution staff at Nuremberg.

Evidence against Göring was raked together from the most eclectic sources. British intelligence intercepted a letter in June 1945 from Stockholm to London in which a Mrs. Anna Morck wrote that Göring had given jewelry to Carin's sister Lily Martin—"Things stolen from Poland and other places, which ought to be given back." Hidden microphones installed in a special prison camp outside London recorded Göring's generals in, as they thought, private conversation. Bodenschatz was heard telling Milch that Göring was "the most ungrateful man in the world!" "Always was," agreed Milch. "A rotten character." When he described the Reichsmarschall's mauve-painted fingernails Galland corrected him: "It wasn't paint, it was a transparent varnish." "Bodenschatz," said Milch, "you say the Führer gave Göring a monthly allowance of thirty thousand Reichsmarks. Do you imagine he met all his expenses out of *that*? . . . The three hundred and sixty thousand marks he received each *year* wouldn't last him even a month!" Each scrap of conversation was transcribed and sent secretly to brief Göring's interrogators.

Now calling himself "Major Emery," Ernst Englander visited this camp on June 5 and told Milch, Koller, and Galland that Göring was blackening their names. The angry generals exchanged more scuttlebutt about him. In his private diary Milch jotted down what the others told him of Göring's sleazy dealings with Heinkel, Siebel, Koppenberg, and aluminum factories in Norway. Told of Göring's apparent interest in Professor Morell's pharmaceutical empire, General Kreipe chimed in that the Reichsmarschall had also been the majority shareholder in a certain brand of contraceptives. "Do you know," replied Milch, capping that tidbit, "that our commander in chief received money personally for each picture hanging in a barracks?!" He banged his first on the table. "Do you know that our commander in chief pocketed a fine of fourteen million Dutch guilders imposed for a rebellion somewhere in Holland and transferred them to Switzerland for his personal use?* The SS told me all this, and backed it up with evidence. But there is such a thing as poetic justice, gentlemen! . . . Göring's chauffeur made off with a case containing all Mrs. Göring's jewelry."

Emmy Göring had been allowed to return to a little cottage near Veldenstein. One day an American army sergeant arrived and told her in confidence that her husband had been secretly tried and acquitted, and would be released the next day. Emmy had never been noted for political acuity. She happily gave the messenger a precious emerald ring, scraped together some victuals for a welcoming feast, and waited for several days before she could accept that the man had been a trickster.

Confined at Mondorf still, Göring paced his cage like a trapped lion. For a man born and bred in the mountains, who had spent his youth in the skies

---

*General Christiansen, military commander of the Netherlands, had imposed a 14-million-guilder levy on a Dutch community. The British informed Allied officials at Nuremberg of the overheard allegation, namely that Göring had given 1 million guilders of this fine to Christiansen and transferred the remainder as Swiss francs to Switzerland. Challenged about this on December 22, 1945, Göring dismissed it as "nonsense" and pointed out that "Krischan" came directly under the high command, not the air force.

and his manhood at the wheel of a sports car on Hitler's autobahns, every moment of this confinement hurt. He was wasting away. Front and profile mugshots taken on June 22 show him glowering and drawn. On July 10, similar photographs show the cheekbones protruding almost like when he was a young lieutenant in the Richthofen Squadron. But he was still defiant. "Except for a considerable loss in weight," the interrogators reported after seeing him on the seventh, "Göring's detention has not affected him very visibly. He is . . . very wary. Göring knows that we are trying to convict him of something, but he is not quite sure what that is."

The commandant, Colonel Andrus, ordered the paracodeine dosage reduced. On July 19, Göring counted the pills, noticed there were only sixteen, and complained, "Each day less and less." A German doctor had by now been introduced to the prisoners—Dr. Ludwig Pflücker, a mild-mannered urologist of the type that Göring had often noticed at health spas. Göring complained of headaches, and asked for a sedative. Pflücker, avoiding problems, applied heat therapy instead.

"Send up Fat Stuff!" The cry became routine that July and August in Mondorf, and Göring would attempt a pixie smile as he loped off to the interview room between two guards. On July 19 and 20, 1945, several U.S. Army historians came to talk with him. Their chief, Dr. George N. Shuster, had no axe to grind and allowed him free rein in venting his spleen about Hitler and Bormann. "Once," reminisced Göring, "we had to make four thousand phone calls to answer one single question from the Führer"—he still called Hitler that—"about an airplane engine." His real bête noire was Martin Bormann. "I can't conceal that Bormann was the Führer's evil genius, and I couldn't wish anything sweeter than to shoot the dog down myself. I haven't the slightest doubt that there would have been a reconciliation between the Führer and myself once we had begun winning in the air again."

To Kenneth W. Hechler, one of Shuster's team, such an interview was like reeling in a big fish—playing out just enough line to bring him in eventually. "*Morgen, Herr Reichsmarschall!*" he would greet him ingratiatingly, and listen with apparent sincerity to Göring's recital of the humiliations he was suffering and his role in the 1940 Nazi victories in France. Once Hechler tried to ask about the far more interesting 1944 Ardennes offensive, but Göring began by comparing it at length to the great Nazi lunge through Sedan in 1940 and never reached 1944 in his narrative.

"Göring," the interrogators warned on July 17, "has the happy faculty of believing his own fabrications, which upon repetition become more and more plausible to him." Hechler found he could detect when Göring was about to tell a whopper. His smile twisted, his words became more guttural, his hands swept fractionally wider; he tossed in more humorous quips too, as though to throw dust in his interrogators' eyes.

"If we had not invaded Normandy," he asked, "do you think you could have beaten Russia?"

Göring leaned forward and whispered in mock confidence that if Eisenhower had given his *personal* guarantee, the Germans would have socked the Soviets so hard that they would have seen the sun (he jabbed one finger skyward), the moon (another jab), and the stars (a whole galaxy of jabs). Hechler roared with laughter.

That Monday, July 23, a Soviet officers' commission arrived. Bellowing, "The Russians are coming!" Göring vanished into his cell. The next day he saw them nonetheless, and Hechler heard the Russians screaming at him.

> Suddenly [wrote Hechler four years later in a private memoir] I heard Göring starting to answer the interrogators. I couldn't distinguish what he was saying, but it was interrupted repeatedly by chuckles from the Russians. Soon Göring's voice rose, and the chuckles swelled to roars of laughter. For two hours the noise of guffaws echoed down the halls, and then the Russians came out slapping each other on the back.

Afterward, Göring came in to see the major and hitched up his baggy pants with a swagger. "I really had those Russkies rolling in the aisles, didn't I!"

Undoubtedly Fat Stuff was coming back fighting, and the Americans only had themselves to blame. On July 23, 1945, Colonel Andrus recorded a further cut in the paracodeine dosage. "He looks very good, is losing much weight [and] has apparently no other ill effects—except that he would like to get larger doses."

He still worked off his old grievances. He told Ribbentrop impolitely where he could file an eighty-five-page memorandum he had just composed. He still insisted that *he* was Hitler's surrogate, and nobody else. "Dönitz," he complained once more to Shuster on the twenty-third, "just took command on the basis of a radio message that was never confirmed in writing. Bormann signed it 'p.p. the Führer.' "

He had shed seventeen pounds already and was still losing weight. By July 26, his dosage had been cut to fifteen pills. Andrus noticed his disgust at "being short-changed," but that was all. On August 4, the colonel reported, "Göring states that his health is better now than it has been for years." He explained to his superiors, "It is our purpose not only to keep Göring well, but to eliminate any possible bar to trial or punishment."

Göring had already made the simple decision that eluded his co-defendants in the coming trial: to die like a man. He had never been afraid of death. As a lad, he had stood his ground when an Austrian avalanche had crashed around him. "The true German," he had sermonized to his staff on November 25, 1944, "faces up to the ultimate sacrifice with a certain sovereignty and peace of mind. . . . For me, life on this planet has just been an intermission during which I have had to perform as best I could. No more, and no less. . . . The devil take it, before I allow any man to drag me down and make me grovel just to cling on to this tattered thing called life!''

On August 5, the U.S. Army sent to SHAEF headquarters the formal list of prisoners to be turned over to the control of prosecuting counsel. Göring's name headed the list. He had become number-one man in Nazi Germany at last. Five days later his paracodeine medication was stopped for good.

Unwell once again, he remained upstairs in the Grand Hotel, suffering the old heart trouble, while his more fortunate fellow prisoners were mustered and left. All came to say their farewells except for two Staatssekretäre who churlishly refused. Dönitz's adjutant was the last to come up. Göring received him esconced at the head of his bed in a heap of blankets that he had contrived to convert into a kind of throne, as though sitting in the high chair at Carinhall. The naval officer could see he was in a brilliant mood, having obviously found his old form and vitality. "Whatever happens," the Reichsmarschall promised him, with the glint of coming battle in his eye, "you can count on me. There're one or two things I'm going to say at the coming trial."

That afternoon, August 12, 1945, an American C-47 transport plane flew him from Luxembourg to Nuremberg. Perhaps unaware that it was to be the last airplane journey of his life, he thoroughly enjoyed the trip and chattered keenly about the flight. "His health is probably not very good," warned an American officer three days later, "and on two recent occasions he was to be found in his dressing gown and pajamas in bed, as a result first of a slight heart attack and . . . bronchitis.''

Nuremberg was a landscape of ruins surrounding the Palace of Justice and its adjoining detention block. The cells were low-ceilinged cubicles barely thirteen feet by seven. Göring would sleep on a metal cot bolted to the floor along the left wall. Just to the right of the narrow doorway a porcelain toilet bowl was set in an alcove to afford minimal privacy. As his eyes took in the fresh plaster patches where iron hooks had been ripped out of the wall, the lack of electric wiring, and the Perspex freshly installed in the tiny windows high up the end wall, he must have smiled. He had no intention of ducking out of this last battle prematurely. He placed his few possessions on the little table—so flimsy that no prisoner, let alone a Hermann Göring, could stand on it—with pride of place going to a snapshot of Edda. "Dear Daddy," she had written on the back, "come back to me again soon. I have such longing for you. Many thousand kisses from your Edda!!!!"

Tight security precautions were also taken with medication. Pflücker injected daily Vitamin B and provided Seconal tablets to help him sleep despite the harsh new jail regime. Tormented by rheumatism, Göring was also occasionally allowed one aspirin, but he was watched to ensure that he swallowed it.

Colonel Andrus had ordered pencils and paper provided so that the prisoners could write private letters. These, Andrus reported, were "promptly sent to the chief of interrogation," Colonel John H. Amen.

One of Göring's first letters was to Helga Bouhler:

> Dear Heli!
>   As I don't know where Emmy and Edda are, please tell me their address if you know it. Are they still at Fischhorn? How are things with you? Where is Ango? Not very much I can tell you, we've all just got to grin and bear it. But I wish you all the best from the bottom of my heart.

Andrus could not have forwarded this letter even had he wanted to. "Ango" Bouhler had taken cyanide in U.S. captivity, and Helga had leaped to her death from a high window at Fischhorn.

The Americans pocketed these early letters and sold them off privately years later.

Of course, the prisoners were puzzled about the lack of any response. "We've been permitted to write letters and postcards for two months," wrote Keitel on October 10, "but no replies have been received."

Göring's blue luggage had been stowed in a baggage room to which only a few named officers held the key. "There was one item," Andrus would insist later, "that belonged to Göring which he was never allowed to go into, and that was a vanity case containing bottles, jars, nail file, scissors, etc. To the best of my knowledge this vanity case was never opened until it was searched for some salve"—a search that was a consequence, in fact, of the last posthumous shaft that Göring would loose off at the colonel, his detested jailer.

At the end of August 1945 Andrus asked Pflücker why the prisoners' condition was deteriorating, and the doctor pointed to the poor food and lack of human contact (so he testified to the later board of inquiry): "The colonel ordered better food. I was permitted to speak to the prisoners more."

He testified further that Göring suffered frequent heart attacks.

"I am not a heart specialist," he warned the colonel. "I have no heart instruments to make a proper examination."

The daily routine began at 7:00 A.M. with a prison trusty handing breakfast and a spoon through the Judas hole in Göring's cell door. A barber came and shaved him while a truncheon-wielding sentry ensured that no words were exchanged. "Sentinels moving back and forth on the catwalks," Andrus reassured Justice Robert H. Jackson, the chief American prosecutor, "view the prisoners every half minute." By five-thirty it was dark. At 6:00 P.M. he was given supper. His eyeglasses, pen, and wristwatch were taken away, and the cell light turned off at 9:30 P.M.; a spotlight then beamed through the hole in the door onto his face all night.

There was one episode on August 21 that suggests that Göring's health was indeed less robust than people believed. At 3:00 P.M. that day American officers performed the (wholly meaningless) ritual of discharging him from the German armed forces in an upstairs interrogation room, and he suffered yet another heart attack after being marched up the three flights of stairs. He was short of breath and exhausted when returned to his cell at 4:00 P.M., and complained of heart pains. The crisis lasted all night. His heart action became irregular, his pulse increased. An American army doctor administered a cardiac drug and phenobarbital both then and at 11:00 P.M. Attributing this crisis to the exertion as well as the ugly implications of the "discharge" charade, the American doctor ordered the Reichsmarschall to bed for two days. He confidentially warned Andrus that unless their prize captive was allowed thirty minutes of exercise outdoors each day, the next heart attack might be Göring's last.

The interrogations resumed, this time on a different tangent. Several times a week armed sentries handcuffed him and marched him down the stairs and along the covered catwalks to the interrogation rooms on the second floor of the Palace of Justice. Meetings with Allied questioners were conducted face to face across an open table. But to consult with his own counsel (the insipid, prim former patent and labor attorney Dr. Otto Stahmer had been assigned to him), he was taken behind a partition with windshield glass to bar any physical contact. Documents were passed through a slide after a sentinel had sniffed them to make sure they were not steeped in poison.

On August 28, Colonel Amen grilled him about Hitler's aggressive plans against Austria, Czechoslovakia, and Russia. "Considering that it is eight years ago," Göring said, playing for time, "it is almost impossible for me to pin down what the Führer said in 1937." He refused to co-sign the transcripts, thereby rendering them useless. Questioned on October 3 about allegations that the German Aviators' Club had paid Major Alexander Löhr 5 million Reichsmarks for information about the Austrian Air Force, he laughed incredulously. The Austrian Air Force had only one squadron, he pointed out. "I would probably have told him that for five schillings I would give *him* all the intelligence he needed about his own air force!" Asked by the humorless Amen on the eighth about alleged links between his Reich Forestry Administration and plans for a postwar Nazi guerrilla movement, Göring retorted with a grin that he couldn't imagine "what they could have done with my trees." Five days later Kempner took over the interrogation and claimed that both Diels and Gritzbach had incriminated Göring in the Reichstag fire. Göring called his bluff, demanding to be confronted with the two supposed witnesses. Kempner meekly put the allegations away.

Göring was worried about the silence surrounding his wife and daughter. On October 12, Dr. Douglas M. Kelley, the junior prison psychiatrist, took a letter to Emmy at Neuhaus, near Veldenstein. She asked him how Hermann was. "As firm as a rock in a raging sea," was the kind reply. She wrote him on the thirteenth and fourteenth, but the letters were not delivered.

To turn the psychological screw on the defendants, their families were now arrested. Even Göring's indignant brother Albert, whom American Special Intelligence had only recently contemplated using as an agent, was incarcerated. At 11:30 A.M. on October 15, Paul H. Goldenberg of the CIC arrested Emmy together with her niece, sister, and the nurse Christa Gormanns. The women were imprisoned in Straubing Jail, and Edda was put in an orphanage.

On October 19, Colonel Amen served the formal indictment on Göring. The transcript shows that he asked only for a trustworthy interpreter and an interview with his old lawyer, Hans Frank. But Frank was in the same boat as Göring now. Others proved more fragile, under this mounting pressure. Ley went insane and strangled himself with a wet towel on October 25. Göring expressed heartless satisfaction. "It's just as well," he told the psychiatrist, "because I had my doubts about how he would behave at the trial." He detected signs that Ribbentrop was cracking up too. "I'm not afraid of the soldiers," Göring remarked. "They'll behave themselves."

After Ley's suicide, Andrus redoubled the security precautions. Göring was repeatedly strip-searched, his private effects were picked through zealously, and he was often moved without warning to a different cell. Asked by Andrus to report, the new psychiatrist Dr. Gustave M. Gilbert assured the commandant that Göring was a very low suicide risk. At 138 Göring's I.Q. was inferior only to Hjalmar Schacht's (143) and Arthur Seyss-Inquart's (141). In fact, Göring's morale was so high that he was likely to prove their most troublesome defendant. When Gilbert remarked that the German public now openly regretted that the attempt on Hitler's life had failed, Göring roared at him. "Never mind what the people say *now*! I know what they said before! I know how they cheered when the going was good."

He looked forward to the trial with undisguised relish. "I can answer for anything I have done," he told Gilbert on November 11, but he added uneasily, "I can't answer for anything I haven't done." And he concluded, "I know what is in store for me."

That day he wrote a farewell letter to Emmy—just in case—and signed a new will. He handed the will to Otto Stahmer. The attorney revealed now that Emmy was being held in prison. Tears in his eyes, the Reichsmarschall told the other prisoners, "You see, the Americans are just as bad as the Gestapo. What have women and children got to do with this?"

On the nineteenth, he wrote Emmy a letter:

> My dearest,
>   Major Kelley still has the last letter I wrote you. If you've got
> back to Edda at Neuhaus, he'll drive out to give you the letter. . . .

If you're not back at Neuhaus, another letter will go to you at
the [Straubing prison] camp. . . .

The Nuremberg Trial began formally the next day, November 20, 1945.
Quietly regretting that he had to share the limelight with crackpots and
criminals, Hermann Göring asked for permission to get a change of uniform
from his baggage. He wanted to make a neat impression in the courtroom.

44
ON TRIAL

"As Reichsmarschall of the Greater German Reich, I assume political responsibility for my own acts." Thus Göring began the written declaration that he had planned to read out as the trial began on November 20, 1945. "Although answerable for these acts only to the German people and to the German courts," the statement continued, "I am nevertheless willing without recognizing the jurisdiction of this Tribunal, to provide it with any explanations that are desired and to speak the whole truth. I do however . . . refuse to accept responsibility for acts committed by others—acts of which I was unaware and which I would not have approved of or been able to prevent had I known of them. Hermann Göring."

Justice Robert H. Jackson, the U.S. chief prosecutor, had always regarded Göring as his principal adversary in the coming trial. They came from different worlds—the "Renaissance" figure from the bomb-devastated land of political assassins and military gangsters would be jousting with the wing-collared East Coast representative of the neat-lawned legal democracies. Jackson was a brave champion of human rights. It was he who had fought for a tribunal in the first place, whereas Roosevelt and Churchill had argued alike for a "political solution"—the liquidation of Göring and his consorts without even the pretense of a trial.

As Göring took his prominent place at the front and right-hand end of the dock, Jackson studied his face intently. He realized that so long as this Nazi leader did not choose to upset the procedure, none of the others would.

Called upon now to enter his plea of Guilty or Not Guilty, Göring stepped to the microphone, clutching his proposed declaration. "Before I answer—" he began.

The British presiding judge, Sir Geoffrey Lawrence, interrupted him. Göring doggedly began again, and Jackson caught his breath. But Lawrence firmly halted the defendant.

Göring murmured, "Not Guilty," adding quickly, "in the sense of the indictment." His declaration remained unread.

After the charges had been read out, Jackson opened the prosecution case with a major speech describing the Nazi crimes that had killed an estimated 5.7 million Jews. During the adjournment, somebody asked who had ordered these things, and Göring said, "Himmler, I suppose."

He was uncomfortable. "The German people will forever be condemned for these brutalities." He strove to achieve a monolithic defensive front, but these atrocities rendered that almost impossible.

On November 29, the court rang with laughter as his boisterous phone conversations with Ribbentrop and Prince Philipp during the Austria crisis of March 1938 were read out. But his pleasurable nostalgia was poisoned as awful film sequences were shown that afternoon of scenes in the concentration camps. "It just spoiled everything," he complained to Dr. Gilbert. Worse followed on the last day of the month. A prosecution witness, General Erwin Lahousen, the Abwehr department chief responsible for subversion and sabotage operations, described his own acts of treachery against Hitler. "That traitor!" thundered Göring during the lunch adjournment. "That's one we overlooked on the twentieth of July. Hitler was right—the Abwehr was a traitor's organization. No wonder we lost the war!"

The possibility of bribing somebody to help him was never far from Göring's mind. He eyed the American guard officers in particular. Probably it surprised—even annoyed—him that they were not of the highest caliber. (Colonel Andrus repeatedly complained of their low standard, in letters to his superiors.) But in Germany the Nazis had had the same problem. In 1944 the Reichsmarschall had urged Hitler to provide better guards for the Allied prisoners of war than the "old Santa Clauses" then being used. "You see," he reminisced in a revealing moment to Colonel Amen, "those prisoners received a large number of Red Cross parcels . . . with chocolate and food, and they were very successful in bribing the guards."

Somehow, Göring struck up a friendship with Lieutenant Jack G. Wheelis. A hard-drinking six-foot-two Texan, Wheelis impressed Göring for two reasons: He was an impassioned huntsman, and he held one key to the baggage room. Göring was photographed next to him, showing him a sheaf of papers; he signed one photo, as "Reichsjägermeister," dedicated it to "The Great Huntsman from Texas," and gave it to Wheelis.

Who can say what emotions seized the U.S. Army lieutenant? Perhaps it was pity for the caged lion. He agreed to carry letters to Emmy and little Edda—who had joined her mother in Straubing Jail on November 24. Göring rewarded these favors with gifts of valuables, presenting to Wheelis the solid-gold Mont Blanc fountain pen and Swiss wristwatch engraved with his signature, the gold cigarette case that Goebbels had given him, and the gray suede gloves he had worn at Augsburg. Somehow Göring retrieved from the locked baggage room other valuables like his gold epaulets and a swastika-embossed gold matchbook cover, and used them to reward other American officers.

It was indeed the Last Battle, albeit on a minuscule scale, and each side used its own dirty tricks. A Jew who had fled Germany before the war, the psychiatrist Dr. Gilbert overrode the dictates of medical ethics to submit to the prosecution team regular notes on what he had overheard. Then prosecutor Jackson would telegraph this intelligence to Washington, as his papers show. "Göring's defense against proposal to seize Atlantic islands for war against United States," read one Jackson wire, "apparently is that Roosevelt speeches indicated attack from us. . . . Also reported Göring will testify to statements by Bullitt and Davies [the American Ambassadors William C. Bullitt and Joseph Davies] in support of Roosevelt threat of aggression against Germany."

Cynical and realistic alike, Göring declared to Gilbert that the victors would always be the judges. "He constantly drums into the others the idea that Germany was a sovereign state, Hitler a sovereign ruler, and the court has no jurisdiction." Commenting on the charge of waging "aggressive war," Göring maintained that Britain, America, and Russia had all done the same. "But when Germany does it, it becomes a crime—because we lost!" Aware of Churchill's own plans to invade neutral Norway and Sweden, which the Germans had learned about from documents captured in 1940, defense counsel for Keitel, Jodl, and Göring all challenged the British government to produce the relevant telegrams. Their request caused acute embarrassment to the new, left-wing foreign secretary, Ernest Bevin, in London. Sir Norman Brooke, the British Cabinet's secretary, agreed that the defense's allegation about Churchill was true but warned against allowing the production of isolated documents at Nuremberg—"especially when we do not know precisely what captured [British] documents the other side may have."

In this unequal battle the Reichsmarschall's only supporters were Rosenberg and Ribbentrop. Former Nazi youth leader Baldur von Schirach was wavering, reported Dr. Gilbert, and Field Marshal Keitel was "afraid to talk up." The psychiatrist advised Jackson to concentrate on winning over banker Hjalmar Schacht and Hitler's young arms minister Albert Speer, using two

chinks in the Reichsmarschall's armor—the Nazi atrocities, and his acquisition of art treasures. "They spoil his pose as a hero-patriot and model
officer."

The damning evidence of the concentration-camp atrocities flabbergasted
Göring. "I still can't grasp all those things," he admitted. "Do you suppose
I'd have believed it if somebody came to me and said they were making
freezing experiments on human guinea pigs, or that people were forced to
dig their own graves and be mowed down by the thousands? I would have
just said, 'Get the hell out of here with that fantastic nonsense.' "

The Nazi newsreel film of people's court judge Roland Freisler screaming
at once-respectable general staff plotters turned Göring's stomach. But when
the psychiatrist mentioned Röhm, Göring erupted about the "dirty homosexual swine" and angrily paced his tiny cell in shirt sleeves and slippers.
"It was a damned good thing I wiped them out," he roared. "Or they would
have wiped us out!"

Two days before Christmas Gilbert found him brooding on the future.
What was his own fate compared to such a tide of history? "If I have to
die," he pondered out loud, "then I'd rather die as a martyr than a traitor."
He brightened, and said, "Don't forget that the great conquerors of history
are not seen as murderers—Ghenghis Khan, Peter the Great, Frederick the
Great!" Five years hence, he predicted, Hitler would be the idol of Germany
again, and with a rueful laugh he invited Gilbert to mark his prophecy.

The new year, 1946, began with fresh unpleasantness for Göring. SS
General Otto Ohlendorf testified on January 3 with apparent sincerity about
mass liquidations that he had himself directed; worse, that afternoon Speer's
defense attorney calmly invited the SS officer to testify whether he was aware
that Speer had plotted to kill Hitler.

Göring choked. A major breach was appearing in the defense front line.
He flounced over to the ex-minister as the session ended, but Speer pointly
ignored him.

"Gott im Himmel!" Göring exclaimed to Gilbert that evening. "I nearly
died of shame. To think that a German could be so rotten, just to prolong
his wretched life—to put it crudely, to piss in front and crap behind a little
longer. Herrgott! Donnerwetter! For myself," he barked, "I don't care if I
get executed. . . . But there is still such a thing as honor."

A few days later, on January 12, Colonel Andrus heard from Gilbert of
the uproar among the prisoners caused by the arrest of their next of kin by
the CIC. Andrus had little sympathy for the CIC officers, most of whom had
only recently been German citizens themselves. "Göring's wife," he protested in a secret letter to the tribunal, "was reported to have been arrested
and the child taken from her. . . . She has not written to him and it may be
that she is not permitted to do so." Fearing that the defendants might bring
this painful matter up in open court, "which would place the Americans on
the defensive," Andrus demanded that the womenfolk be released at once.

That day, his final birthday, Göring also complained to the tribunal, writing in longhand to Judge Lawrence that he had received only three letters from Emmy and Edda since his capture and asking the tribunal to order the authorities to allow them to exchange letters again.

> Before my voluntary surrender to American custody [he explained] I wrote asking General Eisenhower to take care of my family. Upon arrival at Seventh Army headquarters (General Patch) I was expressly promised that my request would be honored. My wife, daughter, relatives, and next of kin were taken to Veldenstein Castle, my family property north of Nuremberg, and interned there. They were able to move around the castle freely, though isolated from the outside world, which was very satisfactory to me.

But since their arrest on October 15, he complained, neither his wife nor daughter had been allowed to write to him.

Evidently in consequence of this complaint, the American chaplain, Henry F. Gerecke, a fifty-four year old Lutheran from Wisconsin who spoke fluent German, visited Emmy at Straubing. Afterward, Göring wrote to her, using prisoner-of-war notepaper:

> My darling Emmy!
> Yesterday the chaplain came back from visiting you and brought me your good wishes. How very happy they made me, thank you. Now I am feeling calmer.
> It's obvious why you're all in custody—just because you are mine. As the Führer is dead, I am the No. 1 principal war criminal, and you are my relatives. The hatred and the thirst for revenge —you can imagine whose—are boundless. . . . But I am not going to let them bend or break me. . . .
> How often I go to you in my thoughts and try to imagine the life you are leading! Have you enough books? My treasure, I cannot express how much I love you. You and Edda have always been my pride and joy. I am filled with gratitude to you both. Regards to Else, Ellen [Kiurina], and faithful [nurse] Christa. Why on earth did they arrest Christa?

She sent him a four-leaf clover for good luck. It was removed before Göring got the letter, but he thanked her all the same. "Luck—ours has run out now," he commented. They now allowed him to write one letter and one postcard each week.

> You know how unutterably it hurts [he wrote] to know that you, my only beloved, are suffering all of this because of me! Just

because you are my wife you have to suffer this persecution. You only did good to people, but what does that matter? You are my wife, and that's enough.

I wanted to bring you happiness forever, but I brought you misfortune. And yet you know how immense is my love for you and how much I long for you. I am keeping my chin up although things are looking grim. Greetings to Else and everybody. Kiss my little Edda. A big hug and kisses, and endless love, from your Hermann.

"Day and night," he wrote in another letter, "two eyes stare at me through the porthole in the cell door. A spotlight shines on me all night. . . . Your letters are the only sunshine in my life."

On the last day of February 1946, Emmy and Edda left Straubing Jail. They were permitted to move into a cottage deep in the forest at Sack-dilling, near Veldenstein. The cottage had neither water nor electricity, but it was home. Once or twice Jackson's oily ex-German aide Kempner called on them out there. Edda, grave and unsmiling, declined the oranges that he offered.

"You will see," Göring predicted to Dr. Gilbert that month. "This trial will be a disgrace in fifteen years' time." A few days later Field Marshal Paulus took the witness stand. Acting now as a witness for the Russian prosecution team, the former Stalingrad commander testified that Hitler had begun planning *Barbarossa* in 1940. "Ask that dirty swine if he knows he's a traitor," shouted Göring to his defense attorney, Stahmer. But it was Himmler's murder operations that still haunted Göring. "Anybody can make an atrocity film," he sniffed on February 15, "if they take corpses out of their graves and then show a tractor shoving them back in again."

Over lunch he scurried to repair the breaches torn in their front line by Speer's self-serving "treachery," bullying the other defendants like a sheep-dog chasing errant sheep. He urged the craven homosexual Walter Funk to stop worrying about death—in fifty years' time Germany would recognize them all as martyrs and heroes, and they would put his (Göring's) cadaver into a marble mausoleum like Napoleon's. Alerted by Gilbert to Göring's intensive canvassing, Jackson persuaded Sir David Maxwell-Fyfe, the British prosecutor, to agree to Göring's being isolated over lunch. Dr. Gilbert himself drafted the new seating plan: Göring would sit in a cold, dim room for lunch alone, separated from the other twenty defendants. The order went into force at lunchtime on February 18. Speer crowed, Gilbert found Göring dejected and tremulous like a rejected child. In the even greater solitude of his cell, later that day the Reichsmarschall came close to contrition. "Don't think," he pleaded to Gilbert, "that I don't reproach myself in the loneliness of this cell for not having lived my life differently, instead of coming to this end.''

"Effect of separating defendants & isolating Göring marked," reported Gilbert to Jackson, "and on the whole favorable for trial.''

On the twentieth, the court was shown a Soviet-made atrocity film. As the images of torture instruments, mutilated bodies, guillotines, and baskets of decapitated heads flickered and danced across the movie screen on the far wall to their left, Göring yawned demonstratively. "They could just as easily have killed a few hundred German prisoners of war and put them into Russian uniforms for the atrocity picture," he scoffed to Kelley's successor, Major Leo N. Goldensohn, that evening. "You don't know the Russians the way I do!" He shrewdly pointed out that the corpses had obviously been filmed before rigor mortis had had time to set in. "It is not that atrocity films leave me stone cold," he felt compelled to explain to Dr. Gilbert a few days afterward. "But I have seen so much already . . . women and children burned alive in air raids.'' Embroidering on the facts, he continued, "All that [Hans Fritzsche] had to do was *broadcast* that Berlin or Dresden had suffered another terror raid. But I went and *saw* the corpses—sometimes still burning— because I was air minister.'' When a woman who claimed to be an Auschwitz survivor started a moving testimony (the American judge Francis Biddle wrote, "This I doubt," in his diary), Göring took off his earphones in disgust. "The higher up you were,'' he explained to Dönitz's attorney as they rose for the adjournment, "the less you saw of what was going on.''

Göring was now back in his physical prime. On March 6, 1946, as he passed Field Marshal Milch in a corridor, they exchanged illicit salutes, and Milch noted in his diary that the Reichsmarschall was fitter and slimmer than he had ever seen him before. It boded ill for Jackson and the prosecution.

On Friday the eighth, the defense called Bodenschatz into the box. Jackson made mincemeat of the servile, elderly general, and Göring felt sorry for him. "Wait till he starts on *me*," he boasted, as he accepted a cigarette from Dr. Gilbert with trembling fingers. Milch followed Bodenschatz to the microphone that afternoon, and Göring murmured to his counsel, "Now I'm for it—we weren't on the best of terms." But the field marshal, despite a clumsy attempt at blackmail by Major Englander in November, did his best for Göring.

Sworn in [Milch recorded in his diary], everybody wearing earphones; then examination by attorney Stahmer. . . . When I was asked about Göring's attitude to prisoners of war Jackson interrupted, "We've shown enough patience, but this is going too far. I object!"

The Tribunal sustained his objection and poor Stahmer, somewhat confused, asked me one more short question and sat down. . . .

An hour later the court adjourned for the weekend. "The defendants were mostly very crushed," Milch described. "When I saw Jodl being led away, his eyes were filled with tears."

That Saturday morning Göring lay in bed, fully clothed, brooding. "Knowing what I know now," he confided to Gilbert in a low, serious voice, "I wish I could have Himmler here—just for ten minutes—to ask him what on earth he was up to out there."

For a few more days he was compelled to listen. On Monday, March 11, Jackson cross-examined Milch. The field marshal now put up a stout defense of Göring—whom he had only three weeks before raged at in his private diary as "this idiot . . . this antique dealer and yellow-belly." *The Times* of London, reporting on his testimony, complained, "For nearly five hours he was engaged in a battle of wits in which the prosecution was apparently at such pains to discredit his evidence that it often seemed that Milch, rather than Göring, was the accused man." (Reading these lines, Milch bragged in his diary, "I must have knocked their plans into a cocked hat!") "Unless means is found," warned the British newspaper, "of keeping witnesses to the point, the Nuremberg defense will become an opportunity for Nazi polemics and false trails." Displeased with the stocky field marshal, the American Army tossed him into their notorious punishment bunker at the Dachau concentration camp a few days later, as a warning to others who still had to testify.

On March 13, 1946, the five months of enforced silence were over. There was not an empty seat in the courtroom as Göring took the stand. Unable to control his trembling hands, he glared at the microphone and newsreel cameras. Jackson knew that the next hours would make or break one or the other of them—perhaps both. He anticipated that the Reichsmarschall might appeal over the heads of the tribunal to the confused and baffled German public. The trial might even fuel renewed anti-Semitism and pro-Nazi sentiments.

The tall, red-faced British judge, Sir Normann Birkett, wrote in his private manuscript on the trial that Göring was the man who really dominated the proceedings. He had followed the evidence with great intentness when the evidence required it, and had slept like an infant when it did not. Nobody, reflected Birkett, seemed to have been quite prepared for Göring's immense ability and knowledge, or for his mastery and understanding of the captured documents.

Göring was stripped of his finery but still noble in manner and now handsome in feature once again. As he began to speak—hoping that somewhere, out there in the depths of the Bavarian forest, Emmy and Edda might be listening to his voice—he gained in confidence and assurance with each answer. Even Speer was moved by the spectacle as this lion of a man fought back. He began to pump out resonant oratory, scattering immortal lines before this last arbitrary tribunal of mortal enemies. He embellished his replies with repartee, attracting gales of laughter from the public in the courtroom, then subtly hushed the listeners with some throwaway self-incrimination of apparent sincerity.

Millions of listeners around the world were hearing the trial broadcast. It was relayed by loudspeaker over prison camps all over Germany, the United States, and Britain. The effect was not what the victors had desired at all. Meals halted, the prisoners poured outside to listen, as Hermann—"Just Hermann! Never anything but Hermann!"—began this last battle for his country. In the courtroom itself the newspapermen were stunned by his performance—they had swallowed their own reports, believing, as Jackson wryly commented later, that the Reichsmarschall was indeed a dope fiend, a physical wreck, a neurotic.

Too excited to eat, he sat on his cot afterward, unwinding; he smoked his long meerschaum pipe, and held out an arm to Dr. Gilbert to show how steady he now was. He had mapped the broad outlines first, while digging in for the main attack, so he explained. He ruminated out loud about man as the world's most fearsome beast of prey, and about the inevitability of war. Perhaps, reflected Gilbert, the great music of Richard Wagner's *Götterdämmerung* was pounding through the chords of his brain; more likely, the Reichsmarschall's mind was prowling on ahead to the moment when he, the beast of prey, would liberate himself from this earthly cage.

On the next day, March 14, he testified with frankness and candor on how he had consolidated the Nazi stranglehold on Germany, and once more made no bones of his role in the Röhm massacre. Gilbert asked him, as they adjourned for lunch, what he proposed to say about the SS atrocities.

Göring threw him an uneasy look. "That I didn't take the rumors seriously," he said.

Once that afternoon he noticed the American judge, John J. Parker, nodding affably to him, and he knew that he was making headway.

"Now you see why he was so popular," lamented Schirach to Dr. Gilbert.

"That Göring is quite a guy," said Speer's attorney admiringly. "A *Mordskerl* [a real killer]!"

Chagrined, Speer expressed the wan hope that Justice Jackson would "show him up" when his cross-examination began.

That historic duel began on Monday, March 18. Göring stepped into the box, his hair slicked back, his eyes gleaming with insolent defiance. He sensed that the terms of trade were in his favor, and indeed they were. Accustomed to the U.S. district courts—to harrying and crowding hostile witnesses—Jackson was out of his depth at Nuremberg. Here, he would have to wait while each question and response was ponderously translated into the trial's four official languages. Göring had a good grasp of English; not only did Jackson have no command whatever of German, but more than once he was extremely embarrassed by the faulty translation of documents that he had submitted as key exhibits.

His original plan had been to deflate Göring by asking about his anti-Jewish decrees and art collection. Fatally, he changed his mind at the last moment and leveled the more general political accusations first. He found to his consternation that Göring, far from denying these charges, went way beyond mere admissions in his answers. No, he had always *intended* to overthrow the Weimar republic, to end parliamentary government in Germany, and to suppress the opposition! Once, when he launched into yet another long discourse, Jackson ordered him to answer yes or no. Too late, he saw the American judge, Parker, lean over and whisper something to the president, Lawrence. "Mr. Justice Jackson," interrupted the latter, "the tribunal feels that the witness should be allowed to make whatever explanation he cares to make in answer to this question."

Jackson blushed. Grinning broadly at Jackson's humiliation, Göring continued.

Worse was now to come. Jackson challenged Göring on Tuesday, the nineteenth, about the extreme secrecy of the Nazis' planning. Göring smirked, and answered that he could not recall having seen the U.S. government *publish* details of its own mobilization plans. There was loud laughter. Jackson tore off his earphones and appealed to the judges for protection—in vain. "Göring's answer," he caviled to his learned colleagues afterward, "was impudent and argumentative and the court should have used its gavel."

There were extraordinary scenes at the prosecutors' secret meeting that night, as the shorthand record shows:

> JACKSON: The arrogance of Göring in today's session supports what opponents of this Trial have always said: if you give these people a chance to speak they will propagandize and make it a farce.
>
> When I objected to Göring's attitude [and] requested the Court to instruct him to answer responsively, [the American judge] whispered in the ear of the presiding judge, and thereupon the Court overruled me on its own motion without even hearing an objection from Göring's counsel.
>
> If Göring is permitted to get away with this he will encourage all the defendants to do the same thing. I have never heard of such a rule for cross-examination. The witness should be compelled to answer the question and to reserve his explanations for later (re-direct). It is utterly impossible to cross-examine unless the Court controls the witnesses, and Göring knows he has the Court in his corner.

Quite openly sulking, Jackson proposed abandoning the cross-examination of Göring altogether. Maxwell-Fyfe was aghast. "To cease now," he interjected, "would be interpreted as a victory for Göring's obstructive tactics."

"Göring is being permitted to preach," objected Jackson. "He is becoming constantly more arrogant, and if this goes on it will do our countries more harm than good."

Maxwell-Fyfe agreed. "We must tell the court that we are dealing with an experienced politician. He will make the proceedings ridiculous unless the tribunal cooperates. The result will be that the trial is a disaster."

He recommended that they unofficially convey this to "our own judges." "The Allied Control Council, for instance," he continued, "is apprehensive lest Göring's examination-in-chief do a great deal of harm in restoring Nazi prestige."

"This," agreed Jackson, "is a critical point of the trial as far as achieving its objective is concerned." If this remark did not unmask the true, political face of the trial, Jackson's subsequent outburst did. "Göring is permitted to become a hero of the Nazis because he dares talk back to the United States. This wins him admiration from all the Nazis who remain in Germany, and he will influence the other defendants to do likewise. I almost felt this afternoon that it would have been wiser to have shot these men out of hand."

The British prosecutors were more fortunate than Jackson. Maxwell-Fyfe, an incisive, bullying barrister who would rise to the very pinnacles of the British legal establishment, brought beads of perspiration to Göring's brow over the Gestapo's execution of the escaped British aviators. When the Englishman asked if he was still loyal to Hitler despite the atrocities that had now come to light, Göring hesitated, recognizing the lethal burden of the question, then answered true to form—he believed in being loyal in times of hardship as well as in the more golden years. Most likely, he pointed out, the Führer had known as little of the atrocities as he himself had.

After that, the show ended rapidly. The Russian naïvely inquired why Göring had not refused to obey Hitler. "If I had," replied Göring with easy humor, "I certainly should not have had to worry about my health."

"If you handle yourselves half as well as I did," Göring bragged to the other defendants, resuming his place in the dock, "you'll be doing all right." It had thrilled him to see his own ability to withstand the taunt and thrust of his prosecutors without crumpling. "Don't forget," he reminded Dr. Gilbert in his cell some days afterward, "I had the best legal brains of Britain, America, Russia, and France arrayed against me. And there I was—alone!"

His bearing in the witness box had impressed friend and foe alike. Fan mail from Germany and abroad poured into the prison for Göring—letters reading, "Keep your chin up, Hermann," and "Good for you!" (He was not allowed to get them, of course.) "Göring had nothing to lose," Keitel's veteran attorney said in private, shortly before the final act. "That's why he played the part to the very end—with élan and shrewdness, and dialectically adept. He won round after round against Jackson, much to the glee of the other Americans. But he's as self-centered, vain, and pompous as ever."

Dr. Gilbert went out to see Emmy at Sackdilling, and returned on March

24—her birthday—with a letter from her and a postcard from Edda. Göring's letters to Emmy show, however, how the continued restraints and captivity were preying upon his nature. "I keep thinking about the onset of spring out there, bringing those wonderful woods alive," he wrote in one letter to Sackdilling. "You can imagine how I am seized by yearning for you—how I long to walk through this awakening forest with you. God protect you and Edda and you all! Although we have to be apart, believe me that my love and longing for you have never been greater." "My dearest," he wrote on another card to Emmy, "heartfelt thanks for yesterday's dear lines. I hope you're getting on and keeping together at Sackdilling—you, Edda, and Elses big and small. Today my counsel Dr. Stahmer is allowed to visit you. I trust him implicitly. Talk about everything with him. Best wishes to everybody at the cottage. You know how endless is my yearning, and how powerful my love for you. I hug you and kiss you all fondly. Your Hermann."

Then Wilhelm Frick's defense witness, the Abwehr/OSS double-agent Hans Bernd Gisevius, took the stand. Through his purposeful distortions, he did far more harm to Göring's case than good to Frick's. "In ten or twelve years," snorted Göring on April 25, "history will take an entirely different view of these traitors." Jackson was delighted, however, and thanked OSS chief Allen Dulles three days later for making Gisevius available. "[Gisevius] fulfilled the expectations stated in your letters," he added. "Göring is in a badly depressed state."

Despite threats from Göring, loudly uttered to Schacht's attorney, to get even, Schacht testified on May 3 that Göring used to appear dressed as the emperor Nero, wearing lipstick, rouge, and nail polish. (Göring hotly denied the lipstick, talking that evening with Dr. Gilbert.) Schacht was fighting to save his skin; but then Grand Admiral Dönitz testified, and he was fighting for Germany. "Now I am ready to listen to some more treason," said Göring, relieved, during the recess afterward. Schirach followed, and "sold out" like Speer; and these, Göring commented ironically, were both men whom their Führer had favored to the very end. "Rather die like a lion," he philosophized to Werner Bross, Stahmer's deputy, "than survive to scamper like a rabbit."

Die, yes—but not by the hangman's hand. Göring let it be known to Jackson that if *guaranteed* a firing squad he would give the prosecution some *real* dirt on Schacht. Jackson, foolishly as it turned out, did not heed him. Göring then intensified his contacts with the American Army's Lieutenant Wheelis. To make doubly sure, he evidently removed one wafer-thin metal diaphragm surreptitiously from his earphones in the courtroom. The loss was discovered and his cell minutely searched, but the sliver of metal was never found.

"My darling," he now wrote to Emmy. "Today the birthday letter for Edda goes off. So this week I can only send you a postcard. Heartfelt thanks for [letter] No. 19. What the newspapers are writing is a matter of supreme indifference to us. Never let it get you down! I've been in bed for three days, sciatica in my right leg. Now I can understand what you must have been through. In passionate love, I hug and kiss you. Your Hermann."

The "birthday letter" to Edda has survived:

> My darling, sweet child! My golden treasure!
> Now's the second time that your birthday has come around and I can't be there. And yet, my darling, today I'm especially close to you, and send you my warmest and most heartfelt greetings.
> I pray to Almighty God from the bottom of my heart to look after you and help you. I can't send you any gift, but my boundless love and longing is all around you and always shall be!
> You know, my little sparrow, how fond I am of you! You are always so sweet and tender. You'll always be our happiness and joy.
> Mama has told me what a brave little helper you are everywhere and how good you are being. I'm proud of you.
> I hope the weather's fine so you can spend your birthday outside in the wonderful forest. My little sweetheart, once more all my warmest wishes for today and always: fondest hugs and kisses from your Papa.

The letters from them, he wrote to Emmy a few days later, in June 1946, were the "only ray of sunshine in my solitude." He went on:

> So the darling child's birthday went off well after all. I thought it was going to be almost impossible for you to get hold of any present for Edda.
> Just imagine: Ronny [probably his adjutant Ondarza] is in Hamburg but refusing to have anything at all to do with me, even a written statement. He hasn't even replied to Stahmer. There's gratitude! . . . I am in better health again. . . . In the prison yard three jasmine bushes are in blossom. You've realized my yearning to be out in the forest and breathe free air again. But even greater is my longing for you and Edda, and greater still my love. . . . Is Teske [Major Werner Teske, another adjutant] a free man?

He wondered if he would ever see Edda's golden curls again.

45
RELEASE

Allowed to make a closing address to the Nuremberg tribunal, Hermann Göring declared on August 31, 1946, "The German people trusted the Führer. Given his authoritarian direction of the state, they had no influence on events. Ignorant of the crimes of which we know today, the people have fought with loyalty, self-sacrifice, and courage, and they have suffered too in this life-and-death struggle into which they were arbitrarily thrust. The German people," he pronounced, "are free from blame."

Fighting here on their behalf, Göring had accepted blanket responsibility, and thereby rendered his last useful service to the German nation. By his execution—by firing squad, he confidently expected—he himself would expiate all crimes.

He expected no earthly reprieve. Because he had been number-two man to Hitler, the prosecution had attributed to him comprehensive knowledge of every crime in Nazi Germany. Thomas Dodd, one of Jackson's prosecuting staff, had alleged that Göring had directed Heydrich to kill the Jews and had ordered Allied airmen shot. To challenge the incriminating stenograms of his war conferences, Göring argued that the tribunal's own shorthand record showed how inaccurate such transcripts could be. As for the administrative crimes of the Nazi forces in occupied Europe, Göring scoffed that these were no more criminal than those of the victors now—in suspending the Geneva Convention, dismantling industry, confiscating property, and enslaving millions of Germans.

A letter arrived from Edda, stamped CENSORED & PASSED—CENSOR, IMT. She had enclosed a pressed flower plucked from their forest.

> My darling Daddy!
> How happy I was when the chaplain visited us, he was kind and nice but sadly he couldn't stay long. Aunt Fanny [Carin's sister] and Aunt Erna were here too and brought me crayons and a coloring book and I was very happy. . . . Aunt Else brought me a few pictures, including one of you, that was the most beautiful present! . . . If only you could come here quickly and walk through the forest with me, how beautiful it would be!!! The forester's puppy is much bigger, I play with it all the time, it's so sweet.
> Mama was sad she didn't hear you on the radio. I would have given up all my toys just to hear your voice. Mommy has told me she's going to be allowed to see you. I'd like to see you frightfully too. Can't I come as well? I'm *sooooo* fond of you and it's so awfully long since I saw you. Oh, Papa, if only I could come too!
> Mommy has taught me almost the whole of [Friedrich Schiller's ballad] "The Bell," and I learned the rest by myself and recited it to Mommy and she was very pleased.
> Aunt Thea sent us a packet with a bar of soap, two little candles, some cotton, four buttons, and a washcloth, we were very happy about that.
> I promise you, Papa, that I always try to comfort Mommy and I'll always protect her. How much nicer it would be if you were there to protect us!!!
> I pray every evening to dear God that Mommy and I can see you soon and give you a big hug.
> Darling Papa, in my heart you are always right next to me and whenever I'm doing anything I tell myself you're looking on and that way I only do nice and good things.
> Now I throw my little arms around your neck and give you a big kiss. Your Edda.

Emmy Göring implored the tribunal to let her see the imprisoned Reichsmarschall for a few minutes. "I haven't seen my husband for a year and a quarter," she wrote, "and I am longing so terribly for him that I don't see any way out. I need strength to carry on without my husband. A few minutes when I could see him and hold his hand would help me no end. . . . My husband is very much worried about my child and myself, as we are without protection and help."

Softened by her solicitous feelings, the tribunal authorized the meeting. But for several more weeks Colonel Andrus disallowed it. Looking much thinner, she was finally allowed to come for half an hour on September 12, 1946. Hermann sat on the other side of the partition's glass window, hand-cuffed to a guard. He told her to write a list of things to say next time. "Otherwise we will forget too much that is of importance."

Five days later little Edda was led shyly in, unannounced. She was eight years old now. "Stand on a chair," commanded Hermann, weeping freely, "so I can see how you've grown." Edda recited the ballads that she had learned, and a famous poem containing the lines, "Above all, child, be loyal and true / And never, lips, be sullied by a lie." Göring tapped the glass and softly interrupted, "Yes, remember that, Edda: all your life long."

"Papa," she squeaked, "when you come home, will you please put on your rubber medals in the bath like people say you do?"

He never saw Edda again. When the world speculated how he had obtained the poison, later, she clasped her mother's hand and said, "I know! A window opened in the ceiling of his cell, and an angel of the Lord came down from heaven and gave it to him."

Since sentencing was postponed, the daily half-hour visits were continued. So near and yet, with the glass plate separating them, so far: He asked Emmy once what she did all day long (she was staying with the Stahmers) and she smiled. "For twenty-three and a half hours each day," she replied, "I look forward to seeing you." On September 29, the wives were ordered to leave Nuremberg. "Don't you believe," she pleaded at their last meeting now, "that we three shall, one day, be together in freedom?"

"I beg of you," Göring replied fervently, bending close to the glass, "give up hope."

As the sentinel led him away, he turned and called out, "Don't write anymore. I shan't either."

Judgment day, Tuesday, October 1, came. The execution team—four generals—had demanded privileged seats in the courtroom that day, but Jackson primly refused, arguing that it was always possible that there would be no death sentences whatever. More realistically, the world's newspapers published photographs of the chosen hangman, Master Sergeant John C. Woods, fingering his heavy hempen rope. Woods boasted that it would soon hang Hermann Göring.

Fifteen miles away, out at Sackdilling, Emmy and Else sent their little girls out to play in a forest glade, then clustered around the white portable radio set that an American girl had given them at the courthouse.

There, the president summed up the case against Göring first. The Reichsmarschall watched gravely, shaking his head in barely perceptible disagreement. "His guilt is unique in its enormity," Sir Geoffrey Lawrence concluded. "The record discloses no excuses for this man. The court finds the defendant guilty on all four counts of the indictment."

Not a flicker of emotion had crossed Göring's brow. But when Biddle now announced Schacht's acquittal, he slammed down his earphones in disgust.

At 3:00 P.M. he stepped alone from the elevator at the courtroom's rear, to hear sentence. He came to attention, and Lawrence read it out, in the oddly disembodied voice of the English upper crust. "Defendant Hermann Wilhelm Göring, the International Military Court sentences you to death by hanging."

As he was led back to his cell, Göring was astonished to see *German* police mustering to rearrest Schacht and the other two who had been acquitted. He loathed Schacht now, but he gagged at the humiliating spectacle.

He found Dr. Gilbert hovering near his own cell door.

"Death," said Göring, reaching for the book that he had left on his cot. His eyes blurred, and he asked to be left alone.

The prisoners had been notified that they had four days to petition the Control Council for Germany for clemency, and that the hangings would take place fifteen days (excluding Sundays) after sentencing. Now that Göring was formally a condemned criminal, Andrus intensified security precautions—he wanted nothing, but nothing, to go wrong. He denied Göring all outside exercise, and he refused him permission to shower on the fourth and eleventh. Göring wrote two letters between the first and fifth: Andrus seized them both.* On the morning of the fifth, he ordered the straw pallette in Göring's cell changed without warning. He ordered the prisoner manacled to a cell guard and escorted during each of the remaining seven interviews over the next two weeks—Göring was taken to Room 55 on October 2 to sign papers, and then again to see his attorney on the 3rd and 4th as well as (finally) twice on the 5th, their 144th and 145th meetings.

He had instructed Stahmer not to submit any plea for mitigation of sentence. Nevertheless, Stahmer formally petitioned the Control Council on October 4, requesting it to commute the death sentence or at least to alter it from hanging to the firing squad. Stahmer pointed out that Göring had been a brave officer in World War I, and one universally respected for his chivalry. He also referred to Göring's then little-known efforts before the war to maintain European peace, and argued that there was not the slightest evidence that Göring had even known of "the extermination of the Jews carried out by Himmler."

---

*According to Dr. Stahmer. In later years an impudent "last letter" allegedly composed by Göring to Churchill and dated October 1, 1946, was widely circulated in right-wing circles. It was probably a forgery, emanating from South Africa.

A last letter had now come from Emmy, written, despite his veto, on the fourth. "My beloved," she had written:

> . . . today suddenly a great calm has come upon me. I am close to you. You are near me, whatever happens! God grant that I am allowed to come once more to Nuremberg. Every second that I can gaze into your beloved face is a joy to me. I sometimes can't understand how I survived Tuesday without dying from the fearful fright! But one can suffer more pain than one supposes. I wonder what you are going through now. You must sense how the multitudes are with you in their boundless love.
>
> How endlessly happy we were. Again and again I review our blissful marriage in my memory. Blessings be upon you, my love, forever.
>
> Words cannot express my love for you. Your Emmy.

With time now running out, Göring wrote across the page, "Thank you, darling! Eternally yours, Hermann." Seeing his attorney for one last time, he gave him through the sliding panel his wedding ring and his blue-leather attaché case to hand to Emmy.

Before leaving the city, Stahmer phoned Emmy that Sunday, to say that she would be permitted one last hour with her husband the next day.

Thin and handsome again, like the lithe, upright aviator and politician of the early thirties, Göring strode into the partitioned room at 2:45 P.M. that last afternoon, October 7, 1946. His right wrist was manacled to Private First Class Russell A. Keller, and three men stood in a semicircle behind him holding Thompson submachine guns. Through the glass he could see Emmy sitting next to the American chaplain Gerecke, nervously clutching the wedding ring. He asked how Edda had taken the news. "I hope life won't be too hard on her," he sighed.

"You may die with your conscience pure," she replied. "You have done here in Nuremberg all that you could for your comrades and for Germany." In a way, she added, he too would be dying in battle.

His face cleared; he found that the lump in his throat had gone. "I had no idea you were so brave."

"Listen closely," she said, inclining toward the glass. "Do you still have your comb?"

"Yes."

"And brush?"

"Yes."

Without changing her tone, she whispered, "Do you still have what Ango gave you?"

"No," he replied, then hesitated. "I would like to have said yes, because that would make it easier for you. Do you have yours?"

She shook her head.

"They won't hang me," he assured her, choosing his words carefully. "Not that. It's *the Bullet* for me. They won't hang a Hermann Göring."

She was feeling faint. "Shouldn't I go now?" she asked. He smiled. "I'm quite calm, Emmy."*

He left, thinking most probably about that bullet. Since cameramen were waiting out front to film her sorrowing departure, the chaplain opened the back door and let her through behind the partition. She stroked the chairback where Hermann had been sitting, as they walked past—it was still warm.

Hermann had returned to his cell, in mental turmoil. As Dr. Pflücker came in with a sedative, the prisoner said, "I've just seen my wife for the last time, my dear doctor. Now I am *dead*. It was a difficult hour, but she wanted it. She bore up magnificently. She only faltered toward the end."

He looked at the sedative pills. Once, during the summer, he had casually asked Pflücker how many of these might be dangerous. The doctor had replied that even twenty or thirty would only induce a deeper sleep. "It isn't easy to die from sleeping pills," he said, reading the prisoner's mind.

They shook hands—the first time that the normally taciturn Reichsmarschall had done so with him. "If *you* had been with this man for fifteen months," the doctor reproached the Board of Inquiry, "you would understand."

Now Hermann Göring was isolated, except for his friendship with the Texas lieutenant. For a few days he waited to learn the outcome of Stahmer's unauthorized plea for clemency.

That outcome was not in any doubt. Fearing that the Allied Control Council in Berlin might make the wrong use of the powers granted under Section 29 of the London Charter of August 8, 1945, to "reduce or otherwise alter the sentences," the British Labour Cabinet decided late on October 7 to instruct the British member, Air Marshal Sir Sholto Douglas, that "from a political point of view it would be an advantage if there were no alterations of the [Nuremberg] sentences." And so it came to pass. The Control Council met in Berlin on the ninth; they heard that Raeder, Göring, and Jodl had all asked for execution by firing squad. The American member briefly favored Jodl's petition, but in the end all were denied.

Göring somehow learned that newspapermen and photographers would be invited to watch the hangings; and it did not take an Albert Einstein to calculate that the hangings would probably take place on the sixteenth. These two pieces of information were vital to his plan.

There are certain extraordinary documents that suggest that somehow Gö-

---

*After a period of internment Emmy Göring was cleared by the denazification courts in Bavaria and her remaining property was restored to her; she died in 1974. Edda married a dentist and lives in Munich.

ring had by now reassured himself that at least one lethal cyanide "bullet" was still in his baggage—and that somehow too, he had obtained a firm promise from a third party to smuggle one of these brass capsules into his cell. These documents consist principally of three taunting letters, all dated October 11, that he wrote, perhaps as a final prank. It is improbable that he would have risked leaving these letters lying around his cell for five days— their premature discovery would have resulted in the immediate search of his locked-away belongings and the painful frustration of his plan. So it is a reasonable deduction that he entrusted the letters to some officer whom they were also designed to reassure and protect: an American, no doubt, who would see that they were restored by trusted hand to the cell at literally the last moment—two men who would between them extricate the cyanide bullet from the baggage room, and smuggle it in to the prisoner. It is likely that the American officer was Lieutenant Wheelis (he died in 1954), and that the trusted hand was that of Doctor Pflücker (who is also now dead).

The letters still survive, in an American army safe in Berlin, and are published here for the first time. The first, cross-folded to fit into an upper pocket or very small envelope, was clearly intended to attract ridicule to the pompous little colonel's security measures:

Nuremberg, October 11, 1946
To the Commandant

I have always had the poison capsule with me, ever since my delivery into imprisonment. On delivery into Mondorf I had *three* capsules. I left the *first* in my clothing so it would be found upon inspection. I put the *second* under the clothes rack when undressing and retrieved it when dressing. I concealed it so well at Mondorf and here in the cell that despite *frequent* and *very thorough inspections* it could not be found. During the court hearings I kept it with me in my high riding boots.

The *third* capsule is *still* in my little toilet case, in the round pot with the skin cream (hidden in the cream). I could have taken this twice at Mondorf if I had needed it.

None of those entrusted with the inspections is to blame, as it would have been almost *impossible* to find the capsule. It would have been pure chance.*

---

*Andrus erroneously claimed in his memoirs that Göring admitted in this suicide note that he had concealed the brass capsule "in his anus and in his flabby navel." Since the capsule and enclosed phial subsequently found in the hand cream were identical to the capsule and phial found on his corpse, the latter clearly came from his baggage (and not from outside the prison). Laboratory inspection tentatively found fecal traces on the brass capsule taken from the corpse. This suggests that he may have placed it briefly in his anus—perhaps to confuse the investigation—but given its size (35mm long, 9mm caliber) he could not comfortably have retained it there for long. Postmortem examination showed his fingernails to be clean and free of odor.

Suffice it to say that it would have been impossible for Göring to have secreted the brass, bullet-shaped capsule in his cell as claimed. The cell was liable to random change, and he was often strip-searched without warning. He would not have risked forfeiting the capsule so carelessly. Besides, without damage to his purpose the letter could easily have revealed the *precise* hiding place if it had indeed been hidden in the cell.

He added a postscript to the letter. "Dr. Gilbert told me the Control Council has refused to convert the manner of death to firing squad!"

He now took one of his sheets of notepaper with the heading "The Reichsmarschall of the Greater German Reich," carefully dated this one too—"Nuremberg, October 11, 1946"—and wrote:

To the Allied Control Council

I would have let you shoot me without further ado! But it is not possible to hang the German Reichsmarschall! I cannot permit this, for Germany's sake. Besides, I have no moral obligation to submit to the justice of my enemies. I have therefore chosen the manner of death of the great Hannibal. Hermann Göring.

Turning the page, he continued the letter on the back:

It was clear from the outset that a death sentence would be pronounced against me, as I have always regarded the trial as a purely political act by the victors, but I wanted to see this trial through for my people's sake and I did at least expect that I should not be denied a soldier's death. Before God, my country, and my conscience I feel myself free of the blame that an enemy tribunal has attached to me.

Finally, he wrote a last letter to his wife and enclosed it in an envelope with a letter to the chaplain:

Nuremberg, October 11, 1946

Dear Pastor Gerecke!

Forgive me, but I had to do it like this for political reasons. I have prayed long to my God and feel that I am doing the right thing. (I would have let them shoot me.) Please comfort my wife and tell her that this was *no ordinary suicide*, and that she can rest assured that God will still gather me up in his great mercy.

God protect my dearest ones!

God bless you, dear pastor, evermore. Your Hermann Göring.

My only sweetheart!

Upon mature consideration and after profound prayers to my God, I have decided to take my own life and thus not allow my enemies to execute me. I would always have accepted death by firing squad. But the Reichsmarschall of Greater Germany can not allow himself to be hanged. Moreover, the killings were to be carried out like a spectacle with the press and film cameras there (I assume for the newsreel pictures). Sensation is all that matters.

I however want to die quietly and out of the public eye. My life came to an end the moment I said my last farewell to you. Since then I am filled with a wondrous peace and I regard death as the final release.

I take it as a sign from God that throughout the months of my imprisonment He allowed me the means to free myself from this mortal coil, and that this means was never discovered. In His charity, God thus spared me the bitter end.

All my thoughts are with you, with Edda, and all my beloved friends! The last beats of my heart will mark our great and eternal love. Your Hermann.

When the American prison surgeon, Lieutenant Roska, came to his cell and talked about literature, for want of any other topic, he remarked that Göring seemed remarkably cheerful. Referring to the coming event, Göring remarked that his father had once told him to do anything he wanted—but to do it with a smile.

The psychiatrist Dr. Gilbert made his last visit to the condemned men on the thirteenth. "Only Göring seemed to be deliberately holding out," he reported to Andrus, "because he did not want to admit any more guilt than had already been proven by the prosecution." The Reichsmarschall had mentioned somewhat bitterly "that the Control Council might at least have given them another method of execution."

That night, October 13–14, the condemned men heard heavy trucks backing into the prison yard less than a hundred feet away—the gallows equipment had arrived. Göring heard former Reich manpower commissioner Fritz Sauckel screaming loudly, but there was nothing he could do to help. First Lieutenant John W. West searched his cell, ransacked his belongings, and removed and shook all the bedding while Göring talked volubly and "seemed very happy," as West later testified. He found nothing. Late on the fourteenth, as the hammering from the gymnasium filled the cellblock two hundred feet away, the chaplain came into the cell. Göring asked Gerecke if he knew the execution hour—Gerecke said he did not, and to Göring's distress also refused him Holy Communion. "I refused him the Lord's Supper," the pastor testified a few days later, "because he denied the divinity of Christ who instituted this sacrament. . . . He became more discouraged because I insisted he couldn't meet Edda, his daughter, in heaven if he refused the Lord's way of salvation."

Thus the different men faced up to the last day in different ways. An enterprising American officer at Nuremberg issued a philatelic "first day cover" to mark the coming executions. Andrus ordered tanks and anti-aircraft units to guard the prison against last-minute liberation attempts. It was now October 15, 1946. At 8:30 A.M. Dr. Pflücker slipped into Göring's cell, checked his pulse while an American private looked on, and talked for ten minutes. Göring was seen reading out some papers to the doctor in German, and the two men laughed. An hour later the prison barber came, again escorted by a private. At 3:15 P.M., prison trusty Otto Streng brought Göring a book from the library—*With the Birds of Passage to Africa*. Göring also asked Streng to fetch some writing materials. At three-thirty, while he was writing, a white-garbed kitchen attendant came in with a mug of tea.

What was he writing? Among the letters found in the cell afterward was one undated item that appears to fit the bill:

> I find it tasteless in the extreme to stage our deaths as a show for sensation-hungry reporters, photographers, and the curious. This grand finale is typical of the abysmal depths plumbed by court and prosecution. Pure theater, from start to finish! All rotten comedy!
>
> I understand perfectly well that our enemies want to get rid of us—whether out of fear or hatred. But it would serve their reputation better to do the deed in a soldierly manner.
>
> I myself shall be dying without all this sensation and publicity.
>
> Let me stress once more that I feel not the slightest moral or other obligation to submit to a death sentence or execution by my enemies and those of Germany.
>
> I proceed to the hereafter with joy, and regard death as a release.
>
> I shall hope for my God's mercy! I deeply regret that I cannot help my comrades (particularly Field Marshal Keitel and Colonel General Jodl) to escape this public death spectacle as well.
>
> The entire effort to stop us from doing harm to ourselves was never motivated by concern for our welfare, but purely to make sure that all would be ready for the big sensation.
>
> But *ohne mich* [count me out]! Hermann Göring.

That afternoon Pflücker returned—he had just been told that the condemned men were to be awakened at 11:45 P.M. and notified that their execution was imminent. He was seen to give Göring a white pill—the usual sedative—and place a small white envelope on the table. Göring felt inside the envelope, then poured some white powder from it into his tea. Perhaps what he was looking for was not inside it. (At least two envelopes would be found in his dead hands. One, marked with his first initial and name, contained the empty brass capsule and had had a corner torn off; it is unfortunately no longer in existence—did it spell his name "Goering," the American way?)

A few minutes before 6:00 P.M. *Daily Express* reporter R. Selkirk Panton, one of the eight newspapermen privileged to watch the hangings, cabled to his editor in London: "Eight reporters to witness hangings. Am now being taken into prison whence I unpermitted file anything until hangings over."

The prison block was now a blaze of light; it was obvious that tonight was the big night. When the chaplain came at seven-thirty that evening, the Reichsmarschall complained that he had not been allowed to see poor Fritz Sauckel, to help him through these days. After talking of the dishonor of hanging, there was a silence. "I broke in to ask him once more about his complete surrender of heart and soul to his Savior. [Göring] again claimed he was a Christian, but couldn't accept the teachings of Christ." He expressed the hope that he could rest during the evening—"Said he felt at ease."

At 8:30 P.M. the guard changed. Private First Class Gordon Bingham took up his station at the peephole and noticed that Göring was lying on his cot, wearing his boots, pants, and coat, reading the book. Twenty minutes later the prisoner got up, urinated, and changed into his slippers. Two or three times he went over to the table and looked inside the eyeglass case. Then he tidied the cell, moved his writing materials to the chair, and changed into pajamas—pale blue jacket and black silk pants. After that he lay back on the cot, pulled the khaki blankets up to his waist, and appeared to doze.

He had arranged his clothing into neat heaps—the silken undershorts, sleeveless woolen sweater, breeches, coat, and cap. His overcoat and silk robe were folded under his pillow, his bedroom slippers and high dress boots on the floor.

The sentinel could see both arms outside the blanket, as regulations prescribed: his left arm stroking the wall, while his right hand once massaged his forehead. At five past nine Dr. Pflücker made his third round. "I'll see him later," he said, indicating No. 5—Göring's cell.

First Lieutenant James H. Dowd, passing by, saw Göring lying on his back, seemingly asleep. The eight newspaper correspondents were allowed a final peep at the condemned men. Kingsbury Smith, the only American, reported an hour later to his newspaper that he saw Göring slumped on his small iron cot, his heavy shoulders sagging against the bare whitewashed wall, reading a well-thumbed book about the birds of Africa. "[I] stood looking at Göring over shoulder of the prison sentinel whose duty it was to observe Göring constantly. . . . With the eyes of an American security guard watching him like a cat watches a rat, Göring had little hope of emulating Ley's act [i.e., suicide], even if he had entertained such an idea." Struck by the prisoner's "criminal features, the mean and mad face, the lips with a rat-trap tightness about them,'' Kingsbury Smith calculated in his cable to New York that Göring would have the longest walk to the gallows, as the No. 5 cell was at the far end of death row.

Perhaps Göring was recalling the words he had once muttered to Dr. Friedrich Bergold, Bormann's attorney—an old but particularly apt German proverb: "These Nurembergers hang no one before they get their hands on him." At half past nine Dr. Pflücker came back to give him and Sauckel their sleeping pills. He did not however want Göring to fall asleep—now of all times—and admitted later that he had in fact filled Göring's (but not Sauckel's) pills with baking soda. He explained in evidence a few days later that he had not wanted Göring to have to be awakened for the execution.*

Be that as it may, as Pflücker entered, escorted by the duty officer First Lieutenant Arthur J. McLinden, Göring sat up immediately. The doctor spoke with him in a low voice for about three minutes. He later testified—for what it is worth—that Göring had told *him* that tonight was the night. The doctor was seen to hand over something, which Göring put in his mouth there and then. After a few more words Pflücker took the pulse of the Reichsmarschall's far (left) wrist, straightened up, shook his right hand ("because, the last time, it was difficult for a doctor *not* to shake hands") and left, followed out of the cell by McLinden.

"*Gute Nacht*," said Göring. Pflücker had been his last visitor. The poison capsule was now in Göring's possession. He lay still for fifteen minutes, his head turned to the wall—calculating, perhaps, how much longer he dare wait. Once he clasped his hands over his eyes for a few minutes. Twice more Lieutenant Dowd peeped in, at 9:35 and 9:40, but Göring had not moved.

Ten-thirty P.M. came. Did Göring perhaps now hear, straining his ears, the sounds down in the yard as chief prison officer Captain Robert B. Starnes met the six-man hanging team and let them into the gymnasium? Göring heard the guard changing, glanced up, and saw a new man—Private First Class Harold F. Johnson—taking Bingham's place at the peephole.

He casually lifted his left hand and clenched it to his face as though to shield his eyes from the spotlight. "He lay perfectly motionless, till about ten-forty," was all that Johnson would later admit having seen, "when he brought his hands across his chest with fingers laced and turned his head to the wall. He lay that way for about two or three minutes, and then placed his hands back along his sides. That was at ten-forty-four P.M. exactly. I looked at my watch to check the time."

---

*Most suspiciously, it was Dr. Pflücker who drew the attention of the Board of Inquiry to the "toilet bowl" theory, which they subsequently adopted. "You can hide poison in the toilet," he testified. "The toilet has a rim and this is hollow. . . . But," he continued, mentioning the obvious drawback to this theory, "how could Göring know he would always have the same cell?" The detailed testimony of the sentinels shows that Göring *at no time* on that final day sat on the alcove toilet.

* * *

It is D-Day for Hermann Göring: he is about to make his one-man crossing to eternity. The brass bullet is undone, concealed in one fist. The phial of cyanide is in his mouth, its fragile nipple is poised between his teeth. Daring to wait no longer, he clamps his jaw shut. The glass splinters between his molars, and a stinging, acrid taste of almonds strangles him. A blowing, choking noise escapes his lips.

As a darkness more infinite than any morphia enfolds him, he perhaps hears the hoarse shout of the sentinel, the rattle of the cell door being unlocked, the metallic ring of boot studs pounding along the catwalk outside. His brain certainly flickers long enough to sense Gerecke coming in and feeling his pulse—his struggling eyes focus sufficiently to see the American chaplain's mouth forming the words "This man is dying!"

Perhaps, seconds later, as Dr. Pflücker too comes in, Göring can still feel his right arm being lifted back onto his pajama'd chest, and an envelope being placed under his fingers.

"Remember—I found this in Göring's hand!"

If the dying man hears these words—uttered by Dr. Pflücker to the chaplain—this will explain what the photographs now show: that Hermann Göring dies with one eye winking open and one eye winking shut.

ACKNOWLEDGMENTS

No serious attempt has been made until recently to document the life of Hermann Göring, although he was from first to last the second man in Hitler's Germany. Since 1933 there have been attempts, ranging from unashamed hagiography to unabashed plagiarism; the earlier biographies suffered from the lack of primary material, the more recent, of which those by Stefan Martens (1985) and Alfred Kube (1986) are the most outstanding, are embarrassed by the wealth of archival material now available.

Given that Göring's life, although spanning only fifty-three years, would have sufficed for half a dozen lesser men, this is not surprising. Not only are his own archives now beginning to resurface, having been looted in 1945 and sold off by their illegal owners; but the secondary materials relating to him—in particular the interrogation reports on everybody who had to deal with him—have been accessioned by public archives in London, Canada, and Washington from the government agencies that held them secret until now. I would mention in particular the ADI(K) and CSDIC series of reports at London's Public Record Office (PRO) in record-class WO/208 and in the Washington Federal Records Center at Suitland, Maryland—primarily in record groups RG153, RG332, and RG407 (boxes 1954A–M). Surprisingly none of even the latest biographies makes use of the shorthand records of the Reich Air Ministry conferences (so-called Milch Documents, now held at the Bundesarchiv in Freiburg, Germany); none of the biographers is aware of the official records of Göring's World War I exploits at the U.S. Army Military History Institute (where my special thanks go to Professor Harold F. Deutsch, and to archivists Dr. Richard J. Sommers and David A. Keough); few of them had uncovered more than a dozen of the Carin Göring letters, which hold the vital clues to the strains of his young manhood and his growing megalomania.

I have donated all the records of this biographical research to the Institut für Zeitgeschichte in Munich, Germany, where they are freely available subject to the institute's conditions. May I express my thanks to the institute's director, Martin Broszat, and to Hermann Weiss for allowing me to become one of the first researchers to use the Hermann Göring diaries, which came to them as a "windfall" result when the state of Bavaria intervened to stop their sale at Sotheby's (on behalf of an unnamed French ex-officer) in London in 1977. I am also indebted to Edda Göring for permission to quote these diaries, and trust that I have used them fairly in accordance with the terms of that permission. Special gratitude also is owed to Colonel James W. Bradin, U.S. Army, for allowing me the first privileged use of his late father's "scoop," the Bormann bunker file with which my narrative opens.

I express my thanks to the staff at the Public Record Office in London, which benefits at last from one of the world's most advanced archival systems; and to the Borthwick Institute, York, for access to the papers of Lord Halifax, and the RAF Museum at Hendon; and to Churchill College, Cambridge, England, for access to the Malcolm Christie files.

In Washington I owe thanks to John Taylor, Robert Wolfe, and George Wagner at the Modern Military Records Section of the National Archives, as well as to the late John Mendelssohn, who devoted his last years to producing a fine catalog of war-crimes records (and helped me toward several little-known deposits of Göring archivalia); to J. Dane Hartgrove and John Butler of the Civil Archives Division; and to Amy Schmidt and Richard Olsen of the Modern Military Field Branch, at the Washington Federal Records Center, Suitland, Maryland. Thomas F. Conley, of the U.S. Army's Intelligence Security Command, Fort C. Meade, Maryland, provided me with their intelligence dossier on the Reichsmarschall. More general thanks are due to the Office of the Chief of Military History, Washington; to Helen Pashin at the Hoover Library in Stanford, California, for showing me their Göring Collection; to Raymond Teichman (supervisory archivist) at the Franklin D. Roosevelt (FDR) Library, Hyde Park, N.Y.; to Robert J Smith (chief, Office of History) at Wright-Patterson Air Base, Dayton, Ohio to the director of the Albert F. Simpson Library, Air University, Maxwel Air Base, Alabama; to John E. Wickman (Director), Dwight D. Eisenhowe Library, Abilene, Kansas; to John Dojka, librarian at Yale University, fc

access to the Stütz collection of Göring letters; to Robert W. Fisch, curator
of the museum at the U.S. Military Academy at West Point, N.Y., where
the Reichsmarschall's baton is housed; to Geoffrey Wexler of the State
Historical Society at Madison, Wisconsin; to James H. Hutson and the staff
of the Manuscript Division of the Library of Congress, for access to the
papers of Generals Carl F. Spaatz and H. H. Arnold, and to the private
papers and diary of Justice Robert H. Jackson. The librarian of Old Dominion
College, Norfolk, Virginia, provided me with a copy of Lieutenant General
Beppo Schmid's manuscript.

Over in West Berlin Dr. Daniel P. Simon, director of the U.S. Mission's
Berlin Document Center, in addition to granting access to Nazi party files
on Göring and his staff, also permitted me the first-ever use of the final
letters found in Göring's dead hand (and allowed me to inspect them again
when I decided that the exact folds in the letters might provide important
clues).

In Ottawa John Bell, of the Prime Minister's Archives section at the Public
Archives of Canada, once more allowed me to read the remarkable diaries
of Prime Minister William Mackenzie King.

Among the West German institutions consulted were the Bundesarchiv in
Koblenz (for civil records) and Bundesarchiv-Militärarchiv in Freiburg (military files); the Militärgeschichtliches Forschungsamt (by kind permission of
the Wissenschaftlicher Leiter, Dr. Horst Boog) in Freiburg; the Politisches
Archiv des Auswärtigen Amtes in Bonn (diplomatic files); the Staatsarchiv
Nürnberg (trial and some attorney records); the Bayerisches Hauptstaatsar-
chiv, Munich (early police records on the Nazis and the 1923 beerhall putsch),
and the Geheimes Preussisches Staatsarchiv in Berlin-Dahlem.

Among many scores of individuals to whom I am indebted I make mention
only of Richard J. Giziowski, who passed on hints about unknown collections
of Göring materials; Reinhard Spitzy, who provided copies from the papers
of Prince Max von Hohenlohe; Oberstleutnant a.D. Hans-Joachim Kessler,
who supplied material from his father's papers; Nerin Gun, Gerd Heidemann,
Billy F. Price, Charles E. Snyder, and Keith Wilson, who all supplied copies
of Göring's Nuremberg letters, which his next of kin had regrettably sold
off (most of the other letters have vanished irretrievably); Freifrau Jutta von
Richthofen, who permitted me to quote from her late husband's diaries (to
which Oberst a.D. Dr. Karl Gundelach provided access); Ursula Backe, who
let me use her diaries and Herbert Backe's letters to her; Lev Bezymenski,
who furnished copies from the Fritsch papers; Lieutenant Colonel Burton C.
Andrus, Jr., who allowed inspection at Colorado Springs of his late father's
Nuremberg prison files; Walter Lüdde-Neurath, who sent me the manuscript
of his prison memoirs; Philip Reed, of the Foreign Documents Centre at the
Imperial War Museum; the family of *Daily Express* journalist Ronald Selkirk
Panton, who let me consult his papers in the National Library of Australia,

Canberra; Ben Swearingen of Lewisville, Texas, who showed me his convincing researches on Göring's suicide. My gratitude also goes to Susanna Scott-Gall for her assistance and support through trying times, and to Harriet Peacock for translating the Swedish raw material.

David Irving
London

NOTES

PROLOGUE: ARREST THE REICHSMARSCHALL!

11   Martin Bormann's handwritten drafts of the signals and diary, and his letter to Heinrich Himmler, were
     provided to me by Col. James W. Bradin, U.S. Army. The originals will go the USAMHI; I have deposited
     copies in my collection at the IfZ, Munich, along with all my other research files. (See my microfilm list on
     page 549.)
13   *The events after Apr. 22, 1945:* In Berlin, Koller's diary and his telegram to Hitler, Apr. 25 (BA,
     Schumacher/366; NA film T32/9/5929ff; DE426/DIS202; and BA-MA, RL/5); and Koller, SRGG1284 and
     1293. I also used Hermann Göring's (HG's) version under interrog. at "Ashcan" (Mondorf on June 3, and
     Lammers' version in telegram to Hitler, Apr. 24, 1945 (Lammers Papers, NA film T580/265; ND, NG-1137;
     DI film 64).
13   *Apr. 23 on the Obersalzberg:* Koller diary, and diary of Col. Berndt von Brauchitsch, read out in SRGG1342.
     There are two versions of HG's Apr. 23 telegram to Hitler in Bradin's papers and the Berlin Document
     Center (BDC) file on HG, and a different text in DE426/DIS202; Bradin's file contains HG's messages
     to Keitel, Below, Ribbentrop, and Himmler. I also relied on U.S. interrogs. of HG's personal staff:
     Archmann, Görnnert, Brandenburg, and Lau (University of Pennsylvania Library and SI) and HG's re-
     marks on May 24 (SAIC/X/5). Steenracht's (X-P/18, and a memorandum by Lammers, Jul 27, 1945 (OCHM,
     and SI).
14   *Testament:* Lammers Papers, NA film T580/266.
15   *In Hitler's bunker:* Bradin Papers; my interview of Below, 1972; interrog. of Speer, June 1, and (BAOR)
     Sept. 11, 1945; CSDIC interrog. of SS Obergruppenführer Jüttner, May 14, 1946, and of Below, Mar. 18,
     1946 (both TRP).
16   *"Prevent" his flight:* Speer to Galland, Apr. 23 (NA film T77/775/1194f; Beppo Schmid, SRGG1311).
17   *Arrest:* Hitler to HG, Apr. 23 (war diary, WFSt North); diaries of Koller, Brauchitsch, and Bormann; interrogs.
     of Görnnert; Prof. Richard Suchenwirth, interview of Ondarza (BA-MA, Lw.104/3); SS Obersturmbannführer
     Dr. Bernhard Frank, interrog. in SAIC/PIR/186, AND 1984 book *Die Rettung von Berchtesgaden und der Fall
     Göring* (Berchtesgaden); interrog. of SS Brigadeführer Dr. Ernst Rode, NA, RG226: OSS file XL29950), and
     letter of Oct. 16, 1951 (Lw.104/3). In general, Maj. Ernst Evans (a.k.a. Ernst Englander, major in U.S. Air
     Force), "Göring–Almost Führer," in *Interavia* (1946), nos. 4 and 5; and "The Flight of the Culprits" (Hoover
     Library, Germany, F621).

21 I found HG's hitherto unpublished letter to Eisenhower and Devers, May 6, 1945, in the files of Mrs. Ardelia Hall, OMGUS (NA, RG260, box 395, file HG3); there is no copy in the Eisenhower Library, Abilene, Kansas.

22 *Capture:* For American portrayals, see *The Fighting 36th: A Pictorial History of the 36th Div.* (Austin, Texas: 1946); Capt. Harold L. Bond, "We Captured HG," in *The Saturday Evening Post*, Jan. 5, 1946; Robert Stack, "Capture of Göring," in *The T-Patcher*, 36th Div. Journal, Feb. 1977; and *T-Patch*, special edition, May 8, 1945.

22 *Twelve years run:* Suchenwirth interview of Gen. Paul Deichmann (BA-MA, Lw.104/3).

PART 1: THE OUTSIDER

1: THE TRIANGULAR AFFAIR

25 *Genealogy:* Prof. Frhr. von Dungern, "Family Trees of Famous Germans, Generaloberst HG" (Leipzig: 1936). This displays odd omissions like Emmy Sonnemann's first marriage and divorce. Also useful: the chronological table of genealogical research on eight hundred ancestors from Charlemagne to HG (undated, BA, R39/254). The (now missing) Veldenstein family documents folder listed in Feb. 1944 a baptismal certificate dated Rosenheim, Apr. 24, 1893; a confirmation baptismal certificate dated Rosenheim, Feb. 12, 1908; and a confirmation certificate dated Mar. 20, 1908 (NA, RG260, box 395). Cf. HG to Franz Gürtner, minister of justice, Dec. 7, 1937, re transmittal of marriage certificate of HG's grandfather, Wilhelm G. (now in Stütz Collection, Yale University).

26 *German South-West Africa:* For Dr. H. E. Göring's service as first imperial commissioner ad interim in G.S.W.A., from May 1885 to Aug. 1890, see Horst Gründer, *History of the German Colonies* (Paderborn: 1985); J. H. Esterhuyse, *South-West Africa, 1880–1894: The Establishment of German Authority in South-West Africa* (Cape Town: 1968), 99ff; and *The Colonial Reich*, vol. 1 (Bibliogr. Institute, Leipzig and Vienna: 1909); *History of German Colonial Policy* (Berlin: 1914).

26 *Psychiatrist:* Dr. Gustave M. Gilbert, "HG, Amiable Psychopath," in *Journal of Abnormal and Social Psychology*, vol. 43, no. 2 (Apr. 1948). Report by psychiatrist Dr. Paul L. Schroeder, Dec. 31, 1945 (Library of Congress, R. H. Jackson Papers, box 107).

26 *Albert Göring:* See his interrogs., SAIC/PIR/67, SAIC/FIR/48, and at Nuremberg on Sept. 3 and 25, 1945 (NA, film M1270); and his letter to Col. John H. Amen (NA, RG238, R. H. Jackson office files, box 180); Bodenschatz, GRG318. HG's relations with his half-brothers, the "Rhineland Görings," was frigid as they were Freemasons. See too HG interrog. by SHAEF, June 25, 1945 (USAISC).

27 *Burg Veldenstein:* Dr. Wilhelm Schwemmer, typescript history, "The Castle and Former Parish of Velden- stein" (undated, NA, RG260, box 359, iv). The Feb. 1944 Veldenstein listing mentions "deeds of conveyancing of Veldenstein castle, Dec. 23, 1938."

27 *Romantic youth:* Olga G., cited in Rudolf Diels, *Lucifer ante Portas* (Zürich: undated), 63.

28 *As a cadet:* The BA-MA at Freiburg archives has a "listing of the most important dates" from HG's personnel file (MS1g.1/13); much more informative is the file plundered from HG's special train at Berchtesgaden in May 1945 and now in the USAMHI, Carlisle, Pa.: "Military Personnel Files of the Reichsmarschall Since 1905, Collated by [Dr. Erich] Gritzbach." Together with the collections mentioned below, these were drawn upon in Oct. 1941 by the Luftwaffe's military history division to provide a basis for "a military biography" of the RM. For reference to Capt. Richard von Keiser, by Feb. 1942 a major general, aged 75, see Görnnert's file, NA, film T84/8/7591).

29 *Italian journey:* HG's travel journal, Apr. 1–3, 1911, is in USAMHI. Three earlier 1911 journals by HG were sold in Apr. 1988 by a Munich auction house; two related skiing jaunts, the third the first part of this Italian journey. See too HG's curriculum vitae (ibid.) and K. Höhler and H. Hummel's official history, "The Organization of the Air Force, 1933–39," in *Handbook of German Military History, 1648–1939*, vol. 4 (Munich: 1978), p. 507.

29 Professor John K. Lattimer generously made the diary available to the author of this book.

32 *Personal papers:* for a box listing of the documents at Veldenstein in Feb. 1944, see NA, RG260, box 395, folder 2.

32 Also in USAMHI archives are three green Leitz-type binders of documents collated by the Luftwaffe historical divisions from war diaries and other files, entitled, "The RM's Combat Flights," Nov. 3, 1914, to July 8, 1918 (incorporating extracts from war diaries of HG's units); "RM's Combat Reports," Oct. 3, 1915, to July 18, 1918; and "44 Photo Recce Reports by the RM," Mar. 4 to June 20, 1915. Seven of HG's World War I diaries, covering his dramatic experiences as an aviator, 1914–1918, surfaced in Aug. 1988 in a Pennsylvania auction house, offered for sale by a Mr. Irwin, along with a 1910 HG journal.

36 *Combat victories exaggerated:* Loerzer in conversation with Maj. Gen. Wolfgang Vorwald, reported in Milch diary, Apr. 5, 1947 (DI film 58); and U.S. interrog. of Gen. Ulrich Kessler (NA, RG238, R. H. Jackson office files, box 210).

38 Göring's Aug. 2, 1919, pilot's license is noted in the Veldenstein list.

38 *Candidate for Reich president:* Dispatch by German legation, Stockholm, Sept. 28, 1923 (German F.O. archives, file: Referat Deutschland, Pers.1). HG's correspondence with the demobilization office (*Abwick- lungsstelle*) is in BA-MA file, MS1g.1/13, and USAMHI archives.)

39 Carin Göring's stolen letters were last seen in private hands in 1955 in the United States. In the summer of

1988 they resurfaced, purchased by a Pennsylvania auction house from a Mr. Irwin. In the USAMHI there is a 108-page translation of the most important letters by Robert G. Hacke; others were published by her sister Fanny von Wilamowitz-Moellendorff in *Carin Göring* (Berlin: 1934). Only a few letters were found in the possession of Carin's son, Thomas von Kantzow, by Björn Fontander (*Göring och Sverige* [Stockholm: 1984]), and Leonard Mosley (*The Reich Marshal* [London & New York, 1974]).

2: STORM TROOP COMMANDER

44 HG interrog. by Dr. George N. Shuster, U.S. Army Historical Commission, July 20, 1945. I have deposited a comprehensive collection of HG interrogs. at the IfZ, Munich (SI). For Hitler's version of their first meeting, see his *Table Talk*, Jan. 3–4, 1942, and HG at International Military Tribunal in Mar. 1946 (*IMT*, ix, p. 64f), and in his book, *Aufbau einer Nation* (Berlin: 1934), and Gilbert (see note to p. 32), 211ff.

45 *History of the SA:* See BA, Schumacher/403.

45 *Villa in Obermenzing:* Munich police HQ, file #10061 (Munich State Archives).

46 *Married Carin:* On Feb. 3, 1923. The date was confirmed to me by Munich's Pasing registrar's office on May 23, 1986, and by documents listed in the Veldenstein listing. The marriage certificate is now in the IfZ archives (donated by an anonymous French officer). Recent HG biographers Martens (p. 16) and Kube (p. 7) are wrong in saying that HG married in 1922.

46 *Aunt Mary:* Swedish text in Fontander, 44, who also describes an episode witnessed by Bertha Fevrel, wife of a friend of Nils, in 1923, when Nils lunged at Emil Fevrel after he mentioned HG, grabbed him by the neck, and then leaped out of the train. After this, Nils was suspended from his teaching post.

47 To establish HG's role in the famed Beerhall Putsch I read the 3,000-page transcript of the "Treason Trial of Adolf Hitler, et al.," Feb. 26–Apr. 1, 1924 (NA films T84/1, 2 and 3) with the particularly valuable testimonies *in camera* of Hitler, Lossow, Kahr, Seisser, Röhm, Ludendorff, and others.

48 *The "Vollmacht"* of Aug. 24, 1923, has not survived but is referred to in the Veldenstein listing as having been "granted by the Führer" on that date.

48 *Italian correspondent:* Leo Negrelli (see note to p. 68).

48 *March on Berlin:* See E. Deuerlein (ed.), *The Hitler Putsch: Bavarian Documents on November 8–9, 1923* (Stuttgart: 1962).

3: PUTSCH

55 Witnesses at the treason trial agreed that the reporting by *Münchner Neueste Nachrichten*, No. 304, Nov. 9, 1923, was impeccable. My version is knitted together from the eyewitness evidence at the trial. Cf. too Karl-Alexander Müller, *Im Wandel einer Zeit* (Munich: 1938).

61 *Bodenschatz:* GRGG306.

61-2 *Escape route:* Carin's letter to her mother, Nov. 13, 1923; reports by Thanner, Feb. 1, 1934, and Feb. 15, 1935 (in HG's personnel file, formerly NSDAP Central Archives file 1225, then NA, film T581/52, now BA, NS.26/vorl.1225). Thanner wrote his report in support of a lawsuit brought by HG against Fritz Gerlich (the journalist whom he would order liquidated on June 30, 1934) on account of Gerlich's claim that HG had broken parole to escape. Cf. *Bayer. Staatszeitung*, Nov. 14, 1923 (BA, Hans Frank Papers, NL.110/AH.3).

63 *Mercedes:* Deuerlein, doc.258.

4: FAILURE OF A MISSION

68 Mr. Ben E. Swearingen of Lewisville, Tex., provided to me the file of original HG correspondence that he purchased from the estate of Dr. Leo Negrelli (copy in SI). Some of these items were used by Michael Palumbo in his paper "Göring's Italian exile" in *Journal of Modern History* (1978), no. 50, special edition D, 1035ff, though without being able to correlate them with the all-important Carin Göring letters. Cf. too K. P. Hoepke, The *German Rightwing and Italian Fascism* (Düsseldorf: 1968), 301ff; and Giuseppe Bastianini, *Memoirs* (Milan: 1959).

69 The Veldenstein listing refers explicitly to "copy of a letter from the Führer, May 14, 1924; first Vollmacht issued by the Führer on Aug. 24, 1923; general pass, signed Hossbach, Salzburg, on May 12, 1924; second Vollmacht issued by the Führer on May 14, 1924." Unfortunately, all were looted in 1945 (NA, RG260, box 395, folder 2).

70 *Hotel de Russie:* HG interrog. by Shuster, July 20, 1945.

71 *Secret deal:* The reports of Guido Renzetti, later Italy's consul general in Berlin, are in Mussolini's private papers (NA, film T586/419/9467).

72 The surviving text is in Italian; Goring probably used the German, *Sudtirol*.

77 *Press clippings:* For example, from the *Münchner Neueste Nachrichten*, Oct. 25, 1925.

5: ASYLUM FOR THE CRIMINALLY INSANE

83   *Förster,* SRGG1206. For FBI reports on HG's drug problem, see FDR Library, file OF.10b.
84   *Ossbahr:* These and other Swedish eyewitnesses are cited by Fontander's fine recent study, *Göring och Sverige* (Stockholm: 1984).
84   *Letter to Capt. Lahr:* June 26, 1925: Copy in Prussian secret state archives, Berlin Dahlem, inventory 90b, no. 286.
86   This author is indebted to Harriet Peacock for these translations from the Swedish.
88   *Certificate:* This document is one of six items plundered from Göring's personal effects and recently returned to Munich by a French officer (IfZ's HG Collection, ED.180). All six figure in the Feb. 1944 Veldenstein listing.
89   *Second stay:* BA, NS.26/ vorl.1225.

6: TRIUMPH AND TRAGEDY

90   *Paul Körner:* BDC file on Körner and his testimony in postwar trials (e.g., Case XI, 14,133ff) and Emmy Göring (ibid., 19, 538ff); and interview with Körner published in *Essener Nationalzeitung* (a newspaper under HG's control), no. 211, Aug. 3, 1933.
92   *Turkey:* HG interrog. June 3, 1945; and curriculum vitae, in IfZ file, Fa.190.
92   *Morphinism:* A fascimile of the affidavit submitted by court doctor Lundberg was published in the *Communists' Brown Book on the Reichstag Fire and Hitler Terror* (Basel: 1933), 57; and Olof Kinberg's certificate was quoted by K. Singer in *Göring, Germany's Most Dangerous Man* (London: 1940), 98. For rumors on the morphine addiction, see the FBI files referred to (see note to p. 83) and *OSS Current Biography 1941,* prepared by OSS R & A CEu Section, Dec. 16, 1941 (DeWitt C. Poole Papers, DI film 36a).
92   *Blackmailed:* HG's letter to Lahr (see note to p. 84); and Otto Strasser's book, *Hitler and I* (Konstanz: 1948), 119.
94   *Bribery:* Milch, SRGG1279; further, my interviews of Milch in 1967, and his memoirs (SI and DI film 36a).
94   *Spoke only once:* Wilhelm Frick, *The National Socialists in the Reichstag, 1924–1931* (Munich: 1932). Killinger, GRGG1243. Under § 331ff of the Reich Penal Code, the bribery of *Reichstag deputies* was not a criminal offense.
94   *One time dispensation:* My interview of Messerschmitt directors Rakan Kokothaki and Fritz Seiler, 1969.
95   *Milch diaries:* I had these microfilmed when preparing Milch's biography: 1912–19 (DI film 54); 1919–24 (DI film 55); 1924–35 with notebooks (DI film 56); 1936–45 with notebooks (DI film 57); 1945–51 (DI film 58), and made a selective transcript of the years 1921–50 (DI film 59).
95   *Lufthansa:* HG interrog. at Nbg., Oct. 13, 1945; letter Deutsche Bank to Deutsche Lufthansa, June 6, 1929 (Deutsche Bank archives in East Germany, cited in Karl-Heinz Eyermann, *The Great Bluff* [East Berlin: 1963], 320; Milch letter to Deutsche Bank, May 30, 1936 (ibid., 356f). Milch, confidential study on HG, May 17, 1947 (DI film 37).
96   *Hess:* Letter to Franz Xaver Schwarz, Feb. 6, 1934 (BDC file on Milch). Further closet Nazis: BDC file on Theo Croneiss.
96   *Prince Auwi:* Interrog., Nbg., May 14, 1947.
97   *Groener:* Files of HG's attorney, Hans Frank (NA, NL.110/AH.2); judgment in BDC file on HG.
98   *Carin's health:* A loose page to be found in HG's so-called *Game Diary* (Library of Congress) certainly dates from these Jan. 1931 days: "1.) health cure; 2.) Engadin; 3.) Doorn; 4.) Reichstag, Feb. 3; 5.) Munich Hitler; 6.) Important conferences; 7.) BMW files Munich (Hochkreuth); 8.) Munich advertising-contracts and -potentialities; 9.) Dirksen 2,000.00; 10.) Frau von S.?; 11.) Thomas press; 12.) [Thomas] Sweden; 13.) [Thomas] land; 14.) general customer planning; 15.) Carin health cure; 16.) [Carin] Sweden; 17.) Carin Engadin; 18.) [Carin] Doorn; 19.) Dortmund, cash; 20.) L.—H.; 21.) Cn.-Mai!; 22.) bank (general purpose account); 23.) me in Sweden; 24.) Hi. [Hitler?] book in America.
98   *Doorn: The Kaiser in Holland* (Munich: 1971) by the kaiser's A.D.C., with its diary entries for Jan. 8 to 30, 1931. HG visited the kaiser again May 20 to 21, 1932.
99   *Orsini:* Transcript of Orsini's dispatch to Rome deciphered by the Abwehr in papers of Maj. Gen. von Bredow, IfZ film MA.23; and see Schleicher's letter to Brüning, Mar. 13, 1931 (BA-MA, NL.42/25); and in general HG's correspondence with Renzetti, in Renzetti Papers (BA).
100   *Pizzaro:* E. Deuerlein, ed., *The Rise of the Nazi Party in Eyewitness Testimony* (Munich: 1974), 351ff; and J. Petersen, *Hitler-Mussolini: The Origins of the Berlin-Rome Axis, 1933–1936* (Tübingen: 1973), 42f. Neither author was aware of the unpublished Carin Göring letters, however.
102   *Carin's death:* Sister Märta Magnuson (quoted in Fontander, 139ff) and Birgitta Wolf. The railroad platform scene is described by Mosley, 130.

7: THE SPEAKER

104   *Emmy Sonnemann:* Testimony in the "Wilhelmstrasse Case" (Case XI), 19,538ff; memoirs, in *Revue* (Munich), no. 49/1950 through no. 5/1951; and book version, published in Oldendorf, 1967.

105   *Dissolution:* HG interrog. by Shuster, July 20, 1945; and Hans Frank Papers in BA, NL.110/AH.2.
106   *Sommerfeldt* published memoirs as *Ich War Dabei: Die Verschwörung der Dämonen, 1933–1939* (Darmstadt: 1949).

PART 2: THE ACCOMPLICE

8: BONFIRE NIGHT

111   *Reichsminister without Portfolio:* The decree appointing HG as such and as Reich commissar for civil aviation will be found in BA, R43I/1483. I have also used the Reich cabinet minutes, R43I/1458ff (in part on DI film 72).
111   *Schwerin von Krosigk:* Diary, Nov. 5, 1932, to Feb. 5, 1933 (DI film 39, and file DE433/DIS202).
113   *Papen:* Often interrogated, but see especially interrog. of July 12, 1945 (SI), and of HG, Aug. 15 and Nov. 6, 1945; and Hitler, *Table Talk*, May 21, 1942 (from Heinrich Heim's original note in the possession of François Genoud).
113   *Aviation:* Presidential decree of Feb. 2, 1933, in *Reich Law Gazette*, 1933, I, 35.
118   *Dimitrov:* HG interrog. by Shuster, July 20, 1945.
119   Dimitrov, et al., were deported to the USSR despite strong protests by HG and Diels; Hitler informed HG on Apr. 26, 1934, he had ordered the men sent quietly away (BA, RG43II/294). For the trial of Dimitrov, see the report in the *Neue Zürcher Zeitung*, Nov. 6, 1933.

9: GÖRING'S PET

121   *Concentration camps:* On May 22, 1933, HG allowed foreign journalists to tour his camp at Sonnenburg, where 443 "leftists" were held without trial. AP's chief Berlin correspondent, Louis Lochner, satisfied himself that the cruel treatment had now stopped and that the prisoners were being treated humanely. Lochner, letter to daughter Betty, FDR Library, Toland papers, box 53.
121–22 *Diels:* I have used (with proper caution) his affidavits of Oct. 30 and Nov. 1, 1945 (ND, 2460-PS and 2544-PS), and above all his BAOR interrog. in 031 Civilian Interrogation Camp and his manuscript, "The Prussian Political Police and the Founding of the Gestapo," both in NA, RG332 (series MIS-Y), box 49. Decree of Apr. 26, 1933, in Prussian Law Collection, 1933, 122.
123   *Chief architect:* Heinz Tietze (of Berlin's Dept. of Buildings and Finance), interrog. by SHAEF PWE ("The Rebuilding of Göring's Apartment"), May 26, 1945 (NA, RG226, OSS file 132120). Floor plans of Göring's official residence are in the Hoover Library.
123   *Forschungsamt:* Diels called it "Göring's darling" (BAOR, *see* note to 121). HG himself was interrogated about the FA on June 10, July 7, 19, 1945. The only history of the FA is my own *Breach of Security*, with Prof. D. C. Watt (London: 1968). For the current work I interviewed FA officials Dr. Gerhard Neuenhoff, Karl-Anton Loibl, and Milch; David Kahn interviewed Walther Seifert (head of section Vb, evaluation.) See too Ulrich Kittel's study on the FA in IfZ, ZS.1734, and BA, K1.Erw.272, and the affidavit of the FA's legendary chief Gottfried Schapper in Case XI, Nbg., Mar. 2 and June 7, 1948. For documents on FA operations see: security directives, 1938–45, in BA-MA file RL.1/25; correspondence files of the Führer's adjutants in the BA, NS.10/35, /36, and /89, and with HG's ministerial bureau, in the Hoover Library, HG Collection, box 1. Scattered "research reports" (i.e., wiretap reports) will be found on NA film T120/723 ("from the Munich Agreement to August 1939"); HG in the Anschluss crisis (ND, 2949-PS); Beneš in the Sudeten crisis, Sept. 1938 (PRO file FO.371/21742): Ciano phone call on Aug. 26, 1939 (NA film T77/545).
123   *Gisevius treachery:* HG stressed (under interrog., June 10, 1945) that the deciphered dispatches of the American legation in Berne had "proved especially helpful"; confirmed by Körner, interrog., July 18, 1945. On Gisevius's role as an OSS agent, see Allen Dulles's letter to R. H. Jackson, in Library of Congress, R. H. Jackson Papers, boxes 101–102.

10: RENAISSANCE MAN

129   *Most powerful in the world:* Lutwaffe G-2, "The Air Situation in Europe," May 2, 1939 (app. to ADI[K] 395/45).
130   *Blomberg* held a conference on "the proposed development of the air force" in Oct. 1933 (Liebmann Papers, IfZ, ED.1). On the rebirth of the Luftwaffe, I have used mainly the personal and official papers of Field Marshal Erhard Milch: his diaries (see note to p. 95), interrogations (DI film 36), selected Reich Air Ministry files (DI film 53), trial documents from Case II (DI film 67). The voluminous collection of Milch documents from the Reich Air Ministry has now been repatriated to Germany by the British government: among them, the verbatim records of the most important conferences held by Milch, HG, Director of Air Armament, Fighter Staff, Central Planning, and other agencies; for a listing of these volumes (cited below as MD-) and documents, see ADI(K) report 414a/1945 DI film 16; or SI); I have deposited in the IfZ my

own index to the conferences. Of major importance is the volume *Conferences with the Reichsmarschall and Führer, 1936–43* (DI film 40).

130 *Loerzer and Kesselring:* Quoted by Prof. Richard Suchenwirth. Suchenwirth's well-constructed interviews with Milch, Roeder (Judge Advocate General), Loerzer, Ploch, Kreipe, Stumpff, Körner, Bodenschatz, HG adjutant Brauchitsch, Schmid, Seidel, Student, Kesselring, Hammerstein, Ondarza, Klosinski, Knipfer, and Jeschonnek's colleagues Lotte Kersten, Leuchtenberg, Meister, and Christ are in the BA-MA, file Lw.104.

131 *Croneiss:* BDC file on Croneiss. In 1945 Croneiss was still cited in overheard prisoners' conversations as being the authority for Milch's "Jewish" descent. His true parental background, of which I am aware, shows that Milch had no Jewish blood.

132 *Letter to Rust:* Quoted by Oskar Söhngen in *Arbeiten zur Geschichte des Kirchenkampfes* (Göttingen: 1971) vol. 26, 55f.

133 *Martin Niemöller, Hitler, and Protestant Church Leaders: What Happened on Jan. 25, 1934* (Bielefeld: 1959); Bishop T. Wurm, *Memoirs* (Stuttgart: 1953); Jörgen Glenthöy: *Hindenburg, Göring, and the Protestant Church Leaders* (Göttingen: 1965), vol. 15, 45ff. On Hitler's confrontation with Niemöller, see especially *Table Talk*, Apr. 7, 1942; Alfred Rosenberg, diary, Jan. 19, 1940; HG interrog. by Shuster, July 20, 1945; manuscripts by Lammers, Dönitz, and Schwerin von Krosigk, July 1945 (OCMH), and a letter from Niemöller to myself (SI).

134 *The Forschungsamt report* of Jan. 25, 1934, is in HG's file, "Political Excesses by Protestant Clerics," Jan. 9–25, 1934 (BA, R43II/163; and cf./156 and /161). Also the news item in *Allgemeine Evangelische Landeskirchenzeitung*, Feb. 23, 1934. For a letter from HG to Franz Gürtner about Niemöller and the Confessional Church dated July 28, 1937, see the Stütz Collection at Yale University.

135 *Galland;* Interrog., "Birth, Life, and Death of the German Day Fighter Arm," ADI(K) report 373/1945. See also Galland's papers in the BA-MA.

135 *Koppenberg:* His preface to a history of developments at Dessau during 1934 (written 1935); in Junkers Papers, SI.

136 *Carinhall expenses:* HG interrog. at "Ashcan," June 2, 1945; Bodenschatz, GRGG306, and see note to p. 123 (Tietze).

136 Lists of gifts in RG260, box 260, folders xv and xvi.

136 *"His staff":* For the files of Göring's "Stabsamt," particularly those of his P.A., the engineer Fritz Görnnert, see NA films T84/6, /7, /8 (thus the file on C & A Brenninkmeyer is on T84/7); further files on the Stabsamt, particularly its espionage activities abroad, are on NA film T120/2621 (film of German FO file 5482H, relating to special missions carried out for HG in London by the duke of Coburg, Prince Max von Hohenlohe, and in Sweden by Prince Viktor zu Wied, the later ambassador in Stockholm. In June 1935 HG set up an attaché section in the Reich Air Ministry under Maj. Friedrich Karl Hanesse: the air attachés (Wenninger, Waldau, and others) reported primarily to HG and not to the F.O. from their new vantage points in Rome and London, to which were later added Warsaw, Moscow, Washington, and Tokyo. Some of the papers of Staatssekretär Ludwig Grauert's office (Prussian ministry of the interior) and of the Prussian State ministry are now in the Prussian secret state archives in Berlin Dahlem (inventories 77 and 90 respectively). An overview of the Stabsamt is gained from its telephone book (now in Hoover Library), while the Stabsamt organization plan will be found on NA film T84/6/6008ff. See also the interrogs. of Limberger at Nbg., May 19 and July 29, 1947, and of Gritzbach, May–Sept. 1947; and Robert Kempner's evaluation of HG's staff in "The Case Against HG" (NA, RG153, Records of Judge Advocate General, box 57).

137 *Gifts and donations:* There were allegations that after Hugenburg's resignation as minister of economics on June 26, 1933, HG maneuvered his old friend and benefactor Dr. Kurt Schmitt of the Allianz insurance corporation into this office—ignoring the claim of the old party veteran Otto Wagener to the post—and that Schmitt paid RM100,000 into HG's bank account on June 15, 1933, as a reward. (See Kurt Gossweiler's East Berlin dissertation, *The Roll of German Monopoly Capital in Procuring the Röhm Affair* [East Berlin: 1963].) This is highly plausible, given that HG's bank statements, preserved in OMGUS files (NA, RG260, box 395) record regular annual deposits by Schmitt rising from RM50,000 in 1936 to 100,000 in 1942. Among other benefactors was Dr. Herrmann, whom HG had appointed "State Privy Councillor": On Jan. 3, 1942, he paid RM 1 million into HG's account at the Thyssen Bank ("Herrmann," HG conceded under interrog. on May 29, 1945, "was a publisher of insurance periodicals." Göring, states his report, "helped him a great deal.") The Allianz corporation and its directors, Herrmann and H. Hilgard, also made costly gifts to HG—hunting pictures by Ridinger at the end of 1937, two silver cutlery services, a large vase of May flowers and orchids (on his first wedding anniversary in 1936), two silver candlesticks and a flower vase on his 1937 birthday, a baroque angel and antique silver goblet when Edda was born in June 1938, plus a gift of RM50,000 for the child. Aircraft manufacturer Fritz Siebel donated a porcelain "stag at bay"; Schmitt, a bronze stag cast in China in the seventeenth century; director Friedrich Flick gave HG a "Gothic hunting chamber" for Carinhall; on Jan. 12, 1940, Walter Hofer (acting on HG's behalf) purchased with funds of C & A Brenninkmeyer (RM18,000) an altarpiece by Cornelius Engelbrechtsen, and with funds provided by the Reemtsma Cigarette corporation an "early Renaissance tapestry."

11: MURDER MANAGER

138 *Blaschke:* Interrog., Nbg., Nov. 19, 1947. Backe's words are quoted from the diary of his wife, Ursula, May 15 and June 13, 1934.

139 *S.A. crisis:* See Heinz Höhne's excellent investigation in *Mordsache Röhm* (Hamburg: 1984).

140 *Darré:* Overheard in CCPWE, no. 32 X-P6, May 16, 1945. In general on the Röhm crisis, I used the Liebmann Papers in IfZ (ED.1), Milch's diaries and notebooks (DI film 56), the papers of Eduard Wagner (SI), of General von Fritsch (see note to p. 194), and Klaus-Jürgen Müller's authoritative history of the Reichswehr and the Röhm affair in *Militärwissenschaftliche Mitteilungen* (1961), 107ff.

141 *Landespolizei:* Initially the Landespolizeigruppe Wecke (Special Purposes); then, from Dec. 12, 1933, the Landespolizeigruppe "General Göring," and from Sept. 23, 1935, incorporated as the HG regiment into the Luftwaffe.

141 *Phipps:* Dispatch to F.O., June 10, 1934, in DBFP (2) vi, 749ff; diaries of Milch and Darré.

142 *Mussolini:* Graham to F.O., Oct. 11, 1933, in *Documents on British Foreign Policy* (DBFP) 2 vols., no. 44. And Pompeo Alois diary, Nov. 6, 1933, French edition, Paris 1957. Decrypt of Italian ambassador's dispatch of May 13, 1933, in German Central Archives, Potsdam, file 60952.

142 *Lipski:* See Marian Wojciechowski's book on Polish-German relations, 1933–38 (Leiden: 1971), and Lipski's diary, now in his papers in the Pilsudski Institute, New York. I also used HG interrog., U.S. State Dept., Nov. 1945, and by Shuster, July 23, 1945.

143 *Renzetti:* Letter to Mussolini, June 16, 1934 (NA film T586/419/9467ff).

144 *Managers of June 30:* Darré, in X-P4, May 14, 1945.

145 *Lutze:* Viktor Lutze's diary was published in the *Hannoversche Presse* in 1957.

145 *Popp:* Information from Neuenhoff (see note to p. 123) and Milch memoirs (SI).

146 *Brückner:* His affidavits dated May 28, 1949, and June 25, 1952, are in my collection (SI); I also interviewed Hitler's private secretary, Christa Schroeder, about the events of this day.

146 *Göring in Berlin:* HG in conversation with Werner Bross: *Gespräche mit Hermann Göring,* p. 18; Papen in conversation with a British officer, May 16, 1945 (X-P6); my interview with Milch, Dec. 1, 1968 (SI); Blomberg MS (SAIC/FIR/46). Further detail on June 30, 1934, in Berlin from Meissner, interrog., July 23, 1945 (OCMH), HG interrog., Nbg, Oct. 13, 1945; Frick interrog., July 20, 1945 (OCMH); Darré conversation, May 14, 1945 (X-P4), and diary; letter from Renzetti to Mussolini, July 13, 1934 (NA film T586/419/9439ff).

147 *S.A. headquarters:* HG interrog. by Shuster, July 20, 1945. He added that Ernst was arrested "as he was about to take a powder with RM80,000." Cf. Gilbert, op. cit., 79, and Bross, 18.

147 *Schleicher's murder:* The reports by the district attorney of the Potsdam Assize Court, Tetzlaff, are to be found in *Vierteljahrshefte für Zeitgeschichte* (VfZ) (1953), 71ff; for HG's role, see OSS R&A Branch report, "HG as War Criminal," June 25, 1945 (DI film 34).

148 *Gerlich:* For HG's lawsuit against, see Hans Frank's files, BA, NL.110/AH.2; Gerlich's defense lawyers introduced homosexual letters written by Ernst Röhm, and the suit was dropped. (See BA, Reich Justice Ministry files, R22/5006, and Schumacher/402.)

149 *Darré:* Diary, June 30, July 1, 1934; and Milch diary.

149 *Moulin-Eckart:* HG interrog. by Shuster, July 20, 1945. Leon Graf du Moulin-Eckart, doctor at law, was chief of the Nazi party's information service in the Brown House in 1932, and Röhm's adjutant. Born Jan. 11, 1900; indicted for procuring and for unnatural sexual intercourse on Oct. 21, 1934, having provided his apartment to Röhm for homosexual activities; acquitted (BA, R22/5006).

149 *Next of kin:* See Himmler's note for a meeting with Hitler on Aug. 14, 1944, item 3: "Provision for next of kin," i.e., of the executed plotters (NA film, T175/94/5329); in the files of party treasurer Schwarz is a letter from Himmler to Lammers and others on Aug. 27, 1944, reporting that at their meeting the Führer had ruled that the next of kin were to be provided for "as in the case of the Röhm putsch of June 1934" (IfZ file, Fa.116).

12: OPEN DOOR TO A TREASURE-HOUSE

150 *Rewarded the Gestapo:* Görnnert, note for Gritzbach, Nov. 5, 1942 (NA film, T84/6/5450).

151 *Croneiss:* See note to p. 94.

152 *Swearing in:* Lt. Gen. H. J. Rieckhoff's memoirs, *Trump or Bluff, Twelve Years of the German Luftwaffe* (Zürich: 1945), 55f.

152 *Belgrade:* Sir Nevile Henderson's dispatch to the F.O., Oct. 29, 1934 (PRO, FO.434/1); Heeren's dispatch to German F.O., Oct. 22, 1934 (ADAP, C, iii/1, no. 265).

153 *Thomas von Kantzow:* Diary, Dec. 23, 1934 (Fontander, op cit., 181f).

153 *Air Ministry Building:* RAF Air Central Interpretation Unit, report K.110(R), "Berlin Main Air Ministry Building," Feb. 8, 1945.

154 *Expansion in the East:* Lipski, memo cited in Wojciechowski, op. cit., 245; and cf. memo by Lt. Gen. Schindler, the German military attaché in Warsaw, Feb. 22, 1935 (BA, Beck Papers, NL.28/1).

155 *Don:* The interpreter at HG's interview was the then C.O. of the Flying Training School at Warnemünde, Col. (later Lt. Gen.) Ulrich Kessler: Kessler interrog. Sept. 20, 1945 (NA, RG238, box 210), and Kessler's private papers, kindly made available to me by his son.

155 *Little dinner party:* Letters from Phipps to John Simon and Orme Sargent, Mar. 22 and May 5, 1935 (PRO file FO.317/18879).

156 *Twelve rings:* Darré, overheard describing this on May 14, 1945 (X-P4).

156 *Rug:* Tietze (see note to p. 123).

156 *Medals:* Reich cabinet meeting, Apr. 7, 1933 (BA, R43I/1461). Schacht, interrog by Maj. Tilley, in *IMT,* xiii, 14.

157 *Fat-Arsch:* Lt. Fiedler, an FW 190 pilot shot down on Jan. 1, 1945, overheard relating this, in CSDIC report, SA draft 1197.
157 *Wedding ceremony:* Ibid., Apr. 11, 1935 (/9451f); letter from Louis Lochner to his daughter, Apr. 20, 1935 (FDR Library, Toland Papers, box 53); William C. Bullitt letter to Roosevelt, June 3, 1935 (FDR Library); Phipps dispatch to F.O., Apr. 15, 1935 (FO.371/18879).
158 *Gifts:* Schacht, *Revue,* no. 45/1953. Gift of Reichsgruppe Handwerk is referred to by Otto Ohlendorf in PW Paper 133 (PRO file WO.208/4176).
158 *Prince of Wales:* PRO file FO.371/18882.

13: GETTING READY IN FOUR YEARS

160 *Vicar Schulze:* Franz Gürtner diary, Feb. 26, 1936.
160 *Göring Standard:* Dispatch of British embassy in Berlin to F.O., Nov. 9, 1935 (FO.371/18880).
161 *Homespun:* Letter from Himmler to SS Obergruppenführer Oswald Pohl, Sept. 30, 1942 (NA film T175/43/5427).
161 *Snide remarks:* Reich Ministry of Justice circular to senior judges and D.A.s, Sept. 25, 1935 (BA, R22/996); and Neumann to Gürtner, Aug. 17, 1935, letter about prosecution of utterances against the RM (/845). Dr. Robert Kempner, a senior U.S. prosecutor at Nuremberg later wrote on May 10, 1945, to Col. Melvin Purvis recommending interrogating HG "to soften him up" about "the former intimate friendship of [Emmy] with a Jewish theatrical man" (NA, RG153, Judge Advocate General, box 1390).
161 *Genealogical brochure:* Prof. Otto Frhr von Dungern, *Ahnentafeln berühmter Deutscher,* Generaloberst HG (Leipzig: 1936).
162 *Secret conference:* Letter from HG to Neurath, May 21, 1935, and minutes of staff conference of May 20 in *ADAP,* C, iv/1, no. 97.
162 *War inevitable:* Phipps to Vansittart, F.O., Jan. 23, 1936, in *DBFP* (2), xv, no. 474. Lord Londonderry, *Ourselves and Germany* (London: 1938), 80ff.
163 *Economists:* On HG's role in the German economy, see particularly the well-researched accounts by Alfred Kube, *Pour le Mérite and Swastika* (Munich: 1986), and by Stefan Martens, *Hermann Göring* (Paderborn: 1985). On the arbitration issue, see Friedrich Gramsch's manuscript of Aug. 1, 1947 (ND, NID-12616), and letter of Darré to Schacht, Jan. 14, 1936 (BA, R43II/331).
163 *Currency decree:* In BA files on the Four-Year Plan, R26/35; DNB-agency dispatch in *The Times,* Apr. 28; Phipps to Eden, F.O., Apr. 30 (in *DBFP* (2) xvi, No. 282). Letters from Blomberg to HG, Apr. 4 (BA, WiIF.5/433) and May 7 (/405), and Reich Finance Ministry memo of Aug. 5, 1936 (BA, R2/19542). HG interrog., June 25, 1945 (USAISC), and Aug. 15, 1945 (SI).
164 *Currency conferences:* May 12, minutes in BA, R26I/36; cabinet of May 12, ND, 1301/PS; see also diaries of Milch and Darré, and Neurath's memo of May 13 (Wiehl Papers, NA film T120/3137/E.513894f). May 15: minutes in R26I/36; conference of experts on May 26 (among those present being HG's cousin, Herbert L. W. Göring, "General Counselor in the Reich Ministry of Economics") R26I/29; and June 30, 1936: R26I/36.
165 *Economic staff:* Prussian cabinet, Lists of Participants and Minutes, 1936–37, in Prussian secret state archives, Dahlem, Inventory 90. Backe: diary of his wife, July 15, 1936.
165 *Keppler:* HG interrog., Nbg., Sept. 13, 1946 (Hoover Library, HG Collection). Memo on conference with HG, July 6, 1936 (BA, E26I/Ia). HG, undated memo of July 1936 (ND, 3891-PS).
165 *Bodenschatz* memo in ND, 3890-PS. For the history of the Four-Year Plan, see Wilhelm Treue, "Hitler's Memo on the Four-Year Plan," in *VfZ* (1955), 184ff; and HG, manuscript OI-RIR/8 of Oct. 24, 1945, and interrog. of Nbg., Oct. 17, 1945. Wiedemann: note dated Mar. 28 [1939] in his papers in the Library of Congress.
165 *Franco's letter:* See the account by Angel Viñas in *La Alemania Nazi y el 18 de julio* (Madrid: 1974), 408ff, based on the testimony of HG's man Johannes Bernhardt and Spanish archives. Other details from Speer interrog. by FIAT, June–July 1945; Milch diary, July 26, 1936, and HG interrog., July 27, 1945 (OCMH).
165 *Lindbergh:* Letters to Lt. Col. Truman Smith, June 5, July 3, Aug. 6, Sept. 8 and 16, 1936 (Hoover Library, Truman Smith Papers, box 1); Harold Nicolson diary, Sept. 8, 1936.
166 *Written submissions:* Letter of HG to Schacht, Aug. 22 (BA-MA, WiIF.5/203); reports of the R & E Section of HG's Raw Materials and Currency Unit, July 21, 1936 (BA, R25/18).
166 *Four-Year Plan* memorandum: In *ADAP,* C, v/2, no. 490; cf Treue, Gramsch (see above) and Esmonde Robertson, "The Four-Year Plan," MS in IfZ (Ms.94).
167 *Cabinet* on Sept. 4, 1936: BA-MA, WiIF.5/3614; cf. ND, 416-EC; Georg Thomas, note of Sept. 2, 1936 (ND, 1301-PS); Darré, diary, and Herbert Backe, letter to his wife of Sept. 7, 1936 (kindly provided by Frau Backe).
167 *Vansittart:* Report of Sept. 10, 1936 (Vansittart Papers, Churchill College, Cambridge). For summaries of the payments to HG, July 12, 1937, to Oct. 17, 1943, see SAIC/31 dated May 29, 1945: "HG—Financial Report." HG's account books are in NA, OMGUS files, RG260, box 395. Cf. Gritzbach interrog., Nbg., Sept. 9, 1947.
168 *Limberger:* See her interrog. in NA, RG239, box 84. She was born Aug. 30, 1893, in the Saar, served as a librarian in the Prussian State Library in Berlin, joined HG's staff in 1935; her sister, a doctor, emigrated to London.
168 *Reemtsma* himself was interrogated at great length by CSDIC (WEA), FIR report 56, Mar. 18, 1946: He stated that HG agreed to stop the prosecution in Apr. 1933 in return for a RM4 million "donation" and

1 million per annum in quarterly installments (NA, RG332, Mis-Y, box 18). My narrative is also based on HG's account books (see above); affidavit by Körner, Oct. 14, 1945 (ND, NG-2918); HG interrog., Nbg., Dec. 22, 1945; Milch diary, Jan. 12, 1950; report on Reemtsma trial in *Rhein-Neckar Zeitung*, Jan. 19, 1948. Görnnert, note for RM's talk with Führer, July 29, 1942 (NA film T84/8/7882); HG conf. with the Reich commissars of the occupied territories, Aug. 6, 1942 (ND, exhibit USSR-170). The Reemtsma receipt is in NA, RG239, box 78, "Art Fund" folder. Under § 331 (simple passive bribery) and § 332 (serious passive bribery) Reemtsma payments to HG were criminal offenses under the Reich Penal Code.

169　*Göring's advice:* Ordinance of Oct. 18, in *RGBl*, 1936, I, 997; executive decree, Oct. 22 (BA, R43II/353a); HG speeches of Dec. 17, 1936 (ND, NI-051), and Apr. 13, 1937: "Apart from this bargain orally and don't write things down!" (BA-MA, WilF.5/1196). HG quotation is from his interrog. on June 25, 1945 (USAISC).

14: THE BRIDGE AT GUERNICA

172　*Burckhardt*, Prof. Carl F.: *My Danzig Mission* (Stuttgart: 1960), 106f. And telegram of British delegation in Geneva to British F.O., May 27, 1937 (PRO, FO.371/20711).

172　*Seasick:* Kessler interrog., Sept. 20, 1945 (see above).

172　*Backe:* Frau Backe diary, Dec. 12, 1936. Vansittart: report (see note to p. 167).

173　*HG staff conference:* ND, 3474-PS. Udet's planning: memo of Jan. 11, 1937 (MD.65, p. 7529).

173　*Udet:* I have used a chronology drawn up by his adjutant, Max Pendele (BA-MA, Lw.104/15), and Udet's conference notes in MD.65. On the cancellation of the four-engined bomber project, see Milch to Adm. Lahs, Nov. 1, 1942 (MD.53, pp.0780ff), and his testimony in *IMT*, ix, 72.

174　*Visit to Mussolini:* See Malcolm Muggeridge, ed., *Ciano's Diplomatic Papers* (London: 1948), 80ff. There is a German transcript of HG's talk with Mussolini on Jan. 23, 1937, in the German Central Archives, Potsdam (DZA file 60952).

174　*Guernica:* Richthofen diary, Apr. 26, 1937 (extracts in SI). Maj. Klaus Maier, Guernica, Apr. 26, 1937. *The German Intervention in Spain and the Guernica Affair* (Freiburg: 1975); and Siegfried Kappe-Hardenberg, "Guernica—and No End" in *Deutschland in Geschichte und Gegenwart* (1980), 19ff.

175　*Lothian:* Report of May 4, 1937 (PRO file FO.371/20735); on the general antipathy to HG in Britain, /20734.

175　*Henderson* reported his talk to F.O. on May 25, 1937 (/20735). See especially Nevile Henderson, *Failure of a Mission* (London: 1940).

177　*Iron Ore:* For materials on Germany's native iron ore resources, see BA, R25/180 through /185. Protest by the steel bosses: see the facsimile in T. R. Emesen, *From Göring's Writing Desk* (East Berlin: 1947).

177　*Brassert:* Hermann Alexander Brassert, of H. A. Brassert & Co., Chicago. Cf. HG interrog., Dec. 22, 1945. For an analysis of the HGW's pan-European tentacles, see FBI report to FDR, Feb. 16, 1940 (FDR Library, file OF.10b).

177　*Reichswerke Hermann Göring:* Göring MS, OI-RIR/8, Oct. 24, 1945 (SI); interrog. at Ashcan, June 2, 1945.

178　*Carinhall:* HG to Hitler, July 21, 1937 (BA, Führer's adjutants' files, NS.10/13).

179　*Second Henderson interview* on July 20, 1937: reports by Sir G. Ogilvie-Forbes and Henderson in FO.371/20750 and /20736.

15: THE VERY PRIVATE KINGDOM

180　*"That green Freemasonry":* See above all the papers of Oberstjägermeister Ulrich Scherping (BA file K1.Erw.506).

181　*Swiss diplomat:* Burckhardt (see note to p. 172).

183　*Reich Game Law:* in *RGBl.*, 1934, I, 534. Cabinet meeting of July 3, 1934: Papen in X-P6, and Darré diary.

183　*Austria:* HG interrog., Nbg., July 6, 1945 (in *The Treason Trial of Dr. Guido Schmidt before the Vienna People's Court* [Vienna; 1947], 299ff; cited hereafter as Schmidt Trial); also, testimony of Seyss-Inquart, July 6, 1946, and Dr. Kajetan Mühlmann, Mar. 25, 1947 (ibid.); the proceedings also reproduce HG's correspondence with Schmidt.

184　*Ward Price:* Report in PRO file FO.371/20710; for his other conversations with HG, see Eden Papers, PRO, FO.954/10 (Mar. 25, 1936); and Halifax Papers, PRO, FO.800/313 (Nov. 19, 1936, and Mar. 23, 1938).

184　*Mackenzie-King:* Diary, June 29, 1937 (Public Archives of Canada, Ottawa, MG.26/J.13). Henderson to Eden, June 27, 1937 (PRO, FO.954/10). Sir Francis Floud would write from Ottawa on Aug. 8, 1937, that Mackenzie-King thought that HG resembled "a large and friendly Newfoundland dog" (PO, FO.371/20750). Four years later, on Aug. 30, 1941, King George VI would relate to the Canadian PM that he had at one time "invited Göring to England."

185　*Bugged the conversations:* HG freely admitted this under pretrial interrog. at Nuremberg, Oct. 3, 1945.

185 *Party rally:* Henderson memoirs, and letter to Eden, Sept. 12, 1937 (PRO, CAB.21/540).

187 *Lloyd-George:* Telegram of Phipps to Eden, Oct. 21, 1936 (PRO, CAB.21/540).

188 *Hunting diary:* Sept. 26, 1936, through Oct. 6, 1937 (Library of Congress, Ac.9342). The many remnants of the famous green-and-gold Sèvres porcelain "hunting service" (now owned by Mr. Keith Wilson of Kansas City) also act as a kind of diary. Each piece commemorates particular trophies like "The High and Mighty of Gilge," Sept. 14, 1934; Kastaunen, Sept. 13, 1934; Finohr, Rominten, Sept. 29, 1934; "The High and Mighty of Schuiken," Rominten, Sept. 27, 1936; Farve, Oct. 24, 1936; Springe, Nov. 18, 1937; Basedow, Oct. 22, 1938; Reichenbach, June 21, 1939; Schorf-Heath, Feb. 11, 1940; and "Matador," Rominten, Sept. 22, 1942.

189 *Henderson at Rominten:* Henderson, 90f; and letter to Eden, Oct. 10, 1937 (PRO, CAB.21/540).

190 *Game exhibition:* Final program printed in Schmidt Trial, 310f. See also Scherping Papers, and Henderson's report of Nov. 2, 1937 (PRO, FO.371/20750).

191 *Hossbach conference* of Nov. 5, 1937: Hossbach's text is ND, 386-PS. See Walter Bussmann's paper in *VfZ* (1968), 373ff. For the arms-production background of this conference, see Milch's letter to HG, Oct. 30, 1937 (MD.53, 0849), and the paper by Dr. Treue in BA-MA, M.1690/33966a. Blomberg's invitations to HG and others to attend this conference will be found in BA-MA file WilF.5/1196. Cf. HG testimony in *IMT,* ix, 344f; interrogs. at Nuremberg, Aug. 8 and Nov. 28, 1945, and Bross, op. cit., 69.

192 *Lord Halifax:* Diary in Halifax Papers, Borthwick Institute, York University. For a partial transcript, see PRO file FO.371/20736.

16: THE BLOMBERG-FRITSCH AFFAIR

194 This chapter, the inside story of the scandal, is largely based on the private papers and draft letters of Gen. Baron Werner von Fritsch, which were seized by Soviet authorities in 1945 and are now in private hands in Moscow. The author has deposited copies in the BA-MA (archived there as N.33/22). In reconstructing the chronology, the author has used the diaries of Keitel's adjutant, air-force Capt. Wolf Eberhard (DI-film 74), Jodl (DI-film 84), and Milch (DI-film 57); he has also used narratives written by Keitel, Milch, Bodenschatz (IfZ, ZS.10), Lt. Gen. Biron (PWB/SAIC/18, of June 9, 1945) and a memoir written by Puttkamer for him in June 1979. Cf. Ministerial Direktor Heinrich Rosenberg, "The Dismissal of . . . Fritsch," *Deutsche Rundschau* (1946), 93ff; Blomberg's own version (SAIC/FIR/46) and confidential memoirs, now in the hands of his heirs. Police file no. 7079 on his bride, Erna Grühn, is now held by the IfZ. See too the interrogations of Blomberg at Nuremberg, Aug. 29, 1945 (NA, RG.165) and (in confidence) of HG, Nuremberg, Nov. 6, 1945).

195 *Blomberg:* Bodenschatz, ZS.10; Lehmann, cited by Bross, 170f; Puttkamer, ZS.285, and in interviews with the author in 1967–68 and 1971.

195 *"Battle against the Jews":* Private letters from Fritsch to his friend Baroness Margot von Schutzbar; the originals are in the Wheeler Bennett Papers, St. Anthony's College, Oxford.

196 *Hitler's dissertation* of Jan. 21, 1938: Milch diary, and text in BA-MA file RH.26-10/255.

197 *"For three hours I sat":* HG interrog., Nuremberg, Oct. 20, 1945. HG's question to Henderson: see *DBFP* (2) xvii, nos. 536 and 550. Göring wanted to succeed Blomberg: Bodenschatz in conversation with Suchenwirth, June 22; von Below, ditto, July 26, 1954 (BA-MA, Lw.104), and in IfZ, ZS.7; Bodenschatz, ZS.10; Blomberg, affidavit of Nov. 7, 1945 (*IMT,* xxxii, 465).

200 *Gestapo interrogation:* The text is on NA film T84/272/0536ff, and in BA-MA, Fritsch Papers, N.33/7. Werner Best's diary unfortunately has vanished: In 1945 it was in the Royal Danish State Archives in Copenhagen, where British officers used it during their interrog. of this top Gestapo functionary.

201 *Attorney von der Goltz:* See his papers in the BA, Kl.Erw.653/3. Information on Heitz is in Weichs's memoirs, BA-MA.

202 *Court opening:* Goltz (see above and SAIC/13); Keitel, interrogated by U.S. State Dept., Oct. 12, 1945; letter from Fritsch to Hitler, Apr. 7, 1938.

17: THE WINTER BALL

204 *Pecking order:* Letter from Meissner to Brückner, Feb. 10, 1938 (BA, NS.10/5).

204 *Austria:* Tauschitz's dispatches to Vienna were captured when Hitler annexed Austria in 1938. See Serial 2935 in the Political Archives of the German Foreign Office, on NA films T120/1447 through 1449; a few were cited in the Schmidt Trial. See too HG interrog., Nuremberg, Sept. 13, 1946, and ND, 3473-PS.

204 *Berghof confrontation* with Schuschnigg: Bross, 70; HG interrogs. of Oct. 9 and 20, 1945, and Milch diary, June 24, 1946.

205 *Dictated a letter:* HG to Schmidt, Mar. 8, 1938, draft reproduced in Emesen, op. cit. In the winter of 1948–49 Nicolaus von Below (Hitler's Luftwaffe adjutant, June 16, 1937, through Apr. 30, 1945) wrote a 254-page memoir, *From Rise to Fall: Hitler and the Luftwaffe;* he kindly made this available to the author.

206 *Forschungsamt* transcripts of HG's phone conversations with Vienna and London are in ND, 2949-PS; see too his interrogation at Nuremberg, Oct. 1, 1945.

207 *Winter ball:* Himmler pocket notebook, Mar. 11, 1938 (NA film T84/25); Milch testimony, Case II, Mar. 12, 1947, p. 1810; and Bross, 116f. See too the contemporary account of the U.S. chargé d'affaires, Hugh R. Wilson, in a letter to President Roosevelt dated Mar. 12, 1938. Wilson described how HG had done over the old Herrenhaus "in a form both garish and beautiful" for the event: "In his ability to handle great shows he would strike envy in the hearts of any of our Hollywood directors. There was a huge orchestra from the opera, the best singers of Germany, the best dancers gathered together, supper and wines were of superlative quality. We were at Göring's table. He entered late amid a blare of trumpets, followed by a burst of music from the orchestra. A fat round figure in resplendent uniform with a striking, clean-shaven face, he strode into the room saluting and taking the salutes of everybody present. Like wildfire, rumors went around the room that the break into Austria had occurred. There was apparent on every German face a mighty satisfaction and intense pride of power. . . . Göring talked to the ladies while [the show] was going on. As soon as it was finished, he seized the British ambassador by the arm and disappeared. . . . I supposed everyone in the room had in their consciousness the memory of the Ball of Brussels on the eve of Waterloo." FDR Library, PSF box 45.

208 *Hitler's letter to Mussolini* with the omissions proposed by HG is reproduced in facsimile by Emesen, 108ff. See the interrogs. of Prince Philipp of Hesse, Nbg., Mar. 1 and 6, 1948.

208 *The promise to Mastný* is mentioned in telegrams from the French envoy in Vienna and François-Poncet to Paris, Mar. 11 (*Livre Jaune*, nos. 2, 3, and 4); letter of Jan Masaryk to Halifax, Mar. 13 (PRO, FO.800/309); Mastný, phone call from Berlin to Prague, Mar. 12 (Václav Král, *Das Abkommen von München, 1938* [Prague, 1968], no. 34); and in the testimonies given by Tauschitz and Schmidt (Schmidt Trial, 132, 222).

211 *Schwarzenberg:* Testimony of Mar. 19, 1947 (Schmidt Trial, 200f).

213 *Pumped Fritsch's hand:* Author's interview of court reporter Dr. Ludwig Krieger, May 12, 1972.

213 *Ought to have been shot:* Letter of Himmler to HG, July 7, 1942, with HG's handwritten comment (NA film T84/7/7215). Fritsch, note of Jan. 18, 1939 (Fritsch Papers).

PART 3: THE MEDIATOR

18: BLAME IT ON NAPOLEON

219 *Jewish employees:* Affidavit sworn by Hans Malzacher, Körner's PA, for Case XI.

219 *Case green:* The original case file "Chefsache Fall Grün" is still in Washington, D.C. The author had it microfilmed (DI film 78, NA film T77/1510).

219 *Testament:* Führer decree of Apr. 23, 1938, in Lammers Papers (NA film T580/266; ND, NG-1159, -1161; NA: RG.226, OSS-file XL.33360). Cf. decree of Dec. 7, 1934, in BA, NS.20/129.

220 *Income tax declaration* and other documents, reproduced by Emesen, op. cit.

220 *Britain among our enemies:* Telegram from Puttkamer to German Naval Staff, May 24, 1938, in BA-MA files PG/34162, /33535, and /36794.

220 *Hitler conference* of May 28, 1938: Wiedemann note of Mar. 28, 1939, in Wiedemann's Papers, Library of Congress, box 604; and interrogs. of Sept. 30, Oct. 3, Nov. 10, 1945; Milch diary, and Col. Gen. Ludwig Beck Papers, BA-MA, N.28/3.

221 *Bridges:* Tietze (see note to p. 123 above). Copenhagen: Fontander, 199ff.

221 *Skat:* G. Heidemann's interviews with Kropp, Aug. 7, 1973, and Görnnert, Sept. 2, 1974.

222 *HG conference* with the gentlemen of the aviation industry, July 8, 1938 (ND, R [= Rothschild] -140); and Milch diary.

223 Extracts were published in the *London Daily Herald* and *The New York Times* in July 1945; the diary has now vanished.

223 *Pariani:* Rintelen, report of July 14, 1938 (in Hoover Library, Daniel Lerner Papers, box 24).

224 *Wiedemann visit* to London: Wiedemann's Papers in Library of Congress (DI-film 19); Halifax Papers, Borthwick Institute, York, and official files in PRO, FO.800/313 and /314; BA, ZSg.101/90; Wiedemann interrog. at Nuremberg, Oct. 24, 1945. Letter of Duff Cooper to Lord Halifax, Aug. 12, 1938 (FO.800/309).

224 *Vuillemin's* journal of Aug. 12 through 21, 1938, was provided to the author by the Fondation Nationale des Sciences Politiques in Paris: Edouard Daladier Papers, file 4DA19 Dr 3, no. 327: Vuillemin. For François-Poncet's report of Aug. 23, 1938, see *Documents Diplomatiques Français, 1932–1939* (2) (Paris), x, nos. 429, 440, and 444.

225 *Edgar Mowrer:* PRO file, FO.371/21738.

225 *Conversations with Henderson:* See Henderson's dispatches of Sept. 13 (PRO, FO.800/269 and /314) and Sept. 17 (FO.371/21738). Cf. Ulrich von Hassell diary, Sept. 17, 1938.

226 *Rutting season:* Ulrich Scherping memoir in BA file Kl.Erw.506/4. For a typical briefing by Udet out at Rominten, see that of Sept. 24, 1938, in MD.57, 3227.

227 *Forschungsamt:* The "Brown Pages" transcribing the phone conversations between Beneš, Masaryk, and Osuský will be found in PRO file FO.371/21742.

228 *Junkers 88 history:* In Imperial War Museum, Koppenberg Papers, box S.377; and MD.57, 3239ff.

229 *Interpreter:* Air force Col. Peterpaul von Donat, "The Munich Agreement of September 29, 1938," in *Deutsches Adelsblatt* (1971), 126ff.

19: SUNSHINE GIRL AND CRYSTAL NIGHT

230 *Bridal silk:* Reader's letter in BA, ZSg.101: Göring. Trouble with the Nazi party: HG talking, May 24, 1945 (SAIC/X/5).

231 *Emmy not a party member:* Nazi party correspondence, in HG's BDC-file (see note to p. 61 above).

231 *Goebbels's "confession":* Rosenberg diary, Feb. 6, 1939; and Bormann diary, Oct. 21 and 23, 1938.

232 *Henderson on the Jews:* Letter to Halifax, July 1938 (PRO, FO.800/269). Letter of HG to Imhausen, June 23, 1937, reproduced in Emesen, op. cit. HG talking, May 24, 1945 (SAIC/X/5). Re *Albert Forster:* Burckhardt, 106f. HG's ordinances on the exclusion of Jews from German economic life: Bormann letter in BDC file 240/II.

233 *Petschek:* H. Wohlthat, final report on the "de-Jewing" of the Ignaz Petschek Group, May 3, 1940 (BA, R.22/5005); and files of the Czecho-Slovak Financial Claims Office, British Treasury (PRO, T.210/18).

235 *Outraged at Goebbels:* Likus report, Nov. 30, 1938 (NA film T120/31/29067). Wiedemann interrogs. Sept. 30 and Oct. 9, 1945; HG, quoted by Bross, 21ff, and diaries of Hassell, Nov. 27, and Groscurth, Dec. 21, 1938. Manuscript memoirs of Luftwaffe judge advocate general Christian Baron von Hammerstein, *Mein Leben,* in IfZ. Darré talking, May 16, 1945 (SAIC/X-P5).

235 *Crystal Night:* The crimes are catalogued in a report of the Supreme Party Court, Feb. 13, 1939 (ND, 3063-PS), and in the transcript of a conference in the Reich Air Ministry building on the Jewish problem, Nov. 12, 1938 (ND, 1816-PS); letter of Heydrich to HG, Nov. 11, 1938 (ND, 3058-PS).

237 *Two laws:* Published in *Reichsgesetzblatt* (Reich Law Gazette), 1938, I, 415 and 1579; cf. the interrogs. of HG, Funk, Schwerin von Krosigk by SHAEF officers on June 26, 1945 (USAISC). Further HG ordinances of Dec. 14 and 28, 1938, are in BDC file 240/II and BA file K1.Erw.203, and of Jan. 24, 1939 (ND, MG-5764): and cf. the memo by M. Luther, Aug. 21, 1942 (ND, MG-2586), and HG's directive that all Jewish war veterans be released from custody, Dec. 2, 1938 (BDC file 240/II).

237 *Ilse:* Cited in Hassell's diary, Apr. 3, 1939.

237 *Guidelines:* HG circular letter, Dec. 28, 1938, in BA, K1.Erw.203, and ND, 069-PS.

238 *Central Reich office:* HG order of Jan. 24, 1939 (BDC file 240/II; ND, NG-5764). Hitler's speech: *Völkischer Beobachter* (VB), Jan. 31, 1939 (its headline read, *One of Hitler's greatest speeches: prophetic warning to Jewry.*)

20: LOSING WEIGHT

240 *Hitler speeches:* Transcripts in BA file NS.11/28 (DI-film 88).

240 *Göring diary:* In an A4-sized notebook (now held in the Library of Congress), on which HG had entered his Berlin address as No. 7, Badensche Strasse, he listed twenty-two different diaries that he intended to keep simultaneously. This was probably written new year, 1930–31. The total contents of one of HG's diaries, *Besprechungen* ("Conferences"), Oct. 3, 1938, through Aug. 8, 1942, were published in the London *Daily Herald,* July 7–14, and the *New York Herald Tribune,* July 6–24, 1945; the original diary has vanished since then.

242 *Increasing the Air Force:* Thomas, conference with HG, Oct. 14, 1938 (ND, 1301-PS). Eberhard diary, Oct. 21 and 25, 1938 (DI film 74); cf. Milch diary, Oct. 15 ("Mid-day to see Göring on Schorf Heath"); Oct. 17 ("Basic conference on decimetric [radar] wavelengths"); Oct. 25 ("Reich Air Ministry, conf. with Udet and Stumpff on Britain"); and Oct. 26 ("Carinhall for major conf. on Luftwaffe expansion"). Cf. Karl-Heinz Völker's official history, *Dokumente und Dokumentarfotos zur Geschichte der deutschen Luftwaffe* (Stuttgart: 1968), nos. 89 and 135. On Oct. 18, 1938, Charles Lindberg recorded in his diary a stag party at the U.S. embassy in Berlin attended by HG, Milch, Udet, aircraft designers Heinkel and Messerschmitt, and U.S. military attaché: "Marshal Göring of course was the last to arrive." HG awarded to Lindbergh the order of the German Eagle, on Hitler's orders, asked him about his recent trip to Russia and talked about the Ju 88. HG "said that at one time he knew so little about finance that he couldn't even keep his own pocketbook filled. Göring said he told Hitler he would be willing to take on any problems in Germany except the religious problem. . . . He spoke at length, then sat and frequently closed his eyes while the translation was going on."

243 *Reich Defense Council:* Woermann's notes on the first session, Nov. 18, 1938, are on NA film T120/624/ 0347ff; for a different version, see ND, 3575-PS. Darré recorded in his diary that day, "Reich Defense Committee. The cabinet had gradually fallen asleep. The Four-Year Plan is devolving into individual commissions, hence this attempt to reactivate the Reich Defense Committee which last sat in 1934. Göring attacks me unfairly, and I reply in kind."

243 *Losing weight:* Letters of Henders to Halifax, Feb. 15 and 22 (PRO, FO.800/315), and to the F.O., Feb. 18, 1939 (FO.371/22965).

244 *San Remo:* Lt. Gen. Josef (Beppo) Schmid, "Reichsmarschall Hermann Göring [and] His Position in the Conflict between Germany, Britain and the U.S.A., " a memoir in Rear Adm. Walter C. Ansell's Papers at Old Dominion University, Norfolk, Virginia; further, Schmid's conversation with Suchenwirth (see note to page 130) and interrog. report, "GAF Intelligence in the War," ADI(K) 395/45 (in SI). Also, testimonies of Fritz Görnnert and Emmy Göring in Case XI, pp. 19,546 and 21,103.

244 *"Old woman":* Letter of Ivone Kirkpatrick to F.O., Feb. 20, 1939 (PRO file FO.371/22965).

245 *Forschungsamt:* David Irving, *Breach of Security* (London: 1967), 51.
245 *Threats to Hácha:* Hewel note in *ADAP* (D) iv, no. 228; U.S. State Dept. interrog. of Keppler; Meissner, memoir of Oct. 1945, and interrogs. of the interpreter Paul Schmidt, Oct. 19–26, 1945 (all on DI film 34).
245 *Disapproved:* HG interrog. OI-RIR/7; Körner testimony, Case XI, p. 14,284. The FBI document quoted is in FDR Library, file OF.10b.
245 *Lookout:* Milch diary, Mar. 21, 1939 (DI film 57).

21: OUT OF FAVOR

248 *Trip to Libya:* Reports of British consul in Tripoli in PRO file FO.371/23808. For HG's talk with Mussolini, Apr. 15, 1939, see NA film T120/624/0479ff.
248 *HG's dinner with Hitler:* HG, interrogated by U.S. State Dept., Nov. 6–7, 1945 (DI film 34).
249 *Weibisch:* Letter of Henderson to Halifax, May 3, 1939 (PRO, FO.800/315); and see note to p. 245 above. *Hitler's brief pep talk of Apr. 20:* Letter from Wolf Eberhard to the author, May 8, 1971, and interviews with Gerhard Engel and Ottomar Hansen (SI).
249 *French air attaché:* See the French *Livre Jaune*, no. 123: Coulondre's dispatch to Bonnet, May 7, 1939, and Paul Stehlin's memoirs, *Auftrag in Berlin*, 180ff.
249 *Rendezvous with Franco:* Ribbentrop memo, and letter to HG, May 16 (NA film T120/617/0313ff), and Rosenberg's diary, May 20, 1939; Schmid wrote a vivid account of the fiasco (see note to p. 244 above).
250 *Schmundt record* of May 23, 1939: ND, L-79; for the controversy on this document, see the testimonies of Vice-Adm. Schulte-Monting at Nuremberg, May 22, 1946; of General Schniewind, Case II, p. 1,312f; of Warlimont, ibid., p. 1,300ff; of Raeder, ibid., p. 1,497ff; of Engel, p. 1,362. Also the affidavit sworn by Below, June 14, 1948 (ND, NOKW-3516); the entries in Milch's diaries for Jan. 17, Jan. 19, Feb. 19, Mar. 12, May 30, and Nov. 18, 1947; and the interrogs. of Bodenschatz (Nuremberg, Nov. 6, 1945) and HG (Sept. 24, 1945).
252 *Wenner-Gren:* Born on June 5, 1881. FBI and other reports on him are in the FDR Library, file PPF.3474 (in connection with his well-documented plea for "de-listing" dated Jan. 4, 1943: He explained that Count Eric von Rosen had introduced him to HG, their first meeting had been on Sept. 11, 1936, the second at the end of May 1939); see too FDR's file OF.10b, and NA, RG.226, OSS file XL.13225. For Wenner-Gren's meeting with Chamberlain on June 6, 1939, see PRO file FO.371/23020.
253 *Reich Defense Council:* Second session, June 23, 1939: ND, 3787-PS.
253 *Rechlin display:* There are several documents on this in MD.63, 6185ff, and MD.51, 0329. For HG's speech of Sept. 13, 1942, see note to p. 356 below. Warsitz described his pay bonus in a letter to the author, Jan. 26, 1970.
254 *Wohlthat's* talks in London are recorded in PRO file FO.371/22990; his own report on July 24, 1939, is on NA film ML.123. For an early analysis, before the F.O. files were available at the PRO, see Helmut Metzmacher's paper in *VfZ* (1966), 370ff.

22: HOPING FOR ANOTHER MUNICH

255 *Dahlerus:* The author is grateful to Prof. Bernd Martin of the University of Freiburg for making available to him in 1973 a listing of the visa stamps in Dahlerus's passport from Feb. 18, 1939, through July 4, 1943. German records of Dahlerus's negotiations are on NA film ML.123; the most important files on Dahlerus in the PRO are: his first approaches, July 1939 (FO.371/22974); the main Dahlerus file (/22982); the "D. file," July 1939 (/22990); the embarrassing dossier, "Translation of Report of Negotiations Between Great Britain and Germany . . . ," with comments by Sir A. Cadogan, E. L. Woodward and Frank Roberts, Nov. 16, 1942, through Apr. 16, 1943, is in FO.371/34482; the attempts to blackmail D. into silence, in FO.371/39178. For Halifax's papers on D., see FO.800/316; for Chamberlain's, PRO, PREM.1/331a.
256 *Carin II's* logbook for 1939 from the collection of G. Heidemann. HG's conference of July 25, 1939, is noted in Milch's diary.
256 *Sönkenissen-Koog:* Narrative by the British participants in this meeting, PRO, FO.371/22976.
258 *Leslie Runciman:* Letter of Wohlthat to Hohenlohe, Aug. 1939 (Hohenlohe Papers, in the collection of Reinhard Spitzy); for R.'s conversation with HG, see PRO, FO.371/22976.
258 *Hitler's Berghof speech:* Diaries of Gen. Halder and Milch, Adm. Albrecht and Boehm (latter, ND, Raeder exhibit 27), Gen. von Bock and Adm. Canaris (ND, 789- and 1014-PS), and Manstein (latter kindly provided to the author by the field marshal's son). No credit can be attached to the version in ND, 003-L; see Winfried Baumgart's essay on this speech in *VfZ* (1968), 120ff.
259 *Cabinet meeting:* Based on Darré's diary and the private letter written by Herbert Backe on Aug. 31, 1939 (kindly furnished to the author by Frau Ursula Backe).
261 *"Is this just temporary?":* HG interrogated at Nuremberg, Aug, 29, 1945.
261 *Italian raw material demands:* For the Forschungsamt's "Brown Page" intercept of Aug. 26, 1939, see NA film T77/545.

262 *Dahlerus:* His negotiations and telephone calls in the final days of Aug. 1939 are recorded in PRO files FO.371/22982, /22991, FO.800/316, and the British cabinet minutes of Aug. 28 and 30.

263 *Vormann:* Copies of the diaries and private letters of Col. Nikolaus von Vormann, the liaison officer of the Army High Command to the Führer, were provided by his widow to the author, who has deposited them in the SI at the IfZ. Vormann would write later, "During all those days I did not hear one bellicose word uttered by [Göring]; in fact from all his remarks it was clear that he viewed the situation as deadly serious and was racking his brains for a better way out. And Göring had no reason at all to try and fool me, an old cadet comrade of his."

264 *Disembodied voice:* See the Forschungsamt's dossier, N140098, "On British Foreign Policy from the Munich Agreement to the Outbreak of War," on NA film 120/723/3510 (DI film 28). A transcript of this phone call is also on NA film T120/32/9636.

PART 4: THE PREDATOR

23: DOCTOR READY TO BECOME BOSS

271 *Schmid:* See note to p. 244 above.

272 *Wiegand:* Quoted in FBI report, FDR file OF.10b.

272 *Warsaw:* See the captured dispatch of the French air attaché in Warsaw, Gen. Armendgaud, reproduced in the German White Book no. 8, *Dokumente über die Alleinschuld Englands am Bombenkrieg gegen die Zivilbevölkerung* (Berlin: 1943), especially document no. 46, dated Bucharest, Sept. 14, 1939: "The German air force has not attacked the [Polish] civil population. I must emphasize that the German air force has acted in accordance with the laws of war; it has attacked only military objectives . . . It is vital that people in Britain and France hear of this so that nobody exacts reprisals where there is no cause for reprisal, and so that we are not the ones to unleash total air warfare."

272 *Dahlerus:* Reports from Sept. 3, 1939, are in PRO file FO.371/23098.

273 *Bialystok:* Von Vormann, unpublished MS (IfZ).

273 *Ministerial Defense Council:* See the handwritten memoirs of Lutz Count Schwerin von Krosigk in the IfZ archives, ZS/A.20. During one session on Sept. 8 the OKW's legal chief, Lehmann, briefed Field Marshal Göring on a disciplinary case. Afterward a memo went to the army's commander-in-chief, Brauchitsch: "Although SS Gruppenführer Heydrich expressed the subsequent view that the Reichsführer [Himmler] has the right to order the immediate shooting of Germans in such cases, Field Marshal Göring has laid down that death sentences are never to be executed without proper adjudication" (BA-MA, file RH.1/vorl.58). See too Heydrich's departmental briefings of Sept. 7 and 19 (NA film T175/239/8226f, 8499ff, 8516ff), and Thomas's minutes on the Reich Defense Council sessions, Sept.–Nov. 1939 (on NA film T77/201/7516ff).

274 *Hertslet,* Dr. Joachim G.A.: Had been sent to Mexico on behalf of the Reich Economics Ministry in July 1939, according to his interrogs. by the Americans, SAIC/PIR/194 of July 19, and SAIC/FIR/43, Sept. 11, 1945.

275 *William Rhodes Davis* met with FDR on Sept. 15 (according to FDR's appointment book and Adolf A Berle's diary of that date, FDR Library). He told the president he had "developed close personal relations with Marshal Göring and Herr Hertslet," and added that "immediately prewar Hertslet had cabled Davis through [the] German embassy in Mexico saying Göring was now in effect the Reich government, that Hertslet should become ambassador in Washington." Two or three days before, Davis continued, he had received a telegram from HG "again stating that G. was in effect Reich government, desired peace, asked if FDR would act as arbitrator." "FDR," noted Berle, ". . . replied that he thought it unlikely the British and French would agree; FDR empowered him [Davis] only to feel out the situation." For further FDR files on this odd episode, see OF.5147 and PPF.1032 and 5640.

275 *Two British aviators:* Documents in BA-MA, RL.1/9, and PRO, FO.371/23098.

276 *Christie, Malcolm:* Former British air attaché in Berlin; for his long conversation with HG on Feb. 3, 1937, see Christie Papers, Churchill College Archives, Cambridge.

276 *Dahlerus* talk with Hitler, Sept. 26: Minutes on DI film 26; his subsequent visit to Lord Halifax in London: PRO files FO.800/317, FO.371/23011, /23097, /23098, /23099.

276 *William Rhodes Davis:* Wohlthat, minutes on talks with Mr. W. R. Davis on Oct. 1, 1939 (NA film ML.123; Cabinet Office file AL.1506). This document was submitted to HG "with the request that he take note, Oct. 2." See the mentions of this episode in the diaries of Groscurth, Oct. 3 and 5, and Rosenberg, Oct. 5, and Davis's own letters to FDR dated Oct. 11 and 12 in FDR Library, which were shown to Adolph Berle, who now rebuked Davis for having spoken to FDR about the imminent "probability of General Göring's taking over the government." Davis conceded "that in Berlin, while Göring's word is law, he [Davis] had not found any immediate indication that this was going to occur." Roosevelt now withdrew, apprehensive about falling for a Göring or Himmler trap. See Berle's diary, Oct. 5 and 6; on the seventh he noted, "So FDR has evidently ordered the whole [Davis] mission squelched."

276 *Dahlerus visiting Hitler on Oct. 9:* For a minute on this, "written by an officer" on Oct. 11, and supplements of Oct. 17 and 25, see NA film ML.123.

277 *"Declaration of war":* Milch wrote in his diary, Oct. 12: "Evening to see Führer with Göring and Udet. Manufacture bombs—the war goes on!"

277 *Mooney:* The PRO file on this is FO.371/23099. On Mar. 7, 1940, Mooney had a further private meeting with Göring, who displayed a "most friendly and sympathetic" attitude toward Roosevelt and explained that

his own adjutant's brother and sister were U.S. citizens living in Kentucky: letter of Mooney to FDR, Mar. 19, 1940, in FDR Library, PSF box 4.

278 *Dahlerus:* Writing on Oct. 26, 1939, Dahlerus observed: "The Field Marshal [Göring] can be so cool and objective, but toward the Führer's person he is instinctively a boundless admirer even when common sense might call for a different judgment. On the one hand the Field Marshal assuredly still wants to bring about an honorable peace, but on the other hand he shows willing, if the Führer does not approve of this course, to subordinate himself without question and perhaps without sufficient willingness to defend objectively his own point of view as he ought, being the principal advisor." (BA-MA, Groscurth Papers, N.104/3) and see Darré diary, Oct. 26.

278 *Leaflet attacking Göring:* FO.371/23056.

279 *Supplies to Russia:* See too HG's letter to Ritter, Nov. 16, 1939 (NA film T120/740/7111).

279 *Rainmaker:* Milch's diary recorded on Nov. 7: "Göring, met. conference, then Schwefler the rainmaker"; further meteorological conferences were held on Nov. 8, 10, and 20.

24: *YELLOW* AND THE TRAITORS

282 *Freemasons:* HG related this to G. M. Gilbert, *Nuremberg Diary* (New York: 1947), 16.

282 *Oster's treachery:* See the correspondence between Weizsäcker (Berlin) and Mackensen (Rome) from Jan. 1940 through July 1941, in German F.O. archives: DI film 100, NA film T.120/102/4885ff); further details in Huppenkothen's interrog., in BDC special file, "Canaris"; and the diaries of Groscurth, Jan. 2; Halder, Jan. 7–8; and Tippelskirch (the Army's chief of intelligence), Jan. 22: BA-MA, III.H.36/1.

282 *Hammerstein:* Op. cit.; and affidavits by him, May 16, 1946 (NA, RG.238, R. H. Jackson Papers), and Lehmann, *IMT*, x1, 256f.

282 *Hirschfeld* case: BA files R43II/1411a and 4087; and Hammerstein (see above note.)

283 *Bishop Berggrav:* Conversation with HG, in PRO file FO.800/322.

284 *Command conferences at Carinhall:* Milch diary. For an important file of Hilter's and Göring's decrees on air-force production programs, see Karl-Otto Saur Papers, FD.3049/49, file 2, in Imperial War Museum, London. Thomas's notes on these conferences are on NA film T77/441.

285 *Dahlerus to Berlin:* Evidenced by entries in his passport dated May 6 and 11; cf. West, op. cit., 201 and 221. On May 11 Dahlerus brought an official Swedish delegation to discuss German transit rights with HG; the latter expressed optimism about D.'s Narvik plan, as the Swede subsequently, on May 19, reported to the British legation in Stockholm.

286 *Special operations:* Minutes of a Führer conference on operations by [Special Unit] 100 and D-Day, Nov. 20, 1939 (Canaris/Lahousen Papers, IWM, CO file AL.1933 and ND, 3047-PS).

25: VICTORY IN THE WEST

287 *The Train,* Asia: See, e.g., the loading manifest for HG's trip to Paris, Nov. 22, 1942, on NA film T84/5/5280ff; for the bathroom coach inventory, T84/6/5382ff.

288 *Rotterdam* air raid: The most reliable analysis is that by Prof. Hans-Adolf Jacobsen in *Wehrwissenschaftliche Rundschau (WR)* (1958), p. 257ff; cf. Kesselring, interrogated by USSBS.

288 *Unrepentant:* HG interrog., May 19, 1945: SAIC/13. Churchill routinely wrote of "thirty thousand dead" in Rotterdam, e.g., in his letter to the king of Sweden, Aug. 2, 1940.

289 *Fritz Görnnert:* Born Mar. 18, 1907; became HG's personal assistant in Jan. 1937; he had until then been assistant to Prof. Töpfer, who held the chair for aircraft construction at Karlsruhe University. See Görnnert's interrog. in May 1945 (DI film 13), his testimony in Case XI, Nuremberg, and interviews by G. Heidemann in 1974 and 1977. The testing of the air-raid warning procedure was described to the author by Col. Hans-Karl von Winterfeld, Milch's adjutant, in 1969.

289 *Swedish consul general* was Raoul Nordling. Cf. Paul Reynaud, *Mémoires,* ii, 363 and 509.

290 *Mopping up at Dunkirk:* Quoted by Gerhard Engel, MS (IfZ). On MAy 23 Richthofen (CO of VIII Air Corps) noted in his diary instructions received that the British in the Dunkirk pocket were to be "annihilated." On HG's personal role: Below, MS (see note to p. 205 above).

290 *Milch lectured Göring:* Milch, SRGG.1313.

290 *Charisma:* Overheard in SRA.4842. Squadron commander: SRA.640, of Sept. 29, 1940. SRA.1459 of Mar. 19, 1941.

291 *A bit ridiculous:* SRA.364, Aug. 20, 1940. A deer from Carinhall: Winterfeld (see note to p. 289 above). Shot-down pilot: SRA.926 of Nov. 8, 1940.

291 *Trawling for art in Amsterdam:* "Shopping list" from the papers of Walter Andreas Hofer, "Curator of the Art Collections of the Reichsmarschall," in OMGUS files: NA, RG.260, box 396.

292 *Compiègne:* Diary of Gen. Otto Hoffmann von Waldau, June 23, 1940; kindly placed at the author's disposal by his daughter (DI film 75b).

292 *"Sea Lion" a bluff:* Schmid (see note to p. 244 above). General of Signals Wolfgang Martini "had the impression" for a long time that the whole Sea Lion plan "was a feint," according to the interrog. report ADI(K)334/45. The letter from Maj. (G. S.) Baron Sigismund von Falkenstein to von Waldau, June 25, 1940,

is reproduced in Karl Klee, *Dokumente zum Unternehmen Seelöwe* (Göttingen: 1959), 296f., and he enlarged on it in an interview with the author, May 11, 1971.

293 *Reichstag and Reichsmarschall:* HG interrogated by Shuster, July 19–20, 1945. The Reichsmarschall's baton was an ivory wand 19 inches long, 1¼ inches thick, covered with an alternating pattern of eagles, military crosses, and iron crosses all worked in solid gold; there were solid-gold coronets at each end, encrusted with diamonds, HG's name, and the date July 19, 1940. HG also carried a 34-inch interim baton, again of ivory, furnished with fittings executed in gold and platinum.

293 *Carinhall inventory*, dated Feb. 1, 1940, in OMGUS files, NA, RG.260, box 395.

294 *Luftwaffe war conferences:* Recorded in Milch's 1940 diary and notebook and HG's file on the Battle of Britain, now in the Library of Congress, Ac.10,253 (DI film 20); and see the Hoover Library microfilm D787.G373, "Reich Air Ministry: Briefings and Conferences with Reichsmarschall," July–Aug. 1940.

295 *Battle of Britain:* From Sept. 1940 through Feb. 1941 the diaries and notebooks of Field Marshal Milch are particularly useful (on DI film 57). On Sept. 4, 1940, he wrote: "Then to see Göring with Luftflotte commanders Jeschonnek, and Bodenschatz. 1. 'When [can we bomb] London?' . . . 6. Göring [will visit] Holland Friday, spend Saturday, Sunday at Ghent. Göring's going over there for about fourteen days to exert stronger influence on the commanders." And on Sept. 16: "Conference with Göring in his train near Beauvais . . . Thinks the British are scraping together their last forces. British [have] issued tough operations orders—[our planes were] rammed twice." After the same conference Milch noted: "Luftwaffe has jurisdiction over everything connected with the Luftwaffe. Death sentences to be executed by hanging in the village concerned; leave them hanging twenty-four hours. Death sentence too for cases where our prisoners have been badly tortured." For a lower-level chronicle on the Battle of Britain, see the lecture given on Feb. 2, 1944, by Capt. Otto Bechtle, operations officer (Ia) of KG.2 bomber wing (based in Holland), in NA, RG.407, box 1954m.

296 *Fascinated by the Soviet Union:* Based on the war diaries of the High Command (OKW), Naval Staff (SKL), and of Halder, Leeb, and Bock, and notes taken by George Thomas (ND, 1456-PS).

26: THE ART DEALER

299 *The Art Dealer:* Göring's "art dealing" activities were fully investigated for years after the war by the British Monuments and Fine Arts Commission (see the files in PRO class T209, and IWM, FO.645, box 349) and by its American counterpart, the Commission for the Protection and Salvage of Artistic and Historic Monuments in War Areas (records in NA, RG.239). The latter retained the files of "Orion," the OSS Art Looting Investigation Unit, especially its draft report (box 42) and interrogs. (box 84); see further the report, "Works of Art Mentioned in Various Transactions on Behalf of Göring during 1943 and 1944" (box 26), the files of the Einsatzstab Reichsleiter Rosenberg, ERR (box 75), of Hitler's dealer Karl Haberstock (box 79), of Hermann Bunjes (box 82), of Alois Miedl (box 80), and of Walter Hofer (box 172). Some of this material is duplicated in the OMGUS Property Division records (NA, RG.260, Mrs. Ardelia Hall Collection), *Interalia*, box 395: HG's financial records and inventories; box 396: correspondence of HG and Miss Limberger, notes on purchases; box 397: HG's jewelry, dispatch lists, correspondence; boxes 398, 399, and 400: chronological HG files, 1940–45; boxes, 401, 402, and 403: numerical HG files. In general on HG's art activities, see his remarks on May 24, 1945 (SAIC/X/5), and interrogs. at Nuremberg, Oct. 6, 7, and 8, and Dec. 22, 1945 (NA, RG.260, box 172), and Aug. 30, 1946 (box 183); and in particular the OSS Consolidated Interrogation Report, No. 2, "The Göring Collection," Sept. 15, 1945 (Hoover Library, HG Collection, box 1).

299 *Looted:* Under § 259 of the German Penal Code, HG's acquisition of the works of art from the ERR was certainly "receiving stolen property." See the memo by D. Loofer of MFA&A, Control Commission for Germany, Dec. 10, 1945 (NA, RG.239, box 82). The quotations are from HG's interrog. on Dec. 22, 1945; cf. that of June 2, 1945 (USAISC and NA, RG.153, box 1534).

299 *Miedl*, Alois: Born in Bavaria on Mar. 3, 1903, and introduced to HG by the latter's brother-in-law, Fritz Rigele. For Miedl's business interests in Berlin, see OSS report XL.2771 (NA, RG.226). The Katz Case: FBI and other reports, 1944–45 in NA, RG.239, box 80.

299 *Goudstikker:* In general, NA, RG.239, box 25, 41, 70, and 77, and RG.260, box 387. Miedl himself escaped to Spain with twenty-two valuable paintings, some of them from the Goudstikker Collection. On Apr. 23, 1945, he wrote from Madrid to Goudstikker's widow that he had fled Amsterdam with his Jewish wife and two children on June 28, 1944, "as I didn't want them to be exposed to the risk of being deported by the Germans after all" (NA, RG.239, box 80).

300 *Cheating:* Maj. Gen. Edgar Petersen, former CO of Luftgau XXX, overheard in SRGG.1218. Seyss-Inquart, interrogated on Aug. 31, 1946 (NA, RG.260, box 172).

300 *Hofer*, Walter Andreas: Born in Berlin on Feb. 10, 1893; for his interrog., see NA, RG.239, box 84. Ribbentrop: interrog., Aug. 31, 1946.

300 *Einsatzstab Rosenberg:* Report INTR/6922/MA, "The Einsatzstab Rosenberg," an analysis of the captured letter-register of the ERR, Oct. 29, 1940, through Mar. 9, 1941 (IWM, FO.645, box 349); Orion report CIR no. 1, "Activity of the ERR in France," Aug. 15, 1945 (NA, RG.239, box 75); Rosenberg interrogs., CCPWE/DI-13, June 20 (ibid., box 76) and Aug. 30, 1945 (RG.260, box 183); and HG interrogs. SAIC/14, May 19, and SAIC/X/4, May 21 and June 3, 1945.

301 *Inspector Dufour:* Dr. H. Bunjes, Situation Report, Nov. 20 through Dec. 20, 1940 (NA, RG.230, box 70).

301 *Jeu de Paume:* Bunjes (see above); CIR no. 1 (see note to p. 301 above). HG's order of Nov. 5, 1940, is

in Bunjes Papers (NA, RG.239, box 74; and see box 78, "HG, France.") HG swooped on the ERR's art depot at the Jeu de Paume twenty times: on Nov. 3 and 5, 1940; on Feb. 5, Mar. 3, 11, and 14; Apr. 7; May 1 and 3; July 9; Aug. 13, and 15; Dec. 2, 3, and 4, 1941: and on Feb. 25, Mar. 14, May 14, and on Nov. 24 and 27, 1942, on which latter occasion he acquired a Van Gogh landscape worth 1 million francs, from the Weinberger Collection, for only 100,000 francs, thanks to Lohse's haggling (NA, RG.153, Records of Judge Advocate General, box 1390: OSS X-2 "Interim Report on the Art Activities of HG," June 12, 1945). For the HG order of Nov. 5, 1940, see PID report 119, Oct. 18, 1945: "The History of the Battle for the Preservation of German Works of Art" (Hoover Library, Daniel Lerner Papers, box 20).

301 *Lohse,* Dr. Bruno: Born in Westphalia, Sept. 17, 1911; joined the Nazi party in 1937; commissioned into the Luftwaffe, appointed to the ERR in Feb. 1941. On Apr. 21, 1941, HG issued him with these credentials: "Dr. Bruno Lohse has been instructed by me to acquire objets d'art from art dealers and private collectors and at public auctions. All agencies of the State, Party, and Wehrmacht are directed to assist him in the execution of his office" (NA, RG.239, box 84).

302 *Party treasurer:* HG's correspondence with Rosenberg, Nov. 1940, is in ND, 1736-PS; HG's letter to R., Nov. 21, 1940, is in PID report DE.426/DIS.202 (Hoover Library, Lerner Papers, box 2). The correspondence between ERR and Party Chancellery, Dec. 1940, is in NA, RG239, box 74.

302 *Cartier:* Numerous visits are recorded in HG's diary; and see his interrog., SAIC/14, May 19, 1945. *Cash:* Col. Pasewaldt overheard in SRGG.1187 ("I heard him [HG] say that with my own ears.").

303 *HG's visit to the Wilkinsons:* Wilkinson letter to HG, Dec. 22, 1941 (NA, RG.239, box 78).

304 *596 paintings:* Rosenberg report, Apr. 16, 1943 (ND, 015-PS). After Prof. Voss inspected the ERR's "salvage depot" at Neuschwanstein castle, he reported on Apr. 19, 1943, to Hitler, with the result that Bormann transmitted a Führer directive to Rosenberg ordering him to hand over all works of art to Voss; when Rosenberg protested, he was informed that the reason for the directive was that "a major part of the seized works of art" had found their way into HG's collection.

304 *Italy:* For Mussolini's files on HG's purchase of Italian art treasures between May 1941 and June 1943, see NA film T596/1287.

304 *Harassed secretary:* Gisela Limberger, interrogated at Nuremberg on May 19 and July 29, 1947 (IWM files).

305 *Forged Vermeer:* See the list headed "Swap of Vermeer (Miedl) and Seven Pictures from Renders Collection, Brussels," in NA, RG.260, box 396; and Limberger, memo for Dr. Lohse, July 18, 1942 (ibid.). HG originally purchased the "Vermeer" for 1,650,000 guilders. Since Miedl refused to identify the seller (in fact the forger Van Meegeren), HG kept him waiting six months for payment, then converted the deal into a swap (OSS report, July 23, 1945: NA, RG.239, box 42; and Miedl dossier in box 80). For the unmasking of Jan van Meegeren, see the British United Press report, July 20, 1945.

306 *Final interrogations:* HG interrog., Nuremberg, Aug. 30, 1946 (NA, RG.260, box 172).

27: THE BIG DECISION

307 *Winter at Rominten:* HG interrogs. July 19–20, 1945.

307 *Bodenschatz:* GRGG.306

308 *Molotov visit:* HG interrog., Nuremberg, Aug. 29, 1945. For the British ("Ultra") decrypt of Schulenburg's Moscow disptach to the German F.O., Nov. 18, 1940 (reporting Gustav Hilger's notes on HG's meeting with Molotov), see FDR Library, John Toland Papers, box 53.

309 *Von Waldau:* Diary, 1940–43 (DI film 75b).

309 *Doctors:* From a list in Miss Limberger's files (NA, RG.239, box 395); Dr. Gehrke was at Bad Gastein, Stubenrauch at Nuremberg.

309 *Letter to Eric:* Letter from HG to Count Eric von Rosen, Nov. 21, 1940, in PID report DE.433/DIS.202 (Hoover Library, Lerner Papers, box 2).

311 *Göring diary,* 1941: The original diary was read in 1986 by the author at the IfZ, Munich (ED.180); measuring 7 inches × 5¼ inches, it was marked HG *persönlich.* It has now been restored to Edda Göring's possession, but the author has deposited a typed transcript at the IfZ.

311 *Cigarette case:* Emmy Göring, writing in *Revue;* HG diary, Jan. 12–13, 1941

312 *Count Knut Bonde:* Letter to Anne Barlow, Jan. 20, 1941 (PRO, file FO.371/26542).

312 *Opposition to Russian campaign:* HG claimed this in several interrogs., e.g., on May 10 (by Spaatz); on June 17 (by Soviets, in *WR* [1967], 524f); on July 19–20 (Shuster); July 25 (ETHINT, on DI film 8); at Nuremberg on Aug. 29 and Oct. 11; on Oct. 24 (OI-RIR/7); on Nov. 6–7 (U.S. State Dept.); and cf. Bross, op. cit., 16, 78, and 81, and Emmy Göring, testimony in Case XI, Sept. 2, 1948 (p. 19,534).

312 *Student:* GRGG.354; HG diary, Jan. 25, 1941, et seq. Körner, testimony in Case XI, p. 14,272.

313 *Hanesse:* CSDIC (UK), PW paper no. 27, Oct. 16, 1944: "German Treatment of Works of Art in Occupied Territory." Josef Angerer: see his files in NA, RG.239, box 74. The footnote to this page is based on HG's interrog. by E. E. Minskoff, Dec. 22, 1945 (NA, RG.260, box 172).

313 *Kurt von Behr,* Oberführer: For his wrongdoings in Paris, see the conversation (overheard) between Gen. von Choltitz and von Schlieben, GRGG.185. Behr killed himself in May 1945.

314 *Jeu de Paume:* See Franz Count Wolff Metternich's manuscript, "On My Activities as the German War Department's Officer Responsible for Protection of Works of Art from 1940 to 1942" (ND exhibit RF-1318); letter of Bunjes to Harold Turner, Feb. 1941 (ND, 2523-PS); the report in Bunjes's papers (NA, RG.239, box 70); Hofer's report in RG.260, box 182; and HG's diary, passim.

28: WARNING BRITAIN ABOUT *BARBAROSSA*

317 *Raeder:* C-in-C Navy, conference with the Führer, Feb. 4, 1941. For the German text of Hitler's naval conferences, see DI film 44; English translation on DI film 66.

317 *Dönitz:* Memo on Dönitz's talk with HG, Feb. 7, 1941 (BA-MA, PG.31762d).

317 *Schnurre:* Julius Karl Schnurre. See Körner's testimony in Case XI, p. 14,275, and Marotzke's testimony, p. 22,558; Schnurre's files are on NA film T120/1373.

317 *Göring up at the Berghof:* Feb. 19, 1941. See HG's diary, and that of Walther Hewel (German F.O. liaison officer to Hitler), kindly provided to the author by the widow of Hewel, who had killed himself in the Berlin bunker on May 1, 1945 (DI film 75a).

318 *Thomas:* Memo of Feb. 27, 1941 (ND, 1456-PS).

318 *Antonescu:* Memo on his talk with HG, in papers of Hasso von Etzdorf (on DI film 61).

318 *Nathan Katz:* HG interrogs., Dec. 22, 1945, and Aug. 30, 1946; and Schmidt, memo for the Stabsleiter, dated The Hague, May 10, 1941.

318 *Dahlerus:* According to his passport (see note to p. 255 above), he arrived in Berlin on Mar. 24, departed Mar. 27; further information was provided by D.'s widow. *Milch:* Diary, Mar. 26, 1941, and interrog. in Nuremberg, Oct. 18, 1945, and testimony in *IMT*, ix, 57ff, and in Case II (Mar. 12, 1947) p. 1,839, and handwritten memoirs (IfZ, SI); see too his statement at the GL conference on Dec. 9, 1942 (MD.17, 3669).

319 *Oshima:* For the American or British ("Magic") decrypt of his dispatch to Tokyo on Mar. 26, 1941, see NA, RG.457, SRDJ.10,684.

320 *Hitler's speech* on Mar. 30, 1941: See the diaries of Von Waldau, the Naval Staff, the High Command (OKW), and Halder.

321 *Schwenke:* See Schulenburg's dispatch to German F.O., Moscow, Apr. 8, 1941 (NA film T120/105/3325); Below MS, and Schwenke, interviewed for the author on Aug. 10, 1971, and his letter to the author on Dec. 12, 1970. Georg Thomas, "Replies to English Gentlemen's Queries," Aug. 16, 1945 (OCMH files).

321 *Fight against the Jews:* HG order dated May 1, 1941, in Bunjes files, NA, RG.239, box 74.

322 *Speer-Model:* HG diary, and Speer's 1941 Office Chronicle, May 5, 1941.

323 *Hess's flight:* Bodenschatz, talking in SRGG.1236, and to the author on Nov. 30, 1970; and Hewel diary (DI film 75a); Messerschmitt, interrogated by USSBS on May 11–12, 1945, and private papers (IWM file FD.4355/45, vol. 4); HG interrog. on June 15 (CCPWE, DI-15) and July 23, 1945 (Shuster).

325 *"If I had any say in it":* HG interrog. at Nuremberg, Oct. 3, 1945.

325 *"Hermann":* Captured Luftwaffe officers' conversations, reported in SRA.1727, SRA.1844, and SRA.3121 (all in PRO file WO.208/4128).

325 *Crete:* HG interrog., SAIC/13. Maj. Gen. Conrad Seibt, "Air Supply Problems of the Crete Campaign," Sept. 1, 1945 (APWIU, 9th Air Force, report no. 97/45); Gen. Meister, in SRGG.1306, and Student in SRGG.1338.

325 *British code breakers:* In May 1940 the British cryptanalysts had used computers to break the German air force's operational code, with the result the British and American archives today contain thousands of signals that were lost or destroyed at the time of Germany's collapse. See, for example, the British analysis, "Use of CZ/MSS Ultra by the U.S. War Dept., 1943/45" in NA, RG.457, SRH-005. The most important source used by this author, apart from the few Ultra decrypts released to the PRO in London (class DEFE.3), was the long narrative written in June 1945 by the American Lt. Col. Haines, "Ultra—History of U.S. Strategic Air Force Europe versus German Air Force" (NA, RG.457, SRH-013).

326 *Luftwaffe overextended:* Hewel diary (DI film 75b). For Stalin's secret speech, see HG's interrog. at Nuremberg, Aug. 29; by the U.S. State Dept., Nov. 6–7, 1945; Bross, op. cit., 81; and Ribbentrop's meeting with the Bulgarians Cyrill and Filoff on Oct. 19, 1943. Soviet prisoner interrogations confirming the Stalin speech are on NA films T120/695 and /1017.

326 *Broad hint:* Hewel diary, June 3, and Oshima dispatch to Tokyo, June 4–5, 1941 (Hillgruber, *WR* [1968], 329ff); cf. letter of Hitler to Mussolini, May 25, 1943 (Mussolini Papers, NA film T586/405/0600f).

326 *June 15, 1941:* Meanwhile HG had summoned Dahlerus once more to Berlin: The passport shows his arrival on June 9, departure on June 16, 1941. Mallet's dispatch to the F.O. reporting the "cryptic" message from HG, June 9, is in PRO file FO.371/29482; two days later he confirmed, "My informant was Dahlerus." Dahlerus also must have informed the Americans, because late on June 9 Sumner Welles, in Washington, notified Lord Halifax, the British ambassador. From London Vincent Massey (Canadian high commissioner) cabled to his government in Ottawa on June 13 the same information (Mackenzie King Papers, file MG 26, J1, vol.312: Public Archives of Canada). But Hitler's preparedness to attack the Soviet Union was known to Churchill from Ultra code breaking in any case, and on June 13, Foreign Secretary Anthony Eden passed a warning to Soviet ambassador Ivan Maisky (FO.371/29482). Sikorski's warning is quoted in Biddle's letter to Roosevelt, June 20, 1941 (FDR Library, PSF box 34, file: A. J. Biddle, 1937/410).

29: SIGNING HIS OWN DEATH WARRANT

328 *Jeschonnek:* Beppo Schmid, interviewed by Suchenwirth, Feb. 22, 1955 (BA-MA, Lw.104/5). *Planes shot down:* Milch diary (DI film 57); HG interrog., May 29, 1945; the figures are confirmed in the official Soviet *History of the Great Patriotic War.*

328   *Secret decree* of June 29, 1941: Lammers Papers, NA film T580/255.
329   *Diamonds:* SS Obergruppenführer Berger, SRGG.1299. *Heydrich:* HG interrog., Dec. 22, 1945.
329   *Heart specialist:* HG diary, passim. *Stumpff:* Related in interview by Suchenwirth, Nov. 22, 1954 (BA-MA, Lw.104/5).
329   *Führer conference of July 16, 1941:* Bormann, "Memo on the Definition of German Objectives in the East" (ND, 1221-PS); cf. Thomas memo, "Outcome of the Discussions with HG and Keitel," July 17, 1941 (NA film T77/771). In his memoirs, 174, Rosenberg would describe Koch as "a favorite of Göring, who set great store by Koch's business acumen." Rosenberg managed to keep Koch out of the Baltic provinces, but not out of the (more important) Ukraine.
330   *Bräutigram, Otto:* The quotation is from the handwritten diary kept by him from June 11, 1941, through Feb. 8, 1943 (DI film 97).
330   *Dahlerus:* HG told him "that Japan had been granted a free hand in east Russia," that despite the surprising Soviet tank strength HG "felt that power of Russian armies will be crushed in about six weeks," and that "it is then planned to divide Russia into small states, Göring to be economic dictator and Rosenberg political dictator." Telegram of Greene (Stockholm) to Hull, July 27, 1941, in FDR Library, PSF box 4.
331   *Instruction to Heydrich:* Photocopy (with HG's signature) in BDC file on Heydrich, attached to latter's letter to chief, SS Main Office, Jan. 25, 1942 (DI film 81); further copies: unsigned, ND, NG-2586; undated, ND, 710-PS.
331   *Palace of Minos:* Roeder, cited in Milch diary, Oct. 6, 1947 (DI film 58).
331   *Italian tapestries:* Limberger note for HG, listing purchase in Italy, Oct. 8, 1942; letter of Ondarza to Limberger, Aug. 28, 1941; note by Angerer to HG, Sept. 12, 1941 (NA, Angerer Papers, RG 239, box 75). *Rothschild treasure:* Letter from Naval Signals Command West, Apr. 26, 1941 (ibid., box 70).
332   *Ramcke:* SRGG1065.
333   *No comparing . . . :* Waldau diary, Sept. 9, 1941 (DI film 75b). On the following, I have used primarily Suchenwirth's study on Udet (DI film 15b), Col. Max Pendele's chronology (BA-MA, Lw.104/13), and Milch's 1941 diary (DI film 57).
334   *We have won the war:* Jodl, cited in Hewel diary, Oct. 8, 1941 (DI film 75a).
335   *Canaris:* Lahousen, memo in Canaris/Lahousen Papers (CO file AL.1933 in IWM).
336   *Communiqué:* Telegram of Ondarza to Witzendorff, Nov. 18, 1941 (MD.51, 0444f).
336   *Pétain:* HG meeting with Duce, Jan. 28, 1942 (NA film T120/59/7585ff); shorthand diary of Gen. Karl Koller, Dec. 1, 1941 (DI-film 17).
339   *Hitler takes command of the army:* Hitler telegram to HG and Raeder, Dec. 19, 1941 (BA-MA, Raeder Papers, PG.31762e).

PART 5: THE BANKRUPT

30: THE "INSTRUCTION" TO HEYDRICH

343   *Railroads clogged:* See Görnnert's briefing notes for HG re transport bottlenecks, Apr. 3, 1942 (NA films T84/8/7585, /8024ff, /8039f, /8050ff). *Hans Frank* is quoted from the stenographic record of his government session proceedings, Dec. 16, 1941 (Frank diary, IfZ).
344   *Auftrag:* HG instruction to Heydrich, July 31, 1941: a photocopy, including HG's signature, is in BDC-file "Heydrich," as an annex to H.'s letter to the chief of the SS Hauptamt, Jan. 25, 1942 (DI film 81); further copies are ND, NG-2586, and (undated) ND, 710-PS. Cf. HG's testimony at Nuremberg, *IMT*, ix, 574f, and Dieter Wisliceny's report, Bratislava, Nov. 18, 1946 (IfZ, F.71.8).
345   *Oranienburg concentration camp:* Ondarza interviewed by Suchenwirth, Apr. 17, 1956. HG interrog., May 24, 1945 (SAIC/X/5). *Low temperature experiments:* See Himmler's letter to Dr. Sigmund Rascher, Oct. 24, 1942 (ND, 1609-PS).
345   *Relations with Himmler:* Letter of Himmler to Scherping, Sept. 12, 1942 (NA film T175/62/8465). Re Herbert Göring: Himmler to chief of RSHA, Feb. 8, 1943 (T175/21/5933); Albert Göring, interrog. at Nuremberg, Sept. 3, 1945 (see note to page 26).
345   *Forschungsamt* official: Based on the author's interview with the official's son, Klaus Scholer, on Aug. 17, 1985. *Disposal squads:* HG interrog. SAIC/X/5. *Hitler's conferences:* Memoir by Ludwig Krieger, one of the Reichstag stenographers assigned to the Führer's HQ, Dec. 13, 1945 (IfZ, SI).
346   *Göring's role:* See in general M. Luther's memo of Aug. 21, 1942, in the file kept by Section II Inland of the German F.O. on "Final Solution of the Jewish Problem, 1939–43" (Serial 1512, on NA film T120/780/1976ff, = ND, NG-2586).
346   *Geographical solution:* Letter of Heydrich to Ribbentrop, Jan. 24, 1940 (ibid., /2047).
346   *Invitation:* Letter of Heydrich to Luther, SS Gruppenführer Hoffmann and others, Nov. 29, 1941 (ibid., /2043; ND, 709-PS; BDC file, Heydrich).
346   *Wannsee conference:* Summary minutes (NA film T120/780/2024ff); and see Luther's memo. Lammers, testimony in Case XI, Sept. 23, 1948. Himmler, telephone log, Jan. 21, 1942 (NA Film T84/25).
346   *Letter of Heydrich to Luther:* Feb. 1942 (NA film T120/780/2023). *Jewish homes:* Note from Görnnert to Schrötter and Brauchitsch, Jan. 24, 1942 (T84/8/8190 and /7647).
347   *Reich Research Council:* A shorthand record of this opening session on July 6, 1942, is in Milch's papers: MD.58, 3640ff. For the *Gauleiters' Conference* of Aug. 6, see the shorthand record (ND, USSR-exhibit 170) and M. Bormann's diary, Aug. 5–6, 1942 (DI film 23).

347 *"All cruelty":* HG interrog., SAIC/X/5. And see HG's diary, e.g., Apr. 16, 1942 (see note to p. 240 above). According to a newspaper item of Nov. 1939 ("Göring's job for Bouhler") on NA film T84/8/8035, HG, acting as chairman of the Ministerial Defense Committee, had given B. the task of "examining all tips and complaints coming in from ordinary members of the public." Typical samples of HG's office (Görnnert) passing on to Bouhler's such cases are on film T84/8/8028ff, /8459; the Greim case, T84/7/6786f; the Stengl case, T84/6/6012ff; the Waizer case, T84/6/6527; the Manasse/Cohn case, T84/9/8693, T84/6/5758, and T84/7/7159. Körner's statement about Auschwitz at the Central Planning session of July 2, 1943, is in Milch's papers, MD.48 and ND, R-124; cf. Körner's testimony in Case XI, Aug. 3, 1948, p. 14,664.

31: THE THOUSAND-BOMBER RAID

351 *Sponeck:* Waldau diary, Jan. 1942 (DI film 75b). See particularly the paper by Dr. Günter Gribbohm in the *Deutsche Richterzeitung,* May 1972, p. 157ff, and Feb. 1943, p. 53ff. For Himmler's speech of Aug. 3, 1944, see *VfZ* (1953), 382f.
351 *Heat packs:* Hitler's *Table Talk. Code breakers:* NA, RG.457, SRH-013 (see note to p. 325 above).
351 *Robert Ley:* See too Ley's personal files in Library of Congress, R. H. Jackson Papers (DI film 79).
351 *Visit to Rome:* Itinerary on NA film T84/8; Paul Schmidt minutes, Jan. 28, 1942 (see note to p. 336 above); and Ciano's diaries. In Rome HG also spoke with Japanese Gen. Oshima, whose Jan. 31 report to Tokyo was intercepted by "Magic." HG asked for Japanese expertise in designing landing craft. "I feel," he added, "that I have made a great mistake in not giving more study to the matter of launching aerial torpedoes." FDR Library, PSF box 5.
352 *Appointment of Speer:* Milch diary (DI film 57) and memoirs; Speer office chronicle.
353 *Milch documents:* Offer a full account of his expansion of Luftwaffe production during 1942: correspondence between HG and Milch, MD.57; HG conferences, 1942, MD.62; General Luftzeugmeister (GL, director of air armament) conferences, 1942, MD.13–14; and Central Planning, 1942, MD.46. All these volumes are now archived at the BA-MA; for an index to them, see DI film 16. See too the Messerschmitt Papers in IWM, FD.4355/45 and 4924/45.
353 *Reprisals against London:* HG conference, Mar. 21; and shorthand diary of Koller, Mar. 1942 (DI film 17). See too the Milch file, "Briefings of Reichsmarschall and Führer, 1936–43" (DI film 40).
354 *Ohlendorf:* See note to p. 158 above. *Hans Lange:* RG.260, Hofer Papers, box 182.
355 *Veltjens, Josef:* Richthofen squadron veteran, later SA Oberführer; evicted from the Nazi party in 1931 for participating in the "Stennes Putsch," and not readmitted despite HG's personal efforts (a letter of Sept. 17, 1937, in BDC files). Adolf Galland interrog., ADI(K) 373/45. For Veltjens's agency in Holland, "Aussenstelle West," see HG's diary, Apr. 14, 1942—a discussion with V.,—and Görnnert's files, NA film T84/6/5856, black market purchase of machine tools, and /5281, /5908, purchase of canned meat and five hundred thousand woolen blankets for the Eastern front. Further documents on V.: see *ADAP (D)* ix, no. 313; x, 330 and 366; xi, 139f, 162, 213, 258, 274, 411, and 542.
355 *Horcher:* Port wine: letter of Brauchitsch to Görnnert, Aug. 19, 1942 (NA film T84/6/5348); automobile gas, T84/7/6749ff.
356 *It's a disgrace:* HG conference, Sept. 13, 1942 (NA.62, 5277ff).
356 *Trip to Paris:* itinerary, etc., on NA film T84/8/7573ff. *Anger:* See note to p. 361 below.
356 *Transportation problem:* Conference at Führer's headquarters, May 24, 1942 (Milch Papers, DI film 36a).
356 *Thousand-bomber raid:* German report on the effects, in MD70/71. *Hitler* quoted from the war diary of the OKW's Historical Section.

32: THE ROAD TO STALINGRAD

359 *The Road to Stalingrad:* In general, this chapter is based on the verbatim records of the GL conferences (MD.14 through MD.17), the GL-Development conferences (MD.34), the GL-Supply conferences (MD.17), and the Central Planning conferences (MD.46–47). *Table Talk,* July 4, 1942 (Heim, op. cit.).
359 *Petroleum fields:* Statistics as of Jan. 1, 1940, on NA film T84/7/6630.
359 *Petroleum conference* of July 10, 1942: Verbatim protocol, T84/6/5605ff.
359 *Knochen:* Note in Hofer Papers, NA, RG.260, box 183.
359 *Château de Bort:* Maj. Drees, report of June 26, 1942 (NA, RG.239, box 76); letter of French education minister to SHAEF, Mar. 6, 1945 (box 77); HG's nephew, cited in SRA.4821; and Gen. von Thomas, in CSDIC (UK) report SRM.83, and PW paper 27 of Oct. 16, 1944.
360 *Production comparison:* HG conference, June 29, 1942 (MD.62, 5235).
361 *Gauleiter conference:* Shorthand minutes of HG's conference with the Reich commissars for the Occupied Territories and the military governors, Aug. 6 (ND, USSR exhibit 170); cf. von Etzdorf's notes, Aug. 7 (DI film 61); Görnnert's memo of Aug. 11, 1942 (NA film T84/8/7923ff, 7871ff, and 7666ff), and Bormann diary, Aug. 5–6, 1942.
362 *Schmid:* Interrogation report, ADI(K) 395/45 of Oct. 16, 1945.
362 *Partisans:* Dr. Günther Joel, memo, Sept. 24, 1942 (ND, 635-PS), and HG interrog., Nuremberg Oct. 8, 1945. *Sausage fingers:* Halder in GRGG.3266 and Gen. Kurt Dittmar's diary, Aug. 1945 (DI film 60) and GRGG.346.

363 *Caucasus crisis:* Helmuth Greiner, private diary (SI) and draft war diary of OKW operations staff (DI film 91); and HG testimony, *IMT*, Mar. 15, 1946; Milch diary, Sept. 7, 1942.

364 *Luftwaffe field divisions:* See Field Marshal von Manstein, diary of Nov. 16, 1942; and the report of Lt. Gen. Eugen Meindl, May 15, 1943 (MD.51, 551ff).

365 *Kesselring:* His phone conversations with HG are reproduced in Ugo Cavallero, *Diario* (Rome: 1948).

366 *Mundane duties:* See, e.g., Görnnert's files, NA film T84/6/5269 and 5870ff. A typical day, Dec. 7, 1942, saw lined up for HG a list of twenty-four appointments listing fifty names of people, some of whom had been waiting for weeks to see him: Frau Mölders Jr., Gauleiter Forster, Reich Minister Rüst, Dr. Popitz, Dr. Ley, von Hammerstein, Dr. Richard Conti, Milch, Himmler, Sauckel, followed by a board meeting of H.G.W.-Romania.

367 *Stalingrad airlift decision:* The best study is by Johannes Fischer, in *Militärgeschichtliche Mitteilungen* (Stuttgart; 1969), 7ff; Fischer, however, did not have access to the Milch documents and diaries or those of Richthofen, Manstein, Pickert, and Fiebig (DI film 15a) upon which this author partly relies. HG interrog., SAIC/13, and especially his remarks to Richthofen (diary, Feb. 10) and his secret speech to the other Luftwaffe commanders on Feb. 15, 1943 (Koller shorthand diary, DI film 17).

367 *Oil conference:* Shorthand minutes, Nov. 21, 1942, on NA film T84/6/5661ff.

368 *Special train "Asia":* "Itinerary for the Trip from Berchtesgaden via Munich to Paris," Nov. 22–23, 1942, on NA film T84/6/5280.

·33: FALL FROM GRACE

370 *Shopping in Paris:* The receipts, extimates, and dispatch lists are in the papers of Prof. Jacques Beltrand, dated Paris, Nov. 24–28, 1942 (NA RG.239, box 74).

371 *Jewish brothers Löbl:* Orion interrogs. of Walter Hofer and Bruno Lohse (NA, RG.239, box 84); Lohse, memo (ibid., box 76); Limberger, note of June 22, 1943 (box 78).

372 *Rommel appears at headquarters:* Rommel diary (shorthand text on NA film T84/259, transcribed by author on DI film 160) and journey report (NA film 313/472/1016ff).

372 *Trip to Rome:* See interpreter Eugen Dollman's report to Himmler, Dec. 16, 1942 (NA film T175/68/42411ff); Lt. Alfred-Ingemar Berndt, briefing note for HG, Nov. 30, 1942 (T313/473/1026ff); and diaries of Rommel, Milch, and Greiner.

372 *Mussolini reception:* Cavallero diary.

373 *Rommel weeps:* Milch diary, and handwritten memoirs (DI films 57 and 36a).

373 *Ciano and Cavallero arrive:* Italian minutes in Comando Supremo files, Dec. 15, 1942 (NA film T821/457/0409ff), and Cavallero diary.

373 *Stalingrad:* Zeitzler Papers (BA-MA class N.63) and files of the Sixth Army and Army Group Don in BA-MA.

374 *Luftwaffe production:* Records for 1943 will be found in the files of GL conferences, MD.17; GL-Development conferences, MD.34; Central Planning conferences, MD.46-MD.47. The author also relied on HG's appointment diary, Jan. 1–June 5, 1943 (IfZ, Ed.180), and a more comprehensive notebook written up by HG from late May to July 3, 1943; as the IfZ's Hermann Weiss has observed (*VfZ* [1983], 365ff), these are worthwhile sources only when used in conjunction with the Milch diaries and documents.

375 *Stalingrad mission for Milch:* Diary of Task Force Milch, Jan. 15–Feb. 2, 1943 (DI film 15a; MA-MA, Lw.108/7 and III.L78/1-5); Maj. Werner Beumelburg, study on the Stalingrad airlift, June 8, 1943 (Milch Papers, DI film 36b).

375 *Failure of transport squadrons:* See particularly Milch's acid comments at his GL conferences on Feb. 9 (MD.18, 4336ff) and Feb. 16 (/4438ff), and the telephone conversations logged in his task force's diary.

377 *Richthofen diary:* Feb. 10–13, 1943; this historically important diary was kindly provided to the author by Col. (Ret.) Karl Gundelach by permission of Baroness Jutta von Richthofen.

378 *Paulus was too weak:* From Feb. 15–17, 1943, HG had summoned the Luftflotte commanders to a situation conference: transcript in MD.57, 3046; and shorthand minutes taken by Koller, diary.

34: JET-PROPELLED

380 *Seversky:* HG interrog., May 10, 1945 (Library of Congress, Spaatz Papers). A shorthand record of HG's conference with Milch, on Feb. 22, 1943, is in MD.62, 5353ff.

381 *On the Obersalzberg:* Goebbels diary; for his talks with Speer, see the latter's office chronicle, 1943: original IWM file FD.3037/49 on DI film 41; an imperfect copy "sanitized" at Speer's direction after the war is in the BA, Koblenz.

381 *In Italy:* Letter from Hofer to Ventura, Mar. 1943; interrog. of Hofer by Giorgio Castelfranco of the Missione della Republica Italiana per le Restitutione dalla Germania e dall'Austria, Dec. 4, 1946 (NA, RG.260, box 396); Dr. Gottlieb Reber, HG's art agent in Italy, stated that HG often spent hours with art dealer Count Cortini to the despair of his Luftwaffe commanders. "Contini," HG once raged. "It's too bad you're not a Paris Jew, then I'd just take them all away from you" (NA, RG.239, box 77). For HG's art payments to Italy, via his official *Amtsrat* Gerch—8 million lire on Feb. 25, 2 million on Mar. 3, 1943, etc, see ibid., box 76.

382 *Jeschonnek:* Suchenwirth, conversation with Lt. Col. Werner Leuchtenberg, Jan. 24, 1955 (BA-MA, Lw.104).

382 *Reichsmarschall arrives back:* Diaries of Goebbels, Greiner (DI film 91), and Rommel (shorthand on NA film T84/259, transcript DI film 161). *HG appoints Pelz:* MD.65, 7071f.

382 *HG tirade* of Mar. 18, 1943: Verbatim in MD.62, 5461ff; summary minutes in Messerschmitt Papers, IWM, FD.4355/45, vol. 2.

383 *Can't find London:* In general on the air war, 1943–45, see Col. (G. S.) Greiff (operations officer, Luftwaffe operations staff), interrogated by APWIU, 9th Air Force, report no. 85/45 (NA, RG.332, box 46). *Electronic warfare:* Interrog. of General of Signals Wolfgang Martini, ADI(K) 334/45, June 21, 1945.

384 *Dittmar, General Kurt:* Diary of May 19, 1943 (DI film 60).

384 *Me 262 decision:* Report from Galland to Milch and HG, May 25, 1943 (MD.56, 2620); GL conference, May 25 (MD.20, 5430ff); Milch diary (DI film 57); Galland, SRGG.1305. Prof. Messerschmitt kept a special file on the Me 262 controversy (IWM, FD.4924/45); see too Hans Redemann's article, "Messerschmitt 262" in *Flug Revue* (1970), 119ff.

35: EXIT JESCHONNEK

385 *"Bigger barrage balloons":* All these observations are quoted from HG's 1943 handwritten notebook (IfZ, ED. 180).

386 *Heavy raids on Russia:* See the paper by Herhudt von Rohden in *WR* (1951), 21ff.

387 *Fi 103 robot plane conference* with HG: June 18, 1943, transcript in archives of Führungsakademie der Bundeswehr, Hamburg.

388 *Göring's stock is low:* Goebbels's unpublished diary (DI film 52).

389 *Aircraft designers visit Hitler:* Capt. Wolf Junge, typescript memoirs (IfZ, SI); USSBS interrog. of Messerschmitt, and his briefing notes for the conference in IWM file FD.4924/45; and Bormann diary, June 27, 1943.

389 *Hüls:* Milch to HG, June 23, 1943 (MD.51, 0426).

389 *Herrmann* conference with HG, June 27, 1943 (MD.63, 5842ff) and interview with the author; Milch telegram to HG, June 29, 1943 (MD.51, 0514).

390 *Hitler's speech* of July 1, 1943: Summary in Gen. Johannes Friessner's papers, BA-MA, RH.24-23/1; partial verbatim record on NA film T77/783 (= ND, 739-PS); referred to by Gen. von Knobelsdorff, in report X-P4, May 14, 1945, and a paper by Gen. W. E. Kempff in BA-MA, N. 63/12.

390 *Ruhr inspection by Milch:* Milch, report dated June 29, 1943 (MD.51, 0512ff); diary, July 2–3, 1943, and testimony in Case II, Mar. 14, 1947. Axthelm, SRG.1302.

392 *Euphoria about Citadel:* Rommel diary, July 6, 1943 (DI film 161).

393 *Hitler furious:* Hitler at war conference, July 25, 1943; Helmut Heiber, *Hitlers Lagebesprechungen* (Stuttgart: 1962), 309ff.

395 *Bodenschatz:* In SRSGG.1222; Milch diary, Aug. 3, 1943; cf. Wilfried von Oven, *Mit Goebbels bis zum Ende* (Buenos Aires: 1949). HG phone call to Milch, July 28, 1943: MD.51, 0421.

395 *New Night Fighter tactics:* Milch telegram to HG, Aug. 3, 1943 (MD.56, 2590). See too the interrog. report on Galland and Gollob, "The Birth, Life, and Death of the German Day Fighter Arm," ADI(K) 373/45; and that on Schmid, Kammhuber, Stumpff, and Ruppel, "The History of German Night Fighting," ADI(K) 416/45. Both are to be found in NA, RG.407 box 1954m.

396 *HG unpopular:* Letter from Berger to Himmler, July 30, 1943 (NA film T175/124/9100).

396 *Jeschonnek:* Suchenwirth's interviews of Lotte Kersten, Kurt Student, Hans-Georg von Seidel.

396 *Jostling for position:* HG interrog. July 20, 1945, by Shuster.

397 *Peiner:* Letter from Limberger to HG, Aug. 16, 1943 (NA, RG.260, box 396). *Ondarza:* Interview with Suchenwirth, Apr. 17, 1956.

397 *All night fighters to Bear:* Telegram of Weise to HG, Aug. 21, 1943 (files of the Führungsakademie der Bundeswehr, Hamburg); author's interview of Kammhuber, Nov. 6, 1963. *Raid on Peenemünde:* David Irving, *The Mare's Nest* (London: 1964).

398 *Suicide of Jeschonnek:* See notes to pp. 396 and 397 above; and Suchenwirth's study, "Hans Jeschonnek," on DI film 15b.

36: SCHWEINFURT

400 *Statistics on flak and fighter defenses:* Milch speech to Gauleiters in Posen, Oct. 6, 1943 (NA film T175/119/5054ff).

400 *Glider pilot:* GL conference, Sept. 14, 1943 (MD.25, 7634ff).

401 *Park Hotel:* Bodenschatz, SRGG.1238.

401 *The Korten era:* USSBS interrogation of Koller, May 23–24, 1945. In general, on Luftwaffe production problems in the second half of 1943; see the verbatim minutes of the GL conferences in MD.21-MD.26; GL-Development conferences, MD.38; GL conferences with Speer (from Aug. 25 onward) MD.30 and MD.31; GL-Night Fighting conferences, MD.30; GL-Flak conferences, MD.41; and Central Planning conferences, MD.48 (all at the BA-MA).

404 *Bombing Brindisi:* HG conference, Oct. 14, 1943 (MD.63, 6228); and cf. Oct. 8 (/5722 and 5775f).

404 *"I would far prefer . . .":* Hitler at war conference of Oct. 3, 1943.

404 *Galland:* HG in conference on Oct. 7, 1943 (MD.63, 5665).
405 *What on earth is Milch thinking of?:* HG in conference, Oct. 9, 1943 (MD.63, 6309). *The greatest battles:* HG in conference, Oct. 7, 1943 (MD.62, 5652).
406 *Schweinfurt:* HG in conference on that day, Oct. 14, 1943 (MD.63, 6252ff). On the Schweinfurt air battle, see Galland's words in GL-Speer conference, Oct. 27, 1943, MD.31, 0751), and HG at Arnhem-Deelen, Oct. 23, 1943 (MD.63, 6133f).
407 *"You fat old Lump!"* HG speech in canteen at Arnhem-Deelen airbase, Oct. 23, 1943 (MD.63, 6119ff). Cpl. Schürgers, overheard in SRA.5022, Feb. 26, 1944 (PRO file WO.208/4133).
408 *Dornier observer:* SRA.5065 (ibid.) The British raid on Kassel is analyzed in the night operations report of the Operational Research Section RAF Bomber Command, Oct. 22–23, 1943 (Air Ministry files).
408 *Hitler's top-level conference:* Naval Staff war diary, Oct. 27, and transcript of the same date on DI film 44; HG in conference, Oct. 28 (MD.63, 6080) and Nov. 2, 1943 (/5961ff); author's interview of von Below, Nov. 19, 1969.

37: THE BLIND LEADING THE BLIND

411 *Gauleiter conference:* HG speech of Nov. 8, 1943 (MD.63, 5859ff, and BA-MA RL.l/1); quotation used is from a letter by Herbert Backe to his wife, Nov. 15, 1943.
411 *Production program:* See the GL conferences in MD.26 through MD.29; GL's conferences with Speer, MD.31 and MD.32; the GL-Development conferences, MD.38, MD.39, and MD.43; the GL-Flak conferences in MD.41; and Central Planning conferences in MD.48 (all at BA-MA).
411 *Me 262:* Messerschmitt's file FD.4355/45, vol. 3, at IWM; HG at conference, Oct. 14, 1943 (MD.63, 6261f).
411 *Regensburg:* HG in conference, Nov. 2, 1943 (MD.63, 5961ff); HG at Desau, Nov. 4, /5923ff; at Brandenburg, Nov. 5: /5706ff.
411 *Galland order* of Nov. 8, 1943: Decoded English text in SRH-013; copy sent to FDR on Nov. 24, 1943 (FDR Library, file A16/Germany.)
412 *Air-raid damage of Nov. 22. 1943:* Milch, in SRGG.1323; Naval Staff war diary, Nov. 22, and Milch at GL conference, Nov. 30, 1943.
412 *Invited to Carinhall:* Transcript of this conference of Nov. 23, 1943, on MD.64, 6636ff.
412 *Insterburg:* Program, MD.51, 0416ff; Kröger's remarks at GL conference, Feb. 1, 1944; and author's interviews with Milch, Petersen, and von Below.
413 *Reprisal raids:* HG conferences of Nov. 26 (MD.64, 6632ff) and Nov. 28 (/6694ff); HG operations order, Dec. 3, 1943, an annex to the war diary of the Luftwaffe High command (OKL) on NA film T321/10.
413 *Jet bombers:* See von Below's telegram to HG, Dec. 5, 1943 (MD.53, 0725), and GL conference, Dec. 7, 1943. *To Paris:* Goebbels diary, Dec. 7.
413 *Basel altarpiece:* HG interrogs. at Nuremberg on Oct. 6 and 8, 1945.
414 *Cuckoo's egg:* Reports by MFA&A, June 29, 1945 (IWM file FO.645); war office, art looting report, Feb. 2, 1945 (NA, RG.239, box 42); for pictures of the loot from Monte Cassino, see box 49. The MFA&A report dated July 20, 1944, lists the crates and contents that did arrive at the Vatican (box 62).
415 *To the Wolf's lair:* Führer naval conferences, Jan. 2, 1944 (DI film 44), and Jan. 3, 1944 (MD.64, 6568ff). *U-boats:* Central Planning conference, Dec. 21, 1943 (MD.48, 10,126), and GL conference (MD32, 1073).
415 *Underground factories in the Harz mountains:* For Allied investigation reports on "Central Works Inc.," see file FD.194/46 (A4 production records), FD.3268/45 (tour of the tunnel complex), and DI film 24. In general, see the testimony of Xaver Dorsch in Case II, Feb. 24, 1947.
415 *Me 410:* Telegram of HG to Milch, Jan. 12, 1944 (MD.51, 0414f).
415 *Ramcke:* Overheard in SRGG.1065.
416 *Turning point:* War diary of First Fighter Corps. *"Big Week":* U.S. Army Air Forces in World War II, vol. iii, 30ff; British Air Ministry, *The Rise and Fall of the German Air Force,* 206 (PRO, AIR.41/10).
416 *Fighter staff:* HG conference, Mar. 4, 1944 (MD.64, 6511ff); Milch, speaking at Fighter Staff conference, Mar. 6 (MD.1, 0375ff); Saur at Central Planning conference, Mar. 11 (MD.48, 9874); and Milch diary (DI film 57).

38: IMMINENT DANGER WEST

419 *Japanese ambassador:* Morale report, radio to Tokyo; quoted in "Magic" summary of May 7, 1944 (NA, RG.457, SRS1286-1307). *NS Indoctrination Officers (NSFO):* HG interrog. July 20, 1945, by Shuster.
419 *Concentration camp prisoners:* Letter of Himmler to HG, Mar. 9 (ND, 1584-PS); and see Himmler's diary, Mar. 9, 1944. *Slave labor:* GL conference with Speer, Aug. 25 (MD.30, 0418) and Nov. 10, 1943 (MD.31, 0711).
419 *Sagan camp:* Jodl, trial notes, Apr. 5 and 8, 1946 (Jodl Papers); HG interrog. at Nuremberg, Oct. 8, 1945; Luftwaffe Gen. Förster, overheard in SRGG.1239; CSDIC(UK) interrog. of two Sagan camp guards, SIR.1170; Milch diary entry for Feb. 23, 1946 (DI film 58). Indignantly asked: HG interrogated by Eric Warburg, May 29, 1945.
420 *"Dr. G West":* Paper by K. Gundelach, "Imminent Danger West," in *WR* (1959), 299f; and W. Gaul, "The German Air Force during the Invasion of 1944," ibid. (1953), 134ff.
420 *Ju 188 pilot:* Overheard on Apr. 20, 1944, in SRA.5166 (PRO file WO.208/4133). For general sources on

Luftwaffe production in the first half of 1944, see GL conferences, MD.29; Fighter Staff conferences, vols. MD.1 through MD.6; and in particular Milch's four trips to inspect the savaged Luftwaffe industrial base ("Operation Hubertus") from Mar. 8 to 13, 14 to 15, 21 to 22, and Apr. 3 to 4, 1944; and Central Planning sessions recorded verbatim in the vols. MD.48 and MD.55.

420 *Suicide squadron:* Interrog. of Hanna Reitsch by AIU/IS, report no. 10, dated Nov. 28, 1945 (Hoover Library, Lerner Papers, box 21). And see note to p. 427 below.

420 *Over Stuttgart:* NCO Kugler, overheard in SRY.1978.

421 *Mountain stroll:* Saur, speaking at Fighter Staff conference, Apr. 8, 1944 (MD.5, 2388f).

422 *Underground factories:* See HG conference, May 1, 1944 (MD.64, 6400ff); and Oct. 28, 1943 (MD.63, 6040); Saur at HG conference, Apr. 19, 1944 (MD.64, 6480), and his notes after meeting Hitler, Apr. 6–7, 1944 (IWM file FD.3353/45, vol. 68); also Xaver Dorsch's conference with HG on Apr. 14, et seq., reproduced in Willi Boelcke, *Deutschlands Rüstung im Zweiten Weltkrieg* (Frankfurt: 1969), 349ff.

422 *Speer:* Office chronicle entry for Apr. 19, 1944; Führer decree, Apr. 22, 1944 (IWM, FD.2049/49). On May 25, 1944, Speer would remark at a Central Planning session, "If we've not seen anything [i.e., any invasion] by June or July, we can assume that the whole winter will pass off quietly" (Md.55, 2170).

422 *Smashing oil production:* See HG's interrog. by APWID (9th Air Force) on May 29, 1945; Milch, overheard in SRGG.1313; USSBS interrogation of Karl Koller, May 23–25, 1945. *The radio signal* is quoted in SRH-013 (see note to p. 325 above).

423 *Enemy terror fliers:* Milch, statement in Fighter Staff conference, May 3, 1944 (MD.6, 2974f); and Wehrmacht High Command (OKW) documents on NA film T84/331/0832ff; Führer decision, May 21, 1944 (ND, 731-PS); HG interrogated on July 20, 1945, by Shuster and at Nuremberg on Sept. 22, 1945; Jodl, memos dated May 20–22, 1944 (on NA film T77/778).

424 *HG's production program conference:* Held the morning of May 23, 1944, verbatim text MD.64, 6832ff; diaries of Milch and Richthofen; interrog. of Galland, ADI(K)373/45. The controversy centered on Koller's secret study, "Requisite Minimum Strength of German Air Force Flying Formations if Central Europe Is to Be Retained," dated May 19, 1944 (in Koller Papers, on DI film 17; copy in MD.53, 0706ff).

424 *Up at the Berghof:* See HG conferences, May 24 (MD.64, 6900ff), May 25 (/6718ff), and May 29 (6323ff); Fighter Staff conference May 26, 1944 (MD.7, 3646ff), and author's interviews with Milch, May 14, 1968, and Petersen, June, 28, 1968; and the report to Bormann on BA file NS.6/152. Interrogated on May 29, 1945, as to the reason why the Me 262 was operated as a bomber, HG retorted: "The lunacy of Adolf Hitler!"

425 *Führer order:* Telegram from HG to Milch, Galland, et al., May 27, 1944 (MD.53, 0730f).

425 *"To avoid misunderstandings":* HG conference, May 29, 1944 (MD.64, 6323ff).

39: TOTAL SACRIFICE

426 The initial quotation is from HG's interrog. SAIC/X/5, dated May 24, 1945. The II Air Corps radio message is in SRH-013 (see note to p. 325 above). The author has also relied on the war diaries of C-in-C West, the OKW, the Naval Staff, and Army Group B, and the interrogs. of HG and von Brauchitsch quoted by Ernst Englander in *Interavia*, July 1946.

427 *Karl Koller's papers:* Primarily the series of "Daily Records" dictated by him throughout June 1944 (DI film 17).

427 *Decoding:* A study well founded on the Ultra files now in the PRO is Ralph Bennett, *Ultra in the West: The Normandy Campaign of 1944–45* (London: 1979).

427 *Suicide pilots:* Reitsch (see note to p. 420 above); Koller's daily records, June 9 and 18; Milch diary, July 29 and 31, Aug. 1; Speer, second memo on hydrogenation plants, July 28; memo on conference with SS Col. Skorzeny, July 31, 1944 (MD.53, 0691), and letter from him to the author, June 11, 1970.

428 *Galland:* Overheard in SRGG.1248.

429 *Poltava:* Koller daily record, June 21 (DI film 17).

429 *Luftwaffe production* in summer 1944: GL conferences, MD.29; Fighter Staff conferences, MD.7 and MD.8; Central Planning conferences, MD.55.

429 *Radio signal* by HG, July 9, 1944: English text in SRH.013 *Berghof conference of June 29, 1944:* War diary of Army Group B (on NA films T84/281 and T311/278), and the notes taken by Dönitz, Koller, and Jodl (whose diary for this period has been largely disregarded by historians).

429 *Art treasures:* Correspondence between Bunjes and Hofer, July 7–17, 1944 (NA, RG.260, box 172). The "Diana" was from Château Anet, sculpted in marble probably by Jean Goujon; the French sculptor G. Chauvel had been commissioned to make a copy for HG, who had a special truckload of marble brought up from Italy. (Letter Bunjes to Limberger, Feb. 16, 1942, in RG.239, box 78.)

430 *Hitler's strategy:* Koller daily record, July 9, 1944 (DI film 17).

430 *HG on morning of July 20:* Letter from Maj. Gen. Friedrich Kless to the author, Oct. 19, 1987.

430 *Couldn't stand Mussolini:* HG interrog., SAIC/13.

430 *Bomb attempt on Hitler's life:* The author has used, in particular, the file of documents collected by Maj. Hugh Trevor-Roper for British military intelligence after the war (DI film 38). *HG's presence at Hitler's that day:* Letter from Martin Bormann to his wife, July 19 (original in the possession of François Genoud; cf. *The Bormann Letters* [London: 1954]). The most reliable eyewitness accounts are by Bodenschatz (SRGG.1219), Dollmann (CSDIC/CMF/X-194), von Below (BAOR report, Jan. 23, 1946), and Buchholz (DI film 13). See Paul Schmidt's note on Hitler's conference with Mussolini, and the Naval Staff war diary, July 20. *HG's views on Beck:* HG interrog., SAIC/13.

431   *Secret speech:* Verbatim record of HG's speech, Nov. 25, 1944, is in Koller's papers (DI film 17). "*No officers of my Luftwaffe . . .*": Quoted by Heydt, GRGG.205.

431   *Barsewisch:* Handwritten memoir in Trevor-Roper's papers (DI film 38). *Involvement of Herbert L. W. Göring:* Handwritten testimony of SS Maj. Dr. Georg Kiessel, Aug. 6, 1946 (ibid.); and more especially the BAOR interrog. of Rudolf Diels at 031 Interrogation Camp (NA, RG.332, MIS-Y, box 49). *Concerning Luftflotte Reich and the Putsch:* Manuscript by Lischka, Apr. 10, 1946 (DI film 38); and radio message, July 20, 1944, in SRH-013 (see note to p. 325 above).

432   *Clique of generals:* Letter of Von Osten to Lina Heydrich, Oct. 29, 1944 (Hoover Library, Lerner Papers, DE.424/DIS.202).

432   *Helldorf:* Interrog. of his son, Cpl. Joachim Ferdinand Count von Helldorf, who had been captured in Normandy on July 11, 1944: PW paper no. 12, dated Aug. 4, 1944. *Hit lists:* Reich Main Security Office (RSHA), Dept. IV memo: "Documents . . . Found in an Envelope Left for Dr. Goerdeler," dated Berlin, Aug. 3 (DI film 38).

432   *Fighting speech:* Speech on a visit to the HG Escort Regiment, July 21, 1944 (annex to war diary of HG Panzer Corps, BA-MA, RL.32/37).

433   *One of Hitler's stenographers:* Karl Thöt diary (IfZ, SI); telegram from Dönitz to naval commands, July 23, 1944 (BA-MA, H.3/463), and telegram from HG, July 23 (BA, Schumacher Collection, file 117). See Karl Raeder's memoir, "My Relations to [*sic*] Adolf Hitler and to the Party," Moscow, Aug. 1945 (DI film 48).

433   *Successor to Korten:* The author follows the diary kept by Lt. Gen. Werner Kreipe from July 22 to Nov. 2, 1944 (NA, MS #P-069; copy in SRGG, SI), and Kreipe's interviews by the IfZ (ZS-87) and Suchenwirth, Nov. 22, 1954 (BA-MA, Lw.104/5); and the diary kept by Werner Beumelburg, July 18, 1944, to July 12, 1945 (the "male friend" referred to).

435   *Under house arrest:* OSS report L.44952, dated Aug. 29, 1944 (NA, RG.226).

40: WITCH HUNT

437   *Evacuate works of art:* Rosenberg minute to Lohse and others, Aug. 14, 1944 (ND, exhibit RF-1346); and see Lohse's interrog. (NA, RG.239, box 84).

437   *WL prefix:* Letter of Berger to Himmler, Sept. 26, 1944 (ND, NO-1822). The scandalous behavior of some Luftwaffe officers in France is described in Suchenwirth's interview with Hammerstein, Sept. 5, 1955, and the Bormann dossier (BA, Schumacher Collection, file 315). *Horsedrawn vehicles:* II Fighter Corps signal quoted in SRH-013.

437   *Bachstitz case:* See Hofer files, NA, RG.239, boxes 74, 75, and 78; the detective was Kriminal-Obersekretär Franz Brandenburg, interrogated by 101 U.S. Airborne Division, July 4, 1945 (DI film 13).

442   "*Disgraceful failures*": HG order no. 3, Oct. 17, 1944 (Hoover Library, Lerner Papers, DE.337/DIS.202).

443   *If Hitler died:* HG interrogs., July 20 and 23, 1945, by Shuster.

443   *Trakehnen:* Related by HG on Nov. 25, 1944 (see note to p. 431 above).

443   *Fighter squadron commanders:* Galland, overheard in SRGG.1229; Capt. Pliefke, SRA. 5828; and Lt. Col. Kögler, SRA. 5813.

444   *Spaatz warning:* Spaatz diary entries for Oct. 21, 1944, and Jan. 5, 1945 (Library of Congress, Spaatz Papers, boxes 16 and 20).

445   *Darré:* Diary, Nov. 7, 1944, and see his remarks overheard in X-P4, May 14, 1945. *Klosinski:* Interviewed by Suchenwirth, Feb. 1, 1947 (BA-MA, Lw.104/14).

446   *Bormann dossier:* BA, Schumacher Collection, file 315.

41: ZERO HOUR FOR HERMANN

448   *Figher offensive:* Interrogs. of Brauchitsch, Aug. 20, 1945 (APWIU, 9th Air Force), and HG, July 20, 1945 (Shuster).

448   *Christmas at Carinhall:* Ondarza, interviewed by Suchenwirth, Apr. 17, 1956 (BA-MA, Lw. 104/3); Emmy Göring, memoirs.

448   *Galland:* Cpl. Reuthers (of HQ, 2nd Fighter Division), overheard in SRX.2123 (WO.208/4164); Galland, overheard talking to Herget in SRGG.1211; Milch, in SRGG.1250; Galland himself in SRGG.1226 and SRGG.1229; Lt. Col. Kögler (who had commanded *Jagdgeschwader* 6) in SRA.5813; Capt. Pliefke, in SRA.5828; and Galland Papers, BA-MA, N.211/2, and his file on "The Luftwaffe in Crisis Situations," Oct. 15, 1944, through Apr. 20, 1945 (BA-MA, RL.1/4).

448   *Bodenplatte:* APWIU (9th Air Force), report no. 2/45: "New Year Greetings from the Luftwaffe," Jan. 5; and no. 4/45, of Jan. 9, 1945 (NA, RG.332, box 46). Interrogs. of HG, May 10 and May 29, 1945; Koller, May 23–24, 1945; von Greiff, June 29, 1945; Christian, May 19, 1945; and Maj. Karl Heinz Sandmann, of the Luftwaffe High Command (OKL) plans division, by APWIU (2nd Tac. Air Force), no. 77/45 (NA, RG.332, box 46). For differing summaries of the results, see the war diaries of the Naval Staff, Jan. 2 and 7, and the OKW, vol. iv, 1359; the 3rd Fighter Division claimed the destruction of 398 enemy planes on the ground, but conceded "considerable own losses" out of the 622 sorties flown (Bennett, op. cit., 203); the author of SRH-

013 estimated nine hundred German fighter-bomber sorties were flown that day, of which "at least" three hundred were shot down; sixty fighter pilots were taken prisoner.

449 *"Zero hour for Hermann"*: These German signals had been deciphered at 3:08 and 3:29 A.M. respectively, but their significance had not been appreciated (PRO file DEFE.3/DT.878 and 879).

451 *Something of the old ruthlessness*: HG order no. 11, Jan. 16, 1945 (BA-MA, Lw.104/3; NA film T177/3/5007ff; and Hoover Library, Lerner Papers, box 21). *Waber case*: See too Kreipe diary, Sept. 28, 1944.

451 *His detectives heard him exclaim*: Brandeburg and Lau, interrogated on July 5, 1945 (DI film 13).

451 *Galland's philandering*: "Typical of the Party gentry!" Milch was overheard exclaiming on May 20, 1945: "Saying this about Galland, when there's not one of them who hasn't got at least two tarts himself—the swine!" (SRGG.1250). HG's order no. 12 of Jan. 23 is in BA-MA file Lw.104/3 and (deciphered by the British) in SRH-013 (see note to p. 325 above).

452 *Family problem*: Interrogs. of Albert Göring on Sept. 3 and 25, 1945 (NA film M.1270). In general, for this chapter the author has drawn upon the surviving war diary of the Luftwaffe High Command operations staff, Feb. 1 through Apr. 7, 1945 (NA film T321/10/6800ff).

453 *"Ridiculous excursions"*: HG interrog., July 20, 1945, by Shuster; and Bross, op. cit., 193.

453 *Trip to Veldenstein*: Minute on HG's conference with Prof. Hetzelt, Feb. 7, 1945 (NA, RG.260, box 395).

454 *Goebbels quotation*: From his diary.

454 *Target was Dresden*: OKL war diary, Feb. 14; in general, David Irving, *The Destruction of Dresden* (London: 1963), and DI films 10, 11, 12 and 35.

454 *British code breakers*: Himmler's message is quoted in SRH-013 (see note to p. 325 above); and see his subsequent telegram to Alvensleben, Feb. 15, 1945: "My dear Alvensleben! Received your telex report of Feb. 15. 1: Approve relocating your office but only to suburbs of Dresden. Any further would make a rotten impression; 2. Now is the time for iron steadfastness and immediate action to restore order. 3. Set me a good example of calm and nerve!" (NA film T175/40/0553).

454 *Bodenschatz to report*: Bodenschatz, overheard in SRGG.1222.

454 *Flying Fortress unit*: Interrog. of the survivors by APWIU (9th Air Force), report no. 18/45, and by APWIU (1st Tac. Air Force), report no. 19/45 in NA, RG.332, box 46; further on KG.200's special operations in ADI(K) report 512C/1944, and HG interrog., June 4, 1945, at "Ashcan"; also the overheard remarks of survivors Lt. Magdanz (SRX.2077), Capt. Pliefke (SRA.5811 and 5825), and Helmdach (SR draft 2234).

455 *Admitted to Görnnert*: Görnnert interrog. of May 12, 1945 (DI film 13). HG interrogated on July 20, 1945, by Shuster.

455 *Cargo of art treasures*: Party Chancellery report in NA, RG.260, box 182.

456 *"Stark staring mad?"*: Koller, letter to Exner, Mar. 25, 1946 (Salmuth Papers), and memo on this case by Hitler's stenograhers Heinz Buchholz, Dec. 13, 1945, and Gerhard Herrgesell, July 19, 1945 (IfZ, SI).

456 *Mistletoe project*: Koller papers (DI film 17) and interrog. by USSBS, May 23–24, 1945; OKL war diary and annexes; and HG interrog., SAIC/X/5, May 24, 1945

456 *"Imagine," he told Koller*: Koller Papers, "War conf., F. 26.3.45'" (DI film 17). *Lammers*: Overheard talking with HG, May 19, 1945 (SAIC/X/3).

457 *Movie director*: Dr. Otto Stahmer, application for witness, Mar. 8, 1946 (NA, RG.238, box 180).

457 *Concerned to end the bloodshed*: From Koller's diary (DI film 17); a later shorthand diary kept by him has survived only in English translation as ADI(K) report 348/45 (DI film 39); a copy is also in Sir Norman Bottomley's papers, AC71/2 file 40, at the R.A.F. Museum, Hendon.

457 *Suicide missions*: Goebbels diary entries for Mar. 15, Apr. 1; OKL war diary, Mar. 18; HG's message to Geschwader commodores, Mar. 15, is in SRH-013 (see note to p. 325 above); Galland, SRGG.1248.

458 *Werewolf*: For British reports on this little-known operation, see ADI(K) report 294/45, and Gollob's views in report 373/45. That the operation *was* attempted is evidenced by the OKL war diary, Apr. 4 and 7, 1945.

458 *The deserter Henry Fay*: See his explicit interrogs. by APWIU (9th Air Force), nos. 49 and 50/45, and the scathing entry in the diary of Gen. Hap Arnold, Apr. 4, 1945 (Library of Congress, Arnold Papers).

459 *Letters to the bank*: Carbon copies in HG's papers in NA, Ardelia Hall Collection, RG.260.

459 *Hitler's birthday*: BAOR interrogation of von Below, Jan. 23, 1946. Soviet interrogs. of Otto Günsche and Heinz Linge (IfZ, SI); Koller diary; Julius Schaub, typescript memoirs (IfZ, SI), and author's interview of Rear Adm. von Puttkamer, 1967. In general, Walter Baum's essay, "The Collapse of the German Military Command in 1945," in *WR* (1960), 237ff.

459 *Hitler splits the High Command*: Hitler order, Apr. 20, 1945 (NA film T77/775/1189f); and Grand Adm. Dönitz's war diary (NA film T608/1/0018ff).

460 *The curious discussion with Himmler* on Apr. 20, 1945: HG, overheard relating this to Lammers, May 24, 1945 (SAIC/X/5); interrog. of Gerda Christian, Apr. 25, 1946 (DI film 39). British files contain a telegram from the British minister in Stockholm dated Apr. 13, 1945, reporting that Count Bernadotte had spoken "last week" with Himmler, who, however, still felt bound by his oath of allegiance to Hitler to whom he owed everything. "Göring, it is said, has taken to cocaine [sic] again, dressed up in a toga, and paints his fingernails red." See too Ohlendorf, SRGG.1322.

460 *Göring visits the shelters*: Brauchitsch diary (narrated in SRGG.1342); HG overheard in SAIC/X/5; Milch in SRGG.1249. In general, with caution, see Koller's edited text of his 1945 diaries, *Der letzte Monat* (Mannheim: 1949).

461 *Pilsen*: Milch, SRGG.1249.

PART 6: THE SURROGATE

42: INTO THE CAGE

465 *HG's capture: The Fighting 36th: A Pictorial History of the 36th Div.* (Austin, Texas: 1946); Capt. Harold L. Bond, ''We Captured HG,'' in *The Saturday Evening Post*, Jan. 5, 1946; Robert Stack, ''Capture of Göring,'' in *The T-Patcher*, 36th Div. Journal, Feb. 1977; and *T-Patch*, special edition, May 8, 1945.

467 *Dahlquist:* Reports in *The New York Times*, May 11, 1945: *The Washington Post* , May 12, 1945; and albums in John E. Dahlquist Papers (USAMHI).

467 *Spaatz:* HG interrog., May 10, 1945 (Library of Congress, Spaatz Papers, box 21). Criticized later for having saluted HG, Spaatz stoutly told Charles Lindbergh—who noted it in his diary on May 15—that he had returned HG's salute as one officer to another, in accordance with proper military customs.

468 *Barcus:* Lt. Gen. Glenn O. Barcus's description of the interrog. in Oral History, Aug. 10–13, 1976 (Maxwell Air Force Base, Alabama, archives).

468 *At Augsburg:* Reports of HG's ''press conference'' are in *The New York Times* and others on May 12, 1945. ''Shaking Hands with Murder,'' *News Chronicle*; ''Coddling of German War Killers,'' *New York World Telegram*, May 14 (Dahlquist Papers); and telegram from Gen. G. C. Marshall to Eisenhower, May 12 (NA, RG.153, box 1476).

469 *Sidestepped all knowledge of atrocities:* Eric Warburg, interrog. of HG, May 29, 1945; and HG interrog. SAIC/X/5.

469 *Hidden microphones:* HG overheard talking with Lammers, May 19, 1945: SAIC/X/3, and with Ohnesorge on May 21, 1945: SAIC/X/4.

470 *Art collection found:* Report by Lt. Charles L. Kuhn, in NA, RG.260, box 172; inventories and lists in box 396. And report by Lt. R. F. Newkirk, Aug. 1, 1945, in NA, RG.239, box 77.

471 *Rothschild painting:* HG in conversation with Anton Zoller, reported in *Hannoversche Presse*, Oct. 7, 1948. HG interrog., May 19, 1945: SAIC/X/3.

471 *Wall Street financier:* Letter from Lt. Col. Ernst Engländer to Justice R. H. Jackson, May 18, 1945, in R. H. Jackson Papers, NA, RG.238, and see the articles by ''Evans'' in *Interavia*, July 1946: ''Göring, Almost Führer.''

472 *Not a man to be underrated:* SAIC/13. The list of fellow Nazis at Grand Hotel is the SAIC Weekly Roster of Internees, June 30, 1945, and passim (PRO file WO.208/4153). Walter Lüdde-Neurath kindly loaned the author the memoir he wrote in 1947.

472 *Found brass cyanide cartridge:* Testimony of Col. Burton C. Andrus, annex to ''Report of Board of Proceedings of HG (Suicide),'' Oct. 1946 (copies are in BDC Director's Safe; NA, Records of OMGUS Allied Control Council, RG.260, file 2/92-1(2); and in the Wheeler Bennett Papers at St. Anthony's College, Oxford). The receipt signed by Emmy Göring is now in the Andrus Papers, which his son, Col. B. C. Andrus, Jr., kindly made available for this biography. Cf. B. C. Andrus, *The Infamous of Nuremberg* (New York: 1969), p. 32f.

43: FAT STUFF

476 *The cause:* Quoted from SAIC/13. *Protest to Eisenhower*: Letter of HG to Eisenhower, and covering letter of May 25, 1945, in Andrus Papers.

476 *''Two thousand pills'':* Correspondence between Andrus, SHAEF, and the FBI in USAISC file on HG.

476 *Hiram Gans:* HG interrog. June 2–3, 1945 (ibid., and RG.153). *The Americans found it hard*: HG interrog. June 25, 1945 (USAISC).

477 *Kempner:* Letter of R.M.W. Kempner to Col. Melvin Purvis, May 10, 1945, in NA, RG.153, box 57. The *special prison camp outside London:* This was the CSDIC(UK) at Latimer: Here, the overheard remarks were by Bodenschatz, SRGG.1238, and Milch, SRGG.1279; cf. Milch's diary, June 5 and July 29, 1945.

478 *Scuttlebutt:* Milch, Kreipe, and Schmid overheard in SRGG.1311 (PRO file WO.208/4198).

478 *Footnote on Christiansen:* File A.100-569 in NA, RG.153, box 1534; HG interrog., Dec. 22, 1945 (RG.260, box 172).

479 *He was wasting away:* CCPWE no. 32 (= ''Ashcan'') report DI-36.

479 *Pflücker:* See the memoirs of Ludwig Pflücker, published in Oct. 1952 in the *Waldecksche Landeszeitung*.

479 *Hechler:* Maj. K. W. Hechler, ''The Enemy Side of the Hill,'' in Library of Congress, Toland Papers, box 12; HG's interrog. by Hechler, July 25, 1945, will be found in NA, ACSI ID files, no. 364812.

480 *Being shortchanged:* Andrus's reports of July 26 and Aug. 4, 1945, are quoted from the Andrus Papers. HG's speech of Nov. 25, 1944, is recorded on DI film 17 (Koller Papers).

481 *His health is probably not very good:* Report on HG, Aug. 15, 1945 (U.S. State Dept., DI film 34).

482 *Helga Bouhler:* Letter of HG to Helga Bouhler, undated, reproduced as a facsimile in Charles Hamilton, *Leaders and Personalities of the Third Reich* (San Jose, California: 1984), 108.

482 *Tight security precautions:* Listed in Col. Andrus's papers and his weekly reports to Jackson (R. H. Jackson Papers, NA, RG.238) and Board of Inquiry (see note to p. 472 above).

482 *Andrus asked Pflücker:* Pflücker testimony to Board of Inquiry (see note to p. 472 above).

483 *Kelley:* As a result of petty jealousies that arose between Kelley and his superior officer, Gustave M. Gilbert,

Kelley left Nuremberg "under a cloud," and published a book based on Gilbert's consultation notes, *22 Cells in Nuremberg*. The author has relied on Gilbert's original notes (in the R. H. Jackson Papers).
484   *Ley's suicide:* Ley had spoken of HG with profound contempt in his interrog., SAIC/30, on May 29, 1945.

44: ON TRIAL

486   *Written declaration:* The German text was circulated among the Allied newspapermen attached to Nuremberg. The author found it in the papers of R. Selkirk Panton of the *Daily Express* (National Library of Australia, Canberra, Collection 5808, file 3).
486   *Jackson:* The author has relied on the stenographic notes of the behind-the-scenes meetings of the Nuremberg prosecutors (Library of Congress, R. H. Jackson Papers; DI films 70 and 71), his diary (ibid.), and his 1952 Oral History interview on the Nuremberg trial (DI film 92); and on the diary and papers of Judge Francis Biddle, Syracuse University Library, box 3.
487   *"Old Santa Clauses":* HG interrog. at Nuremberg, Oct. 8, 1945.
487   *Jack G Wheelis:* See the well-researched investigation by Ben S. Swearingen, *The Mystery of Hermann Göring's Suicide* (New York: 1968). Swearingen did not obtain access to HG's last letters, with their vital clues as to his mode of suicide. Andrus's papers show that on at least two occasions Wheelis had caused minor disciplinary problems.
488   *Jackson would telegraph:* Telegram of Jackson to U.S. State Dept., Feb. 13, 1946 (NA, RG.238, R. H. Jackson Papers).
488   *Churchill's plans to invade Norway:* The Germans had captured the files of the Allied Supreme War Council in France in 1940. *Cabinet embarrassment:* PRO file PREM.9/393.
489   *Andrus protest to Tribunal:* Letter of Andrus to Commanding General, Headquarters, IMT, Jan. 12, 1946 (Andrus Papers); and handwritten letter, HG to Tribunal, Jan. 12, 1946 (BDC file), with covering letter from Andrus to Tribunal, Jan. 14 (Andrus Papers).
491   *HG isolated over lunch:* Andrus's directives to this effect are in the files of 6850 Internal Security Detachment (NA, RG.238, entry 199, box 7). Thus he informed the prisoners on Feb. 16, 1946: "You are hereby notified that neither the Tribunal nor any other authority has required that the defendants be allowed to remain in constant communication with each other."
495   *Extraordinary scenes at the prosecutors' secret meeting:* The shorthand record is in R. H. Jackson's private papers (Library of Congress).
496   *Hollywood-size fan mail poured in:* Referred to in one dispatch by Selkirk Panton (see note to p. 472 above).
497   *Allen Dulles:* Letter of Jackson to Dulles, Apr. 28, 1946 (Library of Congress, R. H. Jackson Papers).
497   *"Rather die like a lion":* HG on May 14, 1946, quoted by Bross, op. cit., 196.

45: RELEASE

502   *Fifteen days after sentencing:* Andrus, testimony to Board of Inquiry (see note to p. 472 above). *Göring wrote two letters:* Reported by Stahmer to the British authorities in 1947 (PRO file WO.208/3785).
502   *Stahmer formally petitioned:* Stahmer, petition dated Oct. 4, 1946 (NA, OMGUS, RG.260, box 15; and papers of Judge Francis Biddle, Syracuse University, box 15).
502   *"Last letter":* Copies of HG's "last letter to Mr. Churchill" are in BA-MA, MSg.1/161; Julius Schaub Papers (IfZ, SI); Salmuth Papers (ibid.); BA-MA, Keitel Papers; the papers of General Ulrich Kessler, etc.
503   *Farewell visit from Emmy:* Telegram from Selkirk Panton to *Daily Express*, 5:45 P.M., Oct. 7, 1946; Milch diary, Dec. 10, 1947.
504   *Pflücker:* Pflücker, testimony to Board of Inquiry.
504   *British Labour Cabinet:* Telegrams in PRO file PREM.8/392. Minutes of the Allied Control Council in Berlin, Oct. 9 (ibid.) and Oct. 10, 1946 (NA, RG.153, box 1561).
505   *Three taunting letters:* The three letters were generously made available for the first time to the author by Dr. Daniel P. Simon, director of the Berlin Document Center. On Oct. 31, 1946, *The New York Times* reported that the Allied Control Council had ruled that the three letters left behind by HG would never be published.
506   *"Dr. Gilbert told me . . .":* Andrus would write later to prison surgeon Dr. William H. Dunn, "I have every reason to believe that Gilbert notified the condemned men . . . as soon as he learned of it through the newspapers and several days before the official notice arrived for me to publish to them. This, of course, gave Göring a good deal longer to make his plans" (Andrus Papers). Gilbert's last formal report to Jackson is dated Oct. 16, 1946, and states: "The writer's observations terminated on 13 October 1946" (Library of Congress, R. H. Jackson Papers).
507   *Lieutenant Roska:* Roska, testimony to Board of Inquiry.
507   *"I refused him the Lord's Supper":* Gerecke, testimony to Board of Inquiry. The book, *Mit den Zugvögeln nach Afrika*, was still in the Nuremberg prison library in 1949 (see note to p. 491 above).
511   *D-Day for HG:* The final scene is based on the precise testimonies rendered to the Board of Inquiry by Roska, Gerecke, McLinden, Johnson, Pflücker, Starnes, and the American corporal Gregory Tymchshyn. The fatal cyanide capsule is today (1988) the property of a New York urologist.

SELECT
BIBLIOGRAPHY

Abendroth, Hans Henning. *Mittelsmann zwischen Franco und Hitler: Johannes Bernhardt erinnert 1936* (Marktheidenfeld 1978)

Adám, Magda (ed., with G. Juhász, L. Kerekes). *Allianz Hitler-Horthy-Mussolini: Dokumente zur ungarischen Aussenpolitik* (Budapest, 1966)

Andrus, Burton C. *I Was the Nuremberg Jailer* (New York, 1969)

Assmann, Heinz: *Deutsche Schicksalsjahre* (Wiesbaden, 1951)

Baumbach, Werner. *Broken Swastika* (London, 1960)

Baur, Hans. *Ich flog Mächtige der Erde* (Kempten, 1960)

Bekker, Cajus. *Angriffshöhe 4000* (Oldenburg, 1964)

Bewlay, Charles. *Hermann Göring* (Göttingen, 1956)

Bezymenski, Lev. *Die letzten Notizen von Martin Bormann* (Stuttgart, 1974)

———*Sonderakte Barbarossa* (Stuttgart, 1968)

———*Der Tod des Adolf Hitler* (Hamburg, 1968)

Blau, George E. *The German Campaign in Russia, Planning and Operations (1940–1942)* (Washington, 1955)

———*The German Campaign in the Balkans, Spring 1941* (Washington, 1953)

Blunck, Richard. *Hugo Junkers: Der Mensch und das Werk* (Berlin, 1942)

Bodenschatz, Karl. *Jagd in Flanderns Himmel* (Munich, 1935)

Boelcke, Willi A. *Deutschlands Rüstung im Zweiten Weltkrieg* (Frankfurt am Main, 1969)

———*Kriegspropaganda 1939–1941* (Stuttgart, 1966)

————*Wollt Ihr den totalen Krieg?* (Stuttgart, 1967)

Bormann, Martin. *The Bormann Letters* (London, 1954)

Bross, Werner. *Gespräche mit Göring während des Nürnberger Prozesses* (Flensburg, Hamburg, 1950)

Bullitt, Orville H. *For the President* (Boston, 1972)

Burckhardt, Professor Carl F. *Meine Danziger Mission 1937–1939* (Stuttgart, 1960)

Burdick, Charles. *Germany's Military Strategy and Spain in World War II* (Syracuse, N.Y., 1968)

Caidin, Martin. *Black Thursday* (New York, 1960)

Cavallero, Ugo. *Diario* (Rome, 1948)

Collier, Basil. *The Defence of the United Kingdom* (HMSO, London, 1957)

Dahlerus, Birger. *Der letze Versuch* (Munich, 1973)

Danners, Russell. *Goering ante sus jueces: apuntes secretos* (Madrid, 1946)

Deichmann, General Paul. Unpublished study: "Why did Germany have no four-engined bomber in the Second World War?" (Archives of Militärgeschichtlichtes Forschungsamt, Freiburg, MGFA)

Detwiler, D. S. *Hitler, Franco und Gibraltar* (Wiesbaden, 1962)

Diels, Rudolf. *Lucifer ante Portas* (Zurich, undated)

Dietrich, Otto. *Zwölf Jahre mit Hitler* (Köln, 1955)

Dilks, David (ed.). *The Diaries of Sir Alexander Cadogan, 1938–1945* (London, 1971)

Documenti Diplomatici Italiani (Rome, 1954 et seq.)

Documents Diplomatiques Français 1932–1939, Vols. 3–6 (Paris, 1968–70)

Documents on British Foreign Policy, Third Series (HMSO, London, 1950 et seq.)

Documents on German Foreign Policy 1918–1945, Series D (HMSO, London, 1950–64)

Domarus, Max. *Hitler: Reden und Proklamationen, 1932–1945, Vols. 1, 2* (Neustadt an d. Aisch, 1962–63)

Dönitz, Karl. *Zehn Jahre und Zwanzig Tage* (Bonn, 1958)

Erickson, John. *The Soviet High Command* (London, 1962)

Eyermann, Karl Heinz. *Der Grosse Bluff* (East Berlin, 1963)

Fabry, Philipp W. *Die Sowjetunion und das Dritte Reich* (Stuttgart, 1971)

Fenyo, Mario D. *Hitler, Horthy and Hungary* (New Haven, 1972)

Fontander, Björn. *Göring och Sverige* (Stockholm, 1986)

Foot, M.R.D. *S.O.E. in France* (London, 1966)

Frank, K. H. *Confessions of Karl-Hermann Frank* (Prague, 1946)

Galland, Adolf. *The First and the Last* (London, 1953)

Germany. Auswärtiges Amt. *Weissbuch Nr. 3: Polnische Dokumente zur Vorgeschichte des Krieges* (Berlin, 1940)

————*Weissbuch Nr. 4: Dokumente zur englische-französischen Politik der Kriegsausweitung* (Berlin, 1940)

————*Weissbuch Nr. 5: Weitere Dokumente zur Kriegsausweiterungspolitik der Westmächte: Die Generalstabsbesprechungen Englands und Frankreichs mit Belgien und den Niederländen* (Berlin, 1940)

————*Weissbuch Nr. 6: Die Geheimakten des französischen Generalstabes* (Berlin, 1940)

————*Weissbuch Nr. 7: Dokumente zum Konflikt mit Jugoslawien und Griechenland* (Berlin, 1941)

————*Weissbuch Nr. 8: Dokumente über die Alleinschuld Englands am Bombenkrieg gegen die Zivilbevölkerung* (Berlin, 1943)

Germany. Oberkommando Der Wehrmacht. *War Diaries, 1940–1945*. Published as *Kriegstagebuch des Oberkommandos der Wehrmacht* (Frankfurt am Main, 1961–1965)

Gilbert, Dr. Gustave M. "Hermann Göring, Amiable Psychopath," in *Journal of Abnormal and Social Psychology*, Vol. 43, No. 2, April 1948

————*Nuremberg Diary* (New York, 1947)

————*The Psychology of Dictatorship* (New York, 1950)

Goebbels, Joseph. *Tagebücher aus den Jahren 1942–1943* (Zürich, 1948)

Göring, Hermann. *Aufbau einer Nation* (Berlin, 1934)

Görlitz, Walter (ed.). *Generalfeldmarschall Keitel: Verbrecher oder Offizier* (Göttingen, 1961)

Great Britain. Air Ministry. *The Rise and Fall of the German Air Force* (London, 1949)

Gregory, Frank Hutson. *Goering* (London, 1974)

Gritzbach, Erich. *Hermann Göring: Werk und Mensch* (Munich, 1940)

————(ed.). *Hermann Göring: Reden und Aufsätze* (Munich, 1938)

Groscurth, Helmuth. *Tagebücher eines Abwehroffiziers, 1938–1943* (Wiesbaden, 1951)

Guderian, Heinz. *Erinnerungen eines Soldaten* (Heidelberg, 1951)

Halder, General Franz. *Diaries*, published as *Kriegstagebuch* by Hans Adolf Jacobsen (Stuttgart, 1962)

Hammerstein, Baron Christian von. *Mein Leben* (IfZ, 1962)

Hassell, Ulrich Von. *Vom andern Deutschland: Tagebücher 1938–1944* (Frankfurt, 1964)

Heiber, Helmut (ed.). *Hitlers Lagebesprechungen: Die Protokollfragmente seiner militärischen Konferenzen 1942–1945* (Stuttgart, 1962)

————*Reichsführer! Briefe an und von Himmler* (Stuttgart, 1968)

Heinkel, Dr. Ernst. *Stürmisches Leben* (Stuttgart, 1953)

Hesse, Fritz. *Das Spiel um Deutschland* (Munich, 1953)

Hilger, Gustav. *Wir und der Kreml* (Frankfurt, 1956)

Hill, Leonidas E. (ed.). *Die Weizsäcker Papiere, 1933–1950*

Hillgruber, Andreas. *Hitler, König Carol und Marschall Antonescu* (Wiesbaden, 1954)

————*Staatsmänner und Diplomaten bei Hitler, 1939–1941* (Frankfurt, 1967); *Vol. 2: 1942–1944* (Frankfurt, 1970)

Hoensch, Jörg K. *Die Slowakei und Hitlers Ostpolitik* (Cologne and Graz, 1965)

Hoffmann, Peter. *Widerstand, Staatsstreich, Attentat* (Munich, 1969)

Höhne, Heinz. *Mordsache Röhm: Hitlers Durchbruch zur Alleinherrschaft* (Rowohlt, 1984)

Homze, Edward L. *Foreign Labour in Nazi Germany* (Princeton University, 1967)

Hubatsch, Walther. *Hitlers Weisungen für die Kriegführung, 1939–1945* (Frankfurt, 1962)

Jacobsen, Hans-Adolf. *Fall Gelb* (Wiesbaden, 1957)

Jansen, Gregor. *Das Ministerium Speer* (Berlin, 1968)

Johnson, Lt. Col. Thomas M. *Collecting the Edged Weapons of the Third Reich* (South Carolina)

Kehrig, Manfred. *Stalingrad: Analyse und Dokumentation einer Schlacht* (Stuttgart, 1975)

Kehrl, Hans. *Krisenmanager im Dritten Reich* (Düsseldorf, 1973)
Kelley, Dr. Douglas McG. *22 Cells in Nuremberg* (New York, 1947)
Kempka, Erich. *Ich habe Adolf Hitler verbrannt* (Munich, 1948)
Kesselring, Albert. *Soldat bis zum Letzen Tag* (Bonn, 1953)
Klee, K. *Das Unternehmen Seelöwe* (Göttingen, 1958)
Klein, Burton H. *Germany's Economic Preparations for War* (Harvard University Press, 1959)
Klink, Ernst. *Das Gesetz des Handelns: Die Operation Zitadelle 1943* (Stuttgart, 1966)
Koller, Karl. *Der letze Monat* (Mannheim, 1949)
Koppenberg, Dr. Heinrich. *The Development of [Junkers works] Dessau during 1934;* an unpublished report of January 1935
Kotze, Hildegard Von (ed.). *Es spricht der Führer* (Gütersloh, 1966)
Krecker, Lothar. *Kriegstagebuch des Oberkommandos der Wehrmacht (Wehrmacht-führungstab) 1940–1945, Vols 1–4* (Frankfurt, 1965, 1963, 1963, 1961)
Kube, Alfred. *Pour le mérite und Hakenkreuz: Hermann Göring im Dritten Reich (Quelle und Darstellungen zur Zeitgeschichte, Bd. 24)* (Munich, 1986)
Lange, Eitel. *Mit dem Reichsmarschall im Kriege* (Linz, 1950)
Lee, Asher. *Goering: Air Leader* (London, 1972)
Lipski, Josef. *Diplomat in Berlin, 1933–1939: Papers and Memoirs of Josef Lipski, Ambassador of Poland*, ed. Waclaw Jedrzejcwia (New York, London, 1968)
Lüdde-Neurath, W. *Regierung Dönitz* (Berlin, 1964)
Ludendorff, General Erich Von. *Vom Feldherrn zum Weltvrevolutionär und Weg-bereiter Deutscher Volksschöpfung* (Munich, 1940)
Maier, Major Klaus A. *Guernica 26.4.1937: Die deutsche Intervention in Spanien und der Fall Guernica* (Freiburg, 1975)
Manstein, Erich von. *Verlorene Siege* (Bonn, 1955)
Manvell, Roger, and Heinrich Fraenkel. *Göring* (London)
Martens, Stefan. *Hermann Göring: "Erster Paladin des Führers" und Zweiter Mann im Reich* (Paderborn, 1986)
Martin, Bernd: *Deutschland und Japan im Zweiten Weltkrieg* (Göttingen, 1969)
———*Friedensinitiativen und Machtpolitik im Zweiten Weltkrieg, 1939–1942)* (Düsseldorf, 1974)
Meinck, Gerhard. *Hitler und die deutsche Aufrüstung, 1933–1937* (Wiesbaden, 1959)
Meissner, Otto. *Operationsgebiet östliche Ostsee und der Finnisch-Baltische Raum, 1944* (Stuttgart, 1961)
———*Staatssekretär unter Ebert-Hindenburg-Hitler* (Hamburg, 1950)
Milward, Alan S. *The German Economy at War* (London, 1965)
Mosley, Leonard: *The Reich Marshal* (London, 1974)
———*The Reich Marshal: A Biography* (New York, 1974)
Müller, Klaus-Jürgen. *Das Heer und Hitler* (Stuttgart, 1969)
Namier, Professor Sir Lewis: *Diplomatic Prelude*
Neubacher, Hermann. *Sonderauftrag Südost, 1940–1945* (Göttingen, 1956)
Nuremberg: *Trial of the Major War Criminals before the International Military Tribunal* (Nuremberg, 1947–48)
Orlow, Dietrich. *The Nazis in the Balkans: A Case Study of Totalitarian Politics* (Pittsburgh, 1968)
Oven, Wilfried Von. *Mit Goebbels bis um Ende, Vols. 1–2* (Buenos Aires, 1949)
Overstraeten, General Van. *Albert I–Leopold III* (Brussels, no year)
Overy, R. J. *Goering the "Iron Man"* (London, 1984)

Paget, Reginald T., QC. *Manstein: His Campaigns and Trial* (London, 1951)

Papen, Franz Von. *Der Wahrheit eine Gasse* (Munich, 1952)

Picker, Henry. *Hitlers Tischgespräche im Führerhauptquartier, 1941–1942* (Stuttgart, 1963)

Price, Alfred. *Instruments of Darkness* (London, 1967)

Der Prozess gegen die Hauptkriegsverbrecher vor dem Internationalen Militärgerichtshof Nürnberg, 14 November 1945–1 Oktober 1946 (Nürnberg, 1947–49)

Raeder, Erich. *Mein Leben, Vol. 2* (Tübingen, 1957)

Rieckhoff, General H. J. *Trumpf oder Bluff?* (Geneva, 1945)

Röhm, Ernst. *Die Geschichte eines Hohenzollerns*

Schacht, Hjalmar. *Account Settled* (London, 1948)

————*Memoirs* published in *Revue* (Munich, No. 45, 1953)

————*76 Jahre meines Lebens* (Bad Wörishofen, 1953)

————*Wie eine Demokratie stirbt* (1968)

Schröder, Josef. *Italiens Kriegsaustritt 1943* (Göttingen, 1969)

Seraphim, Hans-Gunther (ed.). *Das politische Tagebuch Alfred Rosenbergs* (Göttingen, 1956)

Siegler, Fritz von. *Die höheren Dienststellen der Deutschen Wehrmacht, 1933–1945* (Munich, 1955)

Skipper, G. C. *Goering and the Luftwaffe* (Chicago, 1980)

Skorzeny, Otto. *Geheimkommando Skorzeny* (Hamburg, 1950)

Speer, Albert. *Erinnerungen* (Berlin, 1969)

Stehlin, General Paul. *Temoignage pour l'histoire* (Paris, 1964)

Sündermann, Helmut; *Deutsche Notizen, 1945–1965* (Leoni, 1966)

Thomas, General Georg. *Geschichte der deutschen Wehr- und Rüstungswirtschaft* (Boppard am Rhein, 1966)

Thorwald, Jürgen. *Ernst Udet: Mein Fliegerleben* (Berlin, 1954)

U.S. Army. *U.S. Strategic Bombing Survey: The Effects of Strategic Bombing on the German War Economy* (Washington, D.C., 1947)

U.S. Strategic Bombing Survey. *Aircraft Division Industry Report (No. 4)*

————*British Experience During German Air Raids (A British source document, filed as 64.b.q. (15))*

————*The Defeat of the German Air Force (No. 59)*

————*V-Weapons (Crossbow) Campaign (No. 60)*

Völker, Karl-Heinz: *Die deutsche Luftwaffe, 1933–1939: Aufbau, Führung, Rüstung* (Stuttgart, 1967)

————*Dokumente und Dokumentarfotos zur Geschichte der deutschen Luftwaffe* (Stuttgart, 1968)

————*Die Entwicklung der militärischen Luftfahrt in Deutschland, 1920–1933* (Stuttgart, 1962)

Webster, Sir Charles, and Dr. Noble Frankland. *The Strategic Air Offensive Against Germany* (London, 1961)

Weizsäcker, Ernst Von. *Erinnerungen* (Munich, 1950)

Ziemke, Earl F. *The German Northern Theater of Operations, 1940–1945* (Washington D.C., 1959)

Zoller, Albert. *Hitler privat: Erlebnisbericht seiner Geheimsekretärin* (Düsseldorf, 1949)

AUTHOR'S MICROFILM RECORDS

The author has deposited copies of the papers used in this work in the Irving Collection of the Institute of Contemporary History, Leonrodstrasse 46b, Munich, West Germany. He has prepared microfilm copies of some of the files, and these can be ordered from Microform Ltd., East Ardsley, Wakefield WF3 2JN, Yorkshire, England (telephone 0924-825 700).

DI-1: U.S. Peenemünde report, interrogations, etc.

DI-3: U.S.S.B.S. interrogations, and ADI(K) report, "Birth, Life, and Death of the German Day Fighter Arm" (by Galland and others).

DI-8: ETHINT interrogations of OKW and other officers.

DI-13: Interrogations of personal staffs of Göring and Hitler, Berchtesgaden, May 1945.

DI-15: Professor Richard Suchenwirth: studies on Göring, Udet, Jeschonnek, Milch, and others.

DI-16: ADI(K) index to Milch documents; U.S.S.B.S. index to U.S.S.B.S. source documents.

DI-17: Papers and diaries of General Karl Koller.

DI-19: Papers and manuscripts of Fritz Wiedemann.

DI-24: Papers and investigations of Central Works (Mittelwerk G.m.b.H).

DI-25: Diary of Hans Junge and Heinz Linge (Hitler's personal staff).

DI-35: Author's collection of latest British and German records on the Dresden air raid, 1945.

DI-36: Papers and diaries of Field Marshal Erhard Milch (and see DI-53 through DI-59).

DI-37: Nuremberg interrogations of Milch.

DI-38: Professor Hugh Trevor-Roper's papers on July 20, 1944.

DI-39: Professor Hugh Trevor-Roper's papers on the last days of Hitler; includes ADI(K) version of Koller's 1945 diary.

DI-40: RLM file of Göring and Hitler conferences, 1936–43.

DI-41: Speer chronicle, 1943 (the authentic one).

DI-44: Führer naval conferences 1939–45, German text.

DI-52: Goebbels diary, September 1942, February and June 1943 (original fragments).

DI-53: Selected documents from private papers of Field Marshal Erhard Milch.

DI-56: Milch diaries, 1933–35.

DI-57: Milch diaries, 1936–45.

DI-58: Milch diaries, April 1945 through December 1951.

DI-59: Selected extracts transcribed from Milch diaries.

DI-60: Original diaries of General Kurt Dittmar, 1939–45.

DI-66: American translation of Führer naval conferences, 1939–45.

DI-67: Court documents on Milch Case, 1946–47.

DI-72: Selected Reich Cabinet minutes, 1933–38.

DI-74: Diaries of Luftwaffe Hauptmann Wolf Eberhard, 1936–39, as Keitel's adjutant.

DI-75a: Diaries of Walther Hewel, 1939 and 1941 (Ribbentrop's liaison officer on Hitler's staff), and souvenir album.

DI-75b: Diary of General Otto Hoffmann von Waldau, 1939–43, and reports as Fliegerführer Afrika.

DI-78: Colonel Rudolf Schmundt's file, *Case Green* (April through October 1938).

DI-84: Transcript of diaries of General Alfred Jodl, 1937–45 with commentary and analysis by his deputy, General Walter Warlimont.

DI-87: Justice Robert H. Jackson, Oral History, 1952: Memoirs of Nuremberg Trial.

DI-91: Original draft by Helmut Greiner of OKW war diary, August 1942 through March 1943.

DI-88: Texts of selected secret speeches by Hitler, mostly unpublished, 1937–39.

DI-97: Diary of Otto Bräutigam, 1941–42.

DI-121 through DI-128: Author's collected research files on the 1944 Normandy landings.

DI-150: Rommel's personnel file, battle reports, diary of his Italian interpreter in North Africa, and further transcripts of Waldau diary (see DI-75b above).

DI-151: Diary of Vice-Admiral Friedrich Ruge, December 1943 through October 1944; telephone log of Rundstedt's G-2, Meyer-Detring; diary of Captain Hermann Kaiser, January through August 1943.

DI-154: Diaries, etc., from the papers of Generaloberst Hans von Salmuth; documents on the Speidel and Hofacker affairs.

DI-159: Rommel diary, original and transcript, summer 1941 through September 1942.

DI-160: Rommel diary, original and transcript, October 1942 through March 1943.

DI-161: Rommel diary, original and transcript, November 1942 through May 1944.

DI-170 through DI-176: Author's collected research files on Reichsmarschall Hermann Göring, including:

DI-170: Complete collection of Allied and Soviet interrogations of HG (excluding those at Nuremberg, for which see NA film M.1270).

DI-171: transcripts of HG's personnel files, private letters, and diaries; the Bradin collection of Bormann notes from the Führer bunker.

DI-172: transcripts of letters between HG and Carin; HG's letters to Leo Negrelli 1924/25; dossier on the Forschungsamt.

INDEX